BAX
A composer and his times

Other books written or edited by Lewis Foreman

Havergal Brian: a collection of essays (1969)
The British Musical Renaissance: a guide to research (1972)
Discographies: a bibliography (1973)
Archive Sound Collections (1974)
Systematic Discography (1974)
*Factors Affecting the Preservation and Dissemination of Archive Sound
    Recordings* (1975)
British Music Now (1975)
Havergal Brian and the Performance of his Orchestral Works (1976)
Edmund Rubbra: composer (1977)
Dermot O'Byrne: selected poems of Arnold Bax (1979)
Arthur Bliss: catalogue of the complete works (1980)
The Percy Grainger Companion (1981)
From Parry to Britten (1987)

BAX

A composer and his times

LEWIS FOREMAN

Foreword by Felix Aprahamian

Second Edition

Scolar Press

First published in 1983
This second edition published in 1988 by
SCOLAR PRESS
Gower Publishing Company Limited
Gower House,
Croft Road
Aldershot GU11 3HR
and
Gower Publishing Company
Old Post Road
Brookfield, Vermont 05036

British Library Cataloguing in Publication data

Foreman, Lewis
    Bax.
    1. Bax, Arnold   2. Composers — England — Biography
    I. Title
    780'.92'4   ML410.B275
    ISBN 0-85967-643-9

Library of Congress Cataloging in Publication Data

Foreman, Lewis.
    Bax: a composer and his times.

    Bibliography: p.
    1. Bax, Arnold, 1883–1953.   2. Composers — England —
Biography.   I. Title.
ML410.B275F7   1983   780'.92'4 [B]   82-19150
ISBN 0-85967-643-9

Printed in Great Britain at
the University Press, Cambridge

by Felix Aprahamian

In relation to his true stature, Arnold Bax is now far and away the most neglected British composer who flourished in the first half of this century. Those fifty years were a Golden Age of English music. The tonal system had reached its zenith, all valid harmonic resources had been uncovered, and a magnificent native school, from Elgar to Britten, rivalled any precursor in its variety. The harmonic riches available gave its members so wide a choice as to enable each of them to present a personal, instantly recognisable musical physiognomy to the world. Whereas only a real specialist, or one-time cathedral chorister, might distinguish, say, Tallis, Taverner or Tye, my musically untutored Californian students have no difficulty at the end of a single term in telling Elgar from Britten, Delius from Holst, or Vaughan Williams from Walton. Somehow or other, Bax lost his place among these Titans. Perhaps the fine composers were too numerous at one time. Just as in France, in the same period, two names – Debussy and Ravel – overshadowed the rest, relegating important figures like Roussel and Schmitt to the background, so, in England, Bax and many lesser composers suffered the same fate. With Bax, the process of rediscovery has already begun, and, in this volume, the fruit of long years of devotion to Bax's music, Mr Foreman has supplied its essential handbook.

Bax, although an inspired and compulsive composer, did little to promote his music. Intensely shy and retiring, he was a very private person whom I venerated at a distance in the Twenties and Thirties, when he really resembled his portrait by Herbert Lambert. Those sensitive features became progressively bloated in post-war years when the uneasiest of all musical Laureates paid a weekly visit to London from his country refuge. But my earlier memories of him and of performances of his music are the most precious. One that was crucial dates from November 1929, when at one of the Sunday evening concerts at the Working Men's College in Crowndale Road I first heard Bax's Second Sonata for violin and piano. Played by Bessie Rawlins, who had given the first performance with Bax in 1922, it left an indelible impression on a fifteen-year old who had just glimpsed 'modern' music through the Ravel *Sonatine*. From that time, I sought out performances of Bax's music, and those in which the then extremely beautiful Harriet Cohen ceded the piano part to the composer and acted as page-turner were especially memorable.

I remember Bax as a superb pianist, not only in his own music; I have never forgotten his song-accompaniments at the Wigmore Hall Peter Warlock Memorial Concert in 1931. By then I was a Bax-addict, rushing into print with a Letter to the Editor, when a critic wrote about the 'curious noises' opening the Third Sonata for violin and piano, and buying all the Bax scores I could. Too shy to approach the Master myself, I asked a tall young violinist in the then recently-founded BBC Symphony Orchestra to get Bax to sign his Second Sonata for me during a Prom interval, which he very kindly did; but I dare say Harry Blech has probably forgotten this. I marked Bax's fiftieth birthday by inscribing the Epilogue from his Third Symphony on a large sheet of parchment, thonging it as a standard lamp-shade, and delivering it anonymously with a birthday-card to his place in Fellows Road. I had previously sounded out Arthur Alexander, who at the time shared Bax's reputation as a prodigious score-reader and was a mutual friend, as to whether it would be acceptable. 'Yes, he'd appreciate anything like that', had been the reply. Years later, I learned from Tania that Bax had been so terrified of reaching his fiftieth birthday that no one was allowed to mark or celebrate it. He wanted it kept as quiet as possible: he had been horrified to think that someone outside his immediate circle should have remembered the depressing landmark he would rather not have been reminded of.

Much longer than half a century ago, the tunes that haunted me were the cello phrase opening Bax's Piano Quintet and the viola tune from *Tintagel*. The critic-dedicatee of the former, Edwin Evans, I already knew, but I was impatient to visit the site that had inspired the tone-poem. And so my first holiday away from the family was to visit a friend in Cornwall who had promised to drive me to Tintagel. Many years later, I was to persuade Gillian Widdicombe to drive me from Cork to the Old Head of Kinsale, so that I might gaze on Bax's own last view of the Garden of Fand.

It was dear Frank Merrick, another Bax dedicatee, who introduced me to him in 1934, after which we were on greeting terms, but I was still too young then to really know him. Our closest encounter was in 1949 when Tania invited me with a few others to their run-through at Gloucester Place Mews of the Left-hand Concerto he had just written for her. I turned over for Bax who was playing from his manuscript full score at the second piano. After a break, it was decided to go through it again. At the end of the first movement, Bax slipped off to the bathroom, unnoticed by Tania, who began the piano solo opening of the second movement. As Bax had not returned, I carried on with the orchestral part which, after all, I had heard half an hour earlier, and got through several pages. When Bax came back, I think his surprise almost equalled his resentment that my playing had taken Tania in, and that his particular role had been duplicated.

Like Bartók and Szymanowski, whom I also met in the Thirties, Bax seemed not only a shy but a worried and preoccupied man. Years later I was to learn what good cause for worry the two Central Europeans had. Now Mr Foreman's book makes clear that Bax's worries went back even further. It has shed light on the man as well as the music that has been so shamefully overlooked in recent years. In the year of the centenary of Arnold Bax's birth, the publication of this valuable volume should play its part in the long overdue revival of interest in his work.

Felix Aprahamian
Muswell Hill
March 1982

CONTENTS

PLATES
(*between pages 266 and 267*)

1   *a* Bax's parents; *b* Francis Colmer; *c* a group at Ivy Bank.
2   *a* Ivy Bank from the garden; *b* Maids prepare children's party at Ivy Bank.
3   Ivy Bank (Ordnance Map).
4   *a* Irene Scharrer; *b* Myra Hess; *c* Thuell Burnham, Arnold and Evelyn Bax.
5   *a* Lionel Tertis; *b* Frederick Corder; *c* Tobias Matthay; *d* Sir A. C. Mackenzie
6   *a* Arthur Alexander; *b* Olga Antonietti; *c* Dolly and Paul Corder.
7   *a* Glencolumcille; *b* Balfour Gardiner, Bax, Frank Hutchens (?).
8   *a* Bax, Elsita Bax, Phyllis Russell; *b* Ernest Belfort Bax; *c* Luisa Sobrino
9   The painted frontispiece to *Tamara* (*King Kojata*).
10 *a* The Old Broughtonians, 1912; *b* The Old Broughtonians, mid 1920s.
11 *a* George Russell; *b* Philip Heseltine; *c* Winifred Small; *d* May Harrison.
12 *a* Bax, his mother, Clifford and Evelyn; *b* York Bowen; *c* Sir Thomas
    Beecham.
13 *a* Mrs Christopher Lowther with Miss Billie Carleton;
    b Peter Warlock Memorial Concert, 1931, programme; *c* Beatrice Harrison.
14 Harriet Cohen and Bax, 1920.
15 *a* Bax, Eugène Goossens, Arthur Bliss, Dorothy Moulton; *b* Tamara
    Karsavina.
16 *a* Morar River, 1938; *b* Bax with Aloys and Tilly Fleischmann.
17 *a* Bax with his mother; *b* Bax and Harriet Cohen; *c* Sir Henry Wood and Bax.
18 Fragment of a possible sketch for an unfinished violin sonata.
19 Mary Gleaves.
20 *a* Ethel Bartlett and Rae Robertson; *b* E. J. Moeran; *c* Bax with Basil
    Cameron.
21 *a* Bax with Mr and Mrs Stanley Fitch; *b* The White Horse; *c* Memorial
    plaque.
22 The unused orchestral storm in *Oliver Twist*.
23 *a* Muir Mathieson, Harriet Cohen and Bax; *b* Bax with Mary Gleaves, 1953.
24 Bax in 1947.

INTRODUCTION
to the first edition

This book has been fifteen years in the writing, and over such a long time there may be a tendency to remember more clearly those who helped in its later stages, at the expense of those who were involved at the beginning. All have been important to its progress, however, and I have tried to ensure that those who set out with me on the voyage into Bax's then unknown musical wonderland are duly remembered in the notes that follow.

I have tried to write about the music after performance, rather than by merely studying the scores, and although I have not succeeded in hearing everything that Bax wrote I think I can honestly claim to have heard a high proportion of what is a very large corpus of music. Rigorous analysis of a large number of works has not been my primary aim, although I have discussed a broader sweep of his music than has been attempted by any previous commentator. I have been more interested in attempting to discover Bax's motivation in writing music which is patently a subconscious expression of his personality and his emotional life. In doing so I have attempted to introduce as much commentary as possible in Bax's own words, for along with his other gifts he had a marvellously idiosyncratic use of the English language, which gives his remarks, particularly when unguarded and in personal letters, a flavour all his own. In presenting a large collection of previously unpublished source material I hope I may stimulate others to draw on it and explore other facets of this fascinatingly complex man and his music.

Additionally, I have attempted to set Bax into his period, and at least put a little flesh on those skeletal figures whose names head small entries in the reference books, but whose music, though less expansive than Bax's, also deserves performance and evaluation:

what we have here is not just an unjustly neglected composer, but a forgotten generation. But Bax is, by a long chalk, the most fascinating and rewarding of them all.

Bax's spelling of names, particularly of Irish names, and of certain words (such as 'extasy' or 'Roussalka') is often individual or old-fashioned. However, his spelling has been retained in quotations, giving, as it does, a special flavour to his highly personal use of language. Outside quotations I have tried to standardise spelling for use throughout the remainder of the text, making a compromise between what Bax used and current usage where it is greatly different. Thus Bax sometimes writes Glencolumcille and sometimes Glencolmcille; I have retained the former in preference to the Irish Ordnance Survey map's Glencolumbkille or the Irish Gleann Cholm Cille. Where Bax writes in Irish I have retained his spelling with only a few exceptions.

Lack of space precludes giving special mention to all who merit it, but I would like to single out Graham Parlett and Stephen Lloyd who not only generously shared the fruits of their own research into the British music of the first half of the twentieth century, but also read and commented on my work. Patrick Piggott, too, devoted much time to the script and made invaluable suggestions, while Tony Payne's attention to matters of literary style and presentation has been an education. Fionnuala Cullen gave advice at a late stage on questions relating to the Irish language and its dialects, while Stephen Banfield, John Bishop, Garry Humphreys and Burnett James also provided valuable advice as readers.

Leslie Howard and Harold Truscott played the music for me on the piano, Tom Tatton on the viola, and Leslie Head and Joseph Vandernoot on the orchestra. All the time I was working on the book Vernon Handley was making his own performing exploration of Bax's music – at Guildford, on the radio, and on record – and thanks are also due to him for his enthusiasm and pioneering investigation of the repertoire.

The latter part of my narrative is also Mary Gleaves' story, and I would particularly like to thank her for her co-operation, her memories, and access to her magnificent collection of the letters Bax wrote her, as well as photographs and other Bax documents in her possession.

The following have all contributed in their various ways, and are listed here in alphabetical order. I have to thank: Felix Aprahamian, Annabel [Farjeon] Arney, the late A. L. Bacharach, the late Alan

Barlow, Barbara Bax, Evelyn Bax (Sir Arnold Bax's sister), Judge
Rodney Bax, Anne Baynes, Donald Beswick (sometimes Hon. Sec.
of the Oriana Madrigal Society), Trevor Bray, the late Havergal Brian,
Mr N. Bruce, Lionel Carley, Tom Clarke, the late Harriet Cohen, Eric
Cooper, Ian Copley, Peter Craddy, Sister Kathleen Cronin, the late
Anne Crowley, Shiela Larchet Cuthbert, Oliver Davies, Beryl Davis,
Geoffrey Dearmer, Eva Eckersley, Joan Farjeon, Eric Fenby, Professor
Aloys Fleischmann, C. M. Francis, the late David Garnett, Clifford
Gillam, Cloë Green, Hilda Goldstein, the late Patrick Hadley, the
late Mrs Dorothie Harrison, Jack Henderson, Clare Hope, Herbert
Howells, Derek Hudson, the late Harry Isaacs, Richard Itter,
Christopher Johnson, Michael Kennedy, the late Maria Korchinska,
the late Vivian Langrish, John Lindsay, George Lloyd, Richard
MacNutt, Meta Malins, the late Muir Matheson, John and Laurie
May, the late Marjorie McTavish, Rodney Meadows, Jessica Morton,
Pauline Myatt, the late Boyd Neel, the late Vera Newman, John and
Sylvia Nicole, Christopher Palmer, Peter J. Pirie, Paul Podro, Michael
Ponder, Mervyn Roberts, Mrs Maeve Rosenberg (Sir Arnold Bax's
daughter), Dr Edmund Rubbra, Edward Sargent jr, Mrs N. Sargent,
Colin Scott-Sutherland, John Simons, Frank Solano (executor of the
estate of the late Winifred Small), Kaikhosru Shapurji Sorabji, Justice
Sir Melford Stevenson, Patric Stevenson, G. R. Strong, Freda Swain,
Robert Threlfall, Fred Tomlinson, Viscount and Lady Ullswater,
Henri van Marken, Myra Verney, Mrs Eve Vypan, Malcolm Walker,
Richard Walker, Mrs C. Wallers, Guy Warrack, Michael Webber,
Christopher Whelen, Dorothy Wilson, and Tony Wood.

In addition many institutional libraries and collections gave
invaluable assistance. Probably the bulk of my requirements were
met by the Central Music Library, London, but in addition the
following public libraries provided invaluable help: Blackpool,
Bournemouth, Bradford, Bristol, Ealing, Gloucester, Hampstead,
Hertfordshire (and especially my local branch at Rickmansworth),
Islington, Lambeth, Liverpool, Manchester, New York, Norwich,
Philadelphia, and Portland (Oregon). Other institutional libraries
include the universities of Cape Town, Columbia (New York),
Indiana, Leeds, London, Reading (Finzi Room), Texas (the
Humanities Research Centre at Austin), Yale and the University
Colleges of Cork and Dublin. Other institutional sources were: the
Army Records Centre, the BBC (Music Library, Scripts Registry,
Sound Archives, and the written Archive at Caversham where
Jacqueline Kavanagh and her predecessor Mary Hodgson were

particularly helpful), British Film Institute, British Institute of
Recorded Sound (Eric Hughes), British Library (Pamela Willetts,
Dept. of Manuscripts), British Piano Museum, College of Librarian-
ship Wales, Det Kongelige Bibliotek (København), Library of
Congress, Mander and Mitchinson Theatre Collection, Performing
Right Society, the libraries of the Royal Academy and Royal College
of Music, and the Sibelius Museum (Åbo, Finland). Orchestras were
also a valuable source of information and particularly the staffs of
the Boston, Chicago, Cleveland, London Symphony and New York
Philharmonic Symphony orchestras, and the Royal Philharmonic
Society.

The staff of Bax's main publishers were always more than helpful,
specifically Peter Todd at J. & W. Chester, and successively Danny
Inman, John Devereaux and Kathy Copisarow at Chappell & Co.

Some material was previously published in *Recorded Sound,* the
*Bax Society Bulletin, Records and Recordings, Audio and Record
Review, Musical Opinion, Current Musicology,* the *RMA Research
Chronicle,* the *Proceedings of the Royal Musical Association, Music
and Letters* and as programme notes for various concerts and for
Lyrita records, and I would like to acknowledge the use of this
matter which while not extensively quoted verbatim is drawn upon
from time to time.

Thanks are also due to the authors, publishers and copyright
owners of all material quoted, and in this respect I have to acknowl-
edge the co-operation of Anton Bax and Mr A. B. Rye for the
Bax Estate; Chappell & Co. Ltd. in respect of quotations from Bax's
music which are their copyright (*Lyrical Interlude, In the Faery
Hills,* Violin Sonata No. 1, *Enchanted Summer, Nympholept, Red
Autumn, The Garden of Fand,* Piano Quintet, 'The Well of Tears'
from *The Bard of the Dimbovitza,* Symphonic Variations, *The Truth
About the Russian Dancers, Mater Ora Filium,* Viola Sonata,
Symphonies Nos 1, 2, 3, 4, 5, 6 and 7, String Quartet No. 2, *Cortège,*
Piano Sonata No. 3, Two-Piano Sonata, *Winter Legends,* Nonett, *The
Tale the Pine-Trees Knew, Northern Ballad No. 2,* Violin Concerto,
Malta GC, copyright in the name of Murdoch Murdoch & Co.,
assigned to Chappell & Co. Ltd., reproduced by kind permission of
Chappell Music Ltd.); Ascherberg Hopwood & Crew Ltd. in respect
of *A Romance* (© 1919, reproduced by kind permission); J. & W.
Chester/Edition William Hansen London Ltd. (*Fatherland,* 'Eilidh
My Fawn' from *A Celtic Song Cycle,* Trio in One Movement, *Dream
in Exile* by Bax, and Symphony No. 5 by Sibelius); Oxford University

Press (*Watching the Needleboats*); and Breitkopf & Härtel (London) Ltd. (*Tapiola* by Sibelius).

I am grateful to all copyright holders of textual matter quoted, who have given permission to quote from their work. Sources of brief quotations and references may be found in the notes (pp. 388–401); otherwise I am pleased to acknowledge the following: Mr Anton Bax and the Bax Estate for all Bax copyright material used (including quotations from *Farewell, My Youth*, originally published by Longmans); Felix Aprahamian; Barrie & Jenkins Limited (in respect of *Music Magazine*, edited by Anna Instone and Julian Herbage, and Norman Demuth's *Musical Trends in the 20th Century* – both published by Rockliffe); the BBC (for quotations from material in the BBC Written Archives, Caversham, BBC scripts, and items first published in *The Listener* and *The Radio Times*); Blackie and Son Ltd (for Margaret Morris's *The Art of J. D. Fergusson*); The Bodley Head (for the 1952 edition of Peter Warlock's *Frederick Delius*); the estate of the late Joseph Campbell for four lines from his poem 'As I Came Over the Grey, Grey Hills'; Chatto and Windus Ltd and Constance Garnett for the extract from Constance Garnett's translation of Gogol's *Evenings on a Farm Near Dikanka*; the estate of the late Richard Church (for quotation from his *The Voyage Home* published by William Heinemann Ltd); Martin Cooper; *The Daily Telegraph*; Gerald Duckworth & Co. Ltd and Christopher Palmer (for *Delius – portrait of a cosmopolitan*); Margaret Dobson (for a quotation from Wilfred Mellers' *Studies in Contemporary Music*); Faber and Faber Ltd (for quotations from *A Bundle of Time* by Harriet Cohen); the estate of the late Eleanor Farjeon (for extracts from her *Edward Thomas – the last four years*, published by Oxford University Press); Gervase Farjeon (for permission to reprint Herbert Farjeon's *The Happy Forest*); *The Financial Times*; Aloys Fleischmann (in respect of his mother's unpublished memoir of Bax); the estate of the late Oliver St John Gogarty; Hamish Hamilton Ltd (for a quotation from Jerrold Northrop Moore's *Music and Friends*); Vernon Handley; Ibbs & Tillett; Harrap Ltd (for a quotation from Hubert Foss's *Ralph Vaughan Williams*); *The Irish Times*; John McCabe; Macmillan (for a quotation from Mary Colum's *Life and the Dream*); the editors of *Music and Letters, The Music Review, The Musical Times*; Michael Joseph Ltd and G. P. Putnam (for *Jung, His Life and Work* by Barbara Hannah); the editors of *The New Statesman* and *The Observer*; Oxford University Press (for E. R. Dodds' *Missing Persons*); various writings of Clifford Bax are reprinted by permission of A. D. Peters & Co. Ltd; Peter J. Pirie; Derrick Puffett's contribution to *Art Nouveau, Jugendstil and Musik* is quoted from with acknowledgement to the publisher Atlantis Musikbuch-Verlag, Zürich; Dr Edmund Rubbra; the estate of the late George Russell (for his poem 'parting'); Colin Scott-Sutherland (for his book *Arnold Bax*, published by J. M. Dent and Sons, and other writings on Bax); Kaikosru Shapurji Sorabji; Patric Stevenson; *The Sunday Times*; Freda Swain (for Arthur Alexander's writings on Bax and on Matthay); the Humanities Research Center of the University of Texas at Austin (permission given only as owner of physical manuscripts of letters of Arnold and Clifford Bax); University of Cape Town and the estate of the late W. H. Bell (in respect of W. H. Bell's unpublished memoirs); Ursula Vaughan Williams (for a letter of Ralph Vaughan Williams); extracts from the poetry of W. B. Yeats and from his preface to *Cuchulain of Muirthemne* by Lady Gregory are printed by permission of A. P. Watt Ltd; Christopher Whelen; Patricia Weir (on behalf of Dr Margaret Sutherland); Dr Percy Young (literary executor of the estate of the late Harriet Cohen, in respect of unpublished writings by Harriet Cohen).

Sources and permissions for illustrative material used (except for the musical examples, acknowledged above) are as follows – Collection author: 1a, 1b, 1c, 2, 4c, 5a (from *Musical Times* December 1906), 5b, 5d, 8, 11c, 12, 15a (an unidentified cutting), 17, 20a (from *The Gramophone* July 1928), 20b, 21, 23, fig. 2, fig. 3; John Bishop/Peter Warlock Society: 11b; British Library: rear endpaper; Camden Public Library Local History Department: 3; J. & W. Chester/ Edition William Hansen London Ltd: front endpaper; Aloys Fleischmann: 16b; Clifford Gillam: 18; Mary Gleaves: 16a, 19, 20c, 23b, 24; Christopher Johnson: 4a, 4b; Keystone Press Agency Ltd: 21; Stephen Lloyd: 7b, 13d; David Loeb: 14; Raymond Mander and Joe Mitchensen Theatre Collection: 15b; Rodney Meadows: 7a; Jessica Morton: 6b, 6c, 10a, 10b; Oliver Neighbour: 22; National Portrait Gallery, London: 11a; Graham Parlett: 11d; Royal College of Music: 5c; Colin Scott-Sutherland: fig. 1, fig. 4; Freda Swain: 6a, 13a, 13b; Fred Tomlinson: 13c; University College, Cork: 9.

Finally my agent, Andrew Best of Curtis Brown Academic Ltd., and my editors Martin Bailey, Judith Donnington and Dee Cook all contributed to smoothing the path to publication, while my typist Charmian Angelo has performed wonders with my second, third and subsequent thoughts, and has, in fact, typed much of the script several times. At the beginning Vera Bawden typed much of the bibliographical matter that is still present in the final version. Last, but by no means least, Robin Crofton, who prepared the musical examples.

While Bax's life and personality are fascinating, the music is the main call on us, and I hope I may have persuaded performers to investigate Bax's music and provided them with the data necessary in planning performances. If I have succeeded in that, while instructing and entertaining my readers, and provided documentary evidence for other, future, writers about Bax, then I shall be well satisfied. I will always be delighted to hear from any reader who can add to the story told in these pages, or can trace the missing scores: please write to me care of my publishers.

Lewis Foreman
Rickmansworth
November 1982

INTRODUCTION
to the second edition

It is now four years since the first edition of this book was passed for press, and in that time remarkable strides have been made in the performance and dissemination of the music of Sir Arnold Bax. Much of the impetus behind this activity came, in 1983, from the BBC's centenary series of twelve programmes of Bax's music, which concentrated on the unperformed and lesser-known works. At about the same time there came the first of a quickly-growing catalogue of fine recordings from the Chandos Record Company, many recordings from other sources (during this time nearly 100 recorded performances of Bax's music have appeared, including 37 of works not previously recorded), and the emergence of the Sir Arnold Bax Trust as an active organisation promoting knowledge of Bax's music. Thus many of the orchestral and choral and orchestral works that were unknown to most music lovers are suddenly accessible in good performances: the result has been a revelation even to Bax's best-informed and most-committed admirers. The new perspective gained from this activity has allowed me to amend one or two of my more tentative judgements in the first edition, in each case in the music's favour. Probably the works for chorus and orchestra have gained the most. Bax's vocal scores are difficult to assess at the piano, and the impact made by the BBC's choral concert conducted by Vernon Handley (at which *Enchanted Summer, Walsinghame* and *To the Name Above Every Name* were played) was electrifying. *Walsinghame* in particular stands out as a work of passionate engagement, one of the high-spots of Bax's achievement in the period after the Second Symphony. We have been able to go back even earlier, to demonstrate, as never before, the quality of the young Bax's achievement. He was in advance of most of his British contemporaries and his luxuriant pre-1914 scores, including *Enchanted Summer, Spring Fire, Nympholept* and various works for solo voice and orchestra, far from being promising prentice works can now be seen as being among his most significant achievements, and coming as they do from his youthful maturity, they have a glow and an optimism that is missing from his, albeit powerful, later music. Our dating of his mature achievement now demonstrates it to have begun ten years earlier than has previously been generally accepted.

This investigation of unknown music has also brought to light a number of delightful shorter pieces, including the comparatively well-known *Summer Music*, as well as such things as the enjoyable dance-fantasy *The Dance of Wild Irravel*, the ebullient and virtuosic *Symphonic Scherzo*, in which so many Baxian finger-prints are to be found, and the vigorous, compact *Northern Ballad No. 3*, which Bax called *Prelude for a Solemn Occasion*.

I have taken the opportunity to correct a sprinkling of literals and other mistakes, and have introduced some new material into the text where opinion is now easier to focus in the light of fine performances. Bax's letters continue to come to light, and examples seen have included those written to May Harrison, Herbert Howells, Eric Chisholm and Stewart Deas. Three of the missing scores have also been located, and the Discography is growing very quickly indeed. Thus, in the light of the many performances that have taken place, both the Catalogue of Works and the Discography are very considerably changed from their appearance in the first edition. Additions to the Bibliography, however, have been made in a supplementary sequence to avoid re-setting.

Time flies, and it is now my sad task to mark the passing of several contemporaries of Bax who helped me with the first edition. It has been my privilege to have known them and to have been able to set a tiny fragment of their personal stories in the amber of the printed page. They include Arnold Bax's sister, Evelyn, his daughter, Maeve Rosenberg, and his nephew, Judge Rodney Bax, as well as the composers Freda Swain and Edmund Rubbra. September 1984 brought a tragic bolt from the blue with the premature death of the violinist Ralph Holmes, at the age of 47. During 1983 he had widely toured a recital programme that included the Bax Third Sonata, and had been preparing the Violin Concerto and Viola Phantasy for recording, having given a couple of concert performances of the latter.

Finally thanks to those who helped by providing amendments, corrections and comments for the revision. In particular, I am grateful to Stephen Lloyd and Graham Parlett, but also to Patrick Piggott, Christopher Palmer, Connie Mayfield, Chris King, Gloria Bax and Stephen Banfield, and to Cecile Kelly of Chandos Records. All those who have performed the music since the first edition have provided an invaluable body of experience with which to confirm impressions or reconsider judgements. Chief among these splendid artists are the conductors Vernon Handley and Bryden Thomson, and the pianists David Owen Norris, Margaret Fingerhut, Noemy Belinkaya and Martin Roscoe.

Lewis Foreman
Rickmansworth
October 1986

For Susan, Tamsin,
and my parents

That is no country for old men. The young
In one another's arms, birds in the trees
— Those dying generations — at their song,
The salmon-falls, the mackerel-crowded seas,
Fish, flesh, or fowl, commend all summer long
Whatever is begotten, born, and dies.
Caught in that sensual music all neglect
Monuments of unageing intellect.

W. B. Yeats

A composer is unable to hide anything — by
his music you shall know him.

Yehudi Menuhin

The background

When two brothers each achieve a national reputation in different arts, it is natural enough to look at their forebears to see if there has been any family tradition in either art. In the case of Arnold Bax, one of the major British composers of his period, and of his brother Clifford, who achieved a similar if short-lived reputation in belles-lettres and as a playwright, there appears to be no such long-standing tradition. The only earlier manifestation of artistic talent in the Bax family had been shown by their uncle Ernest Belfort Bax, who was a well-known socialist author, and had also studied music at the Stuttgart Conservatorium during 1875–6. In the late 1880s and early 1890s he practised as music critic, sharing the columns of the *World* with the young George Bernard Shaw, using the pseudonym of 'Musigena' in rivalry with Shaw's 'Corno di Bassetto'.[1]

In 1880 the writer William Sharp, better known as 'Fiona Macleod', who later was to influence the young Arnold Bax, showed Ernest Belfort Bax a sonnet he had written called 'Religion'. This deeply impressed Arnold's uncle, and he subsequently set it to what Sharp thought 'very beautiful recitative music'. 'There are some fine chords in the composition,' Sharp noted, 'preluding the pathetic melody of the finale'.[2] This music does not appear to have survived.

The Baxes came from Holland, probably in the sixteenth century, and were important farmers in the Ockley district of Surrey. By the late nineteenth century they had become a wealthy middle-class family, their income being derived from the manufacture of Mackintosh raincoats, in the patent of which they had an interest, and from the ownership of a sizeable plot of land in Oxford Street, roughly where Selfridges stands today. In the 1890s Arnold's father is also known to have been financially involved with property development.

Alfred Ridley Bax was born on 25 April 1844. He was a barrister-at-law of the Middle Temple, though he did not practise. Of apparently more interest to him was his hobby of antiquarianism and family history, and he devoted a good deal of time to it. He was a Fellow of the Society of Antiquaries and a member of the Councils of both the Surrey and the Sussex Archaeological Societies. He also collected brass rubbings with great zeal and accuracy. A mild tempered man, he kept aloof from the running of his household, leaving all day-to-day domestic matters to his determined young wife.

On 7 November 1882 he had married Charlotte Ellen Lea, the daughter of a Congregationalist minister and one-time missionary to China, where she had been born in 1860. The contrasts that might be expected between a somewhat retiring man nearing forty and his strong-willed and vivacious twenty-two-year-old wife dominated the conduct of their household for the remainder of Alfred's life – some thirty-six years – though for his last fifteen years 'Old Ridley Bax', as he was generally known, became increasingly feeble.

Alfred Bax and his young wife had four children, and in due course appointed a tutor to look after the education of their sons Arnold and Clifford. At the end of his long life the tutor, Francis Colmer, described[3] how the boys' father 'had lived a very restricted life at his paternal home' and 'was thoroughly imbued with the narrow view of life held by his Quaker ancestry, and was unfamiliar with any of the common pleasures, or any form of art save that of music.' Colmer expressed surprise at the way his employer, in whose house he lived for many years, 'having no particular desire for marriage had been induced to enter into a union with a woman seventeen years his junior!' 'It is scarcely surprising', continued Colmer, 'that he was really unfitted for paternity and had so little communion with his children that they grew up without having the proper intercourse expected from a father.' The Baxes' mother on the other hand, although from a similar background, was very much more outgoing. 'A sweet and lovable woman' was how Colmer remembered her, feeling that her dominant influence over Arnold and Clifford was ultimately the basic force that shaped their later characters and latent talent. She reacted to her own narrow childhood and youth, 'with little opportunity and no encouragement to take part in the pleasures incidental to early years', by adopting a lax regime as far as her offspring were concerned. She 'was full of vitality, highly sexed, anxious to gain some knowledge of aspects of social life of which she had been deprived, and always taking a warm maternal interest in the youthful members of the other sex' who came into her children's circle.

Arnold was born at Heath Villa, Angles Road, Streatham,[4] on 8 November 1883, a year and a day after his parents' marriage had been celebrated. This building has now been demolished, but we may assume the household to have been a fairly large one, including Eleanor Bax, Arnold's grandmother, who was living with the family, as well as a considerable number of domestic servants.

Alfred Bax's father, Daniel Bax, continually moved house, an almost nomadic trait that Arnold inherited from his grandfather, and Daniel died at Kenmure House, Streatham Road. After his death, which happened to be in the year of Arnold's birth, grandmother Bax went to live with her son. Indeed, as Victorian custom would have it, she took over control of the household, servants and daily running of the establishment. She was a woman of narrow and puritanical upbringing and her influence dominated Alfred Bax and his wife for the remainder of her life.

Two brothers for Arnold — Aubrey and Clifford — and his sister Evelyn were born during the next few years. This expansion of the family at Angles Road, and the death in November 1890 of grandmother Bax, precipitated the first of two moves in which the family was involved during the young Baxes' childhood. They first moved locally, and took a large and rambling residence called Marlborough House, at the corner of Clapham Common. However, this was to be an unhappy house and, after Arnold's brother Aubrey contracted meningitis and died in March 1895 at the age of ten, the family moved again, to the 'far more interesting social milieu'[5] of Hampstead.

Alfred Bax had purchased a large house standing in extensive grounds on Rosslyn Hill, the continuation of Hampstead High Street, in 1893. At that time Ivy Bank, as the house was called, and one or two other fine houses set in almost park-like grounds, had been encircled by new streets, though not far to the north Hampstead Heath 'was itself the frontier between town and country', 'stretching away to the villages of Finchley, Hendon, Edgware, Kingsbury and Wembley'.[6] Arnold's father had mixed motives in purchasing so large an undeveloped site in an area where property development was in a comparatively advanced stage, and he started to build houses along the bottom of his extensive gardens. Ivy Bank had been rebuilt by its previous owner as recently as 1875, and so the fabric of the building was comparatively new. Between 1893 and 1896, when the Baxes moved in, considerable renovation and decoration took place.[7]

The large house with its rambling and beautiful gardens was to be of great importance to the development of Arnold and his brother Clifford. Much of the Hampstead that the Baxes knew then (and indeed later) is now no more, and this includes Ivy Bank. But for a very important fourteen years, during their artistic development, their studies, and their early creative years, the house was a place of much happiness and it exerted an influence which lasted all their lives. The first summer at Ivy Bank Arnold suffered an attack of sun-stroke, and when he recovered wrote what is said to have been his first composition, the song *Butterflies all white* (which appears not to have survived).

The boys' schooling appears to have been somewhat intermittent. A school report survives from 1892 showing Arnold top of a rather small class. Later, in Autumn 1896, they went to Heath Mount School, only a short walk from Ivy Bank (incidentally, later attended by Evelyn Waugh and Cecil Beaton). Arnold stayed until December 1898, having made his name on the cricket field and become a pre-fect. At home Alfred Bax employed a tutor for the boys, and after leaving school Arnold passed the Cambridge junior local examination in March 1899. In the summers of 1899, 1901 and 1902 Arnold's cricket team played the school eleven.

Alfred Bax's choice of tutor to educate his sons was a crucial factor in their development, probably even more so than their physical situation in Hampstead. Francis Colmer was an exhibitioner from Exeter College, Oxford. Like all the Bax circle he was quickly dubbed with a nickname, though in this case the obvious one of 'Col'. He remained in association with the Bax household throughout the Edwardian period and after. A later friend of Arnold, Arthur Alexander, met the eccentric Colmer just after Bax's parents had moved to Cavendish Square in 1911, and has left this vivid portrait:

He seemed uncertain of the exact position of the floor for his long legs worked spasmodically and nervously. He spoke in abrupt jerks and appeared to possess a series of voices at different pitch levels. These he often tried out before he decided which one to use. He had a great deal of general knowledge, but more especially of books and painting and he was pathetically short-sighted ... He taught painting to Clifford. At one time, feeling his position a trifle insecure he began his comment on one of his pupil's pictures thus: 'Awfully jolly, old man — I rather like that er - er foreground, but your choice of colours for that er - er - er. And the relationship of the er - er - er - to — As a matter of fact, old man, *it's all wrong*!'[8]

Colmer's sympathetic and indeed lax regime, combined with the indulgence of their mother, allowed the boys to develop as they wished. Yet, as Clifford Bax has recorded, he and his brother were still absorbed by the usual boyish pursuits, and neither could be considered in any way a prodigy. Clifford Bax wrote: 'Until I was fourteen I cared only for cricket, chess and my coin-collection ... Ladysmith and Mafeking might hold out or surrender: to me their fate was of slight importance compared with the difficulty of bowling out my brother'.[9] Arnold was beginning to seek wider horizons and, as Clifford observed, was 'already alive to the interests of music or of love'.

Francis Colmer's assessment of the developing personalities of Arnold and Clifford showed an acute awareness, in pre-Freudian days, noting as he did the influence that the character of their parents had on their developing artistic and sexual make-up: the two facets closely intertwined. 'Both Arnold and Clifford had an undeniable feminine streak in their character which they certainly derived from their mother', he wrote.

This is a most precious gift when allied with unusual intellectual power. It is a quality invaluable to those who devote themselves to any branch of art, informing their work with tenderness and the perfection of beauty, and coming sometimes into sharp conflict with the more violent emotions of the masculine mind. These diverse contrasts are strongly exhibited in both the music and stories of Arnold; and the poems, plays and stories of his brother. In both are found the mystic and haunting glamour of unearthly things, and the barbaric violence of the ancient world. Both brothers were under an obsession which was part of their beings and which it was not of their power to control.[10]

Arnold's musical development was a very gradual process. The Baxes were a cultured family and so it was quite natural that, writing later in his life, Bax should be unable to remember a time when he could not play the piano, just as he was unable to recall when he could not manage at least a 'miserable smattering'[11] of French. Playing in the family circle, particularly in competition with his father's brother Ernest Belfort Bax, encouraged him to develop, for his uncle was efficient at the keyboard. Arnold had no formal musical education before 1898, but certainly his interest had a firm hold about the time of the move to Ivy Bank. His father began taking him to the Crystal Palace Saturday Concerts where the conductor was August Manns, whose imposing figure attracted Arnold's interest. Looking back through his father's bound set of concert programmes kept Arnold occupied for hours, amusing himself 'by improvising absurd symphonies and overtures from the musical excerpts'[12] printed in them.

Gradually other musical experiences were added. One September evening in 1896 he was taken to a Promenade Concert by an aunt. 'The decision to go was made on the spur of the moment and we arrived late' to find the second movement of Mozart's G minor symphony playing at 'the exact point when the violins begin that Tannhäuser-Overture-like figure'. Two years later Bax stole off alone from Hampstead to attend his earliest regular symphony concert. 'Though still super-human the conductor's stature had slightly diminished. Sir Henry [Wood] has always seemed a little touched that I recall my first hearing on that occasion of Brahms's Third Symphony in a programme concluding with the "Prelude and Liebes-tod". I had never yet heard this adored work either, but dared not stay for it for fear of reprimand at home. (I was supposed to have gone with my brother and tutor to a Memorial Exhibition of the paintings of the recently dead Burne-Jones.)'[13]

Chamber music remained something of a closed book until he heard the Joachim Quartet at Hampstead Town Hall, the occasional visit from the Bohemian Quartet and, on trips into town, the 'Satur-day Pops' at St James's Hall.

Arnold's father cherished a private choral society, to which the young pianist acted as accompanist from the age of thirteen, acquir-ing a decidedly jaundiced view of the intellectual accomplishment of most singers, amateur or professional. The repertoire consisted of 'long-outmoded British works from the back shelves of Messrs Novello's'. Father Bax could 'seldom be induced to stray from these innocent pastures, although Mendelssohn's *Lauda Sion* and *Walpurgis Night* were tackled, and once *Acis and Galatea*'.[14] The choir was directed by John Post Attwater, to whom Arnold owed a considerable debt, for it was he who ultimately persuaded his father that Arnold should train professionally at the Royal Academy of Music. By that time, however, Attwater had retired from being choirmaster of Alfred Ridley Bax's choir, and had been succeeded by another local organist, Dr Arthur Greenish who also taught at the Academy.

By this time, Arnold was beginning to compose. These youthful attempts prompted his father after a year or so to seek professional advice as to whether a musical career was possible for his son, and on being advised that it was, he sent him to study at the Hampstead Conservatoire, 'an institution ruled with considerable personal pomp' by Cecil Sharp.

Arnold's prowess at the piano developed quickly in his mid-teens, by which time he could attempt most of the Beethoven piano sonatas. His experience of music revolved around the piano, and his earliest surviving compositions date from this period. In a notebook containing 'Clavierstücke by A.E.T. Bax 1897–8' are twenty-eight pages of music comprising a Minuet in E minor, two Hungarian Dances ('Ra's Dance' and 'On the Mountains'), three Mazurkas, two Scherzi, a Prelude in G major, Nocturne in B major, Minuet in E minor (written out in eight instrumental parts: flute, oboe, clarinet, bassoon, strings) and a Sonata in D minor (No 5, unfinished). Of these pieces the Nocturne in B major (Ex. 1) is probably the most

Ex. 1

assured, though clearly inspired by Chopin's E♭ Nocturne. But the two Hungarian Dances show how, even at this embryonic stage in his development as a composer, he was thinking in terms of programme music, while the opening of *On the Mountains*, clearly takes as its model a passage in the first movement of Schumann's Sonata Op. 11. It is interesting to note that Arnold's most cherished birthday present in 1898 was a vocal score of *Die Meistersinger*, one of only two scores that he kept until his death (the other being *Tristan*).

Life at Ivy Bank at the turn of the century seems enviable to us today. In the summer of 1900 Arnold was sixteen, Clifford thirteen and Evelyn twelve, and so the children would have dominated the life of the household. The boys were under the personal supervision of 'Col', who joined them in cricket and boyish games on the huge lawns. Also present would have been 'Col's' delicate wife, conspicuous with her bright red hair. It was a typical Edwardian house, finely appointed, and requiring a large staff to run it properly.

Alfred Bax was rather distant except at family prayers, which
were held daily. The whole household would file in, father Bax
following, often wearing a velvet jacket. Tall, with silvery-grey hair
and moustache, and his face dominated by the prominent Bax nose,
he would enter slowly, with great dignity, and speak in a far-away
detached voice. On special occasions he would wear a red tie. His
was a strict sect, yet it was not an authoritarian household — quite
the opposite. His manner was very gentle.

There were often visitors staying, friends of the boys or Evelyn
as they grew older, but before this, as later, Mrs Bax had compassion
on a constant stream of waifs and strays who were taken into the
circle. There was always a large family party at Christmas and on
Boxing Night forty people or more would sit down to dinner, Mrs
Bax always taking care to invite those who might be alone during the
festivities. Games were *de rigueur* at these family parties, and little
prizes were always forthcoming for the winners. Even later, when
they moved to Cavendish Square, Mrs Bax was noted for her superb
children's parties. The servants were not left out of this atmosphere
of goodwill. Many became more family friends than domestic servants
and were looked after financially once they had left the Bax employ.

Where the Baxes lived there were several other large houses, all
standing amidst extensive gardens. And it was the garden that went a
long way towards making Ivy Bank so important an influence on the
lives of Arnold and his brother. In a radio talk Arnold remembered
the 'large and beautiful garden, whilst the long rambling house
certainly seemed to belong to the country rather than to a London
suburb'. Through the window of Arnold's small study the onlooker
was faced with 'a density of trees and shrubs, through which not a
sign of a house could be seen'.[15] Clifford later described it in the
following terms:

How many acres did our 'well-stocked garden' comprise? Was it five? Was it six?
I forget: but I remember with delight the row of tremendous trees — chestnuts
and sycamore — that towered diagonally across its length; and the three large
lawns and the one that was smaller; and how in Spring the apples and cherries
in the orchard were so lavish of blossom as to seem at times impossibly beautiful;
and how, though we were always many in the house, no one had any difficulty
in finding a shady solitude. Most clearly of all I remember those ancient trees —
the last survivors, I imagine, of Belsize Park — and the largest of those lawns: for
it was that lawn which we used as a cricket field and it was in front of those
trees that we pegged our net. Here for a number of years, while adolescence led
onward to early manhood, we played matches of three, of four, or sometimes of
five men aside. Our struggles were strenuous and protracted. The greenhouses at

deep mid-off were punctured so frequently by mis-hits that the gardener, an enthusiastic cricketer from Yorkshire, had to roof them with wire. A strong drive over the bowler's head would carry the ball distractingly into the strawberry-beds; and a really big hit, if it did not quite land in Belsize Lane, would crash with an inebriating report against the far-off fence that bounded the estate .... .

Occasionally, when the sun had gone down, when the clouds were apocalyptic, when the chestnuts were glowing like bronze, and when our match had come to its climax, we should hear the peremptory noise of a distant gong summoning us to supper. My mother had so lively a sympathy with our interests that she restricted us as little as possible. Presumably she hoped that we should wash our hands, but she permitted us to sit down in our flannels, just as we were. After supper we would break up into groups. My brother and a girl-visitor would play, perhaps a sonata for violin and piano: and most of the household remained in the music-room to hear it. A few might wander about the dusky garden, or attempt a game of croquet by starlight: indicating the hoops by holding hand-kerchiefs above them.[16]

That circle, of the children of relatives and family friends with whom the brothers grew up, also strongly influenced the way they developed. It was a closed group with whom they associated. Until they went, in their late teens, to college in London, these were al-most the only contemporaries they knew. They were very fortunate in their domestic circumstances and this childhood at Ivy Bank was almost continuously a happy one. Families with whom they associated included the Lowes (Rudolph Lowe played cricket with them for many years); the Angoves (Mr Angove became Alfred Bax's secretary, and Ivy Angove, three years Arnold's junior, was a brilliant young violinist and Evelyn's greatest friend; Arnold was never much attracted to her but Clifford once imagined himself in love with her); the Rueggs (three sisters, beautiful little girls, who were brought up by a governess, and were always at Ivy Bank Christmas parties; their father, who was not English, was a banker); and the Lees (Gladys Lees also played the violin, and became very closely involved with Arnold a few years later). Uncle Ernest Belfort Bax, ten years younger than Arnold's father, was usually present, and his five children (of whom Elsa died in April 1901 before her twenty-first birthday) would swell any family gathering.

In the summers, extended holidays were enjoyed, and the family would take a house and move *en masse*. In the early spring of 1900 they went to Freshwater, Isle of Wight. They arrived at sunset, as Clifford later remembered, only seeing the wood thick with prim-roses behind the house and the broad sands awaiting their cricket on the morrow. The cricket, however, was not to be the whole matter

of the holiday, for when rain intervened Arnold turned his attention
to his music, and Clifford, leafing through a volume of Keats encountered *Lamia*, and found that within a quarter of an hour the
direction of his life had changed.

A number of songs written in 1900, immediately before Arnold
started at the Royal Academy of Music, are now preserved among
the papers left to the British Museum by Harriet Cohen. They show
a considerable advance over his previous attempts at composition,
and we can see the gathering complexity of the piano parts as his
technique grew. Indeed over-elaborate piano parts mar many of
his early and otherwise successful songs.[17]

There was to be another holiday later that year — with a large
family party in North Wales — before Arnold began his daily trip by
horse-bus to the Royal Academy of Music, for which he had passed
the entrance examination. The summer of 1900 was the brothers'
last together before Arnold's new colleagues from the Academy
brought them new friends and widening horizons.

The Royal Academy of Music

In September 1900 Arnold became a student of the Royal Academy of Music. For a tutor-educated young man this must at first have been much of an adventure and a significant broadening of his experience, even if it did not involve leaving home. The RAM was then still in Tenterden Street, off Oxford Street, and, as Bax later observed in his autobiography, was architecturally a rabbit-warren. 'Somewhere about 1850,' he wrote, 'I suppose, the three eighteenth-century houses which the institution comprised were departitioned, one conjectured with fearsome violence. Even dynamite could be hazarded. Wherefore else the need for those tortuous tunnellings, that labyrinthine intricacy of passages, the cul-de-sacs, and follies? The bewigged and decorous soul of the original designer must surely have writhed in its rococo heaven (or maybe hell) when the fell deed was done. It took the average new student about a month to get his or her bearings.'[1]

The Royal Academy of Music was by far the senior of the main London musical institutions, having been founded in 1822. Sixty years had elapsed before its principal competitor, the Royal College of Music, had been founded in South Kensington, and although negotiations had taken place with the object of uniting the RAM and the RCM they were unsuccessful. By the time Bax attended the Academy the two encompassed marked differences in philosophy, which distantly reflected the very real musical conflict that had been fought on the Continent twenty years before between the partisans of Brahms and those of Wagner. At the College, composition was taught under the gimlet eye of Stanford, reflecting the Brahmsian approach. The Academy tended to be freer and more Wagner-orientated. Yet we do well to remember the influence of Liszt in both College and Academy circles. Calum MacDonald has reminded us of the otherwise unremarked influence of Liszt on the works of Parry,[2] while Bax's composition teacher, Frederick Corder, was the author of one of the first English-language studies of Liszt;[3] and of course through Corder the influence was felt by Bax and his fellow students. Sir Alexander Mackenzie, the principal of the Royal Academy of Music in Bax's day, had known Liszt personally, and during Bax's second winter as a student Frederick Corder's arrangement of Liszt's *Orpheus* for organ, strings and harp, was given a noted performance.

Another influence on the students at both institutions, also unremarked, was that of Tchaikovsky and Glazounov. This can be seen reflected in the piano music that was soon beginning to be written by Bax and his contemporaries.

Bax found himself starting at the Academy on the same day as Benjamin Dale. Dale quickly established himself as a precocious young composer, and his once celebrated Suite for viola is particularly interesting, in that the *Romance* from it starts in a style that foreshadows Bax's Sonata of a decade and a half later, an idiom that contrasts curiously with its middle-section melody which looks back to the Raff-dominated sentimental melody of their Academy principal Mackenzie's *Benedictus*, of twenty years earlier. Dale was celebrated in 1905 – the year in which Bax left the Academy – for his large-scale and assured Piano Sonata; a sonata, what is more, that was one of the *raisons d'être* for the foundation of a co-operative publishing scheme, from which Bax was also to profit, a few years later (see p. 37). History has not been kind to Dale, and his work has not received its due. As well as music for viola and for piano he also wrote a short choral work, *Before the Paling of the Stars*, which was once widely sung. His most extended orchestral composition, a tone-poem called *The Flowing Tide*, has only once been played – during the Second World War.[4] He eventually became Warden of the Academy. Once or twice Dale joined Arnold, his brother and their friends at cricket on the lawn at Ivy Bank.

Although Dale's fine Piano Sonata achieved an early familiarity among followers of the then new in music, by the mid-1920s its charms had begun to appear faded. At that time Clifford Bax wrote how 'years may have outmoded its manner, but, in my lay judgement, it is so vibrant with the Arcadian romanticism of early youth that it may well last as long as *Endymion*. Indeed, if any one who is now eighteen were to ask how we at the same age felt toward life, I should willingly let that Sonata stand for my answer.'[5] Today we are at sufficient a distance from its period for it to be enthusiastically received again by audiences and pianists alike.

Bax and Dale found themselves fellow composition students of Frederick Corder, with many others who later achieved considerable reputations as composers. They included Montague Phillips, Harry Farjeon and York Bowen. Paul Corder, the son of their teacher, was also a student, and remained a good friend to Bax until his premature death in 1942. W.H. Reed (later a celebrated violinist) had been a composition student of Corder, and Eric Coates studied under him shortly after Bax left the Academy.

During Bax's time, Myra Hess and Irene Scharrer, both to become famous pianists, arrived to study with Tobias Matthay, who also taught Bax. Bax remembered them as very small, eternally giggling girls. As early as November 1901 Scharrer appeared in an Academy concert at St James's Hall, playing Chopin's *Rondo in E♭*, Op. 16.

While Bax's musicality was certainly never in doubt, he had found himself in very talented circles, where young composers like Benjamin Dale already had real achievement to their credit, which Bax had not. An even more brilliant talent was a young man a year Bax's junior who had already made a reputation both as composer and performer. This was York Bowen, whose string of prizes and scholarships, coupled with public performances of several ambitious works while he was still in his teens, secured him gushing publicity in the musical columns of the society papers. A symphony, a piano concerto in E♭, and a tone poem — *Lament of Tasso* — were all heard, the latter at the 'Proms', before Bowen was twenty. Two more piano concertos and a second symphony quickly followed, although it was to be nearly forty years before Bowen wrote his delightful Third Symphony. Composed in 1951, it was not heard until 1954, after Bax's death. An unperformed fourth symphony is lost. There was also a Fourth Piano Concerto. Bowen was soloist at Queen's Hall in Mackenzie's *Scottish* Piano Concerto in October 1904 during that year's Proms. Although Bax was soon noted for his sight-reading skills at the piano (see Bowen's comments on Bax, pp. 33–4), and for what then appeared to be his advanced compositional style (Parry referred to Bax's early songs as sounding like 'a bevy of little devils'),[6] he did not then seek public performance, and so was a long time in demonstrating his talent to a wider public.

Having arrived at the Academy Bax was stimulated to write a string of youthful works. The earliest extant piece to date from his

Academy period is the 'Fantasia in A minor' for two pianos, dated 28 October. It shows the young composer's immediate realization of the possibilities of this hitherto unfamiliar medium. The day after finishing the Fantasia he started a March which was completed, for piano, by 3 November. It is interesting that the young Bax should conceive of a concert March a year before Elgar created a vogue for such things with his *Pomp and Circumstance*, though admittedly it was three years after the success of Elgar's *Imperial March*. Bax's was a funeral march, written in memory of Tchaikovsky, and quotes from the *1812 Overture.*

Although Frederick Corder was highly thought of by many commentators at the time, conventional wisdom would now have it that his liberal attitude was, as is so often the case, but a recipe for sloppiness on the part of many of his pupils. They achieved some short-term notoriety, but appear to have lacked the staying-power and technique of their more rigorously trained contemporaries at the Royal College. At the time it appeared differently. Writing in 1912, Raymond Tobin sang the praises of Corder's major pupils in extravagant terms:

Perhaps when we have examined or listened to the works of Granville Bantock, Hubert Bath, Paul Corder, York Bowen, W.H. Bell, A. von Ahn Carse, Arthur Hinton, Benjamin J. Dale and Joseph Holbrooke we have mentally decided that these composers were all, more or less, especially gifted and naturally endowed with remarkable powers; and of course to a certain extent that must be granted. But these men, who seem to embody the hope and glory of our present English school of composition, received their instruction in the art of composition from Mr Frederick Corder, Professor and Curator of the Royal Academy of Music: we then realise that there must be something more than natural aptitude to account for their achievements. It is in fact an unique and all-sufficing testimony to the excellence of the teaching methods of their master; a result of which we must all be exceedingly proud.[7]

Of note is Tobin's exclusion, in 1912, of Bax, who was just beginning to make an impact as a widely-known figure. Yet all these composers are now forgotten (with the exception of several works of Bantock) and totally unplayed. In several cases so complete has been the eclipse that even the manuscripts and orchestral materials have been lost, rendering performance impossible. In one or two cases there are certainly particular works by these composers that should be revived, and they may yet maintain a small niche in the more specialized repertoire of individual instruments, but whether to have hailed them as 'the glory' of English music was a mistake or not, must await further investigation. Corder's orchestral music itself, mainly influenced by middle-period Wagner, Dvořák and other continental models, was not only derivative but not even good of its type. The writing tended to be episodic and its composer was content to illustrate as he went along. Typical in this respect is the overture *Prospero*, the only piece by Corder to have been recorded (by Henry Wood in 78 rpm days). The dim recording exemplifies the faults implied by this account of Corder written by a pupil, Arthur Alexander.

This very unconventional pedagogue, looking not unlike a Chinese mandarin, a fanatical Wagnerite (with his wife he had translated the opera libretti into mostly execrable English, some of the worst lines of which Arnold delighted in quoting), was quite without system in his teaching methods. One might take along a harmony exercise to one lesson; a piece of orchestration or a fair sized chunk of composition to the next and nothing at all to the one after, when, after a prolonged sigh, he would produce the inevitable Dvořák duet — and that was that. Yet in spite of this kind of thing, one learnt much, although it must be confessed that very few of his pupils acquired a really first-class technique.[8] His musical taste, alas, was not of a very high order, and should one get stuck in a composition, the almost inevitable recipe for its continuation was a long and slowly ascending series of Wagnerian sequences. Brahms was his *bête-noire* — perhaps because his opposite number at the Royal College (Stanford) was a whole-hearted Brahmsian. Nevertheless I recall Corder's delight in the opening bar or two of the Brahms Fourth Symphony (the D and C naturals took his fancy) and in just eight bars in the Finale of the Second Piano Concerto.[9]

The publisher Joseph Williams brought out a set of piano pieces by Corder which could be accompanied by Czerny's *School of Velocity* played on a second piano. This appears to have been a typical Corder method, for York Bowen wrote a second piano part to accompany Beethoven's *32 Variations.*

Alexander's opinion that Corder 'influenced Bax much less than any of his pupils' is probably true. Yet a glance at the various books Corder published on the art of composition show that he approached his task in a practical way. 'The student finds the idiom of the past irksome and repellent,' he wrote, 'it is the vernacular he desires to learn'.[10] And in one respect at least Bax himself might have echoed Corder's words: 'Beauty is our one aim: purely scientific compositions — the Fugue, the Canon, the Motet and the Madrigal — no longer appeal to the modern mind, and the goal of our ambition is the orchestral tone-poem ... but ... there is a technique for everything ... and no amount of "inspiration" or mental fine frenzy can obviate the necessity of learning how to handle the tools of one's trade, or employ the resources of one's art.'[11] Although demonstrating a natural flair in the matter of orchestration, Bax for long remained a novice. Corder's thorough way of dealing with the practicalities of this important skill must have long placed Bax in his debt. In particular Corder did not ignore the then more obscure extras such as cornet, celesta and exotic percussion.[12] Yet in a letter to Edward J. Dent, written in the early 1920s, Bax said of his old master:

I think you are a little hard on poor old Corder, who really had no sympathy with ... vague rhapsodising. As a matter of fact he was of course an arch-Wagnerian and anti-Brahmsite and had very little sense of symphonic form, and it seems to me — none of orchestration (strange in a Wagnerian). But his faults were all negative, and attributable to a rather disorderly romantic temperament — not to any evil convictions.'[13]

Nor in his memoirs was Bax kind in his remarks about his piano teacher, Matthay, and yet he owed him a lot (and elsewhere wrote of him with affection), although Arthur Alexander tells us that 'no pupil could have been so un-Matthay-like in his approach to the keyboard and in his playing'. Tobias Matthay exercised an enormous influence both on the piano technique of his students and also on the composition students. Alexander has published a vivid vignette of Matthay as Bax would have known him:

Taking one of London's last horse buses from Westbourne Grove to Finchley Road, I climbed up the steep incline of Arkwright Road to his house, and rang the bell. From within came an unearthly clanking. This was followed by a slow and mysterious opening of the door — but there was no one to be seen. I was terrified. At last a pupil appeared and said: Mr Matthay says you are to come in. I did so. It was then that I noticed a peculiar wire contraption, and a few cocoa tins along the wall. By the piano, close to this wall, was a heavy lever that set wire and cocoa tins in motion. This was Uncle Tobs's contrivance to spare the old servant in the basement the trouble of coming upstairs.
    Matthay was tall, but very stooping — his arms were long and he had enormous hands. His bald and quite flat head was fringed at the back with long — and for many years — light-coloured hair. His complexion was youthful and healthy, and it seemed that only his chin ever required shaving. He wore a moustache and glasses (he was very short-sighted). His brown velvet coat, oatmeal tweed trousers and Harris tweed overcoat were particularly noticeable in the days when professors wore frock coats and silk hats. (My composition professor Frederick Corder relaxed a little in the summer — *he* wore a dingy straw boater with *his* frock coat.) Matthay's expression was that of a kindly German professor of the old school. His movements were quick and shuffling — his entry into a room blowing kisses, was *allegro agitato murmurando*. In cold weather he wore an overcoat as a rug when the rug was not handy, and on his hands, mittens. After my first visit, I told my mother that not only was he mad, but that he was shaky and frail, that it was unlikely that he would last more than a month or two. In actual fact he enjoyed almost perfect health for another

thirty-five or forty years. His strange husky voice was unforgettable. From a long series of buzzing sounds (*legatissimo*), accented words stood out here and there. At first (hence my comment above), I could understand almost nothing, however, once accustomed to those strange mumblings, I found them both expressive and helpful. Uncle Tobs was capable of the amazing feat of giving a whole lesson without the use of a single intelligible word.

His greeting and farewell took the form of a brushing glissando kiss. I well recall my embarrassment at being kissed in Oxford Street at a busy time of the day, and worse, the terrible occasion when he rushed on to the platform of the Queen's Hall and embraced me as I left after playing *The Emperor*. And I remember 'V.W.' telling me with amused horror, that he was once kissed by Uncle Tobs! I should like to have seen that.

Matthay's patience and kindness were inexhaustible, and his explanations of musical and technical problems could not have been more lucid (so unlike some of his books).[14]

What Bax obtained through his masters, in particular Corder, and which was of greatest value to him, was a sympathetic environment, talented musical friends of his own age, and the companionship of established figures on the musical scene who gave him an entrée for his own work. Otherwise he developed on his own, using this growing band of contacts when necessary. He quickly achieved an enviable piano technique, and for quite some time before the First World War was regarded in some quarters as the best sight-reader in the country. In March 1903, Bax and York Bowen at two pianos accompanied the operatic class in performances of Act I of Gluck's *Orfeo* and Acts I and II of *Der Freischütz*. In July of the same year Bax accompanied performances of the third act of *Orfeo* and the second of *L'Amico Fritz*, and the *RAM Club Magazine* found he 'succeeded in imparting to his playing a broad orchestral style which assumed very well in the absence of a band'.[15]

Rather more laboriously, he emerged as a composer with an individual mastery of the orchestra. Yet he was in many ways a dilettante. He always had the firm bedrock of absolute financial security, and only wrote or played while the passion for music was on him. After he discovered Ireland in 1902 he travelled or devoted himself to literature as the whim took him. It was surely Corder's example, too, which discouraged Bax from teaching: he just did not know how to give an effective lesson, and when all his colleagues, in their turn, became teachers to earn their living, Bax was enjoying the easy life of the wealthy middle class to which he belonged.

Arnold had always been a somewhat delicate child, suffering from a heart murmur which ultimately (some fifty years later) may have contributed to his death. In 1901 the family went for the summer to Malvern, where a momentary panic was caused when a local 'quack' diagnosed Arnold's condition as advanced and terminal heart disease. Though Bax could laugh about it in his autobiography, one can well understand his parents' motivation in visiting a spa, and endeavouring to ensure their brilliant though wayward son his life and health, after their trauma with Aubrey only five years before.

This holiday was also the occasion of Bax's celebrated meeting with Elgar. At the Academy he had become friendly with a horn player, George Alder, who lived nearby and was long acquainted with the composer. During August, Bax saw much of his new friend and later wrote that

one day he perturbed and delighted me with the proposal that we should walk over to Birchwood, the woodland cottage where *Gerontius* had been scored and where the composer was still living, and pay him a visit. We set out on a sultry afternoon, our heads in a cloud of gnats which we tried to disperse by energetic smoking, and as we approached the unpretentious but charming cottage I almost regretted my temerity in coming. My tongue and throat were dry and my heart a-flutter with nervousness, which was part allayed and part aggravated when we were told by a maid that Mr Elgar was at present out somewhere in the woods. But he would be back at tea-time or soon after, and meanwhile would we sit in the garden where the mistress would join us at once?

The composer's wife, a pleasant-looking fair-haired lady, with – it struck me – rather an anxious manner, welcomed us very kindly in her gentle, slightly hesitant voice. Almost at once she began to speak enthusiastically and a little extravagantly about her wonderful husband and his work.

'Oh, here he is!' cried Mrs Elgar, and I rose and turned with suddenly thudding heart to be introduced to the great man. Hatless, dressed in rough tweeds and riding boots, his appearance was rather that of a retired army officer turned gentleman farmer than an eminent and almost morbidly highly strung artist. One almost expected him to sling a gun from his back and drop a brace of pheasants to the ground.

Refusing tea and sinking to a chair he lay back, his thin legs sprawling straight out before him, whilst he filled and lit a huge briar, his rather closely set eyes meanwhile blinking absently at us. He was not a big man, but such was the dominance of his personality that I always had the impression that he was twice as large as life. That afternoon he was very pleasant and even communicative in his rumbling voice, yet there was ever a faint sense of detachment, a hint – very slight – of hauteur and reserve. He was still sore over the *Gerontius* fiasco at Birmingham in the previous autumn, and enlarged interestingly upon the subject. 'The fact is,' he said, 'neither the choir nor Richter knew the score.' 'But I thought the critics said ...' I started to interpose. 'Critics!' snapped the composer with ferocity. 'My dear boy, what do the critics know about anything?'

Knocking out his pipe, he suggested that we might like to have a glance at a huge kite that he had recently constructed.[16]

In late August and September the family again went to North Wales, the last holiday they all enjoyed together. While there Arnold wrote the first movement of a Piano Trio in B♭ minor. This *Allegro Appassionata* [sic] is in ternary form with a slow — *molto più lento* — middle section. The title-page of the manuscript lists three succeeding movements: *Scherzo, Elegy* and *Allegro Vivace*, although these have not come to light and may possibly never have been written.

Thus he entered the second year of his career at the Academy. The autumn saw renewed application to composition, which, while still clearly student work, was beginning to achieve some individuality. In the output of a young composer we may differentiate between three stages. First, the projected major work, which, although conceptualized, fails to materialize on paper in the way intended and dries up or is superseded by another. Second, a completed score, which is probably played through within the student's circle, giving confidence because it is finished and heard, but which is no doubt quickly recognized as jejune and naive, and leads the composer on to further work. Finally, the completed music which, no matter how derivative it may be, is all of a piece, a finished and viable work of art. It took Bax a long time to get beyond the second of these stages, which is particularly exemplified in two works written in the autumn term of 1901. These were a violin sonata dated 'November', which was played in the family circle, and a set of *Songs of the Four Seasons*.

On 21 October, two days after their successful première in Liverpool, the first two of Elgar's *Pomp and Circumstance* Marches were given at Queen's Hall under Henry Wood's baton. This was a 'memorable evening' that Bax often recalled with apparent affection. He wrote: 'The hall was inspissated (a word at one time dear to musical critics and ever associated with "gloom") by one of London's most masterly fogs. The contrast between those slowly shifting nebulous veils choking the audience and the blare and glare of Elgarian brass was never to be forgotten. The famous and now much debated tune was greeted by thunders of applause.'[17]

Bax continued to write music and very gradually began to find a way forward. On 21 February he finished — in piano score — a *Love-Song for Orchestra* which, though never orchestrated, demonstrated a personality beginning to emerge. His harmony was becoming more confident, and moving away from the simple octaves and triads in the left hand that characterized much of the very early writing.

The growing contrapuntal and harmonic complexity of his piano
writing was a direct measure of his progress both as composer and
pianist, a trait which, by the time he left the Academy, had become
in many ways a handicap to be consciously overcome. Possibly the
Love-Song was the outcome of a youthful passion such as Bax has
described.

And the lovely, bewitching entanglement of sex! It was all about us. Its unseen
meshes were electric in the air through which we moved. I don't suppose there
was any student who did not love, sentimentalize over, or lust after someone
else in the place, and the accidental contact with the knee or shoulder of the
girl of one's own (or even of some other's) choice would set live fire jetting
through one's whole body. This it is to be young and still virginal.

No more than the next lad did I escape, nor did I wish to do so.

I found her almost at once amongst the second violins in the orchestra,
sitting next to the aged and peering Polish professor with the unpronounceable
name. Instantly I was enslaved. Every Tuesday and Friday rehearsal I would
make, rather shamefacedly, for the same seat in the hall immediately below
her and watch her every glance and movement. I never thought of speaking to
her or seeking for an introduction. I was too shy for that. Enough for me that
when she was there those drear autumn days would turn to spring, whilst her
absence made black midwinter shroud my heart.

And then, sitting in my usual place in the hall a little before the end of term,
I started with furiously beating heart, for amazingly her eyes and mouth were
smiling down at me over the bridge of her fiddle — requital for my weeks of
silent but, I suppose, obvious adoration. So it began, and at home that evening
my lonely bedroom faded out and I wandered dizzily on the floors of heaven.[18]

One is certain that Bax had countless college romances during the
five years of his formal musical education, and indeed a few very
flowery adolescent letters have survived, written by Bax under the
pseudonym 'Dermid'. But his most serious attachment while at the
Academy was to Gladys Lees, a student violinist who, with her
family, was already a frequent visitor at Ivy Bank. His relationship
with her eventually developed into his first serious love affair.

Much of 1902 was devoted to writing a lengthy String Quartet
in A major. When the work had been forgotten and Bax had achieved
some reputation as a composer, legends persisted in Academy circles
of an 'unplayable' quartet he had written as a student. However,
the manuscript survives, and the work, while difficult and perhaps
uncharacteristic of the later Bax, is by no means unplayable.
Indeed the slow movement was successfully performed at an
Academy student concert on 23 November 1903. The *RAM Club
Magazine* reported it 'a composition of considerable merit'.[19] This

work (*Allegro con fuoco ma moderato in tempo* — *Andante con moto e cantabile* — *Scherzo finale*) is notable for its three-movement form. At the beginning of the last movement Bax has indicated that 'this movement is intended to serve both as Scherzo and Finale so that the Quartet will consist of three movements instead of the customary four'. Thus in his first completed full-length work Bax had already set the formal pattern of the future development of his music in the symphonies. The music just pre-dates his discovery of things Irish, and bears a quotation from Shelley's *Ode to the West Wind:*

> Be thou, Spirit fierce,
> My spirit! Be thou me, impetuous one!

Sometime during the Spring of 1902, Bax happened upon the poetry of W.B. Yeats. Opening a volume of poetry during a dull afternoon he read:

> Sad to remember, sick with years,
> The swift innumerable spears,
> The horsemen with their floating hair,
> And bowls of barley, honey and wine,
> And feet of maidens dancing in tune,
> And the white body that lay by mine.

It is not difficult to appreciate what young men found so heady about Yeats's early poetry, in a world whose innocence the First World War was yet to shatter. Clifford Bax has recalled that Yeats's example 'was far stronger than we realised. For a few years Ireland swept the board. No poet was much praised in the press if he did not write of Cuchulain or the fairies.' The Irish influence was an important but passing one on Clifford, but for his brother it engendered a lifelong vision of ecstasy which never failed him. In a broadcast talk in 1949, he made the incredible statement that 'Yeats's poetry means more to me than all the music of the centuries'.[20]

It was *The Wanderings of Oisin* that he was reading that day in 1902, and the discovery of Yeats was followed by visits to Ireland. Those first trips to Ireland were made in the company of his brother and, later, his sister. Quite when he went on his own is not known, but it was while he was still at the Academy. He describes this journey of discovery as might a convert encompassing a new and all-embracing religion. It was the wildest part of Ireland that he visited 'in great spiritual excitement'. Once there, he later recalled, his 'existence was at first so utterly unrelated to material actualities' that he found it difficult to remember it in any clarity. 'I do not think I saw the men and women passing me on the road as real figures of flesh and blood; I looked through them back to their archetypes, and even Dublin itself seemed peopled by gods and heroic shapes from the dim past. I spent most of my time in the west, always seeking out the most remote places I could find on the map, lost corners of mountains, shores unvisited by any tourist and by few even of the Irish themselves.'[21]

In a letter written to a girl-friend in 1903 or 1904 from the Glencolumcille Hotel, Carrick, Co. Donegal, Bax wrote of the Ireland that 'as usual is all so heart rending and so beautiful, and she seems more like a living being to me than ever ... I bury my face in the grass and dream fiercely in the dear brown earth ... What of Irish Dermid [i.e. Bax himself] and his homeland ... I wonder if I should seem the same through the peat smoke and blue mists of Eire. This is the real Dermid at any rate and the English edition is only a reprint somewhat soiled and very much foxed.'[22]

At the beginning of the century the far west of Ireland was already established as a tourist attraction, though the lack of high-class facilities, particularly in Donegal to which Bax went, meant that some parts were little known and therefore very wild and cut off. The Donegal Railway Company was so poor that it had 'no spare capital or profits to divert to the building or supporting of hotels, much though they might be needed to augment traffic.'[23] The young Baxes did, of course, travel by rail, where it was available, but much of their touring would have been by bicycle.

One well-established, and by the standards of those times, expensive hotel Bax came to love was south of Donegal. He wrote how he spent

many April weeks over a stretch of years at Renvyle House, at the south-western corner of lovely Killary, the ancestral home of the Blakes, one of the Twelve Tribes of Galway. The last remnants of this immemorial clan, finding themselves like so many ancient Irish families in much reduced circumstances, had years ago turned the place into a hotel – of sorts. And a bizarre enough hostelry it was! The house was very old, standing in a neglected demesne and surrounded by tall trees, raucously clamant all day with the voices of tumbling and volplaning rooks. Beneath the trees was a glory of daffodils curtseying to the winds of spring, the only season of the year in which I ever visited Renvyle.[24]

After the Blake family left Renvyle House it belonged to Oliver St John Gogarty, the writer-surgeon and politician, who described it

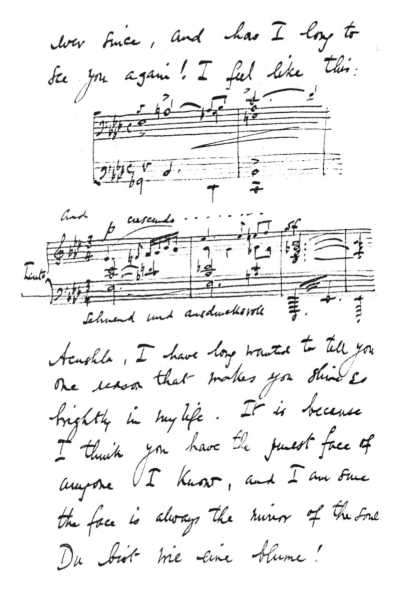

ever since, and how I long to see you again! I feel like this:

And crescendo ... sf

Sehnend und ausdrucksvoll

Acushla, I have long wanted to tell you the reason that makes you shine so brightly in my life. It is because I think you have the purest face of anyone I know, and I am sure the face is always the mirror of the soul Du bist wie eine blume!

Fig. 1 A typical page from a letter written by Bax to an Academy girl-friend (ca 1903–4). The second musical quotation is of particular interest as it is the same as the opening of *In the Hills of Home* (or *Irish Landscape*) from the Four Orchestral Sketches, ostensibly composed in 1912–13, though there it is given the time signature $\frac{4}{4}$ and is in E major.

as 'the long, lone house in the ultimate land of the undiscovered
West'. Gogarty went on:

my house, too, stands on a lake, but it also stands on the sea. Water-lilies meet
the golden seaweed. It is as if, in the faery land of Connemara at the extreme
end of Europe, the incongruous flowed together at last; and the sweet and bitter
blended. Behind me, islands and mountainous mainland share in a final recon-
ciliation at this, the world's end ... In the evening the lake will send the westering
sun dancing on the dining-room panels, the oak of which the sun and age have
reddened until it looks like the mahogany of a later day.[25]

Small wonder that Bax was enchanted by the place.

Bax's espousal of things Irish extended to calling himself 'Dermod
McDermott', even in letters, and addressing his lady friends of the
moment as 'Eilidh', 'childeen', 'birdeen', or 'In'Endail', though
these Irishisms rub shoulders with occasional Germanic words, a
favourite in Bax's vocabulary at the time being 'schusüchtig'. Bax
immediately began to attempt to write 'Irish' poems and stories,
the poems particularly under the influence of early Yeats and often
conceived during dreams. In one of his later Irish stories he adopted
an autobiographical tone which must have closely reflected these
early experiences, though one imagines the date to be part of the
fiction:

The other day I was looking through a spasmodic journal that I kept about ten
years ago during a stay in South Connemara. I was just beginning to write at the
time, and the pages of this little book are full of my first faltering and uncertain
attempts to seize some broken echo of the deep and solemn music that Ireland
was pouring into my wakening ears. My boy's mind was like an Aeolian harp,
swept through mightily by all the eight coloured winds of Erin, and giving forth
but a confused and many-toned murmur from amid which it was difficult for my
untrained artistry to call forth a coherent music. My diary of that period is filled
with the beginnings of numberless poems and stories, nearly all of which seem to
have become hopelessly distraught at the end of a page. But, turning over the
leaves of this bewildered phantasmagoria, I found a few notes which recalled to
my memory an incident that at the time made a very deep impression upon me.

The page was dated 'Roscarn, April 16th, 1902', and the sight of these words
evoked at once and with startling vividness the nondescript little room in the
house where I lodged, – the only slated house in the street, – the peculiar tone
of the evening sky, faces long since forgotten in the mists of time, and in fact
almost every circumstance that enshrined that arresting experience.

I suppose that evening I must have become particularly downcast and impatient with the result of some verse that after a day's work appeared ever more
leadenfooted and pallid. At any rate I remember stamping off towards the hotel
in a foolishly reckless mood, my eyes hot and pricking, every nerve tingling, and
my whole being one wicked prayer for any kind of diversion. I knew the hotel
keeper's daughters very well, gentle Gaelic creatures who combined humble

hearts and mediaeval piety with a treasure of local lore and mild scandal that caused them, I believe, an almost physical uneasiness until communicated to some one. Their melodious and vivacious recitals of these domestic sagas always interested me as revelations of the social complexities of a district that at first glance seems like some unhuman lotusland drowsing eternally in a flood of pale jewelled light, and yet on deeper inquiry is shown to be netted in the strands of politics as entangled as those of any great city.[26]

In the last years of his life Bax became very friendly with the young composer Christopher Whelen, who was then assistant conductor at Bournemouth, where a lot of Bax's music was presented. Bax encouraged Whelen to visit Ireland, and, in a letter, reminisced on his own early experiences in the far west: 'There is nothing quite like Connemara and its magical coloured lights. The blue of the Twelve Pins can be completely other worldly. I stayed at Carna very often in my youth — always in the Spring ... and also wrote one of my earliest short stories with the local scene as a background.'

The village of Glencolumcille was soon discovered in West Donegal, and was to be Arnold's spiritual haven for the next thirty years and the fountainhead of much of his music. Its very remoteness must have underlined the attraction of this tiny community, set in a gently sloping valley facing the Atlantic but rising to high and awe-inspiring cliffs of either side. Arnold revelled in the savagery the Atlantic brought to the country of West Donegal. No fair-weather traveller, he found a personal serenity in the fact that wild beauty is rarely comfortable or comforting, and he experienced a fierce exultation in the primitive and untamed which was later to be reflected in his music. He established an enduring and affectionate relationship with the inhabitants of Glencolumcille, many of whom are delightfully drawn in his autobiography,[27] including Paddy John McNelis the publican, seated outside his door upon a pile of empties; the tapping of lame John Gillespie; Cormac Molloy, the weaver; old Peggy, Paddy John's wife, her figure almost as round as she was high; and other wilder characters from the district.

Writing from 'Glen', as the place came to be known to the Baxes, much later in 1929 and 1930, Bax described it as 'primeval' and wrote how 'this place gets all the wind there is ... life is much the same here as it was 100 years ago and there is no civilisation worth speaking of ... all this progress of humanity has not counted for very much'. On another occasion he reported: 'this has been a wild strange day here — wonderful changeful lights — huge cliffs to the North — gentle and innocent people — a great privilege they regard me as one of their own'. This contrasts with a letter written similarly at a later date from the Midland Hotel, Manchester, which he found to be 'really a hellish place — fearful villains everywhere and jazz bands — such horrors. I do so loathe all civilisation'.

Bax quickly came to regard 'Glen' as home and a safe retreat from all the worldly troubles that were to beset him later, finding 'the most amazing peace' there. He placed his story 'Ancient Dominions' in Glencolumcille itself, and also vividly encapsulated its magic in another, 'The Servant of the Bishop', which opens with an affectionate evocation of the place doubtless written while he was actually staying there.

The long-lingering wistful dream of the Northern Twilight had at last faded before the approach of the solemn and vibrant midsummer night. The scraig to the north-west still lifted a throbbing outline against the faint red glow that would scarcely die before the opening of the more fiercely kindling eyes of the dawn. For during the month of June there is but little night in Tir-Connaile. Over the sea hung a few immense unblinking stars, censers of peace that seemed to be swinging in an enormous and languid rhythm, spilling their silver smoke of dreams over the seas and hills of Eire. From my door I could see on the wet sand a faint and exquisite line of white fire trailed from the place where Venus was sinking slowly into the impenetrable dove-grey veils heaped above the western ocean.

About two hours before, the fishermen had passed with their lines on their way to the slip at Lug-na-tsruthain, and half-an-hour later two barefooted Doonalt girls, returning home from the shop in Cashel, had gone by, shyly drawing their shawls more closely over their heads as they wished me a soft and serious 'Fine night'.

From where I stood I could dimly perceive several of the boats, each from time to time showing darkly upon the top of some faintly gleaming swell, and instantly disappearing in the shadow behind it, as though swallowed by the sea.

In this hour the materiality of all the familiar features of earth appeared to be dissolved, even their individuality seemed withdrawn. One might fancy that everything glowed darkly with a common inner essence, palpitated with a more mysterious, august and perhaps more terrible life, the shy and incomprehensible excitement that whispers through the summer darkness. It was the hour in which a man may hear the beating of his country's heart, when ancient songs tingle in his ears, when one's feet yearn into the depths of dewy moss, and the whole body thrills almost to the point of pain with the consciousness of what soil is dim and dark and warm beneath one's tread. In such an hour one may scarcely look at a familiar gap in a stone wall without tears.

Such a mood was mine that night as I stood alone at my door, and looking down at the tingling dimness of the strand allowed my heart and will to sink unresisting into the grey and silver veils of woven star and ocean light. Except for the quiet murmur of the tide and the distant creaking cry of a corncrake singing his strange love-song in the long grasses towards Cashel, the profound stillness was absolute.

Tears stood in my eyes, and I turned to enter my cabin, for in a little time Beauty would have become an agony, burning the soul like a searing flame.[28]

The songs of the peasant people made an immediate effect on Bax, although he did not write Irish folksong rhapsodies as such. (But see p. 56.) The, to him, horrific example of Stanford ensured that he would try to absorb the essence of Irish music into his own without merely quoting it. In the late 1930s Bax listened to recordings of Irish folksongs that had been collected in the early years of the century, and he was able to identify not only the singers but also when and where the songs had been collected, a testimony to the impact they had made on him. Bax always stayed in the same pub, having his own room there, and his sister Evelyn later visited the village and recalled that she stayed in 'a little inn there ... It was then isolated, with scattered houses, but a nice strand along the sea.'

Arnold appears to have reconciled his own affluence with the poverty of the peasants and was quickly accepted by his Irish friends. He travelled all over the west coast of Ireland and visited the Aran Islands just after Synge's book of that name had appeared, and the scene would have been as the Irish playwright described it:

The steamer which comes to Aran sails according to the tide, and it was six o'clock this morning when we left the quay of Galway in a dense shroud of mist. In about three hours Aran came in sight. A dreary rock appeared at first sloping up from the sea into the fog; then as we drew nearer, a coastguard station and the village ... I have seen nothing so desolate. Grey floods of water were sweeping everywhere upon the limestone, making at times a wild torrent of the road, which twined continually over low hills and cavities in the rock or passed between a few small fields of potatoes or grass hidden away in corners that had shelter ... It has cleared, and the sun is shining with a luminous warmth that makes the whole island glisten with the splendour of a gem, and fills the sea and sky with a radiance of light ... The women wear red petticoats and jackets of the island wool stained with madder, to which they usually add a plaid shawl twisted round their chests and tied at the back. When it rains they throw another petticoat over their heads with the waistband round their faces, or, if they are young, they use a heavy shawl like those worn in Galway ... The men wear three colours: the natural wool, indigo, and a grey flannel ... and seem to wear an infinite number of waist-coats and woollen drawers one over the other ... For men who live in the open air they eat strangely little ... no animal food except a little bacon and salt fish.[29]

Under the influence of Ireland Bax's music immediately found direction. His colleagues and masters at the RAM must have been delighted with the way he suddenly blossomed as a composer during the Academic Year 1902/3. In the song 'The Grand Match' (words

by Moira O'Neill from *Songs of the Glens of Antrim*) for baritone
and piano, dated 29 June 1903, we find a tentative, superficial
'Irishry' developing. It was sung by a fellow student, George Clowser,
at a concert in St James's Hall on 23 July and was Bax's first public
performance. The work is quite successful with its jig-like rhythms
and impetuous vocal line, and among the best he had written up till
then.

One strong personality with whom Bax quickly established friendly
relations was the viola player Lionel Tertis. Tertis was seven years
Bax's senior and had joined the staff of the Academy in Michaelmas
Term 1901 as Professor of the viola. Tertis's life-work in championing
the viola and its repertoire is well-known. He badgered the young
composers of his time to write for the instrument, and a number of
them obliged, including York Bowen, Adam Carse, Benjamin Dale,
J. B. McEwen, Waldo Warner, W. H. Bell (who had been appointed to
the Academy staff in 1903) and others. By then Tertis was principal
viola of the Queen's Hall orchestra and was actually able to arrange
for performance of the works written for him. So, with the prospect
of a hearing, the young composers were doubly encouraged to write
for the instrument.

In the spring of 1904, under the influence of Tertis, Bax wrote a
work for viola and piano that at the time was considered revolutionary in Academy circles. After the first performance (in December
1904) at a Patron's Fund concert, *The Musical Standard* critic found
it one of the 'most advanced works in the programme ... Consisting
of one movement only in the usual sonata form, somewhat modified,
it breathes a spirit almost of rebellion and riot throughout its fervid
pages.'[30] In this Concert Piece Bax consciously attempts to absorb
the folk music he had encountered in Ireland, without actually
writing a folksong rhapsody. Throughout the composition free use is
made of the flattened seventh, the falling intervals of the pentatonic
scale, and other features characteristic of Irish folk music. The first
subject group consists of three themes, the third of which Bax himself intended to be an 'unmistakably Irish theme'[31] (Ex. 2). Bax was

Ex. 2

well served by Tertis in this enterprise, and the *RCM Magazine* thought the performance to be the 'finest interpretation of the evening'.[32] Although we would not now regard it as typical of the later Bax, the work could still be an enjoyable addition to the repertoire of its instrument. For its time it was impressive, and indicative of a powerfully developing musical personality.

In the autumn term of 1903 one of the new students at the Academy was Rebecca Clarke, later to be celebrated as a viola player and composer. She was three years Bax's junior and felt herself very much a 'pigtailed nonentity' among the giants, and in her unpublished memoirs vividly records how Bax and his contemporaries appeared to her then.

The bustle of all the students going from class to class, the sounds of the different lessons and rehearsals mingling together, were very exciting. Awestruck, I gazed at composition students whose names were already known to me. They were in person at the fortnightly concerts — Benjamin Dale, York Bowen, and grandest of all, Arnold Bax, resplendent in a pale-greenish suit with a pink carnation in his buttonhole.

The great event of the year at the Academy was the prize-giving. Dressed in white, with the white scarlet ribbon across my breast, I sat on the platform at Queen's Hall with all the others, waiting to be herded past whatever august personage was awarding the medals and prizes. The ironclad rule was that only those who passed the annual examination in Elements of Music were allowed to take an award. The subject was certainly elementary, but it was easy to be tripped up in a viva voce exam by an unexpected question like: 'What key has a flat for leading note?', and the story goes that the great Arnold Bax once flunked his elements and was denied the Certificate of Merit.[33]

Clifford Bax had by this time persuaded his parents that Cambridge was not for him and had entered the Heatherley Art School. Their garden cricket, which until now had formed a continuous summer's background to artistic pursuits, gradually became less important as friend after friend went off to Cambridge, or the Army or, as in the case of a particularly close companion of Arnold, Lynn Hartley, to be 'lost in the labyrinth of the Stock Exchange'.[34]

That autumn Bax was working on another string quartet, this time in E major, an attractive and assured full-length work in three movements. The slow movement (*Adagio ma non troppo*) is headed with a quotation from Yeats (slightly misquoted by Bax):

> Know that I would accounted be
> True brother of that company
> Who sang, to sweeten Ireland's wrong,
> Ballad and story, rann and song.

Thus even a movement from a string quartet was actually a tone poem in Bax's mind, and between December 1903 and July 1905 Bax orchestrated it, giving it the title *Cathaleen-ni-Hoolihan*. (See p. 35.) That quartet movement contains the seeds of many aspects of Bax's later style, but the work appears never to have been heard in public.

In 1904 Mr S. Ernest Palmer (later Sir Ernest, finally Lord Palmer) inaugurated the Patron's Fund. This was an endowment of £20,000 to the Royal College of Music, for the purpose of public rehearsal and performance of promising young composers' work. The music to be played at the first concert – an orchestral one – was chosen as the result of a gargantuan rehearsal session at which Stanford, or the young composers themselves, conducted all or part of some forty-four works. Discussion had obviously taken place on an informal basis between the staffs of the London music academies and colleges, one of whom would have been Bax's composition teacher, Frederick Corder, the professors' various protégés assessed, and possible recent works considered.

On 10 June 1904, Bax had completed his first successful attempt at a really large-scale orchestral work – Variations for Orchestra (Improvisations) – demanding a large, though not excessive, orchestra, and occupying 115 pages. Corder asked Bax to send him the score, and as a result it was included with those works to be run through by the orchestra. Bax's account of the rehearsal, which caused him to resolve never to attempt to conduct an orchestra again (a resolve he never broke), is one of the most celebrated passages in his autobiography:

A letter arrived from the Royal College charging me to present myself there on a certain day ... for the rehearsal of my work.

The day came round (that sort of day always does!) and with it the beginning of a blistering heatwave.

Now, hitherto I had never been near the RCM, and I had no idea of its manners and customs, though I always had a vague notion that it was a more aristocratic and pompous place than our old Academy. Quite likely, baronets and others of high degree abounded there. How, I asked myself, should one be dressed in the presence of Sir Hubert Parry? After careful deliberation I decided to be on the safe side and to array myself in my seldom worn frock-coat and tall hat.

The heat was intense during my journey to Kensington Gore, and I arrived at the intimidating portals of the RCM already perspiring not a little. Shyly entering the concert hall, I started back, appalled at finding the place crammed with students and visitors.

It appeared that I had come in the nick of time, for Sir Charles Stanford approached me at once, and said brusquely, 'So here ye are, you're Bax, aren't you? Well now, ye can go up there and work your wicked will on the orchestra.'

At these dreadful words my knees knocked together and I stammered out in a very small voice, 'But I have never conducted in my life.' 'Never mind that,' retorted the ruthless Stanford. 'You've got to begin some time, my boy. Go on with ye.' There was nothing for it but to obey.

Over-harrowing it would be to resuscitate in any detail the pity and terror of that scene. I would naturally conduct with my left hand, and I probably did so then, but I really don't know, and from these words the perspicacious reader will have aforeseen that in all my life I have never consented to handle the baton again. The embarrassment, the horror I endured on that sweltering afternoon! The orchestra players, I must admit, were stoically long-suffering, and only once did a politely ironic voice query, 'Excuse me, but are you beating in twos or threes?' After some forty-five minutes of mental and physical misery Stanford applied the closure, and I stumbled off the platform, not far from collapse. 'Ye look warm, young man,' observed C.V.S. and taking me aside chatted very amiably for some time, incidentally giving me no doubt excellent advice on the subject of conductor's technique. But I remember nothing of that discourse, nor would it have served me in after life, for as I have said, in that hour I made my firm resolve, 'Never again!' To crown all I had donned the detested garb of bourgeois respectability to no purpose except to make myself almost as hot and uncomfortable as I have ever been in all my days. For Parry was not there.[35]

Needless to say, the final public concert did not include Bax's work, though it had won the RAM's composition prize, the Charles Lucas medal. The score has not been heard since, though the manuscript survives.

We have already noted the second Patron's Fund concert, a chamber concert given at the Aeolian Hall on 6 December, for it included the Viola Concert Piece already discussed, as well as the 'delightful' Preludes for piano by Bax's friend Paul Corder. The autumn of 1904 was something of a high spot, for another work written during the summer of that year, *A Celtic Song Cycle*, had been partly performed at a RAM students' concert, on 21 November at Queen's Hall, by a fellow student, Ethel Lister. This cycle of five songs was criticized at the time for being Debussyesque (before, Bax claimed, he had heard a note of that composer), and later for the over-complexity of the piano parts. Certainly it is indicative of Bax's growing mastery.

The cycle comprised settings of poems by 'Fiona Macleod' — the pseudonym of William Sharp, whom Bax got to know through Sharp's wife, a friend of Mrs Matthay. The five poems Bax chose are: (i) 'Eilidh my Fawn' (*Allegretto impetuoso*), (ii) 'Closing Doors' (*At a slow swinging pace*), (iii) 'Thy Dark Eyes to Mine' (*Allegro appassionato*), (iv) 'A Celtic Lullaby' (*Andante con moto*), (v) 'At the Last' (*Lento*). The prevailing tempo marking for each song is given, so that the reader may understand the pacing of the cycle in the absence of performance. It should perhaps be added that the second song ends with a page and a half of *agitato*. We cannot know how well the work was performed at that concert save to say that one critic noted the performer was 'another of excellent vocal ability, who gave much pleasure by her rendering'.[36] The songs performed were the first, the second and the last, which prompted the same critic to complain of their lugubrious character and remark, 'we have listened to more pleasant themes from the pen of this gentleman'. Certainly the cycle as a whole is worthy to be considered with his later songs and includes some good examples of his work in the medium. In fact it is his earliest single work to have entered the concert repertoire, though no longer sung today.

The settings are remarkably successful, though one can see here the faults that mar many of the other early songs, particularly the over-decoration of the piano parts. However, they do not intrude as much as in works written shortly afterwards. As in later songs, Bax is at his best when his conception is simplest. The texture may be complex but one should not be distracted by it. The best music is to be heard in the first and last two songs. The cumulated effect of the brief grieving 'At the Last', only forty bars in length – in which the whole song is given on the B♭ below middle C rising for the penultimate word to D – is of considerable effect. The other, now less significant, aspect of the work is its dedication to Gladys Lees, whom the family quite expected Arnold to marry when he had finished at college.

However, *A Celtic Song Cycle* has a particular interest to students of Bax, other than for its particular musical beauties. The score was one of his first published works and later, after the First World War, was reissued by J. & W. Chester. For that reissue Bax revised the piano writing by making extensive proof corrections on pulls of the original plates. Those corrected proofs survive[37] and allow us to see how Bax simplified his own piano writing in the light of experience. The amendments, which are extensive, fall into three categories: simplified notation; alteration of the actual notes, retaining the harmonic feel but making the texture lighter and more effective; and rewriting. Typical examples are the alteration, in the twelfth bar of 'Eilidh my Fawn' from Ex. 3a to Ex. 3b; and later in the same song, the right hand of bar 46 (Ex. 4a) became Ex. 4b, thus throwing into relief the high triplets in the bar (bar 47) that follows, making for

Ex. 3a   Ex. 3b

Ex. 4a

Ex. 4b

variety of rhythm and colour. There are very many others but space precludes their discussion here — the interested reader should compare the two editions of the published score, though it should be mentioned that pages 20–27 of the earlier version will be found to be identical in the later.

In 1905 Bax shared the Walter Macfarren Prize for piano playing with another student, Margaret Bennett. He had already been awarded, in addition to the Charles Lucas Medal, in January 1903 the Battison Haynes Prize and a Macfarren Scholarship. His college friend and contemporary, York Bowen, wrote about him in a vein which was repeated by other commentators at different periods of his life.

While still a student, he showed a most remarkable gift and avidity for reading at sight, and after a time there was no one who could touch him in this way. I well remember entering for some prize at the RAM where the requirements were the playing and interpretation of a long slow movement of a Beethoven Sonata plus a sight-reading test. When I found that Bax had also entered for this, I nearly withdrew my name, thinking that his marvellous sight-reading would give me no chance whatever. However, as it happened, the reading test was reasonable enough in difficulty and I did manage to win the prize. It was almost magical to hear Bax trying over something like a piano quintet from a small score and being able to read all the staves at once and giving a remarkably good idea of it at sight, even if it were a modern and complicated work. The other unmistakable sign of his growing creative gift was his power of extemporization, altogether beyond anything I have ever heard since at the piano keyboard. He took little interest in developing his piano technique and gradually dropped it.[38]

In fact the composer George Lloyd tells a revealing anecdote about Bax in this respect, told him by Bax's friend Harry Farjeon. Bax went in for a score reading competition — playing full scores at the piano — but he did not win because at some critical point he doubled the tempo and read the music at twice the correct speed. However, so good was his actual playing that a special consolation prize was awarded.

For his achievements both as pianist and composer, Bax was 'much beloved and appreciated by Matthay',[39] though his technique was far from reflecting Matthay's method. 'He sat very high with his wrists raised and his fingers invariably straight. Bax's playing always sounded orchestral, and he got around — though stiffly — in an amazingly nimble fashion.'[40]

He loved piano improvisation, and we may catch a glimpse of his improvisational style in a work for voice and two pianos that he wrote at the beginning of 1905. Originally written for voice with one piano, the writing was so complex it proved unplayable and had to be recast for the two keyboards. In its headlong cascade of notes one may imagine Bax and, who knows, York Bowen or Paul Corder at two pianos, running through the work with a student singer. This work is a William Morris setting, *From the Uplands to the Sea.* A long programmatic prelude for the two pianos contained many hints of his later style but was rather too superficially chromatic in places for the mature Bax to own.

There is some confusion over Bax's orchestral works at the end of his time at the Academy or just after. Of these, two scores survive: the string quartet movement that became *Cathaleen-ni-Hoolihan* for small orchestra (dated 'Dec. 1903 — July 1905') and *A Song of War and Victory* for full orchestra (dated '1905'). There are no contemporary critical notices of either of these although there are of two other orchestral works, *A Connemara Revel* and an *Irish Overture*, neither of which appear to have survived. In a list compiled in 1907 (see p. 38) they were all catalogued with the exception of *A Connemara Revel*, which would appear to indicate that perhaps this work was, in fact, one of the others in disguise. This possibility is strengthened by the fact that a performance of the *Irish Overture* in 1906 was probably not its first, and *A Connemara Revel* is the only one to have been played previously. It was included in a student concert at

Queen's Hall in April 1905, under the baton of the Principal, Sir Alexander Mackenzie, and was well received, *The Musical Times* describing it as 'a neatly written overture',[41] while the *RAM Club Magazine* noted that it 'consisted of the adaptation of Irish airs'.[42]

Ex. 5a

However, it is *Cathaleen* that is of particular interest, containing seeds of Bax's mature style with traits that later may be traced in *In the Faery Hills* (1909), *Tintagel* (1917–19) and the Third Symphony (1928–29). As we have seen (see p. 30), *Cathaleen* in its original string quartet form was Bax's first extended reaction to his newly discovered Ireland, and the orchestral score (which was not played until 1970) bears the same quotation from Yeats. The work succeeds by its simplicity, the uncomplicated ternary form and the restrained orchestration. And yet the score is astonishingly mature, particularly in the way orchestral colour is applied. The climactic passage (in Ex. 5a), for example, eleven pages from the end, in its use of ostinati sounding simultaneously and in its sure orchestral placing, exhibits much of the mature Bax. (The original string quartet is given in Ex. 5b.)

Ex. 5b

In the summer of 1905, Bax gave up the Macfarren composition scholarship before it had run its course; most of his friends had already left the Academy and he was restless and wanted freedom. His father, in common with other well-to-do parents of talented sons, reimbursed the Academy the 100 guineas studentship he had held.[43] Bax was now to spend 'more and more time alone in places lorded by the Atlantic and the dream-light of old tradition'.[44] It was to Ireland now that he turned, and from Ireland that he was to forge his mature style.

Many influences

As we have seen, during the period in which Arnold Bax was at the Royal Academy of Music an unprecedented number of young composers appeared on the British musical scene. As a result of this it was felt in certain optimistic quarters that perhaps a new school of composers was being born. The machinery for promoting, publishing and performing such composers was at that time almost non-existent and consequently the Society of British Composers came into being.

The Society was a co-operative effort, but the influence of Matthay and Corder was there behind its inception, and Corder became chairman. Its most valuable achievement was a publishing scheme which resulted in a good selection of piano music, songs and chamber works being issued. Publication was under the imprint 'Charles Avison Ltd', selling through and being printed by Breitkopf and Härtel. Later the imprint changed to Cary, and finally to Novello. Bax had several works published in this way. *A Celtic Song Cycle* and some separate songs appeared in 1906, the Trio in One Movement and the vocal score of a choral work called *Fatherland* in 1907. The movement emanated chiefly from Academy student circles once the professors had given life to the idea, and the leading lights included one of Bax's contemporaries, J. B. McEwen, and Stanley Hawley, an earlier student there. Writing of the Piano Sonata by Benjamin Dale, their mutual teacher Frederick Corder recalled the circumstances of the formation of the Society of British Composers and its publications. The problem that faced Dale in promoting his very substantial work was felt by many of his contemporaries. Corder wrote of the Dale piece:

Written in 1902, whilst its composer was yet a student, its merits were so evident to his fellow-musicians that they felt the imperative necessity of having it published. But how was this to be rendered possible? What publisher in his senses would dream of undertaking as a business proposition the production of a Sonata, let alone one of over sixty pages in length and of extreme difficulty, by a totally unknown writer? Several abortive attempts were made, and at last, owing to the fact that there happened to be quite a group of unusually talented young men just then with works of a similar tendency, the Society of British Composers was formed, with the intention of doing for England what Belaieff had done for Russia — undertaking the publication of high-class music of a non-commercial kind, recognising the fact that the sale of such music could only prove remunerative after a long time, if at all. Of the difficulties of his enterprise it needs not here to speak; suffice it to point out that among the first publications were the Dale Sonata, Paul Corder's Nine Preludes, Swinstead's Prelude in D, Bowen's first Miniature Suite, and Bax's Celtic Songs. All works which were artistically far ahead of any pianoforte music hitherto produced in this country. With the limited resources of such a Society the advertising possibilities could never be adequate for the pushing of these works into the reluctant public mind.[1]

In addition to the publication of the music of the participants and to performances of it (not that Bax benefited under this part of the scheme, for 'he cared not a straw for public performance'),[2] the Society issued their yearbooks. The three that were issued (for 1906/7, 1907/8 and 1912)[3] are particularly valuable for the lists of member composers' works, which occupy most of their bulk. Thus we have a means of knowing what Bax wanted to be judged by at the early turning points in his life — and a way of knowing about works that may have been written but have not survived.

The first of the Bax lists, although dated 1906/7, would appear to have been compiled early in 1906. It is as follows (the sequence is that in the Yearbook):

ORCHESTRAL

Variations on an Original Theme
Cathaleen-ni-Hoolihan. Tone-poem for small orchestra
Irish Overture
A Song of Life and Love.   Tone-poem for full orchestra
A Song of War and Victory.   "   "   "

CHAMBER MUSIC

String Quartet in E major
Concert Piece for viola and pianoforte

SONGS

Five Celtic Songs. Pianoforte accompaniment. (Avison edition)

Two Songs with orchestral accompaniment:
(a) 'The Rune of Age'
(b) 'Viking Battle-song'

Six Songs with pianoforte accompaniment:

1. 'When we are lost'   4. 'Leaves, Shadows, and Dreams'
2. 'Green Branches'   5. 'The Grand Match'
3. 'The Multitudes of the Wind' 6. 'The Fairies'

From the Uplands to the Sea. With accompaniment for two pianos.

Six Songs:

1. 'A Song in the Twilight'   4. 'A Hushing Song'
2. 'Golden Guendolen'   5. 'I fear thy kisses, gentle maiden'
3. 'The Fiddler of Dooney'   6. 'Echo'

The Yearbook for 1907/8 added the following:

TWO RECITATIONS WITH PIANOFORTE ACCOMPANIMENT

1. 'The Blessed Damozel'
2. 'The Twa Corbies'

Trio in one movement for piano, violin and clarinet (or viola)
Phantasie for violin and piano

Of these works, the orchestral *Song of Life and Love*,[4] the orchestral score of the *Two Songs* with orchestra and the *Phantasie* for violin and piano, all appear to be lost. We have already discussed the *Irish Overture*, which is also no longer extant. Bax had obviously weeded out a lot of the early music mentioned in Chapters I and II, which he would by then have regarded as juvenilia.

One of the most important contacts Bax made through the Society was Edwin Evans,[5] later a well-known critic and an influential friend. Evans, himself the son of a famous critic of the same name, was just beginning to establish himself when the Society brought them together. Although Evans' series of articles on Bax did not begin until 1918, and his practical influence had also to wait until about that date, he was to be a wise friend and a contact with the day-to-day musical world while Bax was becoming known. His friendship was later repaid with the dedication of the Piano Quintet of 1914/15.

Theodore Holland, an Academy friend of Bax, introduced the Franco-Greek critic M. D. Calvocoressi to Bax's circle in 1905 or 1906. The Avison edition was the visitor's 'first introduction to the music of Bax, Dale, Bowen and McEwen'.[6] Later, through Edwin Evans, Calvocoressi was responsible for Vaughan Williams studying with Ravel. Bax remained a friend, and many years later dedicated his Five Greek Folksongs to the critic, by then a naturalized Briton.

The only work on the Society's list that we have not yet discussed is *A Song of War and Victory*, dating from 1905. It was written out

in full score, but does not appear ever to have been played. This
vivid, though in places too heavily scored, music represents a *genre*
at which Bax was later to excel — the orchestral march. *Roscatha*
(1910), the finale of the First Symphony (1922) and *Cortège* (1925)
were all developments of an idiom that was tentatively explored
here, and in fact the trio theme of the 1937 Coronation March
London Pageant first appears here. However, perhaps the most
significant facet of the score is not the music, but its dedication — to
'Godwin H. Baynes'.

Arnold probably met Baynes during 1905. That winter his brother
Clifford set out upon a journey round the world, and his seven-month
absence left a considerable gap in Arnold's life. Into this stepped
Godwin Baynes, who came from a poor family background, and who
became one of Mrs Bax's protégés. She paid for Baynes's education
and it was while he was an undergraduate that he dominated the
young Bax's circle. Baynes, 'by virtue of his gigantic physique,
omnivorous mind, universal goodwill, and overwhelming vitality,
became an object of hero-worship wherever he went'.[7] He later
became a doctor and assistant of Jung, translating one of Jung's
books for publication in the UK (see p. 206). But before the Great
War, and particularly before Arnold's marriage in 1911, they were
great friends.

Baynes, who had a fine voice, trained for a brief period as an opera
singer before taking up medicine. But he was not a professional
musical friend. There were many others, forming the set based at
Hampstead, where the Baxes kept open house to all clever people.
Grouped under the friendly spire of the old parish church could be
found poet, painter, novelist, as well as musician, and these included
Ernest Rhys, Henry Holliday and May Sinclair at that time. The
Baxes' young friends were drawn from local artistic and musical
circles of varied background. It was never wealth that was the key to
the clique, but rather the ability and inclination to participate.

As well as cricket they played tennis and croquet. The tennis in
particular provided an almost continual summer's background during
the spacious Edwardian days. Clifford remembered how, during a
typical afternoon, through the trees he 'watched four players darting
about the court, my brother and two girls and Maitland Radford,
whose mind has a razor's edge ... The sound of their voices and the
thudding of the ball made a background to my meditation. Now and
again the sound ceased, and looking up I perceived that they were
searching for lost balls in the raspberry bushes.'[8] Maitland Radford

became a doctor and a writer and was to remain a life-long friend. Maitland was the son of Dollie Radford, 'a cheerful and hospitable middle-aged poetess'; mother and son both hovered on the fringe of Bloomsbury circles, and were friends or good samaritans towards D. H. Lawrence, especially during the Great War.[9] Later, on the cricket field and as dinner companions, the two Baxes, Baynes and Radford (by then in their forties), called themselves 'the Four Just Men' and dined regularly together (see p. 205). It was Radford, together with Baynes, who was the political conscience of the group, and turned Bax's circle into Fabians: they were all idealistic socialists, at least in theory. In Bax's tennis-playing years, Herbert Farjeon (writer and dramatic critic) and Stacey Aumonier (short-story writer and artist) joined the circle.

It was not only the Baxes who had their own tennis court, so had the Corders, and from their first days at Swiss Cottage they seem to have become a centre for many of the families in the area. Particularly there were the Farjeons (Harry, Nellie, Joe and Bertie), the Hesses, when young Myra, later to be the famous pianist, was growing up, and an Anglo-Italian family called Antonietti who were all very beautiful in a dark southern style (Aldo, a talented violinist; Romeo, Hilda and Olga, later actors). Dorothea Corder was the oldest of the group. She had the misfortune to be plain in a group of beautiful people; nicknamed 'The Dodds', she was what the French call 'une jolie laide'. She had an immense character, and a wit and charm and a way of dominating a company very gently and keeping them on the boil. She was also a friend of all the mothers, and regarded as a sort of chaperone when the young people gathered at the Corders' — so everything was quite respectable.

The Farjeons participated in the cricket and were roped into the cricket tours that Clifford soon started to organize, while Aldo Antonietti was a particular friend of Arnold, and his sister Olga was later to accompany Arnold to Russia and to have a passionate love affair with Clifford shortly after the latter's first marriage.

In the winter the short walk up to Hampstead Heath meant that it was conveniently near for wild games of hockey. They had appropriated a high piece of ground, and after playing they all 'foregathered round a mountainous tea' in Arnold's study, 'and after the tea ... crowded together over a variety of exciting parlour-games'.[10] Clifford, who appears to have delighted in organizing his friends into teams, formalized the hockey into a team which played on Sundays. David Garnett, remembering that he played once or twice with it, described

Clifford as 'a very violent player' who once broke a rib of a Hampstead doctor on the opposing side. Garnett thought Clifford 'affected and did not like him'.[11]

Although Arnold had found in Ireland a source of musical inspiration that enabled his art to develop in a personal way, he was also, for a brief student period, attempting to reconcile it with a different approach: that of Richard Strauss. Bax remembered, in a broadcast talk on Strauss, how when he first went to the Royal Academy,

all the harmonies we youngsters ever heard could have been triumphantly analysed by Professor Ebenezer Prout, though those of Wagner would no doubt have caused him discomfort and even pain! Then in 1902 the music of Strauss poured into this country in full flood. And what a to-do there was! Each work to arrive proved more breath-taking and controversial than the last. Wagner had made music the language of passion, and now in Richard the Second neurosis became vocal. Ancient and pedantic ears were assaulted by novelties of all kinds. Seemingly perverse progressions – the swaying in and out of keys and back again – titillating wrong notes – melodies in enormous sweeps hitherto undreamed of (e.g. the opening of *Ein Heldenleben*), and beside all these the lusciousness and languor of those delayed cadences creating the effect of long-drawn-out summer sunset. This last invention has proved one of the abiding characteristics of the composer's work, until in some of the later operas, such as *Arabella*, the sweetness becomes cloying and over-ripe.[12]

In the spring of 1906 Arnold went to Dresden and 'battened expensively on the fleshpots of the agreeable Bellevue Hotel'. Across the square from the hotel was the opera house which he visited three or four times a week, and 'came in for about the fifth performance' of the first production of Strauss's *Salome*, which 'seemed the *ne plus ultra* of the art of music' to the young composer.

Among his acquaintances in the German city were two young expatriate English composers, Roland Bocquet (five years Bax's senior, he had been a fellow student at the Academy) and Archie Rowan-Hamilton, to both of whom Arnold dedicated his most recent works (probably written in Germany). To 'A. J. Rowan-Hamilton' he inscribed his Trio in One Movement for violin, viola (or clarinet) and piano. To Bocquet, the ballad-recitation *The Twa Corbies* from 'Border Minstrelsy', which is dated 20 September 1906. (Bocquet reciprocated with the dedication of his song *Sicheres Glück* (Lasting Happiness).)[13] It is probable that the examples of Grieg's *Bergliot* (then very fashionable), and of Strauss's *Enoch Arden* inspired Bax's recitation, while in the Trio, Strauss and Eire maintain an uneasy truce. This is not to imply that the Trio is not worth the occasional performance. Bax himself ended up hating it, but that was only because it tended later to be promoted at the expense of his mature work (which happened just because it became part of the catalogue of the music publishers, J. & W. Chester). But even if we agree that it is not characteristic, it is worth considering in some detail. It is the sort of work that would possibly be appreciated in amateur circles, but (in common with much of Bax's music) it is far from easy. In particular the viola part is set very high, in the treble clef for much of the time, and rising to a high D above the stave in that clef. Presumably Bax wrote this under Tertis's influence, and went some way towards recognizing the problem by agreeing to the alternative of a clarinet in the part.

The work's deficiencies may best be seen in passages where the chromatic writing (particularly in the viola part) jars with the inclination to a pentatonic melodic line. But Bax's spirited, red-blooded treatment of the material still makes this an enjoyable piece. In places we find more than a hint of the idiom of the later works for violin and piano, and the comparison between this and the first two violin sonatas demonstrates how this style and feeling for the instrument was developing (see Ex. 6). The piano writing and a

Ex. 6

passing use of waltz-time are all links with music of the composer's early maturity. Even the excessive use of sequential writing in the Trio can be exciting, though it is also responsible for the work's *longueurs*.

Back in England at the end of the year an orchestral work was played at Bournemouth. Like so many composers of his generation, Bax had good cause to thank Dan Godfrey and the Bournemouth Municipal Orchestra, who performed *An Irish Overture* on Thursday 13 December. It appears to have been favourably received. As the music does not survive, the programme's description of it that follows gives us a tantalizing glimpse:

Allegro Vivace in E minor ...
A brilliant and lighthearted representation of several sides of Irish character, this Overture has much in it that is interesting. The composer is already favourably known as the writer of several Celtic pieces, based more or less upon Folk melodies. In the Overture played today only two actually Irish tunes are used: the well known 'Emer's farewell to Cuchulain' [better known as the *Londonderry Air*] and one of the traditional 'Caoines' or Keens, a kind of wailing chant sung for hours together to the word 'Ochone' by mourners at wakes − at least in former days. The Overture is intended to represent for the most part the lighter side of Irish life, but besides that and the touches of pathos which always underlie humour, there are indications of the fiery and warlike side of the Irish nature.
    The first section of the Music is founded on a theme in typical Irish tonality.
    The middle section in the Major introduces the hearer to a delightful melody, on the first violins: further on the Caoine will be recognised by the descending triplet with which it begins, and by its being given out by Bassoon and Cello.
    The merrier tune soon regains its sway, and the Overture proceeds happily on its way through a clever series of subject management, to its brilliant ending.[14]

The programme (which described Arnold as 'Mr Trevor Bax') also indicated that he would conduct his own work. Later in the concert Frank Merrick gave the first Bournemouth performance of the Dvořák Piano Concerto, and he was later emphatic in his recollection that Godfrey conducted throughout.[15]

    It was probably late in 1906 that Bax first encountered Balfour Gardiner. Certainly Gardiner's notebook records Bax, Hamilton and Dale joining him for dinner on 14 November. H. Balfour Gardiner, six years Bax's senior, was one of the 'Frankfurt Gang' which also comprised Percy Grainger, Cyril Scott, Norman O'Neill and Roger Quilter. A professionally trained musician of considerable personal wealth, he single-handed, over a period of years, enabled many British composers to hear their music through acts of patronage. A patronage, moreover, that was widely disseminated and substantial and not solely devoted to music. His friendship with Bax almost certainly grew out of a brief association with the Society of British

Composers for whom he read some scores including Bax's *Twa Corbies*. However, it was probably not before 1908 or 1909 that Bax and Gardiner became close friends, and began to meet regularly, particularly at the latter's house at Ashampstead. These visits to the Berkshire village were to continue on Bax's part for twenty-one years, and became one of those regular features of his life to which he looked forward with great anticipation.

It was also at about this time that Arnold and his mother visited Norway, though the exact dates are not known. Arnold – and Clifford too – became very interested in northern literature (Scandinavian and Finnish) and both developed a great enthusiasm for it. They were probably influenced in this by a family friend, Arne von Erpecum, to whom the choral work *Fatherland* is dedicated. The original Swedish words of this piece (which appear in the vocal score and may have been actually set by Arnold) are taken from *Fänrik Staal's Saagner* ('Ensign Staal's Tales'), two series of poems published in 1848 and 1860 by the Finnish-Swedish poet Johan Ludvig Runeberg. The words are now those of the Finnish National Anthem, though with music by Fredrik Pacius. Bax made a literal translation which his brother worked into a more poetic English version. Arnold wrote about this work that 'although these poems and the hymn that precedes them have a very particular local significance, it is clear that the latter might appropriately voice the sentiments of any small oppressed nationality'[16] and in this doubtless Ireland was not far from his thoughts. Indeed, later, writing about a possible Irish National Anthem he referred to Runeberg's as 'unquestionably the most moving national poem ever composed'.[17]

Bax's short programme note for the music gives a good idea of his intentions. He was particularly taken with the idea of a strolling ballad-singer 'chanting by a smoky hearth on some northern winter night and surrounded by an entranced audience of young and old. The emotional appeal gradually increases, the listeners participating more and more actively in the music until finally with linked hands and eyes flashing in the flickering firelight, the whole company bursts forth into the song of the fatherland's approaching freedom and glory.'[18] It is an attractive work, and the concept of a strolling ballad-singer unites two very fruitful artistic sources: Elgar (in *King Olaf*) and Irish folksong. Certainly the jump from Irish to Nordic folk tradition is not a difficult one to make in this context. In style *Fatherland* is a much simpler work than others he attempted at this time, and perhaps it is this and its direct melodic appeal that

prompted Sir Thomas Beecham to keep it in his repertoire, last
playing it (in its revised version, which dates from 1934) at the
Royal Festival Hall in December 1954. However, the 'patriotic'
melody (Ex. 7), in particular, would not have been out of place

Ex. 7

in a work of Stanford (such as *The Revenge*), nor would the choruses
that echo the soloist, very much in the style of Stanford's popular
works, and it probably embarrassed Bax in later years.

In January 1907 Bax had returned to Dresden accompanied by
Paul Corder, the composer-son of his composition teacher. Paul
was to be a good friend all his life. He endeared himself to all who
knew him. His accomplishments included the invention of an early
form of colour photography, and the making of a variety of beautiful
craftsman-built furniture which he gave to his friends. The two again
met Bocquet and Archie Rowan-Hamilton, and it would have been
in their company that the score of *Fatherland* was written. Arnold
was by now passionately involved in the second major love affair
of his life. This time the object of his affections was Dorothy Pyman.
His sister Evelyn tells that her brother, in his memoirs, *Farewell, My
Youth*, disguised her as the 'tall, calm-eyed Scandinavian girl' with
whom he fled the town on a snowy March day. It is one of the
most picturesque incidents in that compendium of the picturesque,
his autobiography:

We took the train to the Austrian [now Czechoslovakian] frontier where we
chartered an ancient and tumbledown yellow cab, the floor of the interior
heaped with none too clean straw. It was drawn by a scraggy and pessimistic-
looking horse, and the bearded driver was so heavily swathed in rugs that he
looked like a Russian *isvostchik*.
    Bucketing out of the station yard, the man on the box incessantly jerking out
curses and moaning complaints of the cold, we rolled and creaked into the
woods.
    My companion said she felt that there ought to have been an angered parent,
foaming at the mouth, and brandishing a horsewhip, in close pursuit.
    We huddled together for warmth, stealing rather awed sidelong glances at
the white-drifted rides of that vast and gloomily romantic Bohemian forest.

It was getting towards dusk, and it seemed not impossible that trolls from her country and native kobolds lurked behind every tree, or that — seeing that we were on the verge of Slavonic earth — the Baba-Yaga herself might come blundering through the branches with her monstrous pestle and mortar. However, after bumping through ever deepening snow for some miles, we at last drew up at the warm and hospitable Rainwiese inn, where we reckoned on staying for two or three days.

Unforgettable days they proved to be, poignant — sweet in recollection to my dying hour. By day we wandered in the endless glistening forest, gazed up at the mighty Prebischthur, or were ferried by a silent one, who may have been Charon himself, upon an ice-green water mirror, its breathless surface reflecting the tall frozen cliffs of the canyon through which the scarcely flowing stream sluggishly crept. Later, with the intense silence of the snow-curtained pines beyond the dark blue of the window, we lay wakeful in one another's arms half the night. And then ... and then, no more! I can never discover how it was that during that strange virginal honeymoon — despite the urgencies of youth and unfulfilled desire — I penetrated into a fastness of peace and contentment, to which in all these long years I have never since attained.[19]

Back in Dresden after this expedition Bax has recorded how he was engaged on a 'colossal symphony which would have occupied quite an hour in performance'.[20] There survive in the collection of Colin Scott-Sutherland the manuscripts of two piano-score movements of a 'Symphony in F minor', *Allegro molto vivace* and *Andante con moto*, clearly the first two movements of the symphony. At University College Cork are preserved two further movements, also in piano-score, of a symphony in F, Op. 8 dated 3 April, 1907: the third and fourth movements of a symphony, the first being headed 'III Intermezzo' and the other 'Finale'. The suspicion that these are the remainder of the Symphony in F minor is confirmed by a note in the Appendix to the 1914 edition of *Grove* which refers to 'a symphony in F Minor and Major ...'[21] So the piece, although never scored, was still regarded as a valid work just before the First World War. We thus have a complete symphony by Bax dating from fifteen years before the actual first symphony and worthy of at least passing attention.

Bax gives no hint of a programme, nor of any programmatic origin that the work as a whole might have had. But he does preface the third movement, *Intermezzo*, with a note which implies an overall theme:

The motif of this intermezzo was suggested by, and to some extent based upon, the central idea of 'Der Tor und der Tod' by Hugo von Hoffmansthal. The central idea of this author's play, Claudio (der Tor) is the impersonation of the over-civilized and hypersensitive modern man, the tragedy of whose destiny is to be traced to the super-subtlety and complexity of his emotional life. At the end of life he realizes that he has not really lived in the fullest sense of the word. A perverse demon has haunted him throughout the whole course of his earthly existence preventing him from sounding the depths of any of the great spiritual experiences and mingling them together in such a manner that joy has become confused with sorrow and love with hate and so forth. It is this central conception that this intermezzo sets forth to illustrate. In the scherzo section the demon of unrest and perversity is represented and in that part of the movement usually occupied by the Trio three motivs [sic] are introduced symbolizing respectively (a) Love (b) Religion or Philosophy (c) The Battle of Life. Each of these is interrupted and broken to pieces by the theme of the Scherzo. In the coda the subject of the programme dies returning with a broken sigh to the love of his youth.[22]

Although the conception of the work is Straussian, the musical working out reveals a number of conflicting styles that the young composer has endeavoured to mould together, and they work surprisingly well. The score was obviously conceived in instrumental colours, and indications of the orchestration appear throughout.

In trying to work out what this work may have sounded like in orchestral dress, we are given more than a hint if we look at the chromatic middle section of the full orchestral score of *Fatherland* (front end paper), which is exactly contemporary with it. The theme of the *Intermezzo* itself is in waltz-time, and we find Bax hinting at a Straussian waltz-style before *Rosenkavalier* was thought of (Ex. 8). The three 'trio' motifs are also of interest. The first, 'Love', has previously been quoted by Scott-Sutherland as an example of Straussian writing, but in it we should not miss an 'Irish' melodic line struggling to break through the chromatics that Bax associates with 'Love'. 'Religion or Philosophy' is presented by a hymn-like idea, while 'Battle' really does remind us of Strauss. There are interesting premonitions of the later Bax in this work. The piano style of the sketch is reminiscent of the orchestral Scherzo (1913, orch. 1917), and the use of a waltz theme relates it to the music written (but never orchestrated) for the ballet *Tamara* (1911) and, not surprisingly, to a 'waltz' (though not entirely in $\frac{3}{4}$!) for piano written in 1910, and published by Boosey. The end of the *Intermezzo* is brilliant and thrilling even on the piano, and the movement might well have been viable on its own if it had been orchestrated. It is indicative of Bax's quickly growing sureness of touch in larger forms.

He had returned to England by the beginning of the summer: Here Thomas Dunhill, an RCM-trained composer some seven years

Ex. 8

Bax's senior, was starting his chamber concerts, presenting the newly published *Celtic Song Cycle* in one of them on 14 June. A number of songs were also written during the year, including several Celtic songs – apparently intended to form a coherent set. One of them was 'The White Peace', destined to become Bax's most famous song, and possibly his most performed work. The manuscript is dated 'Sept 30th' and is inscribed 'To Dorothy', but by the time the song was published (in 1919) this inscription was changed in favour of the composer's mother.

These songs form the background for plans to write an opera. We do not know exactly when he started investigating the possibility of an Irish dramatic opera, but the seeds were doubtless sown in the Dresden opera house. Although it was never to come to fruition as Bax intended, there is a good deal of surviving evidence to show how he was approaching the task. More than one commentator has remarked that he might well have been successful as a composer of opera, but later in life he himself was adamant that opera was unsuited to the English as a race, and in a radio talk in 1949 he mentioned two which he had attempted early in his career, one progressing no further than the libretto and the other only to a few sketches. The first of these was an Irish folk comedy, *The Twisting of the Rope*, the second a five-act drama called *Déirdre*,[23] from which two fragments of orchestral music survive in short score. We can gain more than a little idea of the brilliance that a Baxian opera might have had from his reworking of one of the *Déirdre* fragments as the tone poem *Roscatha*, in 1910.

Almost certainly the attempt to write *Déirdre* came first, the typescript being dated 30 November 1907. The two fragments of orchestral music that Bax sketched are of particular interest because of their relationship to completed orchestral works. How *The Gathering of the Chiefs* later became *Roscatha* is described on p. 74. The manuscript of the other, headed 'Cuid 5' (or Part 5), has the following, beginning 5 bars from the end (Ex. 9).

Ex. 9

Thematically this is the same as the opening of the short score of his next orchestral work, a tone poem called *Into the Twilight* (Ex. 10).

Ex. 10

(CONCOBAR goes out quickly. FERGUS has crept out unnoticed at the beginning of the last speech of the king. The sound of distant horns is heard, heralding the approaching company. Servants enter and light great torches all about the hall. They arrange the chairs and stools and smaller tables. A barbaric march tune is heard, and the heroes and nobles of the Red Branch enter in procession. With them come a number of bards with beautifully carven harps, trumpet players with great curved instruments fashioned of bronze with decorated mouthpieces, tympan-players, ollavs (the administrators of law), druids, (CATHBAD amongst them), and other dignitaries. The KING enters last with CUCHULLAIN, CONNALL CEARNACH, and FERGUS MAC ROIGH. CONCOBAR strides to the high seat in silence. CUCHULLAIN and CONNALL take their seats on either side of him).

CATHBAD | (standing fo_ward)

> The blessing of the gods upon this feast.
>
> > (He sits).

CONCOBAR | (rising)

> Welcome, my friends, unto this royal house.
>
> The blessing of the sun and moon and stars,
>
> Of Dagda and Dana and Aengus *of the* birds,
>
> Rest on your hearts. Now let the mead go round
>
> And song and laughter and old tales make glad
>
> My harvesters among the fields of war
>
> In this their time of ease. Forward, ye bards,
>
> And give a laughing music to your harps
>
> And sweetness of old stories.

Fig. 2 Bax's typescript of *Déirdre*, showing the gathering of the chiefs, for which he wrote the music later orchestrated as *Roscatha*. (From Bax's original typescript, scene ii.)

Graham Parlett has argued that this idea might have been used as Déirdre's motif in the opera. *Into the Twilight* was written in the winter of 1908, and the fascinating part of the riddle is that the short score is headed just *'Eire'-Prologue*. Could it be that at that

stage *Eire* would have been synonymous with *Déirdre*? Further
evidence for this comes at the end of the piano score of *Into the
Twilight*, where Bax has written the words 'curtain rises'. The evidence
of a unity running through this early 'Irish' orchestral music of Bax
is underlined when we realize that the main theme of *Cathaleen-ni-
Hoolihan* (and hence the slow movement of the E major quartet)
reappears in *Into the Twilight*, and is hinted at in the tone poem *In
the Faery Hills*, of 1909, which was dubbed the second part of *Eire*.
The fact that the third part of *Eire* is *The Gathering of the Chiefs*
from the opera makes it possible to suppose that the cycle of tone
poems is intimately concerned with Bax's operatic ambitions and
represents all we are ever likely to hear of them. So vivid are they
that we may regret most keenly the fact that he never managed to
complete the project, a regret that is underlined by Graham Parlett's
idiomatic orchestral realization of the second short score sketch of
an operatic interlude ('Cuid V') with the title *On the Sea-Shore*, now
splendidly recorded by the Ulster Orchestra conducted by Vernon
Handley.

Bax's knowledge and experience of Ireland were by now considerable and once or twice in each year with his brother Clifford,
he went to Connemara, Galway, the Aran Isles, and Donegal. Clifford
remarked on the difference between his own and his brother's
approach to natural beauty, for while Clifford found that 'a thought
excited me twenty times as much as a place or person',[24] his brother
dealt in emotional responses. 'My brother did not intellectualise
the mountains,' observed Clifford, and added 'he derived a pure
happiness, I think, from the wild loveliness of the islands and lakes
and windy heights, and from the charm and vivacity of the peasants.'[25] It was a pleasure that Bax never forgot, nor one which ever
failed to excite him.

During Bax's life there were several concerts devoted to his music.
The most celebrated was the one which the publishers of his mature
work, Murdoch, promoted in 1922; but the first took place in the
Aeolian Hall on 16 July 1908 and consisted of the early and overlong
String Quintet and some songs. The notice of this concert in *The
Times* is of considerable interest:

The concert given at Aeolian-hall on Thursday evening showed Mr Arnold Bax
as a composer of great inventive power. In a quintet for strings — using two
violoncellos, which was played by the Wesserley Quartet with Mr R. W. Tabb
as second violoncello, his facility of invention keeps the interest alive, though

it leads him to spin out the work to extreme length. Its four movements are built upon themes which in themselves are simple, and yet have strong character; but the innumerable subsidiary figures with which he continually adorns them sometimes give a rather overloaded effect. The ensemble is difficult, and might, surely, be simplified in many places without musical loss, and, indeed, some moments of repose, especially in the slow movement, would be a gain to the listener.[26]

In November two movements of the Quintet were heard again, and Balfour Gardiner found them 'most imaginative, and beautifully written'.[27] That Quintet was one of two instrumental works completed during 1908 (the other being *Into the Twilight*) and was written at Glencolumcille, the first three movements at least being completed during May. The music is in four movements as follows:

  I Allegro vivace – andante con molto – allegro vivace
 II Lento expressivo [sic]
III Scherzo (allegro vivace – trio – tempo primo – presto)
IV Finale (allegro molto vivace)

The use of a second cello in the scoring, rather than a second viola, makes for a very rich string texture, a feature particularly apparent where there are simultaneous double-stoppings in several parts. After the First World War (during which he thought the score was lost in Germany) Bax edited the second movement as a *Lyrical Interlude*, re-scoring it for a quintet with two violas, in which form it was published. 'Complexity never existed for him', stated Vaughan Williams (to whom the *Lyrical Interlude* is dedicated), and this work is a case in point. But the Quintet is certainly of interest to the student of Bax, for it is his first really extended instrumental work in which a self-evident 'Irish' flavour offers distinctive melodic writing rather than incidental colour. Examples 11a and 11b, from the

Ex. 11a

Ex. 11b

first and second movements respectively, are probably the two most attractive examples of this trait. The first was later re-used by Bax in his piano piece *A Hill Tune*. The chromatic development and over-decoration of this material is not completely successful, and each movement is far too long, the complete work having a playing time of at least forty-five minutes. In performance the outer movements, in particular, sound unexpectedly tame. However, it was a valuable musical experience for Bax, because, in addition to its one public performance, it was played privately, which resulted in a number of cuts and amendments to the score. A separate set of parts of the Scherzo survives, from which it appears the second cello was also used as an *ad lib* double-bass part. It would be interesting to hear the music played by string orchestra.

Bax's earliest musical inclination was to achieve his impressionistic effects with a fine filigree of contrapuntal movement. Considering that Debussy was only beginning to be performed here during this period, this was a considerable achievement, as we can hear in a work such as *Cathaleen-ni-Hoolihan*. But much of this natural intuitive grasp of the medium was lost in his attempts to write an extended work, and certainly the example of Strauss rubs shoulders uneasily with that of the folk-music of Ireland in the Trio of 1906, and the Symphony in F of 1907, while *Fatherland* was only redeemed by its less complex method and the invention of a simple and memorable tune which had to do with neither Strauss nor Ireland.

The Quintet apart, Bax appears to have written comparatively little music after he completed the symphony in piano score in April 1907. There are just seven songs representing the remaining eight months of 1907 and a further five for 1908. Of these half were settings of 'Fiona Macleod' ('Longing', 'From the Hills of Dream', 'A Milking Sian', 'Heart O'Beauty', 'Shieling Song' and 'Isla'), although this was an influence that was beginning to wane. The other songs showed Bax looking to Scandinavian and German authors for texts, as well as setting 'A Lyke-Wake', subtitled 'Border Ballad' by Bax, and much later to be used by Benjamin Britten in his *Serenade for tenor, horn and strings*.

Bax first met Arthur Alexander, a young New Zealand pianist and budding composer, around 1908. In 1907, the sixteen-year-old arrived in England to attend the Academy, where he too became a pupil of Corder and Matthay. Despite the eight-year age difference Bax and Alexander almost immediately became great friends, drawn together by their mutual delight in piano-duet playing, and possibly by the fact that Alexander had rooms on Flask Walk, Hampstead, only a short walk from Ivy Bank at the top of Haverstock Hill. Alexander remembered Bax, when he met him, as:

slender, pale and poetic in appearance, with an expression of refinement and alertness. His walk was very characteristic — one shoulder slightly higher than the other and one hand behind his back. His voice was rather high-pitched and at times querulous. He spoke quickly yet clearly and very much to the point, with a meticulous use of words. He possessed a quick and very apt sense of humour, which was sometimes a little unkind. He enjoyed reading aloud any passage that had taken his fancy, and he had a prodigious and often photographic memory. Once when I was reading something through at the piano, he was standing at the tail end of the instrument gazing at a recently published score; when I had finished, he sat down and played from memory well over a page of the work at which he had been looking.[28]

For years they played through a variety of Russian orchestral music, and were also fond of the music of Dvořák. 'In those days we were looked on as the best sight readers in the country,' claimed Alexander, and added, 'but in reading orchestral mss Arnold surpassed me.'[29]

Bax frequently dropped in on Alexander in his Hampstead rooms. He would seldom ring, but would step into the ground-floor room through the open window. 'If I were out he would say to the landlady's daughter some such thing as "Is the Bishop in? If not, I'll wait", and he would spend the time reading or playing the piano. He was himself almost oblivious of his surroundings — they meant little to him — and he could live and work under conditions of startling discomfort and untidiness.'[30]

These frequent duet sessions, almost always playing from full orchestral scores, quickly assumed a special significance for Bax. Alexander remembered their sheer fun.

In our duet playing we did idiotic things (apart from cutting every rest of long duration): we would, for instance, vie with each other in reading the music from an absurd distance, or we would continue playing as darkness fell, until the music was almost invisible (I once suggested our going on the halls as Bax and Frontz). We raced through the eight Glazounov symphonies (the Scherzo of the eighth was our especial 'tour de force' and the first movement of the second, and all of the seventh we actually played through several times). Then there were the two symphonic poems 'Stenke Rasine' and 'The Kremlin', all Rimsky-Korsakov's orchestral works (the revolutionary march 'Dubinushka' was a great favourite): the two Borodin symphonies — and the less well-known two of Balakirev. The latter's 'Thamar' gave us especial pleasure and we must have been amongst the first to play through the 'Sacre du Printemps'.[31] Dvořák and Strauss were not forgotten, but I don't think we ever played a single duet written as such. It amused me to discover traces of some of these recently-played works in the compositions by Arnold which immediately followed.[32]

Towards the end of 1908, Bax was again attempting an extended orchestral work, and in this case not only was the music quickly completed in full score − quite an achievement in itself − but it was programmed and played by Thomas Beecham in April the following year. This was *Into the Twilight*, after the Yeats poem of the same name (see pp. 51−2). The experience of writing the Symphony in F had shown Bax where his weaknesses lay: in an excess of ambition which caused him to lose his vision in a haze of unnecessary notes. For *Into the Twilight* Bax went back to *Cathaleen* and reworked some of the material for larger forces, ornamenting it and asking for a more elaborate orchestra, including cor anglais, bass clarinet, contra-bassoon, two harps and celesta. No trumpets are required, and there is a mere four-bar entry for *four* trombones. This last point makes one wonder whether such idiosyncratic scoring was the result of Bax's inexperience or, as suggested, of the piece having been intended as the opening of a more extended work. Bax refers to this music in his autobiography as a 'mild and rather hesitant essay in Celticism'. After its first performance in 1909 it was not heard again until Aloys Fleischmann conducted it twice in Ireland during 1971. After one of those performances an Irish critic wrote admiring its 'fresh sincerity' and its clear textures, finding it to be 'the only truly convincing Irish Rhapsody I have met'.[33] It was heard again during the BBC's Bax centenary series and is now recorded by Bryden Thomson (a recording greeted by Michael Oliver in *Gramophone* with high praise, finding its third theme, in particular, 'magical'). The overall impression is of a delicate and finely-spun musical fabric. Bax asks for solo violin and solo viola, and the celesta − one of his favourite 'faery' instruments − is extensively used for the first time. Professor Fleischmann has pointed out that the striking phrases for celesta and woodwind antedate by two years the effect of the 'Silver Rose' motif of Strauss's *Rosenkavalier*.[34]

Bax has described how Beecham's performance of the music was a source of crushing humiliation to its over-sensitive and inexperienced composer. The decision to play the work was taken at fairly short notice, and Bax put the score out to a professional copyist to prepare the parts. He later recalled in his autobiography that no orchestral work of his had been performed since his student days, 'and such was my innocence of all practical musicianly matters that I was unaware that professional copyists have no bowels of compassion and seldom trouble to correct their own careless mistakes. The parts only arriving on the day of the concert at Queen's Hall itself, there was no time whatever for me to go through them, with the result that the rehearsal was a welter of wrong notes, through which Beecham ploughed without comment and utterly unperturbed.'[35] Bax turned for assistance to W. H. Bell, who although ten years his senior, had been a friend of his Academy days.[36] Bax continued: 'with help from Bell, and by dint of hours of labour (unimaginable to anyone lucky enough not to be acquainted with this soul-destroying form of drudgery) I managed to get the thing right by the evening. But any other conductor than the nonchalant Beecham would have declined to take the chance after the chaos of the morning, and I do not know what impish perversity prompted him to leave the piece in the programme. After all it went tolerably well.'[37]

Quite how Bax and Beecham first met is not known, but it was late in 1908, and may have been through Bell, a mutual friend. Beecham had started presenting concerts with what became known as the 'New Symphony Orchestra', and the first concert in which the name was used was in November 1906. Later, in October 1907, the orchestra was expanded to a full-size symphony orchestra. Having achieved something of a reputation for his unusual programmes (and half empty halls), he was already presenting Delius's music, and late in 1908 conceived the idea of producing a series of concerts of new English music. Bax's mother was not only in the habit of indulging her own children but of supporting artistic enterprises that required patronage, and she was interested in the project. Thus formal invitations were issued by Mrs Ridley Bax to 'A Causerie on Modern English Music and the Position today of the English Composer'. This took place at Ivy Bank on Friday 26 March, and Bax remembered in particular 'the abrupt arrival of Ethel Smyth attired in tweeds, heavy boots, and a deerstalker hat'.[38] M. Montagu Nathan, the historian of Russian music, was there and later remembered how

Having been officially received we were first ushered into the music-room, and there, on a platform, lolling back in his chair, sat Mr Thomas Beecham clad, if memory serves me, in a velvet dinner jacket. He addressed his audience some-what nonchalantly on a subject already then, and still now, dear to his heart. I seem to remember his being severely heckled by an argumentative guest; this individual was invited to mount the platform, whereupon they embarked upon a discussion quite heated on one side but conducted on the other with that characteristic bland suavity with which we have since been made familiar.[39]

Late in 1907 and for much of 1908 Bax spent a lot of time in the William Morris circle, visiting Kelmscott House in Hammersmith, and at one point being invited to live there. Possibly his friendship with Harry Marillier, the manager of the Morris establishment in Oxford Street, and the owner of Kelmscott House, had resulted from an introduction by Frederick Corder, one of whose passions was collecting the Kelmscott Press books. Bax's friend Paul Corder, too, was heavily influenced by Morris. Bax became known in Pre-Raphaelite circles, but their influence did not extend to his music, other than to one or two early songs which were suggested by Pre-Raphaelite paintings. Unexpectedly a favourite birthday present in 1907 was a volume of Stefan George's poems, splendidly avant-garde at the time in its sans serif typeface, and even now a satisfying example of the typographer's art in its own right. Any interest Bax may have had with George's poetry was doubtless fostered by George's London Pre-Raphaelite connexions. Certainly Hofmannsthal's association with the George-Kreis, George's literary 'school', may have been the avenue for Bax's earlier interest in him as the source of a theme for the projected symphony of the previous year. And while the young Bax might have been momentarily intrigued by a symbolic art evoking a sense of intoxication, he would not have been by George's new grammatical classicism in German poetry. Bax did not set any of the George poems. His real interest was far away in Ireland.

Three delightful and affectionate letters and three postcards survive, addressed to Mary Field.[40] These date from around 1908, though quite what Bax's relationship was with her, we do not know. She was one of Clifford Bax's theosophical art circle, and a member of the company of the 'Peoples' Free Theatre' that produced classical plays in East End Halls; other leading lights of this organisation were Godwin Baynes and Clifford's future wife Gwendolen Bishop.[41] Years later Bax referred to her, in a letter to a friend, as 'the girl I went wild with years ago'. In one of the letters to Miss Field, Bax writes at length on the art of recitation, which he considers to be in some respects 'the most intimate of interpretive arts, and ... nearest allied to that of the "story-telling" of old times and all its lovely romantic associations of firelight and the rhapsodic interludes on the harp or some other simple instrument, now developed (not altogether to the betterment of the emotional effect) into the Enoch Arden of Richard Strauss and similar complexities ...'. In another he writes a forty-eight-line parody on *The Fighting Temeraire*.

The summer of 1908 also saw the beginning of something that

became a regular feature of Bax's life for some thirty years (with an interlude for the First World War). This was a summer cricket tour in the first week or two of August. When, years before, Arnold's brother Clifford had been cramming for his Cambridge entrance exam he had been sent by their father to a tutor in rural Norfolk. It must have been friendships made then that allowed him now to arrange a tour of eleven matches in the area. In the course of the tour, Arnold took 39 wickets for 272 runs, while Bertie O'Donnell (B. Walton O'Donnell, – known as 'Bandy', later conductor of the BBC Military Band) played 10 innings for 199 and 'the Major' (R. H. Lowe) 12 for 230. The team against Sheringham, on 10 August, which won by 112 runs, included in addition to Arnold, Clifford and their friends already mentioned, 'Tiny' Baynes and two other Baxes, 'R. Bax' and 'C. E. O. Bax', presumably Rodney Bax and Cyril Ernest Orlando Bax, the latter later joint authors of the history of the Eighth Division in the First World War. (The other names in the team did not later become celebrated and cannot otherwise be traced. They were E. C. Woolley, E. Stiehel, 'Rev. Green' and N. Colenso.)[42]

Clifford's interest in theosophy had been responsible for the Baxes starting a modest journal, published in support of the artistic theosophical circle with which Clifford was associated. This quickly developed into a sumptuous quarterly periodical called *Orpheus*, and a series of literary booklets by unknown authors, which, while ostensibly the brainchild of Clifford, included the first publication of verse, and later of stories, by Arnold. Indeed Arnold was to edit one issue of *Orpheus* in 1910, which would otherwise have been delayed by Clifford's marriage.

Ireland and Russia

Bax must have spent much of the first part of 1909 in Ireland. It was certainly Ireland that was the inspiration of the symphonic poem *In the Faery Hills*, completed on 28 June. *In the Faery Hills* is the only one of the early tone poems to be published, and is probably the best. In it Bax takes a very great step forward from its predecessor, *Into the Twilight*, and although he does not achieve the subtleties later to be accomplished in *The Garden of Fand*, many pointers to the later score are to be found. The music was among the first of his maturity to grow, as it were, out of his surroundings. Writing of *Le Sacre du Printemps* Stravinsky said 'I heard and I wrote what I heard. I am the vessel through which *Le Sacre* passed.'[1] In similar vein Bax told a friend, referring to *In the Faery Hills*, 'I got this mood under Mount Brandon with all W.B.'s magic about me, and I know there is no piece of mine quite like it — no credit to me of course because I was possessed by Kerry's self'.[2]

For the first performance Bax wrote a descriptive note, the following extract from which indicated his programmatic intention, in so far as he was prepared to admit it.

'In the Faery Hills' attempts to suggest the revelries of the 'Hidden People' in the inmost deeps of the hollow hills of Ireland. At the same time I have endeavoured to envelop the music in an atmosphere of mystery and remoteness akin to the feeling with which the people of the West think of their beautiful and often terrible faeries — beings very different from the lightsome folk of 'A Midsummer-Night's Dream'. The middle section of the work is based to some extent on a passage in W.B. Yeats's poem 'The Wanderings of Oisin'. In this he tells how the Danaan host give the human bard a harp and bid him sing. The latter sings a song of human joy, which the immortals declare to be the saddest thing they have ever heard. One of them, weeping, snatches the harp from Oisin's hand and flings it away into a pool, whereupon the host surround the harper and whirl him away in a tumult of laughter and dancing.

The piece is heralded by a faery horn-call, used throughout the work in various forms. The gates of the hills are opened, and the revelries of 'the way-ward twilight companies' begin in a maze of shadows and sudden flashings of opal and rainbow light. In the middle section, referring to the incident of the harper, the gloomy caoine-like melody must be understood not as the actual 'song of human joy', but rather as that singing as it sounded in the ears of those 'who fear no dawning morrow', and 'dance like shadows on the mountains'.[3]

The enchanted mood is evoked quite simply in the opening sequence. In a remote part of Kerry the light has almost gone and a faery dusk prevails. In the words of Yeats's poem:

> We ... told the purple deeps their pride,
> And murmured snatches of delight ...
> And Niamh blew three merry notes
> Out of a little silver trump;
> And then an answering whispering flew
> Over the bare and woody land,
> A whisper of impetuous feet,
> And ever nearer, nearer grew.[4]

The romantic horn-calls of the opening (Ex. 12) persist in various

Ex. 12

guises through the early pages. This motif is of particular interest in that it is also heard in Elgar's incidental music to the play by W. B. Yeats and George Moore, *Grania and Diarmid*. It is unlikely that Bax would quote Elgar in quite such an obvious way without acknowledging it, and the alternative is, perhaps, that they were both quoting from a common source. However, Michael Kennedy is emphatic that Elgar wrote the motif, and tells how it began 'with a request from Moore, who had heard Elgar's music at a Leeds Festival, for a horn-call to be used in the play which Frank Benson was to produce at the Gaiety, Dublin, in the autumn of 1901 ... Eventually Elgar wrote the horn-call, incidental music (37 bars), and a magnificent funeral march which ought to be more widely known ... [Yeats] described the *Grania* music as "wonderful in its heroic melancholy".'[5]

In the Faery Hills is designed in the basically ternary form that Bax uses so successfully in his later tone poems and which was to develop in the 1920s into the more complex forms of the first movements of the symphonies. Much of the music is scherzando in character, and this is underlined by a dancing $\frac{6}{8}$ figure (Ex. 13)

Allegro Vivace

mf

Ex. 13

which is developed in long sequences through different parts of the orchestra. The most striking resemblance between this work and the later *Garden of Fand* is Oisin's 'song of human joy', whose immortal singing is evoked in a central passage. Against a harmonic background painted by the winds, various solo instruments recall the enchanted dusk of the opening: first violin, then clarinet and viola. The strings enter tremolando playing muted and against the bridge (*sul ponticello*), while the timpani quietly murmur an F pianissimo, marked to be played *'with pennies'.* This last touch is a practical example of Bax's quickly developing orchestral experience, almost certainly following Elgar's use of the same trick in *Enigma (XIII)*. The faery horn-calls are heard again. Oisin now sings on the cor anglais with gentle harp chords supporting his song (Ex. 14).

Cor Anglais

p molto espr.

Ex. 14

This tune is one of the work's weaknesses, not being in any way memorable, for in the last analysis one of the attractions of *Fand* is the intrinsic melodic beauty of 'Fand's song of immortal love'.

Before publication in 1926 Bax revised the full score, making a ten-bar cut two bars before letter K and sixteen bars at letter N in the published full score. The latter is of particular interest in that the composer Philip Heseltine (Peter Warlock), with whom Bax was staying in 1926 while he was at work on proofs of the full score of *In the Faery Hills*, strongly objected to its being made. In *his* copy of the printed score he noted 'This is where the trombones came in with the excellent tune which Bax cut out in revision because he thought it was "vulgar"! The passage, which was a gay and brilliant climax to the first movement of the piece, is now merely thick and commonplace.'[6] Heseltine transcribed the cut section (Ex. 15) and there is certainly much to support his opinion. Bax's first thoughts were very often his best.

Ex. 15 The passage Bax removed from *In the Faery Hills.* Philip Heseltine's manuscript, pasted on the otherwise blank back flyleaf of his copy of the published full score.

In the Faery Hills is such an important work in Bax's development, particularly regarding his treatment of the orchestra, that we should look at the scoring a little closer, and see how much of Bax's later style evolved from it. The passage that Philip Heseltine illustrates closely approaches his later style in its broad bands of orchestral colour moving contrapuntally against each other. Yet in the later music Bax would not allow each instrumental part to be as static within each band as usually happens here. The woodwind are a case in point. In his climaxes Bax doubles all the wind on the same melodic line, and reminds us of the neo-Straussian scoring of his young contemporaries elsewhere in Europe, such as Bartók in his *Kossuth Symphony*. The irridescent effect of many flashes of instrumental colour found in Bax's later works has not yet been evolved by him, and the separate lines are not sufficiently rhythmically alive. Yet in the chamber-scoring of those quieter moments where solo instruments create a faery landscape, Bax has achieved much of the magic which characterizes his maturity. More important, perhaps, he has created an identity as a composer, and a work that still has a real personality and life of its own, over sixty years later.

We have already seen how the Society of British Composers helped Bax and others gain public recognition. A continuation of this tradition, though on a more prestigious scale, was provided by the Musical League. This organization was conceived in the autumn of 1907. Originating from an idea of Delius, and with the organizational energy of Granville Bantock, the scheme was launched over the signatures of some of the most eminent British musical names of the day — including Elgar, Delius, Bantock, W. G. McNaught (the critic) and Henry Wood. *The Times* reported that the aims of the League were to include the holding of an annual festival 'of the utmost attainable perfection', and to devote the programmes of these festivals to 'new or unfamiliar compositions, English or foreign'. The first festival took place in Liverpool on 24 and 25 September 1909, although a continuing tradition was not established. There were three concerts — one chamber, one orchestral and one choral and orchestral. Bax participated in the first as pianist, and in the last as composer, his *Fatherland* opening the concert. He later recalled that 'almost every English composer and outstanding executant made the pilgrimage to Liverpool' for this loudly heralded event, and it must have been of considerable importance in establishing an awareness of Bax's musical gifts in the profession.

The first concert, a chamber concert in the Yamen Rooms, included string quartets by his friends Balfour Gardiner and J. B. McEwen, a song cycle by W. H. Bell, as well as pieces by Stanford and Cyril Scott performed by the young Percy Grainger. There was also music by Josef Holbrooke, and two songs by composers now totally forgotten, Frederick Nicholls and Edward Agate. Holbrooke's contribution was a piano sextet in F minor, entitled *In Memoriam*, in which Bax played the piano. That was on the evening of Friday 24 September. The following day there was an afternoon orchestral concert, and in the evening the festival ended with a choral concert in which an enhanced orchestra drawn from the Hallé and Liverpool Philharmonic orchestras joined with the Liverpool Welsh Choral Union, the combined forces directed by the Welsh conductor and educationalist, Harry Evans. Bax's *Fatherland* was played first, and was followed by music by Havergal Brian, Vaughan Williams, Ethel Smyth and Bach. As an individual venture the festival was a success, but although there was eventually another festival in 1913 (which also included music by Bax), the Musical League lacked momentum, and was never to become an effective body for the promotion of British music.[7] However, the festival certainly allowed Bax to hear his most extended non-chamber work to date under almost ideal conditions (though *Fatherland* does not show sufficient signs of the way Bax was to evolve to be of other than incidental value in his development as a composer).

Bax's skill at sight-reading meant that he was occasionally called upon to deputize at short notice for other pianists. This happened several times at 'The Music Club'. If he had not written of his relationship with The Music Club ('a dressy concert-cum-supper affair') in his autobiography,[8] we would not know of it. Yet, he tells us, during 1909 the Club entertained the composers Debussy, D'Indy and Sibelius 'to glut them with copious food, strong wines, and selections from their own works'. Bax was not even a member of the Club, but his sight-reading facility was widely known. He recalled how it regularly happened that two days, or even a day, before a Music Club evening an envoy — it was usually Stanley Hawley —

would call upon me, and snapping open a music-case, proceed feverishly to lay the catastrophic facts before me. These songs of tomorrow night's guest had been sent a week ago to such-and-such professional accompanist, and — would I believe it? — that inconsiderate swine had only just returned them with a note to the effect that he was sorry to inconvenience the Music Club, but it would be really impossible for him to get up the music in time. Hawley's eyes and voice would here become imploring and almost tearful. 'Now we know that you can do it on your head, dear boy, if only you will. I know too it's a darned shame to ask you so late in the day, but we may — mayn't we — rely upon you not to let the Club down?'[9]

It is particularly indicative of Bax's accomplishment at that time that a fairly well known professional concert pianist should be asking Bax to undertake such tasks, rather than attempt it himself. Hawley, only sixteen years Bax's senior, had made his debut in 1887 with the Grieg concerto and appeared frequently both as pianist and accompanist. He was also Secretary of the Royal Philharmonic Society until his death in 1916 at the age of forty-nine. But it was not to please a likely patron that Bax agreed to play, but rather that 'being young and a little vain of my one accomplishment as an executant, I never thought of refusing, though I was not offered a fee and was a trifle vexed that not once was it announced that I had undertaken a very responsible task at the eleventh hour.'

Later, in September 1912, Bax was also to encounter Schoenberg at the Music Club under similar circumstances. Bax noted that the 'neurotically emotional early work' which was heard was 'extremely deftly written'. Schoenberg was in London for the first performance of his Five Orchestral Pieces under Sir Henry Wood, the rehearsal of which Bax attended.

In October 1909 Bax was in London working on the short score of the *Festival Overture*, which he had almost completed. This work reveals the festival spirit in a riotous mood, 'somewhat akin', said Bax, 'to that of a Continental carnival'.[10] He went on: 'there is no "realism" in the piece, however, the composer being content to suggest the atmosphere of Bohemian revel in terms of purely absolute music.' Edward J. Dent, with whom Bax was later to be on cordial terms, was very dismissive of the work and its composer after a performance in 1914. He wrote 'Bax is a clever brat; but what has a born Cockney to do with Celtic Twilights? He takes himself too seriously and has no education. His Bohemian overture was like Hampstead people in a Soho restaurant.'[11]

Although the work was played on a number of occasions before the First World War, it is curiously lacking in the personality which distinguished *In the Faery Hills*. Its large-scale and heavy orchestration is more reminiscent of a Straussian tone poem than a concert overture, enjoyable as the music is. However, if we compare it to Szymanowski's similar early and overtly Straussian Concert Overture (which *has* been recorded) the stature and personality of Bax are immediately apparent. He did not quite finish the music of the overture in 1909, and it was not scored or completed until 1911. A two-piano version survives, but whether Bax arranged it then or reduced it from the full score later is not known. It was performed thus during the BBC's Bax centenary series. Shorn of its orchestral colouring it exhibits an unexpected resemblance to Percy Grainger. The same October he also wrote *The Garden by the Sea*, a setting of William Morris, dated the 26th.

In that autumn of 1909, Bax met 'a tragic young girl'[12] from the Ukraine, at the Corders' house in Swiss Cottage. Her name was Natalia Skarginski (dubbed Loubya Korolenko by Bax in his autobiography *Farewell, My Youth*), known to all as 'Natalie'.[13] When he met her, Natalie, who could speak no English, was lodging at the Hampstead home of the Anglo-Italian Antonietti family. She was, Bax recalls, 'like a naiad for beauty – a golden Roussalka with ice-blue eyes!' Subsequently, Natalie and the youngest daughter of the Italian family, Olga (called 'Fiammetta' in *Farewell, My Youth*), took rooms together, and thus moved into Bax's Hampstead circle. Natalie was certainly welcomed by the Bax family, and was liked on her own account, Evelyn Bax in particular having fond memories of her.

At Christmas 1909 Natalie was present at Ivy Bank, and Bax later remembered that 'lured by the fascination of her nationality and history how easily did I slip into absorbing love of her!' That Christmas, Bax composed an elaborate Christmas carol, which was sung in the family party, and a decade later was published as one of the album of Seven Songs.

Up to this time Bax's inspiration for his music had either originated from the legends, scenery and ambience of Ireland, or from literary sources, be they Irish or otherwise. But the love affair with Natalie was to move Bax artistically to embrace a more explicit relationship between experience and its expression in his art, and henceforth for some twenty years his most successful work was written as a direct expression of his deepest emotional experiences. The music was not 'about' anything specific, rather did Bax sublimate his emotions in art. As he wrote later, 'the artist who is truly inspired is possessed by a demon'.[14] The first composition in which this happened to Bax was the First Violin Sonata, the first movement of which in particular was an expression of his romantic attachment: it was a young man's passionate outpouring in which he also sensed the mastery of his art (Ex. 16). Although Bax never admitted its

Ex. 16

passionate programmatic origins in any public pronouncement,
later in the 1920s, after performing it with a 'worthy' lady violinist,
he lamented to a friend: 'I am not sure that middle-aged and unquestionably virtuous virgins ought to play my music'.

The Sonata was constructed in three movements. First an expansive and romantic opening marked (in the original manuscript)
'moderately slow and very tranquilly' [sic], and in all basic respects it
remained the first movement of the version that was later published.
(The Sonata was to be revised on a number of occasions before then.)
The first movement is dated 2 February 1910, and the 'slow and
sombre' middle movement, 8 February. The Finale was a headlong
allegro molto vivace. Bax was long troubled by the problems he had
posed himself in this work. The first movement was undoubtedly a
success, but the other two did not quite add up, and Bax rejected
them long before he finally decided to replace them with two completely new movements (in 1915). The ultimate shape was of two
moderate movements flanking a ferocious scherzo, an approach Bax
returned to again in the Viola Sonata of 1921.

Maybe it is true that this sonata finds Bax in a style much nearer
to John Ireland and to Delius than he is in his orchestral works, yet
it represents a considerable achievement for its young composer, and
marks a real development in his style. The motto theme so impressed
one early reviewer that he wrote, 'Within its two-bar confine is
enclosed a concentrated power of emotional expression which I
have no hesitation in declaring that few men, living or dead, could
surpass.'[15] There is a quasi-folk character to the idea that is later
exploited in a dance-like metamorphosis. The convincing construct-
ion of the first movement, its assured manner and memorable
treatment of the material, all contribute to our recognition of a work
by a young composer which should be judged with his mature output. The glorious outburst into E major, like the sun striking warm
through the clouds, or the misty pianissimo of the coda to the first

movement, in which the texture takes on a fairy quality not far removed from the more atmospheric passages of *In the Faery Hills*, shows that although his heart may have been captured for the moment by a Slavonic nymph, his soul was committed to the blue misty landscapes and the smouldering sunsets of the far west. Certainly there is no mistaking the emotion Bax put into the work, and to have done this so convincingly, in a first movement lasting over thirteen minutes, is no mean achievement. It is perhaps not surprising that in his original second and third movements Bax should not have been so successful.

At this time, Myra Hess appeared on the scene as a young pianist who wanted to play his music. Bax immediately wrote a piano piece for her dated 16 February, and dedicated 'To Myra Hess, most poetical of pianists with admiration and sympathy'. This was the 'Concert Valse in E♭', from the title-page of the manuscript the first of 'two Valses', but apparently the only one to have been written. If today it appears a somewhat naive work, it nevertheless was, for a short time, a piece which Myra Hess championed in the concert hall, and which their mutual piano teacher, Tobias Matthay, persuaded Boosey to publish.

Myra Hess played the 'Valse' in a concert promoted by the Society of British Composers at the Broadwood Rooms on 18 March, again on 19 April at the Hampstead Conservatoire and on 17 May at the RAM Club and Union. But Bax would have only heard the first of these for he was out of the country during the spring and early summer of 1910, for reasons which will be explained below. Finally, Miss Hess crowned this succession of performances by playing the 'Valse' at a dinner in honour of Frederick Corder at Blanchard's Restaurant on 4 July.

A little before Easter, Arnold and his sister went to Ireland and journeyed to Connemara. They toured around seeing Arnold's beloved wild places, much of the adventure, perforce, being on foot. Arnold would stride ahead on these trips with Evelyn running behind trying to keep up. One day Arnold received news from London that Natalie was proposing to return to Russia and, acting on an impulse, he left Evelyn with only sixpence to her name. She had to beg her fare home from friends in Dublin, but Arnold had only one thought, and rushing back through a spring storm arrived in London before Natalie had left. He would go with her! And it was thus arranged that Olga Antonietti would accompany them, for in 1910, even in as liberal a circle as the Baxes', young men did not travel alone with

twenty-one-year-old girls without at least a nod at the convention of
the times. The decision to go to Russia was made in great haste. Bax's
parents were in Italy, and in making the practical arrangements —
visas and so forth — Bax was helped by his friend Arthur Alexander,
who has stated, in his unpublished memoir of Bax, that Bax visited
Russia twice. There is no other evidence in this respect, but it may be
that this was Bax's second visit there and hence he knew the ropes.
Bax recalled the journey to Russia in his autobiography thus (the
girls' real names have been substituted for Bax's pseudonyms):

I met the two girls on the platform at Lausanne — or rather I avoided them there
until the train started, as Natalie was surrounded by her family and friends,
assembled to see her off. We journeyed to Berlin, where Natalie took offence
with Olga over some trifle and would not speak to her for hours. At last I, who
had never yet been sent to Coventry, took it upon myself to remonstrate gently,
and to my surprise and relief Natalie consented to make up the one-sided quarrel.
From Berlin we lumbered over the weary illimitable Prussian plain, and at last
reached Eydtkuhnen — the German frontier town. At the next station we were —
thrillingly to two of our party — in Russia. Truly the stately amenities of a
Russian customs-house afforded an unlikely introduction to a reputedly semi-
barbarous land.

   In one corner was an ikon with a lamp burning before it; conspicuously
displayed on the wall facing the door hung a lifesize portrait of Tsar Nicholas II;
our baggage was politely — almost deprecatingly — examined by elegant young
army officers in grey-blue cloaks and with swords dangling from their hips.
Every single object in our trunks was delicately lifted to the light, whilst sedulous
search was made amongst books and magazines — not a page of the latter left
unturned lest an unflattering caricature of the Tsar or an article derogatory to
the imperial régime should be overlooked.

   But the courtesy of everyone was overwhelming, and I am not certain that we
were not even offered tea.

   When to my serious alarm my passport was temporarily removed by a smirking
official, Natalie told me that he was amused by the shortness of my name, and
certainly when the document was returned to me I noticed that I had become
'Baksi', in Russian script, a more seemly sound, I suppose, to the Slavonic ear.

   We must have been two hours in that place, and it was midnight before we set
out again by the broader-gauged Russian railway through dark leagues of birch
and pine en route to St Petersburg.

   My earliest experience of that great and beautiful city was dramatic indeed,
for we chanced to arrive on the evening of Easter Day. Bells thundered and
jangled from every church with its cupolas and crosses awry; the Nevski Prospekt
was a flooded river of cars and droshkys, pouring steadfastly westward towards
St Isak's Cathedral; every class of the people of the capital was abroad in the
streets.[16]

   Russian opera and ballet had a great influence on Bax's musical
style, and his first encounter with the Russian Imperial Ballet had an

almost physical impact: 'I was so headily excited that I came near to casting myself from the dress circle into the stalls',[17] he wrote. Out of this came various works ostensibly for piano. It is surprising that he did not write a ballet score that achieved any lasting success, for his talents were admirably suited to the task, and as we shall see, when the Russian Ballet came to England the following year he did make the attempt. However, Russia, its life and landscape, as well as Bax's emotional commitment to the expedition, had a profound effect on the young composer — an effect which finally allowed him to write music personal to himself and not dependent on any models.

At the end of April, Natalie and her party set out to join her family in the south. The Skarginski estate at Krouglik, midway between Kiev and Kharkov, in the Ukraine, was to provide Bax with bitter-sweet memories. He spent May and June there, months which were hot by day and 'by night the languors of the not very remote Orient invaded the gardens, woods and hills'.[18] Bax was both attracted and repelled by 'these burning alien lands'[19] as he called them. Possibly Martin Cooper has put his finger on why Bax showed at least some sympathy with the land in which he found himself when he wrote of how, in the great Russian imagination, 'the Ukraine plays a rôle not wholly unlike that occupied by Ireland in that of the Anglo-Saxon peoples: dissident and romantic, easy-going and comical, essentially provincial and the exact opposite of the cold officialdom represented by St Petersburg. Added to this the spell of the exotic exercised by the South over all Northerners ... and the enchantment of the long, hot spring and summer days and scented nights.'[20]

Written in the Ukraine was the work which, when revised some seven years later, became Bax's First Piano Sonata. In early lists of Bax's music appears a mysterious *Symphonic Phantasy* for piano, dated 1910. It was played by Myra Hess as late as 1919 under this title, but is probably none other than the original version of the First Sonata. It is possible that what is ostensibly another Bax piano work, the *Romantic Tone-Poem*, of which no trace has ever been found, may also be another fanciful title for this same work.

Bax's inclination was to write for the orchestra, and in the 'Russian' sonata colouristic effects abound, particularly at the bottom of the keyboard. The dark-hued images that Bax conjures certainly appear to have been written with some other palette in mind than the black and white of the piano. The characteristics of the music that strike one immediately are its passion and its onward sweep — developing the material organically into a large-scale

structure — and yet the absence of specific extended 'tunes' as such.
In this work Bax does not offer us musical picture postcards as he
does in the short, Russian-oriented, *May Night in the Ukraine* which
he wrote in 1912 and dedicated to 'Olga and Natalie'. Nevertheless,
Harriet Cohen has offered a clue to programmatic associations by
referring to a section of the music as evoking the 'illimitable distances of the Russian plain'.[21] The 'broad and triumphant' coda is
punctuated by a vivid pianistic impression of the wild pealing of
Russian cathedral bells — the bells that Bax heard as he first arrived
in the Russian cities of Moscow and St Petersburg. Frank Merrick has
suggested that 'the bells in Bax's coda may well have been inspired
by those of the Cathedral of St Isaac in Petersburg ... I was there for a
fortnight in that very year ... and had hardly reached my room in an
hotel when those wonderful bells did their remarkable performance,
twice in close succession. Bax does not use the actual motif with
which the tiny bells began and ended, but what he has written has
several points which lead me to think that it was from the bells of
this very Cathedral that he was helped to plan his superb ending to
the sonata.'[22]

There are several Russian composers whose style Bax occasionally
draws upon over the next ten years or so, but Balakirev (in works
such as *Thamar* and *Islamey*) and Scriabin (in the *Impromptus* and
Fantasy in B minor) are perhaps the most noted in the Sonata,
though there are overtones of Rachmaninov in the opening of the
recapitulation and the coda. The triumphant peroration of the
version we know today was not added until much later. But the
whole episode which had been thus sublimated in music was a
valuable one for a young composer whose life until then had been
divorced from reality.

Left alone with Olga, he subsequently impulsively proposed to her
while they were in the Ukraine, but not being accepted he left her
there (subsequently having to find her way back alone) and returned
to England 'bruised in spirit, but with a strong sense of relief, a
strange satisfaction that one episode in my life had been rounded off,
irrevocably finished. No soiled rags or withered and sick-smelling
flowers remained littered about my heart to mock me. I was grateful
for this experience, thankful even for the mortification it had
involved. Soon the ache was quite dead, and remembered beauty but
the last pallid ray of a wild star in the rising of a new dawn. I felt
enlarged in my sympathies by the clarifying flame of that almost
forgotten pain.'[23]

Marriage

Bax returned to England alone. It was summer, and although he might have wondered how he would explain his behaviour to his family, the shock he received on arriving home was totally unexpected. Up to this time, Ivy Bank had assumed the character of a refuge to which he could always return. But he found great changes imminent, for the house was becoming unsafe owing to settlement and was to be sold, although the family did not finally move – to 7 Cavendish Square – until February 1911. There were other changes in prospect too. His great friend Godwin Baynes had become engaged to Rosalind Thorneycroft (though they did not get married until September 1913); and, later in the year, Clifford made an impulsive marriage.

These new liaisons began to break up the pattern of life into which Bax's young manhood had fallen. But for an all too short four years until the First World War wiped away all his youthful dreams and aspirations (and many of his friends), he lived in a brief golden age. His was a circle of great artistic promise and many were attracted to it. Typical was Edward Thomas, the poet, who through Godwin Baynes 'got to know Clifford and Arnold ... and a new world of leisured people'.[1] Bax was one of the brighter stars in a 'circle of young people who met regularly on the tennis-court and in the garden-studio of Frederick Corder's house in Albion Road'.[2] This brilliant group were constant companions and several times a week, 'played games, invented entertainments, discussed life, and thronged the theatre galleries to drink in Wagner, dote on the Russian dancers, and adore the Irish players'.[3] In addition to Arnold, the Corders, Harry Farjeon, Godwin Baynes, the Antoniettis and Myra Hess, there was Gertrude Peppercorn. She became a well-known pianist and had been a fellow student with Myra Hess and Irene Scharrer at the

Academy with Matthay, and was to marry another member of the group, the writer Stacy Aumonier. Later they were joined by 'little Harriet Cohen', yet another Matthay pupil at the Academy.

No sooner was Bax back from Russia than musical matters arose to which he had to attend. In particular Henry Wood (at Elgar's instigation, we are told) invited him to submit a work for possible performance at the Proms. He sent *In the Faery Hills*, his most recently completed score, and it was accepted. So there was the necessity of having parts copied and of checking them. A day or two before the concert (on 30 August) Wood invited the young composer round to his house, as was his habit when giving a new work. Bax later recalled how in youthful trepidation he

knocked at his door in Hampstead, wondering what kind of reception I should get from that — even so long ago — almost legendary figure. Almost immediately he hurried into the room and I discovered to my relief that in stature he was actually no more than life-size. Like Elgar, Sir Henry at the rostrum always appeared, by sheer force of personality, to be very much taller than he actually is. (Anyhow, that was the impression made upon one young man.) His hand-shake was firm and genial, and in two seconds my nervousness vanished. Getting to work at once (for as ever there was no spare time to waste) he proved kindness itself, showing the keenest interest in and paying the closest attention to my score. At the concert he gave a beautifully balanced rendering of a piece which was at that time considered dangerously modern and uncomfortably difficult to play.[4]

The work was favourably received. The *Pall Mall Gazette* wrote:

Mr Bax's music proved extremely interesting in its suggestion of a suitable atmosphere by means of skilful instrumentation. The actual thematic material struck one as being a little lacking in individuality of style; indeed, once or twice influences of Wagner and Debussy were apparent ... [yet] ... the composer has not failed to show imaginative power and a feeling for the fanciful and pictur-esque. He certainly scores most effectively, and undoubtedly has an unusually strong sense of colour.[5]

After this Bax must have gone to Glencolumcille, where much of the remainder of the year was spent. Two works occupied him during this time — *Roscatha* and *Enchanted Summer*.

Roscatha is a work orchestrated from the short-score manuscript of *The Gathering of the Chiefs*, an interlude from the abortive opera *Déirdre*, and it was completed in full score in November. Bax intended it as the third part of the orchestral cycle *Eire*. Its Irish title means 'Battle Hymn', and it is martial music of gripping brilliance and vigour. The orchestration is not fully characteristic of the later

Bax, and indeed is less so than that of *In the Faery Hills.* Its brassy sound, a tendency to unison and octave doubling of melody, and its pungent harmony, leaves us in no doubt that the work is his first *orchestral* piece to be influenced by the sounds he had experienced at the theatre in Russia. The brilliant orchestral palette of Rimsky-Korsakov and Borodin combines with a certain Elgarian feeling. Dorothy Wilson wrote that this flavour 'is impressed upon the listener as much by the harmonies as by the mellifluous horn writing in the second section,'[6] adding, 'the rhythmic drive of the opening, with the brittle percussion and surging brass, already suggests the raging seas, which are such an integral part of Bax's tone-poetry.' *Roscatha* is dedicated to 'the "mountainy[7] men" of Glencolumcille', the only work Bax ever dedicated to the people of his 'land of heart's desire'. But it was never played in his lifetime, and its first performance did not take place until February 1974, when Leslie Head presented it in a concert in memory of J. H. Davies, late BBC Music Librarian. Its only performance since is Bryden Thomson's splendid recording; issued in 1985.

This was Bax's eighth orchestral full score, and by 1910 he had only heard three in performance (excluding that 1904 rehearsal as being unlikely to have taught him anything). His relative inexperience is evident when at one point a trumpet phrase wanders below the instrument's range, but in contrast his rapidly maturing ear for orchestral sound is shown by the brilliance he conjures from his orchestra.

It is interesting to note how well the cycle of *Eire* tone poems sounds when played consecutively. Can we begin to see the ground-plan of what might later develop into the shape of a Baxian symphony? The first, *Into the Twilight*, is perhaps not deeply enough argued for the actual first movement of such a work, and the urgent opening side-drum and horn calls of *Roscatha* would indicate the prelude to a separate work rather than a symphonic finale. But *In the Faery Hills* has a scherzando character, with a slow lyrical middle section, which would make it an ideal central movement in such a scheme.

Clifford was abroad at this time and Arnold would not have seen him since setting out for Ireland, prior to his Russian trip. As a result, Arnold was having to act as editor for the forthcoming issue of *Orpheus.* Possibly it was this that brought him back to England at the beginning of October. Just before leaving Glencolumcille he had had a surprise on hearing of Clifford's sudden marriage on 28

September to Gwendolen Bishop, who was rather older than him, and a contributor to the *Orpheus* series. She became known to the family by her second name of 'Daphne'. Considering the high emotional level on which he had been living during much of 1910, Bax's basic attitude to the world was remarkably sane, even if his financial independence did allow him to live a life that was divorced from the common grind. It was certainly a life that we might envy. Arnold wrote to his brother on 7 October:

The Longmynd Hotel
Church Stretton
Salop

My dear old Cliff

As you may imagine your news or rather the drifted news of you was about the greatest surprize of my life, and was hard to realize at first. I was in Glen at the time, and the news caused a sensation in Cashel, being the one topic of conversation during the day. 'That's the boy has the heart in the right place' was the general verdict, and John Beag requested me to 'tender you his congratulations'. Annie McGuire sends the same message clothed in more homely terms. You were also discussed by 'La Kamba' and others entirely unknown to you. I was asked for details of the 'lassie' which I was naturally unable to give. It may be amusing to both of you to hear how you have been discussed and approved of in far-away Donegal and even in the Gaelic language.

It is needless to tell you of course how much *I* sympathize with you in the new delight and romance that has arrayed your life in such strange and lovely hues and veils. As far as I know the whole affair was taken with astounding sang-froid possibly touched with fatalism at Ivy Bank, though of course I did not hear the first crash.

Orpheus XII is going to be a very good number. We are including your fragment of salient Saturday Review journalese [published under the pseudonym 'Anatolius'], which I think very good in its own line, though we are (in Edgar's [Edgar Davies] phrase) 'garbling' the titles of both your contributions, putting 'Artists' in inverted commas and altering the other title to 'Children's Play', as 'child's-play' conveys a derogatory impression owing to the well-known phrase. We are not including either Cousins or Lady Margaret as neither of us can 'close', so to speak, with the latter's contribution. It seems to me very heady. Diana Read's poem does not yield its meaning to either of the editors so that they do not feel justified in including it. The pen of the present writer contributes 'The bluggy story' [*The Death of Macha Gold-Hair*] and 'Glamour' [Bax later set 'Glamour' to music (1921)] while Bertie Beng is represented by that charming Greek poem which you have no doubt seen. Hine's [Reginald Hine] dreams also embellish the page with a pleasant fragrance as of 'The Secret Rose' (do not examine this metaphor), and W. B. Y. is also represented in two poems of C. French.

I like your poem immensely.

The following occurred in a p.c. from Sidley [the Hon. Sec. of the Theosophical Society] the other day 'hoping you are having a good time among the emeralds, and culling many gems of much worth.' I presented the card to Edgar, who wept.

ORPHEUS.

(The Art-Movement of the Theosophical Society.)

' To give unto Them beauty for ashes.'

Isaiah, lxi. 3.

CONTENTS.

The tail-pieces are by Fidus, the well-known German artist.

THE AIMS OF THE MOVEMENT.

(The following statement does not necessarily apply to all who contribute to this paper.)

E are a group of artists who revolt against the materialism of most contemporary art. We are adherents of that ancient philosophic idealism which is known to our time as Theosophy, and we believe that by the breath of that poetic wisdom the arts might be kindled into a new and radiant life. We wish to approach with an equal sympathy the methods of East and West; to combat the conception that beauty of theme is inessential to art; to find expression for the noblest moods of the modern soul, and thus in a complicated and restless age to create an atmosphere in which the spiritual self may breathe, delight, and grow strong.

Anyone who is in sympathy with our aims, whether a member of the Theosophical Society or not, is eligible for membership of its art-movement. Particulars can be obtained from the Hon. Secretary, Mr. Herbert Sidley, Strathleven, Oakleigh Park, London, N.

Fig. 3   Contents page of the issue of *Orpheus* edited by Arnold Bax.

Back in Ireland again until Christmas, Arnold completed a setting of Act II Sc. ii of Shelley's *Prometheus Unbound*, for two solo sopranos, chorus and a large orchestra. Quite when this work was first sketched we do not know, but it is marked by such a passionate and exultant mood that it would seem unlikely that Bax could have essayed it immediately following his Russian experiences. One is inclined to think that he was now orchestrating and completing a work conceived earlier in the year or even in 1909. The Shelley setting is in marked contrast to *Roscatha*, and must be viewed as a seminal work in Bax's output at the time, and together with *In the Faery Hills* is an indication of how he was emerging as a composer. *Enchanted Summer*, as it was finally called, was his longest completed orchestral work at the time (the early orchestral variations excepted) and is also the largest of all his choral works. It is certainly his most complex work up to then, and in addition to the chorus and two obbligato soprano voices there is an extended solo violin part, as well as shorter viola and cello solos. Its importance to the Bax-Gardiner circle must have been considerable, as it was chosen to open the first of the series of concerts that Gardiner promoted during 1912 and 1913, and considerable time and resources were lavished on it. Gardiner's notebook for late 1911 frequently reminded its owner of matters to be attended to in connection with *Enchanted Summer*. A reminder to send 300 vocal scores to the Memorial Hall, Farringdon, where the choir rehearsed, is followed by a note that 'all the brass parts ... have to have tempo marks inserted after 40'. Later he had to 'look through solo and 1st violin part' and then '2nd violin part done'.[8] And so it went on.

It is interesting to note the effect *Enchanted Summer* had on the young Philip Heseltine, for one. Heseltine was then nearly eighteen, and in a letter dated 27 September 1912 he wrote to his former music master at Eton, Colin Taylor, enthusing about it:

I have received this week the vocal score of a work which has thrilled me more than anything I have seen or heard in music since Delius' *Songs of Sunset*, which is saying a good deal ... I am absolutely *enchanted* with it, I play parts of it over and over again and the music haunts me all day. The work is Bax's *Enchanted Summer*. I can find no words that will adequately express my admiration for this perfectly *glorious* music. Surely the man who could write this and the *Celtic Song Cycle* must be *the* coming British composer.[9]

That vocal score was published by Riorden in 1912, although Bax retained the copyright. It is safe to say that such an arrangement meant that Bax (or rather his friend Balfour Gardiner) paid for its publication, presumably to facilitate its first performance in March 1912. Thus the decision to perform it must have been taken soon after its completion, otherwise there would not have been time for the vocal score to be engraved.

The absence of documentation of Bax's continuing cordial relations with the Corder family, makes it possible to forget that he would have continued to be a frequent visitor at Albion Road for comradeship and musical advice, and hence the dedication of *Enchanted Summer*, although misprinted on the vocal score, is a timely reminder: 'To F. Corden [*sic*] Esq FRAM my ever-true friend'.

Bax put everything into *Enchanted Summer*. Lessons learned in works such as *Fatherland* and the songs were thrown into the stylistic melting-pot. The specific models to which he turned are either taken from his earlier works, such as the song 'Golden Guendolen', or from more exotic ones such as Scriabin's *Impromptus*. The orchestration, too, shows the seed of the later style more clearly than *In the Faery Hills* had done. In places it is, perhaps, overdone. To mark *con ultimo forte* twice against passages already marked with three *f*'s is indicative of Bax's state of mind at the time. In questions of musical grammar and in the writing of his music on the page there was always much left to be desired. Bax's genius was aural in character and he tended to write in a free chromatic style oblivious of key signatures. The full score, in fact, does not repeat the key signature (often in six sharps) from page to page, once given. So free is the style that some editing was administered, probably by Gardiner, or perhaps by Corder, in the preparation of the vocal score. At one point, for instance, a key signature is moved back four bars in the vocal score from where it is established in the full score. Some of the individual instrumental lines, too, are almost unplayable as written. A cor anglais part in which unnecessary double sharps and double flats frequently occur, and in which flats and sharps mixed together appear almost at random may be indicative of a certain caste of aural imagination: it shows little appreciation of practical musicianship. (This was a problem that is encountered in Bax's music even as late as the Fourth Symphony in the early 1930s, a work that Paul Corder and Marjorie McTavish went through simplifying the notation – they found a chord of C major written as B♯, F♭, G, C.)

Enchanted Summer is in three parts, which play continuously.

At the beginning of the full score Bax has written Shelley's introductory note to Scene ii: 'A forest intermingled with rocks and
caverns ... Asia and Panthea pass into it. Two young Fauns are
sitting on a rock, listening.' The work opens with a short prelude
in which Bax said he tried to evoke 'the profound depths of the
great summer woodland and of the elfin and unhuman inmates
of this Arcadian world'.[10] It is a mood that he several times dealt
with in the music written in the period up to the First World War,
and in it we see the other side of his musical personality, away from
the direct influence of Ireland. This is the first time he attempted
this mood, but he was remarkably successful, even so.

It really needs a performance to realise how closely the opening
of *Enchanted Summer* (Ex. 17) foreshadows the opening of the later
tone poem *Tintagel*, and perhaps, even more important, how

Ex. 17

the climax of the work parallels that of the last movement of the
Sixth Symphony, that 'passing of worlds'[11] as Peter Pirie has called
it, which would later mark Bax's final acknowledgement of the end
of his creative life.

After the opening bars Bax tells us how the wood-spirits, hovering in a flickering of sunlight and shadow among the heavy green branches, begin to sing softly, entranced by the undreamed-of beauty of the two Nereids who, heedless of all else, drift by, following the voices of their dreams.

In this first section the composer has tried to render the continual interchange of light and shadow among the green forest-aisles, and the eternal youth and Theocritan serenity of the woodland in its early summer foliage.

In the second division of the work, illustrative of the strange and enchanted mood occasioned by the midday singing of the nightingales, the music becomes more impassioned, and the swooning peace and drowsiness is disturbed by the eternal pain of Philomela's age-long complaint.

The third part (Allegro Vivace — and here the full chorus enters for the first time) is chiefly concerned in suggesting the glitter and glory of the strengthening sunlight and the vernal force and surge of the youth of the year.

> As inland boats are driven to Ocean
> Down streams made strong with mountain-thaw.

Finally the Spirits, intoxicated with their own voices, rush headlong and laughing through the leaves into the distances of the forest. Silence falls again. The two little Fauns, astonished by what they have seen and heard, approach one another shyly, and one of them who appears to be somewhat wiser than his companion tells what he has heard of the invisible woodland singers. Finally they remember that the goats of Silenus are not yet milked, and run off to perform their duties, lest they shall miss the tales of the origin of the world and the gods that are their delight.

As regards the general character of the music, it may perhaps be added that the composer has endeavoured to combine the impressionistic manner with a melodic scheme freer in scope than that commonly used in choral writing, and yet of a definite cantabile character. It seemed that an attempt at a musical translation of poetry so spontaneous, and inherent with a quality of ecstasy possibly unequalled in English literature, required a mingling of two elements of music usually divorced from one another.[12]

In his treatment of the illustrative aspects of the score Bax is most successful, especially in the numerous points of delicately drawn instrumental colour. His youthful ardour finds free rein in the headlong passionate climaxes, which are thrilling. Particularly characteristic is the theme which crowns the most purple passages with a romantic ardour that recalls Scriabin. But regretfully this idea also reveals one of the work's weaknesses: the orchestral treatment of much of the vocal part of the work. The critic of the *Athenaeum* wrote with under-statement that the 'vocal parts are not gratefully written for the voices'.[13]

The end of 1910 was the time of the first major impressionist exhibition in London, an event that, in conjunction with the colourful blaze of the Russian Ballet the following year, transformed the artistic climate, not least for Bax. As Virginia Woolf wrote, 'on or about December 1910 the human character changed'.[14]

Another Hampstead family with whom the Baxes were on good terms was that of Carlos and Luisa Sobrino and their daughter Elsa. They lived in the Finchley Road. Carlos Sobrino was a well-known Spanish concert pianist. Born in 1861, he had appeared, aged fourteen, at a concert in co-operation with Albéniz, then also a child. Later he became a friend and student of Anton Rubinstein, and toured extensively both as a solo artist and in association with the violinists Ysaÿe and Sarasate. He had married the operatic soprano Luise Schmitz in 1889, and since 1898 they had lived in London, where Sobrino became Professor of the Piano at the Guildhall School of Music in 1905. His wife had been born in Düsseldorf and was well known abroad as a Wagnerian singer. After taking minor roles at Covent Garden, she sang Elvira in *Don Giovanni* in 1901. She also made the first-ever twelve-inch gramophone record by a woman singer in Italian, *Ernani involami*. This was in 1903 for the Gramophone and Typewriter Company, for whom she also made two other recordings in the same year. But it was as a concert and festival singer that she was best known. Notable festivals at which she sang included Leeds, and The Three Choirs at Worcester and Gloucester. Their daughter Elsa Luisa, or Elsita as she preferred to be known, was a close friend of Arnold's sister Evelyn.

This cosmopolitan and musical family must have had a particular fascination for the young Bax. Elsita's parents premièred his song *The Fairies* in June 1908. Elsita was a 'dark, attractive, warm-hearted' girl with a 'highly generous nature'.[15] Moreover she had a fine voice, and it must have been for her that one or two of Bax's songs were written at this time. As her mother was away on a world tour during 1909 she was probably present at the Bax Christmas party of 1909 and may well have been the intended vehicle for the Christmas Carol that Bax wrote then.

On coming home from Ireland for Christmas the following year Bax encountered her again. He had returned from Russia in a very nervous condition, and it is probable that his mother was anxious to encourage him in a stable relationship, particularly in view of the impending upheaval attendant on the move from Ivy Bank. Various alleged or suspected sexual exploits of Arnold and his brother 'were the subject of a hell of a discussion' between Mrs Ridley Bax and a friend, Mrs Stevenson. The only event to compare in its shockingness was when Arnold started drinking whisky, for it was a very teetotal household.

Arnold himself described his state on returning to England as 'bruised in spirit',[16] and it was not surprising that he should embark quickly on another emotional encounter, on the rebound, as it were, from events in Russia. Elsita spent Christmas 1910 with the Baxes, and sang Arnold's songs. He undoubtedly felt a considerable sympathy with her, and marriage may indeed have appeared a good idea. Events moved quickly and, underlined by the pressing move from Ivy Bank, Arnold's and Elsita's wedding was quickly arranged, taking place on 28 January 1911. Bax's father provided a handsome house in Chester Terrace, Regents Park, and shortly afterwards Arnold's parents followed them into town, living in Cavendish Square.

For their honeymoon Arnold and Elsita went to Ireland, and it was in familiar haunts, particularly Renvyle, Connemara, where Arnold orchestrated the *Festival Overture* of 1909, that they stayed. This preoccupation with work at the beginning of his marriage was a bad omen for the ultimate success of the union. Bax was not a family man by nature but a nomad, and the encumbrances of married life stifled his free spirit. Elsita was a highly strung girl, and one cannot think that Bax would have found himself marrying her if things had been normal. A year or two later, Edward Thomas compiled a list of his friends, 'marking' them out of ten as to their various personal qualities. The list included Arnold and Elsita. He awarded Arnold 9 and Elsita 10 for 'vanity', 2 and 9 for 'Christianity', 8 and 1 for 'fire', 8 and 1 for 'adaptability' and 7 and 0 for *'joie de vivre'*.[17] It was, in fact, the attraction of opposites, and once the initial attraction had passed they were revealed as incompatible. And the speedy breakdown of Clifford's marriage left Arnold with the example that, should things not work out as the faithful and optimistic Elsita hoped, he need not suffer in silence.

All his life Arnold had been cosseted and protected, living in comparative ease and luxury, indulging his whims as they occurred to him, in short doing exactly as he liked. This does not mean he had led a 'soft' life, as his travels testify. But he had never had to take a paid position, had had no ties, and never had to observe any discipline or routine. He was comparatively unprepared for the pressures of domestic ties. Arnold continued his musical activities, and it was notable from the first that Elsita often did not accompany him to concerts and other musical events, occasions which began to assume the nature of all-male affairs. Previously, members of the family would go with him to rehearsals, providing moral support, when he began to suffer from palpitations and anxiety lest his music did not go right. But soon Elsita was unwilling to go to functions anyway: she was pregnant. She was drawn into Mrs Bax's protective orbit but was not to provide Mrs Bax with her first grandchild, for Clifford's wife was in the same condition, and their daughter Undine was born on 6 August 1911.

Since his passing interest in the poetry of Stefan George a few years before, from time to time Bax toyed with settings of German poets, and made a number. He was particularly attracted to words by Friedrich Rückert and Richard Dehmel. Altogether he made four Rückert settings, of which only one — *Spring Rain* (1910) — survives; and eight of Dehmel, of which at the present time we have only two. But in 1911, as well as Rückert's *The Bridal Prayer* and *Faith*, Bax wrote *Flight, The Journey* and *Aufblick* to words by Dehmel. Dehmel was the author of many poems set by Bax's young contemporaries in Vienna, and wrote *Verklärte Nacht* which stimulated Schoenberg and Oscar Fried to ripely romantic scores.

After his marriage, probably while still on honeymoon, Bax started writing a cycle of three *Nocturnes* for soprano and orchestra, and they occupied his attention for much of April. *Aufblick* is the first of these, and is dated 18 April. We might sympathise with Bax's interest in setting so richly passionate a poet as Dehmel at the start of his marriage if it were not for the poem he chose to set. Bax set the German original, and I am grateful to Stephen Banfield for the following translation.

> Over our love a weeping willow hangs low,
> Casting night and shadows around us both.
> Our brows are sunken.
>
> Silently we sit in the dark.
> Once a torrent was raging here.
> Once we saw the stars shimmering.
>
> Is everything then dead and dreary?
> Hark! — a distant sound — from the cathedral —
> Bells pealing — night — and love —

While still in Connemara, he orchestrated an earlier song, *Liebes-ode* (to a poem by O.E. Hartleben), as the second of the *Nocturnes*. The song opens quietly with delicate touches of orchestral colour, and the vocal line which begins in the eighth bar is beautiful and affecting, if not very original (Ex. 18). Bax brings the song to a

Im   Arm____   der__   Lieb - e   Schlief - en wir sch - ig...

Ex. 18

climax with the voice soaring to a high A♭ while the orchestra thunders out a romantic backcloth — woodwind and horns fortissimo, and the violins and violas in octaves moving around the adjacent B♮. It is gloriously effective with a Wagnerian soprano riding the texture, but not altogether characteristic of the composer's mature style. While the expansive writing in both *Nocturnes* comes from Wagner, Bax's harmony and his rich and detailed orchestration proclaim his sympathy with the current European developments in composers such as Schreker and Zemlinsky. At the close of *Aufblick* a passing reminiscence of the climax of his earlier tone poem *Cathaleen-ni-Hoolihan*, and violin solos in both songs remind us that it is Bax writing. Bax appears to have rejected the songs almost immediately, for no third *Nocturne* survives, nor, in all probability, was ever written. Yet their first performance by Rita Cullis in the BBC's Bax centenary series, over 70 years after they were written, was more than an act of anniversary piety, and revealed a delightful, living score.

The couple returned to London, where on 25 April, in a concert at the Bechstein Hall, Myra Hess — to be a great champion of Bax's piano music until the appearance of Harriet Cohen on the scene — played his *Romantic Tone-Poem*. As we have seen, this piano work was probably an early version of his first piano sonata.

There was much musical activity, as always on the London scene, yet this was no compensation for having to stay in town. Bax could settle neither to domesticity nor to life in the metropolis. He wrote to Padraic Colum how 'London seems to me possessed with an absolute whirlwind of excitement, entirely without direction of any kind'. 'I find it impossible even to read for ten minutes together. I cannot imagine any literary person producing anything at all whilst living in this place. I know I never could.'[18]

It seems likely that Bax would have been at the first performance of Elgar's Second Symphony on 25 May, and at the Aeolian Hall on 2 June when Myra Hess played the first movement of Bax's 'Sonata in D minor', one of a number of early attempts at piano sonatas. This performance in fact took place as part of the International Music Congress held in London between 29 May and 3 June that year. The concert in which Bax's sonata was heard was an afternoon affair promoted by the Society of Composers to demonstrate the range of young talent active in the country, and included chamber works by many of Bax's contemporaries.

But the various attractions of London were not sufficient to keep Bax in the city. The decision was taken to relinquish the London house and move to Dublin, or rather to the middle-class suburb of Rathgar.[19] This arrangement may well have been brought about by Clifford, who was acquainted with the Irish poet and mystic 'AE' (George Russell), another resident of Rathgar, and with many other Irish artists and intellectuals of the period. However, before the move could take place, Arnold was to find himself confronted by another important artistic influence and a source of liberating energy for his art. The dominating influence in that Coronation Year was the Russian Ballet. There was a festive atmosphere, and the brilliance of this new art exploited it to the full. Bax, we may be sure, would have been present for most if not all of its repertoire and was quite captivated by 'the divine dancer, Tamara Karsavina'.[20]

'The Summer of 1911', Clifford Bax tells us, 'was a procession of golden days.'[21] In the spring of the year he had become the proud owner of 'an old grey Manor House in a rural part of Wiltshire'. This was at Broughton Gifford, where for three memorable summers, Clifford and Arnold Bax and a circle of literary and artistic friends assembled for a series of 'cricket weeks'. Their team played all the surrounding villages, and the event took on the character of a week-long intellectual house-party.

Clifford Bax's evocation of the first of these events in his book *Inland Far* paints a memorable picture of an Arcadian time. He wrote:

They all took a train from London on the eve of the first match, and arrived at the Manor House when the maid was distributing lighted lamps about the rooms. Throughout the day I had done my best to prepare for their pleasure;

hiring a small fleet of bicycles (but none that was strong enough for Baynes), rolling the tennis-lawn for hard use on Sunday, and superintending the emplacement of a cider-barrel in the ingle-nook. Four of the team could sleep in the normal bedrooms. In order to house the others we had turned the long loft under the gables into a dormitory.

For once at least in our lives, anticipation, experience, and retrospect were to be equally delightful. I doubt if upon that August evening when we sat down to supper at a long table of cherry-wood, under the serried beams of the hall, there was any group of men in any part of the world that was happier than ours. We were young enough to feel an aggressive cricketing spirit; old enough to endure defeat and personal failure, if these were our lot, without the dejection of boyhood. We shared, that evening, a mood that must have resembled closely the mood in which a party of young Vikings assembled on the coast of Norway with the excitement of a sea-raid before them. After supper, when we had adjourned to the music-room, the company indulged in a riot of insolent wagers. Farjeon would bet that Baynes, for all his huge build, would not hit a six. Aumonier, madly vainglorious, would stake five shillings on his ability to take more wickets than my brother. And presently we were prophesying, each in turn, the number of runs that the various players would make on the morrow, the entire team asserting that Aumonier would be out first ball. As balsam for this injury, someone — I think it was my brother — produced a limerick that ran:

> With regard to our free-hitting Stacy,
> It is safe to assert that we may see
> A wire arrive
> Saying 'Lords. Half-past five.
> You are wanted for Test. F. E. Lacey.'

And in a few minutes Baynes, who, like Bully Bottom, could never be left out of anything, had celebrated Farjeon's prowess in the lines:

> There was a young fellow named Bertie
> Who never made fewer than thirty —
> It's perfectly clear
> We could rhyme without fear
> If his father had called him Doherty.

Soon afterwards without suppressing the desultory talk of good friends who had not associated for months, my brother went to the piano and Baynes began singing, — singing ditties from Cecil Sharp's collection, Elizabethan lays, and eighteenth-century drinking-songs. Meanwhile, the cider went round, the pipes were knocked out and recharged, and we all became sleepy enough to wish for bed but too well-content to lead the way.

And then the next morning, we straggled down to breakfast, attired in our flannels. Early though I was, I found Snaith already in his chair and the parlour-maid busy with the coffee. We had lifted the table to one side of the hall in order that the old window-seats might supplement the supply of chairs: and through the open window I could see the green shapes of the garden and the colour of innumerable flowers, now fresh from their nocturnal cooling and at their gayest in the new sunlight. Bees, too, were gloating over the roses on the other side of the wall. A spray or two, in the abundance of August, had flourished across the windows. I suppose it was not until ten o'clock that the whole team had breakfasted; but Hartley and I had already arranged a chess-championship, to be played in the course of the week, and an intensive tournament of lawn-tennis, to be begun at nine in the morning on Sunday and finished at nine in the evening. And that we might set a good example to the others, we started a game of chess in the porch, where, between the original wooden seats, we had just enough room to place a stool with a board upon it. At ten-thirty, however, we had to adjourn our game, for the village wagonette had appeared outside the gates. Cricket bags were hoisted into it: and after some delay, with half the team on bicycles and the other half in the brake, we set off down the fragrant high-hedged lanes. As Hartley and I, free-wheeling down a hill, span past the wagonette we could hear Baynes trolling out in his warm baritone:

> A lawyer he went out one day
> A-for to take his pleasure,
> And who should he spy but a fair pretty may
> So handsome and so clever.

We caught a glimpse, too, of Radford and Farjeon, advancing the chess-tournament by playing their game with a pocket-book set of pieces.

Our homeward journeys were not less happy than our settings-out. The hedges were dustier now. The meadows beyond them, and the elm trees, looked as though they were gladly tired by the long day's heat: and the timbered farms that we passed had an air of saying, 'But the sun cannot burn too strongly for us, us who have known four hundred summers – and the faces of earlier men.' We that rode bicycles were the first to be back at the Manor House, having called out our answer to the villagers who shouted, 'How did you fare?' And we were first in the bathroom. By the time that our baths were over, the sun had set, and a long afterglow ensued: and just when the windows of the Manor House were lighting up, the brake arrived with the rest of the players, and then there was a second race for the bathroom. At length we assembled in the hall, as if by so doing we might hasten the coming of supper: for we were fatigued and hungry, and sometimes there was a choric ejaculation of delight when the parlour-maid set a line of candles down the long table and when the cook followed with the first of her dishes ... [Afterwards,] the night being clear and the air still temperate, we would find our way, by twos and threes, to the little square lawns in front of the house, and slant our deck-chairs at the most luxurious angle, and there – with the sharp stars creeping above us and the lilies that bordered the lawns glimmering like ghostly sentinels – we would smoke our pipes and launch forward into the interminable discussions that arise so plentifully in youth.[22]

The strange fact is, that although Eleanor Farjeon was present and has described the ambience of the Cricket Week,[23] the Baxes in their accounts never mention their women-folk at all. This is all the more peculiar considering Clifford's wife bore him a daughter at the time of this first meeting, and Arnold, only six months married, was also to be a father. They were clearly not interested in − or, more probably, were embarrassed by − the idea of parenthood. Both tended to act as if it had never happened.

In this context, to read Clifford's account just quoted (produced only twelve years, at the most, after it happened) is to hear only an edited version of the story. For it was about this time that Clifford Bax fell in love with Olga Antonietti, a passion that lasted the remaining years of peace and resulted in his leaving wife and child.

Arnold and Elsita now took the lease of a substantial furnished suburban villa, incongruously named 'Yeovil', in Bushy Park Road, Rathgar, where they were to remain for two years.

George Russell ('AE') also lived in Rathgar. He was sixteen years Bax's senior, and a respected figure in Irish literary and nationalist circles. Writer, painter, mystic and protagonist of the Agricultural Co-operative Movement, he was Bax's entrée to that world. As we have seen, Arnold was preceded in Dublin by his brother, and it was Clifford who introduced him to AE and thus to the literary scene of which he became an active part. They also introduced him to republican opinion, for AE's home was the meeting-place not only of poets but of agitators, and whosoever had felt the call to foster 'divine discontent in the under-world'. AE's poetry, in particular, influenced both brothers for a short time. Clifford later described AE's artistic achievements in his poetry anthology *Vintage Verse*, writing: 'All through his life he painted small pictures, when he could find the time, some of them renderings of his visions, others land- or seascapes suffused with pantheistic feeling. He painted rapidly, and perhaps also wrote his verses rapidly: but, caring more for spiritual progress than for artistic achievement, he remained always an amateur. AE's poems, made from his conviction that time does not affect the immortal *atma* in man, must always bring a sense of home to those who can find little in European literature to awaken the deepest layers of the self.'[24] 'In my youth' Clifford wrote elsewhere, 'I had looked upon AE as the man for whom I had been searching',[25] and it was this spirit that his brother reflected. Arnold had, of course, through the good offices of Clifford, already published some of his Irish stories and poems and they stood him in good stead in this Irish literary sphere. He was known as 'Dermot O'Byrne' to many and not by his real name at all. No sooner had the Baxes settled in, than Clifford was invited to stay. Clifford had known AE since 1906, and he and Arnold lost no time in going round the corner to AE's villa at 17 Rathgar Avenue so that Arnold might be introduced. Arnold recalled in his autobiography how they were 'warmly welcomed, and whilst I prowled round the walls of the studio ... I listened for the first time to one of those mellifluous if often almost incoherent rhapsodical monologues concerning the "Gawds".'[26] He went on to describe how 'some of us followed AE's example in keeping open house one evening in the week, and thus one met one's friends almost every day. I remember James Stephens entertained on Mondays, the Colums on Tuesday, myself on Wednesday.'[27]

One young observer of this literary scene was E. R. Dodds, from whose autobiography we can piece together the following evocation which, while being atmospheric is also objective:

AE knew everybody worth knowing in Ireland, regardless of religious or political creed; his little house in Rathgar Avenue was the centre of a web from which filaments ran out in all directions ... The circle of his friends was as wide as his interests. There were Old Testament prophets like Pádraig Pearse and practical men like Edward Lysaght; impish jesters like James Stephens and melancholy jesters like Stephen MacKenna; poets like 'Seumas O'Sullivan' [James Starkey], dramatists like Lennox Robinson, art experts like Tom Bodkin, critics like 'John Eglinton' [W.K. Magee] and Joe Hone, scholars like Osborn Bergin from the National University and Edmund Curtis from Trinity ... If you had the necessary stamina you could listen to the lions roaring almost every night in the week. The entertainment was of the simplest — most often just tea and buns and a fire to sit round ... At most houses general conversation was the accepted rule. AE had two smallish rooms with open folding doors between. When there were too many guests for one room the unspoken convention was that politics was talked in the front room and literature or art or theatre in the back one, with AE himself flitting between the two.[28]

Bax took to this circle like a duck to water, coming back from his favourite haunts in the west with, as Mary Colum, one of his particular audience, remembers, 'an extravagant vocabulary which he turned off on all his friends or in his short stories'.[29] Writing of his literary works this wife of one of the leaders of Irish literature described some of the stories as 'extraordinarily good'. The talk was all of Ireland, as Bax went on to describe in his account of the scene.

I should think that more than half of those long-silenced discussions must have been concerned with Ireland from some aspect or other, for, as in Russia and Poland, the shadow of the nation broods over all gatherings of Irish folk, and the voice of the dark land beyond the window-panes mingles sooner or later in every conversation.

New friends and acquaintances were gradually added to the list of those I originally met in Rathgar Avenue: the O'Rahilly, a striking handsome young man, always dressed in a saffron kilt, who was destined to be killed in O'Connell Street during Easter Week; Professor Rudmose Brown, half-Danish, an inquiring, fatly genial man with a vast pink-and-white face that somehow made you want to laugh; John Eglinton (George Moore's 'contrary John'), curator of the National Library and author of several little books of astute criticism written in a scrupulously fastidious style. John would stand no nonsense from Irish-Irelanders, Gaelic language fanatics, or any sort of 'sentimentalist', and spoke shockingly of Cathleen ni Hoolihan as a 'bedraggled beldam with holy water on her brow and whisky on her breath', but somehow he was universally liked and respected.[30]

Bax's published writings also introduced him to a variety of other literary personalities in Ireland. His book of short stories, *Children of the Hills*, was especially potent in this respect. One particular friend whom this volume attracted was Darrell Figgis, a fervent republican and poet who was only a few months his senior. Arnold reported how Padraic Colum returned from staying with Figgis one day in midwinter, saying that his friend was 'tremendously keen' on Bax's stories. Bax recalled his conversation with Colum:

'Who is this Dermot O'Byrne?' says he, and when I told him I knew you well, 'I must meet that man,' says Darrell. 'Tell him to come over here any time he likes and stay a week.'

'Do you think he meant it,' said I. 'He did surely. Send him a wire today to say you're coming.'

This I did, and next evening found myself in Keel above the amethyst caves and the green Atlantic.

Little did I dream then that within a few years both host and hostess would be dead by their own hands.[31]

Bax's poems, stories and a play were widely disseminated within this circle, but rather than distract the reader by this interesting material in what is intended to be basically a musical study, the literary work is considered separately in Appendix A.

Bax had the headlong enthusiasm of the true convert in all this, and clearly the thought never crossed his mind that he might be incurring any resentment in attempting to be more Irish than the Irish. In particular, Bax was proud of his mastery of the Gaelic language, and insisted on speaking Gaelic until AE irritated for once out of his Olympian calm, told him it was damned bad manners to talk to other people in a language of which they knew nothing.

One of the tragedies of Bax's musical career is the sheer bad luck which resulted in none of his ballets establishing themselves in the repertoire, or indeed being remembered at all. His first music which acknowledges the ballet are two movements of a 'Ballet Suite' which survive in short score, 'No. 2 *Humoreske*' and *Russian Dance*. Both are quick movements, and from the style (confirmed by the fact that Bax signs himself 'Arnold E.T. Bax') we may date this forgotten and apparently unfinished work to his time at the Academy, almost certainly late 1901. Far more important is his reaction to the Russian Ballet's London season in 1911, finding it 'absolutely a new art', in which he was 'indulging deeply'.[32] At the time Arthur Alexander was Bax's constant duet partner at the piano, and vast quantities of music were pounded through by those two young master pianists: shortly afterwards they were to be among the first in England to play through both *Petrushka* and *Le Sacre*, almost immediately they were published. But their real liking was for the more romantic and nationalist Russian repertoire. Having probably seen all the ballets presented in this first London season, Bax went off to Ireland determined to emulate them, and devised a full-length ballet in a prologue and two acts.

For most of the period July to November 1911 while at Rathgar, he worked furiously at this Russian-style ballet to be called *Tamara*, which was completed in short score. (The scenario will be found at Appendix C.) The ballet (Bax does not call it thus, but 'A Little-Russian fairy tale in action and dance') comprises the following. References in square brackets are to later works in which Bax re-used the material from this score:

Prelude (Lento — Allegro vivace)
No. 1 Lento malincolo — Allegro vivace
     2 Allegro
     3 Allegretto vivace [reworked as the 'Gay & finely' dance in *From Dusk till Dawn*]
     4 Vivace — Lento ma non troppo [The tune of *Tamara* in the latter section became the 'Dance of Motherhood' (*Water Music*) in *The Truth About the Russian Dancers*]

Act I Scene I [No scene 2 is specified]
No. 5 Lento moderato
     6 Non troppo allegro
     7 Molto vivace
     8 Allegretto
     9
    10 Lento languido [published as *Naiad* for flute and piano]
    11 Allegro vivace
    12 Allegro furioso ('Dance of the slaves and subjects of the enchanter')

13 Tempo di mazurka ('Un danseur et une danseuse')
14 Moderato – Allegro vivace ('The girls') – Variation (Tamara)
15 Variation I: Allegretto ('Une danseuse')
16 Variation II: Allegretto grazioso ('Danseuse II') [published as *The Princess Dances* for flute and piano]
17 Allegro marcato ('Entry of the Enchanter')
18 Valse ('The dance of the Enchanter's thirty beautiful daughters')
19 Vivace – Allegretto scherzando ('Dance – Igor and Tamara')
20 Valse d'Amour ('Igor and Tamara and the girls')
21 Allegro vivace
22 'The servants of the enchanter dance in savage triumph' (Allegro molto vivace)
    Grazioso e espressivo ('The Girls')
    'Une danseuse seule'

Act II

No. 23 Introduction and Polonaise [includes material later re-worked in Overture (*Ceremonial Dance*) in *The Truth About the Russian Dancers*]
24 'The Melancholy of Prince Igor' (Lento ma non troppo)
25 'The Festivities Continue' (Allegro vivace e molto rhythmico)
26 'Une Danseuse' [published as *Shadow Dance* for flute and piano]
27 'Buffoon's Dance' [published as *Grotesque* for flute and piano]
28   [re-worked in *From Dusk till Dawn*]
29 'General Rejoicing' (Allegro molto) – Tempo di Galop
30 Apotheosis [uses, in augmentation, the theme later given to 'Dance of Motherhood' (*Water Music*) in *The Truth About the Russian Dancers*]

From this account of the plot and the musical numbers which comprise it – ninety-two pages of closely written piano score – the reader may realize that we have here a full-length work: the longest Bax ever wrote. It is also certainly one of his most alive and high-spirited scores, if not exactly the most original.

Bax arranged four movements (Nos. 26, 16, 10, 27 in that order) for flute and piano, giving them the titles of *Shadow Dance, The Princess Dances, Naiad, Grotesque,* and these were played during the First World War but not finally published until 1947. Odd movements were occasionally found in programmes in the years immediately after publication. He did not reveal the source of what became known as Four Pieces for Flute and Piano, and that at least would still make a delightfully modest addition to the flute repertoire if revived today.

Having worshipped Karsavina from afar and having inscribed the score of this new ballet to her, Bax was then rather nonplussed as to how to promote it. In a letter he wrote at the time to Rosalind Thorneycroft he said, 'I am full of dreams about my ballet – as

to the possibility of the Russians taking it up – if only I knew
how to get hold of them.' This seems a little feeble when we remember that Beecham, an acquaintance of Bax, had conducted
during the Summer 1911 Diaghilev Season.

Unfortunately, when Diaghilev came to London in the summer of
1912 (12 June to 1 August), the programme was headed by the
announcement of the first performance in England of a now more
familiar *Tamara* with music by Balakirev, and Karsavina in the title
role. Although the plots were quite different, Bax's dismay can be
imagined. His title was changed to *King Kojata,* but though material
from this score is used most effectively in other scores, Bax's big
opportunity had been lost: there could be no going on with the ballet
and he never orchestrated it. He never mentioned it to Karsavina,
even though he came to know her very well later. She did not hear of
the score until after his death. Yet the surviving piano score contains
many pointers to the orchestration, and it must surely be heard one
day. The effect on Bax's career of the successful production of a
major ballet would undoubtedly have been considerable, and its non-
completion was a major influence, albeit a negative one, on the way
in which he was to develop.

Rathgar and London

Both of Bax's children were born at Rathgar: his son, Dermot Colum, on 22 January 1912,[1] and his daughter, Maeve Astrid, exactly twelve months later, on 22 January 1913. Their names reflected Bax's wholehearted embracing of things Celtic, although later he could be amusing on that topic, observing to a friend about the twenty-year-old Maeve that she had become 'a young Amazon' and concluding, 'that's what comes of giving a girl a name like that'.

They spent much time travelling back and forth between London and Dublin, and his London friends visited them in Rathgar. When in London, Arnold stayed with his parents, while his sister Evelyn was often with them in Ireland to help Elsita look after the children, and was present during both confinements.

Balfour Gardiner also visited him in Ireland, and although not a new friend, Bax along with many others began to see much more of him. The circle which grew up around Gardiner brought Bax into contact with many rising 'names' of the period — including Norman O'Neill and Gustav Holst.

Norman O'Neill was eight years Bax's senior, a pupil of Arthur Somervell in London and Ivan Knorr at Frankfurt, and was with Gardiner a member of the 'Frankfurt Gang'. Known as a composer particularly of theatre music, he was enjoying the success of his music to Maeterlinck's play *The Blue Bird* at this time, and probably encountered Bax in Dublin in October 1911 during the play's provincial tour. Norman O'Neill was also musical director of the Haymarket Theatre, a fact that was to result in a minor commission to Bax in the summer of 1912.

Gustav Holst was a year older than O'Neill and became a greater friend of Clifford than of Arnold. When they met Holst was nearing

forty and apparently a failure. He had a sizeable body of music
to his credit, but this included little of the work by which he is
remembered. He earned his living by teaching music at St. Paul's
Girls School in Hammersmith and at Morley College. It was Balfour
Gardiner who was to give Holst his first artistic successes and remove
the weight of failure from his shoulders.

Charles Kennedy Scott was brought into this circle by Norman
O'Neill late in 1911. Balfour Gardiner was promoting a series of
concerts in London, at the Queen's Hall, and O'Neill thought Kennedy Scott might be of practical value with his Oriana Madrigal
Society, as indeed he was. Kennedy Scott, of the same generation
as O'Neill and Holst, had founded the Oriana Madrigal Society in
1904, and was already established as a choral conductor. He played
an important part in presenting choral music in London, and at this
date was particularly associated with the Elizabethan and Jacobean
composers from Byrd to Weelkes (the latter also an enthusiasm of
Holst). Kennedy Scott later wrote of the period how

Almost without one's being aware of it a great ferment of musical activity had
been taking place in our midst — great in quality as well as extent. We discovered
almost suddenly, that we had produced a veritable 'school' of composers, though
its elements were so diverse and individual: a school already cemented by very
close personal friendships (destined to be further extended) which had arisen
largely through the instrumentality of Balfour Gardiner himself.

Balfour's concerts were probably the most important series of concerts
that we have ever had, not excepting those of the Delius Festival in 1929.
They consolidated English music as never before or since. At that time, though
Vaughan Williams was already a considerable figure, Parry, Stanford, and Elgar
were still in the ascendant. But there were younger composers, well past the
prentice stage, who had by no means had their due — Holst, Bax, Dale, Delius,
Balfour Gardiner himself, and others.[2]

The Balfour Gardiner Concerts of 1912 and 1913 were presented,
in two series, each of four concerts. Short-lived though they were,
these concerts established a new note in the music of the time, the
appearance of a truly English approach. 'A liberation', Kennedy
Scott noted, 'not only of formal processes but, what was of far more
importance, of the imagination itself. Of all this, Delius' music is
a chief example.'[3] While we may not agree with Kennedy Scott's
pigeon-holing of Delius, seen from the vantage point of the 1980s, in
1912 he appeared as a truly British figure, and because of his cosmopolitan background could unite many different tendencies in a
supposedly 'British' art. Kennedy Scott continued about Gardiner:

Many of us are aware of Balfour's exceptional generosity and judgement (which, with engaging independence, has always refused to be taken in by accepted opinion of any kind). No one will ever know the full extent of his benefactions – the perfect gentleman has always been behind them. The tribute must be paid here.

The days of these concerts were satisfying, happy days. Balfour had a small town house in Kensington, off Edwardes Square – Norman O'Neill lived opposite. There his friends gathered; there Percy Grainger would play his own compositions, or Bax, with his unrivalled power of score-reading, the compositions of other members of the circle when their own skill was insufficient; there plans were discussed, programmes settled with eager anticipation. The moving spirit was, of course, Balfour Gardiner; no accredited institution could have supplied the stimulus that he gave.[4]

While the most important source of patronage in promoting his series of concerts was certainly Balfour's, Bax, or rather his father, was also guarantor for relatively small sums. For example, an Oriana Madrigal Society programme for 17 December 1912 shows 'A.R. Bax' as a guarantor for £50, and one for April 1914 shows him guaranteeing £40. Arnold's mother also promoted concerts, which were held in the large concert room at their home at Cavendish Square, though, owing to their semi-private nature, these events were not documented, and so we know nothing about them.

Balfour Gardiner's series of concerts of new music brought many aspiring young composers to the fore, and Bax had four large works played. Balfour also dedicated his own contribution to his concerts, his choral *News from Whydah*, to Arnold when it was published by Novello in 1912. Bax must have had a particularly close influence on the whole aesthetic of these concerts in his capacity as pianist to the unofficial committee that chose the music to be played, and thus heard many works, some later to become famous, before they were publicly performed.

The first concert opened with Bax's *Enchanted Summer* and continued with Delius's *First Dance Rhapsody*, Gardiner's *News from Whydah* and works by Percy Grainger and W.H. Bell. *The Athenaeum* was not impressed by the Bax, and criticized the balance of the performance. Other reviewers were kinder. But *The Athenaeum* was entranced by Percy Grainger, and also found *News from Whydah* 'strong' and Bell's choral ballad *The Baron of Brackley* an 'advance in clearness' on that composer's earlier music.[5]

The second concert opened with another Bax première, that of the *Festival Overture*, which Bax had dedicated to Balfour, who conducted. But Bax's music was rather overshadowed in this concert by

Elgar conducting his own Second Symphony, and Percy Grainger performing the Tchaikovsky B♭ minor Piano Concerto. There was no music by Bax in the remaining two concerts of the first season, but he reappeared in the third concert of the second season, in March 1913. This is the concert that Bax describes in his autobiography (see p. 128) where he names his own music correctly – *Christmas Eve on the Mountains* – but incorrectly remembers the rest of the programme, which actually included music by Vaughan Williams, Grainger, McEwen and Holst's large-scale choral work *The Cloud Messenger*. The last concert comprised Bantock's delightfully rich pot-pourri of contemporary influences, *Fifine at the Fair*, Bax's *In the Faery Hills*, Delius's Piano Concerto, a Symphony in E major by Frederick Austin (later to be famous as the reviver of *The Beggar's Opera*), and ended with Gardiner's own very popular *Shepherd Fennel's Dance*.

Bax has described in his autobiography how the concerts ceased because Gardiner fell out with the orchestra. Yet surviving contemporary records show that Gardiner was to have given a third series at the end of 1914 if the war had not intervened.

The two series were very widely followed and reported. Before the first, *The Times* devoted more than a column to the prospectus, and after, a similar amount of space in assessing what had happened. On the national musical scene the concerts received the highest regard and contributed in a very real way to the development of the concept of a British composer at the very time when post-Elgarian composers were trying finally to establish themselves.

Bax's *Enchanted Summer* was so well received in his circle that it was quickly given a second performance by the London Choral Society under Arthur Fagge, before being forgotten. *Christmas Eve on the Mountains* was never played again (a later revision, unplayed in Bax's lifetime, was premièred by Leslie Head in 1979), but the overture enjoyed a brief spell of popularity before and after the First World War. It is only *In the Faery Hills* that has maintained even a small foothold in the repertoire. It was his earliest orchestral score to be published, along with his later work, in the 1920s.

The overt Irish programmes of many of Bax's pre-war works are either of a literary origin (*In the Faery Hills*), or else – as he developed and came under the influence of the Russians – they are atmospheric. This is evident in a short programme note in which he characterized his tone poem *Christmas Eve on the Mountains*: 'The motif of this tone-poem occurred to me whilst wandering one frosty evening last winter [1911–12] in the beautiful and legended Gleann na Smól, in county Dublin. I hope that the rather mystical mood of which this piece is the outcome may be sufficiently evident in the music to carry its own explanation.'[6] Bax added in his auto-biography that he had 'tried to suggest the sharp light of frosty stars and an ecstasy of peace falling for one night of the year upon the troubled Irish hills, haunted by the inhuman *sidhe* and by clinging memories of the tragedy of eight hundred years'.[7] Bax introduces the traditional plainsong of the Credo (*'Credo in unum Deum'*) into his score. This is also quoted by Richard Strauss in *Also Sprach Zarathustra*, which may well be Bax's source. However, this is probably the least characteristic of Bax's more extended orchestral works, though still with many fingerprints of the mature composer. Contemporary reviewers found influences from Wagner and Tchaikovsky after the first performance. In fact the prevailing feel is of an earlier romanticism reminding us of Liszt's tone poems while possibly the rather four-square writing suggests the German-influenced Russians such as Rubinstein. The climax in which the solo organ appears is quite un-Baxian and strongly reminiscent of a similar moment in Tchaikovsky's *Manfred* Symphony, though many touches of orchestral colour indicate even there the way he was to develop. Its more exotic moments, however, are decidedly Russian, suggesting perhaps a Russian Easter festival rather than an Irish Christmas.

Apart from *Christmas Eve*, 1912 also saw the completion of two overt and more characteristic memories of the trip to Russia – the tone poems for piano, *May Night in the Ukraine* and *Gopak*. The former is dated 10 February and was written after Gogol's *Evenings on a Farm Near Dikanka* in which the Russian author evokes the May night in a famous passage. Indeed, so close is Bax's musical portrayal of this sensual and languorous description, that the various facets of Gogol's picture are to be found in the music, complete after six pages or so, with trilling nightingales.

Gogol wrote, 'the moon comes out from the centre of the sky', and Bax obligingly quickly gives us a spread chord across the keyboard. 'The immense dome of heaven', Gogol continued,

stretches further, more inconceivably immense than ever; it glows and breathes; the earth is all bathed in silvery light; and the exquisite air is refreshing and warm and full of voluptuousness, and an ocean of fragrance is stirring. Divine night! Enchanting night! The woods stand motionless, mysterious, full of gloom, and cast huge shadows. Calm and still lie the ponds. The cold and dark-ness of their waters are gloomily walled in by the dark green gardens. The virginal thickets of wild cherry timidly stretch their roots into the cold of the water and from time to time murmur in their leaves, as though angry and indignant when the sweet rogue − the night wind − steals up suddenly and kisses them. All the country-side is sleeping. But overhead all is breathing; all is marvellous, triumphal. And the soul is full of the immensity and the marvel; and silvery visions rise up in harmonious multitudes from its depths. Divine night! Enchanting night! And suddenly it all springs into life: the woods, the ponds and the steppes. The glorious clamour of the Ukrainian nightingale bursts upon the night and one fancies the moon itself is listening in mid-heaven.[8]

Bax contemplated orchestrating this seven-minute movement, although, most regrettably, he appears not to have done so. It was a mood he had already attempted to evoke in two of the dances in his abortive ballet *Tamara*. The movements in question subsequently achieved performance and publication as the 'Naiad' movement of the Four Pieces for Flute and Piano, and 'Dance of Motherhood' (published as *Water Music* for piano solo) from *The Truth About the Russian Dancers*. In the latter we can hear how gorgeously Bax's orchestration can transform what is already an exotic piano piece.

These early piano pieces by Bax were circulated among his pianist friends in manuscript copies. *May Night in the Ukraine,* and the ebullient *Gopak*, were taken up by Myra Hess and first played by her at the RAM Club and Union on 2 November 1912, and later elsewhere. The following year they were published by Joseph Williams, and appear to have begun the popularity of Bax's shorter piano works (encouraged by his colleagues at the RAM).

In June, celebrations were taking place to mark the centenary of Keats's death. In aid of the Keats-Shelley Memorial House in Rome, the Haymarket Theatre presented 'two special matinées of dramatic, musical and scenic illustrations of the works of Keats and Shelley'. For these Norman O'Neill invited Bax to write a short orchestral overture. The resulting *Prelude to Adonais* was first played on 25 June with O'Neill conducting. Bax did not hear it as he was in Ireland at the time, and no trace of the score has since been found.

In July 1912 Bax wrote an extended descriptive 'poem for piano' called *Nympholept*, which he affectionately inscribed to his piano teacher Tobias Matthay. The following written programme is scrawled across the top of the manuscript. 'The tale telleth how one walking at Summer-dawn in haunted woods was beguiled by the nymphs, and, meshed in their shining and perilous dances was rapt away for ever into the sunlight life of the wild-wood.'[9]

The preoccupations of *Enchanted Summer* are resumed in this score, which again has nothing to do with Ireland. The opening of

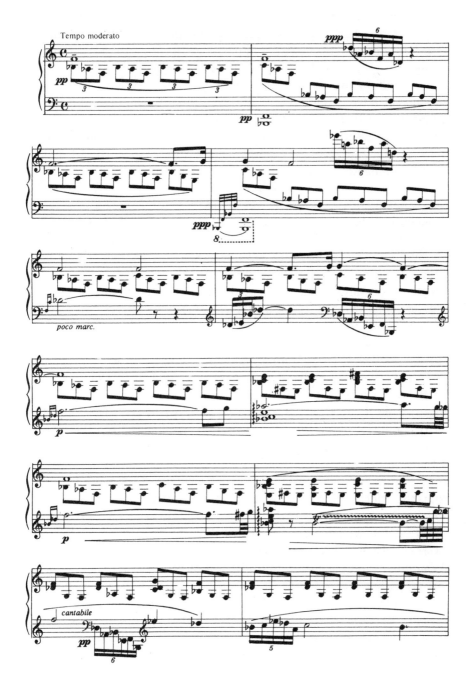

Ex. 19

Nympholept (Ex.19) – nearly three years later to be very successfully orchestrated – has marked parallels with other music of the period. This impressionist approach reappears in *Spring Fire* (1913) and on more sophisticated a canvas in *The Garden of Fand* (1913, orchestrated 1916). On the face of it the music reflects the dawn sequence in Ravel's *Daphnis et Chloé*. A similar technique in Bartók's *Floraison*, the first of his *Deux Images* (of 1910), which anticipates Ravel, reminds us that such a method was very much 'in the air' in 1912, and that Bax was simply being abreast of current trends. Several commentators have remarked on the similarity between certain passages in *Daphnis et Chloé* and Schoenberg's *Gurrelieder*, and how Schoenberg's indulgent farewell to late romanticism arguably shared part of the time of its protracted struggle into full score, as well as the extravagance of its orchestral apparatus, with Ravel's work. Yet although both composers must have been working on their full scores at the same time, the opening sequence of Schoenberg's, so similar to though more complex than the opening of Bax's *Spring Fire*, actually predates Bax's score by over ten years, though Schoenberg's music was not heard until 1913, and did not reach England until the late 1920s. Other composers in this vein included Florent Schmitt, particularly with his *La Tragédie de Salomé*, and Paul Dukas, whose dance poem *La Péri*, with its combination of the impressionism of Debussy and the Russian exotic colour of the Diaghilev Ballet, is very close to the colourful pre-First World War orchestral works of Bax. However, to return to Ravel's *Daphnis*, it is worth remembering that the ballet did not reach England until 1914, although it was first performed in the summer of 1912 in Paris. A clue that Bax might have journeyed to France for the occasion, and thus have heard the music, comes from the fact that we know that in the early summer of 1912 Godwin Baynes went to Paris to study hypnotism at La Salpêtrière, and it might well have been reasonable for Bax to go with him. Alternatively Bax may have had a copy of the original piano score of *Daphnis*, which had been published as early as 1910.

It is, perhaps, of value at this point to reflect on the development of Bax's mature orchestral style during this period, which is strongly marked, as can be seen even from a cursory acquaintance with the scores. The line of development that leads to the mature tone poems (*The Garden of Fand, November Woods* and *Tintagel*) and on to the symphonies, starts with *Cathaleen-ni-Hoolihan* and progresses via *In the Faery Hills, Enchanted Summer* and *Nympholept*. Interpolated into this developing line are brief flirtations with various styles as the young composer responded to different influences. These include *Fatherland* (Elgar and early Sibelius), *Into the Twilight* and *Enchanted Summer* (Debussy and Scriabin), *Roscatha* (Elgar, later Rimsky-Korsakov and Russia), and *Tamara* (The Russian Ballet). The habit of scoring too heavily was a definite problem, especially in the *Festival Overture* and *Christmas Eve*. Like the early over-complex piano parts in his songs, it was a sign of growing self-awareness and confidence as a composer. Although these orchestral works are lusciously scored, they are effective and strong in personality, and for almost the only time in his life Bax was fully of his time: a young lion on the musical scene.

Nympholept is an interesting case in point. It was orchestrated by March 1915, but it remained unplayed until 1961; Bax never heard it. However, it has all the makings of a popular work, and, as the predecessor of *Fand* in Bax's output, exhibits several characteristics of that work. We may wonder with *The Times* critic 'why such a pleasing piece should have to wait over 45 years for a concert performance', for 'in Bax's strong point – colour – it excels'.[10] At the front of the full score he wrote a new and different programmatic tag to that in the piano version, going on to explain a source in Meredith and Swinburne.

> Enter these enchanted woods
> You who dare

The title of this short tone poem comes from Swinburne and the quotation from Meredith's *The Woods of Westermain*. Both poems derive from the same central idea – that of a perilous pagan enchantment haunting the midsummer forest.[11]

Vaughan Williams had also used the tag from Meredith's otherwise leaden-footed poem in a lost orchestral impression called *Boldre Wood* performed in November 1907. *Nympholept*, literally 'caught by nymphs', was the title of a Swinburne poem dating from 1894,[12] and was later the title of a poem in Clifford Bax's *Orpheus* magazine by Margaret Sackville.[13] Arnold Bax himself also wrote a poem with the same title at about this time.[14]

The theme of a haunted wood was pursued in two further works, the 'symphony', *Spring Fire* (1913), and the tone poem *The Happy Forest*, completed in piano score on 13 May 1914, though not orchestrated for nearly ten years. Completed, too, was a smaller impressionistic work, *Red Autumn* (1912), eventually to be recast in 1931 as a work for two pianos, but clearly conceived for orchestra,

indeed crying out for orchestral sound to do its invention justice
(see Ex. 21 on p. 110).

Another work from this period is the *Four Orchestral Sketches*.
Dated '1912–13', the movements are entitled 'Pensive Twilight',
'Dance in the Sun', 'In the Hills of Home' and 'Dance of Wild Irravel'.
At the time, Bax was pleased with the last of them, noting to his
friend Arthur Alexander before the first performance, 'it will sound
like Armageddon – a complete battery of percussion, and castanettes
[*sic*] clucking like a self complacent hen ... [and] the gentle and
refined melancholy of the first piece will set it off well.'[15] There
are remarkable similarities of intent in this work and its immediate
predecessors. Nympholepsy – a condition of frenzy – is very near
to what Bax must have meant by 'Irravel', and I am grateful to
Graham Parlett for an explanation of the probable origin of the name.
The word is an anglicization of the Irish Gaelic *rámhaille* ('mh'
pronounced like a 'v') meaning 'the act of raving in sickness or sleep,
delirium, dreaming' plus the common intensive prefix *ir-*. Thus
Irrámhaille ties in with Bax's description of 'Irravel' as 'a fantastic
dream impersonation of a reckless and irresponsible mood or
whim'. Bax goes on to describe the music: 'the subjects are all dance
rhythms yet the composer has endeavoured to invest the music
with a somewhat veiled and atmospheric quality, and to convey
the suggestion of unreality and strangeness. Attention may be
drawn to the melody of the middle section, which it will be noticed
is really in $\frac{4}{4}$ time against a persistent pulsation in triple measure.
At the close the music becomes more and more remote in mood
and harmonically bizarre, as though the vision were gradually fading
away.'[16] But when in 1928 Bax revised them, he deleted this final
one.

The first and last were played at a Prom in September 1913 with
Sir Henry Wood conducting: a concert also notable for Bridge conducting the second performance of his suite *The Sea*. *The Times*
noted that the hall was 'exceptionally full, even for this season of
crowded houses'.[17] It is of interest to note the reviewer's curious
afterthought about the *Dance of Wild Irravel*: '. . . one is inclined to
wonder whether Mr Bax had been reading Stravinsky when he wrote
this number.' Yet the only composer brought to mind by this
gorgeous and atmospheric waltz is Ravel. It is certainly a viable piece
to be revived on its own account, and has now been recorded.

The four pieces were played as a suite, for the only time, during
one of the Bevis Ellis concerts in 1914. Bax wrote of them that

they had no psychological relationship with one another. So we have neither an early symphony *manqué* nor even a symphonic suite. The first movement, which employs a very small orchestra (the brass being represented by two horns alone), 'is the musical outcome of a romantic twilight mood, melancholy in character, but not gloomy'.[18] The second is a gay dance, the orchestra a little larger than in the first movement. The third movement is scored for strings and harp alone, solos being asked for in the strings, which are frequently divided. The music here deals with two ideas, one passionate and yearning, the other 'a long melody of a folk-song nature'.[19] Finally, there is *The Dance of Wild Irravel*, in which the full orchestra is called for.

Bax tended to act, between periods of apparently happy domesticity, as if he were not married, and went off on his own or with friends much as he had done formerly. This is particularly true of the period in which he lived in Rathgar. Two of these trips have been documented.

In the autumn of 1912 he had gone to Glencolumcille, where he received a postcard from AE suggesting he should join the poet at Breaghy. The latter went there every September to paint. It was a long journey — two days by bicycle, then by train and then 'outside car':

There at the door of a snug thatched cottage on a hill and surrounded by whin-bushes I descried 'AE's' burly and bearded form, his kindly shortsighted eyes peering out in search of me. Within the house we were mothered by a simple apple-cheeked old lady, and fed sumptuously on freshly caught salmon, superb eggs, and a huge and monstrously rich home-made cake.

It was an odd entranced week that I spent there, quite dreamlike in the guttering candlelight of memory. Close by our hillock were the fine house and estate of Sir Hugh Law, a Nationalist MP who, an old friend of 'AE', had loaned him a summer house in the wooded grounds above the sea in which he might paint on wet days.

I have not met with many experiences which cannot be accounted for by a rational explanation, but one of these occurred in that place in the dripping Breaghy woods.

I was reading in the window seat near the door, and we had not spoken for perhaps a quarter of an hour when I suddenly became aware that I was listening to strange sounds, the like of which I had never heard before. They can only be described as a kind of mingling of rippling water and tiny bells tinkled, and yet I could have written them out in ordinary musical notation.[20]

Bax several times tried to capture this experience in his music, probably most effectively in the middle section of the Epilogue of the Third Symphony, written in 1928–9:

Ex. 20

Bax continued the account of his stay:

'Do you hear music?' said 'AE' quietly. 'I do' I replied, and even as I spoke utter silence fell. I do not know what it was we both heard that morning and must be content to leave it at that.

As the dusk deepened many-coloured lights tossed and flickered along the ridges of the mountains. 'Don't you wish you were amongst them?' murmured my companion, and I knew he meant that we were gazing upon the host of fairy. Even under the spell of that lovely hour and with an intense will to believe it seemed to me more probable that those dancing shapes of flame were something to do with the retinae of my own eyes straining into the semi-darkness, and no far-off reality.[21]

To his Irish literary friends Bax made no mention of his music, and many of them did not even know him by his non-Irish identity. This was true of AE during that holiday, and when they returned to Dublin together AE 'listened with amazement when ... [Bax] began to speak about music with Balfour Gardiner.'[22] Whenever Bax and AE met thereafter the Irish poet always made some remark about this incident.

Another adventure took place in the early spring of 1913, and was written up at length by Clifford Bax in his book *Inland Far*. A party of four — Arnold and Clifford Bax, Balfour Gardiner and Gustav Holst (the latter subsidized on the trip by the generous Gardiner) — met at Charing Cross at the end of March 1913 for a month's holiday in Spain and the island of Majorca. Clifford described their departure:

We occupied the four corners of a carriage, and while Gardiner was mastering the enigmas of a Spanish time-table, and my brother remembering all the necessary objects that he had forgotten to pack, Holst informed me that he had just become interested in astrology, and on such a congenial topic I discoursed at length. A frown puckered Gardiner's brow. We could almost hear him muttering, 'Really, really!' And there is no doubt that our conversation grieved him.

None of us had ever visited Spain, and the holiday had therefore a smack of adventure. Gardiner had already acquired some Spanish. Holst and my brother refused to have any contact with the grammar which I offered to lend them. The latter, I fancy, was reading folk-stories in Erse.[23]

The holiday kept them away from 27 March to 21 April, and immediately on his arrival back in England, Arnold went to stay at Petersfield with the Farjeons. Many friends were there, including 'Tiny' Baynes and his fiancée Rosalind Thorneycroft, Paul Corder, Myra Hess and Olga Antonietti. Edward Thomas was also present with this exuberant company. Eleanor Farjeon remembered that Arnold was 'one of our earliest comers and longest stayers':

He brought with him a jet-black cigar of great length and girth, resembling a lumpy stick of liquorice. Installed on the mantelpiece, it became our aim to get it smoked before we left. The men took turns at it several times a day. When Paul paled and succumbed, when Bertie, Arnold, and even Godwin had cried enough, Olga and I weighed in with a few puffs; but the cigar from Majorca defeated us in the end. I think it was left on the mantelpiece as a memento.[24]

Arnold then returned to Ireland. For most of the period during May and June he travelled around between Dublin and the West. When in Dublin he stayed at St Stephen's Hotel, so perhaps his family had already left for England. He returned to England again during the second week in July.

The Baxes were particularly friendly with Padraic and Mary Colum, and the Colums were, in fact, married during the first year of their acquaintance with Arnold and Elsita. Mary Colum describes in her autobiography how, on New Year's Eve 1913, she and her husband 'walked out in the garden in the moonlight at midnight and sang the New Year in. Arnold Bax, AE and Fred Ryan, who was then editor of Wilfrid Blunt's paper, *Egypt*, drank the New Year in on strong tea.'[25] The Colums founded a monthly journal *The Irish Review* which during its brief life — it only ran until November 1914 — provided 'Dermot O'Byrne' with a wider outlet for some of his most vividly 'Irish' writings. Writing from 7 Cavendish Square on 10 September 1912, Bax sent Colum the manuscript of his story 'The Call of the Road',[26] describing it as his 'tinker sketch' and saying 'I think it is a good bit of West Donegal dialect at any rate.'[27] Arnold spent the month from the middle of September to the middle of October at Glencolumcille, where he asked Colum to send the proofs of the story. 'Glencolumcille, Co. Donegal is sufficient address',[28] instructed Bax. Arnold and Elsita were back in Rathgar from the middle of October, doubtless allowing more opportunities for meeting the Colums and other associates of *The Review*, and the commissioning of other writings, including a one act play, also about tinkers, called *On the Hill.*[29]

After he returned from Ireland in the summer of 1913, there was announced a performance of *In the Faery Hills* at a Royal College of Music Patron's Fund concert on 15 July.[30] He asked Balfour to conduct 'as the idea of doing it myself sends the blood to the head.'[31] Bax was not enamoured of his colleagues from the College, and this was always particularly evident on such occasions, referring to 'Stanford with his most Sarcophagus expression in the background ... you might also savour a new rhapsody on Little Puddleswick drinking-songs by R. Vaughan Williams Mus. Doc. ...'.[32]

But the Russian Ballet was still the prime artistic influence. Bax attended at every opportunity. On 27 July Colin Taylor, music master at Eton, wrote to the young Heseltine:

By the way I was introduced to Bax at the Russian Ballet the other night – do you know him? I have always pictured him as a slow speaking dreamy man – dreamy he may be, but in his speech he is short, dry and quite unpoetical. He told me he has a splendid 'Book' for a ballet and he is longing to get to work on it. At present however he is finishing a work for (I think he said) the Norwich Triennial Festival. A ballet should suit him.[33]

What the ballet might have been, unless *Tamara*, we have no clue, but the work for Norwich was *Spring Fire*.

That so brilliant and enjoyable a score as *Spring Fire* should have remained unperformed by a professional orchestra for over seventy years was a major loss to all lovers of the rich balletic music of the period. No prentice work, it succeeds by its sheer exuberance, powerful invention, and colourful orchestration, as Vernon Handley's ebullient recording makes clear. Bax wrote that

the music is an attempt to depict the first uprush and impulse of Spring in the woods, and though deriving primarily from Nature itself, the formal scheme of the composition was influenced in a large measure by the beautiful first chorus in *Atalanta in Calydon* ('When the hounds of spring are on winter's traces'). Indeed, the exuberance and pagan qualities of much of the earlier writings of Swinburne colour the musical content of the fantasy throughout. *Spring Fire* may be regarded as a kind of freely-worked symphony, the four sections linked together without a break.[34]

The four sections are: I 'In the Forest Before Day' – 'Daybreak and Sunrise', II 'Full Day', III 'Woodland Love', IV 'Maenads'. Each has a specific descriptive programme, and is preceded by verses from Swinburne's poem. *Spring Fire*, with its nymphs and fauns, its indolent lovers, its dryads, maenads and bassarids is not the material to stimulate any composer of the later twentieth century to his best work, and it is difficult if not impossible for us today to recapture the pre-First-World War innocence of Bax and his circle. The Somme, Passchendaele and the Easter Rising would remove Bax from his ivory tower all too soon. But through these early scores, and particularly in *Spring Fire*, we may recall some of that neo-paganism which Bax felt then, and which captured so many of his friends and contemporaries including, for example, Rupert Brooke.

The opening section of *Nympholept* is paralleled in the opening section of *Spring Fire*, while the middle section of *The Happy Forest* is also reflected, though not duplicated, in the 'Woodland Love' movement. Once Bax had given up any idea that *Spring Fire* would be played, he quarried the score very successfully for use in other works – the opening reappears in the slow movement of the Cello Sonata of 1923, while the fanfare theme of the Second Section, 'Full Day', reappears as one of the Royal Wedding Fanfares of 1947.

Another work of this time, the short tone poem *Red Autumn*, also started life ostensibly as a piano solo, although in this case it was never orchestrated and was finally published for two pianos. It is a characteristic score of the period and, although only for keyboard, we can imagine a typically Baxian orchestration, so colourful is the writing. Example 21, for instance, suggests the orchestral manner of

Ex. 21

The Garden of Fand, the next work to be completed in short score.

The Garden of Fand is the climax of Bax's first maturity. At the beginning of the score is a lengthy statement of the programmatic origin of the work. The image of Fand was an important one in Bax's imagination not only before the war but after it too (see for example p. 159), but it is difficult to be precise about its significance for him. The central section of the work presents as 'Fand's song of immortal longing' one of Bax's sweetest tunes. In a letter to a friend, he wrote that as he conceived it he 'wept in his Dublin room'.[35] A grown man in his thirtieth year does not weep at the composition of a tune, however beautiful, other than by association. And in Bax's case that association was certainly female. Writing of a performance of *The Garden of Fand* in 1933 at the height of a later passion, Bax wrote 'why do you make me feel such lovely and passionate things? I wish you had heard "The Garden of Fand" as a whole last night because I think it is rather like you — or anyway the mood my delicate passionate little lover brings to me.'[36] Yet the Irish element in *Fand* is strong: Bax said of the work's composition that 'it was all literally given to me by Ireland — I can't remember any work connected with it at all except for the orchestration . . . I remember feeling how almost uncanny it was; I did it partly in Dublin and partly in London but there was no break in the continuity.'[37]

Bax's mention of the orchestration of *Fand* underlines the fact that as far as most of his orchestral works were concerned the orchestral sound was firmly in his mind when he wrote them out in short score, and so the preparation of the full orchestral score was merely a chore: a chore, moreover, which he lightened by having his women-folk — particularly his mother, and later Mary Gleaves — read to him while he was doing it. However, two scores, in which he noticeably achieves a significant advance in technique, were really sweated over, chiefly *Fand*: this is probably why the orchestration was delayed for some three years. The hiatus was probably a necessary one, for the work could hardly have been so successfully realized in terms of the orchestra any earlier in Bax's development.

Fand develops the mood, the orchestration, and much of the figuration of *Nympholept*, as may be seen by the theme in Ex. 22 from *Nympholept* which *Fand* expands into the 'Song of Immortal Love' (Ex. 23).

Ex. 22

Hearing Ex. 22 in the original piano solo version of *Nympholept* one immediately realizes the similarity of the idea to the opening phrase of Bax's song *Roundel*. This work, the first he dedicated to Harriet, sets (in Old English) the words 'Your eyen two wol slay me sodenly'. In the song, too, the accompanimental figures are related to this idea.

Ex. 23

Bax's stated programme for *Fand* is as follows:

The Garden of Fand is the sea. The ancient saga called 'The Sickbed of Cuchulain' tells how that hero (the Achilles of the Gael) was lured away from the
world of deeds and battles by the Lady Fand, daughter of Manannan, Lord of
the ocean; and how in the time of his country's direst need he forgot all but the
enchantments of an immortal woman. The tale goes on to relate that Cuchulain's
wife Emer pursued him to that wonder-land and pleaded with the goddess for
her husband's return. Then, with one of those touches of modern romanticism
which are continually occurring in the Irish pagan tales, the Saga ends with
Fand's pitying renunciation of her human love, and we read, that Manannan
shook his 'Cloak of Forgetfulness' between Cuchulain and Fand, that the memory of each might be blotted out from the mind of the other. This tone poem
has no special relation to the events of the above legend. In the earlier portion
of the work the composer seeks to create the atmosphere of an enchanted
Atlantic completely calm beneath the spell of the Other World. Upon its surface
floats a small ship adventuring towards the sunset from the shores of Eirinn, as
St Brendan and the sons of O'Corra are said to have sailed in later times. The
little craft is borne on beneath a sky of pearl and amethyst until on the crest of
an immense slowly surging wave it is tossed on to the shore of Fand's miraculous
island. Here is inhuman revelry unceasing between the ends of time, and the
voyagers are caught away, unresisting, into the maze of the dance. A pause
comes, and Fand sings her song of immortal love enchaining the hearts of her
hearers for ever. The dancing and feasting begin again, and, finally, the sea
rising suddenly overwhelms the whole island, the immortals riding in rapture
on the green and golden waves, and laughing carelessly amidst the foam at the
fate of the over-rash mortals now lost in the depths. Twilight falls, the sea
subsides, and Fand's garden fades out of sight.[38]

The opening is intended to evoke, as the composer has told us, the
still sea. The gentle ceaseless movement of the water is effected by
'a tissue of shimmering harp and violin figures',[39] over which the
woodwind utter brief fragments. Bax may have had the sea music
from the opening of Frederick Corder's festival cantata *The Sword
of Argantyr* in the back of his mind (probably having attended its
London première at Highgate in November 1900) as he started
writing *Fand* (compare Exs. 24 and 25).

(Bax's short score)

Ex. 24   *The Garden of Fand.*

Ex. 25   *The Sword of Argantyr.*

The layout of a typically Baxian score is finally crystallised in the score of *Fand*. This is not only to do with the very full scoring, but with the contrapuntal elaboration in what is basically a harmonically conceived work. The music is presented in three or four separate bands of ideas and orchestral colour which move against each other, and the way each band reflects the others is the basis of the technique for evoking the sea. Within each of these broad bands there is further detailed contrapuntal movement, the overall effect being kaleidoscopic in effect. What is more, if each section is rehearsed individually it exhibits remarkable musical sense on its own. (This was particularly noticeable to the present writer when, during the recording of *The Happy Forest* in January 1969, it was necessary to rehearse each section of the orchestra separately.) We can see in an example from *Fand* (Ex. 26) the superimposition of unrelated harmonies. Here the three diminished sevenths are grouped together (with the exception of the A♭ in the second), and Bax himself pointed out that 'the harshness of the combination of the first and second is, in actual effect on the ear, mitigated by the "ictus" of the third which distracts the attention until the resolution of the second and third on the first, which has predominated throughout, owing to the insistence of the figure on the strings.'[40] It is this sort of technique which caused audiences of the immediate post-war period to regard Bax as 'modern' and equate him with Debussy,

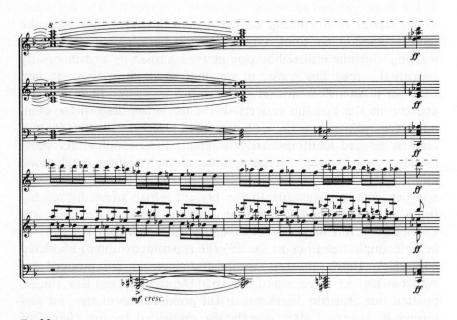

Ex. 26

Casella, Stravinsky and Holst. To these names, too, we might also add Bartók, Kodály and Szymanowski, for all were looking for a way to develop from the vivid language of Strauss allied to impressionism, and finding it in the sublimation of a variety of folk song in their developing personal styles. In this Bax was no different, except that in comparison with his British contemporaries his impressionistic works — with very few exceptions — were more vivid, his assimilation of his chosen nationalism the more complete.

In 1914 Bax gave up his house in Rathgar and moved to Marlow in Buckinghamshire, not far from his brother Clifford who was by then living at Speen — Arnold's first address being Elm Corner, Marlow Common. He still relied on his parents' hospitality, however, and often stayed at 'Cav', as the large house in Cavendish Square was known.

Early in 1914 a newcomer made an appearance in the musical circles in which Bax moved. He was 'a charming young man-about-town and an amateur of all the arts',[41] by name F. Bevis Ellis, only recently down from Christ Church, Oxford. He was one of the De Walden family, well-known as patrons of the arts. Bevis Ellis cultivated a varied circle of musical friends, and was a close friend of the composer and folk-song collector George Butterworth. Butterworth was in turn a friend of Vaughan Williams. So Ellis was in a unique position to bring together Bax and Vaughan Williams, a meeting which he effected by playing their music.

With the apparent demise of the Balfour Gardiner concerts, and Gardiner's ostensible withdrawal from the scene, there was an opening in the London concert world for enterprising promotion. Bevis Ellis put on a series of concerts in March 1914. Bax assisted him, as he had Gardiner, and the two young men became great friends. 'Dear, eager, intelligent, humorous, half-feminine Bevis Ellis!' recalled Bax, 'I became much attached to him ... and almost every evening we spent together either at his highly civilized Albany flat or at Covent Garden or some theatre or restaurant.'[42] There was a series of 'F.B. Ellis Chamber Concerts' at the Aeolian Hall and two notable orchestral ones at Queen's Hall, the latter being given on 20 and 27 March. Programmes for the Chamber Concerts are not available and so we cannot know the identity of the piano music by Bax that Ricardo Viñes (who had given five Debussy first performances between 1902 and 1905) played at one of them, for individual works were not specified in the pre-concert announcements. Both concerts that were heard at Queen's Hall included Bax's music. The first opened with the *Festival Overture*, followed by Butterworth, Dvořák and then the first complete performance of Bax's *Four Orchestral Sketches*. These works were all conducted by Ellis's friend Geoffrey Toye. The second half of the concert was conducted by Ellis himself — Strauss's *Don Quixote*. But the high point of the series was the last concert which included not only three songs — 'Celtic Lullaby', 'Christmas Carol' and 'Lullaby' — that Bax had specially orchestrated, but, more important, the first performance of Vaughan Williams's *London Symphony*.

The *London Symphony* demonstrated a number of valuable lessons to Bax. The example of a non-specifically programmatic symphony was telling enough, and the device of the Epilogue, which is such an outstanding feature of Vaughan Williams's score, was a formal innovation which Bax later used to give balance to the three-movement symphonic forms in which he was to write. Individual points of orchestration in the symphony also provided ready models, notably passages in the first movement, and more importantly the beginning of the Epilogue, which should be compared to the opening passage of Bax's *November Woods* (which, incidentally, Bax always referred to as dating from 1914, although marked 1917 in the score).

Vaughan Williams remembered the occasion as the time when he first got to know Bax well. He wrote:

We were discussing my, then new, London Symphony. One passage disappointed me and I asked his advice. He suggested the addition of a counter melody on the oboe. Indeed he sat down at the pianoforte and improvised one. This actual passage was too obviously Baxian to make its inclusion possible. But, following his advice, I made up another which, though not nearly so good as his, was more in keeping with the rest of the movement.[43]

Bax and Vaughan Williams remained friends, and we shall again see them musically influencing each other in the late 1920s in the context of Bax's Third Symphony and Vaughan Williams's Piano Concerto.

Other events at this time included a supper for Albert Coates at Pagani's given by the Society of British Composers on 19 March 1914 at which Myra Hess played a piano work by Bax. He was also composing the tone poem *The Happy Forest*, and completed the short score on 14 May. Bax categorized his objective in this brief, joyful evocation, by explaining 'in this particular forest humanity takes no place amongst the phantasmagoria of nature. Dryads, sylphs, fauns and satyrs abound — perhaps the goat-foot god may himself be there, but no man or woman.'[44] However, in this Bax had taken a recent literary source as his inspiration, which while partly dictating the music's form was too long to be reprinted in programme notes. Bax referred to it as 'a prose-poem by Herbert Farjeon'. At one time or another most of Bax's literary and musical friends were drawn into supplying Clifford Bax with suitable material for issue after issue of *Orpheus*. Farjeon's *The Happy Forest* was one such contribution.[45] (See Appendix C.)

There was interest too in the work that we now know as the First Violin Sonata. M. Montagu-Nathan, who had been at the 'Causerie' given by Arnold's mother in 1909, wanted to perform the Sonata. In a memorial piece published after Bax's death he recalled how

Early in 1914, P.A. (now Dr) Scholes proposed to organize a visit to Brittany where he planned to hold a musical conference in connection with what I believe was called a Music Study Union, and he invited me to contribute a performance of a modern work by a British composer. Aware that Bax had a piano and violin sonata in manuscript, I asked him if he would lend it to me for this purpose. His reply, from 7 Cavendish Square where the family now lived, was that he would acquiesce with pleasure − adding an opinion that afforded me no inconsiderable satisfaction. 'I have just been reading your very delightful book' (it was my History of Russian Music) 'and am charmed to see that someone has at last put Tchaikovsky in his right place in comparison with Rimsky-Korsakov'. This letter contained ample evidence of his wide knowledge of the subject, gained during travels in Russia. The mooted conference at which his sonata was to have been introduced was, by the way, adjourned *sine die* owing to the ambitions of the last German emperor − happily unrealized.[46]

Later, on 18 June, at the Steinway Hall, Myra Hess accompanied her friend Winifred Smith in the first movement of the sonata. Presumably Bax was already dissatisfied with the remaining two movements, which were discarded, and only later was it completed in its final form.

The summer of 1914 was again dominated by Diaghilev and the Russian Ballet. Bax's friend Arthur Alexander was recommended to Diaghilev by Edwin Evans in the early part of that year, and on several occasions was employed to play through to the Russian impresario and one or two principals of the ballet various manuscript scores with the idea of deciding at which places cuts or extensions might be necessary. Remuneration took the form of free tickets to many of the performances, and doubtless this meant that Bax was seeing or hearing of the doings of the ballet from closer quarters than he had hitherto.

The summer of 1914 was taken up with the writing of the Piano Quintet. This work is on a substantial scale. In the performance

given by Brenda Lucas and the Haffner Quartet in 1973 its movements were timed at 21' 10", 10' 45" and 13' 23" (ten years later
John McCabe's much brisker view of the music took ten minutes off
the total timing). Certainly there are other quintets on this scale, the
near contemporary quintet of Florent Schmitt being but one
example. But in Bax's case the work simultaneously celebrates his
achievement of a fully mature style and exemplifies a minor crisis
in his development — that of over-complex textures. The music
must certainly have been vividly imagined by Bax, for he wrote the
first two movements very quickly, and they are dated 16 and 19
July respectively; but the last movement was not actually attempted
until after the war had been under way for several months, and its
colder atmosphere may well reflect the dark and ominous cloud
that had darkened the sunny landscape of the earlier movements.
The manuscript of the final performing score shows that the composer made many cuts in the last two movements before he was
satisfied. Bax gives us no clue as to any programmatic origin for this
music, but the constant evocative instructions in the score (*Con
passione* — 'precipitately' — 'not humorous' — 'dull and expression-
less' — 'singing gently' — 'strongly sung' — 'distant and smothered')
suggest that there was a non-musical inspiration. It is presented on
a scale similar to that later called upon in the symphonies, and ends
with a 45-bar coda, *Lento con gran espressione*, which acts as an
epilogue to the whole work.

The Quintet was once one of Bax's most widely played works,
but since his death it has only been played four times — in 1954,
1955, 1973 and 1976. Writing of the 1973 performance, Felix
Aprahamian observed that 'after a long period of neglect, certain
performing traditions have been forgotten'.[47] The Quintet is a
passionate and tempestuous work, and the passion of the first
movement is all the more striking for the bereft character of much
of the finale, which, as Christopher Palmer has observed, 'manifestly
fails to find the enclave of serenity it so yearns for'.[48] Recent commentators on this music have found it difficult to find adequate
adjectives to describe it. Anthony Payne singled out the 'crisis-
ridden textures' which 'bring lyrical beauty and destructive elements
into cataclysmic opposition'.[49] Christopher Palmer described it as
'cloudhung' and 'turbulent',[50] while P. J. Pirie compared it to the less
striking Quintet of Bridge very much to the advantage of the Bax.

Frank Bridge wrote a fine Piano Quintet, and is a greatly underrated composer,
but we have only to compare his formally perfect Quintet — strong but rather

colourless and, set against later Bridge, unoriginal — with the smoky blaze, the bursting clumsy invention, the vast stormy landscape and crippled splendour of Bax's Quintet to realise immediately the genius of the latter. It establishes his kind.[51]

The opening of the first movement sets the tone of the whole piece, a romantic sweep of piano figuration over which the cello passionately delivers one of the main ideas of the work (Ex. 27).

Ex. 27

Bax is intent on creating a mood with the flood of piano texture, a fact which is highlighted by his reply to a question put by the pianist Vivian Langrish, who played the Quintet years later. Langrish asked whether a particular note was a misprint and Bax replied that odd notes did not matter so long as the style and atmosphere were right.[52] On his manuscript of the Quintet Bax had written 'passionate and rebellious' against the opening. Later in the movement he introduces a rhythmic idea, as foil to the opening; and then a beautiful lyrical inspiration is first presented as a fragment of typical Baxian piano miniature, 'singing softly'.

Ex. 28

Apart from occasional pre-echoes of the Viola Sonata of 1921/2, the piece looks forward to Bax's orchestral music rather than to his chamber works. Chromatic, running semi-quavers, sometimes in thirds, remind us of the music of turbulent nature in the tone poems, while sudden moments of calm pre-echo similar passages in the symphonies. One sequence, marked 'like a chant' (p. 24), even looks forward to the so called 'liturgical' passages that occur in all the symphonies. In each movement are moments reminiscent of *The Garden of Fand*, usually expressed in a similar texture or figuration. In the Quintet, too, Bax uses a great variety of highly coloured effects in his string writing: arco contrasting with pizzicato, *col legno, con sordino*; double stopping and particularly tremolando. Mixtures of colour too are demanded with, for example, one passage in which the viola and cello are asked to trill *sul ponticello*, while the second violin plays tremolando and the first violin soars above.

In contrast to the richness of much of the texture, Bax also writes some surprisingly cold effects, and in the middle movement, which opens as a glorious Celtic song on the piano accompanied by simple pizzicato chords on the strings, there are interpolated strange 'cold and unemotional' interludes.

The last movement opens with a piano texture, tremolando in the right hand over muffled semiquavers low in the bass, and Bax has added the instruction 'vague'. The themes which are introduced are familiar friends from the first movement. First the opening theme steals quietly in on the strings. Later the second idea of the first movement assumes the character of a wild dance, an approach that Bax uses with success in the First Violin Sonata, and in other works. The third theme from the first movement is heard too before the movement arrives at a climax at the return of the opening subject, and with it there also ensues the extended coda, marked 'Slow and concentrated in expression', which assumes the character of an epilogue.

The last movement does have a different feeling from the first two, and it would be strange if it did not in view of the circumstances of its composition. But through the use of similar textures in the rest of the work, and the cyclic approach to the thematic material, Bax achieves a unity, even though an unsympathetic performance can flaw the overall experience by highlighting the slightly self-conscious effect of the last movement.

In this work Bax has convincingly assimilated the Celtic influence in his music. In the early 1930s the young composer Edmund Rubbra wrote of Bax's music and this work in particular:

Everything in Bax's music subserves the mood: this alone is the agent that instinctively selects from the available mass of scales, harmonies and forms those which will best express the underlying idea.

In classical forms the tension between the subject matter is usually expressed by difference of key, but Bax takes this farther by sometimes opposing two or more scales as well as tonalities, and sometimes by opposing differences of register ... Unity is, however, achieved by the harmonic treatment of these diverse melodic shapes. ... [In] the *Piano Quintet* we immediately see, in spite of the opposing pentatonic and traditional scales in the melodic outlines, wherein lies the secret of the stylistic unity.

Essentially the harmonic basis is a fluid interchange of chords built on the seventh. The possible permutations of this chord are, in Bax's music, seemingly endless, and the subtlety with which they melt and flow into each other is further enhanced by the use of ornamental overtones. The logic of the relationships is often determined by chromatic movement of either the bass or a middle part.

It must not be thought from the above that Bax's music is one luscious variation on the seventh. There is plenty of virile cacophony, the logic of which is often found in contrary motion between the outer parts by intervals following a definite pattern.[53]

The Quintet was first played privately at a meeting of the 'Music Club' at the Savoy Hotel in December 1917. The first public performance, in 1920, was given by the Bohemian Quartet with Fanny Davies at the piano. Writing of that performance in the *London Mercury*, Edward J. Dent observed:

The composer seems often to have been undecided as to what he wished to effect. There are moments when he appears to be aiming at 'atmosphere' and nothing else; then he sheers off and gives us music which must be understood in quite a different way. There is not the least reason why a chamber work should not be 'atmospheric' if the composer can succeed in making it so — Mr Goossens' little sketch *By the Tarn* achieves it with extraordinary charm. But that is a matter of a few minutes, whereas Mr Bax's Quintet lasts about an hour. Mr Bax is a remarkably skilful pianist, and is therefore easily tempted to imagine that whatever his own ten fingers can compass must be perfectly intelligible to an audience. The more I hear of his music (although it invariably gives me pleasure) the more uncomfortably I am forced to admit the truth of a French friend's criticism: 'Your English composers do not know what the word *style* means.'[54]

   Dent is writing as a champion of a new post-war world, of a new
aesthetic, and it was an aesthetic which Bax could not accept. In
the Quintet, Bax celebrates a youthful passion and glory in life. But
over his ecstasy the shadow of mortality falls in the last movement.
Bax's was a philosophy that was expressed through a technique
then just brought to perfection: a technique that, in common with
that of many of his contemporaries, was left dry on the sands of
time, a victim of August 1914. After the war the prevailing view of
life was no longer a romantic one. Bax could not change his musical
idiom, at least not overnight, but he could adapt it, and the conflict
between beauty and horror, between dream and reality generated in
Bax, until the fires dimmed in the 1930s, a powerful body of romantic music in which the old and the new united in a unique art.
It was an art that survives to give us a unique vision of his experience,
and it was the Piano Quintet, straddling the change from peace to
war, that signalled the start of this development and showed the way
it would go.

The Great War

We know, from Balfour Gardiner's notebooks, that Bax was at Gardiner's cottage at Ashampstead on 1 August 1914. On leaving there he went to Cornwall, where he spent the first few days of the war, which was declared on the 4th. He was the guest of Bevis Ellis, his companion during the earlier part of that 'sinister Carnival time, the London Summer of 1914'. The question which immediately preoccupied many a young man, that of enlistment, faced them too, and Bax realized his companion was in the throes of indecision about joining up. 'But', he recalled in his autobiography, 'his reserve kept his mouth shut tight as a clam ... One morning I came downstairs to find that he had gone back to town and the recruiting office without a word of farewell.'[1] Bax had no immediate similar inclination, although the question as to what to do certainly gave him cause for thought. He wrote to Arthur Alexander, 'I have been swaying backwards and forwards between two courses — that of entering the army (and becoming bold and British thereby, or pretending to be) and that of plunging into a narcotic ocean of creative work.'

The holiday with Bevis Ellis in Cornwall was to have been followed by the now customary cricket tour. Clifford Bax had removed from the Old Manor at Broughton Gifford since the 1913 meeting, and was now living in the Buckinghamshire village of Speen. A tour had been arranged and four games were actually played, though the team's poor showing — three games lost to just one win — is indication of the muted character of the proceedings.

Spring Fire was due to have had its first hearing the following month at the Norwich Festival, but the performance and Festival were cancelled on the outbreak of war. The score was not heard at Norwich until Vernon Handley introduced it there in 1985. As the cancellation was so near to the event, orchestral materials must have already been prepared, and Bax's disappointment may perhaps have been somewhat alleviated by his discussions with Balfour Gardiner a few days earlier. For Gardiner was proposing to promote a third series of concerts in December 1914, and one of the works he had in mind was *Spring Fire*. However, the war caused the abandonment of Gardiner's plans later in the autumn. In 1916 and 1919 abortive attempts were made to programme the work, but it was fifty-six years before its first performance, by the Kensington Symphony Orchestra conducted by Leslie Head, and a further thirteen years before a fully professional one, under the baton of Norman del Mar.

For Bax, probably one of the most important events of the summer of 1914 was the decision of his friend Arthur Alexander to return to New Zealand, sailing on the Shaw Savill White Star 'Corinthic' during the last week of July. This was a major blow, for Bax had placed a high regard on his companionship, and especially on their piano duet sessions. A year later Bax wrote to him: 'Do you know I have not played a piano duet since you left — because nobody will do after yourself for that form.'

The vacuum among musical friends left by the departure of Alexander was filled from an unexpected quarter. Sam Hartley ('Tim') Braithwaite was very nearly Bax's exact contemporary, being born on 20 July 1883. Bax would have known him while a student, for Braithwaite held a clarinet scholarship at the RAM in 1902, and they both studied composition under Corder. Braithwaite was talented both as musician and artist. He had succeeded Holst as musical director of the Passmore Edwards Settlement, a post he held from 1910 to 1913. Their re-acquaintance in 1913 was not entirely amicable, Bax referring in a letter to 'the impenetrability of highly respectable Professor Braithwaite'. What changed Bax's opinion is not known, but after coming to stay for a weekend, Braithwaite remained to live with Arnold, Elsita and the children, at Marlow, for the first two years of the war, and Bax accompanied him to see his mother and sisters in Somerset and on holidays to the Lake District. Bax wrote to Alexander in October 1915:

Tim is staying with us and goes up by day to the Abode of Vice (I refer to the RAM). He and I have become great friends. He is really a delightful person and so perversely humorous about his own pessimisms and complaints — one of the few people who have any inkling as to what is worth while in life and what he really wants.

Described by a mutual acquaintance as 'a funny little man' and 'a typical bachelor', Braithwaite was pedantic and finicky, and a great hypochondriac. It was these traits to which Bax's letter alludes. Braithwaite was known for his piano music and orchestral works, two of the latter, a tone poem *Snow Picture*, and an orchestral *Elegy*, appearing under the Carnegie United Kingdom Trust's scheme for publishing works of British composers. However, this publication (in 1923 and 1927) came after he had turned from music to the visual arts. He abandoned music, and became well known for his paintings and etchings. From that time until his death in 1947 he lived in Bournemouth, where he was celebrated for his landscapes of the area, two engravings of which are preserved in the Victoria and Albert Museum collection.

Indeed the war came when many of Bax's immediate circle of the previous years had moved away, and this must have emphasized the feeling of dissolution at the time. Rosalind Thorneycroft and Godwin Baynes were married and living in Wisbech, where Baynes was a 'panel' doctor. Bax certainly visited them there, but attitudes to the war undoubtedly broke up friendships in their circle as they did in many others at the time. Baynes reacted passionately to people and events and joined the RAMC, becoming a major. He wrote to one old friend that he 'spewed him out of his mouth' because he objected to his being a conscientious objector, but at the end of the war told the same friend he had been right to be one. While his reaction to Bax's rather disinterested attitude to the conflict may have been less positive, it was doubtless also the reason why they drifted apart, until, after the war when they were brought together again by Clifford Bax.

Herbert Farjeon and Joan Thorneycroft had also married and they moved into the country on the outbreak of war, Herbert Farjeon joining up, but then being invalided out with severe varicose veins, before eventually becoming a conscientious objector. Clifford Bax's liaison with Olga Antonietti was also coming to an end.

In the opening months of the war, Bax certainly did not identify with the conflict. Writing, again to Alexander, he declared, 'I ... have attempted (and failed) to detect some shadow of sober fact about the War from the wild performances of the English press.' Instead he devoted himself to composition, that 'narcotic ocean of creative work' already mentioned. Within days of the outbreak of the war, he had written a song, *Roundel*, the first of the three *Chaucer Rondels*, which were all completed by the end of October. *Roundel* was, in fact, the earliest piece he dedicated to Harriet Cohen ('Tania'), its opening words, significantly, being:

> Your eyen two wol slay me sodenly:
> I may the beauty of hem not sustene
> So woundeth it throughout my hertë kene.

During October he wrote the second, *Welcome Somer*, inscribing it to Joan Thorneycroft; and then a last setting, entitled *Of her Mercy*.

Having attuned himself to songwriting with the Chaucer songs, Bax then set himself the task of making a series of settings from *The Bard of the Dimbovitza* for voice and orchestra. These poems were published in two volumes,[2, 3] and according to the title pages, were English translations of Romanian peasant verse: 'Roumanian folk-songs collected from the Peasants by Hélène Vacaresco, translated by Carmen Sylva and Alma Strettel'. Carmen Sylva was the pseudonym of Queen Elizabeth of Romania, and it has been suggested that she may have been the actual author of the words. The poems are certainly very vivid, and, published in England between 1892 and 1897, they appealed at once to the same audience that had grown to love Fitzgerald's *Omar Khayyám*, and to the then new interest in folklore and the picturesque. They enjoyed a great success, *The Times* critic observing 'the Dimbovitza is now a classic with which every person of intelligence ought to possess some acquaintance'.[3] The poems certainly appealed to Bax, in whom they provided a stimulus for colour and characterisation. He set six of them, five for mezzo-soprano and one for bass, though the latter has not been performed.

It is surprising that Bax's score has never caught on (only having been played three times, once — in the original scoring — in 1921, and twice — in a revised scoring — in 1949). The vocal score is published, and the orchestra required is a very economical one: in the original, triple woodwind (but only two bassoons), four horns, harp and strings; the revision reduces the woodwind and only requires three horns. The unplayed male-voice song is the vigorous 'The Song of the Dagger', a poem also set at about this time by the American composer Charles Tomlinson Griffes — who also set other poems chosen by Bax. When Bax revised the cycle, not only did he reduce the orchestration slightly, he also changed the order in which the songs were sung.

The second 'The Well of Tears' is particularly interesting because in it Bax introduces a motif (Ex. 29) from *Into the Twilight* into the

Ex. 29

orchestral part, though whether this was a conscious or unconscious association with 'tragic Déirdre' (see pp. 381—2) we do not know. He also quotes from *Cathaleen-ni-Hoolihan* (see last bar of Ex. 29).

Bax and his friend Arthur Alexander were both enormously attracted by this vivid verse, and both attempted settings. Indeed, Alexander observed in his unpublished memoir of Bax that he had been 'not unpleased to find a certain influence of my own settings for voice and orchestra in those that he himself made some years later.'[4] In this Alexander had his chronology wrong. Alexander's settings were made in 1916 quite independently of Bax's, which had been written nearly two years earlier. But Bax did not publish his songs until 1941, when he sent a copy of the vocal score to his friend inscribed, 'To Arthur in memory of younger days'.[5] The style of setting was 'in the air', and reflected their common training at the RAM and enthusiasms during the pro-Russian period of British music. Bax's music in these songs reflects the ornate and decorated style that he adopted in works such as the Second Violin Sonata that he was to write in 1915, and even recalls one of his ambitions to write a work for the Russian Ballet. But in this music Bax makes a marked advance from his rather character-less orchestrations of earlier songs at the beginning of the year. They are vivid in their orchestral dress, and do not work nearly so well with piano accompaniment.

A short piano passacaglia — *In the Night* — also dates from November 1914, though it remained unpublished, and other works followed quickly. Within twelve months he could boast of having had his 'annus mirabilis as far as work is concerned'. He proudly listed the work of this period as follows:

Six orchestral songs from the 'Bard of Dimbovitza'
Three Chaucer songs
The last movement of the quintet
A new last movement to my violin sonata
A Second Violin Sonata
Nympholept 2nd edition (an orchestral effort)
About ten piano pieces
And a longish piece for violin and piano

If we examine the dedication of many of these pieces — the piano
ones especially — we can find at least one of the sources of this
renewed well-spring of Bax's creative art: her name was Harriet
Cohen.

In his autobiography, Bax, during the course of an account of the
first performance of his *Christmas Eve on the Mountains* (on 4
March 1913), wrote of how he looked round the Queen's Hall
audience, and was attracted by a young girl.

Good heavens! the girl I met at that picnic in the Dublin Mountains last spring.
Yes, of course, she told me she was a piano student at the RAM. But it is strange
to see this elfin child here. ... I steal another glance at the girl. She is in profile
to me now, her brow slightly frowning and her eyes fixed serious upon the
orchestra. She is dressed in white, which accentuates her natural pallor, and
looks tired and very delicate. But what a lovely little thing![6]

By the summer of that year (1913), the seventeen-year-old Harriet
Cohen had already become part of that circle which included the
Baxes, Corders, Antoniettis and Farjeons, and had been christened
'Tania', the name by which she was known to her intimates for the
rest of her life. In a letter dated 24 June 1913 written to Arthur
Alexander (who, similarly inspired by the Russian Ballet, had been
dubbed 'Sasha'), Bax revealed his interest even that early by asking,
'How is Tania — that fantastic volatile and delightful creature?
One wishes she would never grow up!' Her transition from being
a delightful child in Bax's eyes, to the object of a passion that was
to influence the rest of his life in one form or another, began during
the autumn and the winter of 1914/15.

Will an objective assessment of Harriet Cohen ever be possible?
Certainly not for some time yet. And as only comparatively little
of her art exists on disc, to judge her as a concert pianist *per se* is
very difficult for those who did not hear her in her prime. But
her success and reputation were dependent on more than just her
piano playing. Many loved and revered her, many appear to have
resented her. She was a most glorious looking woman when young.
However, judged solely as a pianist, she does not now appear to rate
highly among the pianists of this century, British or otherwise.
But how few of those who spring to her defence as they read these
words, or who similarly concur, will do so on purely musical grounds?
For Harriet Cohen was a 'personality'. She quickly outgrew the
delightful naive quality with which Bax fell in love. Yet many
musicians have had cause to thank her, for her work to help the

impecunious up-and-coming was rooted deep in her personal experience of the difficulty of establishing a career. Indeed, Felix
Aprahamian has remarked that he knew from colleagues that she was
'a marvellously intelligent and wise colleague and counsellor in anything that concerned them — their concert careers, their emotional
states. She was an absolute trouper and a good friend.' But he went
on that 'it became obvious to me that, with the passing of the years
she became incredibly stupid with regard to her own career. She was
able to see and pinpoint others' weaknesses and failures and what
they should do. But she simply could not advise herself.'

Her limitations as a pianist had partly to do with the technical
problems arising from her inability to stretch more than an octave
with either hand. Various aspects of Miss Cohen's art and personality
will be dealt with later. But, for the moment, in the winter of 1914
her attraction for Bax was sufficiently strong for him to give up
tentative plans he had of returning to Ireland.

In January 1915, at a tea-party at the Corders she appeared
wearing as decoration a single daffodil, and Bax wrote almost overnight the piano piece *To a Maiden with a Daffodil* in tribute. (One
wonders from the music whether, perhaps, Bax wished the object
of his admiration was crowned by 'cheveux de lin'!) It was the
climax of a number of similar short piano works all dedicated to
her, which he wrote in a mere thirteen days during January, the
others being *The Princess's Rose Garden* and *In a Vodka Shop*.

But he still had time for his family and a wide circle of friends.
At the beginning of the war Bax continued to enjoy an active social
life. We find him invited to the Harrisons at Oxted for 'Nightingales
at 10'.[7] May Harrison was long associated with Bax's violin works,
and her sister Beatrice Harrison, the cellist, was to achieve fame
among non-musicians when she broadcast from her Surrey garden
while a nightingale sang, an experience she later recorded. Between
the wars she was to become a noted exponent of Bax's cello works.
It was during the war that Delius stayed with the Harrisons, and
according to May Harrison 'was very interested in the work of some
of the young British composers.' Delius is reported to have named
Bax as 'by far the greatest, both poetically and imaginatively'.[8]

On another occasion Bax wrote to thank a new friend, the young
composer Philip Heseltine (Peter Warlock) 'for the lively weekend ...
my best wishes to Miss Barbara [Warlock's mistress] and Gray
[Cecil Gray the critic and composer] if he is still with you'.[9] In
March, Bax went to Wisbech to stay with Godwin and Rosalind

Baynes. There too was Eleanor Farjeon, who one day Bax took to Ely, a city that, according to Miss Farjeon, he loved. She recalled how he 'led me round the Cathedral explaining its variety of architecture'.[10]

At Easter he went to stay by Windermere with Tim Braithwaite, from where he wrote to Heseltine:

Firsthwaite Lakeside Windermere
Saturday

Dear Heseltine

Please keep Dermot O'Byrne severely in the background. The musical side of me does not want to have anything to do with him in public as the ordinary mug seems to hold the fantastic and quite ineradicable opinion that it is impossible to express oneself successfully in two different mediums. Of course he may be right, but at present I am not convinced. You ask me about my later work. I have done a good deal since the autumn, including some settings for voice and orchestra of poems from 'The Bard of the Dimbovitza'. (Do you know this book? It is wonderful stuff.) I have also written a piano quintet and finished off a symphonic work called 'Nympholept' both of which I believe to be representative of the best I can do at present. I hope you will hear them soon. Nearly all my longer compositions, the orchestral works at any rate, are based upon aspects and moods of extreme nature and their relation to human emotion & I find this tendency in nearly all the most serious work of the younger English composers and also at times in Elgar. I rather think we may be on the track of quite new discoveries in this field. There is certainly plenty of scope in this direction, as until Debussy's period the treatment of nature in music was almost wholly objective when touched at all. At least, so I feel it. I suppose one of my own most characteristic things is a long orchestral work called 'The Garden of Fand' which is entirely enveloped in the atmosphere of the calm Atlantic off the western shores of Ireland and the enchanted islands of which some of the country people still dream. But this piece is not yet scored.[11]

At this time, it was not Harriet Cohen who was presenting Bax's piano music to the public – her first appearances being some two years later – but still Myra Hess, who at the 'Music Club' at the Grafton Galleries played *To a Maiden with a Daffodil* (the original title of *The Maiden with the Daffodil*), *In a Vodka Shop* and *Nocturne* (i.e. *May Night in the Ukraine*). Myra Hess's playing introduced Bax to Dr L. Strecker, manager of the music publishing firm of Augener. For a short period Bax found Strecker would publish literally any short piano piece he cared to produce, and several appeared in this way, Augener's advertisements declaring Bax's music to be 'remarkable works which are played with extraordinary success by Miss Hess and others'. Myra Hess's performance of Bax at the Grafton Galleries was not an isolated one. For example, in

March she appeared in a concert given by the Classical Concert Society at the Aeolian Hall, playing *May Night in the Ukraine* and *The Maiden with the Daffodil* (the last-named having to be encored). In May she gave a recital on her own account at the Bechstein Hall, and among a group of modern British pieces was *In a Vodka Shop*. Writing about these performances in the *Daily Mail*, Philip Heseltine found that in *May Night in the Ukraine* 'the Russian atmosphere is almost too cleverly caught, with the result that the music sounds more like Balakirev than Bax,'[12] while *In a Vodka Shop* was 'uproarious' and 'stimulating'.[13] Later, Bax acknowledged his debt to Myra Hess by writing *Moy Mell* — 'an Irish tone poem' for two pianos, for her and Irene Scharrer to play together. This was an evocation of the 'pleasant plain' of Irish mythology, one of those pagan places of bliss which Bax evoked in several works. It was first given by them in London on 5 December 1916.

The war was brought nearer for Bax by three separate events. Firstly Strecker, who was a German, was interned as an alien for the duration of the war. Then, what Bax referred to as 'the London Zeppelin event' occurred, and he found the bombing of London 'totally without charm'. Finally the introduction of conscription early in 1916 meant that he had to reconsider the question of military service and ultimately found himself before an Army Medical Board at Reading Barracks, where he succeeded in establishing his unfitness for military service, merely having to suffer 'insolence in full riotous bloom' from the president of the board.[14]

To Mrs Bax, her sons could do no wrong. She adored Arnold and Clifford and was deeply anxious that they keep out of the war. It is perhaps worth remembering the continuing importance of 7 Cavendish Square in the lives of all members of the family and their circle. During the war life at Cavendish Square went on much as it had before. The house was full of the most luxurious Edwardian furnishings. In the drawing-room, Melford Stevenson (a Bax protégé at the time) remembers they had a most lovely Canaletto. There were still an 'astonishing number of domestic servants'. When Melford Stevenson's father fell ill in 1916, Mrs Bax had him taken to Cavendish Square, and provided with the best medical attention money could buy. 'It was the sort of thing she loved to do.' When he ultimately died there, she subsequently provided funds to send Melford Stevenson to Dulwich College.[15]

While Arnold's family were not immediately in sympathy with the war, this was not necessarily true of the rest of the Bax family.

Rudolph Bax (Arnold's cousin), for instance, became a captain in the army, and was then appointed chairman of a board to consider conscientious objectors. Once or twice he put his foot in it at breakfast while staying at Cavendish Square. His observations about people who did not take part in the conflict were not at all appropriate. He was curiously out of place in that household.

Earlier there had been great grief and consternation when Bax's sister Evelyn had become a convert to the Roman Catholic Church. There was much greater consternation when their mother also joined the Church of Rome, though Arnold appears to have accepted it with tolerance and good humour: sectarian differences apparently meant nothing to him – perhaps just as well considering his attachment to things Irish. After Mrs Bax became a Catholic, the number of Catholic beneficiaries of her generosity multiplied considerably. Arthur Alexander described how, when he was at Cavendish Square, 'from its many rooms would emerge at meal times a heterogeneous collection of strange folk, mostly old and mostly uncommunicative. They were mostly pensioners of Arnold's parents. Many of them were quite unknown to Arnold.'[16]

During 1915 and 1916 there was a considerable falling off in recitals and private concert-giving, but orchestral activity was maintained by bodies such as the Royal Philharmonic Society, and the Promenade Concerts continued throughout the war. In London, and later elsewhere, much of this continuity was made possible by considerable injections of private funds into concert-giving bodies, notably by Sir Thomas Beecham (who was knighted for services to music in the New Year Honours of 1916). Bax benefited from the presence of Beecham on the scene, and from the fact that there was a wartime reaction against works by post-1870 German composers, with a corresponding increase in attention given to French, Russian and British music. Beecham seized on two works of Bax, *Fatherland* and *In the Faery Hills.* He gave the former its first wartime performance at Queen's Hall on 24 November 1914 in a Royal Philharmonic Society concert. The programme included music by Handel, Parry, Delius and Berlioz, and was typical of its conductor. The following January, Beecham repeated *Fatherland* in a concert at Manchester. Bax was thus established in the wartime vogue for patriotic works.

In the spring and summer of 1915 Beecham performed British orchestral music on a more substantial scale than appeared to be warranted by public appetite. During May he promoted the 'British Music Festival' at Queen's Hall, the final concert of which included the first performance of Cyril Scott's [First] Piano Concerto, and *In the Faery Hills*. Of the latter Philip Heseltine wrote in the *Daily Mail* that it 'is one of the most original and poetic orchestral compositions penned by a native composer, and, moreover, one which completely fulfilled the object of the festival, namely, to give the stranger a good impression of British music'.[17] Beecham played the work again later in the war, though its most disappointing performance from Bax's point of view must have been at a Royal Philharmonic Society Concert in Queen's Hall in February 1916 when, although *Spring Fire* was announced, a correction slip in the programmes regretted that, 'owing to its exceptional difficulty and inadequate time available for rehearsal', *In the Faery Hills* would be played instead.

Winter Waters is a powerful, sombre piano piece, striking the listener as more imposing than its 6½-minute duration would suggest. 'Tragic landscape' Bax sub-titles this movement, but does not tell us quite what he had in mind. The music is dedicated to the absent Arthur Alexander and dated 5 September 1915, though whether images from the war or something more personal are appropriate one does not know. However, this does not really matter; for the muted power of the writing, the tender and expressive central section that Bax marks 'singing softly', and the quiet poetic fade-out at the end are as effective as any of his orchestral conceptions in a similar mood. The change from the extravagant romanticism of the pre-war tone poems is very striking. *Winter Waters* is of particular interest to the student in that Bax revised the closing bars before publication, and both versions have survived (see Exs. 30a and 30b). Examples of the way in which he would prune his teeming invention to obtain the effect he wanted from the keyboard in the most practical way, and in so doing tightening the emotional effect to its most piquant, are not easy to find in Bax. This is not because he was too easily pleased, or overly facile in his style, but because such working documents have not survived. A comparison of the two versions quoted show quite clearly Bax in full control of his material and its chosen medium of expression.

The Second Violin Sonata came out of a preoccupation with the violin that occurred during the early part of 1915. At this time Bax revised and completed the First Violin Sonata, writing two new movements for it. The new final movement was inscribed with yet another verse from Yeats:

Ex. 30a   *Winter Waters*: Bax's original ending.

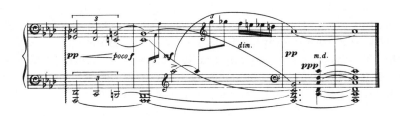

Ex. 30b   *Winter Waters*: the published score (by permission of J. & W. Chester).

A pity beyond all telling is
Hid in the heart of love.

On this occasion though, Bax removed the quotation from the movement on publication. He also wrote two separate movements for the instrument, the *Legend* and the *Ballad*, the former being quickly published by Augener. It seems probable that this activity must have been due to the appearance of a talented player in Bax's circle. It may have been May Harrison or possibly Myra Hess's friend Winifred Smith, to whom the *Legend* is dedicated and who later performed the Second Sonata in public with Bax. But the most likely explanation is the young Winifred Small, who would have been nineteen in 1915, a fine violinist of an arresting appearance with quite beautiful corn-coloured hair and incredible blue eyes. In June 1916 she performed Bax's *Legend*, and the composer confessed himself greatly impressed by her 'beautiful playing'. 'All through the *Legend*', he wrote to her, 'the variety of tone was really remarkable ... All my people', he added, 'were in a violent state of enthusiasm about your playing'. She was later one of the first concert violinists to broadcast from Marconi House in 1920, and was subsequently celebrated as a musical educator and a professor at the Royal Academy of Music. Bax dedicated his *Ballad* for violin and piano to her, and its passionate manner takes account of her highly romantic style of violin playing, of which the opening Allegro, with its marking *energico e tempestuoso* indicates what Bax and his performer had in mind, later describing it as 'a wild stormy thing'.

But most important at this time is the Second Violin Sonata, in which the main romantic theme of the later orchestral tone poem *November Woods* first appears. His champion, Edwin Evans, contented himself by writing that it 'originated during a tragic phase of the war, and is imbued with the thoughts of which many were conscious at the time but the expression of which was left to art'.[18] Indeed, the autobiographical element was so strong that Bax withheld the score, and it was not finally played until April 1922 when Bessie Rawlins was accompanied by the composer. At that time the following note appeared, probably written by Bax himself:

This Sonata was written in 1915 but for various reasons has hitherto been withheld by the composer. Recently it has been considerably revised. The work is in four distinct movements, though the whole is played without a break. The end of each of the first three divisions of the sonata is designed to create an impression of pause and expectancy, so that the plan of the various movements should be clear to the listener. The work is in cyclic form, and the principal motive which dominates the whole sonata, is used also in the same composer's orchestral piece 'November Woods'.

The movements are as follows:

I. Introduction — Fantasy
II. 'The Grey Dancer in the Twilight'
III. Interlude — Lento expressivo [sic]
IV. Allegro feroce — Epilogue

(The second movement, which might also be called 'The Dance of Death', was influenced in a particular degree by the events of 1915.)[19]

The sonata exhibits some of Bax's most florid and ornate writing. It was written very quickly, the autograph being headed 'In Summer 1915' and is dated at the end 'Aug 13 1915'. The music is deeply felt, expression marks such as 'very passionate' and 'very emotional and exuberant' being liberally used. What is perhaps more remarkable is that it fully succeeds in communicating its passion to its audience. It is worth noting that John Ireland's Second Sonata, and Thomas Dunhill's Second Sonata op. 50 were also wartime works in which violin and piano were particularly successful in catching the mood of the time.

Formally the sonata is of considerable interest. First the use of a 'motto' theme — in fact the theme aforementioned that it has in common with *November Woods* — brings a compelling sense of unity. The narrative thread running through the music is underlined by the interludes in which the motto theme is stated. The introductory 'slow and gloomy' prelude to the first movement, and the 'very quiet and serene' Epilogue (though not actually designated thus in the published score) constitute part of this plan, which effectively always returns us to the motto. Bax's revisions before publication were merely intended to try and force these interludes into their adjacent movements of a four movement work. These revisions were largely cosmetic, involving the deletion of some eight pages. There is no harking back to Ireland in this work: far from it. It is a cry from the heart for 'the old values', as Bax called them, for peace and beauty, as well as for a more specific example of beauty, with haunting green eyes and a rope of raven black hair. Suspicions of the latter are strengthened by Felix Aprahamian's observation that Bax alludes to Debussy's *Le Promenoir des deux Amants* in the last movement (a work incidentally that was again quoted in the Fifth Symphony, some twenty years later). Significantly, neither the manuscript nor the printed score bears a dedication.

As he was not conscripted, Bax continued to live a fairly normal life – at least on the surface – with composition occupying much of his time. His attraction to Harriet Cohen was in the open by now, at least as far as his wife was concerned. Yet she appeared unwilling to accept or realize the seriousness of the situation. To her, marriage was, and always would be, sacred, and nothing could justify the breaking of so holy a promise. Arnold had once acted passionately towards her, and she attributed his change to his moody personality.

The summer of 1916 saw them move house again – to another address in Marlow: a grander house, Riversleigh, with a garden that ran down to the river. Bax's daughter Maeve, only three at the time, later wrote that they 'went to live in a house by the river which must have pleased my father since I know he loved to take a boat out and row. There was a boat moored at the bottom of the garden.'[20]

While still at Marlow the Bax family were visited by a variety of friends. Arthur Alexander, back in England, renewed the piano-duet sessions. Francis Colmer, his old tutor, in his absent-minded way would come to stay for a weekend and remain for three weeks, and there would be chess in the garden, or a trip up-river, with Arnold and Elsita, Colmer always getting into some ham-fisted scrape. Eleanor Farjeon recollected in her book on Edward Thomas how she stayed for a week with the Baxes in Marlow.

It was a week of very thick snow, weather that in England and France held back the Spring until April. We walked in the snow between the snowfalls, and at home in the comfortable house sat round the fire and talked, breaking off for music. Elsa sang in her fine voice, and Arnold improvised gloriously – no other musician has ever given me so much pleasure on a piano played in a room.[21]

Clifford Bax had described his brother's early music as 'adolescent dreams, of more than life can give',[22] and it is true that even in his early thirties, with a wife and two children and a European war consuming his generation, he had not fully outgrown such dreams. This immaturity in his personal life is the key to much of his best music – music that was written at this time. Yet there was to be a trauma which was to be reflected in his music almost immediately.

It was not the war in France that removed Bax from the ivory tower of his youth but the Easter Rising in Ireland in 1916. Before he had left Ireland he had met and sympathized with Pádraig Pearse and his aims. Bax wrote:

As he [Pearse] was leaving that night he said to Molly, 'I think your friend Arnold Bax may be one of us. I should like to see more of him.' I was anxious to meet him again too, but somehow it chanced that I never did. I could not forget the impression that strange death-aspiring dreamer made upon me, and when on Easter Tuesday 1916 I read by Windermere's shore of the idealist adventure in Dublin the day before, I murmured to myself 'I *know* that Pearse is in this'.[23]

The trauma of 1916 acted as a catalyst on Bax's creative inspiration, and he wrote a number of works — both musical and literary — in an almost white heat of emotion. Indeed, Bax wrote later of his poems which were printed in a slim volume called *A Dublin Ballad*, and subsequently banned by the British censor, that they were written 'with painful intensity of emotion just after the rebellion'.[24]

Bax attempts to demonstrate himself as a master of rhetoric in a number of poems written at this time, under his pseudonym of Dermot O'Byrne. It is not difficult to see why, twenty years before he was appointed Master of the King's Musick, Bax should have had work of his banned by the censor:

> ('A Dublin Ballad — 1916'):
> O write it up above your hearth
> And troll it out to sun and moon,
> *To all true Irishmen on earth*
> *Arrest and death come later or soon.*

> ('Shells at Oranmore'):
> Never before had such a song been sung,
> Never again perhaps while ages run
> Shall the old pride of rock and wind be stung
> By such an insolence winged across the sun,
> So mad a challenge flung!

Bax had not known Pearse long enough for him to be a great personal friend. Rather was Pearse a symbol, and his death helped to focus the worst of this nightmare for Bax, who attempted an elegiac poem:

> Brother, above the uncertain gulf of death
> I lean and grope to clasp your nerveless hand.[25]

It was not a success. An unequal balance of emotion and technique rarely is.

Also at this time he wrote — in short score — *In Memoriam, Pádraig Pearse*,[26] an orchestral tone poem in the same ternary shape used in the other wartime orchestral poems. In it he characterizes Pearse in a beautiful elegiac tune which he later used to rather less effect in his music to the film *Oliver Twist* (Ex. 31). However, the

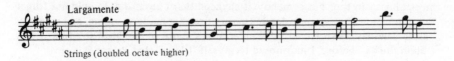

Strings (doubled octave higher)

Ex. 31

work was never orchestrated. In retrospect, it was a wise decision on Bax's part not to promote the Pearse music at the time, for it can scarcely have found a sympathetic audience outside Ireland.

In Memoriam, Pádraig Pearse was Bax's first musical reaction to the Irish tragedy, and was completed in short score on 9 August 1916. But the effects of the incident were long-lasting, and over the next year or two, works were written to which that title might equally have been given. The most substantial of these is the *Symphonic Variations*, completed in short score by 8 February 1917, and clearly autobiographical in a highly specific way. Two chamber works made, perhaps, a more immediate tribute to his Irish friends — *In Memoriam (An Irish Elegy)* for cor anglais, string quartet and harp, and the *Elegiac Trio* (for the same combination as Debussy's Sonata — flute, viola and harp). Possibly the piano pieces *Dream in Exile* and *On a May Evening* were similarly inspired by memories of Ireland, although the former, at least, was dated 'Feb 1916' and thus pre-dates the rising. The sextet, *In Memoriam*, is of particular interest for its folk-like main theme. Later, in 1919, Bax wrote another chamber work with harp — the Quintet — which may also mark his emotional involvement with the events of Easter 1916. With its memorable thematic material, varied and colourful scoring and concise structure (about twelve minutes' duration), it is a work that should not be forgotten.

Dream in Exile is an interesting and haunting work, presenting another theme which later reappears in *November Woods* (Ex. 32).

Ex. 32

This is another of those Baxian piano pieces that are found to be of greater substance, once looked at closely, than one might have thought. The piece is 'affectionately dedicated to Tobias Matthay'.

From its sub-title 'Intermezzo' (it was originally dubbed just 'Capriccio'), and its comparatively simple textures which for much of the time are only in two parts, even if those two parts do expand to include chords and octaves, this piece might be thought to be a typical miniature. In fact it has considerable emotional weight under-lying it. In length too — well over eight minutes — it is comparable in scale to the shorter of Bax's orchestral movements. One presumes that the simple explanation of Bax imagining himself as exile at a time of Irish national troubles might well be somewhere near the truth. And yet, that mysterious thematic allusion that crops up later in Bax's most emotional and conflict-ridden tone poem perhaps makes one pause. There is no solution, and an explanation is un-necessary to the appreciation of the music as music. Yet the use of thematic cross-referencing between works, without disclosure to his audience, is so comparable to similar allusions to personal emotional crises in the piano works and songs of John Ireland — later Ireland was a friend and dedicatee of Bax's First Symphony — that one feels justified in suspecting the romantic artist of using such a subjective machinery to express his passionate thoughts and feelings of the moment.

It was probably late in 1916 that Bax first met Eugène Goossens, later to be a good friend and an important interpreter of his music. Philip Heseltine had published an enthusiastic article on Goossens' chamber music in the monthly journal *The Music Student* (which, incidentally, was the first time that Heseltine's pseudonym 'Peter Warlock' was used in print). Bax confessed himself 'most interested' although he 'had not yet heard a note of it', and asked his young friend if he could arrange for them all to meet 'in town during the Christmas days ... It is certainly quite exciting to hear of anyone who is doing any work that is emotionally honest and who is not content with driving some intellectual theory to death,' observed Bax tartly. 'There is little that amounts to more than this nowadays in any of the arts,' he continued. 'There is plenty of taste — but scarcely any emotional concentration.'

If the Easter Rising had interrupted Bax's preoccupation with Harriet, it had not altered it in any way. On the contrary, in 1917 his adoration now became complete and she took precedence over everybody and everything. She was the 'adolescent dream' that could give relief from war sufferings. For although non-combatant, Bax *was* suffering. A. J. Waugh, a cricketing companion of 1911—14, was killed in 1915; John Eden, cricketer, friend and formerly his father's

gardener had been killed in 1916, as had Bevis Ellis and Edward
Thomas. George Butterworth was to go and, worst of all, his greatest
boyhood friend Lynn Hartley was to be killed in 1918. Balfour
Gardiner joined up in 1916, Vaughan Williams was in France and
Holst was later to go to the Near East, while even Clifford was
employed on war work in the capacity of censor. Yet on a material
plane Bax appears to have suffered neither socially nor financially
through the war, for although no pacifist, he spent it, as he spent
most of his life, doing exactly what *he* wanted to do.

Nevertheless Bax was a delightful companion and generous friend
all his life to those who were close to him, especially in these younger
days before fame gave him artistic targets for which he was unsuited,
and before domestic troubles saddened him. One is sure he would
have been most distressed to read that he was thought selfish. Yet as
a creative artist he was of one mind when the choice lay between his
art and other responsibilities. His wife accurately encapsulated his
personality as 'merely living for the impulse of the moment ... he
does nothing really at once though then when it is done it is always
in a rush!'[27]

Harriet Cohen

The *Symphonic Variations* for piano and orchestra has been something of an enigma. Written during the latter part of 1916, it was complete in short score by February 1917. In it, it would appear, he tried to express his feelings on the passing of the old order. Tangled with this autobiographical concern with love and war are the more specific concerns of Ireland and Harriet Cohen.

The work is in six linked movements, each of which bears a descriptive title. The titles with which Bax adorned each variation have never been satisfactorily explained, although the note for the first performance suggests a programme in Straussian tradition:

The work might not inaptly be compared to some great epic poem dealing with the adventures of a hero round whose dominating figure all the minor incidents are centred ... the hero of the poem passing through a number of different experiences, a clue to which is given in the titles affixed to each variation. The composer wishes to disclose no more than a general outline of the various psychological aspects under which his theme appears ...[1]

More recently, Colin Scott-Sutherland has demonstrated that the work is linked thematically with the song 'Parting',[2] written at the same time with words by AE. Quotations from the piano accompaniment to the song appear with the statement of the theme and at the end of the first variation. The first eight bars of the final variation 'Triumph' are a literal quotation from the song. The following are the verses which were set in 'Parting' and indicate that, far from neglecting his romantic precepts, Bax was restating them even more strongly:

As from our dream we died away
Far off I felt the outer things;
Your windblown tresses round me play,
Your bosom's gentle murmurings.

And far away our faces met
As on the verge of the vast spheres;
And in the night our cheeks were wet,
I could not say with dew or tears.

As one within the Mother's heart
In that hushed dream upon the height
We lived and then we rose to part,
Because her ways are infinite.

As an expert and idiosyncratic pianist, Bax clearly conceived many of his early piano works without regard to technical difficulty, or to the limitations of the pianists for whom they were written, and it was this aspect of the *Symphonic Variations* rather than any intrinsic flaw in the musical scheme which was the cause of Bax's undoing. It is difficult to know how Harriet Cohen, to whom Bax gave exclusive rights in the work, could encompass some of the writing, particularly in the first variation.

After the first performance in 1920, given with Harriet as soloist, Bax was persuaded to make a number of cuts in the score, and by the time it appeared again – in 1922 – the first variation had been deleted and cuts made elsewhere. This shortened a work that played for over three-quarters of an hour to about thirty-five minutes, but in doing so removed one of the most successful movements and made the whole too reliant on slow music. A comparison of the original and revised versions may best be made in tabular form:

Original		Revised	Tempo
Theme:	53 bars	same	moderato
I Youth:	75 bars	deleted	fast
II Nocturne:	89 bars	same	slow
III Strife:	258 bars	15 bars cut	fast
IV The Temple:	138 bars	41 bars cut	slow
V Play:	347 bars	153 bars cut	fast
Intermezzo Enchantment	214 bars	same	slow
VI Triumph:	103 bars	same but 4 bar optional cut	moderato

In this revised version it was widely, if infrequently played by Harriet between 1923 and 1938, including six times at the Proms, and still received the approbation of many critics. For example, K.S. Sorabji wrote:

The *Symphonic Variations* of Arnold Bax is without any doubt the finest work for piano and orchestra ever written by an Englishman ... Elaborate and intricate in texture, both pianistically and orchestrally, it is superbly written for the solo instrument, making full and brilliant use of modern technique ... It is incontestably one of the finest concerted works of the present day ... it is a great pity that the composer has allowed himself to be persuaded into shortening the work by cutting out certain very beautiful and interesting variations.[3]

While its reservation for the exclusive use of one pianist undoubtedly has much to do with its neglect today, the partial destruction in the Blitz of what was thought to be the only score meant that for twenty years further performances were assumed to be impossible. However, in the early 1960s a complete set of parts came to light and Chappell & Co reconstructed the lost section of the score, and in 1963 published it for the first time — in Bax's arrangement for two pianos. This was very well received by the entire musical press: 'A major work, the neglect of which remains a shame on English musical life' (John Weissmann in *Musical Events*);[4] 'Far from being a scented pot-pourri of some minor romantic composer, this is a major — almost the only — British Romantic Piano Concerto of its time' (Colin Scott-Sutherland in *Music Review*).[5]

To give an idea of the actual sound of the work, a comparison with the Grieg or Delius Piano Concertos might be made, and it is true that the theme has been compared to the 'Sarabande' in Grieg's *Holberg Suite* by Colin Scott-Sutherland, who has also noted 'a pointed reference to Grieg's Piano Concerto in bar 6'.[6] However, one does not want to make too much of this, merely to demonstrate that this work is very different in idiom from Bax's later music. In fact, similarity of idiom is most noticeable with the later First Symphony and orchestral *Scherzo*, although Bax's piano style when writing for piano and orchestra is rather different from that used in the extended piano solo works, where many colouristic effects are employed, often low on the keyboard, which are eschewed in the concerted works.

It is interesting to note that the shape of the second bar of the theme in Bax's sketches of the work is altogether different — and less telling — than its ultimate form in the full score (see Ex. 33). Of

Lento espressivo

original version

Ex. 33

much greater interest is the fact that the embryo version of the
theme is the source of some of the later working, for example, that
in the fourth variation.

The first, quick variation, *Youth*, with its surging bravura opening,
is possibly the most purely enjoyable movement of the whole work
and highlights the 'slow and serene' *Nocturne* that follows. 'Nocturne'
is a favourite Baxian title, examples being the slow movement of the
Cello Concerto and *May Night in the Ukraine*, and in such movements Bax creates a romantic, yet wholly individual mood, in no way
Schumannesque. Indeed, he had little time for Schumann, whose Piano
Concerto he described as 'pure sugar water'. Richard Church has
recorded in his book *The Voyage Home* Bax's reaction to that
writer's interest in Schumann: 'Dangerous! Dangerous!' he said, 'the
wrong sort of romanticism.'[7] The writing for horns that leads into
the following movement is a typical romantic moment, evocative
of moonlight and limpid waters, but *Strife*, the last section of the
first part, is a different matter. In this movement, in particular, the
descriptive title is an encumbrance we can well do without. When Bax
attempts real aggression in his music he is sometimes less successful –
the notable exception being the stunning impact made by the First
Symphony. For his *Strife*, Bax writes low in the piano's register,
harmonizes in fourths and moves into the minor, but the comparatively thick piano texture removes any incisive edge from the
sound, and although agitation is evident, the title is misleading. The
movement now closes in G major, the key to which the *Nocturne*
had modulated, and this gives the first part an underlying unity. It is
particularly interesting in view of the relationship of the whole work
with the song 'Parting' that in this third variation Bax makes another
quotation from himself. This time it is from the new last movement
of the First Violin Sonata[8] (with its romantic tag from Yeats – see
p. 136) that he had written in 1915, less than two years before. The
idea from the sonata (Ex. 34) is followed here by its first appearance

Violin Sonata No.1

Ex. 34

in the *Symphonic Variations* (Ex. 35). This is extensively worked in
the *Strife* movement, but always in the orchestra. Reference to the

Symphonic Variations (Variation 3 - 'Strife')

Ex. 35

quotation also appears twice more, in the Intermezzo, *Enchantment,* before Bax launches into his finale with the exactly literal quotation from his song.

The Temple, the 'slow and solemn' movement that opens the second half, is characterized by alternating sections of solo piano and orchestra alone. Quite what the title may refer to is unknown. The music finally leads to a short cadenza-like central section in free time, which indeed Bax had originally intended marking *cadenza,* and a quickening of pace leads into the scherzo, *Play.*

Those who think of Bax as a writer of scores that are either thick and angry or thick and luxurious by turns, will find this movement a surprise. Its deft and infectious good spirits, marked most surprisingly for Bax, 'light and dainty', immediately bring to mind those two favourite concert encores, the Litolff *Scherzo* and the *Allegro scherzando* of Saint-Saëns's Second Piano Concerto.

The triumph of the final section of that name is not one of military splendour, but a musical recapitulation of what has gone before, and a return to the home and 'triumphant' key of E major. Indeed, the pounding chords with which the work closes have little sense of finality and fulfilment, rather a sense of anticipation with an under-lying anxiety, symptomatic of the post-war period to come. Of this closing passage Scott-Sutherland wrote:

The recurrence of the 'theme' at the end of the 'Triumph' variation marks in fact the beginning of the Coda, with its passionate assertion of the essentially transient nature of all beauty. By contrast, the foregoing 'Triumph' is a victory of spirit — of the eternal power of love and beauty over the frailty of created things. The Coda is a cry of agonized passion. There is nothing in British music to compare with these bars for sheer intensity of inexpressible emotion — except perhaps the closing music of *A Village Romeo and Juliet,* where, in almost identical terms, Delius consummates the hopeless passion of Sali and Vreli in the embrace of oblivion. The Symphonic Variations ends with the same kind of finality: 'Heigh ho, Travellers We, a-passing by'. It was a mood both knew well.[9]

A number of works have been suggested that may have program-matic links with Bax's life up to 1917, of which the *Symphonic Variations* is the summation. Shortly afterwards Arnold and Elsita moved to Beaconsfield, and it was from there that Arnold tried to express his feelings in a letter to Arthur Alexander which is quoted in its entirety:

Beaconsfield   Tuesday night very late

My dear old Sasha

This is to say firstly come as early as you like on Thursday for I shall be here all day and not going to London again until Saturday. Also I hope you will stay as long as you care to do so and come as often as you feel that the country would do you good. And now I want to thank you from my heart for all the tacit sympathy and intuitive under-standing that you have been showing to me for a long time. I know that you are in the secret as to the lovely and sometimes rather tragic adventures in which Tania and I are wandering, and your chivalrous affection and kindness to both of us moves me most deeply, dear friend.

It is the most important thing that has ever happened to me and made an unthinkable difference to life. For otherwise I should have stayed in Ireland most certainly, and whilst avoiding the war might have been mixed up in the rebellion. In fact the whole of life has been utterly altered by this wonderful stray creature from the faery hills. She came at a most difficult period when all ideals seemed slipping and now this that has happened has set them like fixed stars in the sky to burn for ever through what ever dangers and troubles may come. And it *is* absolutely impossible to see clearly into the future. This is completely dark and formless. And here are we with our heaven and Earthly Paradise and hell all in one.

Dear Arthur I think we all know one another well enough for you to realize the quality of this love that is between us two, but I do want to assure you that my chief desire is to keep her from all harm and evil, in fact this protective passion is at the heart of everything I feel for her. But I expect you know — I can't write about this. I feel as inarticulate as a schoolboy. But I wanted to thank you for being so true a friend to her; and she needs faithful friends God knows, in this suspicious and mischief-making world — a world that she seems to have drifted to rather by accident. Anyway, her heart is much too pure for its ways.

I am not used to talking about her, so forgive all these clumsy words.

ever your grateful friend Arnold

While at Beaconsfield Bax became friendly with G. K. Chesterton who lived nearby. Chesterton was not musical, but would call and listen to Bax and Alexander playing — confessing that he did not mind their kind of noise.

On 26 March 1917, the Oriana Madrigal Society presented a concert at the Aeolian Hall which included the first performance of Bax's *Elegiac Trio*, with the composer Waldo Warner as the violist. At this concert, too, the flautist in the trio, Albert Fransella, gave a performance of the Four Dances for flute and piano that Bax had rescued from his ballet *Tamara*, and at which he engineered Harriet's engagement as pianist in one of her first appearances on a public platform.

Summer and autumn 1917 saw Bax in an ecstasy of happiness that was reflected in two tone poems, *Summer Music* and *Tintagel*. These were followed in November by *November Woods*, in which the anguish and indecision between domestic responsibility and romantic passion were sublimated in music that evoked the conflict in terms of stormy nature. Bax's mood at this time is expressed particularly well in another letter written to Arthur Alexander:

Beaconsfield   Thursday

My dear Arthur

Would you care to come down here for the week-end either tomorrow evening or Saturday morning? We might perhaps go on the river or something. Isn't this a maddening Spring? Every day seems more golden than the last and makes an almost unbearable extasy in one's being − of what quality one really cannot say. Anyhow I for one am very glad that I am still permitted to be alive. I am doing some extremely interesting work scoring a little ballet I have been asked to write, and which will probably be performed (and perhaps even have a 'run') sometime soon.

Thank God for work say I, for (like most people I suppose in this tantalizing world) I don't get enough of my heart's desire for comfort − and this gets worse in this cruelly lovely season, as you can imagine.

Yours always affectionately

Arnold

Maeve sends you her love. She looks rather wonderful just now.

Summer Music invites comparisons with Delius. With the title *Idyll*, it was written, apparently as a piano piece, in the summer of 1917 and was said by its composer to evoke 'a windless June midday somewhere in southern England'.[10] Before the first performance Bax adopted the final title, observing *'Idyll* is not a little played out'. Writing to Sir Adrian Boult in the 1930s he could still observe of it, 'I am particularly fond of that piece of Southern England under the sun'.[11] It was finally orchestrated, for small forces, in 1920, and revised for publication in 1932, when it was dedicated to Sir Thomas Beecham. Here is a familiar Baxian world and this evocation opens with a haunting horn call which instantly establishes the mood while presenting the principal theme of the piece. Its repetition by cor anglais over a shimmer of strings and harp is very pastoral in feel, and the continuation of the melodic line is certainly Delian in its inflection. But the final exultant orchestral statement of the theme makes comparisons with other composers superfluous: this is Bax

celebrating some personal passionate episode in some of his most
glorious yet economical music. Probably no specific excursion with
Harriet inspired *Summer Music*, but we may be more exact about
Tintagel. Bax and Harriet spent six weeks together at Tintagel in
North Cornwall in August and September. During this time they
spent a week at Trevose, a few miles away, with a Mrs Reynolds. Miss
Cohen wrote about this to Arthur Alexander, lamenting the fact that
their return to London was imminent,[12] for it had 'been so free
here'. Of Mrs Reynolds she wrote that 'she understands about us —
and loathes the stultifying, poisonous conventions by which people
live their lives.' In doing so, she was giving us a hint of the social
stigma attached to a liaison such as theirs in the autumn of 1917. In
his orchestral tone poem *Tintagel*, Bax, while ostensibly writing a
mood evocation of the castle, the sea and its legendary associations,
was in fact celebrating his own passion. Bax provided a lengthy
programme note which is printed in the front of the published score,
but the following is taken from a slightly fuller version that Bax
wrote for a performance at the 1922 Leeds Festival:

This work is only in the broadest sense programme music. The composer's
intention is simply to offer a tonal impression of the castle-crowned cliff of ...
Tintagel, and more especially of the long distances of the Atlantic as seen from
the cliffs of Cornwall on a sunny but not windless summer day. The literary and
traditional associations of the scene also enter into the scheme. The music opens,
after a few introductory bars, with a theme given out on the brass which may be
taken as representing the ruined castle, now so ancient and weather-worn as
almost to seem an emanation of the rock upon which it was built. This subject
is worked to a broad diatonic climax, and is followed by a long melody for
strings which may suggest the serene and almost limitless spaces of ocean. After
a while a more restless mood begins to assert itself as though the sea were rising,
bringing with a new sense of stress thoughts of many passionate and tragic
incidents in the tales of King Arthur and King Mark and others among the men
and women of their time. A wailing chromatic figure is heard and gradually
dominates the music until it finally assumes a shape which will recall to mind
one of the subjects of the first Act of 'Tristan and Isolde' ... Soon after this there
is a great climax suddenly subsiding, followed by a passage which will perhaps
convey the impression of immense waves slowly gathering force until they smash
themselves upon the impregnable rocks. The theme of the sea is heard again, and
the piece ends as it began with a picture of the castle still proudly fronting the
sun and wind of centuries.[13]

The quotation from *Tristan* is the 'Sick Tristan' motif and is first
referred to on page 18 of the miniature score, where it is played by
solo oboe and solo violin, *plaintive and wistful*. It reappears in various

orchestral guises, mainly on the high strings, during the middle section of the work.

As in *Fand*, Bax is inspired by a vision of the sea, but it is a far more vigorous portrait that he gives us in this score: the climax of his several early attempts to depict the ocean in music. *Tintagel* is painted with broader strokes, a less fastidious palette than *Fand*, and in it Bax finally realizes the potential inherent in the juxtaposition of slow and fast moving ostinati in complementary or contrasting colours. He had almost hit upon this in *Cathaleen-ni-Hoolihan*, that first tone poem, and yet had taken nearly fifteen years finally to bring it to perfection. Particularly important in this music is the sense of sheer physical elation and strain that the difficult and often exultant horn parts give to the sound. In fact it is the horns that give us the clue to the passionate and personal nature of both *Tintagel* and its successor *November Woods*.

Bax's technique for writing sea music comes from Wagner and Debussy, of course, but the method is far from derivative, and in many respects quite original, based on close observation, and long experience, of the sound of the element he was trying to depict. Passing similarities with neo-Wagnerian sea music by other composers is also of some significance, particularly the conjunction of seascape and sexual imagery in Chausson's *Poème de l'amour et de la mer*. This imagery is very relevant in the case of Bax who, as we have seen (p. 110), wrote of how he 'wept in his Rathgar room' when composing his earlier seascape, *The Garden of Fand*. Clearly the ostensible legendary nature of his imagery had some more physical nature. In this respect Christopher Palmer strikes to the heart of the matter when he writes, developing Colin Scott-Sutherland's observation, that

the languid, chromatically drooping 'sick Tristan' motif which comes increasingly to dominate the *Tintagel* development section also occurs in Debussy's *La Mer*; he might also have mentioned that it is to be found alike in Delius's *Sea Drift*. Wagner, Debussy, Delius, Bax ... is it mere coincidence that all four composers should have been drawn to the same sea image in the music? We should remember that the chromatic language of *Tristan* was first forged to articulate feelings of sexual desire and passion, and that a shared characteristic of these four great sea-poets in music was the strength of their sexuality. None could be fettered in the usual way to conjugal and family fidelity or responsibility, and it is surely true that any denial of this constant and restless need for gratification of the senses would have impaired the force of their creativity. The sea has always had a Freudian symbolic import – did not Grillparzer once treat the Hero/Leander myth in the form of a play entitled *The Waves of Love and the Sea* – and the *Fand* legend is very explicit.[14]

Bax did not orchestrate *Tintagel* immediately, but went straight on to write his orchestral masterpiece, the tone poem *November Woods*. November 1917 was an unhappy time for Bax. He was faced with making a choice between wife and children, and Harriet. He would meet Harriet at the Crown public house in Amersham from where she returned to London by train and while he was caught in a beech wood near to the station one stormy November day he conceived the idea of *November Woods*.

November Woods is one of Bax's most exhilarating works, and is certainly the best of the nature poems. The music has been more widely known by repute than actual performance, and — like Holst in *Egdon Heath* — has been referred to as bleak and austere. However, concepts of austerity have changed, and *November Woods* is much less bleak than Holst's landscape and could well rival *Tintagel* in popularity.

Bax's inspiration in his programmatic music was almost entirely stimulated by the sea and forests, often interwoven with his literary or personal preoccupations. Nature certainly affected the composer passionately, as he himself once affirmed in a broadcast talk adding, a propos of the later tone poems, that he based his works upon aspects and moods of 'extreme nature'[15] and their relation to human emotion.

Julian Herbage coined the term 'mood-evocations'[16] to describe these mature nature poems, and certainly in this piece in particular the basic mood is as subjective as the pictorialism of the writing is objective. At the time the first performance was being prepared, Bax wrote to Ernest Newman describing the genesis of the music and urging him to play down the strictly pictorial aspect of the writing in the programme note for the first performance. He wrote:

... I don't want it to be considered too seriously in the light of objective programme music. It may be taken as an impression of the dank and stormy music of nature in the late autumn, but the whole piece and its origins are connected with certain rather troublous experiences I was going through myself at the time and the mood of the Buckinghamshire wood where the idea of this work came, seemed to sound a similar chord as it were. If there are sounds in the music which recall the screaming of the wind and cracking of strained branches, I hope they may suggest deeper things at the same time. The middle part may be taken as a dream of happier days, such as sometimes come in the intervals of stress either physical or mental.[17]

The orchestration of this work is typically lavish, but the full tutti is rarely employed, and, like Mahler, Bax is an expert in the weaving of exquisite instrumental detail into the tapestry of the whole. The use of muted instruments and instrumental solos — two of Bax's best-known fingerprints (a muted solo cello is scored at the very beginning) — further enlarge the colour range. Bax paints his scene by means that are obvious to an audience familiar with fifty years of film music, but the runs in the upper wind, ostinati, harp glissandi, and the rest that go to make up the physical side of this aural picture are done with the sureness of touch and the skill of a master. It is, however, the memorable nature of the melodic material with which Bax overlays his evocative orchestral backcloth that makes this work so outstanding.

November Woods opens, as we have already noted, with a vision of a windy day evoked by Bax's usual orchestral palette: harp glissandi, runs in the upper wind, an ostinato figure on the flutes and — more subtly — horns adding to the effect lower in the tonal spectrum. Indeed, as in *Tintagel*, the horn writing is of the greatest importance throughout. Later in the piece, windiness is also created by chromatic descending tremolando figures in the strings, and towards the end by little repeated notes for two or three trumpets. Instrumental doublings and combinations are also of great importance in the creation of this musical fabric, which requires a conductor fully in sympathy with it, for the balance is of great importance. Oboe doubles with cello; a rather subdued tune in the central section of the piece is introduced by viola, bassoon and cor anglais; while the more obvious combination of flute and celesta is used to suggest icy cold when required.

While *November Woods* may be fully appreciated for its surface value as a skilful and evocative symphonic poem, there is clearly more to it, for here Bax brings together themes from works written in 1915 (the Second Violin Sonata) and 1916 (*Dream in Exile*). Do these ideas have some special personal significance for Bax, the more so when juxtaposed in a work deriving from their composer's inner conflict between romantic freedom and domestic responsibility?

In this piece Bax moved further from simple ternary form, as he had begun to do in *Tintagel*, and thus nearer to the sonata design of the symphonies. It was a case of true development which eventually resulted in the first movements of the First and Second Symphonies.

Although most of Bax's major works are substantial in scale and emotional in substance, we do find among his output quite a number of very small-scale works and also a few delightful songs for children.

In February 1918 he produced several vocal arrangements in this vein, using traditional words and music in *The Maid and the Miller, O dear! What can the matter be?* and *I have House and Land in Kent*, in an engaging style, but perhaps with piano parts whose harmonic piquancy and technical difficulty did little to dissuade the average purchaser of them in 1918 from regarding Bax as a difficult modern. Possibly more completely successful are the *Trois Enfantines* written at the same time. These three children's songs, in French but with translations by Edward Agate, consist of the French nursery rhymes 'Jean p'tit Jean', 'Petit enfant, déjà la brume' (called 'Berceuse' by Bax), and, 'Une petite fille âgée d'environ cinq ans'. Their order was changed on publication, for Bax had originally intended to end with the cradle song. These arrangements were commissioned by the publishers J. & W. Chester whose catalogue specialized in French and Russian repertoire, and who were anxious to expand popular lines in the wake of the loss of much of their profitable Russian material after the Russian Revolution. The series of 'Répertoire Collignon' consisted of popular and traditional songs from Britain and France arranged by leading young British composers of the day — in addition to Bax there were Eugène Goossens and Herbert Howells, and one item — *Variations sur Cadet-Rousselle* — in which the song was arranged by Bax, Frank Bridge, Goossens and John Ireland alternately within the same piece. It was later orchestrated by Goossens. The series was hung on the popularity of the singer Raymonde Collignon, a light soprano who was briefly associated with Bax's circle, and with whom Harriet Cohen was to share her concert début.

During the war, various society figures helped in promoting artistic enterprises, particularly on the stage, to raise funds for war charities. Particularly successful in this respect was Mrs Christopher Lowther, who among other coups commissioned and presented Elgar's ballet *The Sanguine Fan*. How Bax was drawn into her circle is not known, but it may have been through their mutual friend Ernest Thesiger.

During the war, Bax wrote two ballets, *The Frog-skin* and *From Dusk till Dawn* (or *From Twelve to Three*), and listed them in the catalogue of his works in *Grove's Dictionary of Music* and else-where,[18] so that there is little doubt that they both did exist at one time. The scores of both appeared to have eluded all research, apart from a few orchestral parts of *From Dusk till Dawn* which showed it as a delightful work, and also demonstrated that more than one number in it was derived from the earlier ballet score *King Kojata*. However, in the spring of 1981, while the present study was being prepared for the press, the autograph score and the remaining missing parts were offered to the library of the Royal Academy of Music by their previous owner who had been unaware that they were considered 'missing'. This at once revealed a delightful score, of 116 pages and perhaps 20-25 minutes in duration, modestly orchestrated though with optional windmachine and clearly with the potential to warrant at least occasional concert performance.

From Dusk till Dawn was written by Bax for Mrs Lowther, and in December 1917 a charity matinée was given at the Palace Theatre, which included the 'graceful little ballet'. A synopsis of the action appeared in *The Stage*, whose critic was 'not by any means clear as to its dramatic action' but found it to have 'some very clever music on the ultra-modern side by Arnold Bax, and with a highly artistic staging ... The action concerns the doings of some Dresden-like figures that on a summer night, moved by the Wind, lose their immobility, and engage in love-making, which appears to have disastrous consequences for the Chelsea Figure, who is stricken down by the Wind for paying attentions to the Dancer, at the expense of the Clown.'[19] In it the influence of Ravel is felt, not only in the music, but also in the subject matter.

In the theatre, Bax's music was conducted by his friend Norman O'Neill, who himself wrote a ballet called *Before Dawn* earlier in 1917. Part of the work was heard once more, when Boult conducted the *Prelude and Dance* from the ballet at a Queen's Hall concert on 4 March 1918. After the concert Bax wrote to Boult thanking him, and observing that 'it went excellently, except for the fact that the side drum was apparently seized with maenad fury, so much so that he was unable to contain himself and poured out his dithyrambic soul in places where his entry was merely on the horizon.'[20]

The ballet opens with a quiet Prelude called 'Summer Night at the Window': atmospheric and evocative, it is also an early example of Bax entwining a number of solo violins — in this case three — above the orchestral texture (see Ex. 36). The full score does not name all the numbers, but the main ones are *The Wind Dances in the Garden, The Dancer and the Clown Dance Together, The Wind Dances Through the Room, The Flowers Dance Again*, and *Dawn*. Towards the end the music quietens down and the oboe sings a sad and beautiful song (Ex. 37), tragically Russian in its folk-like melodic inflexions. This was culled from the twenty-eighth number

Ex. 36   The opening Prelude ('Summer Night at the Window') of *From Dusk till Dawn*.
From a copyist's short score, edited with additional detail from the autograph manuscript
full score, now in the library of the Royal Academy of Music.

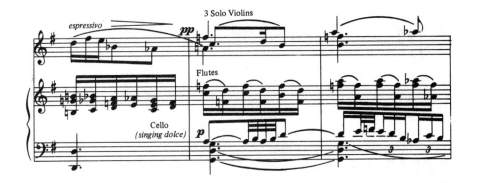

Andante con moto

Ex. 37

of *Tamara*, where it characterised 'a little old woman dressed in green ... carrying a basket of flowers ... she is old and lonely and miserably poor. Will the king buy her flowers?' Although ridiculed by the Court, Prince Igor embraces her, and she 'changes into a beautiful water nymph', who in turn releases the Princess Tamara from her incarnation as a little blue flower.

Bax's other ballet *The Frog-skin* has disappeared entirely, and were it not for its appearance in lists of Bax's works we would not know of it. Soon after composing *From Dusk till Dawn* Bax orchestrated for Diaghilev two movements by his favourite Liadov, which were needed for the revival of the Russian Ballet's *Les Contes Russes* in London in 1919.

Another wartime diversion was the Plough Club which, its first prospectus tells us, 'was formed for the purpose of stimulating interest in good art of an unconventional kind ... Its object is to present dramatic, musical and literary work of merit and originality.'[21] It may be thought that this was hardly the time for such a scheme, yet to its selected membership the Club achieved its aim, setting certain of its members on the road to success when peace came. 'The inaugurators felt that, in respect of dramatic productions, a close collaboration of author, composer, painter, actor and stage-director throughout all phases of preparation – even if the result which they propose be simple – should attain a completeness of aesthetic effect which is impossible if each contributor to the whole is out of touch with his colleagues.' The 1918 committee, on which Arnold and Clifford both served, brought them into contact with a wide circle of 'artistic' people, notable amongst whom was Eugène Goossens, to whom Bax had already been introduced by Philip Heseltine in 1916, and who was to become a close friend in the 1920s and a valued champion then and later. The committee was: 'Granville Bantock, Arnold Bax, Clifford Bax, Laurence Binyon, A. Langdon Coburn, the Baroness d'Erlanger, John Drinkwater, Jacob Epstein, J.L. Garvin, Eugène Goossens Jnr, E.O. Hoppé, Lady Lavery, Charles Mackintosh, Glyn Philpot, George Sheringham and George de Warfaz'.

The first of these functions was a concert which saw the première of Bax's sextet variously known as *Irish Elegy* or *In Memoriam*. The programme, given at 3.00 p.m. on Sunday 10 March was held at the house of George Davison ('32 Holland Park, W') and consisted of music by Cyril Scott, Goossens, Bantock and Bax. Bax's contribution came last on the programme and among the players were many who were to become closely associated with performance of his music after the war. The players were Eugène Dubrucq (cor anglais), Gwendolen Mason (harp) and the Philharmonic String Quartet (Arthur Beckwith, Frederic Holding, Raymond Jeremy and Cedric Sharpe).

The launching of this enterprise coincided exactly with Bax's final break with Elsita. Bax's mother, in particular, was devastated, and certainly Harriet Cohen was not welcome at Cavendish Square ('Cav'), where Elsita went with the children. Arnold left Beaconsfield to stay at The Crown, Amersham, and then, travelling down the Chess Valley, wrote to his brother from the Victoria Hotel, Rickmansworth:

6th March 1918

My dear Cliff

This is a blow, for at present I have no where to lay mine head tomorrow night. (Still Chuck used to do it). [At present it is not possible to explain this, and some other aspects of this letter.] Elsa is coming to Cav besides I am giving Cav a wide berth just now. I cannot bear the morality which accepts me, but will not have a good word for my partner in misdoing, who clearly should be recognised as much less to blame than myself, if blame must be dealt out. This used to sicken me in your case.

We rehearsed the sextet on Monday. I think it will be all right, though that is the only real rehearsal we shall get. Rather awful isn't it?

The subscription shall be sent to-day. It has been on my mind as a matter of fact, but so have a great many things and one ousts the other. I am still in a most infernal muddle and no-one with the exception of Gladys, Kenneth, and yourself shows much insight into the niceties (or rather nastinesses) of the position. If I were to listen to the random voices any movement in *any* direction would find me steeped in crime, or even if I stand still. It is quite comic: as Delius would say: 'there must be somethin' wrong there, Beecham' (this was when the trombones were playing the second movement when the rest of the orchestra were doing the first).

I am (in the moments when the thunders and lightnings and bombs are comparatively reticent) writing a long poem which I find interesting. 'The sickbed of Cuchulain' is the basis of it but it is folded up in a kind of double dream. Fand haunts me at the present time, both my own music and the story — not without reason.

Here is a lyricth. [This would appear to imply a lisp, but to whom Bax could
be referring is not known.]

Learnam – Sídhe

1. There strays a woman here and there
    Who seems to drink unearthly air,
    Whose heart drives through her rarer blood
    Than whips our sluggish multitude,
    And in her tears and laughter rings
    An echo of inhuman things.

2. From him that dreams on such an one
    There is no rest beneath the sun;
    For does a cold wind brush her cheek,
    Shudders a dread he dare not speak,
    And each slow sailing summer cloud
    Trails the shadow of a shroud.

3. Pearl-tissued in the autumn rain
    Are nets to snatch her home again,
    And every stealthy woodland noise
    Is leagued with some disastrous voice
    That jealous of her human breath
    Sighs delightedly of death.

4. Alas! I know this verity,
    For love has done this thing to me.

Tania has been seriously ill with bronchitis and tonsillitis, which fact has some
connection with the above. She is better again, but in rather a risky state.

Well I hope to see you soon. Should letters come will you send them c/o
Tania.

32A Winchester Rd., Swiss Cottage, NW3

Yours A

Harriet was not to give her first extended public recital for over
twelve months, but shortly after this she did again appear on the
concert platform with Bax. This was in an Oriana concert given at
the Royal Victoria Hall (later called the 'Old Vic') on 16 April. The
programme was, of course, mainly choral, including Elizabethan
music, folk-song arrangements by Holst and the conductor Kennedy
Scott, and works by Delius, Elgar, Balfour Gardiner and others.
Towards the end of the evening Bax and Harriet Cohen together
played what was billed as *An Irish Tone Poem* for two pianos, a
work we more commonly refer to today as *Moy Mell*.

The second production of the Plough Club was to be an 'Arabian
Night's Phantasy in Rhyme', *The Sneezing Charm* by Clifford Bax at

the Royal Court Theatre on 9 June 1918. Music was required for a song at the opening of Act II and for a ballet, which Arnold agreed to write, and an announcement to this effect was made in the programme for the first concert. However, coming as it did immediately after the separation, Arnold was unable to fulfil the commission, and in the end Gustav Holst wrote music which he later re-used in the ballet music for his opera *The Perfect Fool*. The Baxes can have had little interest in that particular event for on 4 June their father died, ending the regime at Cavendish Square, and subsequently causing Elsita to find accommodation in Golders Green, where, supported financially by Bax, she lived in an atmosphere of bewilderment and bitterness until her death in 1947. She would have nothing to do with divorce, but clung to the belief that she could pull him through. It was generally believed that she was a Catholic and that this was the reason. However, she was not — although Bax found it very convenient for that impression to be retained by his intimates. In this, one cannot help feeling that she was playing into Bax's hands, as she provided him with an unanswerable excuse for nearly thirty years for not making another legal liaison.

It should perhaps be mentioned that the Plough Club continued with a concert arranged by Eugène Goossens and a play by Emile Verhaeren, *Philip the Second* (for which Goossens wrote a splendidly vivid orchestral *Prelude*). Then on 17 November came a concert arranged by Bax. We do not know the full details of the programme, but it included works by Taneyev, Albert Mallinson, Denis Browne (who had been killed in the war), Ravel, Debussy, Stravinsky, Ropartz, Medtner, Albéniz, Bax himself and a piece composed by Harriet Cohen.[22] It is a pity that we do not have more details about this concert, but the choice of composers shows interests which are reflected in Bax's own music of this time and some time after.

The third concert was probably where Bax first met the composer and conductor Julius Harrison, who was to become a neighbour in Fellows Road, Hampstead, and, in the 1930s in particular, a good friend.

It is not known if Bax's music was presented during the 1919 season (when there were three concerts) but among the members could be noted 'Lieutenant Balfour Gardiner', 'O.M. Kling' and 'Charles Kennedy Scott'. Things were returning to normal, and the first and last, at least, were to be good friends for many years to come, while Kling, as proprietor of J. & W. Chester, was already the publisher of some of his works.

Peace and success

Between leaving his wife in March, and the death of his father in June, Bax produced a score which in its joyous invention and transparent and comparatively uncomplicated textures is in marked contrast to the ever-proliferating decoration in his other music. This was the First String Quartet, the two youthful quartets having by this time been rejected by their composer. The new quartet was dedicated to Elgar and was first performed by the Philharmonic Quartet on 7 June at the Aeolian Hall. The first movement of this delightful music has overtones reminiscent of Dvořák, particularly in the first movement where the Dvořák of the *American* Quartet will be noticed: this is a similar influence to that felt more than once in the slow movement of the Quintet of 1908, which Bax was soon to revise as the *Lyrical Interlude*. In the quartet's slow movement, *Lento e molto semplice*, Bax — for a moment — forgets his new-found exultation in life, and writes a sorrowing threnody, though whether for lost friends, lost youth or something more specifically Irish we cannot tell. In this movement he briefly alludes to the Elgar violin concerto, underlining the work's dedication. That Bax's thoughts *are* in Ireland is revealed by the third and final movement, which opens in the style of a wild jig-like dance, a dance which gives way to a gorgeous and memorable 'Irish' tune.[1]

Bax claimed the tune at the end of the quartet to be original, though Irish audiences were convinced that he had adapted it from the folk-tune *Bán Cnuic Éireann Óg (The Fair Hills of Ireland)*.[2] Bax was a close friend of both Herbert Hughes and the cellist Beatrice Harrison, and Hughes' arrangement of a version of this tune called *The Lament of Fanaid Grove* was played by Miss Harrison as a cello solo, and later recorded.[3] Although differing metrically and in decoration from Bax's usage, this is almost certainly his source.

The quartet ends with the return of the dance, and Bax in high spirits. It was published in 1923, and between then and the Second World War it became one of the most frequently played modern British works for string quartet and was twice recorded.

Having left home, one of Bax's first preoccupations must have been to find somewhere to live. Hampstead, and his familiar old haunts, would certainly have been his immediate inclination, and probably through the Farjeons he took rooms in a villa at 155 Fellows Road, where he stayed until the Second World War. Bax's 'studio' was on the second floor. An interviewer ten years later described it as 'the big, well-lit apartment ... There, across one corner at the back of the room was the tall, upright grand pianoforte [a Bechstein with an extended keyboard]; by the windows papers, music mss and books; books in orderly array on tables ... The many pictures on the walls, the comfortable furniture, the lived-in atmosphere of the place and the blazing fire ... A place inducing intimate thought, and so perhaps a study rather than a studio.'[4]

His accommodation settled, the physical collation of his manuscripts for the move became the probable reason for critically reviewing his output. There was a host of works with which he was not entirely happy, while *Nympholept, Spring Fire, Fand* and *November Woods* were all in full score but unplayed. He was still unsatisfied with the two Violin Sonatas and the First Piano Sonata, while works intended for the orchestra but unscored included *Red Autumn, The Happy Forest, Summer Music, In Memoriam, Pádraig Pearse* and *Tintagel*. The orchestration of the *Symphonic Variations* was in progress. In November, Bax revised the *Festival Overture*, but the revisions were very superficial and it was really the *Symphonic Variations* that took most of his attention.

At 11.00 a.m. on 11 November 1918 a maroon (that doom-laden boom that had formerly announced an approaching Zeppelin) was sounded in Hyde Park to mark the Armistice: the conflict that was the First World War had, nominally at least, ceased. At that precise moment Bax was working on the full score of the *Symphonic Variations*, and was well advanced with the orchestration. He jotted down in his full score the fact of the maroon sounding, and it may be seen in his manuscript 31 bars after GG, near the end of the scherzo

Play. As if prompted by this, he almost immediately introduced a persistent timpani part, suggestive of war, and saying with Housman:

> Far I hear the steady drummer
> Drumming like a noise in dreams.

This is maintained through much of the introspective musing of the following *Intermezzo*. This section is fairly long — 214 bars — yet in the short-score sketch Bax had originally intended making it even longer, and the lead into the final variation, now 27 bars, is a substitute for a more complex draft section of 62 bars. Presumably it was with the pruning of this movement that he would have been preoccupied in the first hours and days of peace.

Bax would have agreed that he was never in any way an adequate businessman, yet with the war over even he would have been hard put to it not to recognize the extraordinary opportunity that was now open to him. He had survived the war and had spent most of it writing music: his colleagues — all competitors for the public ear — had, by and large, been involved in more serious matters during the war. Many were dead, others had written comparatively little during the conflict. Bax, on the other hand, had produced a large body of music, including a significant clutch of works for the piano which had been quickly published and were becoming widely accepted — bringing him his first real income from composition. Not that he needed an income, for with the death of his father he had inherited a sizeable fortune. The opportunity was now to establish himself with his orchestral works.

Bax doubtless did not view the scene in quite this analytical way, but one feels sure that Edwin Evans, to whom Bax turned for advice, did. Bax pressed on and, having completed the orchestration of the *Symphonic Variations*, immediately turned his attention to *Tintagel* which he finished scoring in January 1919, inscribing it to 'darling Tania with love from Arnold'. Meanwhile, Evans wrote a long article — the first to be widely disseminated — on Bax, which appeared in the *Musical Times* in March and April. Evans's opening remarks admirably summarize Bax's situation immediately following the war:

Among the younger British composers, Arnold Bax occupies a somewhat isolated position. In the first place he suffers, perhaps more than any other composer of equal standing, from the disadvantage of being inadequately represented by his published works. He is a copious composer of important orchestral and chamber music, none of which is at present accessible in print except an early Trio for pianoforte, violin, and viola, which has ceased to be characteristic of his writing.

The dozen or so pianoforte pieces and a number of songs which are available are worthy of his pen, but fail to give the true measure of his constructive capacity, which far transcends the limits of these small works, attractive though they be. Although the English publishers have been singularly lacking in enterprise, the burden of blame must in this instance not be entirely placed upon their shoulders. Arnold Bax is of a retiring disposition, not in the least disposed to press his works on unwilling recipients, and he has suffered the fate of those who passively await recognition. It has come to him now, and with the return of normal conditions in the publishing world, it is probable that many of his most important works will come to light.

Another reason for his tardy acceptance is the apparent complexity of his works. As a student he possessed an extraordinary proficiency which made light of every difficulty, and when music like Debussy's 'Nocturnes' and Strauss's 'Heldenleben' were new, he played them to his friends from the score at sight. He could read anything. Such a thing as complexity did not exist for him, and he was unable to realise its existence in his own works when performers complained of their difficulty. As a matter of fact he was right in this matter, for the complexity of his writing, even in those early days when it was most *touffu*, was more apparent than real. His early proficiency tempted him to excessive elaborations, but the structure itself was simple. His music was, however, always subtle, and largely dependent upon the interpretation of nuance, for which adequate rehearsal is indispensable. That is, unfortunately, in this country a costly honour reserved for Strauss or Scriabin, and seldom accorded to a native composer until his name has become a household word. More than once a work by Arnold Bax has been announced and indefinitely postponed at the eleventh hour because the customary 'run-through' revealed that it needed looking at more than once. Hence performances of his orchestral works, except perhaps of the ten year old *Festival Overture*, have seldom if ever been adequate.[5]

Bax appears to have been oblivious of politics during 1919. He resumed the social round cut off in 1914, with the difference that he was now free of domestic ties.

During March, Arnold and Harriet Cohen went to Ireland, a visit that was to extend into the third week of April. Their first port of call was Dublin, where everyone was more than hospitable. They were out with friends or at their houses nearly all the time. The first night they went to see Darrell Figgis and his wife. Miss Cohen described Figgis as

One of the best-looking men I've ever seen — brown hair with red shades — a shapely head — ginger-red beard — olive green eyes, small straight nose and his hat and overcoat match his eyes and his tie and suit his beard — too wonderful! We were overwhelmed!!! He's just been let out of prison.

Another Irish patriot who was there was Frank Fahy, also just released from prison, where he had been sentenced to death and then reprieved.

That first night they also went to see Mr and Mrs Ernest Boyd. 'She was wonderful to us all the time we were in Dublin,' reported Miss Cohen, 'and you'd like *him* awfully I am sure. He looks like the face on a Russian ikon.' The next day they were taken round the Municipal and National Galleries by James Stephens. After tea, Harriet and Arnold went back to the Figgises and then to the Abbey Theatre to see a double bill which included Lady Gregory's *The Rising of the Moon.*

The day after, there were great crowds in the evening to welcome home the Countess Markievicz, but Arnold and Harriet did not go out, for the 'flu was very bad in Dublin in the early spring of 1919. Instead, they visited another favourite pre-war haunt of Bax, Kilmashogue. Miss Cohen reported the occasion in a letter to Arthur Alexander the following day:

[It was] a sweet little mountain outside Dublin. The *Light* was so wonderful — and there I saw the first baby lamb this year. In the morning we had been to see AE at Plunkett House — he's not at all like, but not exactly *un*like William Morris! — We went to his house next evening it was awfully nice — Maud Gonne was there with Iseult who is quite a beautiful person. On St Patrick's Day there was nothing done in the way of Sinn Fein (except that we smoked cigarettes in Stephen's Green and some children called after us 'Sinn Feiners' because of it!!!)
In the evening we went to Maud Gonne's house — AE and Yeats were there and the latter read some of the poems in his new book 'The Wild Swans at Coole' — that was a pleasant experience ... I'm afraid I've become an abject worshipper of Yeats' poetry. He talked to us an awful lot about the 'Noh' plays from Japan ...

This is almost certainly the occasion on which Yeats elaborately praised Bax's wartime 'Irish' poetry (see p. 379).

The naiveté of Miss Cohen which so many found charming at this period of her life is highlighted in another letter written on this holiday, to Arthur Alexander:

I was so pleased, because I looked (so I was told by others than that 'infatuated' Arnold of mine) beautiful on Monday evening. It's so heavenly to be young and look in the glass and see oneself looking like that — I mean. I was so terribly glad for Arnold's sake as you can imagine ... I don't have to apologise for saying those sort of things to you I know because you know they're meant quite simply and with no connection with vanity *etc.*

Later they left Dublin and travelled to the West, to Galway Bay, marvellous with pearly light and calm sea. They slept at Recess in amongst the mountains, at the side of a lake. The wild lonely beauty of the West created a great impression, and they drove sixteen miles through the mountains to Letterfrack only a very few miles from Bax's beloved Renvyle House, with the islands in the sea, the mountains behind and the snug cabins on the shore. From there they went to Glendalough, County Wicklow, for a few days, before going back to Dublin. Bax was to spend Easter with Arthur Alexander and Tim Braithwaite. Miss Cohen wanted to accompany them, but Bax was firm in his resolution not to allow her to do so. Her recital début was scheduled for June, and as she had not worked at her programme for over a month she saw the sense of Bax's stand and acquiesced.

Her début was, in fact, as part of a joint recital with Miss Raymonde Collignon, whose explorations of French folk and children's songs and the less demanding works of the young composers of the day were well received by her recital audiences. The recital was given at Aeolian Hall and *The Times* critic was impressed by the 'air of unmistakable distinction ... Miss Collignon's voice is the lightest of light sopranos − delicate and rarified perfection. Miss Harriet Cohen is a pianist something after the same style.'[6]

Bax now had two female champions, Harriet and Myra Hess, presenting his piano works to the public, and the competition between them undoubtedly caused him to try to define the territory of each. At one point he jotted (on the back of the manuscript of the piano piece *Nereid*) the following brief lists, which are also interesting in that *The Happy Forest* appears as a piano piece and the *Symphonic Fantasy* (later re-worked as the First Piano Sonata, and last played by Myra Hess under the old title at a recital in October 1919) appears under that title. Bax wrote:

Myra	Tania
2 Violin Sonatas	A Mountain Mood
The Happy Forest	Winter Waters
Two Capriccios	Ideala
Moy Mell	Quintet
Symphonic Fantasy	

The marriage of his friend Godwin Baynes and Rosalind Thorneycroft had proved unsuccessful, and in 1919 Rosalind left Godwin and went to Italy. Bax wrote to her in the tenderest terms, his viewpoint being particularly sympathetic after his own marital experience:

155 Fellows Rd
Hampstead NW

Dearest Rosalind
I hear that you are just going away to Italy and I wish I had had an opportunity
of seeing you before you started. Anyway I should like to send you my love and
best wishes, my dear, and hopes that this astounding old riddle of life may
become clearer for us all as years go on. If I can ever be of any help let me know.
I don't think it is very likely, but if you feel lonely or spiritually confused it
might be useful to write to someone who has been through a good deal and can
sympathize with most of the perplexities that beset us in this unguided adventure. I was staying with Balfour Gardiner at Ashampstead in the autumn and
tried to get an opportunity to come and see you, but unfortunately I could not
find one and I was very sorry.
      Dear Rosalind, you will always be in my thoughts and have my love and
sympathy.
      Yours always lovingly
      Arnold

      Musically, for Bax and his circle, and indeed for many lovers of
music and the dramatic arts, the whole of 1919 and 1920 was again
dominated by the influence of Diaghilev. The Russian Ballet opened
at the Alhambra on 30 April and the season ran until 30 July, with a
second season at the end of the year. Not only was this to be a cause
for rejoicing by Bax, who, as we have seen, had been headily excited
by the Russian Ballet at its previous appearance in London, but this
time he was to be musically involved, although only in a small way.
      Edwin Evans was an important musical contact in London for
Diaghilev, and he became musical adviser to Tamara Karsavina,
Diaghilev's prima ballerina. So when Diaghilev produced a scheme
for the first 1919 season involving the use of brief orchestral works
as 'symphonic interludes', there was obviously a need for the young
composers of the day to produce vivid short orchestral pieces for the
theatre. Notable amongst these performances were a suite by Herbert
Howells, the *Four Conceits* of Goossens (who also orchestrated *Clair
de Lune*), and the *Russian Suite* by Bax. The latter was intended to
consist of orchestrations of three piano pieces − *Gopak, May Night
in the Ukraine* and *In a Vodka Shop.* The first and last were certainly
played separately, but when the *Suite* was performed at the Empire
Theatre later the same year, the programme note stated that only
the first and third had actually been orchestrated. However, these
performances meant that Bax was known to Diaghilev, who soon
asked him to orchestrate two short movements by Liadov for the
revival of the ballet *Children's Tales* in the Russians' second season

that year at the London Coliseum. *Les Contes Russes* (as it was first known) had been first seen in San Sebastian in 1916. It was reworked for a further production in December 1918, and expanded again by the addition of Bax's two orchestrations — *Prelude* and *Lament* — for the London production a year later.

If the autobiographical wartime works derive from experiences that are fairly specific, Bax's next major work, the Second Piano Sonata, is more difficult to pigeonhole. Certainly the music has a very considerable emotional power and a form that might be construed as being dictated by extra-musical considerations. That the example of Liszt had been brought before the student Bax by his master Frederick Corder is hardly in doubt, and the device of Lisztian transformation is one that Bax embraced. Yet to see Liszt's Sonata in B minor as the antecedent of Bax's first two numbered piano sonatas, as many have done, is perhaps too glib, though its influence must have been felt. Bax evolved a one-movement form, taking his cue from his own First Sonata, which he had now more or less recast in its final shape, and with at least a sideways glance at his treatment of the material in his orchestral tone poems. All his life Bax tended to develop his material as soon as he announced it, and this caused him to introduce additional material (often derived from the main theme) as a bridge between what one might regard as subjects proper. This he does in the Second Sonata, taking his cue at least partly from the vogue for phantasy-form chamber works promoted by Cobbett and his competitions. Bax was developing a technique that also may have subconsciously drawn on the three-in-one form demonstrated by Benjamin Dale in his flamboyant Piano Sonata in D minor, which spotlights their common origin at the Royal Academy of Music, and in particular their composition lessons with Frederick Corder. It also derives, at least in its sound, from the common youthful enthusiasm of RAM students in the Edwardian age for the piano music of Glazounov, also demonstrated by Dale in his Sonata. It is surprising that some kind friend did not point out to Bax how orchestral a work he had produced (as was to happen later, when he attempted a third sonata and found he had written a symphony). However, Arthur Alexander contented himself by observing that the Second Sonata was 'Liadov-influenced',[7] and presented it in the second of two London recitals, on 24 November 1919. Bax was dissatisfied and withdrew the work, and it was not to make its final appearance in the form we know it now until June the following year.

In evoking the actual sound of this Sonata, Arthur Alexander guides

us in the right direction with his reference to Liadov. The Russian
Ballet had a wide influence while this work was being written, and it
would have been strange if Bax's favourite Russian scores from before
the war had not continued to suggest a mood. He was also interested
in Liapunov's piano Studies, finding *Terek, Carillon* and *The Epic
Poem* 'quite fine' and 'very interesting'.[8] But the actual source of the
Sonata's imagery and inspiration remains a mystery. Frank Merrick
recalled that Bax once told him that it 'in some degree typified a
struggle between good and evil'.[9] Harriet Cohen commented that the
work 'is an epic conception, this time taking the form of a contest
between a legendary hero and the powers of darkness'.[10] Yet in a
man passionately involved with the beauties and identity of Ireland,
Bax's first visit there for years, and the impending blood-letting in
that unhappy land, surely created an overwhelming impression. It
must be of some significance also, that Bax's play *The Grey Swan*
(see pp. 381–2) was written at the same time.[11] So the Sonata is
surely yet another work brooding on tragic Eire, and one of the most
'Celtic' of all Bax's works in its imagery, though not in its overt
language. (Shorter piano pieces from this time celebrated a more
immediate picturesqueness – Harriet Cohen herself in *A Romance*,
later quoted in the Fourth Symphony (see pp. 269–70), and Ireland
again in *What the Minstrel Told Us*.)

It is interesting to consider the reception the Second Sonata has
received from the public, and the ease with which a poor performance can misrepresent it, and at worst make it sound merely dull. In
fact one has to admit that it does not always communicate, yet in a
scorching performance such as that given by David Owen Norris at
the Purcell Room, London, in June 1979, we realise what a great
work it is. After it was published in 1921 the Sonata became comparatively popular and was widely played. One commentator, in July
1926, in the course of a detailed analysis, wrote of it as '... one of the
finest works ever written for the keyboard, a work which for clarity,
directness, and economy of expression, stands almost unrivalled
amongst modern sonatas'.[12] Perhaps Eric Blom's programme note,
written in 1922, best sums up how the work appeared to Bax's own
generation, and how the composer intended it to appear:

This work may be looked upon as the culmination of Bax's pianistic manner so
far. Externally a brilliant exploitation of the instrument's modern resources – as
regards both keyboard and pedal technique – its inner musical content reveals
complete maturity in the use of form and material to a definite artistic end. The
keynote of the whole work is tragedy, but a tragedy that rises above mere

personal grief, and thus touches emotions that are universal. We feel the drama that unfolds itself before us, whatever its hidden significance may be, to have been contemplated by its creator with the serene detachment of the finished artist handling his theme as one who, standing aloof from its tragedy, is able to enlist our sympathy all the more powerfully, precisely because of his aloofness.[13]

Bax's music was already appearing in post-war recital programmes. Myra Hess, for example, included *May Night in the Ukraine* in her 'delightful'[14] recital on 6 February, and the Philharmonic Quartet gave the first public performance of the *Irish Elegy* on 13 February, which was found to be a 'deeply felt work which made a great impression'.[15] It was played again in an Oriana programme in December. Orchestral music, too, was heard, in particular the 'riotous and exhilarating'[16] *Festival Overture*, revived in its revised version on 27 February at Queen's Hall by Boult, in an outstanding concert which saw the first public performance of Holst's suite *The Planets*.

The demobilization of Balfour Gardiner on 25 May was a further indication that Bax's circle was returning to normality. Benjamin Dale had already been released from internment in Germany and Holst came home from Salonika. (Dale had been taken from Ingolstadt where he had been staying on holiday and was initially held at Ruhleben Camp, the internment camp built on a racecourse near Berlin. Later, having broken his arm while playing tennis, he promised not to escape and lived on a farm in Holland. A reception marked his return home.) In the autumn, Bax stayed at Ashampstead, and as Balfour was on the Committee of the Royal Philharmonic Society, and certainly had a hand in arranging the programmes, the question of finding performances for Bax's orchestral music must have been discussed. Balfour's notebook of the period indicates that he had *Spring Fire* and *Nympholept* under consideration, but in the event nothing was achieved until *November Woods* was given the following year. As we have already seen in Chapter VI, neither *Spring Fire* nor *Nympholept* was performed in Bax's lifetime.

In the summer, Arnold and Clifford stayed with their mother and sister, then living in Arundel. Mrs Bax's views on her sons' marital disasters was firm: they came and stayed alone.[17]

Karsavina, whom Bax's circle of friends had revered above all other artists in the Russian Ballet, had been introduced via the all-knowing Edwin Evans. Bax responded to a commission from the ballerina with his *Slave-Girl* for piano, which she danced during a fortnight's season at the Coliseum, creating for it a 'fierce and strange'[18] dance mime, with Harriet at the piano.

It would certainly appear that Bax and Harriet Cohen became well known to the Diaghilev circle. Harriet wrote how

at the Savoy Grill after rehearsal or performance, we would all sup gaily enough and sit later in Diaghilev's suite until all hours making plans and discussing decors. It was through these discussions that I was fired with a love of impressionistic and contemporary art. It was here that incredible drolleries about music were said, especially when Prokovieff was around. I shall ever remember the two Sergeis on the one hand, vying with Evans and Bax in their iconoclasms, on the other. 'Sewing-machine music', said Arnold of Bach's Suites (he did not object to the later Preludes and Fugues, it seemed); but Diaghilev rather shocked the others in his denunciation of Beethoven, whom he described as a 'mummy, a corpse', dismissing the whole of the Violin Concerto, which he said was 'music from the morgue', whereas they said it was only the 'Rondo' they could not stand − 'turning and spinning like some horrible top'. Stravinsky of course, was frequently at hand with wonderful ideas![19]

The scherzo of an aborted piano sonata dating from 1913 had been orchestrated in 1917, and it appeared at a Promenade Concert in September, the *Musical Times*'s critic noting how 'its exciting rhythms and genuine good spirits gave great pleasure',[20] it also gave a foretaste of the orchestral style of the *Symphonic Variations* that was to be played in 1920 and the First Symphony that would appear at the end of 1922. The scherzo created sufficient interest for it to appear − in truncated form − as an invigorating pianola roll in 1920.

Bax numbered Eugène Goossens among his frequent companions at this time, and Goossens remembers in his autobiography how they would return to 'Bax's house, of an evening, eating spaghetti cooked by Harriet Cohen'.[21] Goossens presented *Fand* at Queen's Hall in October 1921, and in December included Bax's *Fanfare for A Hosting at Dawn* in a series of concerts that featured specially written fanfares, in association with the short-lived journal *Fanfare*.

It may have been Edwin Evans who introduced Bax to the firm of Murdoch who were to become his publisher. Already in 1918 his work had been considered in that quarter, and the first publication to appear that year was the piano piece *Burlesque*. In preparing his music for print Bax was still something of a tyro; as he later remarked in a letter to Harry Isaacs: 'I'm correcting my First Violin Sonata for a new edition. It was one of my earliest tunes to be published, and lordy what a host of errors and ambiguities I let pass.'[22]

In his printed music up to that time he had been a rather slipshod proofreader, probably the most unfortunate examples being wrong clefs in the *Concert Valse in E♭* and the vocal score of *Enchanted Summer*, and a missing bar in the violin part of the First Violin Sonata that soon joined *Burlesque* and other works in Murdoch's catalogue.

The end of the year was to be a very busy one. J.M. Barrie had written a one-act whimsical play, *The Truth About the Russian Dancers*, in which Tamara Karsavina — still the prima ballerina of the Diaghilev Ballet (and hence a major box office attraction) — appeared in a dancing role while all the other characters played normal speaking parts, Karsavina even having to dance her responses at her wedding and her participation in a game of golf.

Edwin Evans suggested Bax should write the music; the composer agreed, and started work on it at once. Over forty-five minutes' music was required, and Bax had the piano version ready for rehearsals in six weeks. 'I was soon under the spell of Arnold's music,' recalled Karsavina; 'as I listened ... the shape and curve, the rounds and angles of the movement just sprang as it were from the sound.'[23] At the start Bax played for Karsavina himself, working in the ballerina's large sitting-room at her home in Thurloe Square. 'Arnold was not only wonderfully patient but most helpful, bringing my attention to the uneven rhythm of some of the music ... At this time of his life Arnold looked frail — almost emaciated — but when the tea was brought in and he heartily tucked into sandwiches I became somewhat reassured ... "My people like me to take nourishment", he remarked.'[24] When he was busy with the orchestration he deputed Harriet Cohen to play at rehearsals.

The production was first seen on 15 March 1920 and was a great success. Various old friends wrote to congratulate him. Harry Farjeon was a typical example, to whom Bax replied, 'these little remembrances from one's friends always mean a great deal', and went on to enthuse over Karsavina: 'I think the walking lesson one of the quaintest and prettiest inventions I ever saw'.[25] (Bax remained intermittently in touch with the Corder circle in the 1920s, and after Frederick Corder bought Looe Island in Cornwall in 1925, with the proceeds of the sale of his collection of rare books, Bax would occasionally rejoin his old friends on brief summer holiday visits.)

The Truth About the Russian Dancers was very much a period piece, and would probably not succeed in the theatre today, but the music that Bax produced for this unlikely exercise is of very high quality and is worthy of independent assessment. Indeed it is so good and balletic that one is surprised that companies have not used it for a ballet in its own right, instead of trying to adapt other works (*Fand*[26] and the Third Piano Sonata[27] for example) to this purpose.

The score is in two parts, and in the following list a note is made of those movements which have been extracted as a suite, or published as piano pieces:

The Truth About the Russian Dancers

Part I

1. Overture [published for solo piano as *Ceremonial Dance*]
       [Linking music]: Moderato [solo violin]
       'Rather fast Valse tempo'
       Clarinet cadenza

2. Karissima plays golf
       [Linking music]: Moderato — Valse tempo (with great swing) [The Great
                                   Hall of Vere Castle, entry of Karissima]
       Moderato: Karissima and Lady Vere — Karissima tries to walk on the soles
               of her feet
       Vivace — Andante — Karissima's distress [violin and clarinet soli]

3. Bridal Procession
       The Wedding Ceremony
       Dance
       The Wedding Service
       Allegro molto [A Wild Night — The Maestro]
               Moderato
               Molto Allegro
               Rather fast Valse tempo

Part II

4. Dance of Motherhood   [published for solo piano as *Water Music*]
5. The Funeral of Karissima
6. Child's Dance
7. Karissima's Farewell   [published for solo piano as *Serpent Dance*]
8. Finale

Particularly in the big set-pieces Bax has produced music well able to stand on its own. Indeed it is perhaps better appreciated when divorced from its somewhat strange inspiration. The movements numbered above were all broadcast during the late 1960s and early 1970s, as part of a suite from the whole work, though in no

case were more than five movements done at any one time. This
work cries out for a (preferably complete) recording.

Bax wrote it very quickly and used parts of *Tamara*, though the
quotations are not extensive. A characteristic two-bar phrase appearing in the 'Polonaise' at the beginning of Act II of *Tamara* is used in
the middle section of the overture to *Russian Dancers* (bars 23–4 of
the published piano *Ceremonial Dance*); but the most important link
between the two works is the beautiful invention that characterizes
the Princess Tamara (Ex. 38). This is also the thematic basis – in

Ex. 38

augmentation – of the Apotheosis (No. 30) of that work. In *Russian
Dancers* it becomes the comparatively well-known 'Dance of Motherhood' (or *Water Music* – in its published form for piano solo).

An interesting feature of the Finale is Bax's quotation of a traditional tune, *To the Maypole Haste Away*, at the close,[28] a quotation,
moreover, that has never been referred to by its composer (Ex. 39).

(First time on cor anglais, horns, violas and cellos)

Ex. 39

One has the feeling of recognition as many incidental fragments in
this score pass by, but it is probable that they are not quotations *per
se*, rather clever suggestions of the characteristics of the music played
for the Russian Ballet. One passing musical comment on the composer's part is a conscious quotation, being marked as such in the
short score. This, too, appears in the Finale and is a brief theme from
Balakirev's *Tamara* which had become a favourite work of Bax's and
Arthur Alexander's in their piano-duet days. It was his final acknowledgement to the work that had kept him from the stage in 1912. He
does not tell us of the joke in the final full score, but we may be sure
that he and his friends would have enjoyed it.

Later in the summer, Bax's orchestration for *Les Contes Russes*
was heard again. 1920 was a year of many triumphs including, at last,
the secure establishment of Bax as a figure of national stature on the

musical scene. Not only did he have publishers pressing him for works for publication, but new works were being performed or commissioned. Otto Kling, the proprietor of the publishing house of J. & W. Chester, with the success of *Moy Mell* in 1918 and the album of seven songs issued by Chester in 1919, now took further works and in particular published the *Elegiac Trio* of 1916. Other publishers too were active. Anglo-French issued the piano pieces *What the Minstrel Told Us* and *The Slave-Girl*, and Enoch some songs.

The summer of 1920 was notable for a sudden influx of Polish musicians, 'a deluge of Poles'[29] as Lennox Robinson put it. Among these were the violinist Paul Kochanski and the composer Szymanowski. It is probable that Bax had already met both these figures during the war when they played to private audiences at the Chelsea home of that enthusiastic, rich American music-lover Muriel Draper. Lionel Tertis arranged the 'Chant de Roxane' from Szymanowski's opera *King Roger* for viola and piano, and he and Harriet 'played it everywhere'.[30]

Re-establishing contact with Tertis was inevitably to lead to further works inspired by Tertis's highly individual mastery of his chosen instrument. Two of Bax's most beautiful and rewarding works were written over the next two years or so for Tertis. The first was the Viola Concerto (re-dubbed 'Phantasy for Viola and Orchestra' after the first performance), and this was soon followed by the Viola Sonata, written in late 1921 and completed on 9 January 1922.

The viola Phantasy is divided into three movements which play continuously and are interrelated thematically. The orchestration is light, eschewing the lower brass, and the invention is among the most memorable Bax ever penned. In it he makes the only quotation of an Irish folk-tune that he ever admitted to − in the slow movement − where he uses the tune 'A chailín donn deas na gcíacha bána ('O Pretty Brown-Haired Girl'). The concerto as a whole, with its modal tonality, has an unmistakably Celtic flavour. It was to be Bax's only completely joyous 'Irish' work.

Bax was also persuaded to appear in public as pianist, something that he agreed to from time to time throughout the 1920s. On 22 November he and Paul Kochanski presented the first performance of a revised version of his First Violin Sonata. The violin part was almost certainly edited by Kochanski, and now contained one of Kochanski's own 'discoveries' − a special kind of glissando on two strings combined with tremolo which also appears in Szymanowski's *Fountains of Arethusa* with which Bax was probably acquainted.

When the score was finally published the following year it was now dedicated to Kochanski, and all overt memories of Natalie Skarginski were removed.

Other performers were also allowed to influence particular points of Bax's style. *Whirligig* for piano, for example, that he wrote for Irene Scharrer in 1919, ended with a glissando in thirds, a very difficult technical trick previously asked for by Delius in his Piano Concerto, by Bax's friend York Bowen in the first movement of his early *Miniature Suite* for piano, and (to a rather different effect and in fourths) by Ravel in *Alborada del Gracioso*, as well as, of course, by Liszt.

However, as far as Bax's reputation was concerned, the première of the *Symphonic Variations* at Queen's Hall on the day after the Violin Sonata (23 November) was undoubtedly the most important occasion that year. Bax had inscribed the work to Harriet and it was publicized as having been written for her — whose concerto première this was to be. Harriet Cohen remembered the circumstances of this performance being programmed:

Just about this time, May 1920, I went to an audition held by Sir Henry J. Wood at the Queen's Hall for the Promenade Concerts. This was the most important happening in my musical life so far. There were two other pianists auditioning that morning. Having suffered so much in anticipation of this event I was beyond fright, but noticed with surprise that my legs were shaking as I sat at the piano looking up at the kindly bearded figure who was to become one of the supreme directors of my career from that moment. I played the Symphonic Variations for Pianoforte and Orchestra that Arnold Bax had written for me. This was a monumental work and took fifty minutes to play. Sir Henry was very enthusiastic about the Variations and I think I may say he was pleased with my playing. Anyway, he engaged me to play at a Promenade Concert.[31]

Triumph

There is no documentary evidence to show how Bax reacted to events in his beloved Ireland in the early 1920s. After his spring visit in 1919 it would appear that he did not go there again until after the troubles of 1919–23. It would be strange indeed if Bax just forgot his friends there or had no emotional response to the killings and destruction. Fortunately we have that absolutely reliable barometer of Bax's emotional state: his music. It is not creating a false scent to read an involvement with tragic Ireland in his music of this time. Indeed it is almost impossible to ignore the Irish thread that runs through his work. Yet Bax as a man had grown away from those with a first-hand involvement in the politics of the country, and all he could do was demonstrate his emotional ambivalence in some of his greatest music.

Between 18 February and 1 March 1921, Bax set verses by favourite Irish authors – Joseph Campbell, J.M. Synge and his friend Padraic Colum – and these were quickly published by Murdoch as *Five Irish Songs*, becoming comparatively popular. Bax's reaction to conflict in Ireland was the same as it had been to conflict in France: to escape into dream. Already he was beginning to experience that acute pain at the dissolution of beauty which helped to motivate many of his later works. The second of the songs, for instance, is a setting of Joseph Campbell's 'As I Came Over the Grey, Grey Hills', where he encapsulates this mood at the words:

> The moon is set and the wind's away
> And the song in the grass is dying
> And a silver cloud in the silent sea
> Like a shrouding sheet is lying.

Another set of songs, the *Three Irish Songs* to words by Padraic Colum, was written the following February. These three haunting settings — *Cradle Song, Rann of Exile* and *Rann of Wandering* — underline Bax's concern for Ireland. They also remind us what a considerable songwriter Bax was, though only a few of his marvellous songs have established any sort of niche in the repertoire. The middle song of this group opens with a single melodic fragment on the piano 'in the manner of a caoin', which recurs later in the voice part, and underlines its lamenting character and bitter message. Through his music, with its strongly neo-folksong melodic line, Bax creates powerful and emotional images that far transcend their purely Irish origins. So compelling a songwriter deserves far wider appreciation than has been his lot up to now.

But there were practical musical matters which required attention. In particular his quickly growing fame as a composer meant that opportunities for performance were opening on all sides. Edwin Evans was, of course, still a good friend to Bax in this respect, and was involved when a young conductor, Edward Clark, came to London from Newcastle and began giving 'extraordinary programmes of contemporary music'.[1] Bax was played at one concert which included the first performance of Bliss's then avant-garde storm music for *The Tempest*, with its rhythmic overtones of Holst's only recently heard *Mars*; and the first performance in England of the 1919 version of Stravinsky's *Firebird Suite*. Harriet Cohen took part and, in the Bliss which was 'very strenuous',[2] she smashed a thumbnail.

The Bax work was the 1914 song-cycle, *The Bard of the Dimbovitza*, which received its first performance. Clark preserved the letters that Bax wrote to him during the preparations for this exercise, and they are now in the British Library.[3] They throw interesting light on just how much effort Bax had to devote to his early performances. The problems were all to do with choice of soloist and preparation of materials. Bax much later characterized the sound he wanted in the songs by referring to Oda Slobodskaya, but initially Olga Haley, a well-known mezzo of the day, considered them. Bax played them over for the singer who 'seemed keen to do them', and then there were delays in those pre-photocopying days while the songs were laboriously copied. But, finally the plan did not mature, and so a young unknown, Ethel Fenton, was considered. Bax wrote to Clark that he 'played the songs to Miss Fenton this afternoon and I think we had better decide to have her. ... She very reasonably said that she did not see how I could tell whether she could do them or not, and what I thought was promising was that she appreciated how much there was to be done and is frightfully keen on doing them. We also have a recommendation from Dent.' As late as 17 March the parts were still being copied. For a work that asks for no brass apart from horns, Bax had strings copied out for 5 desks of first violins, 4 of seconds, 4 each of violas and cellos and 3 of basses. He then took himself off to the country and wrote to Clark from the Royal Hotel, Symonds Yat (in Herefordshire) on 29 March, 'I will let Ashbrooke have the book containing the poems on Wed or Thursday, and I myself am going through the songs with Miss Fenton on Wed at 3 at her place ... can you come along too at the same time. I don't suppose she will object and anyway it will be good for her.' Clark evidently did not go, for two days later Bax wrote to say he had 'had a good rehearsal with the lady today and am having another tomorrow at 2. I don't like her voice much, but she has plenty of enthusiasm and really knows the notes which is something anyway. Are the parts done yet? Let us meet soon and go through the score to get the nuances of tempo right.' Bax's score called for instruments not required in the other works in the concert, and he had agreed to pay for the players: it cost him £10.

After the concert Arnold Bennett, who was an increasingly familiar figure in Bax's circle, wrote to Clark to approve of the Bliss which in his opinion 'wiped out members of the French VI'. The next concert, on 20 April, was devoted to the members of Les Six, and Bax attended. Afterwards he wrote to Clark apologizing for his delay in sending a cheque for the extra instruments in *The Bard*. Of the concert he observed, 'I enjoyed *Le Boeuf* [Milhaud's *Le Boeuf sur le Toit*] enormously ... and should like to hear it again. Vulgarity attaining the point of ecstasy is always stimulating.'

Before leaving Clark's concerts it is worth noting some of the artists who were in the orchestra. The violas were led by Raymond Jeremy, who had already played Bax's music and was to remain a good friend. That section also included Philip Sainton, who later made a minor reputation with orchestral works in a very Baxian idiom, of which *The Island* is probably the best known. The cellos included a very young G. B. Barbirolli, and R. V. Tabb who had been the extra cello in the 1908 performance of the string quintet. The oboes were led by the young Leon Goossens, for whom Bax was shortly to write the oboe quintet, and included E. C. Dubrucq, who had played cor anglais in Bax's *In Memoriam* at its early performances. Finally the horn section consisted of that distinguished family Aubrey Brain, 'A. H. Brain (senr)', Alfred Brain and 'E. Brain'.

Bax spent a good deal of time with the young composers who suddenly emerged after the war. Many of these artists reciprocated Bax's friendship by programming his music. The social round continued with endless weekends and parties, which found Harriet in her element. Indeed, Harriet's 'serenades' became celebrated, and she persuaded all manner of famous artistic people to attend. Typical of other hosts was George Davison at Harlech. Margaret Morris vividly evoked his musical evenings in her biography of J. D. Fergusson, the Scottish artist:

GD had a huge electric organ in the big hall, which he loved to play and did very well. Then, Eugène Goossens and Arnold Bax would play their composition and sometimes improvise. I remember one amusing evening just for GD's friends and my Summer School. We did a cod opera — I was the prima-donna, Boonie, tall and handsome (but very well covered!) was the prima ballerina. A Spaniard, a musician but not a singer, called Pedro de Morales, was the hero and Goossens and Bax improvised the music. It was great fun ... Goossens, Fergus and I returned in 1921. I don't remember the other guests, except Arnold Bax again, and Harriet Cohen.[4]

Arnold Bennett has described how, on another occasion, in February 1923, Bax and Eugène Goossens 'sat down at the piano and improvised, without a preliminary word to each other, a Spanish tango which lasted a quarter of an hour and to which Tania danced. It was full of new tunes, and there was never the slightest hitch, discord, or fumbling.'

A composer who later became a very close friend was E. J. Moeran. In a memorial reminiscence Bax recalled how they first met in the summer of 1919 at 'an evening party somewhere in Kensington or Chelsea ... Only a few minutes after my arrival I found myself conversing appreciatively with as charming and as good-looking a young officer as one could hope to meet.' Bax continued:

... he was about to be demobilized after serving in the army all through the War and, in the course of it, suffering a head wound to the after-effects of which may perhaps be attributed a certain instability in his character later on.

He told me that he was a pupil of John Ireland, whom he always declared to be a most painstaking and conscientious teacher. Ireland himself reciprocated Moeran's respect and thought very highly of the latter's gifts as a composer. He had every right to be proud of his pupil.

One of the first of Jack's works to be played and published was the *Sonata for Violin and Piano* given at a recital by Désiré Defauw and Harriet Cohen. It was rehearsed one evening before a small audience in Harriet's music-room in Wyndham Place, and amongst those present was Arnold Bennett ['a lovable sea lion, with chocolate eyes, drooping lids, and a protruding tusk' — Virginia Woolf], a true and sensitive music-lover, though he had, I think, no technical knowledge of the art. There came a moment in the rehearsal when Moeran rose and diffidently interrupted the players in order to suggest some slight alteration in the nuance of their interpretation. Hearing strange sounds beside me I turned to Bennett and found him in the throes of his curious stammer, his head thrown back, eyes closed, and one hand sawing the air gently to assist articulation. Then shrilly: 'He-e-e-e's m-making' (pause — and with a rush) 'a noise like a composer'.[5]

Moeran was another link between Bax and his public, for when shortly afterwards he promoted a series of chamber music concerts of British music Bax's Piano Quintet was included.

With his increasing coverage by the press, Bax was particularly irritated by the journalistic habit of referring to him as 'young' — a practice that continues about established personalities in some quarters even today. In a letter to the *Musical News and Herald* he protested most amusingly:

May I beg the favour of a corner of your paper in which to voice my entire agreement with Mr Bliss when, in almost heart-rending accents, he implores the critics to delete the qualifications 'young' and 'promising' from their references to present-day British composers? Must we always compose adjectively in this country? Recently a distinguished colleague of mine, born in 1874, was characterised as a young writer. This is frankly ridiculous. But worse is in store for Mr Bliss. My old professor used to say that in England creative musicians never 'arrive'. They are either promising or old fogeys, and there is an end of the matter. Apparently there is no estate between the schoolroom and the home for decayed gentlemen. Hitherto the point of life at which the most interesting transformation scene takes place has been unknown, but I am proud to be able to state that it has fallen to my own lot to make this important discovery, for only the other day I found myself suddenly labelled as a representative of the older generation — this in reference to a piece given at a concert in the course of which works by Mr Bliss and Mr Goossens were also performed. Let these two sucklings make the most of their time. The forty-seven-year-old young gentleman mentioned above must have evaded the climacteric by virtue of the sheer energy of his rhythms. As at the age of 37, amid the dust and mildew of my outmoded works, I totter down to musical limbo (to gaze, I fear, upon the scenery of Messrs Novello's top-shelves), may my senile croak join with the infantile pipe of Mr Bliss in a last protest against a very irritating survival of that critical mandarinism once so prevalent in British musical journalism.[6]

However, another foray against the press was not so happy. The First World War had left Bax feeling profoundly anti-German. Tilly

Fleischmann later remembered how he 'wrote a letter to the *Sunday Times* suggesting that all German music should be banned from British programmes and that only English and American music should be performed. He told me, quite innocently, that he was surprised how badly this proposal was received, and that people he knew were so annoyed that they went even so far as to cut him in the street! He got no followers to pursue his idea and added "the English composers were the most indignant of all".'[7]

It was one of Harriet Cohen's 'Serenades' at Wyndham Place that directed Bax to the idea of unaccompanied choral music. At one of these the Tudor Singers sang the Byrd Five-Part Mass, and the experience reputedly 'made a tremendous impression on him'.[8] He had already completed a short choral work the previous year called *Of a Rose I Sing a Song*, a carol for SATB chorus, harp, cello and double bass, which had almost certainly been suggested by hearing the Oriana Madrigal Society. His growing interest and the sudden revelation of Byrd inspired him to set for unaccompanied double choir the carol *Mater Ora Filium* from a manuscript text found at Balliol College, Oxford.

Mater Ora Filium is, without doubt, one of Bax's greatest works, but it is in many ways a work apart from the rest of his music. Although the piece is comparatively short (perhaps twelve minutes), the contrast between the opening tenor solo (Ex. 40) and the final

Fair Mai-den ___ who is this bairn That thou bear-est in thine arm?

Ex. 40

eight-part polyphonic alleluias is most striking. Everything about the work — its pacing, the rich contrapuntal texture, the choral scoring, the strong and memorable material — all contribute to an experience unique in twentieth-century music. The final 'Amen' (Ex. 41) is a crowning feat of contrapuntal writing in eight parts, culminating in a chord spread over three and a half octaves.

At the same time Bax also composed a third carol, a companion piece for *Of A Rose* called *Now is the Time of Christymas* for men's voices, flute and piano.

As far as composition was concerned Bax busied himself with a number of minor tasks. In addition to the *Five Songs* and the choral carols he orchestrated *The Happy Forest*, which had remained in

Ex. 41

piano score since 1914, and revised both the First Piano Sonata and Second Violin Sonata for publication.

The early 1920s were a richly productive time in Bax's life as far as music was concerned. Propelled by his continuing passionate love for Tania, yet troubled by events in his land of heart's desire, he poured out music in an endless stream, and in the short time up to the watershed year of 1924 wrote many of his very best works. The Viola Sonata is certainly one of these. Having only recently come to grips with writing an extended work for solo viola – the concerto, or *Phantasy* – he was obviously inspired by having renewed acquaintance with Lionel Tertis and needed little persuading to write a chamber work for the instrument. The sonata succeeds in a way that the Cello Sonata of the following year could not – Bax fully understood the character of the viola, with its haunting autumnal melodies at once vocal and orchestral in character, and its eloquent timbre.

The Viola Sonata is in three movements – a fast, diabolical scherzo flanked by calmer more reflective writing. Although the work is not cyclic in the true sense of the word, the opening idea is recapitulated at the end of the last movement. The work reveals a genuine poetic vision, and achieves a quiet but intense beauty by comparatively simple means. Of particular importance are leaps of an octave and to some extent those of a fifth – also a rising figure heard at the outset. The juxtaposition of viola and piano tone achieves a poetry which is quite different from that of the admirable Harp and Viola Sonata which appeared five years later. In the earlier work the opening, with its high tinkling piano offsetting the sombre hue of the lower register of the viola, is expertly realized. This first movement is a beautiful meditation which slowly emerges from a tentative opening to a superbly glowing climax. The music seems to embody a magic, passionately romantic view of life. But it is an introverted, almost melancholy world that Bax has painted – a world he seems to frequent more and more in his later works, and it is argued here to perfection. While not overtly 'Celtic' in manner, the sonata and its subject matter (if indeed there is any non-musical source, for Bax has admitted none, even in his letters) is indeed Irish in flavour. For example, the opening theme (Ex. 42) spins out its endless variation in true Celtic fashion, while the vigorous middle movement, *Allegro energico*, has much of the character of a wild, fierce, Irish dance. At its end, after a beautiful rhapsodic central interlude, the movement closes with what Robin Hull calls 'a truly diabolic coda founded upon the first subject ... and gradually working up to a terrific

Ex. 42

climax whose dramatic tension is probably unsurpassed anywhere
in Bax's music.'[9] While Hull overstates the case, this is certainly a
powerful movement. If Bax's music has dated in any respect it is in
his diabolic passages which no longer have the power to frighten a
world that has personally experienced the devil and all his works.

However, the freely chromatic style of writing which is so beautifully sustained in the poignant last movement shows that Bax had
finally forged his mature style. While it may have perplexed some of
its first audience, for whom Bax was then considered a brash modernist, this sonata can be seen today for what it is: a romantic and
individual minor masterpiece.

The rapidly growing audience, at least in records, for Bax in the
1980s derives from his orchestral works rather than his chamber and
piano music. Yet it was the latter which established his name in the
mind of the musical public of the early 1920s, and the orchestral
works were presented to an audience which knew the name but had
only a hazy knowledge of the style. If we think that the name Bax
was associated with the piano music and works like the G major
String Quartet and Piano Quintet, we may understand the perplexity
that some of the orchestral works caused.

Nevertheless, Bax's music was never considered to be technically
easy. In a press interview with Katharine E. Eggar in 1921, this
question was discussed:

A good many people seem to be so pre-occupied with the 'difficulty' of Mr Bax's
music that they never win through to its real musical significance. This is an
attitude which makes a composer a little impatient, for if a musician has given
what is to him the natural and simple and sincere expression of his own clear
thought, it is difficult for him to realise that other people may be puzzled or
confused by it. In preparing this article, the writer and Mr Bax talked over this
matter of 'difficulty' at some length, and he admitted that our method of
notation does make the *reading* of highly chromatic pieces very confusing,

'although', as he had to add with a sly smile, 'I myself can't remember ever having had any difficulty in reading anything'. 'But few people', I protested, 'have what is practically the fairy-gift that you possess. What do you advise the ordinary pianist or teacher to do, so that your music may not remain a more or less sealed book to them?'

He thought a moment, and then said: 'Let them take a course of reading the Wagner piano scores — preferably not the simplified vocal scores with the inner parts taken out, but the piano reductions of the whole thing. There they will find the contrapuntal basis of harmony exemplified, and that, I think, is what bothers them in my music. My harmonies come about as the result of contrapuntal movement. It's no use thinking in up and down blocks of harmony if you're trying to read my things: each part must be taken as a melodic line. But, after all, there's nothing *new* in saying this. These people surely don't think, for instance, of Bach in up and down blocks of harmony. They think in the *lines* of the parts.'

'Ah!' I said, 'there you put your finger on the weak spot. It never occurs to "these people" to think of connecting your music with Bach's. Because you are "modern" you are put in a watertight compartment.'

He looked amused. 'Oh well, if they're going to take "modern" music as a thing apart, without seeing the links by which it is joined to the past, there's not much hope for them. And if they're going to expect to find modern music without chromatics — if they stop short of the Classics — or if they expect it to be like Chopin, shall we say?' A gesture filled in the gap, and then he added: 'Why, what do they make of French writers? Of Mr Ravel? Of Florent Schmitt? If they ever *do* try to know anything of them?'[10]

The atmospheric effects in many of the short piano works might well have alerted the sympathetic listener to a composer of impressionistic orchestral textures. Talking to Miss Eggar, Bax continued about his piano piece *Nereid*, observing that it is 'nothing but tone-colour — changing effects of tone'. But the real clue to Bax's approach to musical sound is given in his introductory note to another piano miniature, *The Princess's Rose Garden*: 'This piece must be played as simply as the elaborateness of its detail will allow. No harmonic points should be emphasized, and the accompaniment figures generally should be kept wholly subservient to the melodic line.'[11] Again to Miss Eggar Bax observed that 'when people see a peculiar combination of notes they poke it out — whereas, the whole thing ought to *float*. There should be no shock of arrival at any particular harmony.'[12]

Bax's mature orchestral works started to be heard in 1920. As we have seen, the *Symphonic Variations* were given at a Prom that year, but it is really with *November Woods* that his mature style began to be experienced. It was first played in Manchester by the

Hallé conducted by Sir Hamilton Harty in November 1920. Commenting on the audience's reaction to the music in his *Sunday Times* review, Ernest Newman observed:

It is strange, by the way, how slow the average mind is to see the imaginative suggestiveness of musical discord. There are things in 'November Woods' that made certain people in the audience look at each other half-protestingly, half-amusedly. The equivalents in an autumn scene — the clashing of different lights, the harshness of line and of sound of trees buffeted by the wind, the discordant cries of birds — would appeal to them at once as full of spiritual beauty and mystery. But let two tonalities clash in an orchestra, and these people hear nothing but the physically discordant effect. It sets up no emotional reaction in them, evokes no imaginative vision.[13]

Nearly a year later, in October 1921, *Tintagel* was first heard, in Bournemouth, and although warmly received by the audience, a local critic found it very difficult:

It would appear, to the uninitiated, to be nothing but a rolling mass of sound, in which only a few passages, most particularly chromatic ones, are emphasised, while the most important melodies are mainly given out by the brass, and a solo violin appears in one place ... This design is, of course, quite compatible with the subject, a sunlit sea, but the opening figure, which stands for the castle, or perhaps the cliffs, is of little consequence, and adds nothing of variety to the music. Mr Bax has chosen a very difficult scene to paint, and his picture contains no variety, nothing but sea, and therefore strikes one as being rather incomplete.[14]

However, it must have impressed Dan Godfrey, for he repeated it during the Festival of British Music that he promoted the following spring at Bournemouth.

During 1922 Bax completed a number of 'Irish' works. As well as the *Three Irish Songs* which were in print before the end of the year, the *Lyrical Interlude* was rescued from the early String Quintet (now scored with a second viola instead of two celli, and dedicated to Vaughan Williams), and the Oboe Quintet, for many years a popular work with its overtly 'Irish' feeling and jig-like finale, was quickly written towards the end of the year.

During the summer of 1922 Bax saw a lot of the violinist Winifred Small, for whom he had written the *Ballad* in 1916. Miss Small played his music on a number of occasions and a good many letters from Bax to her have survived from this time. She first wrote to say that she was to play his First Violin Sonata, and he replied saying that he was also involved in two performances with a violinist called Strockoff, one on 26 May in London and a later one in Paris. It was while he was with Miss Small later in May 1922 that he suffered a severe attack of heart-pain which momentarily frightened them both, and although he could reassure his violinist, 'my silly heart has been behaving much better today', it may well have prompted him to deeper philosophical consideration of the 'ultimate realities of life', as he later put it, in the works that followed.

Himself he appeared to hold in little worth at this time, nor the then current standards of musical performance. To Winifred Small he wrote: 'I have been in North Wales for a fortnight and am up here (with very little enthusiasm) for a performance of one of my things at the Prom on Wednesday. I wonder if you ever get the mood when the whole of professional musical life seems entirely artificial and without any relation to realities — I often feel that. It is very disconcerting!' Subsequently he wrote 'Don't you think everyone plays very badly in these days? Your performance of my sonata was the only good one of anything of mine that I have heard this season. The most horrible things happened at the Oriana Choir concert the other day but no-body seemed to care a hoot.'

In the summer Mrs Ridley Bax decided to give an 'at home' at her new house at 10 Frognal Gardens, Hampstead, and Arnold and his brother Clifford were roped in to provide a lengthy programme of artistic entertainments. Winifred Small played the violin and Bax accompanied her. Mrs Bax did things in style — printed invitations and programmes — and these affairs became regular events for her circle throughout the 1920s. In September Winifred Small performed one of Bax's sonatas and he wrote: 'I can't tell you the extraordinary delight it is to be able to listen to someone playing one's work and to feel that everything is *certain*, and that the player has absolute control of and insight into the mood ... It was wonderful to hear the ponticello version of that little tune so beautifully even and also the same tune in such clear harmonics later in the movement.'

In the summer the dark but short Piano Quartet, written for Bessie Rawlins, was characterised by overtones of satanic power and a rather grimmer language than had been generally expected in Bax's chamber works up till then. These flashes of sombre preoccupations in Bax's imagination are indicative of a major work that possessed him for most of 1921 and 1922. It started as a piano sonata, conceived on the boldest and most dramatic scale: '3rd sonata', Bax wrote at the head of the first page, and he finished the first movement by 27 April 1921. The whole sonata, in three movements, was completed by 30 June. But Bax had created something bigger than a mere piano work, its very opening (Ex. 43) demanding orchestral sound to give it substance. Yet as a heaven-storming piano sonata it still has validity, and Noemy Belinkaya's triumphant performance at London's Purcell Room in October 1983 was hailed by one critic as the high point of the Bax centenary.

Ex. 43

Harriet Cohen claimed that it was she who pointed out to Bax that he had in fact written a symphony. In considering what he had achieved in this work Bax must have realized that the slow movement, which looked back to the romantic piano works, was not appropriate in such a context (Ex. 44).

The great power of the *Lento solenne*, which Bax then conceived

Ex. 44   The opening of the original slow movement discarded by Bax when he orchestrated the piano sonata which became the First Symphony.

in orchestral terms to act as the new slow movement of the symphony, is quite unexpected. It is the most emotional music he ever wrote. And surely the theme of Ireland, by then in open Civil War, is reflected in it. The symphony was a work apart from the rest of Bax's orchestral output up to that time: a work of such aggression and searing passion as to startle previous admirers of Bax's music and make them ask — why? In it the slow movement in particular seems to reflect some of the moods echoed in the poems written during the war. This movement is a highly charged elegy of great power, and towards the end the music seems to suggest the mourner sinking down in numbed despair, as at the end of Dermot O'Byrne's poem 'Kilmashogue — 1916'.

> They are stripped bare of all desire,
> Save to sink down on some green slope
> And snap the chain of nerve and hope,
> And numb the wounds of soul and sense
> In these old hills' indifference.[15]

It is possible, using suitably chosen extracts like this, to make out a persuasive parallel between Bax's fiery music and his emotional poetry which relates to specific events in Irish history — the Easter Rising, for instance, and the events of the following two years. Yet we must not overstate this. In more general terms, too, we certainly should not be surprised at a young man's anger at the folly that had swept away his world and his friends at the beginning of the 1920s. Thus the emotional events of the closing years of the war — the war itself, the Irish rising, the death of his father, the break-up of his marriage, even the Russian Revolution — must have emphasized his feeling of irrevocable change.

It is impossible to ignore the influence all of this *may* have had on the spirited music of the First Symphony. Bax would never admit such specific influences, although earlier in his life he had been quite open about his sources of inspiration and the programmatic nature of his music. But as he grew older he increasingly insisted that what he wrote was 'pure' music, though he betrayed his real musical concerns in occasional asides in letters to his friends. In a programme note on the First Symphony he tried to reject any programmatic intent, as he mentioned in a broadcast talk. Yet ultimately what he said sidestepped the issue. In the talk he recalled how he had written that 'the harsh and stormy music was an example of pure music, unassociated with contemporary events'. 'Whereupon' snorted Bax, a New York critic upbraided me as 'the quibbling Bax' and added 'of course this music from beginning to end represents the reaction of the composer's mind to the Great War'. These are deep matters, and I must admit that scarcely ever in later years have I been tempted to seek again the ivory tower of my youth, even if I could find my way there.[16]

What is certain is that this music was sparked by something other than considerations of 'pure music'. Bax also wrote (to Arthur Benjamin) that he was 'absolutely certain that the only music that can last is that which is the outcome of one's emotional reactions to the ultimate realities of Life, Love and Death'.[17] In so personal a statement as this symphony, one of his most ambitious works, we may be sure that it exemplifies this credo. Whether, however, Bax wanted to admit as much in the context of the sometimes heated debates about 'pure' music and programme music that erupted during the 1920s is another matter. Bax wanted his art judged on purely musical, not programmatic grounds. Anyway, it was probably unwise for a leading young composer of the time to make a public declaration of sympathy with any faction in Ireland; whatever he said would surely be misunderstood. Bax's definition of genius is relevant here:

The smug cliché has it that Genius consists of an infinite capacity for taking pains. I myself think it probable that all that remains really vital in the work of artists throughout the ages, has been given to the so-called 'Creator', with little or no conscious mental effort on his part.

The hour or moment of inspiration conditions a total quiescence of that creaking engine, 'the brain', – a state of mind comparable to that of the religious ecstatic.

It may be true, that 'one must have chaos in the heart if one could give truth to a dancing Star' but no star was ever born of the struggling intellect.

I should say that a Genius may be described as a man possessed of unusually vigorous physical and nervous vitality and awareness of the actualities of the external world, plus an infinite receptivity and sensitivity to those super personal – and other – world ideas capable of being moulded in the crucible of art. Every human being must have occasionally known these moments of fiery enlightenment, but perhaps the only difference between the normal man and the Genius (or even the highly talented) is that the latter experience them in greater numbers and with more intensity.

I believe too, that these visitations are dependent upon nothing but chance.

Every artist must remember mornings when all the conditions seemed favourable – a mood unharassed by any particular worry, and lit by a fire and excitement that promised to be pregnant with creative force. And yet nothing has come, perhaps because the flame was merely cerebral, or because the man's being was preoccupied with some transitory enthusiasm underived from basic emotional life.

We all waste a certain amount of time in the attempt to express states of feeling the depths of which we are temperamentally incapable of plumbing.

On another occasion, when the psychic environment would seem to be more than usually unpromising – it may be in an hour of disenchantment or vexation – the vision may suddenly become blessedly clear, possibly through the lack of consciousness, or because the various conflicting emotional agents cancel one another out, and leave room for the entering of the radiant guest.

But a subject so obscure as this could scarcely be treated adequately in many volumes let alone in a few sentences. All that can be said with certainty is that the truly inspired artist does not possess a gift, but is possessed by it as by a demon.[18]

(In a letter to Watson Lyle dating from the 1930s, Bax was goaded by persistent further requests to comment on the 'difficult enigma of inspiration' to retort that he was 'inclined to doubt whether any composer has been visited by *real* inspiration since Wagner was overwhelmed by Tristan and Isolda'.)

It is apposite to note that early critics dubbed the First Symphony 'The Demon', and on a more general level Bax certainly did not discount the concept of conflict in his music, as his programme note of the time records. In 1925 he wrote how in the first movement 'the fierce, almost defiant character of the first two themes colours the music of this introductory section, and seems to suggest some conflict ... In the development section the music seems to express in still more emphatic a fashion the idea of strife.'[19]

The slow movement is marked *Lento solenne* and is quite unlike anything else in all Bax. 'Here', writes the composer, 'the mood is both mystic and elegiac ... At the outset two clashing tonalities are sounded faintly ... with an accompanying rhythm from side drum (played with snares loosened, as at a military funeral). Then cellos and basses give out a lamenting phrase; the principal subject follows, announced by muted trombones and tuba, with a continuation, a dirge-like phrase for trombones, over a rhythm in lower strings.'[20] This movement is characterized by the hint of bugle calls in almost all its themes, and by the power the composer creates out of solemnly marching trombone chords. Its two shattering climaxes are paced with consummate mastery.

Certainly the technique that Bax used to achieve this work, is far removed from the atmospheric pictures that he was attempting in *Fand, The Happy Forest* and *Nympholept* before the war intervened. Only *Red Autumn*, when later laid out for two pianos (see p. 110), shows the seed from which this style developed (via *November Woods*, if one remembers that this later manifestation uses a more acrid harmony). Writing of the slow movement, one commentator observed:

> There is a different world which Bax sometimes inhabits, and it has been misunderstood by those not in sympathy with it. He is in this dark world in *November Woods* and, most notably, in the slow movement in the First Symphony. Its characteristic is not mere melancholy, but a fierce and tormented sadness. There comes a moment in the latter movement (just before G in the score) where it seems that light is at last going to break through. The full orchestra rises to a vast 4-3 suspension on the dominant of C major (the key of the movement is A flat minor): the suspension resolves and the upper parts play a tremendous chord of C major, fortissimo. But the bass has slipped under it and is on a bare fifth of D flat and A flat, with an effect of overwhelming disaster. Such power as this makes the appellation 'twilight' absurd.[21]

A comparison of *November Woods* and the symphony is striking. In the tone-poem we found that personal emotional experiences were sublimated in an evocation of stormy nature, while in the symphony a personal reaction to contemporary events is sublimated in terms of a universal or archetypal tragedy. Both result in music that is wonderfully evocative. Whatever its imagery for the composer, this music has a mature strength, and is far removed from the Celtic music of his youth, when 'pure and impersonal nature' was the source of inspiration. Now the motivation is anything but impersonal.

After its first performance the *Musical Times* critic characterized its three movements as being of 'battle, of lamentation, and of exultation', and went on to write this remarkable review:

> It is a most magnificent piece of wild music. It shakes a Promethean fist at heaven. It belongs to the great musical order of the frown and fierce stride, an indispensable order, as indispensable as the other, of the philosophic sigh and smile. The temper corresponds with Byron, not Gibbon; Hugo, not Voltaire.
>
> Someone was saying that if art is emotion remembered in tranquillity, then Mr Bax, who has here done powerfully better than before, may be expected one day to do better still, since here he is visibly the prey of his feelings. But there is an art of striking when the iron is hot. Here he has struck in E flat minor to impressive purpose. Whether an artist storms or persuades I take to be no matter for criticism, but one of ingrained temperament, a matter between himself and his Maker. He may carry you with him either way, and the carrying of you is his success. To storm argues the more physical vitality. Few had it like Wagner, and his could flag. Persuasion argues the cooler, less fanatic head and the more playful hand. The ardour of this Symphony ignores the fact that all our battles will be equally unimportant when the next Ice Age comes. A young man's symphony therefore, and a romantic young man's. A hothead and a genius, he compelled us to share at moments his estimate of the importance of his battle, and the drear *Lento Solenne*, ashen in colour, and singularly expressive of the full terror of bereavement, fairly overcame us, however hardened of heart.[22]

Bax's Oboe Quintet followed the orchestration of the symphony in its composer's life. The autumn of 1922 was a very busy one for Bax. Not only did he complete the orchestration of the symphony, on 8 October (for a December performance), but he was also involved in a host of other performances of his works with all the practical problems concerning performing materials and rehearsals that these would involve. Almost as a relaxation, it seems, he wrote the quintet for Leon Goossens to play, the manuscript of the first movement being dated 1 November and the whole work 'Xmas 1922'. It was published in 1925.

The work is cast in three movements, the outer ones quick. The first is prefaced by a rhapsodic *Tempo molto moderato*, and the finale is a wild Irish dance, a jig or reel. In the last movement comes a mysterious *Più lento* interlude in which the strings are all muted, a procedure that is reminiscent of similar moments in some of the orchestral scores. The variety of scoring within the confines of the instruments available is very rich, and often suggests that the orchestra was not far from Bax's mind; indeed Sir John Barbirolli — a noted champion of Bax later in his career — did produce the work as a concerto, in which form it was played several times during 1968 and 1969, including the 1968 season of Promenade concerts. The slow movement is an atmospheric *Lento espressivo*, which opens with a 40-bar passage for the quartet without the oboe. Another, contrasting, feature is the extended *ad lib* cadenza-like interludes in which the oboe plays unaccompanied or against a sustained string chord.

Here and elsewhere appear tunes which sound like Irish folk music. (One only has to compare it with Bliss's similar quintet written five years later, in which 'Connelly's Jig' is quoted, to realise that however delightful Bliss's quintet may be, Bax had seen the real thing; Bliss had merely taken a tune out of a book.) A case in point is the second subject of the last movement of Bax's quintet, where he gives vigorous treatment to what is apparently a variant of the folk tune 'The Lament of the Sons of Usna'. Bearing in mind Bax's personal hostility to the music of both Brahms and Stanford, it is piquant to discover that this tune was included by Stanford in his first collection of Irish tunes, *Songs of Old Ireland*, published in 1882, and subsequently used by both Brahms (opening theme of the slow movement of the Fourth Symphony) and Stanford (accompanimental figure in the strings at the second subject of the slow movement of his *Irish* symphony).

PROGRAMME.

—❦❧—

TONE POEM   -   "The Garden of Fand"
THE GOOSSENS ORCHESTRA

SONGS   -   -   (*a*) "The Market Girl"
                                  (*b*) "I heard a Piper piping"
                                  (*c*) "Green grow the Rashes, O"
JOHN COATES

Piano Accompaniment   -   -   -   ARNOLD BAX

SOLO PIANOFORTE   -   Sonata No. 2, in G major
HARRIET COHEN

CAROL (unaccompanied)   Mater Ora Filium
THE ORIANA MADRIGAL SOCIETY

PHANTASY for Viola Solo and Orchestra
LIONEL TERTIS

FOUR TRADITIONAL SONGS OF FRANCE
                                    (*a*) "Sarabande"
                                    (*b*) "Me Suis Mise en Danse"
                                    (*c*) "Langueo d'Amours"
                                    (*d*) "Femmes, Battez vos Marys"
JOHN COATES

Piano Accompaniment   -   -   -   ARNOLD BAX

SOLO PIANOFORTE   -   (*a*) A Hill Tune
                                    (*b*) Lullaby
                                    (*c*) Burlesque
HARRIET COHEN

CAROLS   -   -   (*a*) "Of a Rose I Sing"
With 'Cello, Double Bass and Harp Accompaniment

         'Cello   -   CEDRIC SHARPE
         Bass   -   VICTOR WATSON
         Harp   -   MARIE GOOSSENS

                  (*b*) "Now is the time of Christymas"
With Flute and Piano Accompaniment

         Flute   -   ROBERT MURCHIE
         Piano   -   ARNOLD BAX
THE ORIANA MADRIGAL SOCIETY

ORCHESTRAL ARRANGEMENT   "Mediterranean"
THE GOOSSENS ORCHESTRA.

Fig. 4   Programme for the Murdoch, Murdoch and Co. concert, 13 November 1922.

Concerts entirely devoted to the work of a living composer, and moreover one still under forty, are unusual. The concert that Murdoch, Murdoch and Co., Bax's principal publisher, promoted on Monday 13 November was a lavish affair, mixing songs and piano music with orchestral works. It was also very long. Many of those who had previously presented Bax's music were involved: Harriet, of course; Tertis; Kennedy Scott; and 'Gene' Goossens conducting. The programme is shown on p. 196.

The programme book was a generous one, almost a monograph in its own right, and was made available in advance of the concert. In his introduction, Eric Blom wrote that even where

a work has an autobiographical significance, Bax is far too reticent an artist to lay bare his feelings to others. He lets them speak to us in disguise: sometimes enwrapped in certain aspects of nature that are attuned to his mood with remarkable felicity, sometimes enlarged into the infinitely more touching expression of the joys and sorrow of mankind at large. Why are such tragic nature impressions as 'November Woods' or 'Winter Waters', and such wistfully bright ones as 'Apple-Blossom Time' or 'The Maiden with the Daffodil' so deeply moving? Why do the sonatas and many of the songs uplift us far beyond their surface impression? Because they speak to something in us that is common to all humanity ... The hidden strength of Bax's music seems to be a preoccupation with nothing but the great and lasting beauty of life and nature, besides which mere personal concerns – essential assets to the romantics – shrink into insignificance. This would explain why Bax, though intensely emotional at times, has never been known to lapse into sentimentality, and why, even when he bases a work on a literary subject, it is never programme music in a descriptive sense ...[23]

However, by its sheer variety the concert might very well have confused its audience if it did not dazzle them. Although written by a friend, Edwin Evans, *The Musical Times*'s review admirably evokes the occasion:

It is raking up an old story to dwell upon the advisability or the reverse of devoting an entire concert to the works of one composer, but in this instance the hero of the adventure has come singularly well out of the ordeal, owing to the unusual variety of the works included in the programme: and his publishers, Messrs Murdoch, who organised the concert at Queen's Hall on November 13, are to be doubly congratulated on its success, and on being able to present such a programme drawn exclusively from their own publications.

Without injustice to other participants, it may be claimed that three events of the evening stand out prominently as in themselves sufficient to make the concert memorable. The first was a performance such as we have not had before of *The Garden of Fand*, revealing all the fascination of its orchestral texture. The second was the choral virtuosity with which the extremely difficult *Mater Ora Filium*, for double choir unaccompanied, was given by the Oriana singers. It is one of Bax's finest compositions, though in a branch of music in which his mastery was until recently unsuspected. The cumulative effect of the elaborate 'Allelujas' was magnificently impressive. The third was Lionel Tertis's playing of the Viola Concerto, now called a Phantasy for viola and orchestra. It was a pity that the orchestra was not more fully occupied, for, returning after a long interval, it did not infuse the same spirit into the performance of an arrangement of the pianoforte piece, *Mediterranean*, which concluded the programme at a very late hour. The Oriana singers, however, showed no signs of flagging when they supplemented their earlier triumph with the two other carols *Of a Rose I sing* and *Now is the time of Christymas*.

Miss Harriet Cohen is a pianist of great musical intelligence as well as technical attainments, but even in the smaller concert-halls the massive Sonata in G taxes her physical strength to the utmost. At Queen's Hall its demands went a little further, and could be met only by occasional sacrifices of rhythm. She was more successful with the smaller pieces, such as *Lullaby* and *Burlesque*. Mr John Coates's contribution to the programme was, as always, entirely admirable.

The effect of the concert as a whole must inevitably be to consolidate Bax's reputation with the general public, in which connection it was gratifying to note the crowded condition of those portions of the hall which are generally held to be the barometer of public interest.[24]

Bax was well and truly launched as a leading – possibly *the* leading – composer of the day, during that winter of 1922–23. On 17 November the Viola Sonata was premièred, and shortly afterwards the famous Flonzaley Quartet took up the G major Quartet and played it in London. Ten days later *Tintagel* first reached London in a Philharmonic Society Concert conducted by Albert Coates and emphasized its composer's mastery of the orchestra. Coates was an important champion of Bax at the time, and between November 1921 and April 1925 he gave performances of the Viola Concerto *(Phantasy)*, *Tintagel*, *The Garden of Fand* and the First Symphony. In December 1922, after the recent experience of Bax's music by Queen's Hall audiences, the announcement of the First Symphony was surrounded with a great air of expectation; and that expectation was more than gratified, though not in the way that many might have expected. The first hearing of the symphony, which Albert Coates conducted on 4 December, must have come as a shock to many who were present: a similar shock perhaps to that which, twelve years later, was felt when Vaughan Williams's Fourth Symphony appeared. In fact the name of Vaughan Williams would have been very much in people's minds in 1922, for his *Pastoral Symphony* had been heard only the previous January and the contrast must have been marked. New

British symphonies were very much to the fore in 1922, a year which also marked the first performance of Bliss's *Colour Symphony.*

Bax's friendship with Karsavina, and his flirtation with the ballet, continued after *Russian Dancers.* He had also written *The Slave-Girl* for Karsavina to dance, and another piano piece, *Lullaby (Berceuse),* which with its haunting though simple melody deriving from ideas in *King Kojata* is suitable for dancing, though it has apparently not been so used. In 1921 Bax orchestrated Chopin's *Ballade* in A♭ as a present for her, and it was presented at the London Coliseum during the first week of July. The number in which Bax's orchestration appeared was announced as 'Mme Tamara Karsavina, M. Laurent Novikoff and corps de ballet in a spectacle designed by C[laude] Lovat Fraser'. A reviewer of a revival in 1931 by Constant Lambert and the Camargo Society mentioned that Bax had transposed the score into A major in his orchestration, though at the time of writing the orchestral score is missing. There were elaborate schemes in the air. Karsavina later remembered how

during one of the Saturday suppers I had in my house, we conceived an ambitious scheme of uniting English composers and artists to establish periodical
seasons of ballet ... None of us had sufficient money for the undertaking. We
thought the idea might appeal to the British public, and decided to circulate
what we joyfully called a 'manifesto'. This manifesto, besides Lovat Fraser and
myself, was signed by Arthur Bliss, Arnold Bax, Eugène Goossens, Lord Berners,
Holst, Paul Nash, Albert Rutherston and others. We expected generous support,
but got none. However, the getting up of the document had afforded us much
merriment. These parties at my house went on far into the night and were often
marked by 'serenades', as Harriet Cohen, to all 'Tania', called the musical
surprises she arranged for me – I was not to know beforehand what they were to
be, whether Eugène Goossens would play or Mademoiselle Collignon sing; most
often it would be Tania herself playing Arnold's compositions.[25]

Arnold also drew his brother Clifford into these schemes, inviting him to join them at Karsavina's house at 44 Thurloe Square, South Kensington. 'The fact is', he admitted, 'I have been bragging about your inventiveness and she [Karsavina] is very much at a loss about some little ballets she wants to do.' These included a short piece out of Schubert's *Rosamunde*, the danced version of Chopin's *Ballade* in A♭ and a short ballet on one of Hans Andersen's fairy tales. 'The Schubert is very urgent', Arnold continued, 'so I should like you to come and let me play you the music and see if anything suggests itself ... In any case she and Bruce would like you to dine there on

Sunday. You will find them both charming, both physically and otherwise ... If nothing comes to you you will be in no worse case than anyone else. The Schubert is a fearful nut to crack. But the attempt may amuse you and anyhow you would like them.'

Another event with vaguely balletic overtones concerned Percy Grainger's 'music to an imaginary ballet', *The Warriors*. Balfour Gardiner wanted to consider this then very innovative score for performance, and early in the summer of 1922 Bax, Harriet, and Frederick Austin played it through to him in Percy Grainger's own version for two pianos, six hands. 'It made an enormous din in the small room' noted Gardiner. 'Soon we all got into it, and liked all that was clear to us very much. The general impression was of jolly, attractive music with plenty of fire in it'. However, Bax never recorded his impressions, and no public performance ensued: it was not to be heard in England until a broadcast in 1966 and a concert performance at London's Queen Elizabeth Hall in 1970.

In 1923 Bax's output was smaller than the almost superhuman achievements of the previous years. Also, apart from the Cello Sonata in E♭, all the works were choral. *The Boar's Head*, a short male-voice carol, was written for a competitive festival — the male-voice classes at the Blackpool Competition — and was first heard on 20 October; and another delightful carol, *I Sing of a Maiden*, was completed though it apparently remained unheard for a year or two. All this had started with a commission from the Three Choirs' Festival, which Bax might well not have wanted to accept. The work, *To the Name above every Name*, a setting in truncated form of Richard Crashaw's long mystical poem, was completed in vocal score on 16 March. Certainly one would have expected Bax to deal with a metaphysical poem sympathetically. But in Crashaw he was confronted with somewhat tortuous imagery, and he responded by dealing with the poem in a sectional way, illustrating and decorating incidents as he went along. While one has to categorise *To the Name* as being among Bax's occasional works, it is by a long chalk the best, owing to its personality and conviction. When Bax tackles a religious subject the most remarkable part of his achievement is the exultant, celebratory note he manages to strike. Certainly this is not a man having to set a mystical poem because the occasion demands it: the world of feeling he underlines is absolutely sincere. Vividly imagined and with tremendous impact, though fairly difficult for the chorus, it is of particular note for its contrasts, which range from the unaccompanied to blazing choral and orchestral textures, its encompassing detailed polyphony, reminiscent of *Mater Ora Filium*, and its brief but beautiful soprano solo, only thirty-nine bars long, which was sung by Agnes Nicholls at Worcester in 1923.

After its first performance it was not heard again for sixty years. Norman Demuth in his *Musical Trends in the Twentieth Century* attempted to put his finger on the reason for its neglect:

Generally speaking, the choral writing is harder than in the motets, probably because Bax knew that the voices would be assisted by the orchestra. The work, therefore, is not particularly approachable. Its ecclesiastical atmosphere precludes concert-hall performance where its use of Gregorian tones would be quite incongruous, and since works commissioned for the Three Choirs Festivals are, for the most part, apparently doomed to one solitary performance, it seems doubtful if we shall ever hear it again.[26]

Whether for these reasons or others, the work was apparently considered and rejected for recording by HMV, as not being 'considered of sufficient interest for recording purposes'.[27] However, there are no grounds for its neglect today, and there can be no question of a modern audience finding it incongruous.

The music written during 1923 shows a decline in quality from that of the previous remarkable years, and this is exemplified by the Cello Sonata. This work, dated 7 November, was written to a commission from Beatrice Harrison, and the variable quality of the material and its treatment makes it patchy in effect. In the middle section of the slow movement, Bax quarries the score of *Spring Fire* and uses the 'Woodland Love' theme from that work. Quoting from previous works was always a sign that Bax was having difficulty ('No star was ever born of the struggling intellect', he said), and there are frequent signs of struggle in the sonata. The last movement is of particular interest because we find one of the first uses there of the term 'Epilogue'. Bax's large-scale works were already demonstrating the need for a lengthy resolution in the form of an extended coda, and had been doing so since the Second Violin Sonata. The use of the appellation 'Epilogue' and its reappearance with increasing frequency henceforth, makes the philosophical and musical weight of these closing passages an important part of Bax's technique: they assume almost the character of small movements in themselves.

The most satisfactory parts of the sonata are the slow movement and epilogue, where a singing line and fine tone from the cello can make their simple and memorable effect. In some ways this is reminiscent of Bax's technique in the Piano Quintet, particularly as regards the cello's relationship with the piano, and the heroic statements of the cello in that work. However, in the sonata many of the elements of Bax's style, particularly the use of different registers in both instruments for colouristic purposes and the frequent changes of tempo and mood, are not well fitted to a medium which cries out for the sustained lyrical line of the Viola Sonata.

Bax's musical climax of 1923 came with *St Patrick's Breastplate*. This fifteen-minute choral work was not announced as celebrating any particular event, but it is surely significant that Bax should choose the moment of the resolution of the Irish Civil War, and the final establishment of a viable independent Ireland, to compose an ecstatic setting of the Irish hymn *Lúireach Naoimh Pádraig*.

There is probably more block harmonic choral writing in this work than in any other by Bax, but that is not to say that there is no variety in the treatment, and its vocal textures do include contrapuntal vocal writing. Of its first performance (on 21 May 1925) the *Musical Times* critic observed that the music 'would have done very well for any other high-flown text, whether a Saint's soul (the Breastplate is the strength and protection of constancy) or a heroic love-tale'.[28] This is a very apposite remark, for Bax's approach to the text is in a vein of passionate mystical fervour. Something Elgarian may occasionally be caught, particularly in the layout of the score, and more than once the actual notes bring Vaughan Williams's 'occasional' choral works to mind – the ending for example, which for Bax is positively conventional. Recalling that he had only recently heard a choral work of his own at the Three Choirs' Festival, one has to admit that *St Patrick* would have been in many ways more appropriate there than its predecessor.

Bax's mood in writing this work was ecstatic, exultant even, and it is impossible not to try again to find an extra-musical reason for his musical high spirits. The resolution of the Irish Civil War is a persuasive one. The 'occasional' feeling of the opening orchestral introduction is vigorous and immediately holds the attention, as does the no-nonsense first choral entry. However, there is something in *The Times*'s observation that 'the work is ... in the predicament of being descriptive without anything to describe'.[29] Bax's illustrative approach to the text is exemplified by his frequent changes of choral texture, including several passages of unaccompanied choral writing, and by frequent changes of key. Tonal ambiguity is a major feature of Bax's style, and we find him modulating from one key to a distant one very quickly, with the familiar Baxian formula of a plagal cadence.

There is no denying the vigour of the music, and in 1925 this upset *The Times* critic who was 'so tired with the roar of sound from voices and orchestra without intermission'.[31] But this is in no way a drawback: for the work is short and the appeal immediate.

Bax finally gives unity to the whole score by repeating the opening choral entry (pp. 20–30 vocal score), and then follows with concluding amens, rather in the manner of an ecstatic coda. This writing is very reminiscent of parts of *Mater Ora Filium*, and Bax produces some beautiful and not at all noisy writing, the voices unaccompanied and the orchestra interjecting muted comments. Throughout, the choral writing is mainly in four parts but divides into as many as eight.

Although Ireland fascinated Bax for the rest of his life, *St Patrick's Breastplate* is his last overt demonstration of emotional involvement with things Irish. He celebrated Ireland's achievement of statehood, and could then relax and divert his energies into other paths which were already opening for him. The dropping-off not only of the quality of his work but also of its quantity, which began to be noticeable in 1923, continued in 1924, when he completed nothing during the first half of the year apart from two songs. The reason for this decline appears to have been his relationship with Harriet, which was deteriorating, and the gestation of the Second Symphony which was its expression. Already Arnold was beginning to look back on the past, with a longing that was later to assume the character of acute pain. Just before Christmas 1923 Clifford injured his leg, and his brother, in writing to commiserate, frankly admitted that he felt 'much the same as you do about the life at Ivy Bank and am not at all ashamed to feel a little sentimental about it ... I, at any rate, was very much happier in those days. I always have the subconscious sensation that a thunderstorm of unprecedented violence may break over my head at any moment – most unpleasant – though it makes one appreciate the sunshine when there is any.' Bax certainly enjoyed his life up to the age of forty. But after this, although he was still to produce several of his greatest orchestral masterpieces, and in particular the symphonies, life gradually saddened for him. Yet for a brief period in the early 1920s he was fêted as one of the great musical figures of the age, at least by British audiences, an indication that beauty and romance had a place in music that was truly modern. If Bax had not lived beyond the First Symphony we should still remember him as a major figure, perhaps remember him better, for he would not have lived beyond his time into a period that was increasingly unsympathetic to his ideals and to the imaginary world he had created in his work.

Crisis

1924 saw Clifford Bax living in London in a tower-like house in St Petersburgh Place, and reacting against his earlier bohemian existence by employing both a cook, and a butler named Smiles. It was doubtless the existence of his factotum which allowed him perhaps once in two months to entertain his brother, and their boyhood friends Maitland Radford and Godwin Baynes, to dinner and leisurely talk. The ambience of these evenings is vividly recorded in Clifford's book, *Ideas and People*, from which a few quotations will give the flavour. 'We were all old friends,' he recalled, 'men who had known one another for at least twenty years. It was Arnold, better acquainted than I was with the works of Edgar Wallace, who termed us The Four Just Men; a description so solemnly adopted by Smiles that he would say to me, while laying out a suit for the day's wear, "No, sir, you cannot go out on Tuesday. We have the Four Just Men." '[1]

Clifford Bax's autobiographical books are notable for their liberal use of dialogue — apparently authentic conversation, of which he habitually kept notes. Of his brother he wrote that he 'was always an impetuous and inconsequent thinker but more likely, nevertheless, than anyone of my acquaintance to throw out some arresting and newly-minted generalisation.'[2] Maitland Radford and Godwin Baynes were both doctors, Radford being Medical Officer of Health for Shoreditch, and Baynes assistant to Jung in Zürich whence he had returned to England in the autumn of 1922. In her 'biographical memoir' of Jung, Barbara Hannah paints a vivid portrait of Bax's old friend who was one of the first English doctors to go to Jung in Zürich where he was always known as 'Peter' Baynes. She recalls that Baynes had soon realized the value of Jungian psychology and, in spite of a rather checkered career, devoted his whole life to it, until his death during World War II ... He was a tall man, even a few inches taller than Jung, a university 'rowing blue', and outstanding in sport and games. He came to Jung originally because his first marriage had run on the rocks while he was in service abroad. One of the first tasks he undertook was the translation of *Psychological Types* into English, so that it was able to appear in 1923, soon after the first German publication, in 1920. Since Peter Baynes did not, at that time, know Germany very well, his translation of this volume has the advantage of being the only translation of any of Jung's books into any language that Jung himself went through word for word.[3]

Baynes's outgoing personality and varied interests meant that he was torn between England and Switzerland, and also spent some time in Africa and America. He felt his vocation was to be Jung's assistant, but this was in short spells which allowed him to be in England, where among many activities he was one of 'The Four Just Men'.

At their first dinner Clifford records his brother as agreeing with his proposition 'that an artist should no more concern himself with the temporary excitements of 1926[4] than with those of 1526, but rather should take an equal interest in both.' In contrast Radford, 'as early a Shavian as his age made possible, was convinced that no artist can stand aside from his age'.[5] At a later meeting of the friends Arnold is reported as passionately arguing that 'any intellectual idea ruins the flow of creative force ... a work of art is good in inverse ratio to its intellectuality.'[6] Clifford also records 'how greatly Arnold surprised us by saying that he did not regard Russian music as important ... "It is all based on folk-music," he declared, "and the Russians can't get beyond the mood of fairy-stories. Their work – Rimsky-Korsakov's, for instance – does not deal with human experience. It's only a kind of objective fantasy. The best of them is Tchaikovsky. He did use music to express his rather turgid personality." '[7]

Certainly the years 1924 and 1925 mark a watershed in Bax's life and in his music. While enjoying a wide circle of friends, and travelling a good deal, he was ceasing to enjoy the serenity that had followed his separation from his wife. The cause of his distress was his relationship with Harriet. Publicly their names were bracketed together, and remained so to the end of his life. But it would appear that Harriet tried to dominate him and there were tumultuous rows. All his life such crises were shattering for Bax, yet he would neither drop the person with whom he was in conflict nor give up his point of view. Harriet had never been strong, and was in poor health, yet in spite of this her manner towards the composer increasingly caused him much anguish. She was becoming possessive with regard to his music too, and tried to organize his artistic life, attempting to forbid him to write for certain instruments. Probably the most significant symptom of this conflict was her insistence that the *Symphonic Variations* should not be published but retained by her for her exclusive use. Bax complied, and this was directly responsible for the work's failure to establish itself, and it was nearly responsible, ultimately, for the destruction of the only score when Harriet's house was bombed in 1941. The whole topic of Harriet's relationship with Bax at this time will doubtless not be finally resolved until her personal papers become available for research (at the British Library) in 1998.[8]

At this time Bax's music overtly reflected his personal emotions, and he was certainly no longer writing 'pure and impersonal nature music'.[9] He sublimated his anguish in music and sketched the Second Symphony in short score, completing it on 10 October. It is *the* most autobiographical of any of Bax's works: as he later observed to Richard Church, 'I was going through absolute hell when I wrote it ... I was certainly not remembering emotion in tranquillity.'[10]

However, 1924 had begun on a high note with a visit to Delius. Bax's friendship with Balfour Gardiner continued, and in January the two arranged to travel to Rapallo where Delius was then staying. The visit was arranged for the beginning of February, and afterwards Jelka Delius wrote about it to Percy Grainger: 'Balfour was here with Bax, they were both very nice – but stayed rather far away on the other side of the Rapallo Bay, so that thin little Bax always looked exhausted when they got here – Balfour doing exercise on principle.'[11]

The composer would have been back in London for the first performance of his Cello Sonata on 26 February, given by Beatrice Harrison and Harriet Cohen. This was the first of a number of appearances by Harriet in Bax's music in 1924, possibly the most demanding of which was the performance of the now cut version of *Symphonic Variations* at Bournemouth later in the year, which she had first played in 1922.

Bax made several more trips abroad that year. In April he was off again, this time with Harriet and, among others, Richard Capel (music critic of the *Daily Telegraph*), the singer Aimée Kemball and her husband E. F. Coccioletti, sailing from Monaco on 6 April for Naples, Sicily, Turkey and the Greek Islands.[12] Then in June the First Symphony was chosen for the ISCM Festival and played in Prague under Fritz Reiner. Later, in August, the Viola Sonata was played at the Festival for Contemporary Music in Salzburg, by Lionel Tertis and Harriet Cohen.

That summer Bax saw a lot of a Danish friend, Christen Pedersen, better known as Christen Jul, meeting him in Europe, travelling to Spitzbergen and returning with him to London. Christen was 'slowly getting Arnold turned towards writing an opera ... he thought that most of his friend's troubles had their root in lack of connection with real life.'[13] Nothing ever came of the opera idea, and by the time Jul became Manager Producer of the Theatre Royal Copenhagen, after the Second World War, Arnold was incapable of obliging.

Early in the summer there would of course be cricket to watch when in London, and cricket to play with Clifford's team in August. The old Broughtonians played at Bath in 1924 for the first time. The four immediate post-war seasons (1920–23) had seen the matches played at Newbury, but now, in Clifford Bax's words, 'the whole scheme and tradition of our cricket-weeks caught new life ... the veteran members were glad to be back in the West Country and to renew old cricket-friendships, in particular, with F. W. Stancomb of Trowbridge and with Dr Keir and the Hurns of Melksham. Secondly, we were joined by Armstrong Gibbs, Ormond, Peters and Jack Squire.'[14]

A growing musical interest of Bax at this time was Sibelius, though there was to be no overt sign of any influence reflected in his music until a few years later. In a letter dated 31 October (1924),[15] Bax writes to Cecil Gray to congratulate him on the publication of his book, *A Survey of Contemporary Music*, admitting to total ignorance of Van Dieren, for whom Gray had made extravagant claims, and confessing to being unconverted to Schoenberg and Bartók. The letter ends by wishing Gray would send him the score of Sibelius's Fourth Symphony, a request that he also made later to Philip Heseltine. However, during the years 1924 and 1925 Sibelius was not making much impact on his musical style, which reflected highly personal emotional issues and, in spite of his reported comments on Russian music, still bore stylistic debts to Diaghilev and the Russians. Other than the Second Symphony all he wrote that year were the settings of Herbert Trench's poems 'I Heard a Soldier' and 'Wild Almond', dated 31 March and 'April' respectively. The symphony continued to cast its shadow over the following year, and the orchestration was not finally completed until 1926. However, during 1925 Bax also completed the gritty Second Quartet, two more songs – 'Carrey Clavel' and 'Eternity' (to words by Hardy and Herrick) – and the orchestral *Cortège*. Except for 'Wild Almond' the songs written in the mid-1920s were dedicated to 'W. Grant Oliver' whom Bax had known when they both lived in Beaconsfield where Oliver was Bax's dentist. Music had brought them together as friends, for Oliver was a fine pianist and often sang Schubert to his own accompaniment. They had continued to keep in touch.

The Second Symphony is one of Bax's very best works. In it considerable emotional forces are unleashed: as he remarked in a letter at the time of the first performance, 'I put a great deal of time (and emotion) into the writing', and, 'it should be very broad indeed, with a kind of oppressive catastrophic mood.'[16] It can be approached at a number of different levels, but at the very least it is music of such evocative power and impact as to make almost all contemporary works, at least by British composers, appear very pale. At the time of its early performances — and it has only ever been played ten or a dozen times — it was found to be an awe-inspiring and difficult work, 'grim' being a favourite epithet. Fortunately today we can enjoy repeated playings as it is available on disc.

Bax calls for a very large orchestra, and although he does not demand all the low woodwind used in the First Symphony (bass — i.e. alto — flute, bass-oboe or heckelphone, and contrabass sarrusophone), his scoring is idiosyncratically colourful through the use of two tubas (tenor in B♭ and bass), orchestral piano, celesta and typically brilliant percussion (including glockenspiel, xylophone and gong) and two harps. Bax also requires organ, although it is very sparingly used, either providing a low pedal, or just once, in the last movement, adding weight and sonority to the great *Molto largamente* outburst before the music gradually fades away to its quiet close.

David Cox has described the prevailing feeling of this work as 'introspective exploration of an inner world of nightmare and frustration'.[17] This may well be true, up to a point, and one has already observed that it certainly seems probable that Bax's personal situation at the time had much to do with it. Yet it should be remembered that it was Bax who later contemptuously dismissed the music of the second Viennese School saying, 'as a means of expressing emotional states [it] must be confined to those deriving from the diseases of soul and body'.[18] So it is unlikely that Bax would write a major work whose basis was merely neurosis. Indeed, even in this tempestuous score, we are allowed flashes of the lyrical beauty that kept Bax in thrall all his life, even if in the last analysis it is the lyricism of the unattainable.

The first movement is in almost direct line from the tone poems, and contrasts with the opening movement of the First Symphony,

which had been a more traditional sonata structure as was in keeping
with its origin as a piano sonata. The mood in this movement is that
of *November Woods* where an emotional crisis was depicted in terms
of stormy nature, and here it is even more convincingly argued. The
symphony opens with a long introduction of some sixty bars, in the

Ex. 45

first ten of which appear four ideas that reappear throughout the work, notably in the outer movements. It is necessary to see (Ex. 45) and hear the opening to appreciate the way in which the music gradually starts breathing, quite differently from any other work of Bax's, starting from the merest whisper and quickly establishing its personality in the distinctive sound and colour. The first of the four recurring themes will be seen starting in the third bar; the mood is gloomy and dark. A backwash of tone is then created by a pedal held on cellos and basses, violas, trombones, bass clarinet and contra-bassoon, gong and rippling piano, all playing as quietly as possible. On to this Bax projects his second idea (Ex. 46), its declamatory, accented character sharply contrasted on bassoons, clarinets and cor anglais.

(Cor anglais, clarinets, bassoons)

Ex. 46

The third motif follows immediately, stalking up from the bass in threatening fashion. It is destined to be important throughout the work, and especially in the opening to the last movement, the sound flavoured by the unusual combination of tuba and euphonium in B♮ (Ex. 47).

(Euphonium, tuba)

Ex. 47

Structurally less important, but for the moment more extended, is the fourth idea, blending the soft sound of three flutes with the more astringent timbre of three muted trumpets (Ex. 48).

(flutes, trumpets *con sord*)

Ex. 48

The bass figure (Ex. 47), rising aggressively, now forces the music towards the *Allegro moderato* of the movement proper. Great waves of sound, ever changing in colour, swell to a huge climax and the *Allegro moderato* is left on clarinets, lightly accompanied, in the

Ex. 49 (i)

echo of the climax. The music is closely reasoned and headlong
in its impact, the argument pressing forward in a sustained span
for almost fifteen minutes. In the First Symphony we saw Bax
using great dramatic washes of orchestral colour to splendid effect,

Ex. 49 (ii)

particularly in the slow movement. The Second Symphony uses this technique even more impressively, and there are several such passages, particularly in the first movement, in which Bax achieves evocative orchestral textures utterly individual among the composers of the time.

The plan of the first movement, while not fully justifiable in terms of classical sonata form, is clearly derived from it, and after the establishment in the introduction of the four recurrent motifs (which determine the emotional ambience of the whole work) the first subject proper is presented and then developed immediately in combination with the opening ideas, particularly the rising bass figure which provides the movement with much of its forward thrust. Into this fast music are interpolated two contrasting slow, melodic episodes, which do duty for a second subject though without extensive working. When recapitulated this material appears, against another typical wash of orchestral sound, launched in irresistible style on viola and cellos (Ex. 49), which momentarily suggests the sound world of Rachmaninov. It is true that the passionate impulse of Bax's work as a whole removes it from that softer world. Nevertheless, where Bax does suggest Rachmaninov, he lends such urgency to his lyricism that he underlines its power. By avoiding the sugar bon-bons of, for example, the slow movement of Rachmaninov's Second Symphony, Bax demonstrates his own strength and authority when a softer episode arises naturally in the argument. We are left in no doubt that ultimately Bax is master of his fate; and this conviction is even more clearly brought home to us in the slow movement that follows.

The second movement makes its effect by almost entirely lyrical means. It is built about three interrelated climaxes. The first of these is a high string passage in running semiquavers over a slow-moving bass (Ex. 50). Although it is only the decoration against which the theme unfolds more slowly on trumpets and woodwind, this running figure signposts the emotional heart of the whole work: an affirmation of confidence in the face of adversity. It has been suggested that this slow movement might be viewed as 'one vast love-song', and certainly the music would seem to support such a view – a passionate and finally exultant outpouring.

The last movement of the symphony is the most 'oppressive' and 'catastrophic' of the three. After a ten-bar introduction (*Poco largamente*) the music erupts with a fury (*Allegro feroce*) that will surprise those who have only previously known Bax in his tone poems and chamber music: a hollow marching is symptomatic of

the prevailing mood. However, the surprise of the whole work is the
literal quotation of some twelve bars from the opening passage of
the first movement, an event – *St Patrick's Breastplate* and the
Third Quartet apart – unparalleled in any other of the composer's

Fig. 50 (i)

scores. This movement in particular demonstrates Bax's orchestral brilliance and resource in a vivid way. The parallel with early Stravinsky and Ravel is particularly noticeable. The use of piano, celesta and glockenspiel, as well as two harps, adds to the composer's

Fig. 50 (ii)

palette a brilliance that tends to be missing from the more Nordic and ruminative later scores. In addition the low piano notes, and those of the organ, add a pagan strength.

The last fifty-nine bars are in fact an epilogue — more formed than in the First Symphony, although not marked as such — and we can witness here Bax tentatively exploring the use of the three-movements-plus-epilogue form that is such a feature of the later symphonies. The music finally fades into silence, and if this is to be taken as an emotional self-portrait it is a frightening one. The desolation that Bax paints at the close will not be more fully explored in music until the last movement of Vaughan Williams's Sixth Symphony some twenty years later.

The despairing mood of the Second Symphony spilled over into the composition of the Second Quartet, another comparatively austere work, which was completed in February 1925. In E minor, the same key as the Second Symphony, the Second Quartet, even if only superficially, frequently resembles it in mood, which is only to be expected with a work written between the completion of the symphony's short score and the commencement of work on its orchestration. Yet the Second Symphony underlines the fact that the symphonies have a character all of their own, particularly in their scale and mode of expression, which makes them works apart in Bax's output. Even though it starts with a movement taking over thirteen minutes in performance, the quartet presents a less epic view of the world in its basically contrapuntal style. In three movements, it is remarkable for its variety of pace and texture: the confidence with which Bax handled the quartet medium in the First Quartet of five years earlier, is here developed with a contrapuntal skill that one might not have expected from him. Yet the work has its problems, particularly in the first movement. It commences with a twenty-one-bar cello solo marked *Allegro*. The cello is expected to declaim a rhythmically awkward theme on which much of what follows depends. There are ten time-changes marked during those bars, which effectively have to be played as though they were not barred at all. This is very difficult to bring off, and if not successfully characterized, can upset the viola that joins in with the same material, and so the prospect of what is to follow can be spoiled. Thus it is thirty-nine bars before we have a full quartet texture, but such is the headlong impetus that Bax gives to the music (an even more exciting feature of the last movement), that its impact when it arrives is quite arresting.

The slow movement of the quartet is fairly chromatic in harmonic style with rich textures. About half-way through the movement Bax makes an undeniable, though fleeting, quotation from the *Romance* for piano, perhaps reminding us that Harriet is still very much in his thoughts. (Compare with Ex. 74, p. 270).

Fig. 51

The last movement is compact (less than eight minutes) and closely argued. The principal idea is a variant of the work's opening cello theme, and is launched with an infectious panache. A fugato, the first of two in this movement, is quite unorthodox in its introduction, yet the gripping way the music communicates during both these passages is sure proof that they were a vital part of the expression of Bax's emotional involvement with the work. The last movement is also of note for the sonorous chords of a typical 'liturgical' theme which provides a slow middle section, and for the brilliant coda.

Little else was achieved in 1925 as we have already seen, and the year was dominated by the orchestration of the Second Symphony which cost him considerable effort. However, a short orchestral work called *Cortège* also dates from 1925. Little is known about the circumstances of its composition, and no evidence has been found of it being played in Bax's lifetime, its first and only performance being given by Leslie Head and the Kensington Symphony Orchestra at a Vaughan Williams Centenary Concert in 1972. Dedicated to Herbert Hughes the critic, composer and arranger of Irish folksongs, this exhilarating five-minute work is brassily orchestrated, its flavour well caught by the opening theme which is first given by two flutes, cor anglais and cornet (Ex. 52). Suitably scored it would make a fine

Allegro moderato e molto ritmico

Fig. 52

addition to the brass-band repertoire. How popular music of this character and vigour could have lain unpublished and unperformed for nearly fifty years is a mystery.

In May, *St Patrick's Breastplate* was given by Kennedy Scott's Philharmonic Choir, and 'of the quality of the choir it would be difficult to speak too highly.' Scott himself conducted, leading his singers 'victoriously through the mazes of ... the cantata'.[19] Two days later, on the 23rd, E. J. Moeran promoted the first in a series of three chamber-music concerts at Wigmore Hall devoted to music by his friends, though starting with the Debussy Quartet. Harriet, newly returned from a successful German tour, played the Bax Piano Quintet in the first concert, and it appeared to have been the most successful work of the three programmes. Music played in succeeding concerts included quartets by R. O. Morris, Arthur Benjamin and Van Dieren, and piano trios by Moeran and Ireland, together with Warlock's *The Curlew*.

Although Bax had no official students, one or two young composers did approach him for lessons, notably the Australians Margaret Sutherland and Arthur Benjamin. Margaret Sutherland had travelled to Europe in 1923, visiting London, Vienna and Paris. She recorded how 'most English Music of the period did not move or hold me ... I actively disliked the dressed-up folk song that was all the rage (preferring it undressed) and the kind of musical inbreeding that was rife.'[20] It is indicative of Bax's musical stature and apparent independence in 1925, that the twenty-eight-year-old Australian composer — having visited Paris and Vienna — should choose to approach Bax in preference to his contemporaries. Her recollections of how Bax reacted constitute a vivid vignette of him at that time:

As a very timid student in London, I plucked up courage to write and ask Arnold Bax if he would give me some lessons in composition. His reply to my inquiry was, as I found later, entirely typical of the man. He wrote: 'I shall be happy to help you at any time; but I am quite hopeless as a teacher.' He meant by this that he had no particular method, and had never given regular lessons. Apart from that fact — perhaps not altogether a drawback either — he was an admirable critic. And his straight-to-the-point comments on any things that I took him have always remained with me as the most valuable advice I ever had. His amazing gift for reading orchestral scores at sight and translating them to the piano facilitated discussion and was, for this reason, of enormous value. He was an extraordinarily fine — if unorthodox — pianist; and I remember asking him one day why he never appeared as pianist in any of his works. 'Oh, I just feel', he replied, 'that once I have written something my job is done. I am already thinking of the next.' He was always a shadowy figure, alone, in the back seats, when his works were played — reflective, withdrawn, extra-ordinarily gentle. And I used to wonder whether his environment at any time made very much impression on him. He was living at that time near the Swiss Cottage station, in one of those nondescript, dreary tenant houses — sad-looking, anonymous places. In the hall downstairs, before one trudged up the stairs to his room, stood a remarkable stuffed cockatoo in a tall glass case — no doubt his landlady's pride and joy. I used to wonder, if he ever noticed it — and if so, did it jar on him?[21]

After leaving Bax, and before returning home to Australia at the end of 1925, Margaret Sutherland wrote a Sonata for violin and piano. Bax was subsequently asked to read the score by Louise Dyer, its intending publisher, and commented, 'It is the best work by a woman that I know.'[22]

Harriet's physical condition was worsening as was her relationship with Bax. The only published source to deal with what now ensued — Harriet's journey to Switzerland to seek a cure for her tuberculosis from Henri Spahlinger — is her autobiography. It is clearly an un-reliable source in describing the emotional atmosphere at the time, but whether it is reliable in its chronology is not known. Miss Cohen does not mention Bax in her account, implying she went to Geneva alone, but this conflicts with the known fact that she actually travelled to Geneva with Bax, and he wrote to his brother Clifford from the Hôtel d'Angleterre after their arrival. The letter is all too clear as to his predicament at the time.

My dear Cliff

If you can spare a half-hour to send me a few lines of gossip or quaint philos-ophy — I shall be most grateful. I feel absolutely marooned in this kultur — which is my idea of limbo — and this is apart from the fact that I am really suffering a great deal in *every* sense (other than physical). Life seems to have landed me in a cul-de-sac, and I see no way out other than blowing up the surrounding edifices; and I have not quite reached this point. But it is really maddening to feel that one ought to be doing one's best work (in one genre or another) and yet one is doing absolutely nothing. My imagination seems to be chloroformed — As Bennett said 'My dear boy these women are the devil' (I have not indicated the stammerings!). And the peculiar devil of it is that I am losing touch with everything and everyone that bring vision and the igniting spark. Fundamentally I appreciate Tania as much as ever I did, but I cannot consent to being absorbed and consumed into the idea of a sick and egocentric mind. I hear you saying that all women correspond to that generalization, and I think you are probably right. The trouble is (absolutely entre nous) that I don't see how I am going to escape from this coil — apart from shuf-fling off the mortal ditto (which is *not* my particular form of vanity and self-advertisement). I think I have rather a morbid sense of responsibility to other people — perhaps just because I find it difficult to believe in the importance of anything or anyone, and *primarily myself* of course — And yet I feel vaguely that I might have done something moderately good in art, if I had been really free — free from any kind of morbidity of conscience or responsibility. As long as this type of existence continues I shall seriously be incapable of anything at all — And yet it is almost impossible to make any change as far as I can see at present. This is a dismal discourse — Cheer me up by writing to me soon, if you are not too much engaged by work — I should really appreciate it.

Clifford Bax evidently responded quickly, for soon his brother was writing again, grateful for correspondence but with no more satisfactory situation to report.

I was delighted to have your amusing and eventful letter yesterday, and I think it was extremely kind of you to write at such length. I am having a perfectly damnable time here — much worse than anything I have imagined possible. There has been a terrible amount of bad luck about it too — needless contretemps making the situation more and more acute. And as you can figure to yourself there is absolutely no relief from this atmosphere of gloom and recrimination. There is not even anyone else to speak to as a rule. When I come out of this predicament — if ever — I shall want to go a long sea voyage with three men.

I envy you so much your successful spell of work and of course am delighted to hear of it. I of course can get nothing done under these conditions — my imagination feels like a dry-sucked lemon — my only resource is an endless (and I fear unsatisfactory) piece of orchestration [presumably *Cortège*].

I am afraid that Tania is really very ill and a good deal worse than when we left England. But naturally she tears herself to tatters in these mad and sometimes frenzied glooms into which she falls. One has to steer the conversation all day long and one never knows what the next quarter of an hour may bring forth. This town — pretty enough to look at — is of monumental and memorable dullness. The women all look like the aunts or nieces of waiters — and indeed they probably are. And all the male population rushes to its duties (napkin over arm) on peculiarly furtive bicycles, which make no sound, nor are they provided with bells — so that one's life is in constant peril. There is a beautiful place rather high on 'La Grande Saléve' (a mountain outside the city) which is really my one and only refuge.

We may possibly go to Montana next week, but it seems there are no decent hotels there, and nothing except sanatoria. This sounds lugubrious, but Tania has been ordered there by her doctor.

I would give much for a dinner of 'The Four Just Men' — but I imagine it will be very long before we shall all be in London again together. That was very sudden about Hilda. I never understood the relation between her and Godwin but I imagine he will get over it.[23]

Tout à toi W.M.[24]

I liked your account of Balfour's Medici-an magnificence.[25]

    Bax resolved his problem by keeping Harriet at a distance, though for the rest of his life — and hers — their names were inseparably linked in the public mind. There was to be a change in Bax's life and in his art, and once he completed the full score of the Second Symphony the following year this began to be evident. He rationalized his emotional entanglements, found a new companion, and established his life on a different pattern which was to encompass the composition of some of his best known music.

New directions

At the end of January 1926, Harriet Cohen returned to London to play in an all-Bach programme that Sir Henry Wood was conducting at Queen's Hall on the afternoon of 6 February. She was to play the D minor Concerto, and then the C major Double Concerto with Arthur Benjamin at the second piano. Bax was doubtless involved as a rehearsal pianist, as he was throughout the 1920s and 1930s. Afterwards Harriet departed almost immediately for Geneva again, and Bax was free to devote himself to a spell of almost continuous work. He did not see Harriet again until April, when they met briefly in Paris while Bax was on his way to visit Delius at Grez-sur-Loing.

While in Geneva Bax had longed for a period of male company, now the opportunity came in the form of an invitation from Philip Heseltine at Eynsford. The previous year Heseltine and Moeran, both friends of Bax, had moved to this Kent village, where they shared a tiny cottage, the lease on which had then just been relinquished by Hubert Foss. Bax's re-introduction to their circle came about when Winthrop Rogers issued two new part-songs by 'Peter Warlock' and sent him complimentary copies. Bax, who had not seen Heseltine for several years, took the opportunity of writing to him:

My dear Heseltine,

I never see you, so I never have the opportunity to tell you what very great pleasure your compositions give me. I don't know a single piece of yours that I don't like, and I am prompted to write to you now since Winthrop Rogers have just sent me your latest part-songs — two of them. I think *The Shrouding of the Duchess of Malfi* is a masterly piece of tragic writing. You are one of the only modern composers in my opinion whose harmonic invention derives from an emotional and natural source. I would rather hear pure diatonic and nothing else than the damnable brain-spun muddle and mess which is the stuff of most modern music. That is why it is exciting to find someone writing harmony that is to my mind obviously sincere and imaginative and flexible.[1]

The period of his stay at Eynsford was an enjoyable one, as well as being musically productive. He wrote the *Romantic Overture* for small orchestra with piano, and dedicated it to Delius who was admired by all three friends, doubtless influenced by the fact that he had arrived straight from his flying visit to Grez. The overture was quickly taken up by the young Barbirolli who played it the following January at one of his short-lived series of concerts at the New Chenil Galleries, with Rae Robertson as the pianist. (This was another fortunate introduction for Bax, since Robertson played the role of a musician in the revival of *Russian Dancers* that summer, and subsequently with his fellow duettist Ethel Bartlett, commissioned and played all Bax's two-piano music.)

We may be sure that Bax joined with zest in the Eynsford atmosphere, encountering the young Constant Lambert for the first time, and probably Patrick Hadley also. It is easy to picture the riotous company into which he had strayed where weekends were devoted to the pub, but weekdays to musical hard work, and to imagine his ease at being able to relax after the strain of the previous year. It was doubtless this atmosphere that encouraged him, in an amusing *jeu d'esprit*, to make a two-bar quotation from the César Franck Symphony in the *Romantic Overture*.[2] The example of *The Old Codger*, one of Warlock's 'Cod Pieces'[3] (where he lampoons the Franck), would have been hard for Bax's sometimes schoolboyish sense of humour to resist.

While he was at Eynsford Bax was preparing the manuscript of *In the Faery Hills* for publication (it appeared in full score at the end of the year), and thus Heseltine had an opportunity to note, and criticize, Bax's emendations to the score (see p. 63).

Their literary sympathies were another bond. Heseltine introduced Bax to Sir Walter Raleigh's poem *Walsinghame*, which found an immediate response and was set for tenor, chorus and orchestra during May. Using a choral style that derives from the narrative passages of *Mater Ora Filium*, the soloist is answered by the unaccompanied chorus. These two elements are punctuated by vocalising, chromatic, contrapuntal choral passages, clearly informed by the example of Vaughan Williams's then new *Flos Campi* (first played the previous October). The three elements combine in an eloquent 18-minute setting generating considerable emotional tension. This is a score whose power is not appreciated from a casual inspection of the vocal score, and deserves to be widely given. However, although published almost immediately, it has only been infrequently played. Bax indicated his gratitude both for hospitality and literary and musical assistance by dedicating the score to Heseltine, and Heseltine reciprocated with the dedication of his *Sorrow's Lullaby*, a setting of Thomas Lovell Beddoes' poem, for soprano and baritone soloists and string quartet, which was also completed during May.

More significantly one wonders if this episode may not have been Bax's introduction to alcohol on more than a social scale. Richard Shead feels 'there can be little doubt that Heseltine did much to confirm [Constant] Lambert in a course that led to his destruction'. During the 1930s and 1940s Bax drank increasingly, and his growing intake of Scotch undoubtedly had much to do with the extraordinary physical change he underwent during his last twenty years. Hints of this enter increasingly into his letters. When the full score of *In the Faery Hills* was published, Bax sent Heseltine a copy referring to an 'evening at Jellineck's' (Lionel Jellineck, a lawyer friend of Heseltine who also appeared at Mrs Bax's parties at Frognal, was later well-known as a circuit judge) and to a 'Rabelaisian Raspberry Saga'.[4] The latter occurred when Bax, Heseltine and Moeran ('Old Raspberry') had become drunk, and Moeran, who had a bad head for alcohol owing to his war wound, was retrieved from the gutter in a comatose state.

That summer, *The Truth About the Russian Dancers* was revived at the Savoy Theatre for the first and last time, Karsavina again dancing Karissima. Bax made minor alterations to the score, and the whole thing was well received, *The Times* finding it 'Brilliant', 'all mockery and magic'.[5]

Five recent songs were printed by Murdoch in 1926 and they were all inscribed 'to W. Grant Oliver', Bax's dentist friend and confidant. One evening that summer, Oliver was due to dine at the Haymarket Hotel with a young friend of his called Mary Gleaves, who was twenty-three at the time. He invited Bax to join them. As they parted after a congenial evening Mary turned round absolutely at the same moment as Bax did and they both waved. Although Bax may not have given any particular significance to this coincidence at the time, it was later to assume a special importance for both of them. Bax was preoccupied and he did not meet Mary again until the following year.

In 1926 there were fewer concert performances of Bax's major works, and for almost the only year between the wars his music did not appear at the Proms, which until the BBC's intercession the following year were in a perilous financial state.

In the autumn he again became interested in the idea of a piano sonata. In contrast to the single movements of the first two published sonatas, he retained the three-movement shape utilized in his previous attempt at a keyboard sonata (which had become the First Symphony). The result was a highly idiomatic keyboard work. Bax had become a symphonist more by accident than by design. But having created two symphonies conceived on a grand scale, and in a variety of language and colour, he must have found what he had achieved in those epic and emotional works very much of a barrier in his mind when he was considering where his music was to go. A crisis of style was upon him before he himself realized it. Yet Bax was becoming impatient with that very element in his art — the long memorable tune — that had until this time been the prime attraction for many of his audience. He had removed the climactic tune from *In the Faery Hills* before publication, and this action was symptomatic of his mood when he came to write the Third Sonata.

The sonata preoccupied Bax during the autumn, and was not finally completed until 23 November. 'It gave me a lot of trouble' Bax wrote later, adding 'and as always when work does not come easily I always felt doubtful about it'.[6] In the one-movement sonatas Bax had been tending to a three-subject form with the least important thematic group making a bridge between the two major groups. In the opening *Allegro moderato* of this work Bax gives us more fragmentary thematic material than in his former, more extended and traditional first and second subjects. The opening of the first group is stated after a two-bar introduction. The music is quiet, and underlined by an ostinato centred on the G below middle C, which hardly changes for most of the first page. The key of the sonata is G♯ minor, although at the outset a subdominant (C♯) pedal-note gives a feeling of ambiguity, indicative perhaps of the fact that although the composer has come through the trauma reflected in the Second Symphony he is still encompassing that emotional world in the music, like recurring, vivid, nightmares.

The symphonic development of four germinal ideas that makes the Second Symphony so unified a work, is also seen in the family likeness of all the thematic material used in the sonata. It is surely no coincidence that Bax's tentative preoccupation with motivic development paralleled his growing interest in Sibelius. There is no extended purely lyrical material in the first movement — no big tunes — though much of the effect is lyrical.

Commentators have tended to bracket the first three symphonies as forming an emotional and stylistic unit, yet extended acquaintance with the music suggests that the expression which is developed in the first two symphonies is continued in this sonata rather than in the later orchestral score. A case in point occurs at the end of the development section, which rises to a frenzied reminiscence of the world of the Second Symphony: arpeggiated harmonic back-cloth in the right hand, dramatic upward-leaping chords in the left.

Ex. 53

A work such as this tends to be underplayed, and suffers accordingly, with its essential drama lost. This is certainly the case on the only two recordings. The first movement of this intense wild score is driven by a passionate and powerful impulse. The sudden juxtaposition of contrasted moods is typically Baxian, and has to be strongly characterized by the performer. After the rising tension of the passage just quoted, Bax recapitulates the opening of the sonata, *fortissimo*, accompanied throughout by untamed arpeggios, but then allows the music briefly to die away, as in a passing dream. The passion then returns only to be effaced again by the dreamlike 'mood of the beginning of the movement', with its quiet evocative chords. A quick crescendo is rounded off with two bars of virile *fortissimo*. A man who emphasised that music should be 'the expression of emotional states' reveals in this score a tormented personality, whose underlying inclination to seek a far-off dream-world is constantly interrupted by passionate and wildly emotional outbursts.

The slow movement proceeds innocently in G major and presents two lyrical inventions, in the first of which a triplet suggests a distant echo of *Clair de Lune*, but is in fact derived from a phrase in the main second-subject group of the first movement. The movement is in typically Baxian ternary form, and the two main ideas

briefly unite at the end. The song-like middle section is one of the
composer's later Celtic inspirations in which the main idea is constantly repeated with changing harmonic dress and with ever more
elaborate decoration. Yet, by virtue of its idiosyncratic flavour, even
the harmonization on its first appearance (Ex. 54) effectively places
the music on a plane of sophistication which one suspects Bax may
not have intended.

Ex. 54

This sonata shows clearly that it was not only in the first two
symphonies that he was leaving the overt Irish characteristics of his
earlier style behind. As Norman Suckling has observed, 'the characteristic Baxian melodies pivoting on a single note, and the equally
characteristic arabesque descending to this pivotal note by means of
an avoidance of any of the upper harmonies implied by it, are miles
away from Dermot O'Byrne.'[7]

If Bax had trouble over the composition of the sonata, it is most
probable that it was most elusive to him in the last movement. In
some ways it has a martial feeling not far removed from the last
movements of the first two symphonies, yet the fact that much of it,
while written in running semiquavers, is also marked to be played
piano or pianissimo makes the pianist's task very difficult. The surges
rising from the bass, together with the semiquavers in triplets, suggest
that this is sea music again, and the swirling triplets underline a certain agitation. The brooding, heroic, *moderato molto espressivo*

middle section might well have been more brilliant if translated on to the orchestra. The return of the quick music makes much play with a rhythmic idea (Ex. 55) first heard in the bass which, punctuated by swirling quavers, seems to catch the distant flavour of his 'Russian' piano pieces from years before.

Ex. 55

In a brief coda, Bax restates the chordal idea that opened the whole work, and then eleven chords quietly rising up the keyboard lead to the fortissimo final chord. Although the key signature in the movement has been four sharps (C♯ minor), the ending is unambiguously in the key from which Bax started out — G♯ minor.

Many of the orchestral works he attempted during this time were exploratory, as he tried to find a way forward after draining himself both emotionally and stylistically in the Second Symphony. Certainly Bax the symphonist, so beloved of certain commentators in the 1930s, did not evolve until he had written the Third Symphony in 1928/29, the work that established a new style which was to inform all the later symphonies. However, at the beginning of 1927 the idea of writing another orchestral work in three movements was clearly attractive to Bax, although there could be no question of risking repeating the Second Symphony. During the year he tinkered with what were to become the *Northern Ballads* and the *Overture, Elegy and Rondo*. If Bax had dubbed the latter 'Sinfonietta' perhaps it would have found its way more successfully than it has. This work, particularly in the opening *Overture*, is the nearest Bax ever came to neo-classicism. The scale of the music in its relation with the symphonies may best be appreciated by a comparison with Schumann's *Overture, Scherzo and Finale* and *his* symphonies. The first movement, the *Overture*, opens with a theme which Bax has described as 'suggestive of an 18th century concerto'.[8] A second, similar idea follows, and these two, together with stalking octaves in the bass, lead to a lyrical middle section in which the horns play a long dreamy melody. This leads to a climax, and the subsequent return of the opening material brings the movement to a strenuous conclusion. Even from so simplified a description, it must be evident that the music does not have the weight for a full-scale symphonic movement.

But in the context of Bax's other occasional overtures it is a worthwhile piece whether played on its own (as it was during the Second
World War and again more recently) or as a part of the whole work.
Bax also authorized the *Elegy* that followed to be played separately,
but his suggestion has never been acted upon.

The *Elegy* opens with a mysterious and sustained orchestral
texture — Bax later referred to the mood created as being 'a little
spectral'[9] — out of which emerges an extended melody for three
trombones and tuba. After a climactic passage another idea appears
'in the nature of a cradle song', and the first returns for a serene close.
This movement in particular shows Bax developing a more austere
harmonic language, or at least a less ripe orchestral dressing from
that which he had formerly used.

The *Rondo* is mainly concerned with the bright tune announced
on the horns at the outset, an idea which much transformed may be
the source of the main theme in the *Rhapsodic Ballad* for solo cello
of 1939, though there to rather more strenuous effect. Barbirolli
certainly thought well of the work for, in a letter written in March
1930, he described it as 'fine stuff, especially the slow movement,
which in its length and concentration of feeling makes me think of
late Beethoven.'[10]

During 1927 Bax began to be interested in Scotland and its
history, and towards the end of the year he sketched several orchestral movements in short score. The generic title of *Northern
Ballads* which he gave to these was indicative of his starting point.
There are three separate movements, which were possibly once
intended as constituent parts of a three-movement work, although
there *is* conflicting evidence. What we have is the *Northern Ballad
No. 1*, known in an untitled short score dated November 1927 and
an undated full score and first performed in November 1931. As the
short score of the second *Northern Ballad* is missing it is not possible
to know definitely whether it was also sketched at this time but
not scored until December 1933 to January 1934 (the date on the
full score), or otherwise. Certainly there must have been a second
movement, for there exists another work in short score headed with
the roman numeral 'III'. This was clearly originally intended as the
third movement of a larger work, for the pagination 31–42 appears
on the manuscript. It is dated October 1927, and thus it would
appear to pre-date the first *Ballad*. It is most probable that these
works originated in the autumn and winter of 1927, but that having
sketched them Bax sensed that they would not make the viable

three-movement quasi-symphonic work for which he was searching. The occasional nature of the third piece was emphasized when in February 1933 Bax finally orchestrated it as the *Prelude for a Solemn Occasion* (unheard until the BBC's Bax centenary series in 1983).

These are all enjoyable scores, though perhaps the first *Ballad* is not quite out of the top drawer. But the fact that before the BBC's centenary it had only been played four times, the second *Ballad* twice and the *Prelude* not at all (though, happily, all are now on disc), underlines the recurring problem: for Bax's reputation has rested on only a small proportion of his total output. This is regrettable, for in the *Ballads* we can see Bax exploring the idiom that would be successfully used in the later Symphonies and the *Winter Legends* for piano and orchestra. The second *Ballad* will be discussed in more detail later, since it is Bax's most successful late tone poem and far removed in idiom from the sensuous decoration of *Fand*.

If Bax's music for the orchestra in 1927 was not altogether satisfactory, his chamber music and songs were. The *Three Songs from the Norse*, settings of J.P. Jacobsen ('Irmelin Rose', 'Lad Vaaren Komme') and Björnstjerne Björnsen ('Venevil'), date from April and June 1927, and are inscribed to 'Lydia', though who she may have been is at present unknown. While plumbing no depths these are attractive and straightforward songs. It is interesting to note Bax setting the poems in their original language. The manuscript was given to the National Library of Denmark, which may indicate that Bax visited Denmark at the time of composition, perhaps to see his friend the Danish play-producer Christen Jul, although no background to the songs is known.

Two Russian emigrés with whom Bax had become very friendly in the 1920s were the Count and Countess Benckendorff. They arrived in England in 1924 and Bax got to know them well in 1926 and 1927, and he and Harriet Cohen were constant visitors to their home near Ipswich in Suffolk. Countess Benckendorff was possibly the leading harpist of her day, and achieved considerable fame under her professional name of Maria Korchinska. Her husband played the flute, and when he appeared on a public platform was billed as Constantin Kony. Bax wrote works for them both, but principally for Korchinska, whose harp technique is reflected in his music, for she had a definite influence on the way Bax wrote for the instrument. Never a composer to worry unduly about the difficulty of his music for the player, he was encouraged in this direction by Korchinska making him aware, even more than he had been before (for he had already written for the instrument with distinction) of what was possible in the hands of a great player. She henceforth performed almost all Bax's harp parts at first and important performances. The manuscript of the *Fantasy Sonata* (Bax spells it 'Fantasie' on the manuscript) is dated April 1927, and gives the instrumentation as 'viola and harp'. When published (later the same year) this had become 'harp and viola'! A full-length sonata, the harpist is in a true duet with the viola. It was his most important work to be stamped with her technique. The work is in four movements – *Allegro molto* – *Allegro moderato* – *Lento espressivo* – *Allegro*. The harp participates as an equal partner, and carries the argument for much of the time. Although there are overtones of the earlier viola sonata in the writing for that instrument – indeed even occasional phrases that might well have strayed from it – the later work is more relaxed and not so great an achievement. Nevertheless, in a live performance or in a good recording the music has tremendous impact. Those who may be tempted to evaluate it from the earlier 78 rpm recordings, in which Korchinska plays, will find it difficult to assess from the poor sound of the old recordings. A lot of the work's success depends on the glorious sound of Bax's chosen instruments. Indeed, when it was played – in October the same year – *The Times* described it as 'full of characteristic poetic feeling, it is beautiful in sound'.[11]

In the *Fantasy Sonata* there are no explicit Irish fingerprints in Bax's thematic material, and yet the Irish flavour can be clearly discerned in his melodic turns of phrase and dancing rhythms. In the short Third Violin Sonata, in only two movements, which Bax also wrote in 1927, a theme in the second movement is labelled 'Planxty', meaning 'a harp tune of a sportive and animated character, moving in triplets'.[12] One has the feeling that some similar association with the traditional music that was indissolubly wound into his own style underlies the writing for harp in the *Fantasy Sonata*. Immediately after finishing the *Fantasy Sonata* Bax went on to provide another vehicle for Korchinska, though a very different one. He arranged a concerto by Vivaldi for harp and string quartet, and Korchinska played it on several occasions.

There was a flood of performances of Bax's music in 1927. Among orchestral works, the first performance of the *Romantic Overture* in January; *In the Faery Hills* at a Royal Philharmonic Society concert in February, conducted by Frank Bridge (presumably the first performance of the recently published revised version); and the revival of the *Symphonic Variations* by Harriet at the Proms in August (the first performance of the work she had been capable of giving since 1924), were probably the highlights.

In addition Bax accepted an invitation to accompany a Miss Edith Robinson in two performances of his First Violin Sonata in January, though he found her playing to be only 'conscientious' and confessed himself 'extremely bored'. The second performance was in Manchester where Bax contracted a bad attack of 'flu. He returned to London to stay at his mother's house at 10 Frognal Gardens so that he might be 'pampered and spoilt', but his condition deteriorated to pneumonia, and it was 1 February before he could pronounce himself convalescent.

Above all, 1927 was *the* year of chamber and instrumental music as far as Bax was concerned, and in particular it marked his sudden reappearance in the capacity of pianist in public concerts. With May Harrison he played the Delius First Violin Sonata and his own Second. At the Blackpool Festival – probably owing to Harriet's inability to cope with the heavy programme – he played his own Piano Quintet, for the only time in public; while he and May Harrison broadcast the Delius First Violin Sonata towards the end of the year. He also appeared in public at this time partnering Winifred Small whom he chose in preference to all others for a concert in Liverpool. They too played the Second Sonata because Bax confessed, 'the piano part does not give me so much anxiety [as the First Sonata]: besides it is a better work in some respects'.

Bax was anxious not to give the impression that he was wanting to become a professional pianist. On 29 November he partnered May Harrison in a broadcast of the Delius First Sonata, and was so annoyed by the BBC's treatment of his appearance (for which no fee was paid) that he caused the Imperial Concert Agency to write to the BBC in strong terms. They 'had just heard from Miss Harrison saying that both she and Mr Bax were very disappointed indeed at the way in which the concert was announced'.[13] Apparently the announcer twice gave out that Miss Harrison would play the Delius Sonata accompanied by Arnold Bax. 'As you know,' the agency's letter continues, 'Mr Bax came to London specially to play this work at Miss Harrison's request, and because Mr Delius himself would be listening in France, and both she and I asked you to make a very particular feature of it, which you said you would do.' It is difficult to decide whether this is Bax speaking or May Harrison putting words into his mouth. The letter continues uncharacteristically: 'I understand that Mr Bax is very indignant at being treated as an ordinary accompanist, and that there was no special reference made to the fact that he, one well-known composer, was paying such a graceful tribute to another one, who had specially asked that his work should be broadcast so that he could hear it away in France.' The agency concluded by hoping that the BBC would 'make a point of engaging Miss Harrison to give a recital of Mr Bax's work', and perhaps 'include the Delius Sonata again', when the whole thing could 'be given proper publicity and Mr Bax who as you know, gave his services on this occasion for the reason stated would receive a proper fee.'

The BBC responded by asking if Bax would give a recital in a programme planned for 3 January. This time they trod on a real nerve and Bax was very decisive in his reply. The Imperial Concert Agency wrote on 20 December that they had 'heard from Mr Bax who says that he cannot play the piano solos, as he never does anything of the kind. He suggests, however, that he and Miss Harrison should play his "Legende" which takes between 5 and 6 minutes. The Delius Sonata takes exactly 24 minutes, so this would make up the required 30 minutes, and we should be very glad if you would put these two works down for the programme.'[14] Delius listened to these and other broadcasts of his music by Bax, and also to the recording of his First Violin Sonata made by May Harrison and Bax in 1929, and was not entirely satisfied with Bax's approach, finding his playing 'too forceful at times for my music'.[15]

There were a number of occasions in 1927 when major presentations of Bax's chamber music were made. The first was on 19 May when May Harrison was accompanied by the composer in his Second Violin Sonata. This was the occasion of Bax's second meeting with his friend Bill Oliver's young companion, Mary Gleaves. Oliver asked Bax to arrange for Miss Gleaves to have a complimentary ticket for the occasion, and in sending it to her Bax observed, 'I think myself that such entertainments should not be arranged on a (probably fine) May Eve'.[16] Bax did not see her at the concert and wrote afterwards: 'Where on earth were you? There did not seem anyone fat enough for you to hide behind, and yet I could not find you anywhere!'

The Second Sonata was repeated in November that year, but perhaps the most important performance of Bax's chamber music came in October, when the Virtuoso Quartet — with Maria Korchinska, Leon Goossens and Harriet Cohen — presented four works: the

Second String Quartet, the Oboe Quintet, the new *Fantasy Sonata* for harp and viola, and the epic Piano Quintet. The Piano Quintet apart, all these works had been written during the previous five years. *The Times*'s critic noted that 'a concert devoted entirely to the chamber music of Arnold Bax is an event of some importance. A large audience listened at Wigmore Hall on Thursday night with close attention to a programme that lasted 2½ hours.'[17] Certainly much critical attention was devoted to Bax at this time, a typical example being Hubert Foss's long article on this concert,[18] a few extracts from which give some idea of the way Bax was becoming accepted even if his audiences were often as puzzled as they were dazzled. Referring to the 1922 concert as well as the recent chamber concert of Bax's music, Foss observed that

the length and variety of these two solitary exhibitions have been their special value ... They have enabled musicians to stop and make a sudden critical survey of Bax's music; to wonder, could any other English composer produce an equal accumulation of effect? This prolific and varied talent not only survives, but even needs such an ordeal as this for displaying itself; so that these concerts have helped to establish Bax as a big composer. He is not yet fully recognized as a big composer; though some of his works have been performed on the continent (at Prague, Salzburg, Berlin, and Paris chiefly), and at Cleveland, Ohio. One may say he is virtually unknown outside Great Britain, and even here there is a tendency still to regard Bax as a promising young man and not as a real composer. With such a catalogue of works at 44, and one of such a quality, his magnitude must surely be accepted; and any criticism of him must be founded upon this base... Bax's sheer ability to compose music [he went on] is phenomenal, his invention of sounds never ceases. One wonders, vaguely, as one has wondered of Reger, whether there could in the future be another Bax: whether, mathematically, music could stand it. But Bax writes sounds where Reger often writes notes. The thousand and one musicians who so seriously toy with composition might well despair at the score of, say, the second quartet. But it is not a mere collection of counterpoints, a charming interlaced pattern printed upon a leaf. It is a map of effects in sound, planned only by intimate knowledge and imagination. The music in Bax is so essentially on the instruments, and the paper notation nothing but a skilfully used aid to the players — an order of procedure not common enough among composers. Compare in this connexion the opening of the second movement of the quartet, or the lovely end to the first movement of the oboe quintet, the last movement of which shows Bax's capability in a clearer texture than he usually contrives. There are times, of course, when the mere music pleases one more than its presence at a particular juncture; one of these, I think, is the ending of the second string quartet's first movement. The E major statement of the second theme (itself not quite convincing to me) leads so suddenly to an exquisite twenty bars of coda, where the first subject, of which we had hoped great things, dwindles to a slightly acid reminiscence in a passage of exquisite sounds.

In December 1927 Kodály visited England. Bax and he met several times and appear to have got on well. They did not meet again until Kodály's visit in the early 1950s, when he was photographed with Bax and Harriet.

For the next four or five years Bax was at the height of his fame and was accorded the sort of treatment due to a major figure who has truly arrived. That summer he received the award of the Fellowship of the Royal Academy of Music; otherwise he spent most of the time away. However, he certainly joined Clifford's cricket team during August, and also visited his mother's summer home at Arundel. Richard Church has left us an interesting vignette[19] of that Sussex household of long ago, which is of particular note for its atmosphere and accurate description. Church had been invited by Clifford Bax to the tall house near the castle where his mother lived 'tended by a staff of elderly servants who treated her like a Holy Relic. They whispered reverently in her presence, or when mentioning her. She was a devout Catholic, tall like her son [i.e. Clifford], gentle and authoritative. Old silver, gracious period furniture, deep curtains, and a long-established domestic ritual surrounded her, and protected her "from the contagion of the world's slow stain". That is how she impressed our young, naive minds at that first meeting. I sat talking to her, facing the long Georgian windows of her drawing-room, Clifford hovering attentively near her.'

Later Arnold Bax came to dislike Church, but before the Second World War his relations with him appear to have been cordial, and Church's description of Arnold, who came down the next day and stayed over the weekend for his mother's birthday, rings true. 'He was', wrote Church, 'shorter, more incisive than Clifford, inclined to be nervously irritable, rapid in speech, sharp in gesture ... He showed an aloof interest in the literary affairs so important to Clifford and me, but shrank with distaste from the evidences of my family life. He talked willingly and with enormous vitality about music, quizzing me for my interest in Schumann. "Dangerous! Dangerous!" he said; "The wrong sort of romanticism".'

It is interesting to see Bax sharing the attitude to Schumann expressed by Sir Arthur Bliss in his autobiography *As I Remember*. Church continued: 'I was too awestricken to dispute with Arnold Bax. He was the first composer I had met, and I had known his work for the past ten years, introduced to it by my brother, who as an adolescent discovered a passionate interest in what may be called the impressionist composers, Bax and Bliss amongst them. Names that we learn in boyhood keep an aura of sanctity for the rest of our lives. So while I sat with Arnold Bax in the drawing-room of his mother's house in Arundel, he at the grand piano and I beside him drawn up close as though I were to turn the pages of the music score, I saw him as a figure of myth rather than flesh and blood. His playing strengthened that illusion. It was massive, a composer's utilization of the pianoforte, his thumbs translating the deeper strings and woodwind. Bax filled the drawing-room, the house, the streets of Arundel, with his transcription from the orchestral score of Wagner's *Rheingold*, and Debussy's *Pelléas et Mélisande*.'

In November, in addition to the repeat performance of the Second Violin Sonata with May Harrison, Bax had to be in Liverpool, where the local centre of the British Music Society presented Harriet Cohen in the first performance of the Third Piano Sonata on the 18th. In a long notice *The Musical Times* commented on Bax's tremendous run of performance. 'Mr Bax is having a great innings at the moment,' their critic wrote, 'and though we have yet to measure ourselves with his chief orchestral and choral compositions, a considerable amount of his chamber music has been played latterly at Liverpool ... The general features of his style are thus fairly well-known — its rich polyphony, its melodic fertility and its decorative arabesque; finally, its spreading, proliferous form.' Harriet Cohen, too, was in good form, having conquered her illness. *The Musical Times* concluded: 'The Sonata, which bristles with difficulties, was brilliantly played by Miss Cohen ... It was not merely a feat of imagination to comprehend the extraordinary subtlety of much of the writing but a masterly display of keyboard technique.'[20]

Harriet went straight on from the performance of the Sonata to a performance of the *Symphonic Variations* on 20 January at a Royal Philharmonic Society concert, with Basil Cameron conducting. But probably the most important events of the year were the London revivals of the First Symphony. Although there had been performances in America under Monteux and Saffronov, and it was to be played by Kussevitsky also, it had only twice been heard in London. So the composer's indebtedness to Sir Henry Wood must have been considerable when he programmed it in a Royal Academy Student Concert at Queen's Hall in March 1928, and then again at the Proms the following August. Writing of the student performance, one reviewer stated that 'the choice was doubly justified in that Mr Bax is the most distinguished composer of his generation belonging to the RAM and this Symphony of his, first produced in 1922, had been less than fairly dealt with. The enterprise was, for all that, a daring one – for the Symphony is excessively difficult, and might well have been thought unmanageable by a student orchestra. It speaks well for the RAM that so good an account of it was given.'[21]

The Promenade concert was broadcast live from Queen's Hall, *The Times* noting that 'the Symphony is not of a kind that is ever likely to win great popularity. It has a few obviously attractive moments, and these are surrounded by much that is on the surface definitely unattractive.'[22] It is difficult to understand quite what he was getting at, though it gives an insight into the impact and apparent modernity of the score to a 1928 audience. He continued:

Its mood is that of the more gloomy and ferocious pages in *The Ring*, of the music associated with the Nibelungs and the dragon Fafner. But if it is mostly unpleasing to the ear as sound, it has a very likeable strength. It is concise and obviously sincere, though the sequence of ideas is difficult to follow. Perhaps its chief fault is its restlessness, and yet this may be its most essential quality. For the work was written at a time when the ferment of the years after the War was seething in the work of most artists who were not content to go on doing the same kind of thing that had been done a hundred times before. There is no question of the masterliness of the writing, and when the composer consents for a moment to lift the veil of gloom, we are given music of an idyllic beauty, like a fitful gleam of sunshine on a stormy day.

Its impact was even more vividly caught by the *Daily Telegraph*:[23]

It is refreshing now and then to listen to the work of an English composer without being obliged to note this or that influence, this or that derivation. Such a work is Arnold Bax's Symphony in E flat which was performed at Queen's Hall last night under Sir Henry Wood's direction. Diffuseness has been the principal charge laid against this composer's works – justly enough as a rule; but when he came to write this symphony three or four years ago, a complex and elaborate composition, he had learned the value of economy in utterance. A rehearing of the symphony makes this economy seem more apparent than ever, and packed as it is with deep thinking, one cannot see where its elaboration could be simplified or its rhetoric curtailed.

In 1928, Bax established contact with new friends in Ireland, in Cork, who provided him with a regular port of call (other than during the war years) until his death. His new friends were the Fleischmanns. Aloys G. Fleischmann was a graduate of the Staatliche Akademie der Tonkunst in Munich and had studied under Rheinberger, and also at Munich University under Sandberger. In Bavaria he was well known for his nativity plays with music. He had been appointed organist and choirmaster of St Mary's Cathedral, Cork, in 1906. His wife, Tilly, was a noted pianist and teacher in Cork, and had received her training under Stavenhagen, who had been the last pianist to study with Liszt.[24]

Tilly Fleischmann remembered in her unpublished memoirs how Bax came to know her family and visit their home in Cork each year. 'In 1927', she wrote,

a meeting was held of the Father Mathew Feis committee of which I was a member ... Father Michael, OFM, presided. We were discussing adjudicators for 1928. Father Michael suggested Sir Edward Elgar, Sir Henry Wood and various other outstanding English musicians. I was appalled at the idea — orchestral and chamber music were practically non-existent in Cork at that time. 'It is a wonder, Father Michael,' said I, 'that you don't write to Arnold Bax.' 'Who is he?' said Father Michael. I told him. 'And where does he live?' I said I didn't know, but I thought it was in London. Well, we had a good laugh, I'm afraid, rather at Father Michael's expense — but in which he joined merrily. The meeting was adjourned for a fortnight, Father Michael saying in his light-hearted manner on leaving, 'you had all better make up your minds by then, as to whom you are bringing over.'

The Father Mathew Feis was founded by the Capuchin Fathers in 1925, and gave opportunities for local musicians to prove their ability before visiting critics. Most forms of musical activity were covered by this annual competition.

However, to continue Frau Fleischmann's narrative, about a week after the conversation just related she met Father Michael 'sauntering down the South Mall' in Cork.

(Arnold used to say that 'Father Michael always walked as if in a meadow, kicking the daisies before his feet') ... 'He's coming,' said he in great glee. 'Who?' said I. 'Arnold Bax of course. I just wrote Arnold Bax, London, and he got my letter.' I got a shock and was very annoyed too. 'Well, Father,' I said, 'I never thought you would have the courage to write to him, or that he would have the humility to come.' 'Oh,' said Father Michael cheerfully, 'he is delighted to come. Read his letter.' I read it there and then. It was certainly a charming, warmhearted letter, saying how much pleasure he would have in coming, and that from now on he would be looking forward to his visit to Cork.

He came to adjudicate for the Feis for three successive years, during which time we all got to know him intimately. And he was a regular visitor, staying with us or Aloys Og [i.e. young Aloys, the Fleischmanns' son, later Professor of Music at Cork] every year (except 1939—46, when he didn't leave England) until 1953. It was a friendship of twenty-five years. Strange to say, Father Michael was the first to greet him when he arrived in Cork, on the *Innisfallen* in 1928, and the last to leave his grave in 1953.[25]

Bax's lifestyle at this time was vividly described in a widely quoted autobiographical essay in the journal *Music America* that year.

... In recent years I have written very little during the summer months, and lead a more or less open-air life. The last works of any size of which I can speak are two sonatas in which the harp is employed – one for harp and viola, and the other for harp and flute. The first has had a good deal of success, and has recently been published. The flute sonata (only recently completed) has not yet been produced.

The work with flute was given a few performances notably by Maria Korchinska's husband Count Benckendorff – Constantin Kony – but ultimately it was withdrawn and rewritten as the Septet (or Concerto for Seven Instruments) in 1936. The middle movement, the *Cavatina*, was revived during the Second World War as a work in its own right at a National Gallery concert, but with violin in place of flute.

Continuing his essay Bax observed that

As far as I know, the only new tendency in my style is but a modification of the manner in which I have always written ... I am a brazen romantic, and could never have been anything else. By this I mean that my music is the expression of emotional states. I have no interest whatever for sound for its own sake or any modernist 'isms' and factions.

I think the present war-cry 'Back to Bach' must only lead its partisans to a cul-de-sac, for the conscious attempt to go back to anything is a mere intellectual futility. We are modern people and must find modern methods of conveying our own aesthetic life to our audience.

There appear to be certain signs of revolt against postwar fads in all the arts, and for my own part I am heartily glad of it. Those amongst my British contempories whom I most respect and for whose work (notably that of Vaughan Williams) I have the greatest sympathy, have developed their own personal styles, regardless of any of the heady excitements emanating from Austria or Russia. And I believe that the sincerity of English composers is one of the most remarkable features of their work. I may mention too, perhaps, that certain of the younger writers who began their careers with an attempt to imitate and even outdo the fashionable gamineries and jocosities of the Continent, have since settled down and are quite likely to produce works of a serious import in the near future.[26]

Dreams and reality

During the last years of the 1920s Bax's friendship with Mary Gleaves deepened into a real and lasting love. Mary was the exception among his many liaisons, most of which were formed with quite unsuitable women. Like his brother Clifford, Arnold launched too often into relationships which were based, not on reality, but on the vivid fantasies which he imposed on the objects of his desire: a constant searching for an elusive, fleetingly-imagined nymph; an intriguing mixture of child-like, wide-eyed innocence and wanton sexuality. Yet in his relationships with the opposite sex Arnold subconsciously also seemed to need someone who would be willing to assume the function of an emotional sheet-anchor without overtly attempting to influence his life or music, or make extravagant demands on him, once the initial passion had passed. In a way the indulgent mother figure of his youth was constantly recreated throughout his life. He certainly did not attempt to remarry, as his brother Clifford did, and Mary acquiesced in the role which Bax evolved for her. Harriet Cohen remained Bax's companion on public and musical occasions, and she remained unaware of Mary's existence until 1948. It was Mary to whom Bax turned for a relationship at once loving and totally divorced from musical matters. As the demands of fame became more and more onerous, Mary provided Bax's secret retreat from the world. All this meant that his life became more and more compartmentalized, each circle having no contact with the others.

The inception of this stabilizing emotional thread is reflected in three works which are more optimistic in character and in which some serenity is achieved – the still troubled Third Symphony and *Winter Legends*, and the extrovert Two-Piano Sonata. Before we go on to see how Arnold's relationship with Mary developed, we should explore these works which provided the musical framework to his life at that time.

The Third Symphony was conceived during the autumn of 1928, and was completed in February 1929, probably in Morar, Inverness-shire. That winter was the first one in which Bax went to Morar to work at his music free of all distractions. The resulting compositions form an end rather than a beginning, and although several comment-ators have postulated that the first three symphonies comprise a clear group, it is preferable to think of the Third and *Winter Legends* – which are only separated by a mere seven months – as a pair, the one looking back, the other forward.

That first trip to Morar – and nearby Arisaig – was made alone, and in the winter of 1929–30 he went there only briefly if at all. It was not until the autumn of 1930 that he started making a regular annual pilgrimage to the west coast of Scotland in winter-time, tak-ing the train on the wild west-coast line. But henceforth, for the remaining years of peace, Bax always went to Morar, taking Mary with him, to relax and to score his works away from all social and professional demands and obligations.

So, in the winter of 1928–29, Bax quietly faded from the London scene, and established himself at the Station Hotel, Morar, and 'there, sometimes in polar conditions, in a dingy unheated room, working in an overcoat',[1] he proceeded to set out the sketch he had previously written 'with constant resource to the keyboard' at his Hampstead lodgings. 'It was wonderful in the north in spite of a mantle of cloud all the time', Bax reported on one such occasion, 'only two sunny days in three weeks.'

The Third Symphony is in three movements with an elegiac epilogue, and it fixed the use of epilogue in the public mind as typical of Bax, even though the example of Vaughan Williams's *London Symphony* (admittedly in four movements) had already been established for years. To many the Third is the archetypal Bax symphony, owing to the comparative popularity of the work before the war, and because it was for many years the only Bax symphony to have been recorded. It is justifiably cited by admirers for its 'instant appeal to both the orchestra and the listener',[2] and for the 'many passages whose sheer beauty belongs to a level of inspiration hardly equalled in the whole range of Bax's music'. Robin Hull wrote of the symphony that 'although the composer is emphatic in his statement that there is no programme attached, it has been suggested that the symphony possesses the mood of northern

legends. Bax agrees that the interpretation is apt, allowing that subconsciously he may have been influenced by the sagas and dark
winters of the North ... [but] the second movement does not share
this mood in any way.'[3]

Bax wanted the music judged purely as music, but in his mind it
clearly meant a lot more than this, as is evinced by the quotation
from Nietzsche with which he prefaced the short score (but suppressed from the orchestral score):

> My wisdom became pregnant on lonely mountains;
> upon barren stones she brought forth her young.

The symphony was almost immediately followed by *Winter
Legends*, for piano and orchestra, a work of comparable scale to the
symphonies, and inhabiting a similar emotional world. There is
clearly more to these two idiosyncratically passionate works than
just the vague programme of Nordic legends Bax implied about them.
They are the musical expression of one of the major turning points
of his life. In the programme notes about the symphony[4] Bax stated
that 'the work in its formal aspect deviates little from the lines laid
down by the classical composers of the past'. He begs many questions with this pat and, in the first movement at least, misleading
statement. However, it is worth remembering in this respect Burnett
James's illuminating observations concerning Bax and Beethoven.
James wrote that

> Bax was acutely aware of the symphonic achievement of Beethoven. I once
> heard him assert that the first movements of the *Eroica* and the Ninth symph-
> onies represented the ultimate in symphonic thought and construction ... In the
> first movement of the Bax Third the woodwind set up an insistent rhythm at the
> end of the introduction which acts as a bridge to the movement proper. It is
> strikingly similar to the corresponding section of the Beethoven Seventh.[5]

The first movement of the symphony 'is preceded by an introduction in which the basic idea of the music is adumbrated as through
a dark haze', Bax tells us. 'The three notes A, B♭ and C♯, at the
beginning of a long melody here, have the importance of a "motto"
theme throughout the movement.'

Ex. 56

'This section is scored almost entirely for wind, and the entry of
lower strings is the signal for the appearance of a theme of a liturgical
character which occurs frequently during the development of the
movement.'

Ex. 57

'After this the tempo suddenly quickens, and a rhythm is set up in a
vigorous ⁶⁄₈ measure, whilst a new motif is heard in the lower registers.' This is another of those rising figures that come stalking up out
of the bass of Bax's symphonic scores with menacing insistence. Bax's
account of the music continues from the climax that quickly ensues,
with 'the statement of the main theme in its fully vitalized form.
This point marks the true beginning of the Allegro. The first section
of the movement is almost entirely dominated by the rhythmical
figure referred to a moment ago, which is seldom absent from the
score. The motif first heard in the lower registers also plays an important part. A forceful restatement of the "liturgical" theme leads
to a stormy climax, after which a passage for seven solo violins
[actually for five violins, though in its last bar the final chord adds
two more soli and a solo viola] prepares the way for the quieter
thoughts suggested by the second section of the movement.'

Ex. 58

'This and pendant ideas are worked for some time and finally sink into complete tranquillity, interrupted by a menacing re-entry of the three motto notes.

'The sombre mists of the introduction again flood the landscape, though on this occasion muted strings take the place of the wind-instruments employed in the original version. A long climax is built up, and ultimately the three motto notes become established as an ostinato, over which the second subject (Ex. 58) and other elements of the movement pass in dark review. There is a final appearance, as in eclipse, of the liturgical theme (Ex. 57), and then the rhythmical figure goads the music to an abrupt and violent end.' The symphony succeeds by virtue of its memorable invention, brilliant and idio-syncratic orchestration, and an intuitive formal structure, which, even if wayward in the first movement, creates its own inexorable internal logic. The first movement has been the subject for comment, because although the ostensible underlying tempo may be fast there is more slow music than quick in the movement. Whenever Bax gen-erates an exciting stretch of allegro in this work, he usually allows it to dissipate into numerous extended slow interludes which in effect constitute the development of the movement, yet it builds up to what Bernard Shore called 'one of the greatest climaxes in modern music'.[6] A timing of the Edward Downes recording[7] of the first movement shows that the music breaks into passages of slow and fast music as follows:

basic tempo	up to cue	timing
slow	6 after 6	3' 25"
fast	26	3' 25"
slow	43	8' 58"
fast	51	1' 37"
slow	56	1' 25"
fast	to end	50"
	total	19' 40"

For many otherwise sympathetic listeners what is in effect a great, brooding, slow interlude occupying nearly half the movement is a stumbling-block with which they never come to terms. On balance, for all its lovely detail, and although it contains within it its own contrasts, it was surely a mistake. Otherwise, once absorbed, the music grips like almost no other British music of its time.

In the slow movement the horn and trumpet solos are wonderfully evocative, quite justifying Norman Demuth's impression of 'standing

on a rocky mountain overlooking the plains ... primeval hosts assembling in the plains below'.[8] Perhaps the third main theme of the
movement (Ex. 59) is the most evocative of all, exemplifying the
typically Baxian mood of regret, the quality referred to by Bax
himself in the suggestion of the 'tenderness of pain, half cruel, half
sweet'.[9]

Ex. 59

The writing is very chromatic and considerable passion is generated
and at one point we can hear sea music strongly reminiscent of
Tintagel.

After a few bars of introduction, the third movement opens in a
bold Allegro, with a theme on violas and clarinets superimposed
upon a strongly rhythmical figure.

Ex. 60

This gives place to another idea employed later in various forms, a
broad theme played fortissimo. These ideas are developed and then
a fanfare on the brass based upon the opening subject introduces
a third motif.

Ex. 61

The reappearance of the second subject of the first movement
presages a climax which leads to the Epilogue. 'Later', Bax tells
us, 'the opening theme of the first movement reappears, purged of
all its original violence, and the work ends in complete tranquillity.'

The lead-in to the Epilogue is magical, and arrives out of a sudden crescendo which subsides, leaving soaring strings rising on a diminuendo. This reveals the quietly marching chords on strings and harp which sound as if they have been going on for ever, but have only just come into our hearing.

Ex. 62

It is one of those many spine-tingling moments in this work (others include the great anvil blow in the first movement and the trumpet and horn calls in the slow movement). The middle section of the Epilogue has been commented upon earlier in this book (see p. 105), and the sound Bax gives us is quite other-worldly, clearly expressing some mystical aural experience in musical terms. Patrick Hadley remembered Bax's inspiration generally as being 'disembodied, as it were', something which 'subsequently had to be realised, or incarnated, into orchestral terms ... Bax's orchestral sense functioned as a transformation rather than a direct creation'.[10]

The consensus would certainly appear to be that, as another commentator observed 'one is left with the impression that this music, individual to the last degree as it is, is born not out of experiment but out of experience'. The Epilogue transmutes thematic material from the troubled earlier pages of the symphony with its spirit of inner peace. This is a genuinely symphonic process as well as demonstrating poetic imagination of a high order.

John McCabe, a sympathetic composer of a younger generation, and a persuasive interpreter of Bax's music at the piano, encapsulated one's feelings about the work at the time of its first LP recording. 'Bax's music', he wrote,

deserves to have a more permanent place in the repertoire ... He was a composer of great integrity, with a distinctive style and with something to say that is worth hearing; his best music usually seems to move an audience, to enter into their consciousness in the way that good music should. This is not a weak work, there is iron as well as nostalgia in its soul, for the first movement's dance-like sections are characteristically forceful (their frequent relationship with the main bassoon tune is what prevents them from completely effacing the dominant mood), and the slow movement has a different kind of peace, reflective, one of the most compelling musical representations of complete stillness and repose that I know, music of immense beauty. Perhaps Bax's style may have dated, but time has been unkind to him only in the finale's main theme, where the devils are of the pantomime, rather less frightening than of yore. Yet even here there is a tinge of sadness and even desperation about the music which gives it character and force, while throughout the work Bax's lyrical invention is at a sustainedly high level (the first movement's slow string tune is one of his loveliest melodies, second only in my view to the glorious love songs in *The Garden of Fand*).[11]

Spanning the composition of Bax's symphony was Vaughan Williams's Piano Concerto, and the two have a strangely intertwined history. The concerto is in three movements, the first two dating from 1926, the last from 1930–31. Ostensibly it was written for Harriet Cohen who gave its first performance in February 1933. However, the solo piano part was so formidable that Vaughan Williams later recast it as a concerto for two pianos. Hubert Foss, writing of the solo piano version, noted how 'powerful and massive' the soloist's part was. 'I have not yet heard one pianist play it as the notes are meant to sound,' he wrote; 'muscles of steel, a ruthless dominance over the orchestra, no fear of stridency or of ugly hitting ... are essentials for the player of the concerto.'[12] Bax and Vaughan Williams appear to have been fairly close during this period. As originally written, a final cadenza in the last movement of the concerto was followed by a two-bar quotation from the Epilogue of the Bax Third Symphony, with a mysterious note in the score, 'according to my promise':[13] a passage VW wanted played 'quite slow and very far off like a dream'.[14] Later VW removed the quotation, though an episode in $\frac{3}{2}$ in the Romanza would appear to have been derived from it. VW wrote to Harriet Cohen, 'the quotation from Arnold is a mistake for public performance [having] personal rather than musical significance'.[15] Vaughan Williams had persuaded Bax to lengthen by sixteen bars the fortissimo orchestral tutti that ends the first movement of his Third Symphony. Was there any more to the interest each composer took in the other's work at this time? Robert Threlfall raises our doubts:

We now know that whereas the first two movements of the concerto date from 1926, and often veer in style somewhere between *On Wenlock Edge* and *Flos Campi*, the grittier Fuga chromatica evolved four years later, and in its turn looked ahead to the great Symphony in F minor which, Vaughan Williams' next significant work, was openly dedicated to Arnold Bax. Was the theme of the Fuga chromatica, first anticipated during the Romanza on piano and later on the oboe, in this place in 1926, or was it later extracted from the inner voices at cue No. 16 in the same movement? Likewise the Bax quotation was implicit in the preceding noble cadenza, which itself relates back to the central portion of the Romanza of 1926. Yet Bax's Third Symphony was written in 1929 and first performed in 1930.[16]

In a letter to the composer Herbert Howells from the late 1930s Bax wrote 'Personally I love that work of Ralph's and like it indeed better than anything else of his that I know. I don't think it is right formally at the end, for the last cadenza confuses the issue, but in my view that dynamo-like toccata is splendid, and the stretto of the fugue one of the most stimulating bits of primitive violence in all music.'

Kussevitzky in America had shown interest in Bax's music. In 1927 Ernest Newman, recently returned from the States, delivered to Bax a request for a new work from the great conductor. Bax, undoubtedly flattered, proposed his Second Symphony, then existing in only one manuscript copy. (How fragile, before the days of cheap mechanical copying, were the methods of transmission of musical works, and how important was publication!) The problem of there being only one copy resulted in considerable delays before the music was heard. Bax did not preserve his letters from Kussevitzky but Kussevitzky kept Bax's. Bax first wrote on 25 October 1927:

Dear Mr Kussevitzky

Owing to holidays and other confusing circumstances it was only a few days ago that Mr Ernest Newman managed to give me your message. I am so sorry about this delay.

'E.N.' told me that you were good enough to enquire about a work by me which has not been performed as yet in America. As a matter of fact I believe all my published scores have been played in the States, with the exception of a short piece called 'The Happy Forest'.

Apart from this there is only my Second Symphony which is still in MS. I have not tried to get this work played as it is very difficult and requires more rehearsal than can be given at concerts in this country. At present there are no parts of this work and only one score.

Personally I have always felt a great desire that you should take up my first symphony, as it is a work which demands from its conductor the passion and breadth of treatment which are so characteristic of your own splendid style.

I shall be very glad to hear from you if you still consider giving a work of mine. It has always been a regret to me that I was unable to hear your perform-ance of 'The Garden of Fand'.

With kind regards, Yours sincerely,
Arnold Bax

My scores are, I think, obtainable now from the Oxford University Press in New York. If you wish to see any of them I will direct the manager there to send you copies.

In fact the Boston Symphony Orchestra had already given three works by Bax, *In the Faery Hills* in 1920 and *November Woods* in 1922, both conducted by Monteux, and the performance of *The Garden of Fand* mentioned in Bax's letter which Kussevitzky con-ducted in April 1925. Kussevitzky must have replied almost by return, and we next find Bax writing on 7 December to say that he has been 'looking over and considering' his Second Symphony, and is having 'a copy made of the score and parts' ... He feels that it will not be ready for the current season and suggests putting it down for the following autumn. Kussevitzky in fact performed Bax's First Symphony on 16 December 1927, obviously having given up waiting for the later one. Press cuttings were sent to Bax, who replied by re-turn on 4 January 1928, 'delighted to hear of the fine performance'. Bax went on: 'Your oboe player Stanislaus wrote a few days back telling me that you took a great deal of trouble over the work and that the rendering was magnificent. Please accept my warmest thanks and congratulations. It gives me particular pleasure to hear from you that you like the work as I have always liked to imagine a performance under your baton. The public and critics have always been rather startled by the somewhat unbridled character of the symphony – perhaps because contemporary music is not expected to be emotional.'

In his dealings with Kussevitzky Bax was most unbusinesslike. The conductor wrote again requesting the Second Symphony, but there was still no duplicate score or parts. Bax consulted again with Murdoch's, his publishers, and a decision was taken to print the score, 'as they don't want the expense of copying the score and parts and probably publishing later as well'. On 14 September we find Bax suggesting it should be put 'into a programme in the latter part of the season in February or March, so that there may be plenty of time'. But delays continued, and Kussevitzky showed commendable doggedness and persistence on his side of the negotiations. On 2 March Bax wrote from the Cairngorm Hotel, Aviemore, Invernessshire: 'Thank you for your letter which has just reached me forwarded from London. I am very pleased that you propose to play my new symphony in the autumn and I will send you a score as soon as it is ready. I am sorry there has been so much delay but engravers on this side are incredibly slow in their methods.' Finally, two performances were given, with great success on 13 and 14 December 1929. They had taken well over two years to arrange.

A succession of London performances was a major feature of 1929. The Flute and Harp Sonata was played twice by Korchinska and her husband (28 January and 12 June). Kennedy Scott gave *Walsinghame* in June at Queen's Hall, and Tertis a new one-movement *Legend* for viola and piano in July. In March the New Philharmonic String Quartet (whose leader Bessie Rawlins was dedicatee of the Piano Quartet) gave the Second Quartet, and at a BBC Chamber Concert at the Arts Theatre (4 February) Bax's Third Violin Sonata was presented with Bax himself accompanying Carl Nielsen's son-in-law, Emil Telmanyi.

In May, through Ernest Newman's influence he was asked by the Columbia Graphophone Company to record his own Viola Sonata with Lionel Tertis. The sessions were on 27 May, but he was apparently dissatisfied with the results because the records were never issued. They were not finally heard until dubbed onto LP in 1981 by the enterprising Pearl label. What was revealed then was a powerful but highly idiosyncratic performance, which in the outer slower movements was played at very fast tempi, over 3½ minutes being taken off the customary timing of the first movement, and 1½ off the last. Also with May Harrison, Bax recorded, for HMV, the Delius First Violin Sonata, with conspicuous success. The first session had been on 1 February, but a number of retakes that were thought desirable had to wait until 26 June, after the Columbia session. Delius claimed not to like Bax's playing, though this may have been owing to the fact that a cut was made in the first movement.

Otherwise, the music which occupied him at this time was the Two-Piano Sonata — a sunny and extrovert work, involved at least in some measure with an external nature programme, and clearly a musical relaxation between the two major works (the Third Symphony and *Winter Legends*) which dominated the two winters framing it.

Rae Robertson and his wife Ethel Bartlett had formed a two-piano team in 1928 and asked Bax for a work to play. He had responded with *The Poisoned Fountain*, considered in its day an adventurous piece: 'luxuriant and with free and daring harmony', and it was thought 'truly menacing'.[17] Then, after completing the Third Symphony in full score in February 1929, he went on to arrange an earlier Scriabinesque piano piece, *The Devil That Tempted St Anthony*, for two pianos, and then for the same performers wrote the sonata. They were delighted, as, apparently, were audiences all over America round which they were toured. (Bax commented privately to a colleague that he did not like the Robertsons' playing of his sonata — 'much too accurate' he said.) The music was quickly published the following year, and the Robertsons subsequently recorded it, coupled with his earlier 'homage to Grieg', *Hardanger*.

The Sonata for Two Pianos is in Bax's customary three movements, each marked by frequent changes of time signature. The opening *Molto moderato* is qualified by the instruction 'in a languorous sun-stained mood', and Bax commented that his programmatic source of inspiration reflected the time of its conception: the coming of spring, and 'the sea in its many varieties of mood'.[18] On their American tour Rae Robertson introduced the music with a few preliminary remarks in programmatic vein. (In a letter to Richard Church, Bax wrote, concerning this sonata: 'As a matter of fact there are a certain number of people who object to any kind of picturesque commentaries upon music ... Rae Robertson made a short speech about the work ... and there were objections afterwards from some members of the audience (privately expressed). I suppose it derives from the idiotic peculiarly English dread of the outward manifestation of enthusiasm bred in the mind at our glorious public schools.') One presumes that they are to some degree based on what Bax had told him, though perhaps in less definitely pictorial terms. Robertson said:

Though this work is not to be regarded as programme music, each of its three movements expresses the composer's reaction to some experience which has stirred his imagination profoundly. The first movement, in rather free sonata form, might be called a Poem of Spring. Its frequent changes of mood and *tempo* suggest that mixture of languor and ecstasy which we associate with the re-birth of the world of Nature when the sun has conquered the frosts of Winter. It is easy, in listening to this movement, to hear the songs of nesting birds, and to picture the gambols of young lambs, but these are only symbols of the awakening of life, tender and delicate yet at the same time full of power and vitality. The second movement takes us into the world of ancient Celtic legend. From some distant fairy heaven across the sea comes a faint sound of unearthly music, hardly distinguishable from the sea-murmur which accompanies it. As the movement progresses the sea becomes more turbulent, rising gradually till at last it seems to break in a great wave. Then comes again the fairy melody, which slowly dies away into silence.[19]

It was a conception strikingly similar to *The Garden of Fand*. 'The last movement,' Robertson went on, 'is based on the rhythm of an old folk-dance, somewhat rough and fierce in its merry-making. At the end of the movement we hear again the languorous, sun-stained melody which opens the first movement, now, however, transformed [Ex. 63] into a song of joy and triumph, as if the Spring had really come at last, in all its splendour.'

Though not one of Bax's greatest works, in a fine performance the sonata is effective and enjoyable. In the range of sonorities and textures he conjures from the duo he is highly successful and inventive, yet, while writing in a highly characteristic keyboard idiom, Bax writes two real parts for his pianos, and the sonata is not, as might have been expected, a solo work that has outgrown the resources of one player.

Surprisingly perhaps, the work was chosen for the ISCM festival at Liège in 1930, and at the beginning of his programme note on that occasion L. Dunton Green found in the music 'a reflection of the smiling English country side or of the sea'.[20] In fact, at about the time the work was being completed, Bax, in company with Patrick

Ex. 63

Hadley, stayed with Balfour Gardiner at Ashampstead for the last
time. Gardiner was in the throes of moving from Berkshire to Dorset.
The visits to Ashampstead had meant a great deal to Bax, and he
wrote on his return to London:

My dear Balfour

I must thank you again for these lovely days — so full of sunlight and gaiety —
and more than this, I must try to tell you of all my gratitude for your unfailing
friendship and generosity through all the twentyone Ashampstead years. When I
crossed the lawn to the gate this morning I simply dared not realize that I might
never see the dear place again.

I suppose I know and love Ashampstead and the cottage more intimately than
anyone except yourself, and to me the place has always been a refuge in adverse
times, and a beautiful stressing of all the fleeting happiness of this uncertain life.
But I think you know how I have loved it — or anyway guessed — (and this in
spite of my general indifference to *any* local habitation).

Indeed all of me that is English has always thought of the dear little cottage
and its garden as *home*.

I do thank you from my heart for all the serene happiness you have allowed
me to enjoy through these long years.

Yours always affectionately, Arnold[21]

Hadley, too, felt the same and wrote how 'the profound happiness
I always feel at Ashampstead was this time overshadowed with sadness.'[22] Hadley later warmly remembered Bax as a companion during

these friendly gatherings. 'One would always look forward to the delights of the evening,' he wrote, 'which would unfailingly be regaled by his wit and incomparable charm. To the list of his other virtues must be added a prodigious memory for people, places and indeed things in general. His slant upon characters he had known was always highly individual, usually sly, and fortified by a telling talent for mimicry. There was never better quiet company.'[23]

Although Bax joined his brother for their usual August cricket tour that year, another insistent call began to be made on his time. Many happy days that summer were spent with young Mary Gleaves, particularly on the Thames, starting at Marlow and going up-river. It was familiar ground to Bax, who must have fully explored this territory when he lived at Marlow during the First World War. As it was, Bax had felt compassion for Mary the previous year when her father was dying of cancer, and her mother was away and also ill. He had provided practical help as well as sympathy, and through family connections with a young surgeon, Jack Piercy, had Mary's father taken from the Charing Cross Hospital and privately nursed. Bax had at first been prompted by purely selfless motives, but during the summer of 1929, when he tried to help her with the terrible personal anguish which accompanied the deaths of her parents, Bax found himself being strongly drawn to Mary. Little by little during 1929 they grew together, the young girl accepting the emotional life-raft that was offered, the older man committing himself only gradually after his disasters of recent years. Was it not Arnold Bennett who wrote that in affairs of the heart both very young and very old men rush in and make fools of themselves, whereas the man in middle years only slowly lets himself down, testing the water all the way? 'This has been a wild year for you', wrote Bax to Mary on 31 December, and himself admitted that 'generally I *do* feel a little frightened of saying all I feel – just because of the dread I have of hurting you.' In one of his first letters to her, Bax had written from the heart when he said, 'it is damned hard for anyone to pass through the inferno that is on the path between youth with its fairy fantasies and the realization of sad human destiny as it is – without becoming embittered'.

Most of September 1929 Bax spent in Glencolumcille, and this month away from Mary was a crucial turning-point in the development of their relationship, as he wrote to her repeatedly and at length. (Bax wrote to Mary constantly henceforth, until his death in 1953. Although the hundreds of letters are undated they all survive in their original envelopes, and a study of their postmarks documents most of Bax's movements for the rest of his life. This source is the basis for all dates quoted in the remainder of this book unless otherwise acknowledged.) His first letter from Glencolumcille is postmarked 4 September.

Mary, dear one,

It is very late, but I feel I want to talk to you a little ... These chains of time and space are so maddening because I feel so close to you, and yet very likely you don't know it, and you are thinking of me as a far away person hundreds of miles from you. It seems strange that I can't call *you* out of your tired delicate body and take you with me into the hills and fierce clean Atlantic air. Though I would rather have all of you here, body and soul, because in your case I can't imagine one element apart from the other. Somehow, dear, your body seems very transparent, and I see your spirit shining through it. This has been a strange wild day here, rough and violent and healthy, a rampaging wind and wonderful changeful lights ... This glen faces out west to the Atlantic, and there is a small bay with a lovely strand where I bathe every day. There are huge cliffs to the north, and in winter the storm-scuds blow the sea foam right up their 750 feet. You would love the gentle innocent people. I think it is a great privilege that they regard me as one of themselves, and just talk about their own affairs as though I were not there at all. Oh little Mary, darling, I would like to put some enchantment on you and bring you here in dream if it can't be done in reality, because I believe it is just this mood that would help you. This West of Ireland atmosphere is hovering between the world we know too well and some happy otherworld that we begin to glimpse when we are growing up and never reach.

I can't explain it, but it *is* so, and every sensitive person is enslaved by the magic of it. You asked me to write about Ireland, dear, and so I am doing so – I want to send you a sea-wind to comfort your heart, and so I do, but really I wish I could bring you here yourself, and hold you softly in my arms, and let you listen to the sea and the wind and all the voices behind them. There are better things than you know – even real things, and not only dreams – and I *wish* I could take you to find them ...

In fact, because it had to be redirected it was probably a fortnight before Mary received that letter, but she had already written, and Bax wrote again two days later:

Mary dear,

Your letter came today, and I am so happy to hear that anything I said could give you some encouragement. Indeed I feel it is little I can do to help you. This is rather a complex psychological entanglement, for all that came so suddenly in November was such a dreadful shock to me that I still feel a little self-conscious and shy in writing to you at all. But I must tell you that it is wonderful to find you just as strange and rare as a grown-up as you were a child. So try not to mind being grown-up! From the tiny bit that I know of you now you seem to have developed in quite an extraordinary degree, and for heaven's sake don't question as to what purpose you were born! I don't think, Mary, there is much difference between the spiritual evolution of men and women. That is a matter of individual genius. Both sexes are capable of losing all for an ideal, though man's sacrifice is usually more spectacular – for instance – Father Damien, who went out to a leper settlement and finally died of leprosy, and the Irish rebels of 1916, who gave up everything – some of them life itself – for their ideal Ireland – and countless others of course. But oh! my dear. I do want you to go on being brave and hold to your romantic ideals about this terribly difficult matter of sex. There is hardly anyone of either sex who is courageous or imaginative enough to try, and as it is probably the most important thing in our vague and muddled existence, if one does not keep one's belief in the old dear faery-tale one loses one's soul, for I think that this (nowadays) so much derided romanticism is the only wing upon which one can fly to the stars and whatever God may be. This is perhaps not the time – but I am not a monk or an ascetic and still believe that the body can yoke with the soul in equal partnership. It seems to me that in all one's experience it has been impossible to think of one apart from the other ...

More letters followed telling of his contentment in his land of heart's desire. 'I have seen endless beauty during the last week (but only between terrific storms),' he wrote; 'the violent seas crashing in from the Atlantic are overwhelmingly grand ... All is a glitter of sunlight ... gleam on the lakes dazzling to the eyes. What is the good of ... design of such things?' Bax joined the local people hay-making and observed, 'there could scarcely be a saner, happier mood in the world. And the people themselves contented in this part of their work.'

In one letter to Mary he broke into verse recalling earlier summer days spent on the upper reaches of the Thames. Their expeditions were to continue throughout the 1930s and of almost any of them Bax might have written:

Ah why did summer stay so long?
Was it some demon in the sun
Who tossed that net of fire among
The water-dappled leaves, and spun
Those insect webs through all the fair
Tumbled sweetness of her hair?

What was September's dangerous whim,
Within that green and golden place,
To make old Reason's lantern dim,
And glorify the pallid face
And blue-grey eyes so meek and mild,
Of that lonely frightened child?

Why was she given a mouth too sad
And soft to save from kissing? Dear,
Because that threatening beauty had
Our wits an hour in thrall, I fear
More that we may climb the stair
To the topmost tower of care!

Later in the month Bax was still in Glencolumcille. In another letter he wrote: 'The wind is howling in the glen tonight. At the sunset it [the sea] looked like boiling metal heaving in a vast cauldron ... I have sat at the window watching [the storm], in a sort of enchantment ... yet there is always a heart of peace in the midst of the storm watches. One seems to be hovering between a world we all know and another existence and the veil between is so flimsy that it might be blown away at any moment.'

Bax returned to London via Belfast, and found himself there on 26 September at the Midland Station Hotel where he had gone 'to see a boy from Glen who was a rather particular friend of mine when he was a "wee fella" and whom I had not seen since 1913.' But he could not help observing that Belfast was a 'somewhat appalling city. It is not like Ireland at all.'

He was back in London the next day, and the experienced and disillusioned side of Bax was in the ascendant. 'Nothing ever returns, he wrote, 'except in dream and memory'.

During the autumn of 1929 the pace of their passion quickened, yet it is not reflected in any demonstrable way in Bax's most difficult extended work which was written in short score at that time. This was the *Winter Legends* for piano and orchestra, in which Bax first makes use of a noticeable change of style. Writing to Mary in 1931 Bax spoke of 'ordinary life and all the grimness which most of my music deals with'. Certainly it is more Bax's cry of despair, 'nothing returns', that is reflected in *Winter Legends* than any hedonistic celebration of his passion as we saw it reflected in the music of the First World War period. But before looking at the score of this enigmatic work, it would perhaps be appropriate to follow the development of their relationship as it is reflected in Bax's letters to Mary. Bax's philosophy is coloured by the sort of language and imagery that would not have been out of place in his brother Clifford's Theosophical Art Circle twenty years before. By now he had thrown all caution aside and was writing exactly what he felt, as he had begun to do while he was in Glencolumcille. On 14 November he wrote:

I *can* understand the difficulties of this muddled life, though you and I meet in another world altogether and may be you think of me just as an inhabitant of that world and don't want to relate me to ordinary existence. But I am very conscious of you as a lovely stranger in a material world — so much so that I doubt sometime you have enough to eat — and I ask you to try to tell me about *every*thing. I don't wonder at your moods when you think you might as well be dead — for to *me* the only realities are Love (when one is simply lost in it) — and certain mystical moods of nature — and I know I don't have to worry about material considerations and most people think that is *every*thing — but indeed it isn't! Life as most people live it is frightfully boring, and it is only those who seem to bring the glamour and extasy of the dream-world of one's imagination that matter.

Bax's thoughts were by now almost completely taken up by Mary. 'I never cease to think of you morning, noon, and night, I feel that you must know this,' he wrote on 6 December; 'I miss you so dreadfully my darling, and the world seems dark without you.' That autumn friends may have wondered what preoccupied him; a new work perhaps, they may have thought. He described such an occasion to Mary on 31 December. 'Of course I have been thinking of you all evening — I was at a dinner party, and I must have seemed very distracted at times.'

Yet Bax did not attempt to introduce Mary to a wide circle of friends. The compartments into which he was sorting various strands of his life were kept quite separate. As with other female friends, the question of a meeting with his family arose — yet Bax had been hurt too often and too deeply. 'My mother is a darling,' he wrote, 'and I would like you to know her, but it would all be rather difficult and complicated.'

Christmas 1929 was a great anticlimax, for although he had finished *Winter Legends* on 4 December, he had stayed away from the family circle because of Mary and found that, for the first time in his life, he had to have his 'Christmas dinner alone in a restaurant ... I must admit that it was rather depressing,' he wrote.

During 1930 and 1931 Bax's passion reached a climax of happiness and fulfilled desire. His sexual ecstasy is vividly illustrated by a particularly revealing letter he wrote in 1931:

My darling one,

I *must* send you my love tonight. You were so sweet amongst the flowers to-day. If you ever have that inferiority complex again about love, remember that I am an entirely uncivilized person. I think there are only two things that really mean anything to us in our short and enigmatical lives on this earth, and they are sex and love and all their extasy, and just crude physical hunger. There is nothing else really. All the rest is dope and make-believe. And I hate and despise all the silly indecent foolery about sex and when I say 'of course you throw yourself at me darling' I mean it as the most lovely honour I could pay you. Why all these idiotic cruelties about the loveliest thing life can give to man and woman? I am so infinitely grateful that I have found you, my wild young naiad. All my body and spirit send their kisses to yours.

Goodnight, my ever *ever* loved one, A.

Winter Legends is a work of symphonic stature. In it Bax consciously attempts to vary the sound of his orchestral palette: while becoming less decorated and colder in harmonic effect and less reliant on intrinsically interesting melodic material, it nevertheless abounds in Baxian fingerprints. He is almost certainly influenced by the sound world of Sibelius, though not by Sibelius's constructional methods. In fact, Bax first inscribed the score to the Finnish master and only later amended it to Harriet Cohen, its first performer, in 1932. The craze for Sibelius that took firm hold in musical Britain and America in the 1930s had already begun, and Bax, as we have seen already, was very taken with Sibelius's Fourth Symphony and *Tapiola* in particular. The work that grew out of all this, if flawed, is original in conception and large in gesture.

The *Northern Ballads* had already underlined how legendary influences in the North rather than the West had begun to fascinate Bax, but those works — still in short score — were only a step on the road, via the Third Symphony; the first flowering in an orchestral score of this new world of pine trees and snow and heroes, with its much greater contrast between blazing light and winter dark, was *Winter Legends*. In his customary three movements with Epilogue, the music was conceived from the start for piano and orchestra. It was written very quickly, the movements in short score being dated '22 Oct', '30 Oct' and '4 Dec 1929'. The orchestration of the first two movements was completed during February 1930; the whole work by 3 April 1930. Bax wrote one of his typically straight-faced programme notes for the first performance which nevertheless by its evocative language still manages to give a fair amount away without meaning to. As it usefully describes the work as a whole it is quoted here verbatim.

This work, which is designed in three movements and on a symphonic scale, makes no pretence of being a piano concerto in the ordinary sense. The piano is not used as a means of technical display though it plays a difficult part. Neither has the piece any communicable programme. The listener may associate what he hears with any heroic tale or tales of the North — of the far North, be it said. Some of these happenings may have taken place within the Arctic circle.

Legends that once were told or sung
In many a smoky fireside nook
Of Iceland, in the ancient day
By wandering Saga-man or Scald.

There is nothing consciously Celtic about this work.
After the side drum has delivered a rhythmic tattoo [Ex. 64]:

Ex. 64

the movement opens with a kind of whirlwind on the piano, leading directly
to the following subject [Ex. 65]:

Ex. 65

the rhythmic figure [Ex. 64] receives a certain amount of development and then
makes way for one of the most important themes in the work [Ex. 66]:

Ex. 66

These two subjects together with a third rhythmic theme centred on E occupy
most of the attention for some time.

A new melody is interpolated in the form of a duet for cor anglais and piano
after which [Ex. 66] reappears in a more romantic and tender mood than anything that has gone before. This dream fades away and the development proper
begins. The movement is not in sonata form — rather it may be described as an
assembling and fusing of various elements for the forging of a great climax. It is
at this point in the music that the building up of this climax begins and the
section ends with a triumphant and glittering version of Ex. 65.

II

This movement is, generally speaking, darker in colour than the first, though its
conclusion is serene enough. The form may be defined broadly as binary (A-B-A).
The first subject [Ex. 67] is given to the piano and the earlier portion of the
movement may suggest a kind of dialogue between the piano and orchestra.

Ex. 67

Later on the rhythmic idea ([Ex. 64] of the first section) reappears in remote and shadowy guise and serves as a bridge to the second division of the piece which is introduced by a menacing surge of sound derived from the piano whirl-wind of the earlier movement. The ensuing music is based upon this theme [Ex. 68]:

(Threateningly)

Ex. 68

which is revealed for some time in a very harsh and baleful light. However it subsequently softens and grows warmer until the mood of Ex. 68 is transformed into something similar to the dream episode in the Allegro. A long climax is established (and with it the return of the darker elements), but finally subsides towards another allusion to Ex. 64. The first melody returns, again in dialogue form, and the movement ends very quietly.

III

The third part opens with a tuba solo — a figure used frequently during the whole work and derived from the original uprush on the piano. This figure alternates with Ex. 64 invested again with all its pristine starkness. The principal subject of the finale soon appears on the piano [Ex. 69]:

Poco piu mosso

Ex. 69 (cont. overleaf)

Ex. 69 (cont.)

quickly followed by another, equally primitive in character [Ex. 70]:

Ex. 70

These continue for some time varied by quieter episodes based upon [Ex. 71]:

Ex. 71

and after a development of no great length we come to the epilogue starting with a piano solo founded upon Ex. 71. This conclusion may possibly suggest the return of the sun and warm airs from the south after the long northern winter. Ex. 66 finally reappears in a serene form, and the music ends in, as it were, a burst of light.[24]

Bax called the work a 'Sinfonia concertante for piano and orchestra', and it is a curious coincidence that he should have written what was to all intents and purposes his fourth symphony immediately before Szymanowski produced *his* Fourth Symphony, which was also for piano and orchestra. Even more intriguing is the fact that Bax, who had met the Polish composer during the Great War, now met him again at one of Harriet's parties, and five years later was to inscribe the score of his Sixth Symphony to Szymanowski (though changing it before publication to Adrian Boult).

Harriet Cohen has made much play with the fact that *Winter Legends* marks Bax's final rejection of things Celtic. 'I have gone Northern',[25] she quotes him as saying, and it is clear she was trying to make out the case for Bax as a Sibelian figure (a composer she revered almost above all others). In the light of the programmatic nature of the music, at a time when the critics were strongly divided over the question of 'programmatic' as opposed to 'pure' music, Ernest Newman's review in the *Sunday Times* (14 February 1932) is of great interest. Harriet Cohen set great store by this account, and was very disappointed that her publishers deleted it from her autobiography. Newman wrote:

At the BBC orchestral concert on Wednesday Dr Boult introduced us to Arnold Bax's new work, 'Winter Legends' which is described as a symphonic concerto for piano and orchestra. Bax, I am glad to see, is at last mustering up courage enough to admit that some of his later work is programmatic. More composers would be glad to make the same simple admission had they not been scared stiff by the superficial aestheticians who insist on the necessity of music being 'pure', the implication being that any music that has the remotest connection with 'literature' is necessarily impure, and therefore ineligible for admission into the musical heaven. The result of the activities of this self-appointed Vigilance Committee for Musical Morals has been to turn most composers into musical hypocrites. They have indulged in secret in this delightful but forbidden dalliance with 'literature', and then denied in public that they even know the naughty lady by sight; while as for ever having called at the house ...

It is true that Bax does not tell us much about the programme basis of 'Winter Legends'. The work, it seems, 'has no programme which could be set down in words'; each hearer has 'full liberty to associate it with any heroic tales of the far North, even with the Arctic Circle.' Having braved the Vigilance Committee and the Prohibitionists to that extent, Bax really might have dared them to do their damndest and told us outright what were the legends that not only set his imagination at work in the first place, but obviously shaped its course for it at a dozen points. For even after making all allowances for the disabilities under which the listener labours at the first hearing of a long new work, it is manifest that the inner connection of this music will never be perfectly clear throughout as music pure and simple. Any listener experienced in these things can lay his finger on passage after passage and say with confidence that the guiding thread here is not purely musical but a blend of the musical and the literary: and until the composer takes us more fully into his confidence he cannot expect us to see the same organic unity in the work that it has for him.

The music is extraordinarily rich in imaginative suggestion; whatever the legends were that prompted it, they have been seized in their inmost essence by the composer and retold in an orchestral language that is the most subtle and the most varied that Bax has yet given us. Our one trouble in listening to it is that often it is difficult to see just why this passage should follow that or lead into the other, the reason being, as I have tried to indicate, that the connective tissue does not explain itself in terms of music alone.

The performance, so far as one was capable of judging, was excellent; certainly the piano part, in the safe hands of Miss Harriet Cohen, was exactly what the composer meant.[26]

There are typical, elusive, textual problems in the solo piano part of *Winter Legends*. In 1954, Harriet Cohen played a cut version of the score, cuts which were taken into the score and parts normally hired for performance, and indeed observed by John McCabe in his performances in 1978 and 1981. Harriet Cohen appears to have performed from a copyist's two piano version, but this differs in many points of detail from the autograph two piano score, the autograph (complete) full score and the copyist's (cut) full score. The solo piano part normally available with the performing materials differs yet again. It was not until Margaret Fingerhut's recording for Chandos that we had a complete reading which incorporates the 'best practice' in the solo part from each of the five possible sources.

At about the time of the first performance Bax was asked about the programme behind the score in an interview, and responded by saying, 'any programme, and programme remember is a curious thing, any concrete ideas that may be in it of place or thing are of the North — Northern Ireland, Northern Scotland, Northern Europe — in fact, the Celtic North.'[27]

So how are we to rate this enigmatic score? Bax himself agreed that it could have been another symphony, though he underlined that 'the form is free' and he thought the first movement 'too rhapsodic'.[28] In structure, the first movement is unlike any other he wrote: a succession of episodes which always return to the rhythm of the opening and generate exciting passages of virile, astringent allegro, mainly derived from that opening side-drum tattoo. At its heart is an extended piano solo, a wayward dream, which in turn gives way to an extended passage of quick orchestral music. This is sustained over many pages to the closing sequence of *Maestoso — Largamente molto — Trionfale*, which brings this troubled movement to a glorious close. Even more than the Third Symphony, this work's initial appeal lies in a large number of memorable, yet at first sight self-contained, highlights.

The Delius Festival was staged in London during October, with the blind and paralyzed Delius in attendance, and it is improbable that Bax missed it. What is particularly interesting is that, if he was there, he would have heard Delius's short work for string orchestra called *Air and Dance*, which was given its first public performance on 16 October. At about that time Bax was at work on the slow movement of *Winter Legends* in which there appears a remarkably close reminiscence of the dotted rhythm that pervades Delius's score.

Bax's slow movement opens with a wintry bassoon solo, and

introduces the fast rhythmic idea of the final movement at a *Lento sostenuto* tempo. The music certainly appears to be telling some hidden narration. It was originally intended that its first performance would be in Boston under Kussevitsky in December 1931 – a performance which did not, however, take place. Bax's friend the critic Herbert Hughes wrote up a private play-through by Bax and Harriet in the *Daily Telegraph*, noting that Bax had repudiated any hint of a programme and commented 'yet in spite of his specific denial of any romantic or narrative implications, in spite also of all one misses of orchestral colour and dynamic force in a piano version, the music expresses a mental and spiritual experience (and in that sense is narrative) as clearly as any written or spoken legend'.

The solo tuba theme that launches the last movement over rippling piano arpeggios has elicited some comment for the rare opportunity offered to that instrument, and there are brief solos for it in all three movements of *Winter Legends*. Yet the chief characteristic of this movement is the alternation of short passages for solo piano and for the orchestra. Particularly in fast running passages this succeeds very well, although at times it is Bax's orchestral clothing which carries the scheme through. There are some hauntingly beautiful pages of Baxian reverie, typically the idyllic presentation of Ex. 71.

Several times we seem to pass into the world of the Third Symphony – textures, orchestral transitions, actual phrases – and the work ends in an extended epilogue introduced by a long piano solo. This emotional world lacks focus, but on a rising crescendo a stormy climax is started, out of the subsidence of which another calm piano solo emerges to herald a far-off reminiscence on the solo horn of the world of the Third Symphony (Ex. 72).

p cantabile   *dim.*   *pp*

Ex. 72

The work dissolves quietly into hazy fragments, until a final resurgence of energy brings the sforzando final chord. If ever a work needed a living tradition of repeated performance for its assessment, this is it.

Plate 1 *Top left:* Alfred Ridley Bax and Charlotte Ellen (Lea) Bax, Arnold's parents, on the garden steps of Ivy Bank (ca summer, 1901). *Top right:* Francis Colmer in his study at Ivy Bank. *Bottom:* A group on the garden steps of Ivy Bank, some time during Arnold's time at the Royal Academy of Music: (left to right, standing) Aunt 'Molly' Lea, Helen Lea, Freda Bax, Gladys Lees, Arnold Bax; (sitting) Mary Barber, Uncle Harold Lea.

Plate 2 *Top:* Ivy Bank from the garden (ca 1901). *Bottom:* The maids prepare one of Mrs Bax's children's parties in the garden at Ivy Bank.

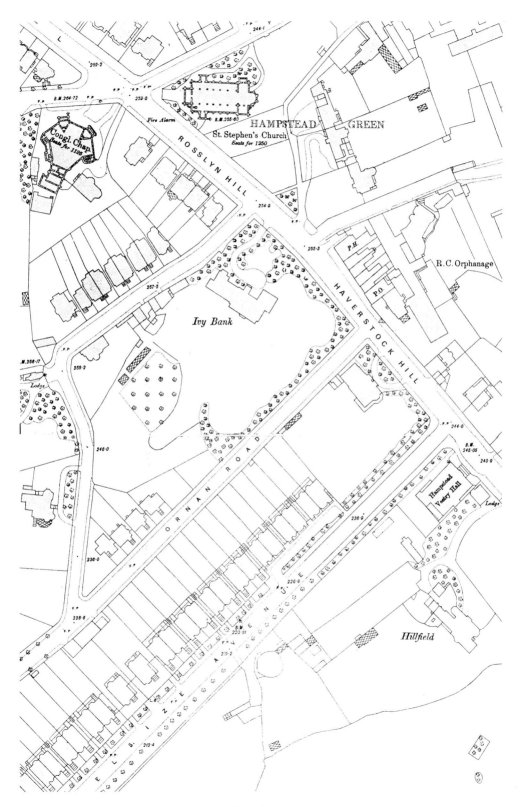

Plate 3 Ivy Bank as it was when bought by Alfred Ridley Bax. (Ordnance Map revised 1893.)

Plate 4 *Top left:* Irene Scharrer at the Royal Academy of Music; sketch by Rebecca Clarke, 1903. *Top right:* Myra Hess at the Royal Academy of Music; sketch by Rebecca Clarke, 1903. *Bottom:* Thuell Burnham (an American pianist friend of Evelyn Bax), Arnold and Evelyn Bax, in the bottom garden at Ivy Bank.

Plate 5 *Top left:* Lionel Tertis, 1904. *Top right:* Frederick Corder, ca 1905. *Bottom left:* Tobias Matthay, detail from the portrait by Kay Robertson (1899) in the Royal Academy of Music. *Bottom right:* Sir A. C. Mackenzie, Principal of the Royal Academy of Music.

Plate 6 *Top left:* Arthur Alexander, ca 1911. *Top right:* Olga Antonietti, ca 1910. *Bottom:* Dolly and Paul Corder, Hampstead, ca 1907.

Plate 7 *Top:* Glencolumcille today. (Photograph by Rodney Meadows.) *Bottom:* Balfour Gardiner's cottage at Ashampstead immediately before the First World War: Balfour Gardiner standing, Arnold Bax on his left. The figure seated on Gardiner's right is believed to be the Anglo-New Zealand composer Frank Hutchens.

Plate 8 *Top:* Elsita Bax, Arnold Bax, Phyllis Russell, in the garden of the Baxes' house in Bushy Park Road, Rathgar, Dublin, January 1913. *Bottom left:* Ernest Belfort Bax. *Bottom right:* Luisa Sobrino, Arnold Bax's mother-in-law.

Plate 9 The painted frontispiece to the short-score manuscript of the ballet *Tamara* (*King Kojata*) – painting by Arnold or Clifford Bax.

Plate 10 *Top:* The Old Broughtonians at Calne, 11 August 1912. Photograph by J. J. Farjeon. (Left to right: Rosalind Thorneycroft, Herbert Farjeon, Lynn Hartley, Godwin Baynes, R. H. Lowe (seated), Stacy Aumonier, Edward Thomas, Maitland Radford, Arnold Bax.) *Bottom:* The Old Broughtonians (mid 1920s). (Standing: R. Straus, C. Palmer, Eric Gillett, Armstrong Gibbs, J. C. Squire, A. D. Peters; Seated: Arnold Bax, Clifford Bax, R. H. Lowe, R. K. Henderson; Cross-legged: P. Knox-Shaw, H. C. Prew.)

Plate 11 *Top left:* AE (George Russell). Lithograph by Mary Duncan, in the National Portrait Gallery, London (Dublin, 1912 or 1913). *Top right:* Philip Heseltine ('Peter Warlock') by John Cooper, 1926. *Bottom left:* Winifred Small ca 1916. *Bottom right:* May Harrison (from a handbill for a Wigmore Hall performance of Bax's First Violin Sonata, 30 April 1927).

Plate 12 *Top:* Arnold Bax and his mother (standing): Evelyn and Clifford Bax (seated). At Arundel, 24 June 1919. *Bottom left:* The young York Bowen, already a celebrity while still a student. *Bottom right:* Sir Thomas Beecham.

WIGMORE HALL
Wigmore Street, W.1

Monday, February 23rd at 8.15

A MEMORIAL CONCERT

of the works of

PETER WARLOCK

ARTISTS:

MEGAN FOSTER

JOHN ARMSTRONG

DALE SMITH

THE ORIANA SINGERS
(Conductor - C. Kennedy Scott)

INTERNATIONAL STRING QUARTET
Andre Mangeot, Walter Price, Eric Bray, Jack Shinebourne

CHAMBER ORCHESTRA

Conductor:

CONSTANT LAMBERT

At the Piano - ARNOLD BAX

Bosendorfer Grand Pianoforte

 Tickets (including Tax): Reserved 8/6, 5/9   Unreserved 3/-
May be obtained from Box Office, Wigmore Hall, or from
THE IMPERIAL CONCERT AGENCY, 175 Piccadilly, W.1
Tel.: Gerrard 9523-4
A stamped addressed envelope must accompany all applications for Tickets by post
P.T.O.

Plate 13   *Top:* Mrs Christopher Lowther, with Miss Billie Carleton as the lily, in a revival of Bax's dance – play *From Dusk Till Dawn* at the Shaftesbury Theatre in July 1918. *Bottom left:* Programme for the first Peter Warlock Memorial Concert, 23 February 1931. *Bottom right:* Beatrice Harrison.

Plate 14 Harriet Cohen and Arnold Bax, 1920. Photograph by Sydney J. Loeb.

Plate 15 *Top:* Eugène Goossens, Arnold Bax, Arthur Bliss, Dorothy Moulton, 1920. *Bottom:* Tamara Karsavina dancing the part of Karissima, on stage at the London Coliseum, March 1920. (Photograph: Raymond Mander and Joe Mitchenson Theatre Collection.)

Plate 16 *Top:* The Morar River, December 1938. (Photograph by Arnold Bax.) *Bottom:* Aloys Fleischmann, Arnold Bax, Tilly Fleischmann (early 1930s).

Plate 17 *Top:* Arnold Bax and his mother in the garden at Frognal Gardens, late 1920s. *Bottom left:* Arnold Bax and Harriet Cohen on the steps of Sir Henry Wood's Apple Tree Farm, at Chorleywood; the figure to the left in the photograph is the writer on music Rosa Newmarch (courtesy Mrs Kathleen Cockburn). *Bottom right:* Sir Henry Wood and Arnold Bax at Apple Tree Farm, ca 1930.

Plate 18 Fragment of what may have been part of the sketch for an unfinished second viola sonata, showing ideas subsequently used in the Sixth Symphony.

Plate 19   Mary Gleaves (early 1930s: photograph by Arnold Bax).

Plate 20 *Top left:* Ethel Bartlett and Rae Robertson, 1928. *Top right:* E. J. Moeran. *Bottom:* Basil Cameron and Sir Arnold Bax at a rehearsal of Bax's Fourth Symphony (mid 1940s).

Plate 21 *Top:* Mr and Mrs Stanley Fitch (proprietors of the White Horse) and Sir Arnold Bax on the steps of the White Horse, Storrington (mid 1940s). *Bottom:* The White Horse Hotel, Storrington, today. *Vignette:* The memorial plaque on the White Horse.

Plate 22 The unused orchestral storm that Bax wrote for *Oliver Twist* (courtesy of Oliver Neighbour).

Plate 23 *Top:* Muir Mathieson, Harriet Cohen and Sir Arnold Bax at the recording session for the film music to *Oliver Twist*, 1948 (courtesy Cloud Nine Records). *Bottom:* Mary Gleaves and Sir Arnold Bax, Summer 1953.

Plate 24 Sir Arnold Bax, 1947.

Going northern

Bax travelled comparatively little in 1930: to Cork to see the Fleischmanns and judge the Feis at the end of April and beginning of May; to Bradford for the first performance of his *Nonett* (the German spelling 'Nonett' is used on the Murdoch full score and is followed throughout, although Chappell, on a later printing, prefer the English 'Nonet'); and with Mary to Morar in the autumn. He appears only briefly to have visited Glencolumcille and, although he did continue to go there until at least 1934, 1930 really marked the break with his habit of spending long periods there. However, most of Bax's attention and energy went into his passion for Mary. '1930 has been as beautiful as anything I can remember', Bax wrote to her in August. There were also important performances – the first of the Third Symphony and the first London performance of the Second Symphony – that kept Bax's name before the public and greatly added to his reputation. He was now one of the leading living British composers, and any new work of his was an important artistic event. So although the public received the impression that Bax was pouring out music, during much of 1930 this was not true – his energies were directed elsewhere. There was the orchestration of *Winter Legends*, of course, which was not completed until April. Concurrently with *Winter Legends* he was faced with how quickly to produce something for a commission from the Bradford Triennial Festival. This he did by scoring a Violin Sonata in F, which he had completed in September 1928 but not brought forward. The resulting *Nonett* was ready in January.

The *Overture to a Picaresque Comedy*, in which Bax consciously parodies Richard Strauss, waltz and all – apparently to win a bet that he could not do it – was also written in 1930. Harriet

Cohen, quite rightly, referred to it as 'uncharacteristic pastiche'.[1] But the most substantial score written that year, one that reflects Bax's happiness and fulfilment, is the Fourth Symphony. This was written between October 1930 and February 1931, almost entirely at Morar, although 'part of the first movement, at any rate, was worked out at Glencolumcille.'[2] There was much publicity for this outgoing work when it first appeared: it was said that Bax recognized the need to avoid writing music that was excessively introspective, and this was a conscious attempt to do so. Certainly the work has a markedly different personality from the three earlier symphonies; perhaps Bax realized this and felt that it required explanation. In fact for the only time in the symphonies he publicly admitted that he had been inspired by the sea, and that the beginning of the first movement meant to him 'a rough sea at flood-tide on a sunny day, and most of the work is nature music.'[3] The score certainly looks back to the approach of his earlier sea music, though nowhere does he essay textures as complex or impressionistic as are to be found in *Fand* or *Tintagel*. Yet, one feels, there is more to it than that. At the height of an earlier passion Bax had produced gloriously ecstatic sea-music. Now, a dozen years later, it is surely no accident that having regained an enchantment he had thought beyond recall, his passion for Mary should be subconsciously celebrated in a vivid and exciting symphonic depiction of the sea. The Freudian sexual imagery of the sea has already been noted in the context of Bax's earlier music, and this could well be a continuing explanation of why the work stands out in comparison with his other music of the period. Bax certainly did think of the sea in this context, and in one letter wrote how he wished he could 'drown with my dearest in the depths of nature and love that we two know are unfathomless [*sic*].'

The work makes a lot of its impact through actual brilliance of instrumental tone, such as the writing for six rather than four horns, and the use of the organ to add depth and resonance to the sound. Typical is the opening which launches a huge paragraph of breezy *Allegro moderato* over an E♭ pedal on basses, bassoons and an organ 16-foot stop, which unambiguously underlines the key and at the same time gives a sense of some deep stirring or undertow. In many ways this is instrumentally the least elaborated of Bax's major orchestral scores, and in this respect stands apart from the other symphonies, eschewing the complex textures of the first three and the detailed working of the Fifth and Sixth. Nevertheless the first movement, although brilliantly painted, is formally the least successful, and in some measure one has to admit the criticism that 'isolated lyrical inspirations lie uneasily beside each other. The development section in the opening movement is typical in this respect, where several sections beautiful in themselves and related thematically do not really flow – the larger structure has not been felt.'[4] Thus noted Anthony Payne when the symphony was recorded. Earlier in the same article Payne had asked, 'how is he to expand architecturally a self-contained item? Self-contained because the idea is such a burning problem that it has to be impulsively pinned down before it disappears. It cannot be left to mature and put out fresh growths, because its very nature is its immediacy – the precise quality of sensuousness and the freshness of the moment must be preserved.'[5] This was not due to Bax's being unable to envisage the plan of an extended work, but because of the programmatic associations evident in this symphony. The slow sections in this first movement certainly take us into a quite contrasted world from the vigorous allegro of the rest of the music. Typical of these is an extraordinary passage of *ppp* chords on strings, all in three parts, over which three muted trumpets play a distant version of the movement's principal theme. Once or twice extended sequential writing or an overworked figure (e.g. around figure 33) suggests that inspiration has sometimes flagged. When it comes the *Molto largamente* coda to the movement brings it to a thrilling, triumphant close. No matter how wayward the harmonic scheme, the final resolution brings it firmly back to the E♭ from which it set out, with the organ adding to the pagan celebration.

It is in the slow movement even more than in the first that Bax writes sea music reminiscent in its technique of earlier scores in this vein. Perhaps most surprising is the ghost of Bax's earlier 'dreamy and passionate' piano piece, *A Romance*, which had been written in 1918 for Harriet Cohen and briefly alluded to in the Second Quartet. The principal motif of that piece (Ex. 73) appears throughout

(harmony omitted)

Ex. 73

the music. Three bars before cue 21, towards the end, Bax suddenly introduces an extended quotation from *A Romance*, starting at the fourth bar on p. 6 of the published score. The quotation – perhaps

Ex. 74 (cont. overleaf)   Fourth Symphony (above), *A Romance* (below).

orchestral realization would be a better description — continues for
26 bars (Ex. 74). Of course as soon as the work was performed
Harriet must have recognized the quotation, yet she can hardly have
guessed its motivation in Bax's mind.

The last movement in some way suffers from the problems of the
first: how to make its slow section flow from the virile, impassioned,
orchestral sweep of its opening allegro. The colour created by trumpets trilling in triads in this evocation perhaps momentarily recalls
the Debussy of *La Mer*, underlining Bax's continued programmatic
point of departure in the work. It concludes with an extended coda,
Tempo di Marcia trionfale, and in 71 bars of gloriously coloured
orchestral tutti Bax ends on a note of confidence and affirmation.
The organ joins this thrilling sound, again with a 16-foot pedal note
underpinning the tonality; indeed, without the organ it is difficult

Ex. 74 (cont.)

for Bax's effects to be fully made. Writing to Christopher Whelen in the late 1940s, when Whelen was assistant conductor at Bournemouth, Bax was emphatic in his ruling that 'No. 4 really *must* have an organ both in the first and last movements'.[6]

In February 1930 HMV issued two 78 rpm records of Bax's *Tintagel* coupled with *Mediterranean* that had been recorded in the Queen's Hall in May 1928, both conducted by Eugène Goossens. These were the first orchestral works of Bax to be recorded, and the importance of recordings to the general appreciation of Bax's music cannot be overestimated. During the 1930s the systematic recording of Sibelius's music was one of the underlying impulses behind the craze for the composer at that time. Bax has only really emerged to anything approaching a wide audience since his major orchestral scores, the symphonies in particular, were recorded in the late 1960s and 1970s – a process that is continuing. *The Gramophone* critic wrote in 1930 of those first recordings: 'To record *Tintagel* is bold and good. The bigger Bax awaits full recognition, and recording will hasten it. So will broadcasting, when Bax can get as much time in the programmes as his stature merits. This is one of the finest suggestions of old scenes and of nature's sway that we have. Much is due to Goossens' sympathy and insight. It should be added that the work is not "advanced" or eccentric in any way.'[7]

In the following issue Compton Mackenzie had to admit that he had found *Tintagel* difficult at first and had only appreciated it on hearing the records. He wrote:

I believe that in some very early number of *The Gramophone* I shall be found to have written in a disparaging way of *Tintagel*, for I heard it some six or seven years ago in Queen's Hall, and then fancied the title a mere excuse to make an unintelligible noise. I had not heard *Tintagel* again until I put it on my gramophone this week, and lo! instead of finding it an unintelligible noise I find it to be one of the most genuinely poetic expressions of the sea's moods that I have ever heard. The lesson is obvious. I need not stress it. And now here is something which may interest Arnold Bax himself. I found that it made the impression on a listener of Hebridean music, although that listener's geography was, I regret to say, not good enough to have any notion at all of where or what *Tintagel* was. Now, if that music was able to suggest the Atlantic and the shores of the Hebrides, it is fairly clear that Arnold Bax has succeeded in expressing the Atlantic round the coast of Cornwall, that he has put into it in fact the very essence of granite and the west wind.[8]

The first performance of the Third Symphony was a major event and elicited wide press coverage. Bax dedicated it to Sir Henry Wood who performed it with the BBC Symphony Orchestra at Queen's Hall on 14 March. Bax was fortunate that Wood took to the score, for during the 1930s he played it many times, not only at home but also abroad. In his autobiography Sir Henry referred to it, not surprisingly, as 'perhaps my favourite'.[9] Incidentally, Bax must have been pleased to read Sir Henry's account of himself: 'We are *very* proud of him. His brilliancy and even his complexity are alluring, and his output is staggering.'[10] Funnily enough, Bax appears to have been caught off balance by the popular success of the Symphony. He wrote to his brother Clifford on 21 March: 'I was very delighted that the Symphony was so much appreciated and somewhat taken aback at its strangely uproarious reception ... I expected it to be a success but not quite as much as that.' Five days later there was another all-Bax chamber concert, at Wigmore Hall, including the

Viola Sonata, Harp Quintet, Piano Quartet, Oboe Quintet and three
short choral works.

Then on 20 May Eugène Goossens, conducting a specially picked
orchestra, gave the Second Symphony its London première — though
to someone observing in the 1970s, the manner of its performance
(as a matinée) was somewhat strange. The concert was very badly
attended, and possibly even in 1930 the hour of the concert may
have had something to do with it. The *Daily Express* wrote:

Debonair Eugène Goossens triumphed at the Queen's Hall yesterday afternoon
with a "nameless" orchestra of 110 performers, magnificent quality and unusually superb balance. There were slightly more than 110 people sitting in the
grand circle; but there looked to be fewer. Row upon row of empty chairs
greeted one of Britain's most brilliant young musicians. Although seats at
Covent Garden are now at an exorbitant premium, and although Goossens'
concerts in New York are packed to the doors, yesterday's event proved one
of the tragedies of the greatest orchestral glut that London has ever known. Yet
Goossens proved a remarkable point: that English orchestral players only need
the proper sort of inspiration to produce brilliant results. Some of them were
BBC men, others from the London Symphony, and most from the Royal Philharmonic orchestras. They had never played as a unit before. And the applause
among the performers themselves at the end was almost greater than that in the
distressingly small audience.[11]

Bax's Symphony was preceded by Brahms's *Academic Festival
Overture*, while the second half presented d'Indy's symphonic
variations *Istar* and three dances from Falla's *The Three-Cornered
Hat*. The *Express* found the Bax 'interesting but inconsistent' and
concluded that it was 'more finely wrought than the Bax Symphony
No. 1' and 'more vital than No. 3'.[12] The *Morning Post* also lamented
that the hall was 'barely a quarter full', finding the concert 'one of
the most exhilarating heard in London recently'. Their critic thought
the Bax symphony 'a work of the highest importance', while wondering if Bax did not defeat his own objective through sheer richness
of orchestral sound. However, from the point of view of Bax's
reputation the concert was certainly a *succès d'estime*, and 'set a
most critical audience, which, containing as it did almost every
musician of note in London, made up in quality what it lacked in
quantity, mad with enthusiasm.'[13]

Most of Bax's time was spent in or near London, meeting Mary
at Kew, or in the Chess Valley, or on the River Thames at Pang-
bourne or Wargrave, where their 'own lovely dream world' dominated his imagination. 'You will always be half-child and half-pagan

nymph — the tenderest wildest lover that man ever found', he wrote.
Perhaps Bax realized that he needed to justify the fantasy world he
had built round a girl half his age, and early in 1931 he did broach
the subject in a letter written late one night.

Dearest sweet

You are asleep, I have no doubt, but I will talk to you for a few minutes all
the same. You must *never* feel unhappy or troubled about love, for you have
brought *me* such unutterable beauty that I never cease to marvel at it, or to
wonder if you can be only a human woman. For I never thought such unself-
ishness and self-surrender could exist on this self-seeking earth.

I know I often ask you if you mind being treated as something between
a faery and a child, and maybe you wish I would sometimes speak of ordinary
life and all the grimness which most of my music deals with. But I can't yet,
my little love. I am so impossibly happy in the faeryland where I first found
you. You are the loveliest thing that ever happened to me.

The summer of 1930 was 'most glorious', and Bax was particularly drawn to the river. 'Those glorious Thames days', recalled Mary
later, and in a letter written in July to Tilly Fleischmann Bax wrote,
'Summer is in full flower here just now ... and I spend much time on
my well-loved river.'

At the end of September the *Nonett* was given at Bradford. This
work often betrays its origin as a violin sonata, with the violin
often assuming the character of soloist rather than an equal partner
in a nonet. Perhaps the music's open-air and serenade-like character
is best demonstrated by the lovely lyrical episode from the first
movement shown in Ex. 75. On 31 March the following year this

Ex. 75

delightful score was played at a private performance in memory of
Eric Verney, Harriet Cohen's brother, who had recently died.

Bax briefly travelled to Ireland early in October, visiting Glencolumcille, and this must have been when the Fourth Symphony

had been started. But he returned quickly and spent most of the month in Morar with Mary, completing the *Picaresque Comedy Overture* in full score on 19 October. Another Irish interlude took him back to Glencolumcille between 17 and 21 November, and then he and Mary returned to Morar for an extended stay that continued with one break right up to March 1931, during which time he completed the Fourth Symphony in full score.

Bax was well connected in the musical world between the wars, though he lacked the sort of professional contacts that a regular teaching appointment at the College or Academy might have given him. He did teach for a time at the Royal Academy but was so often absent that his pupils learned very little. He soon resigned. With the BBC, however, he kept up a frequent correspondence, particularly after Adrian Boult became Director of Music in 1930. Boult was certainly the avenue through which many of his works were successfully promoted, though later in the decade this did not work out so well. Of course it was not only Boult to whom he would write. This letter to Edward Clark is a typical example, written after a promised performance of *In the Faery Hills* failed to take place:

My dear Edward

All right about 'In the Faery Hills'. I was a little disappointed that it was not played, as I still think it is a picturesque piece (and perhaps not bad for 1909) also it has only been done once (by Beecham most *marvellously*) for years and years.

Now about another thing. Would you care to do another early work of mine called 'Three Orchestral Pieces', produced at a Prom in 1912? They have been rescored since and only played once in the revised form. I think they have a certain freshness which might please, although of course they are unfashionably romantic. They are scored for an early 18th century orchestra with the addition of a harp (no brass, except horns). It is a little discouraging that nearly all musical organizations in this country are still only interested in new works by native writers (though the BBC is decidedly better than others in this respect). The consequence is that the public is much more familiar with our names than with what we have written. In my own case even 'Tintagel' (which I know you like, and might easily become, I rather think, a popular piece) is only played about once in two years. However there is so much music in existence now that there is probably no remedy.

Yours Arnold[14]

Adrian Boult was sufficiently punctilious to send an internal memo at the beginning of 1931 to a member of his staff noting that 'Bax

[has] no radio and does not see *Radio Times*. Please send him a pc when any [of his] important choral or orchestral music is noted.'[15]

The composer was, of course, consulted on specific matters of interpretation in his works, and it is interesting to find him writing a letter in this connection which is most revealing about his attitude to points of detail in his own scores. Although the work referred to remains unidentified, it is significant to find him saying that 'it does not matter at all about those [string] tremolos. They are all intended to be as close as possible as a matter of fact, as far as I can remember. I am afraid this is a point about which I have always been rather careless and ambiguous until recently.'[16]

Yet Bax could be most meticulous in preparing the conductors of his music in matters of tempo and orchestral balance. Writing to Adrian Boult about *Summer Music* he asks to

fix up a day to go through 'Summer Music' ... As there is to be only one rehearsal for this concert I would like to discuss this little piece rather thoroughly with you, as it is all solo stuff and needs a good deal of latitude of tempo ... It would be a good thing if the wind players could take their parts home with them before rehearsal (*especially* the cor anglais). I know they are willing to do so, for they were very conscientious about my symphony. (I was very pleased when May [Harrison] told me you had kindly consented to take the place of the recalcitrant 'Tommy' [Sir Thomas Beecham].) I ... enjoyed revising the orchestration. It is practically a new work in a way. Nobody remembers it, certainly. Also there are a few points in 'Fand' that I would like to mention.[17]

During this time Basil Cameron became interested in Bax's music, and Bax gave him the first performances of the Northern Ballad No. 1, first in Glasgow and a few weeks later at Queen's Hall, on 3 December 1931. Cameron had secured the post of conductor of the San Francisco Symphony Orchestra, and he took with him to America the manuscript score of Bax's new symphony, the Fourth, giving the first performance on 16 March before a 7,000-strong audience. This was a work that he championed and gave several times at the Proms in the 1940s. Bax deliberately kept quiet about the new symphony after he had completed it, later saying he wanted the first three symphonies to be given an opportunity to become better known.

Philip Heseltine committed suicide at Christmas 1930: it came as a great blow. Bax wrote to Mary, 'I have had rather a shock for poor Peter Warlock committed suicide on Tuesday night. He must have been preparing to do so at the very time that we were listening to his beautiful "Corpus Christi" carol. He was always a very unhappy fellow and used to try to escape from himself by drug-taking and wild drunken riots and bad behaviour in general. But fundamentally he was an idealist; and in many ways I was fond of him.'

Cecil Gray arranged a memorial concert, which was paid for by a number of well-wishers, and Bax not only agreed to accompany four groups of songs — sixteen in all[18] — but also subscribed to the fund. On 19 January 1931 he wrote to Gray enclosing his 'sub' for the concert and adding: 'As I originally said I am quite willing to go a little further if necessary ... I am so glad that you approve of the idea of my acting as pianist on this occasion. Perhaps I know more about Phil than George Reeves or Charlton Keith, and it gives me a sad sort of satisfaction to be taking an active part in the affair.'

Bax's appearances as pianist in the late 1920s had been in partnership with May Harrison, playing Delius or his own music, and he had accompanied Tertis in the unissued records of his own Viola Sonata (see pp. 251–2). May Harrison doted on Bax at this time. She was always chasing him, and would write to him when he was in Scotland, wanting to join him. So it was not unexpected that when the question of the first performance of Delius's Third Violin Sonata by her was raised, Bax should be first choice as pianist. The Sonata had been dictated by Delius to his amanuensis Eric Fenby, and was finished by Easter 1930. May Harrison was sent for and she and Fenby played it through to the blind composer: not a note had to be changed. Bax held Delius in special affection, as we have seen, and Fenby has recalled Delius saying 'I like Bax', after one of his visits — 'I'm glad he came. If only that boy would concentrate, he'd do something fine. His form is too loose. He should concentrate! ... May Harrison's comment was "Strange! What strikes one most when rehearsing with Bax is his absolute passion for form!" '[19] Bax agreed to give the first performance of the Sonata with May Harrison at the Wigmore Hall on 6 November. To do so he had to return specially from Morar. On 15 January 1931 they played it again, the second concert performance, appearing at the afternoon concert (there had been another at 11.00 a.m.) of the Third Festival of the Federation of Music Clubs at the Grotrian Hall. In the second half Gwendolen Mason and Joseph Slater played Bax's Sonata for Harp and Flute. Other artists in the programme included Helen Perkin, Isobel Baillie and Gerald Moore, Cyril Scott and Esther Fisher. Soon afterwards Bax was back on the train to Morar with Mary, for the completion of the full orchestral score of the Fourth Symphony.

Two substantial works were written almost concurrently during 1931. They were the tone poem *The Tale the Pine-Trees Knew* (short score dated 2 October) and the Fifth Symphony (short score dated 4 November). Both exhibit Bax's preoccupation with Sibelius's music, the Symphony being inscribed to the Finnish master. They must have been gestating in Bax's mind for much of 1931, and possibly he was thinking of one or the other when he wrote to Mary in March, soon after returning from Morar: 'I have been in rather a shadowed mood all day really ... I am trying to begin a new work, and I think it must be rather like the state of mind that a woman knows when she finds she is going to have a child. One feels all nerves and rebellion and egotism, and ready to scream at nothing! It is all such a chaotic mess at present (this piece).' *The Tale the Pine-Trees Knew* was finally completed in full score in December 1931.

In considering this attractive if flawed work, we should remember Harriet Cohen's account of Bax's reaction to the first British performance of Sibelius's *Tapiola* in 1928: 'Half-way through I turned to look at Arnold, and tears were pouring down his face. Years later he was to tell me that he and Cecil Gray had decided that if Sibelius had written nothing else, this would place him among the immortals for all time.'[20]

Bax did write a programme note for the *Pine-Trees*[21] in which he admitted to the fact 'that in planning the composition I was thinking of two landscapes dominated by the pine trees — Norway and the West of Scotland — thinking, too, of the Norse sagas and of the wild traditional legends of the Highland Celt ... But this work is concerned solely with the abstract mood of these places, and the pine-trees' tale must be taken as a purely generic one. Certainly I had no specific coniferous story to relate, and would not have tried to tell it as music if I had, for I do not believe that such a task lies within the province of the art.' In idiom Bax is looking to that chilly yet passionate world he had turned to in the *Northern Ballads*. Superficial comparisons with Sibelius may well be in order, for here we find Bax exploring the textures and formal balance more completely realized later in the outer movements of the Sixth Symphony, in the finale of which he actually quotes a theme from *Tapiola*. Bax would never have been so unsubtle as even to contemplate pastiche Sibelius, and in any case his musical personality is so strong as to stamp his name on everything he wrote. However, it is certainly true that the example of Sibelius prompted Bax to examine certain facets of his own art and to develop in a particular direction. The work begins with a running semiquaver figure on the violas, similar to ideas in the last movement of the Fifth and first movement of the Sixth Symphonies that were to follow. This idea may perhaps suggest, to those who like their music to be pictorial, the wind sighing in the trees. Indeed, at about this time Bax wrote to Mary from Scotland: 'the pine trees in Rothemurchüs sighed and sighed and I longed for you to be with me.' This semiquaver figure certainly creates a restless mood until the appearance of what Bax calls in his programme note 'the principal theme'. The work is flawed by a banal subsidiary subject which soon appears (Ex. 76), and if played

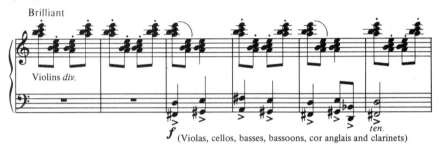

Ex. 76

four-square and emphatically not only dominates the music but also ruins its poetic effect.

What Bax refers to as 'the middle section' of the piece, though in fact the passage following the actual slow middle section, consists of a long climax which occupies twenty-three pages of the full score and leads to a triumphal statement of the principal theme. After this there is a gradual subsidence and the work ends in the fragile mists and shadows of E♭ minor, the opening figure fluttering among the wind instruments. In the published score Bax ends on an E♭ minor chord marked *sforzando* given to woodwind, harps and pizzicato strings. He must have realized that this was too emphatic for the gradual fade-down that constitutes the previous four pages, and in a letter to Julius Harrison written during the 1940s Bax wrote that 'since the printing of the score I have altered the last chord of all to pp, only strings pizz and harps', and concluded 'this sounds much better.' This ending is adopted in Bryden Thomson's digital recording of the music. There is much to admire in this atmospheric work: the evocative and thrillingly romantic horn writing (as always with Bax), the lightly touched palette which provides ever-changing orchestral colours, and the typically tuneful tranquil section with its

passing references to the idiom of other of his orchestral works, as
for example in Ex. 77. Perhaps it is only Sibelian in that it follows

Ex. 77

the Finn's example in its subject matter, for the score might well be
prefaced by the oft-quoted quatrain which Sibelius himself supplied
when asked by his publisher to explain the title of *Tapiola*:

> Widespread they stand, the Northland's dusky forests,
> Ancient, mysterious, brooding savage dreams;
> Within them dwells the Forest's mighty god,
> And wood-sprites in the gloom weave magic secrets.

Like *Tapiola*, Bax's score is notable for his originality in handling
the orchestra, and although he requires larger forces than Sibelius
called for, it finally establishes the sound world he had been aiming
at in *Winter Legends*, and which was to inform the orchestration of
the second and 'third' (see pp. 295 and 230–31) *Northern Ballads* and
the Fifth and Sixth Symphonies. The *Pine-Trees* was first performed
at a Royal Philharmonic Society concert conducted by Sir Thomas
Beecham in April 1934: Ernest Newman for one confessed that he

found it difficult, at a first hearing, to get the hang of Bax's new work 'The
Tale the Pine-Trees Knew' – not that there is anything in the idiom of it, which
is crystal-clear, to puzzle any listener, but that the connection of the ideas
sometimes evaded me ... As with all music of this type, we are conscious of
something having gone on in the composer's mind that would be clearer to us
for a little verbal explanation. The nature-pictures to which Bax confesses a
certain indebtedness have obviously made the music say this rather than that,
go this way rather than that, at more than one point; and until we know why, or
manage to persuade ourselves we know why, the work will not reveal its inner
logic to us. On Thursday I found myself liking what my ear was taking in at the
moment, but my musical imagination was sometimes anything but clear as to
the bearing of one section on another.[22]

During 1931 Bax also produced one or two minor works: the
two-piano version of his unorchestrated *Red Autumn* of 1912,
for the Bartlett-Robertson duo; the delightful if inconsequential
one-movement String Quintet (with a strongly Irish quasi-folk-
tune for second subject), and a *Valse* for harp written specially for

Sidonie Goossens to play at the Wigmore Hall in a programme that was also featuring two Van Dieren first performances.

Having completed *The Tale the Pine-Trees Knew* Bax went straight on to orchestrate the Fifth Symphony, between December 1931 and March 1932. In this work Bax again looks to Sibelius for a solution to his symphonic dilemma. In doing so he was perfectly in tune with his generation, and furthermore he also ensured the approbation of the notably pro-Sibelian critics of the period who saw the Finnish master as marking the gateway to the future. (Burnett James, in a letter to the author, made the following fascinating observation: 'The more I think about it, the more convinced I am that, much though Bax admired Sibelius, it is a red herring. I am convinced the line runs far more accurately from Mahler through Bax to Shostakovich. The famous meeting between Sibelius and Mahler seems to me to put Bax squarely in the Mahler not the Sibelius camp. I think this is important, because the eternal references to Sibelius only work to Bax's disadvantage, since his mind worked in a totally different orbit. Bax, with his confessed Russian affiliations, looks forward to Shostakovich not back to Sibelius, although at the time and for some time afterwards the real connection could not be seen.')

In the first movement Bax attempts a genuine Sibelian growth, into which his penchant for slow interludes in a basically fast movement is made to work convincingly. In fact, this first movement is something of a *tour de force*. It opens with a slow introduction in which the theme on clarinets is closely reminiscent of the opening of the slow movement of Sibelius's Fifth Symphony.

Ex. 78 (a)   Bax

violas, cellos.

Ex. 78 (b)   Sibelius

Although not an exact quotation, the allusion sounds, momentarily, breath-takingly close when heard on the orchestra. Eventually an extended bridge passage gradually increases the tension, and the

tempo, until a climax is reached. There is a pause, and then the
Allegro con fuoco of the movement proper bursts in (Ex. 79). The

Ex. 79

rhythm is that of a cake-walk, and interpreters have clearly had
difficulty in reconciling its awkward accents with the need for a
ferocious forward drive, something not easily achieved. Bax realized
this and wrote 'the most crucial part is the few pages at the beginning
of the first allegro. The strings *must* know their notes and play with
confident ferocity.'[23] The overall shape is not unlike that of the
Third Symphony, but Bax has managed to bring the slower parts of
the movement into proportion, and so the overall effect is of a
virile forward-moving exploration, crowned at the climax by the
cake-walk theme (now 4 in a bar, rather than the 2 at the beginning)
over which the trumpets briefly fanfare in triumph (Ex. 80) before

Ex. 80

the movement subsides to a re-statement of the opening slow intro-
duction and a peaceful close, quite unlike the first movement of the
Third Symphony. Writing from Morar to May Harrison, on 18
December 1931, while engaged on orchestrating the first movement,
Bax described it as 'one of my stormiest and darkest'.

It is difficult to realize how this vivid score could have been the
cause of difficulties to its first audience on account of its modernity.
Yet Ernest Newman wrote after the first performance:

For my part I doubt whether the new work will ever be as popular as either of
its predecessors; it contains too much of the harshness − even ugliness − that the
plain musical man does not like ... We all thought that Bax had exorcised his
spectres in the No. 4; but apparently they still gibber about his bed and will not
let him sleep. But though it would seem, at first, that he has here gone back to
the troubled world of Nos. 1−3, closer acquaintance with the No. 5 reveals
that he has really broken a good deal of fresh ground. His vocabulary is different, his technical procedure is different. For the moment he has turned his
back on all that the casual listener likes in music, especially beauty of colour and
grace of theme. There is not a 'tune' in the whole work that the errand boy

would choose to whistle on his rounds if he could. Bax is now curiously in-different to considerations of that kind; the shape and quality of a melody are of less concern to him than the part it can be made to play, almost in spite of itself, in the building up of a picture.[24]

The question of any programmatic intention in the symphony was also touched on in Robert Hull's enthusiastic review. 'One or two writers', he noted, 'have thought that its music recalls the wild splendour of northern forests which Sibelius captures so strikingly in *Tapiola* ... Bax, on the other hand, makes no mention of a defined programme. We cannot afford, then, to press the comparison beyond saying that the Fifth Symphony, so thrilling is its power, may well turn the listener's thoughts to some vivid scene of primaeval mag-nificence.'[25]

The brilliant pictorial opening of the slow movement – high tremolandi on the strings, running harp coloration and fanfaring trumpets – is breathtaking when first heard, and makes one think this is a deliberate evocation of some long-cherished grand sweep of landscape. In a book review[26] Bax referred to the sensation of suddenly seeing the sea at the summit of Slieve League, a favourite place of natural grandeur in the West of Ireland. To 'anyone going up from the South the sea is hidden by the landward bulk of the mountain itself, so that when it bursts into view at a height of almost two thousand feet, the sudden sight of the Atlantic horizon tilted half-way up the sky is completely overwhelming.' It is some such experience that was being remembered in the splendid and evocative opening to this passionate but autumnal (see p. 314) movement. Years before he had alluded to Debussy's *Le Promenoir des deux Amants* in the Second Violin Sonata, and now in the main theme of this slow movement (Ex. 81) he does so again, an idea echoed in the third of Debussy's orchestral *Images – Rondes de Printemps*.

cant. 3   espress.
Cor Anglais

Ex. 81 (a): Bax

Très modéré

Crois mon con - seil, chère - re Cli - mè - ne;

Ex. 81 (b): Debussy

The finale is really the weakest movement in the work. It opens with a brief introduction in which the hymn-like theme that will blaze forth in glory in the epilogue is first played. It is a forced method of trying to bring unity to a sectional movement, and it does not really work. Yet the fast version of the opening theme of the whole symphony that follows has a panache and vigour often missing from Bax's orchestral movements, and Bax sustains it for twenty-nine pages before it loses impetus and slows to *Lento* and he starts to prepare the epilogue. The two ideas are combined, but the tempo is still basically slow, only the decoration creating a spurious bustle. The climax, when it arrives, just happens. It is impressive but does not flow from the argument. The epilogue that follows presents the opening hymn-like theme as a sort of passacaglia, repeated in various departments of the orchestra in ever more brilliant scoring. In a live performance it can be most exciting, and even on disc sounds very grand. Yet somehow Bax's triumph is forced, and he is again writing music that he has calculated will appeal to a popular audience; it is certainly not an expression of that personal drive that informs the rest of the music.

The work which immediately followed the Fifth Symphony shares certain of its more muted characteristics, yet it has never been played. The impulse which caused Bax to write the *Northern Ballads* and *The Tale the Pine-Trees Knew* did find an outlet in a more

Ex. 82

extended symphonic work, and that was the *Sinfonietta*. The score
is dated May 1932 and is headed *Symphonic Phantasy*. In 1951 Bax
gave the score to Christopher Whelen, still unsure whether he wanted
it to be played, and referred to it as the *Sinfonietta*. 'Arnold's
Sinfonietta,' Whelen wrote on the score. Later the fifth edition of
Grove listed the work by that title. However, Whelen never played it
while he was a practising conductor and it has not been heard since.
The music is continuous but falls into three movements. It opens
Molto moderato with a soft drum roll and a quiet theme on strings,
(Ex. 82) evoking a typical calm seascape. Contrasting colour comes
with the cor anglais' autumnal answering development of this idea
accompanied by other woodwind and harp. The music changes from
the *Alla breve* opening time signature to four in a bar, at the marking
Allegro, but although Bax has noted 'not much faster', the music
becomes dramatic (Ex. 83). A typical *Più lento* is the signal for the

Ex. 83

music to advance quickly into the *Allegro deciso ma moderato* of the
movement proper. There is a strong flavour of the Fifth Symphony
and *The Pine-Trees* about much of this writing and of its scoring.
Bax maintains a convincing fast tempo right through until the coda
of the miniature movement, a big climax marked *Molto più lento e
maestoso*. This rushes straight into the middle movement, *Tempo
Primo (Alla breve)*, where above the entwining wind lines the oboe
sings a northern song of melancholy (Ex. 84), an only slightly altered
version of the opening cor anglais tune.

Ex. 84

The middle movement is predominantly lyrical, while in contrast
the last is a rhythmic *Allegro*. Towards the end the motto theme of
the whole work reappears in a triumphant version in counterpoint
with the rhythmic theme, and that, in augmentation, *Molto pesante*,
marks the close. The *Trionfale* miniature coda with which the work

ends is tinged with that brassy tub-thumping that spoils Bax's last orchestral works, but otherwise it is well worth an occasional hearing.

In this score Bax is exploring a three-movements-in-one form, perhaps influenced again by Sibelius, whose Seventh Symphony, in one movement, was itself originally called *Fantasia Sinfonico*. Bax's dissatisfaction and insecurity over the music was probably due to doubts about its form rather than its invention, which encompasses many characteristic episodes and orchestral delights. Although, perhaps, not of the impact of his greatest works, it would stand up well beside, say, *Overture, Elegy and Rondo* and some of the occasional overtures.

So successful had Bax's appearances been as pianist with May Harrison that the BBC decided to approach him again to give a solo recital, but his refusal was immediate and firm. The Imperial Concert Agency wrote to the BBC: 'We have had a letter from Arnold Bax, in which he says he must decline your engagement ... He says he has never taken himself seriously as a pianist, and the few engagements he has undertaken in recent years were only for the sake of the works of his friend, Delius.'

In March 1932 Bax was asked by his old friend Herbert Hughes to contribute to *The Joyce Book*. Jane Wilson has set this episode in context in her study of the song composer, C.W. Orr, who was also a contributor.

In 1929 friends had felt concern for James Joyce who was facing poverty in Paris, after the scandal caused by the publication and subsequent banning of *Ulysses*. The idea for a Joyce Book arose from conversations between Herbert Hughes and Arthur Bliss when they were in Paris attending the festival of contemporary chamber music arranged by Elizabeth Sprague Coolidge. Joyce was also present at the festival and caused the composers to form an association between chamber music and the poetry of Joyce. It was decided to make a volume of songs by setting the Joyce collection of poems, *Pomes Penyeach*. A different composer was to set each of the thirteen poems, giving his services free so that all royalties could go to the poet. Herbert Hughes agreed to choose the contributors and to edit the book.[27]

Hubert Foss, who by virtue of his membership of Heseltine's circle was known to Bax, designed *The Joyce Book*, an impressive publication in large format, bound in royal blue 'hand-woven silk from the Edinburgh weavers', printed on thick grey paper 'mould-made in Holland',[28] and issued in a numbered limited edition. Augustus John contributed a line drawing of Joyce as frontispiece, James Stephens a verse Prologue, and Padraic Colum and Arthur Symons prose contributions. Bax was allotted 'Watching the Needle Boats at San Sabba', a poem which exactly caught his mood at the time, and which was hauntingly set (Ex. 85).

I heard their young hearts cry-ing   Love - ward a - bove the glancing   oar

Ex. 85

The other composers were E.J. Moeran, Albert Roussel, Herbert Hughes, John Ireland, Roger Sessions, Arthur Bliss, Herbert Howells, George Antheil, Edgardo Carducci, Eugène Goossens, C.W. Orr and Bernard van Dieren.

That summer Bax and Harriet visited Sibelius, travelling with Balfour Gardiner. Bax wrote to Mary constantly on this trip and so one can keep track of his movements. They arrived in Sweden on 27 June on the Svenska Lloyd steamer *Svecia*, after a 'horrid' crossing, and were at the Grand Hotel Stockholm on the 28th and 29th. Bax found Sweden 'an unfriendly sort of place', complaining that the 'country is all the same, so it becomes rather monotonous'. They went on to Helsingfors [Helsinki] later on 29 June and were there from 2 to 6 July. 'It was rather beautiful on the sea coming from Stockholm', Bax wrote to Mary, 'sailing through thousands of fir-covered islands in the sunshine.'

Harriet Cohen was 'not one of Gardiner's favourite women,' Stephen Lloyd tells us, 'and he had to endure one uncomfortable evening alone with her in a restaurant[29] ... He accompanied her and Bax on the steamer crossing to Finland, but then parted company to visit his brother Alan and his wife Hedi who were staying with Hedi's relations. He later rejoined Bax and Cohen for a drive through the Savo province.'

'I remember', Harriet wrote in her autobiography,[30]

that Balfour regaled us with quite incredible stories about Percy Grainger, of whom he was inordinately fond ... He called him the true descendant of Grieg and certainly the tall, fair Percy with his exquisite Norwegian bride seemed the right fairy-tale being to conjure up as we sat on the balcony of the Grand Hotel in the daylit nights of the Aurora Borealis ... In Helsinki I bought a camera and we wandered around. This town rather brought to mind the turrets and towers of Scotland; 'downright Aberdeen', said Arnold with a pleased twinkle. After a short while we decided to take a little trip into the country as Sibelius, who lived at Jarvenpää, could not come into town for a few days. We went to Imatra of the wild, dashing Falls. How we sat and stared at the waters for hours every day — those waters that are known to hold sometimes a fatal attraction ...

Arnold and I had the gayest meeting with Sibelius at an outside restaurant sitting in the sun where I took their photographs, together and separately. We laughed and ate and drank, and the two composers, who liked each other on sight, got on famously. I remember noting how their talk veered round continually to history — a subject in which they were both interested. When the shadows lengthened we went to another favourite haunt of his, the Hotel Kemp and we talked about literature, art and even world politics for hours ...

A few days later I left for a tour of the lakes and forests of Karelia and a drive through the Savo province with Arnold and Balfour, who came with us for part of the time... It was high summer and I shall never forget the marvellous contrast of dark pine forests and fields of bright golden wheat. At night the mist rising from the lakes looked like smoke. We went right up towards the Russian border to the Sea of Ladoga. There, on the island of Valamo, stands the old orthodox Russian monastery, a large building, very old, but without much architectural distinction. The priests were very friendly and sweet to us and allowed us to take photographs of them. They wore long beards and on their heads black brimless hats like tall pots, with a piece of the stuff hanging down their backs ... The little journey in the boat on the pellucid water and in the soft light had a magic and unreal quality. At the entrance to the narrow firth that guards Valamo we saw, as Dumas before us, 'a little church of gold and silver, bright as a jewel, set upon velvet turf in a bower of trees'. There didn't seem to be many birds around, but then, summer in those regions lasts only a few weeks.

Bax was the first to leave Finland, returning via Copenhagen, and by August he was back in Ireland, and probably staying with the Fleischmanns, since he wrote to Mary from Kinsale in County Cork on 6 August. He was definitely feeling he had returned home. 'My Mary', he wrote, 'such a lovely day this has been full of the west of Ireland's marvellous enchantment of sun and sea and that strange feeling that there is only a thin veil between this world and some faeryland where no-one grows old and no beauty can fade.' Bax's mentioning growing old was no chance remark, for the milestone of fifty was only sixteen months away, an anniversary which he increasingly regarded with a dread bordering on the pathological. Then, as if to underline the fear, later in August his 'dear old master Frederick Corder' died, and Bax attended the funeral. 'Really rather dreadful', he noted to a friend.[31]

During that summer Bax revised *Summer Music*, thinning out the orchestration. He also wrote the Fourth, and, arguably, least successful of his piano sonatas. Its first and last movements are much leaner-textured than the earlier sonatas, and less interesting. The slow movement, however, is one of those perfect Celtic jewels which occasionally flowered in Bax's later work, and has been chiefly remarked on for the pedal G♯ that underlies much of the music. It was reputedly one of his favourite piano movements.

Probably the event of the year as far as Bax's public was concerned had been the première of *Winter Legends* in February. He had been leading up to this event for some time, and Harriet had learned the score the previous year. After its première Harriet was due to take the work to America for performance in Boston with Kussevitzky. Bax wrote to Adrian Boult, 'Before Tania goes to America with it – I know it would give both her and myself a great deal of pleasure if you could spare an evening to hear "Winter Legends" on two pianos at her house. It is already going very well, and I am not sure that it is not one of my best things. (The piano is really only an important orchestral instrument, and the work is – in a way – a symphony, except that the first movement is short and rhapsodic.) I would also like you to hear Paddy Hadley play his (as I think) beautiful and individual symphony.'[32]

Hadley's Symphonic Ballad, *The Trees So High*, had been given an amateur performance in Cambridge in 1931. Bax was particularly fond of it and his championship resulted in Boult conducting it in London on 12 January 1934. After its professional première he wrote to Hadley that he was 'tremendously moved by your work ... Really I enjoyed it more than any new work I have heard since *Tapiola*. And I rather suspect that you have been "made" in one evening, and that the next large scale piece you write will be competed for. Anyway, my dear Paddy, you deserve it. That was quite enchanting music. It was a good concert altogether. I found that Ireland's queer and rather sinister piece [the first performance of the *Legend* for piano and orchestra] got me too.'

In 1931, after the death of her brother, Harriet had toured with the cellist Gaspar Cassadó, and it was doubtless during that time that the seeds of a commission from Cassadó to Bax had been sown. The year ended with Bax in Morar. He had accepted the commission from Cassadó for a Cello Concerto, and it was written during the summer and orchestrated in the late autumn. This work was certainly not written out of a burning need to do so. 'Have you considered the horror of trying to write a cello concerto? That is my hideous fate', he wrote to a friend.[33] With this in mind, his letter from Morar to Tilly Fleischmann dated 19 November 1932, explains why performances of the Cello Concerto often fail to convince. 'I am having a lovely quiet time here on the edge of the Atlantic (and with some of the Hebrides over the Sea)', he wrote. 'I have been scoring part of a cello concerto I am trying to write for the Spaniard, Gaspar Cassadó. It is a tricky but interesting undertaking – though I would never have thought of writing such a thing if I had not been bullied into it.' Yet in 1947 Bax lamented to the BBC that it had never established itself in the repertoire, commenting, 'the fact that nobody has ever taken up this work has been one of the major disappointments of my musical life.'[34] But Beatrice Harrison, who gave most of the performances after Cassadó had premièred it, did play it many times. 'I know she must be kept in order about rubatos,' Bax wrote, 'but I do believe she puts the stuff over better than any English cellist.'[35] The Cello Concerto looks straight-forward, and yet is curiously elusive in performance, and can sound routine in less than committed hands. Raphael Wallfisch, its most recent champion, has been most persuasive in his advocacy of it, characterising the first movement with passionate intensity and a sustained command of its lyrical flight. The central *Nocturne* has always been appreciated, but needs a top-flight orchestra to project it, but critical reaction to the throw-away finale has tended to be dismissive. Yet when projected sympathetically it has delights all its own. The middle section's thematic pre-echo of the Seventh Symphony evokes special resonances for the knowledgeable Baxian, while its second subject 'Viennese tune', played by the soloist in thirds with an obbligato viola, has an unexpected character. Listening to the dueting cello and viola one listener remarked that this might be Bax's tribute to Strauss's Don Quixote and Sancho Panza, the swaying tune perhaps evoking the ambling gait of Rosenante. It is also worth noting that Moeran quarried effects in both the second and third movements for his G minor symphony, which was being composed during the time the concerto was first played.

During the winter of 1932–33 Bax orchestrated what had been enigmatically headed 'III' among the short score manuscripts of the *Northern Ballads*. Why he now dubbed it *Prelude for a Solemn Occasion*, and why it remained unplayed for fifty years, is puzzling. Much shorter than the second *Ballad*, this atmospheric tone poem exhibits the authentic Baxian spirit. For its preoccupation with the textures of the second *Ballad* and the *Sinfonietta*, wintry yet passionate, it at least deserves occasional performance.

Now that most of the orchestral works from this period are recorded, we begin to understand Bax's development between the Third and Sixth Symphonies. It is only now that we realize that Sir Adrian Boult's recording of the first *Northern Ballad*, for several years the only one of these transitional scores to be recorded, was not particularly sympathetic to Bax's idiom in this work, and hence a poor yardstick for those wishing to gain a clue to Bax's achievement at that time.

Past fifty

During the 1930s, almost without exception Bax's works were sketched out in London and orchestrated elsewhere, generally at Morar, Inverness-shire. As the decade progressed Bax's life-style became rigid in its overall pattern. Certainly the restless travel continued, his habit taking him to different places at certain times of the year, returning to London in between. Thus he would go to Morar with Mary before or after Christmas, where he would orchestrate the orchestral score of the moment. Christmas itself he endeavoured to spend with his mother in the family circle. This obviously meant a great deal to him, for during the Second World War he wrote that 'Christmas means very little to me today, when Mother was alive there was a real spiritual festivity.'[1] In the early or late summer he would go on the Continent with friends, though, strangely, not with Mary. In April 1933 it was a tour starting in Paris. However, he found the French capital 'so flustered and harassed' that they went to stay in the Forest of Fontainebleau. 'It was a blessing to escape to this quiet little village,'[2] Bax wrote from Bourron-Marlotte. Three days later they were in Venice, but Bax found it 'so dreadfully cosmopolitan and rather like an embalmed corpse.' Then, continuing by boat, they reached Belgrade on 23 April, which Bax insisted on calling 'the capital of Serbia' (they also visited Cetinje 'capital of Montenegro', and Kotor nearby). One sometimes wonders why Bax was persuaded to go on these trips, for he wrote to Mary on the 22nd, 'I keep wanting an English wood near the Thames and the little white body of my secret love ... O how lovely this sweet primitive passion is, and how grateful us two should be that we have found this marvellous accord!' After a 'stormy passage and a still more tempestuous one by car', they arrived at Delphi. On 26 April Bax wrote to Mary from the Hôtel de la Grande-Bretagne in Athens: 'The motor car we were in broke one of its axles on the awful road and we were stranded five hours in the loneliest place in the wildest mountains imaginable. Fortunately we had some food — and at last we were taken in a large lorry with some peasants, banging and jolting over the ruts until we felt as though our bones would crack. But it's fun to look back upon.'

Later in 1933 he went to Amiens; in 1934 to Paris, and several times to Cannes. At the beginning of April 1934 he went to see Delius at Grez-sur-Loing but had to report to Mary, 'the old man was too ill to see me, I don't suppose I shall see [him] again.' When in London, during the summer, cricket became an important topic — to watch, talk about and play. Between 6 and 16 August 1933 he joined his brother Clifford's cricket team for Clifford's last year as a player, and for the remainder of the 1930s Arnold too was score-keeper rather than player.

Later he would go to Ireland and stay with the Fleischmanns, who took him on trips around the south, and Aloys Fleischmann recalled that 'he was a most entertaining companion ... Tremen-dously interested in the people and places he visited, especially in the derivation of place names, he always had a fund of relevant and amusing stories to tell. Some striking quip or other would be seized upon and used as a motif, almost like a fugue subject, with continuing variation throughout the day.'[3] On these trips they travelled widely, for instance, to Lismore Castle in County Waterford, to the Rock of Cashel in County Tipperary, and to the caves of Mitchelstown in County Cork. It was at the caves, Fleisch-mann remembers, that Bax was overcome by an attack of claustro-phobia and had to be almost carried to the surface. 'We visited Herbert Hughes and his wife in their summer place in Cahirciveen, County Kerry, and on several occasions we joined a house party at Lord Monteagle's residence in Foynes, County Limerick. Lord Monteagle was a capable musician, had a fine chamber organ in his house, and he and Bax used to entertain the company playing piano duets.'[4]

Tilly Fleischmann writes: 'Bax had a habit, in company, of suddenly becoming detached and walking away humming to himself — apparently when seized by an idea. But very rarely would he be found writing in his room. Before leaving us each summer he would become acutely depressed, because he regarded his stay in southern Ireland as his annual holiday, away from work. He also greatly enjoyed his visits to the Scottish highlands, but these were mainly working periods.'[5]

Although he kept up the pretence of total severance from his wife and children, in fact he did visit them from time to time, and maintained an interest in the children. One friend recalls meeting him at Golders Green Station at which Bax sheepishly swore his friend to secrecy. Early in December 1933 he was very preoccupied over his daughter Maeve, mentioning her in letters of the time, for as he put it, 'my young daughter had a terrible accident last Tuesday and was nearly killed by a car'.[6]

He was becoming less prolific. In 1933 there was an apparent lack of composition because the Sixth Symphony was already germinating in his mind, yet it would appear that it was not until the autumn that he was able to compose, when he wrote the *Sonatina* for cello and piano, which he dedicated to Casals. Although Harriet Cohen mentions the Spanish cellist several times in her autobiography, there is no documented meeting between him and Bax, so the dedication probably merely reflects the fashionable general admiration for Casals. In three movements, the *Sonatina* was first played on 8 March 1934, by Thelma Reiss accompanied by Harriet Cohen. (It was then called Cello Sonata in D Minor, and the confusion over the name resulted in the erroneous postulation of a 'missing' cello sonata by Bax.) The first performance elicited favourable reviews, *Musical Opinion* for example reporting that it 'was given a good performance and will no doubt prove an interesting and melodious addition to the small repertoire of cellists'.[7]

On 21 October 1933 Harriet Cohen, under Constant Lambert's baton, performed the short *Saga Fragment* for piano and small orchestra that Bax had arranged from the Piano Quartet and then took the work to New York where she played it at Town Hall on 3 December. By then Bax had embarked on the orchestration of the second *Northern Ballad*, completing it in January 1934, although it was to wait another twelve years for a performance. Writing to Julian Herbage at the time of that performance, Bax said that it 'has no special programme attached to it – even less than its predecessor. It suggests merely an atmosphere of the dark north and perhaps dark happenings among the mists. I have never been able to discover whether I like this piece or not – to tell you the truth ...'.[8] Bax's closing remarks give voice to a loss of self-confidence in his own recent works at this time. The *Sinfonietta* and the *Prelude for a Solemn Occasion* were held back by Bax and have never been played;

the second *Northern Ballad* was not performed until 1946; and similar stories may be told of other works from the 1930s, including the one-time popular *Violin Concerto*. The second *Northern Ballad* is without doubt, after the symphonies and *Winter Legends*, Bax's greatest work, dating from the last thirty years of his life. It establishes the instrumental language of the Sixth Symphony in a taut sixteen-minute movement of economy and considerable emotional power. This is the world that Bax had set out to delineate in *The Tale the Pine-Trees Knew*: a very different sound world to *Fand* or even to *November Woods*. The bleak yet strong colours are evident in the opening page, which establishes the mood right from the start (Ex. 86).

Ex. 86

If we next consider the return to *Tempo Primo* (p. 36 of the manuscript score), we may see that it shows the most overt influence that Bax ever allowed Sibelius to have on his actual *sound*, though, as can be seen, Bax's signature is never in doubt (Ex. 87).

Ex. 87

The work relates to the Sixth Symphony not in actual notes but in its exploration of textures and sounds new to Bax's music that are extensively used in the symphony. The dominance of the woodwind and the translucent textures and the horn writing are particularly notable, such as the marvellous example in Ex. 88.

Ex. 88   horns

Stormy seascapes are a part of both the *Ballad* and the Sixth Symphony. But the music is much less decorated than it was even in the Third Symphony, and the pacing of the final climax of the *Ballad* looks forward to the symphony that was to follow. Perhaps the most gripping part of this finally exultant, though far from happy score, is the *Poco più mosso* coda with which it ends. Here in six glorious pages the music ends on a note of affirmation, by constantly resolving upwards, underlined by a side-drum tattoo almost identical with that at the end of the Fifth Symphony. As the music ceases we may imagine Bax gazing at the snowy landscape near Morar still dreaming his indomitable dream of Tír na nÓg across the icy waves, beyond the blue-grey shapes of the islands; the bronze winter sun and purple-grey clouds marking the distant land of eternal youth which he had once glimpsed but could never attain.

During February Bax orchestrated three of his songs, 'A Lyke Wake', 'Wild Almond' and 'The Splendour Falls'. He tried to interest the BBC in these, in a letter dated 9 April to Adrian Boult referring to a 'new work for soprano and orchestra'. However, though they appear never to have been played, the fact that two were later to be memorably set by Britten would make the performance of the Bax songs of particular interest, for they can certainly hold their own against most competition. At present the orchestral scores of the last two are missing.

Of interest from the point of view of Bax's own attitude to his art, and the balance between form and invention in his music, was a performance of the First Symphony given the same month, where for the first time Bax made a cut in the first movement. He explained that 'a cut has been made between the second bar [of] p[age] 37 to the fifth bar [of] p[age] 40 as the composer believes that the shape of the first movement is thereby considerably improved.'[9] It is unlikely that anyone today would countenance such a cut, which demonstrably does the music harm, yet to see Bax so sensitive to criticism of his formal procedures that he should agree to it is further indication of his deep-down insecurity at the height of his fame.

Bax always enjoyed a full and varied social life. Nearby in Fellows Road lived Julius Harrison with whom he had renewed acquaintance in 1929 at the time of Harrison's second marriage, and in the early 1930s they became good friends. It was their common enthusiasm for cricket that initially brought them together. When Bax was invited to dinner at the Harrisons, if Harriet was in town he would always ask if Tania could come too. The Harrisons did not like her, considering her too artificial and shallow both as a pianist and personally. But though her flamboyant style did not find favour with them, she nevertheless usually accompanied Bax on these occasions. Harrison was also conductor of the Hastings Municipal Orchestra at the White Rock Pavilion. There he was able to be

patron to both Bax as composer and Harriet as performer. The
story is told of how, one year, they decided to drop Harriet's engagement. A little later Bax arrived on one of his regular visits, alone. He
was clearly very ill at ease all the day long, and just as he was about
to leave he blurted out, like a naughty schoolboy — 'I say, you
might give Tania a date this year'.

Bax kept up his old friends, too. For example an acquaintance
from the early 1930s encountered him on top of a bus in 1934 or
1935, and he remarked that he was on his way to Lady Cholmondley's for dinner (Mrs Christopher Lowther became Lady George
Cholmondley by her third marriage — see pp. 154–5).

Bax's mother would give family parties at Pagani's, and the reception accorded to her two sons is indicative of their different
characters. Clifford would arrive, very dapper in evening dress with
cloak and stick, and the waiters would all busy themselves round
him. Later Arnold arrived, looking somewhat down at heel in an
ageing raincoat, and was ignored, so that Mrs Bax had to say to the
head waiter, 'That too is my son!'

Harriet Cohen gave a recital at the Salle Gaveau in Paris in May.
Bax was there and they both visited Pierre Monteux's 'charming
little house just outside Paris'. Harriet Cohen, in describing Bax's
visit in her autobiography, told of how he had come over to give her
'what he called one of his "treats", which consisted mainly of
visiting "Boîtes" by night and forests by day; we went to the Trianon
[at Versailles] which he later described had a strangely electric atmosphere. With his innate sensitivity he had immediately felt that the
place was haunted, the strange thing being that neither of us had
then read *An Adventure* by Miss Jourdain and Miss Moberley.'[10]

In May, the BBC organized the London Musical Festival, and
Adrian Boult gave the Fifth Symphony in the concert which pres-
ented the winning entry in the *Daily Telegraph* Overture competition
— the *Festival Overture* by Cyril Scott. Then on Wednesday 20 June,
Bax was made a Doctor of Music *honoris causa* at the Encaenia at
Oxford, on the nomination of Lord Halifax. *The Times* reported:

Mr Arnold Bax inspired the Orator to a burst of lyric poetry:
> En quem non Polyhymnia
> nec torvis oculis Melpomene videt;
> hunc discordia quae prius
> in cantus docuit flectere consonos
> montis culmine Celtici
> Musa Hiberna novos suppeditans modos.

The names of Mr Bax's chief compositions were ingeniously woven into verse:

> Hoc ducente pius jam didicit chorus
> Aestatis Magicae dies
> et laetis Patriam tollere laudibus
> Loricam et Patrici sacram.

The Chancellor described Mr Bax as:

> Vir Musis amicissime, laurea donande Apollinari,
> citharae et plectri Polyhymniae callidissime.

> *(Here we have a man who is favourably regarded by
> Polyhymnia and Melpomene [two of the Muses]. The Irish
> Muse, rich in fresh harmonies, has taught him, from the
> summit of a Celtic Parnassus, to mould former discords
> into concordant, melodious sounds.*
> *Under his direction, the devout choir has already learnt
> to sing the joyous praises of Enchanted Summer days and
> of our Fatherland and Patrick's holy Breastplate.*
> *You are, sir, a man dearly beloved by the Muses, worthy
> of a laurel crown sacred to Apollo, and highly skilled on
> the lute and lyre of Polyhymnia.)*

(translation by Graham Parlett)[11]

In the early autumn, Bax had two works, *St Patrick's Breastplate* and *Summer Music*, played at the Three Choirs Festival, which was held that year at Gloucester. The weather was good, but he hated the atmosphere of the town, being on his own and 'very considerably bored' and wrote to Mary on 6 September that the Midland and Royal Hotel was no good at all, 'unrelenting turmoil'. More surprisingly, perhaps, he continued that he 'didn't like the music': 'This afternoon I ran away and went to the inviting Cotswolds all in sunshine.' It was to Painswick that he escaped, a place he had not previously visited. Eventually it was the turn of *his* music, and after some initial worry he was able to report that the 'two pieces went better after all.' By then the surrounding countryside had established a compulsive appeal and he 'went everyday to Painswick Beacon ... Somehow,' he wrote, 'I could not keep away from the lovely place.'

In June he finished his short, two-movement Clarinet Sonata, written for his fellow cricketer in the Old Broughtonians, Hugh Prew, who finally gave its first performance at the Aeolian Hall on 17 June 1935. This sonata and the Cello Sonatina are two examples of delightful, enjoyable music written with little thought but giving pleasure. If only they were technically easier they would have proved splendid introductions to Bax's art for the amateur instrumentalist. Unhappily there are all too few works of this nature in Bax's *oeuvre*.

The 1930s saw the appearance of all Bax's mature chamber works for large ensembles. After the *Nonett* of 1930, perhaps the most successful and certainly the most widely known of this group of pieces, there appeared a series of similar works for other instrumental combinations.

In October 1934 he completed the Octet (called *Serenade* in the short score) for the unusual combination of horn, piano and string sextet. Later, the song 'Eternity' was orchestrated (6 November) and *Fatherland* revised. However, the most important work of the year, and the one that must have dominated Bax's imagination over all this time, was the Sixth Symphony.

In the journal *Musical Opinion* in 1934, there appeared an announcement that Bax was writing a second viola sonata for Lionel Tertis. Two fragments of what we can now recognize as material from the Sixth Symphony survive written out for viola and piano. The evidence is too slender to say that the work became the Sixth Symphony, merely that a page or two work well for the smaller forces. (See plate 18.)

In the Sixth Symphony, which many consider to be his finest symphony, and which is certainly the climax of the music written by Bax in the 1930s, he returns to the theme of *The Tale the Pine-Trees Knew* in a thrillingly successful essay in relentless nature-music, which constitutes the main section of the first movement. The opening with its ostinato bass and grinding wind chords is unlike anything else Bax wrote. After the grim opening we are presented with a wild landscape which is finally assaulted by a violent and spectacular musical storm. In this symphony we are in the far north, possibly even in Morar where it was written in the winter of 1933–4. (Certainly Bax is reported as identifying a passage in the slow movement as deriving from a view of the islands across the wintry sea.) This is a more primaeval, primitive vision than that in any of his earlier symphonies, Bax's mood in it perhaps underlining his feelings about approaching old age.

The slow movement is beautifully lyrical with typically simple yet haunting melodic ideas, and with the device of the 'Scotch snap' to remind us that Scotland is its location. After one of the composer's most succinct first movements and evocative slow ones comes his most original finale, having itself almost the stature of a separate work. Perhaps its most original feature is the tripartite form: Introduction — Scherzo and Trio — Epilogue. The movement is derived from the opening clarinet solo; around this the other winds gradually entwine, a conception reminiscent of the opening of the Third Symphony. In this movement Bax alludes to the theme of Sibelius's *Tapiola* — though in a quite un-Sibelian way. He first makes passing reference in the interweaving winds during the slow introduction, but the main quotation is the subject of the passionate high string phrases that follow the Trio.

Strings

Ex. 89   Sibelius, *Tapiola*

Clarinet in B♭

Ex. 90 (a)   Sixth Symphony — slow introduction to last movement

Dramatico

Strings (doubled octave higher)

Ex. 90 (b)   Sixth Symphony — after the Trio

Peter J. Pirie encapsulated the power of this music when he wrote how 'the conflict at the heart of Bax finally explodes in his Sixth Symphony. In no other work does the head-on collision between beauty and brutality express itself more forcibly.'[12] The work culminates in a terrific climax; again quoting Mr Pirie, 'the roots of the earth are being torn up, and we have a sense not merely of the breaking of nations but of the passing of worlds'. This seemingly unresolvable cataclysm is hauntingly brought into perspective by the Epilogue. This luminous half-lit world still has a slight menace about it until the last nine bars, when ethereal horns call over hushed chords on harp and wind to bring Bax's tempestuous vision to a close. The Sixth Symphony marked the very peak of Bax's powers — a peak that he never regained. Over the last twenty years of his life the urge to compose gradually left him and he wrote less and less. The Symphony was first played at Queen's Hall in November 1935 under the baton of Sir Hamilton Harty, for whom Walton had recently written his blazing First Symphony. One critic described the performance of the Bax as 'glowing and extremely effective' and Bax himself was ecstatic about it, writing to Harty, 'you realized everything I wanted and indeed took some of it into a world of beauty I did not know the work compassed'.[13]

The following year, 1935, was a muted one for Bax, as far as composition was concerned. He started what was apparently intended as a multi-movement piano work under the generic title *Legends*, but only the first movement appears to have been completed, and this is now known as just *Legend*. It was written for a young Australian pianist, John Simons, who featured several of Bax's works in Wigmore Hall recitals in the 1930s. Most notable was the Third Piano Sonata, his performance of which '*enormously* impressed' Bax, who was so taken by 'the sensitivity [he] showed towards the inner meaning of the work'[14] that it revived in him his original impulse when writing it. However, somehow Harriet got hold of the manuscript of the *Legend* and did not pass it on to him until many years later when he had given up concert work. He finally played it, on Radio 3 in 1969, and in public at the British Music Information Centre in London, in October 1983.

This was the beginning of a waning of public and official interest in Bax's music, imperceptible at first, more overt towards the end of his life. Typical of the resistance he was finding was the attitude of the BBC, whither he directed an increasing number of letters pleading for this work or that. He wrote to Boult offering the revised version of the three pieces for orchestra ('only once played'), *Cortège* and *Nympholept*, but nothing came of it. He also wrote to the conductor Leslie Heward suggesting *Walsinghame* but no performance ensued. However, the success of his works at Gloucester must have gone down well with the Three Choirs Festival Committee, who decided to commission a choral work for Worcester in 1935.

Bax responded to the commission with *The Morning Watch*, to the poem by Henry Vaughan. It will be noted that for his second attendance at Worcester (his previous one being *To the Name* in 1923), Bax again turned to the metaphysical poets. Although Bax was not a religious man in the sectarian sense, he had a deeply mystical side to his nature. Tilly Fleischmann has written about this aspect of Bax's personality, and though his non-Catholic friends have cynically found much of Mrs Fleischmann's own Catholic attitude embodied in it, it nevertheless rings true. She wrote,

'With all Arnold's outward realism and agnosticism pertaining to religion, he had a peculiar love for anything mystical or deeply religious. And, although he seldom revealed it, when he did so, he was as simple and believing as a child.'[15]

The two poems he chose to set in *The Morning Watch* and *To the Name* were strongly contrasted in idiom, a contrast that was reflected in the finished pieces. The Vaughan, a relatively straightforward lyrical poem, was set in a more straightforward way. The decorative, complex writing and tortuous imagery of Crashaw was reflected in the florid chromatic style typical of Bax's earlier output.

The Morning Watch opens with a long orchestral introduction which occupies more than a quarter of the work. The music starts *Poco lento tranquillo*, and then at the fifteenth bar Bax indicates his descriptive intent by marking 'sunrise' against a rising figure in the bass. The central point of the work is at the words 'Prayer is the world in tune ...', a text that was not lost on those attending the first performance against a background of the emergence of Fascism and, though still distant, the threat of war in Europe. Also of interest at the beginning of this section is a typically Holstian descending marching bass figure, repeated over and over again, although here Bax cannot resist making chromatic changes as the music progresses. However, the work as a whole is remarkably diatonic — the chromaticism that characterized the earlier Crashaw work does not intrude unnecessarily here. The piece ends with an extended Amen, foreshadowing the tranquil epilogue of the Seventh Symphony.

Harriet Cohen and Vaughan Williams were both at Worcester in 1935. Vaughan Williams's *Sancta Civitas* was also to be played, and Harriet remembered in her memoirs how 'VW had a quietening effect on our nervous friend, I noticed, as I sat pinned between them waiting to hear *The Morning Watch*. The setting of the sublime words "Prayer is the world in tune" was as Vaughan Williams said then "of ineffable beauty". We found the "working out" fine chorally, but a little "too exciting, too Wagnerian" perhaps for the Cathedral environment and, to my mind, certainly under-rehearsed and rather ragged orchestrally, in performance: the choir was magnificent.'[16]

During 1935 Bax had been 'recognized' by another university, when Durham gave him an Honorary D. Mus. But these occasions were anguish for him and one suspects that he had to be strongly persuaded to accept. However, that Christmas there came a tribute that meant far more: on returning home to Fellows Road he found a parcel awaiting him. It contained VW's Fourth Symphony, in-scribed to him. He wrote immediately:

Christmas

My dear Ralph,

Coming back from a few days in Devon tonight I found your ever-to-be-honoured present awaiting me. This is the finest tribute of affection and com-radeship that has ever been paid me, and I shall value it all my life. I need say no more than this.

I see you have produced yet another new work in the shape of a ballet. I must say that I envy you, for I am derelict in the doldrums just now and cannot get down to anything. I hope this may be only temporary but you once said 'One is wretched when one is in artistic labour, and still more so when one isn't.' So *you* know how I feel.

Yours most gratefully, Arnold [17]

It was about this time that Bax was paid what he called the 'greatest compliment I have ever received'. This occurred when thirty-seven copies of his published works, including full scores and chamber music, were stolen from Nottingham Public Library.[18]

The composer E.J. Moeran was particularly attracted to Kenmare on the Kenmare river in County Kerry, and Bax would join him there in the early spring, a rendezvous the two continued to keep during much of the 1930s. At that time Moeran was endeavouring to complete his Symphony in G minor, a work that clearly reflects Bax's influence as well as the influence of other composers, notably Sibelius and Vaughan Williams. Yet in the symphony Moeran has welded the clearly discernible contributions from his contemporaries with such memorable style and conviction that it is one of the most glorious of English symphonies. Bax and Moeran would stay at the Landsdowne Arms Hotel in Kenmare, where Moeran lived for part of the year and where he was very popular with the locals. Bax was there in May 1936, when he must have been writing the Third String Quartet. In a programme note Bax admitted that the first movement of the quartet was 'probably influenced by the coming of spring in beautiful Kenmare'.[19] Summer weather was early in that part of Ireland in 1936, Bax writing to Mary on 9 May that there were 'more bluebells and primroses than ever'. He went on to des-cribe how he 'walked alone by the sea last night and it did not seem earthly at all ... It might have been the western faeryland of which the old Irish legends tell. It seems almost unnecessary for them to have invented such a place — Ireland being what it is.'

In August 1937 he visited Kenmare while staying at Glengariff, and described another nocturnal vision of the sea in a letter to Mary: 'the whole world turned olive green with a luminous dark golden glow through it and then the nearly full moon rose and flung a silver veil on the sea. Irish enchantment indeed!'

The year 1936 saw a number of new works, though all have been neglected for many years, and it is doubtful if any of them have received more than two or three performances — with the possible exception of the *Overture to Adventure*. These works were (in order of composition): *Rogue's Comedy Overture;* the *Threnody and Scherzo* (for bassoon, harp and string sextet); the Concerto for flute, oboe, harp and string quartet (or Septet as we shall henceforth refer to it) that he arranged from the Sonata for flute and harp; the Third String Quartet; and the *Overture to Adventure*. The two orchestral overtures were soon played, and the second published.

The String Quartet was first heard in 1937 in a broadcast. The stimulus for the exuberant first movement we have already noted. Although Bax said he wanted the slow movement to speak for itself, he wrote that the third 'consists of two strongly opposed elements — a rather sinister and malicious scherzo, and a dreamy, remotely romantic trio. This contest is finally won by the scherzo, when it converts the subject of the Trio to its own way of thinking.' (Bax had first intended to have the two middle movements the other way round, but changed his mind before the work was heard.) 'The texture of the finale is rougher and more robust than the rest of the work, though there is a softening of the mood towards the abrupt and impetuous closing bars.'[20] In the trio of the third movement Bax makes a fleeting but unmistakable reference to Elgar's *Pomp and Circumstance* March No. 4.

In the autumn, the London Contemporary Music Centre promoted a concert of recent chamber music of Bax, at which the Octet, Septet and *Threnody and Scherzo* all appeared. Bax's old friends Arthur Alexander and his wife, the composer Freda Swain, were also close friends of the composer Medtner, and it was probably they who introduced Bax's music to the Russian emigré, and arranged for Bax to write inviting him to the concert. 'I have heard that you like my music,' Bax wrote, ' and so I have much pleasure in sending you a ticket for a concert of recent chamber works of mine, hoping you may be able to come. I have known your own music for a long time, and have always admired your rhythmical invention, and great contrapuntal ingenuity in writing for the piano. I greatly appreciated

your own and Rachmaninoff's interest in my 3rd Symphony.'[21]
However, a shadow was cast over the concert by the Abdication.
Harriet Cohen wrote that:

On the day of the Abdication, 11th December, I played in a concert given by the
London Contemporary Music Centre at the Aeolian Hall. It was interrupted for
the transmission of the BBC's national programme in which at one minute past
ten King Edward VIII bade farewell to the nation in a speech lasting seven
minutes. This sad event cast a shadow over the first performance of Arnold
Bax's Octet, for solo horn and piano with six other instruments. Arnold had
specially written this work for that divine horn player Aubrey Brain, father of
the brilliant Denis, and myself.

None of these three works was sufficiently strong to establish
itself at the time. The Octet, in two movements, is the best, with its
singing invention and characteristic writing for the horn, and it fully
justifies the title 'Serenade' with which Bax headed the short score.
It really deserves to be better known. *Threnody and Scherzo* is less
memorable, though on a similar scale and also employing string
sextet. It was surprisingly successful when later played by bassoon,
harp and string orchestra. The Septet is longer, being in three
movements: an arrangement of the earlier Sonata for flute and
harp, with its engaging 'Irish' thematic material, it would be well
worth programming again. With, say, the Ravel *Introduction and
Allegro*, it would make a favourable impression, and is for the same
forces as the Ravel, except that Bax exchanges Ravel's clarinet for
an oboe.

'I can't grow up'

Early in the autumn of 1936 the BBC approached Bax and asked him to write the music for a feature planned for Christmas that year on an Arthurian theme. Doubtless *Tintagel* had suggested Bax's name to the producer concerned, but that had been conceived almost twenty years before, and Bax confessed that he would 'find it very difficult to recover the peculiar mood of romanticism required'. He made no bones about declining: 'I am rather tired musically', he wrote to Kenneth Wright, 'and do not want to have to work at all strenuously this autumn.'[1]

The commission for *King Arthur* actually went to young Benjamin Britten – his first – and was finally produced by D. G. Bridson on St. George's Day 1937. Britten's music achieved more permanent status in the revised third movement, *Impromptu*, of his Piano Concerto.

Kenneth Wright's reply to Bax's refusal to consider *King Arthur* hinted that if Bax were to produce a Coronation March for the forthcoming ceremony the following year it would receive wide performance. There was no contract or formal commission, but nevertheless Bax set to work. Bax was not very good at these ceremonial works, and what he produced, while vivid, also tended to be a little mechanical, and too long for an occasional piece. The score was sketched during that autumn, and Bax took it with him when he set out for Scotland in mid-January. He travelled alone, although Mary was to join him later.

On 18 January we find him in Invergarry, but the hotel he was aiming for turned out to be full and so he travelled straight onto Morar. 'It is wildly cold,' Bax wrote to Mary on the 19th, 'and I have never seen such deep snow on the mountains.'

The McKellaigs, proprietors of the Station Hotel, made a point of welcoming Bax as they did every year. They 'look so pleased to see me', he wrote to Mary, adding, 'and when Miss McKellaig said with surprise, "Are you alone?", it was so lovely to say, "only temporarily, I hope".' 'It feels absolutely uncanny to be in Morar without you,' said Bax, 'and I simply would not have come if it were not for the expectation that you will be with me (and *very very* close) in a few days time.' On his first evening Bax was delighted by a friendly surprise that awaited him, when he was presented with a token of his host's admiration of his music in the form of 'a half bottle of champagne with a note from the manageress thanking me for the pleasure my music had given her'. The next day was the coldest Bax could ever remember encountering in Morar and he wrote again, 'the days seem so long without you'.

Once Mary had joined him, Bax set to work to score the march, which he finally dubbed *London Pageantry* (later changed to *London Pageant*, by which it is now known), and completed in full score during February. 'The scoring was a very laborious affair,' Bax later recalled, a point he underlined at the time by writing, 'finished thank God!' in his score. Mary remembers Bax later paraphrasing the Bishop to Mozart when discussing it with his friend John Ireland — 'too many notes, too many notes!'

London Pageant was the only work that Bax completed in 1937, though later in the year he commenced work on his Violin Concerto. But although he may have had high hopes of the march, and fancied 'the piece might make some sort of popular success',[2] it was outshone by Walton's *Crown Imperial*. At the ceremony, a Bax work *was* played, but he can hardly have been satisfied that it was the slow movement of the Third Symphony, a piece which Walford Davies (then Master of the King's Musick) and Dr Ernest Bullock chose: Walford Davies was never on Bax's list of friends! In the BBC's Coronation week programme, *Tintagel* was the only Bax work down to be played, although he did attempt to get the new work substituted. Clarence Raybould had to write to tell him that the march would not be heard. However, it was broadcast under Albert Coates later in the month. A suggestion was made that it should be played at the Proms, and although Bax scoffed at the idea as being too long after the event, it was actually first heard in public at Queen's Hall on 2 October during that year's Proms.

Although Adrian Boult always disclaimed any special interest in Bax, he in fact gave many of the finest performances of a limited repertoire of Bax's music. As Harriet Cohen remarked to him during the war, 'you have a wonderful feeling for AB's tempi.[3] (This is very effectively demonstrated in his recordings on Lyrita SRCS 62, which includes *Tintagel* and *Fand*, and in particular on Lyrita SRCS 37, which offers a memorable *November Woods*.) In November 1936 Boult conducted *The Tale the Pine-Trees Knew*, a rendering which so deeply moved Harriet that she said she 'could not speak about it'.[4] Then in February 1937 Boult presented the Sixth Symphony in a programme which also included the *Chaconne* from Purcell's *King Arthur*, Prokofiev's First Violin Concerto and *The Rite of Spring*. Writing in the *Sunday Times*, Ernest Newman articulated the feeling that he gradually developed throughout the 1930s concerning Bax's hidden programmes. 'The Bax symphony is hugely impressive,' he wrote, 'but I must confess that I still cannot see my way quite clearly through it. I still feel that there is something at the back of it all that controls the substance and the shape of the work but that for the present eludes the most attentive and engrossed listener. Why all this *Sturm and Drang* in one movement after another? And in what sense is the curious ending the "Epilogue" to what has gone before? These are questions we shall presumably have to settle for ourselves in the light of increasing acquaintance with the symphony: but even with these problems unresolved there can be no doubt as to the fine quality and the elemental power of the work.'[5]

Quite why Bax was singled out for a knighthood in the Coronation Honours List is hard to explain. After all, his contribution to the musical life of the country was almost solely as a composer, and one temperamentally far removed from the establishment. Possibly the most convincing explanation is that it was due to determined string-pulling by friends and admirers, and the name of May Harrison has been suggested as a moving light in this respect. Bax always shrank from the limelight and was obviously disconcerted by the offer of his knighthood, which reached him in Ireland. He must have gone there early that year, and was touring with an Irish civil servant friend, who one morning at their hotel persuaded him to open his mail, which Bax thought 'just bills or business letters': a cream-wove envelope turned out to contain the communication from Buckingham Palace. His immediate reaction was to refuse. He made excuses: 'I like peace and quiet ... I hate being sought after ... as plain Mr, I travel about Europe on the cheap and this would be impossible if I was Sir Arnold Bax ... No: I must refuse.' His friend replied, 'On the contrary, you must graciously accept the knighthood. This is an honour not just for you personally but for Irish music in general.

For the sake of Irish music you must accept.' 'Let me think about it,' replied Bax.

When they reached the next village (a remote one in Co. Kerry) the car was stopped and the driver hustled Bax into the tiny rural Post Office where he thrust an Inland Telegraph form in front of him. His friend literally stood over the composer whilst he worded the telegram accepting the offer of knighthood. A perplexed but excited postmistress coped with the unusual situation and the visitors went on their way. Nothing more was said about the episode, but next morning most of the Irish papers carried headlines announcing the news – a striking tribute to the efficiency of the Post Office grapevine in a country where honours and recognition coming from across the Channel received little, if any, attention.[6] He was back in England early in May – and his printed acknowledgements to the many letters of congratulation were postmarked Hampstead on 22 May. In May too, on the 16th, the new Third Quartet was first given by the Griller Quartet in a broadcast on the BBC National Programme.

Another Irish friend, first encountered in 1937, was Anne Crowley. Some part of the summer was reserved for staying with the Fleischmanns as usual, and it was on one of these visits that Anne Crowley recalled she 'first met Dermot O'Byrne, as he would like me to remember him, driving from Cork to Carraigh Bui where the Fleischmanns had taken a summer cottage on the shore of Bantry Bay. I was driving a Morris Coupé. The hood being down I threw my new hand-woven Donegal tweed about him. He looked as happy as if he were entering Tír na nÓg. There was no getting to know each other; we were kindred spirits from the start.'[7] But it was not until Bax sent a Christmas card the following December that a correspondence between them started which was notable for being conducted largely in Gaelic, and they met whenever Bax was in Dublin.

Bax started work on his Violin Concerto during June, completing it in short score at the beginning of October. At the end of that month Harriet Cohen programmed a complete Bax concert at the Aeolian Hall in which the Griller Quartet joined her in the Bax Piano Quartet and Quintet. Harriet Cohen recalls in her autobiography the reception Sir Henry Wood, who had got out of his sick-bed specially to come, gave to the Bax Quintet. He wrote, 'What a really great composer Arnold is. Your balance at the piano was perfect, and so dramatic – do tell the Griller Quartet how fine they are.' Vaughan Williams was also there, Miss Cohen tells us, 'never missing a performance of the work he so adored'.[9]

This was one of only a very few performances Harriet was able to give during 1937, as she was ill for most of the year and not able to accept any public engagements until the following March. She also travelled abroad some of the time, and so Bax saw little of her.

In the Violin Concerto Bax continues to explore the formal innovations that he had started in the last movement of the Sixth Symphony. The concerto is in the customary three movements, but the first is, like the last of the symphony, in a tripartite form, this time consisting of Overture (*Allegro risoluto*), Ballad and Scherzo (*Allegro moderato*). The work is notable for a number of reasons, particularly for thematic quotation and self-quotation in the slow movement. But perhaps most noteworthy is its overall character of extrovert lightweight romanticism which, as William Mann has observed, 'sprang surprises in plenty on those who attended its first performance expecting to hear a thickly-scored, highly-coloured, perhaps diffuse rhapsody — something like a long, accompanied cadenza. There is none of that here. This concerto's three-movement design is concisely organized, its texture clear-cut. The solo part offers opportunities to a brilliant player, but there is something almost classical in the work's avoidance of heavy emotion or anything so loquacious as a cadenza — almost, but not quite, for its amiable lightly romantic freshness rather recalls Mendelssohn's Violin Concerto.'[10] It was probably for this reason that during its composition when a friend enquired what it was 'like', he replied, 'it's rather like Raff',[11] meaning mainly romantic and not expressing a hidden personal programme. In fact, this was 'pure' music — entertaining, delightful, but not expressing Bax's usual emotional conflicts. As such it succeeded with early audiences because they could follow it, and for a time it became one of his most popular works although not exhibiting his, until then, characteristic fingerprints. As Peter J. Pirie has observed, this popularity was unexpected — and so was Bax's reaction to this success. 'Ironically, Bax was so upset by what he thought, undoubtedly correctly, to be the exaggerated praise of his Violin Concerto at the expense of his symphonies, that he thought of withdrawing the Concerto altogether.'[12] After completing the full score in March 1938, Bax did not announce the work's existence until commissioned to write a work for St Cecilia's Day in 1943.

The Concerto was his only completely successful essay in what we can now see as his late style. Most of the rest of his music in this vein added little to his reputation, and in one or two works he actually did himself a disservice. Bax wrote in September 1939 that 'for

several years I have had no joy in my work, well I must go on from
day to day in hope and longing.'[13] There really were only two
exceptions to that generalization – the Seventh Symphony and the
Rhapsodic Ballad, to which we shall come shortly.

The first movement of the concerto succeeds through its attractive
tunes and colourful orchestration – an orchestration, what is more,
that eschews the heavy brass (trombones and tuba) and uses little
percussion. The last movement, a dancing rondo, is also attractive,
with vigorous echoes of earlier 'Irish' music, and a deliciously contrasted slow waltz. These show Bax's mastery of the confectioner's
art at its most inventive. But it is in the slow movement that we find
typically enigmatic textual problems which might not be noticed by
a casual listener. To understand fully the strangeness of Bax's sources
in the slow movement of the concerto, it is necessary to recount an
anecdote told by Alan Richardson – an Academy musician friend of
Bax. Richardson met Bax on a bus some time in the early summer of
1937 and enquired what he was writing at that time. Bax replied
that he was at work on a pastiche eighteenth-century sonata, a reply
which caused much amusement for Bax was well known for his views
on 'sewing-machine music'. However, there survives a manuscript in
Bax's hand of a four-movement 'Sonata in B♭ "Salzburg" – Paris
(conjectured) *circa* 1788' (Allegro moderato – Lento espressivo –
Minuet and Trio – Rondo). At the head of the score Bax has written
'author unknown'. Bax was not completely successful in disguising
his musical personality, however, although the pastiche is delightfully
clever, and various progressions and his use of the keyboard ultimately
give the game away. Quite why Bax should have put himself through
this exercise is unknown. In the slow movement of the Sonata
appears a passage which becomes the decorated 'Mozartian' second
subject idea in the concerto, that has been compared to the 'classical'
writing in the post-Second War concertos of Strauss. (See Ex. 91.)
The opening idea of Bax's slow movement alludes to the Elgar Violin
Concerto, presumably a conscious quotation on Bax's part, although
the shape of the music might also be construed to be a quotation
from Benjamin Dale's Piano Sonata of 1905, in which Dale appears
to anticipate the Elgar. One suspects that both allusions are
conscious. (If the allusion to Dale dated from 1943 it might thus be a
tribute to Dale who had recently died.) Although the direct quotation
may be from the Dale, Bax underlines the fact that he is also making
his fourth Elgarian allusion in a major work by his orchestration –
suggesting the guitar effect in the violins for which Elgar asks in the

Ex. 91   The 'decorated' second subject of the slow movement of the Violin Concerto, and its original appearance in the 'Salzburg' Sonata.

last movement of his Concerto at the appropriate point in the score –
and possibly also by the Elgarian sweep to the opening orchestral
tutti of the first movement. The concerto was apparently intended
for Heifetz, to whom it was dedicated on the manuscript score,
a connexion probably deriving from Harriet's activities and
from the fact that Heifetz transcribed *Mediterranean* as a successful
encore, which he recorded. However, the published violin and piano
reduction bears no dedication, Heifetz never played the work, and
Bax, as we have seen, appeared to lose all confidence in his score.

At the end of November, Bax first encountered Christine Ryan, a
young girl very much less than half his age. They spent Sunday
5 December together, and she immediately caught him up into a
familiar world of romantic make-believe. He wrote to her:

I keep thinking of you, Christine, and feel that I must talk to you for a little.
Sunday afternoon seems like a lovely sad dream (smouldering Autumn sunset,
fallen leaves, blue mist among the trees, drifted scent of wood-smoke) I don't
know why sad – except that *you* are not happy and I could never think of you
lightly.
   We talked of playing chess but it seems funny to think of contending with
you in any way. I doubt whether I could concentrate upon it! Perhaps I will try,
though.
   You asked me what I thought of you and I said silly things in reply. So I tell
you now that I understand and love your fastidiousness and delicacy of thought
and feeling. That is all too rare now-a-days – there are not many faery princesses
exiled in the world of 1937.
   My love to you from A.
   Do you know I was so bemused when I left you that I got into the wrong
train – had to come back and start again, and arrived forty minutes late!

For a short time their correspondence and their meetings became
very frequent. After he was fifty Bax became over-sensitive about his
age. He worshipped youth almost above all else, and opened his
autobiography, *Farewell, My Youth*, a few years later with a 'hard
curse upon increasing old age'.[14] This brief, dreamlike affair was
really his last challenge to inexorable fate that was turning him into
an old man.

On 8 December the Fifth Symphony was played. 'On Wednesday
evening there was a superb performance of my fifth symphony at
Queen's Hall', Bax wrote to Christine on the 10th. 'It was quite
thrilling to hear my ideas so perfectly expressed, and there are some
parts of the work that reminded me somehow of the wistful beauty
of last Sunday afternoon.'

It was a relationship which must have aroused echoes from Bax's past: for the moment it was passionate, but it remained largely innocent. Bax wrote to Christine just before Christmas, which was to be the climax of the affair.

Well my dark flower, I cannot tell how *you* have been feeling during these days and nights, but I have thought of you unceasingly, so that you have been like a burning rose against my heart. I keep remembering your eyes streaming with tears and the sweetness of your little breast under my hand. Oh! darling, that was all so sad and rapturous.

I got your dear letter at last on Friday evening — it was a dear letter in spite of your wanting to send me away — (*no* not 'wanting' I know!) I have read it several times. I wonder did you find some flowers and a small note on your door on Friday morning when you came back from work. I must have put them there about 11 o'clock so there was plenty of time for someone to steal them. I did ring the bell, thinking Joyce might be in, but there was no reply. I don't know what is going to happen to us. We first met in mist and darkness, both temporarily lost — and that seems to be symbolical.

Yesterday afternoon I felt I *had* to come home to this place and play the Prelude to Act III of 'Tristan' again (the one I first played to you the other day). Prelude to what for you and me, I wonder, or not a prelude to anything? (But that seems almost impossible.)

I hope you have managed to get some pleasure out of Christmas, you dear one.

As we have seen Bax could be particularly revealing in his letters to those who held the key to that world of dream, where in many respects he preferred to be. Yet after Christmas he clearly felt things were getting out of hand and explanations were necessary. On 29 December he wrote, 'there is *no* "quiet, ordinary" life for me — never has been and never will be — darling little Christine. That is why I am at last a little careful.' Bax continued: 'My life has always been so fevered that I don't know how I have ever got any work done. And I can't grow up, and long for home and children and settled things. Just now it is all worse than ever, and I can't even get down to work — for the last year it has been like this. All just a fever.' The correspondence continued until the middle of the war but the 'affair' — if ever there was one — was ended by March. And it was in March that the full score of the Violin Concerto was completed.

It was in a strange mood of nostalgia mixed with objective detachment that he came to the Seventh Symphony. The devil that had pursued him through the earlier symphonies had been finally laid to rest in the epilogue of the Sixth. The Seventh is technically the most secure of Bax's symphonies, and at the same time the most relaxed:

the summation of the two main streams of his creative life, the symphonic poem and the symphony, at least as far as orchestral music is concerned. After he had completed the orchestration of the Violin Concerto Bax went straight on to compose this Seventh Symphony, the short score of the first movement being completed on 18 June and the whole work in short score by October.

The early autumn of 1938 was notable for what turned out to be the last performance of the *Symphonic Variations* which Harriet was to give. This was at a Prom on Thursday 1 September, and Bax was in attendance for the piano rehearsal in the Queen's Hall artists' room on 27 August ('at 12.50' – typical of Sir Henry Wood, not a moment to be wasted), for the orchestral run-through the day before the concert and the orchestral rehearsal on the morning of the performance. Earlier, on 24 June, Harriet had given a reception for Edward J. Dent, one of those typical parties which Bax attended with Harriet all through the inter-war years, and of which he would have us believe he hated every minute. Later in the year Harriet went to America for a successful tour, and was away until March 1939. Her subsequent return too was only fleeting, for in April 1939 she was off to Holland and then to the Middle East. Of course, the absence of the artist to whom he had given sole rights in his works for piano and orchestra meant that it was not possible for them to be played.

In November Bax and Mary again took the train to Scotland, following the Mallaig line to Morar where they stayed. Bax orchestrated the score of the Seventh Symphony, and soaked in his favourite scenery, with superb seascapes across to the islands of Rhum, Eigg and Muck. The orchestral score was finally completed during January 1939. The symphony was actually commissioned for the New York World Fair, where it received its first performance in June 1939 under Sir Adrian Boult. As a commissioned work it had to be dedicated to 'The People of America', but it is probable that Bax was at work on it before he received the commission, and his original intention is visible on the manuscript where Basil Cameron's name has been crossed through.

The first movement is a seascape, perhaps more successful than that in the Fourth Symphony. The symphony begins with a magnificent long opening paragraph of 60 bars, followed by a general pause. A pianissimo pedal on A♭ is established by timpani and double basses; a very soft gong roll provides a moment's colouration before the first theme is stated by the clarinets. It is another Sibelian-sounding theme

from the same stable as that at the beginning of the opening movement of Bax's Fifth Symphony, though this time it is *Allegro* from
the start. The theme is four bars long, though Bax extends it by
holding the final chord over a further bar, and it is then repeated in
a higher register, the violas joining in, before a second falling motif
on violas, cellos, muted trombones and bassoons leads to a passionate
re-statement of the opening idea on the violins. The way the falling
motif itself is dressed orchestrally and the colouration given to the
ever-present pedal backcloth by flutes, clarinets, muted trumpets and
harp, gives a fine demonstration of Bax's orchestral technique. Eventually the movement proper begins with the falling idea. The basic
momentum is fast, and though, in Bax's customary symphonic
manner, there are slow interludes, they do not impede the flow or
the impact of the climaxes. Rather are they colourful memories that
occasionally intrude into an ageing man's physical enjoyment of the
waves smashing on to the shore, of the northern light and the wild
coastline with the dim purple shapes of the islands out to sea. The
momentum is maintained as the opening idea is transformed into a
long Baxian tune in the strings, only to be outdone by another slow
tune which first appears on oboe and cellos. Having stated his material
Bax proceeds to weave a varied tapestry from it, more tone poem
than symphony, but fully convincing none the less. Eventually the
long slow tune reappears at a passionate climax (between cues 39
and 42), the music quietens, and a strange closing sequence develops
in which ghostly versions of the opening woodwind idea and the
passionate theme recur before the movement ends in a mood of
quiet regretfulness with muted brass chords, still over a timpani pedal
on A♮.

The slow movement is a clear ternary design, and is thus reminiscent, in shape at any rate, of the earlier symphonic poems. The
opening juxtaposes three ideas in a variety of instrumental colours,
after which follows the more programmatic central section, marked
In Legendary Mood. Finally the theme of the opening returns and the
music ends on a note of autumnal musing. This movement has been
troublesome to its interpreters. Sir Adrian Boult's first performance
in New York was recorded on acetate discs at the time and they were
sent to Bax. He said he found the tempi in the first movement 'exactly right' and the third movement 'perfect', although he added 'the
third movement should start more deliberately — a real 18FORTY
romantic wallow!'[15] But Boult does not appear successfully to have
projected the slow movement. Neither did Rudolph Schwarz who

was later to linger over it. But Bax thought Boult had taken the slow movement too quickly. Later after the first British performance Bax wrote again, saying that he 'was particularly moved by the playing of the second movement which expressed all the heavy summer languor which I meant to convey'.[16] The interpretative difficulties all relate to tempi, handling of climaxes and internal balance of the orchestral sound, and of the six conductors who have ever attempted this work, in the slow movement at least, Raymond Leppard on his recording succeeds in a way that none of his predecessors did. Indeed, why the successful interpretation of the slow movement should be elusive is difficult to place, but is completely dependent on pacing. Previous commentators (notably Payne and Pirie) have both rejected it as a 'dud' presumably on the evidence of earlier performances. Yet in a record review Ronald Crichton described the slow movement ('really a very slow 3/8 scherzo') as 'a charmer, beautifully played'.[17] Crichton also wrote evocatively of the first movement calling it 'both dreamy and storm-tossed, sea-music without hint of human conflict (the same could no doubt be said of *La Mer*, but there one is conscious of Debussy's ordering intelligence)'.

The third movement opens with a 32-bar ceremonial prelude, which alternates common time with $\frac{3}{2}$, thus giving it rhythmic flexibility and just removing it from the arena of the ceremonial march, though its effect is to remind us that soon afterwards Bax's music was to include film scores and music for state pageantry. Having created a sense of occasion, the opening softens over a two-bar timpani roll and then the cellos and basses quietly state the theme, which is then taken up by the higher strings. The theme is repeated in various different sections of the orchestra, and indeed throughout the movement it is varied but little, other than in tempo and rhythmic accentuation. So the effect is rather that of a passacaglia than a theme-and-variations proper. Occasionally the music of the prelude reappears, but this is not surprising because the rising phrase at the very beginning of the theme is derived from the rising tail of the opening fanfare.

Including the variation that continues from the statement of the theme there are seven variations altogether, the last of which is the Epilogue. Previous symphonic epilogues had attempted either an emotional resolution (in the Third and Sixth Symphonies and *Winter Legends)* or a triumphal one (in the Fourth and Fifth Symphonies). The Epilogue to the Seventh Symphony, by comparison with the Third and Sixth Symphonies, is a short one, in which the mood of hushed acceptance is curiously compelling and final (Ex. 92) as if Bax is saying farewell not only to this work but also to his

Ex. 92   The closing bars of the Seventh Symphony in Bax's original short score. The first two rising triplets in bars 10 and 12 become B♮, D♮ and F in the published orchestral score.

whole cycle of symphonies, and indeed to serious composition and his loved wild places. As if to emphasize that his world was at an end, no sooner had Bax written out those quiet chords in full score than W.B. Yeats died. Bax wrote to his brother Clifford, 'I feel a most poignant loss in that the greatest of us all is no more ... It seems almost unbelievable that Willie Yeats will never write another line of verse. As Constant Lambert said to me at lunch today, "He achieved a record in pleasing four generations of poetry lovers; even the most recent (Auden etc) reverenced him". I noted that not *one single* poster proclaimed "Death of a Great Poet". What a crazy world!'[18]

The Second War: Storrington

In April 1939 Bax took Balfour Gardiner on a tour of favourite places in Ireland. One of their ports of call was Mongans Hotel, Carna, Connemara, which Bax had not visited since 1913. He wrote to Mary, 'at one time I used to be here every April ... It has not changed a scrap since I was a boy. This is the place I describe in "The Sisters".' In fact their host was the Deputy for South Connemara in the Dail, the Irish Parliament, and on 29 April Bax wrote how he had subsequently 'been taken into the Parliament House in Dublin and introduced to some of the deputies which interested me very much and I found that on the following day I was referred to in an Irish speech by the Deputy for South Connemara'. He was also relieved to be able to report that 'Kerry is passing with credit, I am glad to say, in the eyes of Balfour Gardiner. Hitherto at least he seems to take a lenient view of the country.'

The one-movement *Rhapsodic Ballad* for unaccompanied cello was completed on 3 June 1939. It was written for Beatrice Harrison, but she never played it in public, though during the war she performed Bax's music on several occasions, including the Cello Concerto twice at the Proms. It is said that the reason for Beatrice Harrison not playing the *Ballad* is that she was afraid it would make her sister May jealous. The existence of the work, which was not listed in the fifth edition of *Grove*, only came to general notice when Bernard Vocadlo, then the cellist of the Radio Éireann Quartet, gave its first performance at the Cork Municipal School of Music in May 1966, and Chappell's published it early in 1969. It was subsequently taken up by the fine young Sinhalese cellist, Rohan de Saram, who more recently has recorded his passionate performance. The *Ballad* is Bax's only work for any unaccompanied instrument (discounting the brief Valse for harp) other than piano. The composer's style is usually dependent on a wide range of orchestral colour to make its full effect, yet in this cello piece he succeeds brilliantly in achieving a cogent and forceful extended argument over fifteen minutes' or so duration.

Up to 1939 Bax had remained supremely indifferent to world events, but this time the threat of war depressed him considerably and he stopped writing. In particular, he lost heart in two works he was attempting to complete. He wrote to Edwin Evans, who was convalescing after a serious illness, asking if he might be released from his 'undertaking to write a work for strings for the CMS concert in December'. 'The reason', he wrote, 'is that I do not feel that I could do myself justice at the present time. The perpetual political tension is scarcely conducive to concentration upon creative work, and apart from this I feel that my imagination is getting somewhat weary and needs a rest: I have been trying to perpetrate a small concerto for Tania, but it is heavy labour.'[1] The 'small concerto', or *Concertino* as it is entitled in the surviving manuscript, was sketched in short score only, and was never completed.

On the afternoon of 3 September Bax wrote to Mary of the 'awful state of war in London. It was an awful shock when I accidentally overheard the twelve o'clock news and at first could not take it in.' He immediately went to Sussex, staying first of all at the Roundabout Hotel, Storrington. On 9 September he wrote again to Mary, who was still in Chorleywood near London, 'I want to carry you away from this awful time in an enchanted cloud of love and beauty.' He had a number of addresses in the vicinity over the next few weeks, writing on 29 September from Warnes Hotel, Worthing. 'Of course it is hideous for everyone,' he wrote, 'but if one is dissatisfied and troubled about one's work all this disturbance is just paralyzing.' However, he obviously felt that at a time of uncertainty he should make clear his personal commitment, and he wrote quite unambiguously, declaring, 'My love you must not think that you are only complementary in my life, for I cannot imagine it without you ... You are youth and Spring and love to me and the only woman I ever wanted to marry.' Bax had discovered a convenient hotel at his ancestral village of Ockley and he and Mary started to meet there on a fairly frequent basis during the early period of the war. 'I think it is certainly our home in England and every time we go there it becomes more so.'

Early in October he went to Bournemouth where his friend

Richard Austin was to conduct the last concerts of the Bournemouth Orchestra at full strength. The concert in the afternoon of Thursday 12 October included *The Garden of Fand*. 'It has been quite gay here,' Bax wrote, 'and I have braved several tirades and invectives with success. It was strange and a little unreal to be making remarks at a rehearsal once again.'

At the beginning of the war Harriet Cohen briefly moved to Slindon, near the Downs. Mary later lived at Fittleworth, where Elgar's late chamber works had been written, and Bax's sister Evelyn and his mother were also living in the vicinity. Bax's movement round Sussex ceased when, for a while, he stayed at the Railway Hotel, Pulborough. Various friends lived nearby, including Cecil Gray, John Ireland and Julian Herbage, and it was not long before he discovered a congenial hostelry, the White Horse in the nearby village of Storrington. Eventually he went to stay there and remained for the rest of his life.

In December 1939 Harriet Cohen, having broadcast a recital of short pieces by Suk, Janáček, Novák, Smetana and Dvořák intended to show her solidarity with the Czechs, set off to the USA for a long tour, from which she did not finally return until July 1940. On her American tour Harriet played two ensemble works by Bax (as well as, presumably, others for solo piano), the Octet and *Saga Fragment*. The Octet was heard at a Library of Congress concert and was subsequently broadcast throughout America, while *Saga Fragment* was taken up by the enterprising conductor Bernard Herrmann, later to be famous for his film music. On 21 April Harriet wrote to the BBC enthusing over her reception in the United States. 'I have had a *terrific* success!' she wrote. 'I am still rather dazed by it all ... Our Consul-General said I have done "inestimable benefit to British Government propaganda" and have "put British Music on the map in USA". But I'm a wreck. Haven't let up on working 5-7 hours every day for 3 months. And one gets asked everywhere if one has a really great success, and one must go for *propaganda reasons*! ... Have had 7 invitations to stay – over the summer – but feel that with real danger now [facing] the British Isles my place is at home with my people, and playing for those that need me, in the summer and autumn.'[2]

For Bax the will to compose did not quickly return. He wrote to Tilly Fleischmann on 27 December 1939, while still living at Pulborough, that 'all these fearful events are very distracting ... I cannot adapt myself very well to the conditions. I have written nothing at all since August and I doubt if anyone else has either.'

Gradually the idea was born, probably at Clifford's instigation, that Arnold might write his memoirs. Early in January 1940 he went with Mary to Morar for the last time, sending Cecil Gray a postcard which was postmarked 18 January. 'There is much more snow about than is shown in this photo, and winter has a hard grip on this country', he noted, and continued: 'We enjoy the most dramatic skyscapes up here ... Am having a try at those memoirs, but they are very frivolous! Self defence against the present.'[3] He found the book 'fun and easy to write in the unruffled calm of Morar'. Fundamentally Bax was a kindly man who would not willingly reopen old sores if the protagonists could still be hurt, and this resulted in his memoirs being a succession of delightful, short vignettes, stopping with the outbreak of the First World War. The publication of *Farewell, My Youth*, as the book was called, in 1943, was a great and popular success, being twice reprinted in the first year. Yet in spite of repeated requests for a sequel Bax always declined, for he could not truthfully tell even a part of his story after 1914 without hurting someone. Shortly after the visit to Morar that part of the Scottish coast became a closed area, and he did not return.

The summer of 1940 saw Bax unable to visit Ireland (he was not to return there until 1946), and so with Mary he visited Devon and Cornwall, being at Lynmouth on 8 June and Newquay on 10 July.[4] In Tintagel he encountered Marjorie McTavish, friend of Paul Corder, whom Bax had not met since the days of the Corders' Sunday evenings many years before. 'I went to the hotel bar to have a drink and there was Arnold and we greeted each other with joy', recalled Miss McTavish: 'We went out for a walk and I asked about Harriet.' 'It's so nice to hear someone talk about Harriet who is kind in their remembrance of her', remarked Bax. 'I got the impression', added Miss McTavish, 'that Arnold was drinking too much.'

If the war had brought a sense of change to Bax's life, the death of his mother was a very great blow, for she represented the only real stability he ever knew. She had been ailing for some time and the end finally came at the beginning of November. As Bax observed in a letter to the composer Richard Tildesley (later a double-bass player in the Hallé Orchestra), 'My mother was a remarkable personality beloved by hundreds of people of all classes. But it was better for her to go when she did as had she lived longer she would only have been a helpless invalid. She was gradually fading away for a month before she died.'[5] To Aloys Fleischmann he wrote:

My dear Aloys,

I was deeply touched by your beautiful letter about my mother. I am so glad that you met her and had an opportunity of recognizing her very remarkable qualities. I don't think that any more unselfish and wildly generous person ever lived. She would have made a marvellous queen. I shall always keep your letter, my dear Aloys.

I have been in this village for four months — a beautiful part of the country under the Downs. But I would find it very dull if it were not for some very nice people who haunt this hotel. I cannot do any work under war conditions. It was very different during the last war. But then I was young and on fire creatively. Nothing could stop me in those days, and from 1914 to '18 I did some of my best things.

For many reasons I would love to come to Eire, but I fear it is morally, if not physically, impossible at present. I am looking forward to visiting you in your new — and seemingly — charming home. I regard you as one of my best friends, dear Aloys, and am ever grateful for all your lavish kindness and hospitality in the past.

My love to the family   from Arnold

In March 1941 the BBC programmed the *Overture* from *Overture, Elegy and Rondo* to precede the first broadcast performance of Edmund Rubbra's Third Symphony under Sir Adrian Boult. Writing to Sir Adrian before the performance Bax pressed the claims of the *Elegy*, saying 'I believe [it] ... is one of my better pieces.'[6] But nevertheless it was the *Overture* that was broadcast on 20 March.

Also in March Walford Davies, the Master of the King's Musick, died and, after a hiatus, Bax was offered and agreed to accept the post. Quite why he accepted it is impossible to say, but one again suspects May Harrison's influence in the matter. Bax was not temperamentally suited to a court appointment: he let himself in for a lot of unnecessary correspondence, and produced few works for official functions. He answered Richard Tildesley's letter of congratulation on 10 February 1942 with an implied swipe at his predecessor, saying he was 'very pleased to be following Elgar — even at one remove', and added, 'but do not feel I know much about the duties involved — except that I may have to wear Court dress on occasion ... I am glad', he continued, 'to hear that you are doing some work — somebody has got to carry on in these distracting times.'[7] To his brother Clifford he admitted, 'it is true that the notion of court-dress is a little daunting ... I believe it includes silk breeches and a sword! But sufficient unto the day is the embarrassment thereof.' Having accepted, Bax was duly summoned to Buckingham Palace for a Royal audience. 'The King and Queen were perfectly delightful,' he reported, 'making it so easy that I left feeling that I had talked far too much. But as they kept me for quite a long time I suppose they were not embarrassed or bored.'

Reactions to Bax being honoured by the Mastership of the Musick were mixed. Bax was quite hurt that the musical 'establishment' at the Royal College of Music appeared to resent his being honoured. Patrick Hadley's letter of congratulations was delayed in reaching Bax, who observed in a letter to his brother, 'I am a little surprised that Paddy has not sent me a line since I became the "King's music master". Or is he as Royal College as all that? I doubt it! I had a note from the principal of the RCM the other day. Not a word about my, as you know, utterly unsolicited honour! It seems to me very silly and petty. (Whereas I had charming messages from John Ireland, Adrian Boult, and of course "VW").' The popular press gave Bax good coverage, and he records particularly enjoying the *Daily Telegraph*. 'But', he noted to Clifford, 'the penny rags perpetrated amazing inanities ... According to the *News Chronicle* I am "ruddy-cheeked, grizzle-haired, and dressed habitually in tweeds look to the villagers the typical country squire!" I am also apparently devoted to *beer* (of all detestable beverages).' There was some excuse, at least, for thinking that Bax drank beer, as on 28 March *Picture Post* published a photographic feature on him showing him drinking with the locals at the White Horse. 'Any day of the week', the accompanying text gushed, 'at the White Horse Hotel in the Sussex village of Storrington, a square-cut, tweedy figure is to be seen taking a pint of beer with the local inhabitants ... This is Sir Arnold Bax, the new Master of the King's Music. He went there for the week-end one fine day in autumn, 1940 – and has stayed there ever since. To-day, the appointment of Sir Arnold marks yet another step in the history of the office – for far from being a conventional composer, he is one of the leaders of the modern school. Paradoxically, he rarely listens to music. Once a month he attends the Chanctonbury Music Society's concerts in a Sussex country house. His more frequent recreations are billiards, crossword puzzles, village cricket, and a drink and a gossip with the locals in the bar.'[8]

Yet, in truth, the appointment was a strange one. At the time Wilfrid Mellers accurately summarized what might have been expected in such an appointment in wartime Britain and realistically, Bax did not properly have a place there. Mellers wrote:

To-day, the Master of the King's Music should act as a focal point of the musical life of our society. ... To Elgar as Master of the King's Music the obvious successor was, and is, Vaughan Williams – not such a great composer, but an equally great personality, and a more intelligent man, as benefits our greater sophistication. Vaughan Williams is so much the most commanding personality in English music over the last thirty years that it is difficult to imagine that the English musical renaissance could have happened without him. He is still writing 'household' music and unison choral songs of courage and victory and has virtually been Master of the King's Music for the last twenty or more years. Why he has not officially received the title I do not know. Maybe he was not offered it, not having quite the right kind of friends; maybe when it was offered he wouldn't accept. But if the office means anything it is one to be filled by a man with Vaughan Williams's record, and with his capabilities. In lieu of VW, I should have thought that William Walton was the obvious choice, especially considering the depressingly well-meaning self-conscious Elgarizing in which Walton indulges in his own occasional music. I suppose Walton stood no chance because of the curious notion, nurtured in the nineteenth century, that no one is capable of mastering the King's Music until he has reached the age of sixty; however this may be, I must admit that the appointment to the office of Sir Arnold Bax seemed to me both surprising and perverse.

I do not intend this as a reflection on Bax's talents; merely it seems to me that he has played no part in English musical life, that he has done nothing to mould the English renaissance, and that in his creative work he is neither altogether a contemporary composer nor representatively an English one. All the qualifications that make Vaughan Williams so obvious a candidate, Bax lacks; almost his only qualification is his prodigious facility, and this is a somewhat dubious asset except in so far as it will enable him, if necessity arises, to produce occasional works almost without noticing and therefore without dissipating energies that might be more profitably employed.[9]

Bax's problems while receiving the Mastership of the King's Musick would undoubtedly have made headlines if they had been known, which fortunately they were not, for he was engaged in a dispute with the Inland Revenue. Bax was always casual and negligent about the demands of the real world, and doubtless precipitated 'a super tax demand for £1087'. He lamented to Clifford on 16 July 1941, 'at present [I] can only scrape up about £450 to carry me (Elsa, etc) up to March without paying any of the tax at all!' After receiving his new honour he still owed 'the rapacious government some seven hundred pounds, but as yet they are not pressing me unduly.'

While having many musical friends in or near Storrington it is worth noting that among his non-musical acquaintances was Jomo Kenyatta, his wife and young child, who had a house at Heath Common, above Storrington. Bax and Mary went to tea one day, and arrived early. Kenyatta surprised them, jumping out of the bushes wearing a bright yellow jersey.

All this time Bax was not writing music. On 1 January 1942 he wrote: 'I am very deep in a dump at the moment, and never did I wear so melancholy a hat! I am sick of being idle, but feel no impulse towards any sort of creation. If only there were more encouragement everything might be different.'[10] In fact, Bax did not write any music between August 1939 and the summer of 1942. But during that summer the Crown Film Unit was preparing a documentary about the battle for Malta, and he was persuaded to undertake the score. Bax was probably chosen purely because he was the new Master of the Musick, and he completed the work in September. It was, he noted to Clifford, 'music totally unstimulated by self', and he wondered if 'it may well be different from the rest of my work' adding, 'I can't say I derived much pleasure from the writing'. Eventually the original manuscript, sumptuously bound in red leather was presented by Bax to the Governor of Malta, Lord Gort, at a ceremony in London in February 1943. It was, Bax noted, 'somewhat of an ordeal for a mere "countryman" '.

Today the original score that was presented to Malta is preserved in the National Library in Valletta. On opening the heavy front board, one reads a printed title-page:

This original manuscript of the music specially written for the film *Malta GC* is dedicated to the heroism of the Maltese people by the composer, Sir Arnold Bax, Master of the King's Musick.

London Feb 1943

To which the composer has added in ink:

To Heroic Malta, GC. Arnold Bax [11]

The manuscript score is just headed 'Malta'. Bax gives each new section a descriptive title in ink, other notes have been added in pencil. The pages are marked as follows:

p.1 Maestoso
  3 [in pencil] Convoy
p.9 [in pencil] Entrance into harbour [Ex. 93]

As may be seen from Bax's laborious sequential writing in this example the music did not come easily to him.

Ex. 93

p.11 [in pencil] Ruins [later published as *Funeral March*]
13 [" "] Valletta as it was
p.23 [in blue pencil] (Part 1) Malta contd.
26 [in pencil] Air Raid
36 [" "] Ruins and sorrows after the raid

This continues to p.46. Pagination now returns [reel 2] to 1:

p. 1 Malta Pt II. Quick march
p. 7 [pencil] Quiet street scene
11 Moderato molto energico [pencil] work and play
14 [pencil] Children walking and at school
18 ["] Children's dance

Much of the music is very effective. Bax was obviously quickly learning to comply with the demands for exact timing made by the film; at the end of p.19 appears the following note: 'The eight bars between 13 and 14 can be repeated here if possible to the timing.'

p.31 Moderato march tempo [Ex. 94]

p.45 end.

Ex. 94

Bax must too soon have realized that his 'big tune' in the final march began with strong overtones of 'Men of Harlech', and by changing the two notes marked in the second bar he saved the day. Later, in 1945, when a *Victory March* was required, he elaborated this final march from the film into an independent work. It is indicative of his lack of inspiration at the end of his life that, when he came to write the obligatory *Coronation March* in 1953, he again re-wrote this *Victory March* complete with its feeble tune. However, the music of *Malta GC* was well received at the time, and a suite and three marches – *Victory March, Quick March* and *Funeral March* – were widely played and favourably commented on. In the context of an island at war this was to be expected, yet Bax was wise to mistrust anything that was, for the first time, 'entirely impersonal', for the music adds nothing to his reputation, and its wide appreciation over the next decade detracted from his more important and 'personal' works, and temporarily diminished his true stature in the history of British music.

Having been tempted back to composition with film music, Bax soon received a number of commissions. It was probably late in 1942 that the cellist Florence Hooton asked him for a work, and he responded with the *Legend-Sonata*, which he completed in February. He wrote to Aloys Fleischmann:

My dear Aloys,

I feel much ashamed of myself for not replying to the charming letter you wrote me in the New Year before this. Anyway let me tell you that all the kind wishes in *your* letter are fully reciprocated. I am longing for the day when we can all meet again in Ireland and in peace.

I have been quite busy again since Christmas and have finished a very romantic sonata for cello and piano which gets about as far away from present day realities as it possibly could. I enjoyed writing it and perhaps because of my long rest from responsible composition it all came very easily.

The music I wrote (with much labour) for the 'Malta' film (Ministry of Information commissioned it) appears to be a success with the musical public. Last Friday I presented the score (magnificently bound *not* by myself) to Viscount Gort, Governor of the Island, to be forwarded when the opportunity occurs. I don't like the lime-light but everyone was very pleasant indeed and in retrospect I enjoyed the event.

I don't know whether Balfour Gardiner found employment for the man you recommended to him. He said he was going to try to get him into his nephew's forestry plantations but was not sure whether there would be a vacancy. I have not heard from him since then.

I hope you are all keeping well and not finding difficulties about food. I expect drink is just as scarce as it is over here.

My love to Tilly, Aloys Og and yourself
Arnold

The three-movement *Legend-Sonata* is delightful in performance, but it lacks the power of the earlier music because it lacks its motivation, and ultimately we must recognize that it is the music of an old man who, in trying to regain his former style, can only achieve its manner and not its content. Symptomatic of this malaise is the slow-movement tune which opens with a quotation from 'Fand's song of immortal love', but Bax is unable to carry on into the rest of the movement the ardour which flickers briefly in that opening memory of thirty years before. 'I wrote it with so much hope for a better world', said Bax in the programme for the first performance, but did not go on to explain what he meant.

During the war, Bax's music came into demand. He was an important national figure, and in wartime, not only were materials for performing native works more easily available than those of their contemporaries abroad, but, of course they were promoted to project a national character. However, Bax held aloof from the back-room work that goes into the programming of one work rather than another. He had many friends in the performing and administrative sides of the profession who looked after his interests fairly satisfactorily: in particular, Sir Henry Wood, Basil Cameron, John Barbirolli – recently returned from the USA – and Sir Adrian Boult. However, in spite of all his well-wishers, the picture of him that emerged was a distorted one, for few of his really great or most characteristic works were played. Under pressure to produce a commission for the BBC's St Cecilia Day concert in 1943, the six-year-old Violin Concerto was brought out for Eda Kersey to première, and was a great – and to Bax an embarrassing – success. It was the Fourth Symphony, the Violin Concerto and feeble wartime works that tended to be heard. And of course Harriet Cohen, who was tireless in her championship of Bax's music, was unwittingly the cause of the major piano works not being frequently played, because only she was associated with them. Bax hated the London scene, and he commented at this time in a letter to a friend, 'there are awful and sickening intrigues in the London musical world and they go from bad to worse, not that I think very much about them or their originators.'[12]

Much of Bax's intelligence as to what was afoot in London must have come to him through Harriet. After her return from America in the summer of 1940 she was inexhaustible in the ways she tried to help the war effort. Then came the blitz and disaster, for her 'house and entire possessions including music and piano'[13] were burnt out by incendiary bombs. Harriet was 'prostrated with shock' and cancelled her engagements until November. However, although not playing she remained very active and vocal during this time, seeing herself as a champion of Britain on the BBC Overseas Service, and as a broadcasting personality. But the BBC Music Department was beginning to be critical of her playing, and as early as December 1940 one finds a memo on BBC files observing,'her playing has not improved in recent years'.[14] During the war others also voiced this opinion. But Harriet did not appear to realize this fact, and felt she was the subject of internal BBC intrigues – about which she doubtless made Bax aware. He was unable, however, to secure her engagement, as his influence on the output of Broadcasting House was by no means strong. In 1942 the minutes of a BBC meeting noted that 'Mr Bliss felt the time had come to inform Miss Cohen that the real reason for her "neglect" has been the growing conviction that her pianistic

performances since her return from America do not qualify her to
be included in the very limited number of first class British
pianists accommodated in the Overseas Service.'[15]

Towards the end of 1940 Harriet performed Bax's Piano Quartet
at the Royal Academy of Music with Frederick Grinke, David Martin
and Florence Hooton, and the following May was able to broadcast
the work. She was also involved in an Overseas Service scheme for a
programme of Bax's piano music with the overall title 'Water Music'.
It was not a very long programme, finally consisting of *Winter Waters,
Nereid* and (inexplicably) *Mountain Mood*. Bax was emphatic that he
did not want *Water Music* included, and *Mediterranean*, which had
been tentatively put down, was also omitted.

At the end of 1941 she was prevented from getting the Kabalevsky
First Piano Concerto ready for performance by a sprained wrist, in
spite of having enthused to the BBC about it for years ('Arnold
thinks Kabalevsky the best modern Russian composer'[16]). In fact the
orchestral parts could not be procured from Moscow at the time.[17]
The letter she wrote to Julian Herbage in mitigation is worth quoting
to show the load of provincial touring that was the lot of many
performers in the dark days of the war, and which meant,
incidentally, that she and Bax met quite infrequently at this time.
'I am so terribly sorry that I have not yet got the Kabalevsky
Concerto ready for you,' she wrote,

but I have never had so many concerts before, and as you know, I had already
started my season of playing and dashing round the country when the BBC
asked me to learn the work; one really learns new works in the late spring and
the summer when concerts have stopped for the most part.

Conditions are such that with the blackout and the greatly lengthened hours
of travelling (the trains are always being late) and having a woman only two
hours a day instead of a full time maid, and a secretary only about twice a week,
you can imagine how difficult it has been for me to get through my ordinary
programmes; for instance I will give you an example of the kind of week I have
and you will see there are only about two days in London at the piano. This was
in October, but it has gone on like this ever since the end of August.

Leicester	Sunday	Afternoon concert 2 Concertos.
London	Monday	Preparing for Tuesday's Recital programme.
		Weekend letters attended to.
		Ordinary things such as buying rations.
S. England	Tuesday	Packed. Practised a little.
		Caught lunch time train.
"		Tuesday evening. Concert in the South-West of England.

,,		Wednesday evening. Concert in another town in the South of England.
To London		Thursday morning. Came back to London. 1.30 to 2.30 letters.
London		Thursday afternoon. Practising concerto for Saturday.
To Nottingham		Friday morning. Practised concerto and worked on something for gramophone records.
	Afternoon	Packed. Took train to Nottingham.
Nottingham	Saturday	2 Orchestral concerts with Dr Malcolm Sargent.
To London	Sunday	Returned. Tried to snatch a little time at the piano. Repacked, to Bournemouth.
To Bournemouth		in the afternoon with two Orchestral concerts with Sir Adrian Boult next day.
		N.B. Different concertos from the ones I played on Saturday.

This is the sort of life I have been living, and when you think that this season I shall have played 7 concertos with a possibility of two more, you will agree that my time is absolutely full. However, things are much better this month, especially the first part of the month, and I am trying to devote all of the next fortnight or three weeks to knocking this lovely little work into my head, so it ought to be ready at the end of February or the beginning of March. If there is any chance of getting it done sooner I will hasten to let you know. I think a work ought to be absorbed by one a little while before playing it.[18]

On 3 February 1942 Harriet wrote to Julian Herbage, 'I know Arnold will tell you when he sees you, if he has not already written, that he very much wants me to play his Symphonic Concerto "Winter Legends" at a Symphony Concert with Adrian if possible, as it has not been done for ten years.'[19] Nothing happened immediately, but as soon as Bax's Mastership of the King's Musick was announced she wrote again, to another BBC official, suggesting that she should revive *Winter Legends* arguing that 'it seems the right moment to celebrate his new honour.'[20] She kept up the campaign, writing to Sir Adrian Boult on 2 July,

It is about ten years since you and I produced Arnold's marvellous piano concerto, 'The Winter Legends'. As we all know, his third and fifth symphonies are considered his greatest works, and this work was written between these two, at the peak of his powers, and the best of his work, which he himself also thinks. I am very anxious to play this with you at a Symphony Concert next season, and I would very much like to ask for this great pleasure in this letter, and hope that you aid me in getting the engagement. Not only for my sake but for Arnold's and the work which has been so long neglected. The public is much more educated now musically and I think will welcome it. The violin concerto having been done twice I feel sure that you will consider this.[21]

The matter must have appeared to have lapsed, and neither Harriet nor Bax heard any more about a revival of *Winter Legends* until perhaps a year later, when Julian Herbage suggested informally to Harriet that she should start working on it, as a performance was likely later in the year around the composer's sixtieth birthday. However, Harriet appears not to have taken him seriously, and when Herbage rang in the summer to find how the work was progressing, she had to tell him she had not worked on it at all and could not possibly prepare it before the New Year. However Herbage minuted Bliss, then Director of Music at the BBC, suggesting it should eventually be placed in a symphony concert to be broadcast from the BBC's wartime concert hall at Bedford. Bliss was keen: 'Yes — a good idea — a finer work than the Variations I should say.'[22] It was finally December 1944 before Harriet was ready and the work could be programmed, with Boult to conduct. On 6 December, seven days before the performance, Harriet injured her arm and had to cancel. She wrote to Victor Hely-Hutchinson: 'I am heartbroken about not playing "The Winter Legends" as you can imagine, and have been working on it, except when on tour, for 5 or 6 hours a day since August.'[23] The work was replaced on that occasion by Bax's Sixth Symphony. Towards the end of the war Kussevitsky came to London, and Harriet lost no time in trying to get him to programme herself and Bax's score as he had done in 1933, but to no avail. However, it had not been forgotten, and finally the BBC successfully put the work on in one of their postwar concerts at the People's Palace, Mile End Road, London, in December 1945. There were still reservations in the BBC about Harriet's playing but the consensus of opinion appeared to be that 'in spite of her limited technical equipment she can always pull off this type of music'.[24] From Bax's point of view this whole situation, which had underlain the presentation of a number of his best works, was disastrous. To what extent he was aware of it is difficult to say, but so expert a pianist as Bax himself, even if badly out of practice, cannot have been unaware of Harriet's problems, whether she confided in him over them or not.

After her house was bombed, Harriet did not stay in the country, but moved into the Dorchester Hotel. Bax had originally bought Harriet's house and given her free use of it. Early in 1944 he now bought a West End mews cottage just off Portman Square in Gloucester Place Mews for her, although she only used it as a studio to start with. During and just after the war she went away on the frequent provincial tours which continued to provide her with a considerable public.

During 1943 Bax wrote a short overture for the ENSA (Entertainments National Service Association) concerts. Called *Work in Progress*, it sounds perilously near to Eric Coates in style (perhaps emphasizing their common origin at the RAM), and makes a satirical reference to *Deutschland über Alles* just before its middle section. Nevertheless, with its extended passages of bracing, brassy *Allegro* it is a successful piece, and although plumbing no depths is entertaining. It achieved its purpose as well as did Rawsthorne's *Street Corner* overture, another commission in the same series, but although it had many hearings immediately after its introduction, it has only been heard once (in a broadcast) since the 1940s. Another short work, *Salute to Sydney*, dates from March 1943. Bliss had requested that Bax write a 'special fanfare' for the Overseas Service programme 'Calling Sydney' on 19 April. Bax was not particularly pleased with his work, referring to it as 'this brassy flourish (I cannot call it a fanfare)'.[25] Also in 1943 a suite was extracted from *Malta GC* for concert performance, and remained popular for a time.

Having revived his interest in composition during 1943 Bax developed it in 1944. *To Russia* is a *pièce d'occasion* – a short choral work on a Masefield text for the Albert Hall presentation of *Salute to the Red Army* – and was completed in February. Clearly the Master of the King's Musick and the Poet Laureate were expected to rise to the occasion for an emotional and topical wartime celebration, but neither were on good form in this rather laboured piece.

Later came the *Legend* for orchestra, his last full-scale tone poem, which was finished in May. It was first heard in a BBC broadcast and later at the Guildhall, Cambridge, on 28 October the same year, and was described by one commentator as 'an old Bax-o'-tricks'.[26] Bax wrote to Ralph Hill on 8 October to explain 'the meaning of my piece ... or rather its lack of meaning'. This is the last programmatic programme note that Bax wrote, and in it he varies his approach little from that he had been adopting for many years before. He wrote: 'this piece is not a musical version of any particular story; it merely purports to evoke certain characteristic elements in the tales of some northern land – a matter of the atmosphere of strangeness and remoteness inherent in the word "legend". Mountain landscapes, wild weather, wind-swept castles, shadowy battles and finally triumph in a barbaric setting may perhaps be suggested by this series of musical episodes.'[27] The music, which is well worth reviving, again presents the sound world of *The Tale the Pine-Trees Knew*, though Bax rather spoils this characteristic canvas by ending with a triumphal marching passage in the idiom of the occasional music of *Malta GC* or *Work in Progress*.

Considering he is not normally thought of as a choral composer, it is worth noting that most of the works produced in 1944 should be for that medium. The *Five Fantasies on Polish Christmas Carols* in fact date from November 1942, but were first heard in 1944. They are effective arrangements of five Polish carols for unison children's voices and strings. Dedicated to the Children of Poland this work was first performed at a benefit concert which was to have been conducted by Basil Cameron. In the event Cameron was indisposed, and so the performance was under the baton of the Principal of the Guildhall School of Music and Drama, Edric Cundell. The *Five Greek Folksongs* are complex arrangements for *a cappella* chorus, and are worthy to be considered beside the masterpieces of his earlier style for this medium. Two small pieces for church performance, *Nunc Dimittis* and *Te Deum*, were also completed although neither is successful and they have not been taken up by church choirs. A further unsuccessful ecclesiastical piece, the *Gloria*, appeared in 1945. Otherwise Bax was involved in writing piano music. The rather laboured *Suite for Fauré* was written between April and June 1945. It consists of five extended variations on a theme derived from Fauré's name, and was scored for strings and harp four years later. At the end of the year he wrote a brief set of variations on the North Country Christmas Carol *O Dame Get Up and Bake Your Pies*, written for 'Anna and Julian Herbage in acknowledgement of pies baked and enjoyed on "Christmas Day in the morning" 1945'.[28]

He also revised the First Violin Sonata, making one or two cuts, for re-publication by Chappell, and wrote incidental music for his brother Clifford's play *Golden Eagle*, of which he thought 'the architecture of the drama is most excellently designed',[29] and which was to be produced in January 1946. (Unfortunately it was not a success, and only ran for three performances.)

During the war Bax lost many old and dearly loved friends. Apart from his mother who had died early on in the war, Paul Corder had gone in 1942, Godwin Baynes and Benjamin Dale in 1943, and, perhaps worst of all, Maitland Radford, whose passing in March 1944 came as a great shock. Almost all the friends of his youth had gone, and at this time Bax had a habit of turning up at Eric Coates's London flat on festive occasions — looking for some peace and quiet. He was there on VE day. Although he was achieving performances and was a famous and fêted name on the British musical scene, he was fully aware that he was lauded for the wrong reasons, and although he would survive for another eight years, he had contributed to his art all that he had to say. It would be many years before the full range of his music and his achievement would even begin to be appreciated.

It was at about this time that Bax resumed writing verse. He showed his attempts to only his most intimate circle, and never made any effort to give them wider circulation. The verse is again auto-biographical, and encapsulates his mood of longing and regret. This example, dated August 1945, is entitled 'Thunderstorm'.

> All through the storm the heedless blackbird trills;
> While thunder rocks and tears the coppery sky
> And lightning splinters fleck the curtained hills
> Persists his melody.
>
> So when your body pitches in the trough
> Of bitter tides of longing may you know
> Some solace of the careless lilt of love
> I sang you long ago.

Last Years

Immediately the war was over in Europe, Bax was asked by the pianist Harry Isaacs to write a piano trio for inclusion in a series of six Wigmore Hall concerts being planned for early in 1946. At first he refused on the grounds that the medium was an impossible one, citing Dvořák in the 'Dumky' as the only composer to have tackled it successfully. However, during the year Bax gradually changed his mind and started writing. By 4 December he could tell Isaacs: 'I was thinking that you will be pleased to hear that I have finished two movements of the trio and am in the middle of the last. I am pleased with the work so far.' It was finished on 9 January 1946, and Bax wrote characterizing the first two movements as being 'severely classical'. 'As to the last,' he continued, 'it might have a quotation from Hamlet [III. ii. 148–9]. "This is miching mallecho – it means mischief"'. Possibly Bax was thinking of what for him was an unusual time signature in the last movement: $\frac{5}{8}$.

The work was very popular for a short time and was published soon after its first performance, which took place on 21 March 1946, and received very favourable notices. While indisputably of his late style, the work has a mellifluous turn of phrase which prompted *The Times* critic to write: 'the new work created an immediately favourable impression ... Its themes are vigorous and clear cut in the first and last movements, and their development is less apt to wander vaguely than in some other of the composer's works. The Adagio is one of those quiet contemplations of beauty such as we have come to expect of his slow movements. The texture of the music is exceptionally clear; even the pianoforte part is free from harmonic thickness. Altogether this compact and confidently written work makes a valuable addition to the literature of the form. Its performance was excellent.'[1]

The Trio had a good press, most of the dailies devoting some space to it. 'The themes seem inspired by a deeper emotion than usual', wrote the *Telegraph*, 'and fit their frame more easily ... Nothing is redundant and the three movements give an impression of a composition admirably constructed, characteristic and meticulously balanced in the instrumental parts. Played by the Harry Isaacs Trio confidently and with understanding, the work had a very warm welcome from the audience.'[2]

Scott Goddard, one of Bax's champions in the 1940s, wrote a particularly interesting appreciation in the *News Chronicle* which shows, as in the Violin Concerto, how successful Bax could be in producing late romantic music of little personal consequence, but delightful to hear and to play. Goddard wrote, 'How exciting it is to hear a new work by an old hand that has the freshness of a revelation. Such was the feeling engendered by Saturday's performance of Sir Arnold Bax's latest Piano Trio. The work was played magnificently by the Harry Isaacs Trio at the Wigmore. I imagine that technically it was an almost flawless performance; certainly it made the music vivid. Bax takes in a much wider range of musical experience than before. For instance, there are hints of older styles which I had thought foreign to his nature; also others from contemporary sources. And all transformed into an exquisite personal utterance. A great little masterpiece.'[3]

In August 1946 Bax made his first visit to Ireland since 1939. He stayed at his old haunt the Gresham Hotel, Dublin, and was welcomed with great warmth by all his old friends. The ostensible reason for his visit was to teach at a summer course in Dublin. This was not the sort of thing that Bax could have been persuaded to undertake in England, but in Ireland it was different, and he reported to Mary, 'my pupils are all very charming and attractive, with voices from all over the country, and I feel quite at home in the job.' To his friend Cecil Gray he wrote, 'my work is quite light, and as casual as I choose'.[4] On the mutually interesting subject of liquor — still in short supply in England, but more freely available in Ireland — he reported a happy situation: 'there has been no whisky at all in the bar here since I arrived, but private bottles flow in upon me in spate ... The Department of Education must be rotten with the stuff. I am even asked how many would I like! And there are other sources too.' A footnote to his letter records 'a Lucullan debauch at Jammet's last night'.

However, his visit also provided him with an opportunity for rediscovering all his favourite places of scenic beauty, including many he had not seen for a very long time. On 14 August he described a trip the previous day to the Dublin Wicklow Mountains and the Hellfire Club. 'These mountains', he wrote, 'are as wild and lonely as any in Ireland ... The air up there was like a cool intoxicant ... and for the first time ever I saw the Welsh mountains from Ireland. At first I could hardly believe my eyes ... It was really a great half melancholy glory. I had not been on that road since 1913 and it was rather a wistful experience.' Writing again the following day he was in even more reminiscent mood. 'Yesterday I was taken into the mountains and over roads that I bicycled over so many times when I lived in Rathgar. The ghost of the boy that was then seemed to be at my side, full of impossible dreams and ambitions of youth.'

There was no escaping the welcoming hospitality that was offered on all sides during this first time back in Ireland after so many war-torn years. 'On Thursday evening', he wrote to Mary, 'I was taken to a small party (about nine people) and enjoyed it more than any such affair for many years. All the people were really musical, and I played the piano part of some of my songs for a very good soprano singer ... Our host was a young engineer whose father was executed by the English after the 1916 rising. I found that he knew Co. Donegal and even Glencolumcille very well and we had a joyous conversation about those parts.'

Bax's letters to Mary at this time include examples that are very passionate. Although it is not necessary to reproduce the most personal of these, his references to them in his letter of 15 August are perhaps of interest. 'It is such a cosy thought that you are sleeping in my bed and surrounded by my books and belongings', he wrote. 'O my meadow-sweet, the last note I wrote to you was full of passion, and indeed I am feeling like that all the time ... I feel more lonely without you than ever before ... What is this strange magnetism between us two?'

Bax was back in Storrington on about 26 August but returned to Dublin during the third week of September to examine at University College. 'On the high seas it was rather rough at first', he wrote to Mary, adding that it had not affected him at all, and ending characteristically 'the Irish coast in the pale gold sunset was an enchantment.' Shortly after arriving he went to buy a new suit, as clothing was still subject to coupons in the UK, and his tailor advised him to go in his books under a pseudonym. 'What name do you suggest', asked Bax; and back came the answer 'O'Byrne'. 'What an amazing coincidence', he observed to Mary.

From Dublin Bax went to stay with Dr Tyrell at Comeragh View, Waterford, and then on 30 September to Cork to stay with the Fleischmanns. 'I feel I have been away for weeks and weeks instead of twelve days', he wrote to Mary, adding, 'the overwhelming hospitality that was showered upon me in Waterford and Dublin is being continued here.' They went to visit Professor Daniel Corkery, the author of the celebrated book, *The Hidden Ireland*. 'He lives', wrote Bax, 'in a perfectly peaceful place with a wonderful view some miles out of Cork. The strange thing (and so characteristic of unhappy Eire) is that in the "bad times" (1921–22) people were taken from both *his* and *this* one and murdered by political opponents. And now there is absolute dream and tranquillity upon both!'

After the initial success of the Piano Trio and with the coming of peace, Chappell's, Bax's new publisher (Murdoch had been bombed out and then taken over in 1943), issued the Trio and also the voice and piano score of the song cycle *The Bard of the Dimbovitza*, written long ago in 1914, but recently revised and with the songs in a new order. At about this time Bax received an enquiry from Victor Hely-Hutchinson, Director of Music at the BBC, asking whether he had any new works that might be considered for broadcasting. Although Bax complained about being neglected he received a good number of performances of a limited repertoire of his music, and did well by the BBC, the Proms and many provincial orchestras during the remainder of the 1940s. This was possibly one of the most conservative periods of the century, as far as British public taste in music was concerned, and some of Bax's least demanding works were given a very good innings. Bax wrote to Hely-Hutchinson:

Dear Victor

Thank you so much for your letter of enquiry. Yes I have one work which is virtually a novelty, anyway it can be remembered by no-one and has since its sole performance been drastically revised. This is 'The Bard of the Dimbovitza' an orchestral song-cycle based upon Roumanian folk-poetry. I wrote it about the time of The Garden of Fand but have just finished re-orchestrating the whole work. I should like Oda Slobodskaya to sing it (I have already mentioned it to her). I believe it to be one of my better things. I think it requires more rehearsal than is possible at a Promenade and would occupy about half an hour in performances, I should suppose. Another piece I should like to hear is 'Winter Legends' a sort of three movement concerto with Harriet Cohen as pianist. This has only twice been performed in London – (also given by Kussevitsky in USA). And if I may mention other works I would be glad if the violin concerto (Grinke) were kept in the repertoire and 'The Tale the Pine-Trees Knew' (symphonic poem) which has not been played for a long time.

My apologies for this self advertisement, but you *did* invite it![5]

Probably the most successful work of the year was the inconsequential if delightful aubade for piano and orchestra called *Morning Song: Maytime in Sussex*. This short movement was written in Bax's capacity as Master of the King's Musick to celebrate Princess Elizabeth's 21st birthday in 1947. In scoring it for piano and small orchestra, he must have been influenced by Harriet who gave the first public performance at a Robert Mayer children's concert in the presence of the Princess in October 1947. It had already been recorded on 7 February, and was issued in June 1947, before its first public performance, to mark the Princess's birthday. The review in the *Gramophone* gave it a vigorous, though not uncritical reception, finding it a 'wee bit stiffly shaped ... and perhaps not very new' but nevertheless concluding that it was 'a cordial to the weary heart'.[6] With its almost Mozartian delicacy and poise the music suggests, like the slow movement of the Violin Concerto, a parallel with those works of Richard Strauss's old age, the Oboe Concerto and Duet Concertino. Harriet played the work delightfully, and although the score was published no one else appeared interested. The composer Herbert Murrill noted, in a BBC memorandum, 'it struck me she is definitely useful for such work, being the only pianist who really tackles it with conviction.'

Early in 1947 Bax again turned to the piano and produced a suite of four miniatures — *Fantastic March* (dated 30 January), *Romanza* (11 February), *Idyll* (19 February) and *Phantasie* (12 March). But, for a composer who was notable for his quick-witted and fast-working methods, they were laboriously produced and were not played in public until 1983, and have never been published.

Also early in that year, John Masefield was commissioned to write a play to celebrate the 600th anniversary of the Foundation of the Order of the Garter which fell in April 1948. Masefield's response was called *A Play of St George*, and Bax was asked to write music for it. The whole project was referred to as the *Pageant of St George*, and was intended for production in a Cathedral, and it appeared that after Windsor, Exeter was intended to have seen it first.

Bax sketched quite an extended score for this enterprise, altogether some 558 bars being written. The sketches survive in the British Library, and show a work in nine movements (presumably separated by speech in performance). I list the number of bars in each section to give some idea of the substantial nature that the work, if finished, would have assumed:

I	Allegro Moderato	29 bars
II	Ceremonial Dance	36
III	Chorus of Ecclesiastics	89
IV	Allegro	28
	Interlude	14
V		124
VI		54
VII	Dragon's Song	11
VIII	In Time Long Past	31
IX	The Coming of Spring	44
	Extra Music	98

He wrote on 24 October, 'the Windsor Pageant has been abandoned owing to the financial and political situation, so my almost completed music is a dead loss as it cannot be adapted to any other purpose. A little saddening for the time being.' The administration of the project was mishandled, the cost of the orchestra not being included in the budget. Bax had expended considerable effort on the work, and he was very annoyed at the débâcle. There were several attempts to get a performance, but none came to anything. It was about one of these that, in August 1948, Bax wrote to Masefield: 'I should of course be delighted if my music could be used at the performance of St George at Exeter. But I am afraid the matter of the expense of an orchestra has been forgotten. I went into this matter when a performance at Exeter was suggested some time ago, and found out that at least £200 would be required. I wrote to the Dean explaining this and he replied that the price was prohibitive (as I expected). The music is quite unsuited to the organ and the choral element needs women's voices — so I don't see what can be done as far as the music is concerned. There are some nibblings from another cathedral and perhaps if this should come to anything, they would care for the full performance.'

In the summer of 1947 he went to Ireland to receive an honorary degree from the National University of Ireland, which greatly pleased him. He had, in fact gained an inkling of this honour the previous autumn, observing to Mary at the time, 'if it comes off [it] will please me more even than Oxford or Durham ... It would make me feel that I am taking an authentic place again in the cultural life of this beloved land.' As soon as Bax arrived at the Gresham Hotel he had his wallet stolen, which in the days of restrictions in the avail-ability of travel documents and currency was even more of a disaster than it would be today. Money, tickets, and a cheque from Bucking-ham Palace were all taken, and created a slight stir as some sharp-eyed Irish reporter picked up the story which appeared in the 'Peter-borough' column in the *Daily Telegraph*. The ceremony was two days later. 'There were three "victims" (as the University Registrar called us)', Bax noted, 'Jack B. Yeats, a Celtic professor and myself ... We wore red robes, a different coloured hood, and a velveteen "Sir Thomas More" hat.' Altogether Bax found the ceremony an ordeal which he was glad to get behind him. One can see from the press photographs of the time that he looked dejected; it was 'very hot', he wrote, 'and the clothes mighty heavy'. The ceremony consisted of a tribute in Latin followed by a eulogy in English lasting about a quarter of an hour. 'Then', Bax wrote, 'Mr de Valera handed me the official testimonial.' He was 'very impressed by de Valera', he told Mary. Later he went to a rehearsal of *Tintagel* and *In the Faery Hills* by the Radio Éireann Symphony Orchestra. Bax must have been particularly pleased by this official recognition from his adopted country. He wrote to the *Irish Times*:

A TRIBUTE

To the Editor of the *Irish Times*

Sir, – At the end of a week of fêting and hospitality such as I have never before enjoyed, I feel more than ever that I have once again returned to my own place. From earliest youth Eire has been my Land of Heart's Desire. I want to render enthusiastic thanks to Radio Eireann Orchestra for their patience at rehearsal and magnificent work in the concert generously devoted to my music on Thursday last, and to pay a particular tribute to the conductor, Dr Arthur Duff, who gave one of the most moving performances I have ever heard of my best-known orchestral piece, 'Tintagel'.

I must also praise Miss Maura O'Connor's always sensitive singing of my songs at the less advertised chamber concert on July 9th. And what shall I say of Ireland's most imaginative pianist (it is superfluous to mention the sheer brilliance of his technique), except that Charles Lynch played one of my piano-forte sonatas with a mastery that can only enhance his fame? I am happy to be able to look forward to another visit to Dublin in September –

Yours etc   Arnold Bax

Dublin, July 12th, 1947.[7]

No sooner had he returned for his second visit to Ireland than, on 27 September, while staying with the Fleischmanns in Cork, Bax heard from his son Dermot that his wife Elsita 'died the other night'.

He wrote to Mary, 'I feel in the most awful confusion ... I feel I want to stay in Ireland and tell you to come to me. But alas! things are not so simple as that.' But for the moment Bax did stay in Ireland as he had planned to do. The death of his wife did not materially affect Bax's life. Moreover, he was not to marry Mary, and for the moment did not even tell Harriet about his wife.

Bax's letters resume their description of his travels. On 2 October he went on a car drive through the Knockmealdown Mountains and on to the Rock of Cashel in Tipperary, 'rather a creepy place inhabited by rooks which clamour ceaselessly ... Then home with the sunset red gold on a big river. Of course I longed for you as always.'

Bax had been looking forward to visiting Killarney, 'the loveliest lake in the world under the moonlight', which he reached on 6 October. Writing to Mary the following day after returning to the Larchets' house in Ballsbridge, Dublin, where he was now a guest, having deserted the Gresham Hotel, he reported: 'Killarney was all I anticipated and more. The ethereal lake and dim pearly mountains under the moon were quite unearthly ... On such a day as yesterday it must be one of the loveliest places on earth. But such perfection can only come about once in a lifetime.' On the way back they motored amongst the highest mountains in Eire all day long, and lunch was taken at Bax's favourite Kenmare where he had spent so many peaceful spring days. 'It was all very good for me', he wrote, 'in my very disturbed state of mind.'

His position as Master of the King's Musick again required his attention in November, when fanfares were needed for the wedding of Princess Elizabeth and Philip Mountbatten. 'I have been writing three [only two were actually used] raucous fanfares for the WEDDING at Westminster,' he wrote. 'I have scored them for ordinary orchestral brass but now they have gone to the Military School of Music at Kneller Hall so that the disintegrating din may be keyed up still further. I hope they will not cause too much damage at the ceremony.'[8] 'The Royal Wedding was a sumptuous display', Bax wrote to Meta Malins, 'with a real enchanted faery-tale feeling ... I was in the Abbey and had quite a good profile view of the whole affair. The two Fanfares I wrote for the occasion were considered a great success – indeed I have become not a little sick of the subject. This morning I received a letter from Kussevitsky asking for the scores of them, though what he could do with them in Boston I don't quite know.'

Bax's fanfares are extended, almost symphonic in their effect, and fill a whole side of the 10 inch 78 rpm record that appeared almost immediately after the wedding. But their composition must have been a labour for him, for the effect of vitality is obtained by the use of the fanfare-like theme from *Spring Fire*. Also at this time, though apparently not for the royal wedding – or more probably written but not used – he set part of Spenser's wedding text of 1594, *Epithalamium*, with an organ accompaniment.

In September 1947, the fifth concert of the Norfolk and Norwich Triennial Music Festival included Bax's *Walsinghame* with Peter Pears as tenor soloist, an event that was noted by the BBC, though no action was apparently taken by them to broadcast the performance.

One of Bax's most popular and most played works from his last years was the music for David Lean's celebrated film, *Oliver Twist*. This was a major project that was to give Bax much publicity, and more financial reward than he had received from almost any other of his compositions. At the time of the composition of *Oliver Twist* there was something of a vogue in the cinema for neo-romantic scores for piano and orchestra, and this may explain much of the music's success. Yet Bax initially viewed the prospect with a sinking heart. 'I have been inveigled (not to say bullied)', he wrote in December 1947, 'into writing music for the Oliver Twist film ... It is the book of Dickens that I most dislike, and there is no music in the subject at all. So I must think up counterparts in sound of Gillray's and Rowlandson's savage cartoons. The première is supposed to be at the beginning of March (the usual inconsiderate rush) but I was *not* to be stampeded.'

Bax originally opened his score, after the titles, with a brief but evocative orchestral storm, intended as the background to the opening sequence of Oliver's mother staggering through a storm immediately before she was to die in childbirth. But Bax's music was dropped to make way for the very effective opening sequence without any music at all. The film did not actually open until June 1948, and in April he again complained, 'I am still plagued by the "Oliver Twist" film for which I struggled in agonies to provide music – a very thankless task as there is no music in the subject. I cannot imagine any subject more unsuited to me.'

Easily the best review of the music was by Hans Keller in the *Music Review*.[9] Devoting so detailed an account to film scores in the musical press is a practice we should aspire to today. Keller wrote:

BAX'S OLIVER TWIST

Odeon Theatre, Leicester Square
Press Show: 22nd June
Philharmonia Orchestra, c. Muir Mathieson
Solo Piano: Harriet Cohen
Recorded by Stanley Lambourne and Gordon K. McCallum

There is only one previous film score by Bax, i.e. for the documentary *Malta GC* (1943; written 1942). Why not more? Sir Arnold himself would seem to have supplied the answer:

> I do not think the medium is at present at all satisfactory as far as the composer is concerned, as his music is largely inaudible, toned down to make way for — in many cases — quite unnecessary talk. This is, in my opinion, quite needless as it is impossible to pay attention to two things at the same time if they appeal to different parts of the intelligence.

Of late, however, more attention has been given to the fact that 'the quality of dialogue and its level must be considered in relation to the orchestration and musical balance'. And although, only a few months ago, Sir Arnold repeated his above-quoted opinion to a friend of mine, he has now given us another film score which — thanks perhaps to Muir Mathieson's musicianly attitude — bears no trace of his resentment against film music.

I gather that David Lean, the film's director, suggested to the composer that the title-figure's loneliness might be rendered distinct by entrusting the Oliver themes to a piano. This idea would have killed itself if it had been applied too lavishly, but Bax makes the most of it by putting it into practice at only a few important junctures in Oliver's story. The first (E minor) of the five piano entries is impressively prepared, in the relative (G) major, by variational treatment of the title theme. (The title-music itself is in F minor.) In the sharpest contrast to this E minor section, the then following 'number' again associated with Oliver, is in E flat minor, which is also the key of the third piano entry (the second being, like the first, in E minor, in whose dominant the film ends). The piano's fourth appearance, in E flat major, is not quite happily integrated with the talk above it — this is one of the few points which may annoy Sir Arnold.

Like Walton, Bax avoids the usual film-musical pitfall of treating the visual pleonastically. Oliver's sad pickpocket lesson with Fagin, for instance, is anticipated, rather than merely emphasised, by a relative minor version of the C major tune heard during the boys' (more amusing) pickpocket practice on the previous night. (The actual pickpocket episode, which ends with a 'Stop thief!' chase and with Oliver being knocked out, is in F minor, the tragic title-key.) In C major, too, is the piece that foresees Oliver's first encounter with Fagin. In the scene, on the other hand, where Mr and Mrs Bumble are conspiring with Monks, and Mrs Bumble's tale is illustrated by retrospective 'intercuts', the D minor backflash to the corresponding D minor passage does not seem to add much to the story — or have I missed the point? The utilisation and elaboration of the thematic material is, throughout the score, arresting. One hopes indeed that Bax will now continue to contribute to the film, ideally suited as his work is for exciting the cinema-goer's interest in good film music. For he is able to avail himself, to quite an extent, of a good old idiom, and yet to write good music.

The 'big tune' at the end — 'Mr Brownlow's tune' — was quarried by Bax from the score of the earlier music for *In Memoriam, Pádraig Pearse* (see p. 140). This resort to earlier works for thematic ideas makes one wonder why he did not bring forward some of the earlier, unplayed works that remained in a large trunk in his room at the White Horse, instead of labouring over new scores in which he did not really believe.

Immediately after *Oliver Twist* had been recorded for the cinema sound track, the most notable parts of what were to become the suite from the film, with Harriet at the piano, were recorded by Columbia on 1 September at EMI's Abbey Road Studio No. 1, for issue on two 12-inch 78 rpm discs. The recording of the *Oliver Twist* music was the occasion of Harriet's discovery — through the publication of the will — of Bax's wife's death. She immediately imagined that Bax would marry her. 'All she wanted was to be *Lady* Bax', a friend remarked. He resisted the suggestion, and eventually had to disclose the fact of Mary's existence. A tumultuous, histrionic row ensued, but Bax wrote to Mary, telling her that he was not proposing to anyone, but if he did it would be to her. Later that autumn, while carrying a tray of glasses, Harriet fell and severely cut her right wrist. Her ensuing incapacity as a pianist directly affected her ability to perform Bax's music. This fact and the watery Left-Hand Concerto that he subsequently wrote for her did his own reputation considerable harm.

Bax persisted in using ideas from earlier works. Another example is the choral *Magnificat*, which is merely a choral arrangement of his Pre-Raphaelite song of that name published over forty years before. Another work written for a well-wisher — this time Dr Harold Darke — it was mechanically produced and adds to Bax's reputation not one iota. Nor was it of any value to Darke, who did not like it, thinking it unworthy of its composer.

The revised score of *The Bard of the Dimbovitza* was due to be programmed by the BBC, but it had to be scheduled several times before the performance took place. On 29 April, Humphrey Searle wrote to Bax to say that owing to indisposition, Miss Flora Nielsen, Bax's first choice after Slobodskaya, would not be able to sing. Later, on 8 September Searle wrote again to say that Janet Fraser would now sing it with the BBC Symphony Orchestra under Boult on 2 October. However, this did not suit Bax, who was going to Ireland, and he asked that it might be 'put off for a few days'. In the event it received two performances by Emelie Hooke with the BBC Symphony under Boult on 26 March 1949, and again the following day. It has not been heard since.

The *Concertante for Three Solo Wind Instruments and Orchestra* was Bax's response to a commission to write a work for a concert to commemorate Sir Henry Wood, a request that he could hardly refuse, nor did he wish to. The concept of a 'kind of triple concerto in four movements — (a) cor anglais and orchestra (b) clarinet and orchestra (c) horn and orchestra and (d) all three used as soloists to-gether' — is original, and the approach to each movement through the character of the solo instrument makes for a delightful work. On 18 November he reported that the composition was 'giving me a good deal of trouble'.[10] Nevertheless, the first movement, an *Elegy*, was completed on 23 November, and the other three followed shortly afterwards: the *Lento* (horn) on 29 November, the *Scherzo* (clarinet) on 7 December, and the final *Allegro ma non troppo* on New Year's Day 1949. Writing to John Horgan about the work, Bax underlined the programmatic nature of the first movement, at least. 'The first movement is really entitled "Lament for Tragic Lovers 1803" ', he wrote, referring to the ill-fated love of the Irish patriot, Robert Emmet, and Sarah Curran, adding 'There is a two bar quotation played by solo violin at the end taken from "She is far from the land" [Moore's *Irish Melodies*]. (I wonder if you have read John Brophy's excellent recent novel "Sarah").'[11] The least successful movement is the last, which while enjoyable is still laboured by the standards of his best orchestral music. It is unlikely that the work as a whole will be played often owing to the need for three instrumental soloists, and for a large orchestra only in the last movement. However, the first three movements would work well if promoted separately, when one suspects they would make their way more effectively.

For the remainder of his life Bax continued the pattern of visiting Ireland twice in the later summer — in August and then in late September. While there in August 1948, he declared to Mary, 'what I feel about you is simple and primitive like a fire or a wind and when I dream of you (I did last night) the November fog lifts for that time.' In September it was the familiar round of examining in Dublin, and then on to Waterford and Cork. While staying at Waterford on 1 October, he reported a strange experience to Mary. 'I was half-awake this morning in my bed, when you came in bringing me a drink of water. I saw you quite clearly and spoke to you in, naturally, a surprised voice and then I saw that there was no-one there.' Four days later he wrote from the Old Ground Hotel, Ennis, in familiar vein. 'I have seen so much beauty in the last few days', he wrote, 'that I feel really bewildered. We have been all through the wildest and most remote parts of Connemara. Places where no-one ever goes.'

One of the high points of Bax's life during his last few years was the friendship of a young musician who was setting out on a career as conductor, and who championed Bax's music. This was Christopher Whelen who, for some three or four years in his late teens and early twenties, was assistant conductor to Rudolph Schwarz at Bournemouth. During this time they steeped the Bournemouth audience in Bax; never in his career had one orchestra devoted so much energy to him over so short a period. Now that his music was gradually being played less, this gave Bax much cheer. He would often complain that people only wanted new works, but Whelen and Schwarz gave a wide range of the music, which caused Bax to begin to suggest candidates for revival. A vigorous correspondence ensued, of which the following is a typical example:

I am very much pleased and encouraged by your delightful enthusiastic letter and to hear that you are to conduct Tintagel ... [It] is always well played – I suppose on account of its broad lines. Even the Dublin radio orchestra under a not very experienced conductor gave it a fine performance. I certainly hope to hear it at Bournemouth as well as the symphony in March, and shall look forward to meeting you there.

I think if you are able to give either the second or seventh symphony it would be better to choose the latter as I think it is more accessible than any of the others to those who are unfamiliar with my work. The last time No. 2 was played in England was about 17 years ago – and most magnificently – by Koussevitsky. A work I would like to hear again is the practically unknown Overture, Elegy and Rondo. The score and parts of this are in print, but I believe the work has never been played since it was published. (This is quite enough advertisement of *my* own music!)

I quite agree with you that there is every excuse for the over-worked conductor for not tackling difficult scores which have never received more than luke-warm attention from the critical hacks. VW's works are always received with reverence (and quite rightly too) and are played so often that the orchestras really know them, and consequently they give comparatively little trouble. I am really tremendously grateful to you for your eagerness to make my work better known.

Tintagel went well. In encouraging his young champion Bax agreed that 'the rising wind and sea in the middle is certainly the most difficult to manage'. The Sixth Symphony was also suggested for performance and Bax was enthusiastic, confiding 'it is the symphony of mine which I know least myself ... When I heard it played by Boult about two years ago there were times when I could not remember what was coming next – a very curious experience. I don't think any of my symphonies have been played more than about ten times in this country – a somewhat discouraging fact! So all the more am I happy to find new friends.'

If Christopher Whelen's activities in playing Bax's music were a source of great pleasure and satisfaction to the composer, his activities as an author also received Bax's approval. He was particularly complimentary about an article in the local Bournemouth musical journal, the *Mercury*. The following extracts are quoted to give the flavour of Whelen's assessment, and because this journal may not be generally available to interested readers.

In an age that prefers experiment to invention, an age that encourages the composer to make the counterpoint in his fugues fit like the Edwardian waistline, Sir Arnold Bax describes himself as a 'brazen romantic'. Yet this romanticism of his, which does exist in all his work in a very real way, is not juicy, as is that of César Franck; nor is it of a weird Sibelian harshness or full of a Tchaikovskian self-pity. It is as if Bax has been looking on at experiences and events rather than taking part in them; and Yeats – who created for himself a similar world apart from the mythology of Ireland – possessed just this same sense of detachment, his own startling advice being:

> Cast a cold eye
> On life, on death.
> Horseman, pass by!

Emotionally, then, Bax projects his music for us, as if on a screen – where we can watch it and listen to it objectively. There is no self-pity, and no brooding melancholy – the two emotions with which romantic music is usually so saturated. There are one or two notable influences at work in Bax, among them, I think, a distinct Byzantine strain. When Byzantium became the capital of the Roman Empire, richness of material and decoration was the sole aim of the artist, and Bax's music has always seemed to me to possess this splendid and large influence; a luxurious influence possibly, and one which depends much on colour and surface ornament for its effect. Instead of an equal proportion of parts, the stiff outline and the severe lines of the modern Classicists, Bax gives us extravagant splendour, ornamentation, and superbly chiselled detail. Lack of frequent performance of his larger works is in part due to the fact that no conductor has specialised in them, while such often-performed pieces as *Mediterranean, Overture to a Picaresque Comedy* and *Romantic Overture*, although pleasant enough works, are entirely unrepresentative.

It is to the seven great symphonies that we must look for the kernel of the composer's mind. In several of these, Bax uses a 'motto' technique which tends to make the themes themselves as classical as any; but because of rich and fully sonorous writing his symphonic style is sometimes said to be rhapsodic and shapeless – but only by those who speak first (and loudly) and think afterwards (or not at all). Certainly these symphonies are, formally, episodic and dramatic, rather than argumentative and logical – but they have a very logic of their own, and although they are apt to *sound* dramatic, and even (to the more imaginative listener) pictorial, this does not mean they are unsymphonic nor does it imply any lack of design ...

This [the Fourth Symphony] is music crammed with excitement and drama; when angry, it grinds no axe, for it has no message – only statement; while I think its most lovable feature is the happiness and serenity that shines from the best of it. This particular quality of gaiety (rare as gold in our time) results most often in one of two moods, the one rhythmically adventurous and exciting, the other a mood of supernal calm. Bax's symphonic movements are like tapestries depicting spacious and heroic events, and if the events are of the past (unlike Vaughan Williams' Sixth), if the music itself *sounds* pictorial and legendary, it is because Bax's art, though technically speaking of our time, is ageless.[12]

Bax recommended the author to Alfred Bacharach who was looking for someone to write the article on him in the Penguin 'Master Musicians' series. A book on Bax was also planned, with the collaboration of the composer himself, but it was abandoned in the end because Harriet was continually interfering and attempting to influence what was written.

Harriet's right hand remained disabled for several years, and it was natural she should look for repertoire to play with the left hand only. Bax was persuaded to write a left-hand concerto for her, and in 1949 he was largely preoccupied with it. The *Left Hand Concertante*, as it became known, is not a successful work, and unfortunately for Bax's reputation had the misfortune of being widely played for several years. The critical sneers that it received were, by implication, extended to the rest of his music. It was a pity because it over-shadowed Bax's greatest works for piano and orchestra, in particular the *Symphonic Variations* which Harriet did not play after 1938, although, later in 1954, after Bax's death and after her wrist showed some recovery she very successfully broadcast the *Winter Legends*. Nevertheless, *Left Hand Concertante*, patently Bax's worst extended work, was widely heard. The first movement is laboured although there are some attractive ideas. The slow movement is probably the best; beautiful if limited, it was published in an abridged two-hand arrangement as a piano solo. But the theme of the finale, a rondo, is tawdry. His heart was not in the work. He wrote to the Dutch cellist-composer Henri van Marken during its composition: 'I find it terribly difficult to think of anything effective for the one hand. But then I am very much out of practice in writing for the piano at all.' The last movement opens with a rhythmic idea beaten out by percussion alone, a conception that may well have been suggested by the opening of the 'Adam's Fates' movement of Bliss's *Adam Zero* which was topical in the late 1940s. But except in the finale, Bax seldom brings the soloist away from the lower half of the keyboard, and so the left-hand limitation is thus rather more pronounced than it might have been. Ravel, in his left-hand concerto, which Harriet never played, allowed his soloist a much wider compass, but that work was little known in England in the 1940s. The *Concertante* was first heard at Cheltenham on 4 July 1950 under Barbirolli, and Harriet made a great splash with it, and subsequently with Prom performances.

During 1949 and 1950 there were two crises in Bax's relationship with Mary. In 1949 the opportunity arose for her to go to her sister in New Zealand, and, possibly feeling somewhat insecure in her position, she seriously considered it. But eventually Bax bought a detached house in Fern Road, in the southern part of Storrington, near the convent, to which Mary moved. Here she lived during the remainder of Bax's life and for many years after his death. The second crisis was when she had to undergo a serious operation. 'You shall go into a *good* nursing home', wrote Bax. 'I won't have you enter a public ward in a hospital.' In 1951 she went to Switzerland to recuperate, and Bax amusingly referred to Balfour Gardiner's dislike of the mountains and his favourite phrase 'those regrettable shapes': 'I want you to see the real "regrettable shapes" at Interlaken and Lucerne.'

During 1950 Bax wrote no music at all, and during 1951 only two fanfares for the BBC programme, 'Show Business 1851–1951', which were wanted in March. As Master of the King's Musick he had been commissioned to write a Festival of Britain overture, but nothing came of it. Perhaps there was some truth in his statement to Kenneth Wright of the BBC, in a letter dated 9 August 1951, in which he said that he did 'not write much these days, being comfortably off and lazy'. In October 1950 Bax visited Sligo from where he wrote that he had 'scarcely been there since I was 22 years old and it was inclined to bring back my youth with rather poignant sensations.'

The death of E. J. Moeran on 1 December 1950 was a great sorrow. Bax was appointed executor of the will with Moeran's brother, and wrote a reminiscent appreciation for *Music and Letters* noting to Mary, 'once I had started I found it much easier to do than I had expected. I have made no reference to alcohol!'

In June 1950, Balfour Gardiner also died, and at the memorial concert 'given by his friends at the French Institute, Queensbury Place, London' on Monday 23 April 1951, Bax accompanied Rowland Jones in three of Gardiner's songs – 'Rybbesdale' (to words by his brother Clifford Bax), 'The Quiet Garden' and 'Winter'. The concert does not appear to have been a great success: the singers appeared under-rehearsed, Bax himself was very ill at ease, and Steuart Wilson's address was facetious and struck quite the wrong note. Bax had not seen his old friend for two or three years, for on his last visit he had had to witness a young man whom Gardiner had befriended behaving abominably towards him. Bax was deeply anguished by it all.

Another of Bax's old friends, John Ireland, was well known in musical circles in the Storrington area, ultimately moving to Rock Mill – a converted windmill at Washington with a view over Chanctonbury Ring. Ireland could be bitterly sarcastic at Bax's greater formal recognition than his own. 'The great Mr Bax!'[13] he would drawl; and to Mary 'How is M.K.M., Knight?'

In 1952 Bax was involved in a move to try and obtain a knight-hood for Ireland, writing to the Prime Minister and receiving a reply that his friend's name was already on the list for consideration. 'It seems quite promising,'[14] commented Bax, though it was never known why Ireland was not so honoured. (Muriel Searle in her *John Ireland* tells a different story, reporting Bax as saying, 'I haven't put you up for an honour, old man, as I know you don't like that sort of thing'.)[15]

That year Bax reported that he found his examining duties in Ireland 'more boring than usual'.[16] While in Dublin he 'saw a terrible play about Soviet Russia very well acted on Thursday night, so well done that I should not like to see anything so impressively awful again'. He added 'the work part of this holiday is now over, so I can just relax and lose myself in the Connemara dream'.[17]

On 6 October he was staying at the Banba Hotel, Salthill, Galway, and described how 'yesterday afternoon in perfect sunlight we visited the strange Connemara islands, so unlike anything else in the world: the landscape is all stony flat without one tree ... Long arms of the sea come in everywhere and behind all the quite unearthly looking mountains, literally like gigantic pearls.'[18]

Why Bax now allowed himself to be tempted by a commission to write the music for another film it is difficult to decide, but one imagines it must have been purely for the money. This was another documentary film, the British Transport film, *Journey into History*. Bax turned in the very fragmentary brief score in just two weeks.

Although he was Master of the Queen's Musick, Bax was largely ignored over the music for the Coronation in 1953. As far as the musical arrangements for the Coronation itself were concerned, Bax reported that 'the Archbishop of Canterbury has, as it were, issued an edict to the effect that *all* the Coronation music is to be controlled by Dr McKie, the organist of Westminster Abbey. I am supposed to be consulted, but I shall merely be in the position of a yesman.'[19]

Two new works appeared in 1953, both of them in his official capacity for the Coronation. Firstly, for the anthology *A Garland for the Queen* that Boris Ord prepared and recorded for the Coronation Year, Bax contributed *What is it like to be Young and Fair?* to words by his brother. While purely an occasional piece, it is hard for the listener who knows the history of the two brothers' lives not to find the simple setting and heartfelt sentiment affecting.

Bax's other piece for the Coronation was the *Coronation March*. But he was obviously feeling tired. It was said he had already decided to resign the Mastership of the Queen's Musick and retire to Cork, and for the Coronation had already merely re-written the *Malta GC Victory March*. Although Walton had been commissioned to write his march *Orb and Sceptre*, a contribution from the Master of the Queen's Musick was *de rigueur*.

But Bax had lost none of his quiet wit with those in his circle. He wrote to Christopher Whelen about his appearance in the Coronation Honours List, where he was created the KCVO: 'as a chess player of my acquaintance said "It constituted a fine example of the two knights' defence". The whole thing surprised me a good deal, I must say.'

A lot of Bax's time during his last years was spent in writing letters associated with his official post. He lost no opportunity in telling friends and correspondents how he enjoyed the frequent holidays that he took with Mary in Devon and Cornwall, 'away from music and correspondence'. His lack of creative spark became a familiar cry to his friends. For example he wrote in November 1952 to Henri van Marken, 'I doubt whether I shall write anything else. Nearly everyone has written their best work before reaching my age. I feel that I have said all I have to say and it is of no use to repeat myself ... I really have no impulse to compose in these days, and anyhow I have written a devil of a lot in my time.'

Bax aged very rapidly in his last years, physically changing from the thin, elfin-like figure which he had presented until well into his fifties. Certainly in his sixties he became stout and ruddy complexioned. Eric Fenby called him 'owl-like',[20] hardly recognizing him after a break of several years. Clifford Bax noted to Julius Harrison on 'Shakespeare's Birthday '52 ... Arnold turns up now and again, but I don't like the colour of his complexion.' Much of this trouble must have been due to the amount of whisky that Bax consumed. He was already drinking before the Second World War, but not to the detriment of his faculties — he never appeared drunk. During the war — in so far as he could get any whisky at all — he fraternized with a fairly heavy-drinking set, but afterwards, and particularly towards the end, one gains the impression that he came to rely on it. He certainly had trouble in sleeping, and for this reason, at least, he may have drunk. Yet he tried not to inflict this despairing side of his personality on his family and those close to him. He remained a kindly and human figure, as Richard Walker found when he visited him at Storrington in the summer of 1952. 'He came shuffling down the corridor to meet me,' Walker wrote,

and immediately I sensed a certain reserve and shyness in the manner of his greeting. Bax was dressed in the well-known and tightly buttoned lounge suit ... He was of medium height, with head well sunk into shoulders, and an appearance of what I can most closely describe as bagginess in both build and clothes which was entirely dispelled once he became animated in conversation. Indeed his face, though not I suppose a conventionally handsome one, showed so much of deep sensitivity and incisive intelligence that one soon forgot outward forms and surroundings and became engrossed in his personality and charm. This very compelling and interesting face had as focus very piercing light grey-blue eyes, a short nose, and a most individual downward-slanting slit of a mouth which nevertheless suggested alertness and humour, and was in no way unkind or hard. Bax perched himself on the high fender of the fire in the inn parlour, sitting very squarely and symmetrically, with his head thrust well forward. Conversation was at first of a very general kind, a verbal circling of the subject of music, which neither of us at first was willing to broach. Bax's voice had a slightly constricted, staccato quality, and I remember that when tea was brought and I had asked the inevitable question about preference for 'milk in first' he gave a high pitched cry of 'Feminine Superstition'.[21]

In August 1953 Bax took Mary with him to a concert — a Prom — for the first time. The first Prom performance of his Sixth Symphony was presented by the Hallé Orchestra conducted by Barbirolli (incidentally, after this, it would be over thirty years before a Bax symphony would again be heard at the Proms). After he had taken a bow he joined Mary at the interval, and surprised and saddened her by asking 'Were you proud of me?' It was the first and, as it turned out, the last time he had ever been able to share a musical success with her. On most occasions he would have been overshadowed by Harriet's possessiveness, for she tended to take his triumphs on herself. Once, when he joined Mary on his return from London, she saw that he was upset, and when she attempted to discover the reason, Arnold disclosed that it concerned Harriet and his music. This was unusual, because he seldom mentioned her name to Mary. Mary being irritated by what he said remarked sarcastically: 'I suppose if it was not for her you would never have composed music.' To which he replied, almost in a whisper, 'Yes I have that too.' Mary was horrified. She believed that the urge to create any form of art is a spiritual one and that all else is simply an influence.

In September he went to Ireland to examine at University College, Dublin. From the Banba Hotel, Salthill, Galway, he wrote to Mary on 19 September: 'There is a wild south-west wind screaming over the bay this morning but I hope it may carry my love to you as quickly as maybe. The first thing that happened to me on my arrival in the west was a lunch with two young priests just outside Limerick City. I say lunch but it turned out to be an advanced debauch. Everything potable was there and never have I *refused* so many drinks ... Yesterday we were out in the car all day ... in Connemara and later round the Clare coast with the Aran Islands in sight most of the time. It was a day of mingled sunshine and cloud and a welter of wonderful colour. O! to have had you with me darling, I always feel this about every kind of beauty you know.' Three days later they were at Keel, Achill Island, Co. Mayo. 'The weather has been frightful. Of course the mountains are very impressive in their folds of storm and there have been sudden wild bursts of sunshine which irradiate everything in wild Irish light.' And then back to Dublin to stay with the Larchets before going on to Cork.

It was in Cork that he died suddenly on Saturday 3 October. He had always wanted to die in Ireland and during his sightseeing holidays in 1952 and 1953, and especially during the last few days of his life, he visited many favourite places in the south and west, almost as if he were saying goodbye. Yet there is certainly no evidence that Bax had any premonition of his death, for he had written in his autobiography, 'if I live to be seventy I shall celebrate that birthday by abusing old age with a malevolence even more savage than that evinced by Yeats'.[22]

His last two letters to Mary are dated 25 and 29 September, and they are reproduced below so that they can speak for themselves. Both were written from Ballsbridge, Dublin.

25 September

I have seen endless beauty during the last week, but only in intervals of terrific storm. Achill island is a giant place, full of huge cliffs and mountains and the violent seas crashing in from the Atlantic were overwhelmingly grand. (As usual I wanted you!) We ended up at Sligo after crossing mile upon mile of desolation in north Mayo, a melancholy wilderness of bogland with scarcely any life, either human or otherwise. Yesterday morning we spent in Yeats Sligo Country, Innisfree etc, all in a glitter of sunlight. The gleam on the lakes dazzling to the eye. But what is the good of verbal description of such things.

29 September

Have just received your letter my sweet. And thank you for your love and caresses enclosed in the envelope. I am sending you £12 to pay for the decorations in case you will be short. The exams here were finished today and mighty boring they were. I am going to Cork on Thursday (Glen House, Bally Valane, Cork) and shall be there until Monday. I expect you and Nora have forgotten about the R. Strauss festival at Covent Garden. Anyway you might have found the opera rather perplexing. I saw some remarkable Spanish dancing again the other night here, and last night "The Love of the Four Colonels" which I had forgotten that I had already seen. I was in a box from which it was only by stretching one's neck sideways that one could see one side of the stage at all.

Dublin is so gay and friendly after London but I want to come back to you and your welcoming arms. Ever my love my dear and darling
   from A.

Four days later, he died. Tilly Fleischmann has written the following account of the composer's death:

I think that Arnold would not have wished to die anywhere but in Ireland. He had a deep-rooted love for the Irish people and their country, and was particularly fond of Cork. A few days before his death, he told me he was resigning his position in England and was coming to live here. A friend of his thought he ought to settle in Dublin but he preferred Cork. 'Dublin has become too cosmopolitan'.

The last of his own music he ever heard, was *The Garden of Fand*. My son [Professor Aloys Fleischmann] gave a Bax evening on Tuesday, September 29th 1953 with the Radio Eireann Symphony Orchestra in the Phoenix Hall, Dublin, Arnold being present. The programme consisted of *Overture to Adventure*, *Concertante for Piano Left Hand* with Harriet Cohen as soloist and *The Garden of Fand*. (The year before my son did Arnold's *Third Symphony*, also in his presence). Arnold was very happy that evening, and told me how delighted he was with the whole performance.

A few hours before his death on the following Saturday, he was at the Old Head of Kinsale looking out into the Atlantic. John Horgan who drove him

there, said he never saw such a glorious sunset! The whole sky was ablaze with
colour of every possible hue; red, deep orange, yellow and far away on the
horizon, there was a pale blue mist. Arnold was lost in gazing at it, and John had
to take him gently by the arm, and remind him that we were all waiting for him.

On arriving back from Kinsale, Arnold seemed to be in great form. He enjoyed
every moment of his trip to the Old Head, and was reminiscing about old times,
and his friends. John was just about to give Arnold a drink, when he stood up
from his chair and said: 'Please take me home'. John looked at him and saw that
he was trembling, and that a change had come over him. He called to his wife
Mary, to drive Arnold to Glen House, my son's home where Arnold was staying
at the time.

Mary was terrified, as she thought that Arnold might die in the car on the
way. She knew that he always suffered from heart trouble. To her amazement,
on their arrival at Glen House, Arnold stepped out of the car just as usual, and
walked quickly up the stairs to his bedroom. Anne, my son's wife, suggested
sending for a doctor, but Arnold wouldn't hear of it. He begged her to wait
until morning.

Anne, however, telephoned to Dr James Donovan, who arrived within twenty
minutes. After examining Arnold he told Anne that there was no hope — he had
had a coronary thrombosis and acute pulmonary oedema.

Arnold was half sitting up in the bed. He had no pain whatsoever and was
very grateful, as was his wont for any little attention, saying 'thank you, thank
you!' Those were his last words. After Dr Donovan's fatal pronouncement, Anne
and Mary Horgan said the prayers for the dying, Anne going in and out of the
room. At 10 o'clock all was over — he just fell asleep.

R.I.P.[23]

Derrick Puffett, quoting W. Y. Evans Wentz,[24] has reminded us[25]
that in Celtic mythology 'to enter the otherworld "before the
appointed hour marked by death", a passport was necessary. "This
was usually a silver branch of the sacred apple-tree bearing blossoms,
or fruit, which the queen of the Land of the Ever-Living and Ever-
Young gives to those mortals whom she wishes for as companions ...
Often the apple-branch produces music so soothing that mortals who
hear it forget all troubles." This useful instrument figures in [Yeats's]
Oisin. Fand would have certainly possessed it. The celesta passage
preceding her song has the effect of putting it in inverted commas; of
signalling that we are about to enter another world. This is the import
of similar passages in the symphonies ...'. The Garden of Fand was the
last Bax heard of his own music before his death. One may wonder,
with Mr Puffett, if he understood the celesta's message.

Decline and revival

'I am sick to death of the BBC's studied neglect of me and weary of the musical profession in general',[1] wrote Bax in an uncharacteristic outburst to Lady Jessie Wood a few months before he died. As we have seen, he was really played quite frequently, but the image that was created by the repeated performance of uncharacteristic works was not one to appeal to a new audience or the new young generation of composers who were just emerging. Bax then appeared as a musical fossil, and the attempts of his old friends to promote his music, while pleasing to the composer and his admirers, did nothing to demonstrate the real Bax, for they were all too close even to try to see him in perspective. In 1950 Bax's Violin Concerto was given at a Promenade concert and the critic who found that 'the nostalgic lyricism of the slow movement is perhaps the finest distillation of Bax's poetic fancy'[2] is typical in this respect. Bax died the same week as Kathleen Ferrier, and the BBC's weekly *Music Magazine* programme for Sunday 11 October carried tributes to both. The Bax tribute, written and spoken by the joint editor, Bax's friend Julian Herbage, included three examples on records: the *Coronation March*, *Overture to a Picaresque Comedy* and the end of *The Garden of Fand*, a collection incapable of telling the audience of the time anything except that Bax was master of the orchestra.

Arrangements had been in hand to celebrate what would have been Bax's 70th birthday, and these celebrations now became memorial tributes. In February 1953 Ibbs and Tillett had pointed out that *Winter Legends*, played by Harriet, would be appropriate to mark Bax's birthday, but Eric Warr at the BBC confessed that he felt 'no great enthusiasm for *Winter Legends*', although he conceded, 'it would be more practicable for the birthday than one of the symphonies'. 'Equally, or more likely', he continued, 'is the violin concerto, pleasant and romantic.'[3] Harriet continued to pester the BBC concerning *Winter Legends*, and although it was not played in 1953 her campaign did result in a performance in December of the following year. However, in 1953 Harriet was disconcerted in the middle of her attempts to get *Winter Legends* performed to be asked to give two performances of the *Symphonic Variations*, on 7 and 8 November. She had to decline, and Ibbs and Tillett, in writing to explain her refusal, pointed out that '(a) she must have a longer time to re-learn them as she has not played them for some years and has a fairly full schedule abroad between now and November; (b) no parts exist because they were destroyed in the war and the only score existing is a rather burnt full one from which a piano part will have to be made; (c) Sir Henry Wood asked for the first, long variation to be cut and the work was therefore modified for this purpose: Sir Arnold wishes to replace this movement (as advised by others – notably Lambert and Moeran) but it will take time to revise ... We suggest therefore that the work should be considered for inclusion some time next year.'[4]

Bax's death was very widely reported internationally, and particularly in Ireland. It is significant that all the reports and tributes were couched in terms of the warmest affection. Representative, perhaps, though better informed than many, was Eric Blom in *The Observer*, who wrote:

The sudden death of Sir Arnold Bax, Master of the Queen's Music, means a great loss to a delightfully companionable man's friends. That it does not mean the same to present-day composition he would have been the first to agree. He made no secret of his awareness that his music was out of fashion. Nor did this worry him, for he knew he was a romantic and had no desire whatever to change his spots, as he might have put it with that ironical humour of his which included a large measure of self-recognition.

To meet Bax was to be sure of receiving mental refreshment and no end of amusement. His music, too, has remained memorable by a special atmosphere that hangs about it. Whether one approves of his idiom and procedures or not, one recognises that there is nothing else to take its place. The best examples should at all costs be kept alive, for later music has entered very different phases and there will never be anything like it again.[5]

Bernard Shore, the violist, and author of a celebrated study, *Sixteen Symphonies*, in which he analyzes his chosen works (including Bax's *Third*) from the orchestra player's point of view, remembered Bax's personal qualities as a friend. 'Like his music', Shore wrote, 'so was the man — difficult to get to know at first but, when intimate terms were reached, a rare companion ... A holiday with him was a delight. On walks he would quote Chesterton and Wodehouse by the page, and his gift of mimicry would reduce one to helplessness. His store of limericks was inexhaustible, and cricket was another of his subjects. Last of all would he talk about himself.'[6]

Eric Coates, another old friend, wrote in similar vein. 'Well — he has gone. The slightly stooping, diffident, shy figure we all knew so well will be seen no more, but the music that came from that imaginative and creative mind will still live on. Dear Arnold Bax — the world has lost a great musician and I, personally, have lost an old and loved friend.'[7]

Bax's funeral, in Cork, was held privately, and on 6 October he was laid to rest in St Finbarr's cemetery. The Very Rev. Dean McAdoo officiated at the graveside, and among the mourners[8] who had specially come to Ireland were Miss Evelyn Bax, the composer's sister; Eric Gillett, Bax's old cricketing friend representing Clifford Bax, who was by then an invalid; and Harriet Cohen, who had only recently returned to England. Irish mourners included John Horgan, Aloys Fleischmann and his son, Professor Aloys Fleischmann, Professor D. Gwynn and Mr Stephen W. Farrington, City Engineer, representing the President and governing body, University College, Cork; Professor J.J. McHenry, representing the President and governing body, University College, Dublin; Professor L. Duggan, Senator Ald. Mrs Dowdall, Gerard Larchet and Miss Sheila Larchet, representing Bax's old friends Dr and Mrs J.F. Larchet, with whom he had only recently stayed, David Horgan, Mrs S. Neeson, Professor D.O'Corcora, Seamus Murphy, and Declan Tyrell, representing Dr Tyrell of Waterford who had taken Bax on his last tour of the West. A death mask had already been modelled by Mr Seamus Murphy, to whom the erection of a tombstone was also entrusted.

A memorial service was held at St Martin-in-the-Fields on 28 October which was attended by a large congregation. The music played included works by Elgar and Holst (Prelude to *The Kingdom* and *Turn Back, O Man*), three pieces by Bax (*This Worldes Joie*, the slow movement from the First Quartet and *Nunc Dimittis*) and Bach's *St Anne Fugue*. But, strangely, nothing by Vaughan Williams nor any of Bax's immediate composer friends.

When Bax's will was published it was revealed that his estate was unexpectedly small, at £11,935 gross, but only £1,627 net. A codicil countermanded his former will which left everything to Harriet

Cohen, now leaving his musical legacy to his executors and trustees, and dividing the income between Harriet and Mary. Harriet's bombed house in Hampstead and her mews flat became her property, while Mary received £500 and the freehold of her house in Storrington. Harriet was also bequeathed 'all my furniture prints plate jewellery and all my articles of domestic or personal use or adornment', and she took all the music and other personal papers still at The White Horse, claiming Bax had left them to her. There were complications with the will. A covenanted annuity given by Bax to Harriet in 1949 was considered to be a debt on the estate, but there were insufficient funds in the estate to cover the capitalized value of the estimated future payments under the annuity. The estate was therefore technically insolvent during Harriet's lifetime. As a result of this and other difficulties it took seventeen years for the estate to be wound up. Mary did not get a penny of income while Harriet lived.

Harriet's ownership of most of Bax's manuscripts, and the fact that she continued to treat the piano works as her own personal property, while not the principal reason, must be an important contributory one for the dramatic fall in the number of performances of Bax's major works after his death. Certainly, while she lived, a proper evaluation of Bax's unperformed and unknown works could not even begin, although in the 1960s she did place the majority of the manuscripts on loan with the British Museum. However, her habit of presenting manuscripts to a variety of institutions throughout the world without keeping a list of where they had gone may still mean that some of the manuscripts are unlocated. After Bax's death there was a flurry of memorial concerts, the Sixth Symphony in particular being given in Manchester, Birmingham and Cheltenham, and Harriet broadcast *Winter Legends* with the BBC Symphony Orchestra and Clarence Raybould in 1954. Yet most of the memorial concerts were of chamber music. At a recital in Cork on 30 March 1954, when Charles Lynch and the London String Quartet played the Piano Quintet, it was announced that a special memorial room was to be established. 'Miss Cohen, knowing the composer's attachment to Cork, generously presented to the College his piano, swivel chair, music cabinet, bookcase, and a large collection of books, scores and personalia, on condition that they would be housed in a special memorial room. To this the College authorities agreed, and the President kindly allocated for this purpose a room in the southern part of the recently acquired eastern wing, as part of the new Music Department.'[10]

The Bax family offered to endow an annual Bax Memorial Lecture
or Recital, to be held in Cork on or about the date of the anniversary.
Vaughan Williams was invited to give the inaugural lecture, and
despite his years the octogenarian composer accepted. Harriet also
agreed to give the first memorial recital, in association with Maura
O'Connor (soprano), who had been one of Bax's Irish friends. On
the afternoon of 15 October 1955 the Memorial Room was opened
by Vaughan Williams. The guests included Ursula Vaughan Williams,
Evelyn Bax, Harriet, C.W. Gillam, founder of the newly-formed
Arnold Bax Society, Mr A.A. Healy, representing the Lord Mayor
of Cork, and members of the Governing Body, together with some of
the composer's Cork friends, Mr and Mrs John Horgan, Mr and Mrs
Sean Neeson, Dr and Mrs Tyrell, Mr and Mrs Seamus Murphy, and
Mr and Mrs Fleischmann (senior). Professor Aloys Fleischmann later
reported that the 'Very Rev Dr James, deputising for the President,
welcomed the guests and said that the Memorial Room would help
to keep alive the memory of a composer whose love for Irish folk
music had been intense, and whose sympathy with Irish ideas and
Irish culture had been well known. In declaring the Memorial Room
open, Dr Vaughan Williams said it was an honour for him to dedicate
the room to one who found such beauty in the country of his
adoption, and he hoped that the room would be an inspiration to
the Music students of the College.'[11]
Vaughan Williams' Memorial Lecture was given to a capacity
audience on the subject of 'Some Aspects of the English Folk Song'.
With a wide range of illustration, he discussed the folk-song element
in the idiom and vocabulary of English music. Much mirth was
caused by his thesis that, whereas the best English folk-songs were
always being claimed as Irish, a number of well-known 'Irish' folksongs were in fact English. The inaugural Memorial Recital was given
by Harriet and Maura O'Connor, with Rhoda Coghill as accompanist.
Apart from a Hymn Tune Prelude by Vaughan Williams, played in
honour of the composer's presence, the programme was an all-Bax
one, 'and included the sombre and turbulent Second Piano Sonata,
the delicately ornate Nereid, and an impressive example of ostinato
architecture in Paean, all of them played with that intensity and
that dramatic bringing-out of inner meaning which is so characteristic
of Miss Cohen's style. Miss O'Connor sang settings of poems by
Colum, Campbell, Housman and MacLeod, her rich voice and fresh,
spontaneous approach to the songs winning the audience's sympathy.'[12] Other recitals were not so successful, often when old

friends of the composer, particularly those not in the first flush of youth, insisted on paying their tribute in less than perfect performances.

In 1956 Harriet gave a Wigmore Hall recital which included the Second Piano Sonata. She adorned the programme with quotations ascribed to Rachmaninov and Schnabel. The former was credited with declaring the Bax to be 'the greatest work for piano since the Liszt sonata', while the latter went one better – 'the greatest piano work of the twentieth century'. Critics were unimpressed. 'It would be interesting to know in what circumstances these gentlemen made the remarks attributed to them', remarked one critic, who found the sonata 'diffuse, laboured, unpianistic and far below the inventive level shown by Bax in his best orchestral works ... Its twenty-seven odd minutes, in fact, were ill spent, and we can name many other works worthier of Miss Cohen's time and talent such as the sonatas of John Ireland and York Bowen.'[13] Clues as to the quality of the performance and the sympathies of the critic come in the last sentence. Yet the Bax sonatas have never been frequently performed and, until they were recorded, were very little known.

The predictable reaction to a composer's music after his death was particularly strong in Bax's case. As his friends and champions retired or passed on, their successors were sweeping in their rejection of Bax's ethos. Possibly one of the most ill-founded was Desmond Shaw-Taylor's vilification of the Fifth Symphony after Barbirolli's memorial performance of it at the 1954 Cheltenham Festival. He wrote of 'the ornate bath filled to the brim with richly scented water, [which] overflowed, and at last glug-glugged to a noisy conclusion' and vowed 'never again, shall British music become so soggy or shapeless as this; whatever we may do we will not wallow in easy sentiment, or saunter down the path of least resistance'. Can he really have been writing of the epic Fifth?[14]

The first anniversary of Bax's death was obviously going to be a date which many old friends would want to mark. Harriet wrote to the BBC on this subject in June 1954: 'Miss May Harrison, an old friend of Sir Arnold's said she wanted to give a Concert on his birthday and would I play in it. I had not the heart to say "no" although, as you can imagine, she just beat me to it as I wanted to give one myself. However, I said that I absolutely insisted on the Wigmore Ensemble being in the programme as they have always broadcast the Birthday concert in other years. I am going to do the Piano Quartet, which is quite short – about 14 minutes I think –

with them and I would be awfully touched if the BBC would let
me play this with these boys, perhaps late at night after the Concert
is over so that we can have a performance for Sir Arnold's birthday.
Madame Korchinska is going to play the harp Quintet at the Concert;
perhaps she could play it also for you. That would make a *dear* little
programme, don't you think?'[15]

As far as Bax's work is concerned, probably the most important
event after the composer's death to ensure the eventual revival of
the music was the complete cycle of the symphonies that was broadcast by the BBC during 1956 and 1957. Not only did this series of
fine performances demonstrate Bax's art to listeners at a time when
they could still remember the man, but, owing to the fact that
domestic tape-recorders were beginning to be widely disseminated
in the mid 1950s, enthusiasts taped the performances off the air.
These unofficial tape recordings were privately circulated, and
were eventually directly responsible for inspiring some of the modern
LP recordings that were made fifteen or twenty years later.

One or two of Bax's major works were heard at the Festival Hall
in the 1950s: *Fatherland* conducted by its old champion, Beecham,
in December 1954; the Sixth Symphony by Sir Adrian Boult, in a
poorly attended concert in 1956; and the Violin Concerto on
6 February 1957.

After the BBC series of symphonies, Harriet suggested she should
'be allowed to perform on the Friday and Saturday concerts all the
works for piano and orchestra (which are all written for me and are
my personal property), starting with the Symphonic Variations (of
course with Malcolm [Sir Malcolm Sargent] if possible, but this
would suit Stanford Robinson I think, or Basil Cameron did them
often in the past), then proceeding to the *Winter Legends* (could I
do that with a conductor other than the one I did it with two years
ago, please)?'[16] However, after the performance of *Winter Legends*
in 1954, and one or two of the *Left Hand Concertante*, Harriet
never again performed Bax's works for piano and orchestra. Plans
went on for a performance of the *Symphonic Variations*, Harriet
producing an undamaged score in 1958, and later Bax's two-piano
reduction which Chappell's published in 1963. A set of parts, too,
turned up, and the BBC eventually recorded a performance in 1963
with Patrick Piggott, who had previously demonstrated his mastery
of the idiom in the Piano Quintet and *Saga Fragment*. Piggott played
the complete original score, and Harriet was far from pleased. She
bullied and wheedled both the BBC and the soloist, and threatened

the publisher with legal action. She offered Piggott one of her medals on the understanding that he did not play the work, but the offer was not accepted, and the performance went ahead. (Miss Cohen established and ran for a number of years her International Music Awards, and the Arnold Bax Medal for promising young artists.) However, the BBC negated any impact it might have had by only broadcasting it on the Overseas Service. Afterwards 'PP', as she referred to Piggott, became a taboo subject with Harriet. However, the lesson was obvious: the works for piano and orchestra from the height of Bax's maturity deserved publication and performance by a variety of young artists.

On what would have been Bax's seventieth birthday, the BBC had devoted the whole of the weekly magazine programme *Music Magazine* to him, the contributors being conductor Basil Cameron, the critic Scott Goddard, and finally Bax's young friend Christopher Whelen, by then Music Director of the Royal Shakespeare Company and still only in his mid-twenties. Whelen is again worth quoting for the concluding case he put for Bax in his talk, as valid now as it was then. Whelen said:

Bax is often quite the reverse of what we have been led to believe ... He is *not* a left-over from the 19th century. Gone is the self-pity and self-dramatisation. *Here* is a British composer who has dared to address us in a spacious and flamboyant manner; one whose splendours are carefully, at times almost severely, curbed by an architectural plainness – for all Bax's works are plainly constructed. Rhythmically he built on the firm basis of the primitive dance. More often than not his harmony is simple and diatonic: when it is chromatic it is diamond-clean, often growing from the meeting of many contrapuntal lines. In their frozen luxuriance these harmonies shift like the changing colours in a mosaic ... There are few limping or leaning melodies in Bax ... They are mostly long-spanning tunes which are not afraid to be recognised as tunes.[17]

In the mid-1950s a Bax Society was founded by Clifford Gillam, with Sibelius as its first president. That its initial objective should now appear so modest – to collect sufficient undertakings from interested music lovers to persuade a record company to record a Bax symphony – shows how far the musical climate has changed since then. Between 1968 and 1973 the Society issued a lively and scholarly *Bulletin*, and in 1973 promoted a noted chamber concert at the Purcell Room on London's South Bank which included a rare performance of the Piano Quintet. In recent years the Society has ceased to be active.

During the early 1960s, Bax's reputation was at its lowest. A less sympathetic regime was installed at Broadcasting House, and while it was introducing the European avant-garde into Britain's musical life, there was less room for Bax and his generation, whose inclusion in the Proms became a rare event in spite of regular letters of protest to the press from enthusiasts.

The critics, too, were becoming less sympathetic. Those with influence on the big dailies were more concerned with the cause of Mahler and of the progenitors of the Second Viennese School. 'Alas, poor Sibelius', wrote one misguided commentator at this time, and in such an atmosphere it is obvious that Bax was unlikely to have a fair or sympathetic hearing. After Sir Adrian had conducted *The Garden of Fand* at the Festival Hall in January 1962, one critic wrote that the work 'attempts to disguise the banality of its material behind a screen of purple chromatics', and felt that it 'offered a most embarrassing glimpse of one aspect of English musical culture'.[18]

In 1965 Harriet wrote a notable letter to the *Daily Telegraph*[19] which eloquently pleaded the cause of Bax's music, and although it achieved no practical outcome it found many sympathizers among her readers who could not understand Bax's banishment by the musical establishment.

Sir — Mr John Tebbit's letter (July 28), complaining of the diminished interest in the works of the late Ralph Vaughan Williams and of the omission of his opera from Covent Garden, noted the almost inevitable decline of interest in a man's work after his death.

May I draw your attention to an equally bitter and perhaps more tragic omission at the Promenade Concerts and other symphonic events held in London these last few years, *i.e.* that of the great symphonies and tone poems of the late Sir Arnold Bax?

I have in my possession a criticism by your (late) distinguished music critic Richard Capell, after the first performance of Sir Arnold's Fifth Symphony under Sir Thomas Beecham before the war. Using nearly two thirds of a column he called the Symphony an 'imposing work' and wrote: 'The performance made an effect of great mastery and splendour and by the end the audience was roused to give the composer the most enthusiastic appreciation one could remember his receiving.' He continued the eulogy for three or four more paragraphs.

I, in company with dozens of people all over the country, consider it a grave wrong for the BBC musical authorities to have omitted ever since Sir Henry Wood's death (so far as I remember) the yearly performances of the Third Symphony — played to packed houses and to scenes of incredible enthusiasm — that took place under the masterly and loving baton of Sir Henry, who told me, as did Vaughan Williams and Sibelius, that the work was one of his favourite modern symphonies. And what of the Tone Poems? Constant Lambert particularly loved 'The Tale the Pine Trees Knew' and all of the above-mentioned gentlemen dote on 'November Woods'.

Might I beg that while the fashionable Schoenberg and other 'Serialists' are performed as much as they are, a great Englishman (late Master of the Musick) should not be kicked down in his grave.

Yours faithfully,
Harriet Cohen
London, W.1.

In 1960 the first seeds were sown of a venture that was eventually to result in the recording of a wide range of Bax's music including the symphonies. This was the foundation of the Lyrita record company by Richard Itter, initially as a limited venture, recording piano music which was only available on mail order. At the beginning of 1960 there were only three Bax works in the record catalogues: the *Coronation March, Tintagel* and *The Garden of Fand*. The appearance of a Bax piano recital played by Iris Loveridge, including the First Sonata, was the start of a venture that over twenty years has recorded ten major orchestral works, including five of the symphonies, four works for .cello and piano and twenty-one for solo piano including all four sonatas. Other companies have also added to this corpus, but it was Lyrita that pioneered the field. Writing of that first piano record, Andrew Porter found that, 'in the case of Bax's first Piano Sonata, enthusiasm grows warmer ... There is something of Balakirev in the music. Rich turbulent ideas are here organised with a power that we do not associate always with Bax; it is not a diffuse work, but a cogent sonata in one continuous movement, on a grand scale, that holds the attention. This takes one side of the record; the other is made of shorter pieces that are all agreeable. A *Hill-Tune* and *Country-Tune* are both beautifully written; and *Mediterranean* is rich and sensuous.'[20] Soon after, writing in *Music on Record: a critical guide*, Burnett James described the situation when the fortunes of Bax's music were at their lowest: 'Few composers', he wrote, 'are more completely out of fashion today than Arnold Bax ... Not that he ever stood very high in the public favour. Professional musicians admired and respected him (and some still do); but his music never struck the general response which, in view of its warm, generous, and often noble nature might reasonably have been expected. He enjoyed (and perhaps enjoys) a certain *succès d'estime*; but if you go to a record company with the suggestion that they should record some Bax, you will get the sharp answer — "Why?" Few English composers have been less well treated by the gramophone. And yet Bax's music has many of those qualities that ought to ensure success.'[21]

The influence of the Lyrita piano records was very important, particularly when they were joined a few years later by Frank Merrick's performances of the Sonatas. None of them are, perhaps, ideal performances, but they were sufficiently good to put the works firmly back into circulation. Harriet, again, was not amused, and it was unfortunate that the notion of recording them came just too late to capture her in the art she had espoused for so long.

At the beginning of the 1960s most of Bax's music that had been published was still in print, and at very reasonable prices. One night in 1964 Chappell's premises in New Bond Street caught fire and were completely gutted. Most newspaper reports concentrated on stories of burnt pianos and made no mention of the disaster that had over-taken Bax's music. Overnight almost all his music was out of print, two manuscript scores were destroyed (*Spring Fire* and the *Concert-ante for Three Wind Instruments*) but fortunately nothing was gone for good, for another score of *Spring Fire* was later found among Harriet's papers after her death in 1967, while a photographic print of the *Concertante* was held elsewhere. Many sets of parts survived, and others were recalled from Chappell's agents in America and Australia.

The name of the conductor Vernon Handley was first heard in London at a concert in December 1961 when he was the first to benefit under the Morley College Symphony Orchestra Conductors Scheme, and was hailed next morning by the *Daily Telegraph* as a 'musician of unusual talent'.[22] In that early programme he cond-ucted music by Milner, Holst and Delius, and Bax's Third Symphony. The following year he became Director of Music at Guildford, and developed the Guildford Philharmonic Orchestra from a mainly amateur and student body into a fully professional band. His en-thusiasm for Bax resulted in his programming many orchestral works over the years, three of which were recorded, and important pioneering efforts his recordings were. The works played between 1963 and 1979 were: *Tintagel* (1963), *The Happy Forest, Paean* (orchestral version) and Symphony No. 4 (1964), *The Tale the Pine-Trees Knew* (1965), Symphony No. 6 (1967), *Symphonic Variations* (1970), *The Garden of Fand* (1972), Symphony No. 3 (1974), *Phantasy for Viola and Orchestra* (1978) and *Northern*

Ballad No. 1 (1978). A wide range of Bax was also conducted by him with BBC orchestras, and with the Royal College of Music's first orchestra he gave an eye-opening performance of the First Symphony in 1967. *The Times* critic found the First 'a really splendid work − packed with strong and memorable incidents', and felt that 'we owe a debt of thanks' to Handley and his student orchestra 'for shaming the better known orchestras' neglect of such a complex and rewarding symphonist as Bax'.[23] Yet of the three major Bax scores that Handley has committed to disc, the Fourth Symphony, although revealing and pioneering in its time, suffers from not being played by a top-line orchestra, from the use of a feeble electronic organ and from only adequate recorded sound. *The Tale the Pine-Trees Knew* is the least impressive of Handley's Bax recordings, but the *Symphonic Variations* is very fine, excellent playing well caught, and clearly conveys why the Guildford concerts no longer draw their followers only from the immediate local area, but regularly attract substantial parts of their audiences from London and further afield.

Once the Fourth Symphony had been recorded in 1964, it was probable that others would follow. Three years later the first fully professional LP of a symphony of Bax was recorded by Lyrita. It was of the Sixth conducted by Norman del Mar, the same conductor who gave that work its fine performance in the BBC cycle in the 1950s. When welcoming the recording in *Gramophone*, Robert Layton noted that it was not surprising 'that Bax should have suffered from the usual reaction that overtakes a composer in the decade or so after his death ... What is surprising is the extent of the reaction.'[24] Two years later the Third Symphony, at one time Bax's most popular, was recorded by RCA. This was not, however, the result of long and detailed planning, but of a last minute substitution for another recording session that had been cancelled, together with some financial inducement on the part of Bax's publishers, Chappell and Co. When it was first issued it was not a great success commercially, probably because the most influential of record magazines, *Gramophone*, chose an unsympathetic critic to review it, a critic who began his review, 'I had better say right away that I find myself unenthusiastic about Bax − the basic trouble is surely a lack of memorable ideas.'[25] The record was quickly deleted, but later reissued on a cheaper label, when another critic in the same journal received it as 'one of Bax's most imaginative and enduring scores'.[26]

There has been little comment in print on that curious feature of our times concerning the promotion of the music of British composers now dead but still in copyright: the composer trust. Our evaluation of the music of many, until recently, forgotten composers has been dramatically changed by a great stream of marvellous records over the past few years, as the trusts representing Vaughan Williams, Delius, Frank Bridge, John Ireland and Gerald Finzi have used their income from the promotion of the works of 'their' composers to help finance LP recordings (and incidentally make more income). But of course, all this creates a great imbalance in our assessment of the other composers of the same period who did not leave money to promote their music on disc. Probably the composer who was suffering most in this respect was Bax, for whom there was no trust until 1985. Yet the activities of Chandos in recording Bax, at first with the Ulster Orchestra, have demonstrated that there is a ready market for Bax's music on record, and especially on compact disc.

The revival of interest in Bax's orchestral works has been a gradually cumulative process. Very little has been played in central London by the major orchestras, but in the provinces, at Manchester, Birmingham, Bournemouth and Liverpool in particular, conductors such as Maurice Handford, Sir Charles Groves, Rudolph Schwarz, and David Measham have programmed works in which they believed, in public concerts. The BBC, too, have kept up a representative flow of some of Bax's music, though not in big public concerts or at the Proms.

The crux in the revival of Bax's music was the first two symphonies, and it was clear from the BBC cycle onward that only when these two epic works became generally known in fine recordings would the rest of Bax's output fall into perspective and begin to be understood and appreciated. In 1970 Ken Russell, the film director, suddenly showed an interest in Bax's life and orchestral music, and as well as reading *Farewell, My Youth* and Bax's 'Dermot O'Byrne' stories and poems, was played tapes of the BBC performances of Symphonies Nos. 1 and 2. (Conducted by Stanford Robinson and Eugène Goossens, they were possibly the best performances of the cycle.) Russell's enthusiasm was immediate, although he was less interested in other Bax works he listened to at the same time, including the Fifth Symphony. Russell was keen to arrange and finance a recording session as quickly as possible, and Lyrita was chosen as the issuing label because they could offer a far quicker response than the internal bureaucracy of the larger companies – Decca and EMI – would allow. Orchestra and conductor were chosen at very short notice, on the basis of availability. Myer Fredman, who apparently did not know the Bax symphonies, learned them at ten days' notice, and in the circumstances did a superb job. Russell's ideas on packaging the recordings did cause some raised eyebrows. The first was reputed to have been a close-up of eight battle-stained soldiers wearing gas masks, eyes staring; and the second, a soft-focus snowscape with a naked girl astride a white horse. In the event Russell lost interest and the standard plain packaging used for the Sixth Symphony was adopted for the whole series.

Another orchestra that has done much pioneering work as far as Bax is concerned is the Kensington Symphony Orchestra. This is basically an amateur or student orchestra, based at an evening institute, but regularly stiffened with professionals for its enterprising series of public concerts. In its early days the orchestra tended to bite off more than it could chew, but as it has developed, particularly during the 1970s, the standards have risen so that rarely does a performance drop below professional quality, and many concerts have been broadcast on BBC Radio London. Leslie Head, the orchestra's founder and conductor, in spite of the difficulties attendant on actually getting his performances launched, had shown notable sympathy for Bax's style, and a missionary zeal in undertaking performances of many long-forgotten works. He first gave *Overture to a Picaresque Comedy* in 1962 and later three of the symphonies (Fifth, Second and Seventh), the Second in particular being the first public performance for thirty-five years. At the time these performances were widely noted in the press because of the music's unfamiliarity. Writing of the Second Symphony, John Christopher in the *Liverpool Daily Post* found Leslie Head's conducting 'was admirably idiomatic ... and the many students in the orchestra clearly revelled in the demands of this difficult but finally most rewarding music.'[27] Anthony Payne in the *Daily Telegraph*, while admitting that 'the work needs a virtuoso professional orchestra and Bax's extremely taxing writing was palpably too much for the players on this occasion', conceded, 'but it would be cruelly ungrateful not to warm to the effort involved in putting on this magically beautiful, sometimes cataclysmic work',[28] and nevertheless clearly felt the effort had been worthwhile. It was the strength of the music, then practically unknown, that caught the attention of critics. Reviewing an earlier Leslie Head performance, of the Fifth Symphony, Bill Hopkins was gripped to write that, 'the long-breathed argument of its first movement is truly monumental ... That it is a work that ought to be heard again and again is something of a truism: it is one of the very finest achievements of English symphonic music – indeed of English music of any type.'[29] It is difficult to recall the circumstances which even as recently as the late 1960s made Bax's symphonies such rarities that any expedient to present them in performance was worthwhile. Subsequently the KSO have revived *Overture, Elegy and Rondo, Rogue's Comedy Overture, Enchanted Summer* and *Northern Ballad No. 2*, and have given strongly idiomatic first performances of *Spring Fire, Cortège, Roscatha* and the revised version of *Christmas Eve on the Mountains*. Russell Keable, Leslie Head's successor with the KSO, continued the tradition by reviving the Cello Concerto in 1985 with Lionel Handey as soloist.

Other non-professional organizations, too, have been responsible for Bax revivals. Before Leslie Head became interested in Bax, Terence Lovett and the Strolling Players gave the first performance of *Nympholept* in May 1961, while later the Fulham Municipal Orchestra in west London, under their conductor Joseph Vandernoot, performed *Festival Overture* and the *Concertante for Three Wind Instruments*; and the Royal College of Music Student Association Orchestra under David Chatwin gave the première of the early tone poem *Cathaleen-ni-Hoolihan*.

Valuable pioneering has been done by such organizations, yet the true measure of the extent to which Bax's music has returned to the repertoire is whether any of the major orchestras perform it in their most prestigious concerts in London. And the answer is, they do not – with the occasional exception of *Tintagel*, the work that kept Bax's name before the public when the rest was largely forgotten. The appearance of Bax on disc means that his style is now known and that he has a strong following among young music lovers. Yet if at least some of his music is not in the *regular* repertoire, then orchestras do not know how to play it. This was demonstrated only too clearly when the Seventh Symphony was recorded. The recording was tied in with three public concerts which preceded it. Yet at the first of these, at the Festival Hall, it was notable how unsure and unidiomatic was the string playing compared with that which was forthcoming on disc three performances later. The trouble with such a situation is that most listeners will judge what they actually hear – rather than relating it to what they are supposed to be hearing –

because there is no yardstick against which to measure.

Bax is often compared to European contemporaries such as Strauss and Debussy, and the composer himself tells us one commentator even likened him to Respighi.[30] It is very easy to latch on to the most superficial stylistic features of his music and make a misleading assessment. He drew much from his contemporaries, yet to play him in the wrong style can be disastrous, as the conductor Vernon Handley has observed.

Bax has not been over-performed, but when he has been played he has often been made to sound like someone else. Because he uses the romantic orchestra and enjoys an ability to speak with rich harmony, our stylish orchestras, unless they are prevented, will turn his music into Richard Strauss, and conductors will go along with this, especially if they are unaware of what is happening. Sometimes, because of one of the reasons given above they are unaware of what is happening, and encourage it, treating every harmonic point as a moment to be made a meal of, approaching every suspension with a *rallentando*, crowning every resolution with a pause, and worse of all, playing slow melodies with soft-edged ensemble. While such ensemble is desirable in Strauss, Wagner, Mahler and others, it is death to Bax, who found Mahler, we must not forget, 'muddle-headed'. Bax is firmer and more terse in argument than all these composers, and style in the playing must suit this. So many conductors upon reading a score seem to be *looking* for likenesses to other composers, whereas they ought to be *listening* for differences, so that the individual voice can be heard. When one reads a Bax symphony in this latter way, the three most forceful impressions one receives are of clarity of line, polyphony, and a tremendous number of accents: the orchestral colour and harmonic richness are obviously subservient to the argument.

I have always believed that when conducting this composer one should be careful that one's orchestra is aware of that line mentioned above. One needs to be watchful, because when Bax is at his most impressionistic he nearly always has some important melodic material about. Wide spread string chords, or harp arpeggios over tremolandos are often merely the wash in the picture against which a few pizzicato notes have germinal importance.[31]

Probably, the turning point in the wider appreciation of Bax's music came in 1983. Although the centenary of Bax's birth did not promote quite as wide-ranging a revival of public performances of his music as enthusiasts might have hoped, and there was, for example, no cycle of his symphonies, a lot of performances took place. These were particularly interesting for the large number of works which had been previously unheard in professional performances. For most composers this exercise would have just been an interesting airing of minor chippings from the workshop. But in Bax's case the BBC's series, produced by Chris de Souza, encompassed in twelve programmes all the media for which he wrote, and included almost all the previously unheard important works, which were immediately recognised as worthwhile once the performances had been broadcast. This activity, which was concentrated in the last few weeks of the year, together with the Royal Philharmonic Society's pioneering revival of *Spring Fire* at London's Royal Festival Hall, laid the groundwork for a substantial reassessment of the generally accepted view of what constituted Bax's mature achievement. As Anthony Payne wrote in his long review article:

A major discovery, undoubtedly, was the general high quality of his early music ... precise, brilliant, and absolutely personal. ...Given the threadbare 19th-century English tradition which Bax's generation inherited, his discovery of an individual vein, ahead of virtually all his contemporaries, is remarkable. ...One of the chief facts to emerge is that the centre of gravity in his output lies even earlier in his career than we had previously thought.

From about this date, too, came the first interest in Bax of Brian Couzens of the Chandos Record Company. The first Chandos Bax recordings, two records of all the best-known symphonic poems and the Fourth Symphony, all with the Ulster Orchestra conducted by Bryden Thomson, capitalised on the new recording medium of the compact disc, and received high praise. The record of the symphony, *Gramophone* magazine's record of the year for its engineering, had sold in excess of 10,000 units even before winning the prize. Subsequently, Chandos have gone on to make a succession of glorious recordings of Bax's music, now with the London Philharmonic Orchestra, conducted by Bryden Thomson. Also, with the Royal Philharmonic Orchestra, they have recorded Vernon Handley's powerfully idiomatic view of *Spring Fire*, coupled with the *Northern Ballad No. 2* and the previously unknown *Symphonic Scherzo*.

Vernon Handley, untiring in his promotion of Bax, in addition to the concerts he conducted in the BBC's centenary series, gave many public performances, including the Third Symphony; *Nympholept* and *To the Name Above Every Name* at Guildford; and, in the contentious 'Great British Music Festival', the Three Wind Concertante and *London Pageant*. Also, with Ralph Holmes as viola soloist, he conducted the Viola Phantasy, though the postulated recording was never to come to fruition owing to Holmes' tragic death the following year. For those interested in orchestral style in British music, possibly the most interesting of Handley's many performances was that of *The Garden of Fand* with the orchestra of the National Centre for Orchestra Studies, where, with an ensemble of young players with no stylistic preconceptions and a lot of enthusiasm, they produced a performance that was startlingly concentrated and compelling — absolutely gripping in its conviction and inevitability.

The establishment of the Sir Arnold Bax Trust has provided a mechanism for focussing the promotion of Bax's music by assisting with the financing of both recordings and public performances, and also by providing the expertise to obtain scores and performing materials of works in demand. By the summer of 1986, three orchestral records had been produced and others were planned.

As the remainder of Bax's orchestral music is gradually given life again, in public performance, on the air, and on disc, the cumulative effect of a renewed performing tradition is becoming established. As with any composer whose sound world is as distinctive as Bax's, he needs repeated performance for his proper evaluation and appreciation. The parallel with the case of Sibelius is very close. When properly presented by sympathetic players the world he has created quite bowls one over. In the early thirties Vaughan Williams was ready to equate Bax with the leading continental composers of his day: he was no minor master but one of the leading European composers, and it is quite appropriate to end with Vaughan Williams' sentiments as expressed in a letter to the *Radio Times*: [32]

I notice a curious error in your issue of December 16. In discussing a concert of compositions by Arnold Bax and various Continental composers [Szymanowski, Schoenberg, Conrad Beck, Norbert van Hannenhaim, Hindemith, Poulenc and Stravinsky] you state that: 'Arnold Bax is clearly in place in this distinguished company'. I take it that the sentence was meant to express that the other composers were not unworthy of a place beside Arnold Bax. Personally, I do not consider that most of the names on that programme are worthy to stand beside Bax, but this, of course, is a matter of opinion.

Dermot O'Byrne

Writing in March 1902 in his preface to Lady Gregory's *Cuchulain of Muir-themne*,[1] Yeats touched on the revelation of the 'hidden Ireland' that would hold Bax in thrall for the rest of his life. 'We Irish', wrote Yeats, 'should keep these [legendary] personages much in our hearts, for they lived in the places where we ride and go marketing, and sometimes they have met one another on the hills that cast their shadows upon our doors at evening'. 'When I was a child', he continued, 'I had only to climb the hill behind the house to see the long, blue, ragged hills flowing along the southern horizon. What beauty was lost to me, what depth of emotion is still perhaps lacking in me, because nobody told me ... that Cruachan of the Enchantments lay behind those long, blue, ragged hills!'

Bax was writing almost as soon as he went to Ireland, modelling his style not only on the early poetry of Yeats, and on that of William Sharp ('Fiona Macleod') and later 'AE' (George Russell), but on the local speech of the peasant people he grew to know in the far west. At first Bax wrote only verse. But later short stories − probably his most successful literary medium − and plays were written and published.

As we have seen (pp. 22−4), from the first Bax gave himself an Irish name when in Ireland. Then 'the name "Dermod McDermott" began in June 1905 to be recorded under passages of Yeatsian verse in closely written note-books'.[2] In June 1908 Arnold contributed two poems to his brother Clifford's journal, the *Transactions of the Theosophical Art-Circle* (later renamed *Orpheus*), over the pen-name 'Diarmid'.[3] This finally evolved into 'Dermot O'Byrne', the name first used in 1909 with the collection of his poems called *Seafoam and Firelight* that was the second of a series of books which also appeared under the auspices of Clifford's journal. 'Dermot O'Byrne' may well have been inspired by place-names in the district near his beloved Glencolumcille. Rathlin Óbirne Island is just off the coast at Malin Beg, while funeral mounds for Diarmuid and Grainne are nearby.

Bax's fascination with the Gaelic language and his attempted mastery of it put him in some small degree in advance of his mentor Yeats, in that Yeats never had command of the Irish language. In fact, Bax's understanding of it was very idiosyncratic, based on the usage with which he was familiar in the west. In the years immediately before the First World War, Mary Colum − wife of the poet Padraic Colum − remembered how Bax would return from his visits to Gaelic-speaking districts 'with an extravagant vocabulary which he turned off on all his friends or in his short stories'.[4] Bax's translation (in collaboration with a teacher friend, Donall McGillespie) of part of J. M. Synge's play *The Shadow of the Glen* into Gaelic has been noted by other commentators. But, far from demonstrating his fluency in the written language, it tends, in its literal treatment, to be a catalogue of his limitations; more of a student exercise than a flowing and idiomatic version that could be played.

There are four collections of Bax's verse, the first of them surviving only in typescript, for it was never published. This was a collection of fifty-two poems, over his real name, that was typed out, bound and presented to his brother Clifford in 1907. Later, in 1909, Clifford returned the compliment by publishing the second collection, *Seafoam and Firelight*. The third, *A Dublin Ballad and other poems*, while printed and bearing the imprint 'The Candle Press, 44 Dawson Street, Dublin' and the date 1918, was never formally published, for it was suppressed by the British censor in Ireland, but 'was, none the less, so widely circulated that only two copies remained, the treasured possessions of the printer'.

The nine poems included in *A Dublin Ballad* express Bax's emotional response to the events of Easter week 1916. Later in 1935, five of the poems were included in an anthology of Easter Rising poetry. As soon as it was available Bax sent a copy to Tilly Fleischmann as a Christmas present, and admitted in an accompanying letter that 'the five poems under the name Dermot O'Byrne are by me, written with painful intensity of emotion just after the rebellion ... Willy Yeats told me in public in a Dublin drawing-room that "A Dublin Ballad 1916" was a masterpiece, and this has pleased me more than any praise my music has received!'[5] Bax would have been even more pleased to know that when, in 1966, the Irish Government's weekly *Bulletin of the Department of External Affairs* devoted an issue to the fiftieth anniversary of the Easter Rising,[6] celebrating it in the verse of the period, it would be headed by a verse from the fifth poem in *A Dublin Ballad*, entitled 'Shells at Oranmore':

> Never before had such a song been sung,
> Never again perhaps while ages run
> Shall the old pride of rock and wind be stung
> By such an insolence winged across the sun,
> So mad a challenge flung!

In 1923 Bax published his last collection of verse. This was the elusive *Love Poems of a Musician*, which appeared anonymously. In 1924 Bax sent a copy to AE, then editor of *The Irish Statesman*, asking if he would like to publish any of them in 'The Statesman',[7] — but AE did not do so. The collection includes a poem entitled 'Glamour' that had first appeared in *Orpheus* in October 1910; a poem that Bax had only recently set to music.[8] Perhaps the most difficult of this verse to evaluate is also that which is the least good as poetry *per se*, but valuable for its autobiographical implication. What are we to make, for example, of a poem called 'The Battle of the Somme', which concludes with the following:

> There were a few dreams, he was glad,
> To keep a chap from going mad.
> War was red hell, still he was human,
> And there was such a thing as woman.
> If ever he came out of this
> He'd teach her a new way to kiss,
> And graft on her pale flower of love
> The roots of far more fiery stuff.

God after this unholy push
He might get Leave — aye, leave to crush
Her white warm body up to him,
Strained close till this bad world went dim,
To slake his dusty lips for hours
Upon her crimson bosom flowers.

Dermot O'Byrne's Irish short-stories are remarkably successful, an assessment underlined by several commentators. The idiom Bax employed in them was that made famous by Synge and Lady Gregory. Mary Colum described it as 'a sort of literal translation from the Irish somewhat heightened. Some prosy purists objected to the style and would have preferred a flatter English, but actually it was the only medium for expressing a certain extravagant and fantastic Irish character, the type that Arnold gloried in.'[9]

The idea of informally collecting folk stories, and of deriving his own stories from them, all set against familiar places in the country of the west may well have come in the first place from William Sharp. Sharp, though he died in 1905, influenced Bax during the composer's formative years, not least because Sharp's wife was a close friend of Mrs Matthay (the wife of Bax's piano teacher). The two ladies edited an anthology called *Lyra Celtica*,[10] while the Celtic ambience was underlined by the fact that Mrs Matthay was also the sister of Marjorie Kennedy-Fraser, of *Songs of the Hebrides* fame. Bax, of course, set many 'Fiona Macleod' lyrics in his early years as a composer.

The two stories that make up the volume *The Sisters and Green Magic* exemplify Bax's strengths in this genre very well. The first was sketched in Carna, Connemara early in April 1910, and actually written in St Petersburg later in April and May, during his abortive romance with Natalie Skarginski. It tells of two beautiful peasants, the sisters Sorcha and Noreen who both love the same man. Sorcha marries him before he is drowned, and Noreen transfers her affection to the widow and her unborn child. Noreen has a nightmare about seagulls, and the child is born with a gull's webbed foot instead of a hand. The dénouement is a tragic one. In this tale the vivid description encapsulates Bax's favourite experience in the west:

As I came out into the street the last level and golden rays of the sinking sun were pouring across the house-tops in the west and flooding the commonplace street with their soft and mellow radiance. Through the tears in my eyes I looked into the heart of this still and passionate beauty, and though the broken shafts of light pained me I still continued to stare fascinated at the drooping and splendid disc. In a tender and pensive dream, my heart passed over the savage leagues of hazy rock and heather that rolled away unendingly to the west, and my dream knew that beyond that last bog and tussock Cashla lay, its thousand islands at this moment tranquil and radiant in the golden evening glory as the faery isles of poets' tales, a glory that folded even grey Murrisk and the crumbling walls and boarded windows of that sombre cabin on the sea-ward side. Even further my thought wandered streaming with the dazzling and splendid rain of the sunset out beyond the last limits of our Island of Sorrow, out among the gorgeous twilight fantasies of the ancient and fatal sea, until at last it seemed to pierce with a speed and surety greater than that of the golden bewitched curragh that bore Bran to the isles of the blest, and to come at last to Tír Taingire, to those very shores to the murmur of whose shells the child-ears of my little friend has listened in her last hour upon the bitter brown earth.[11]

Similarly, in 'Green Magic', we are told (in a conversational style strongly reminiscent of Conan Doyle) of a young girl whose mystical fascination for the sea finally results in her committing herself — in an ecstatic love-tryst — to the water, where she drowns. Again the incidental description and evocative use of language is peculiarly vivid. This story dates from September 1909, and was written at Gweedore in Donegal.

Two other collections of short stories were published. First was *Children of the Hills* ('tales and sketches of Western Ireland in the Old Time and the present day'), which appeared in Dublin in 1913, and cemented Bax's growing literary reputation in that city. Then came the war, and with it the dissolution of Bax's literary circle of admirers in Ireland, so that the publication of his last collection *Wrack and other stories* in 1918 did little more than mark the end of an era.

Bax's friend Ernest Boyd was reader to the Talbot Press, and undoubtedly recommended *Wrack* and the play *Red Owen* for publication. Boyd's celebrated book *Ireland's Literary Renaissance* was published in the year of the Easter Rising, 1916, and must have pleased Bax by its assessment of him as an Irish writer. Boyd wrote:

The novel, as such, continues to lack support, and our fiction still affects the form of the sketch and short story. Of the latter, Dermot O'Byrne's *Children of the Hills* (1913) showed unusual qualities, and announced a new writer from whom good work may be reasonably expected. The author is steeped in Gaelic lore, and the old language and history are an essential part of his art. His realism is the realism of Synge, with whom he has many points in common. In such grim little sketches as *Hunger* and *The Call of the Road*, there is something of Synge's manner. The angle of observation is the same as that from which *In Wicklow, West Kerry and Connemara* was seen, while a close study of the West has enabled the younger writer to achieve the same success as his predecessor. The rhythmic, highly coloured speech of the peasants has been caught by an ear no less sensitive than Synge's, and the peculiar atmosphere of the still Celtic Ireland is reproduced. Yet Dermot O'Byrne has resisted the temptation to imitate. If he cared to do so, he could evidently parody Synge in such a fashion as to defy even the expert, but his stories rarely awaken familiar echoes. Even when a turn of phrase reminds us too much of *The Playboy*, it would be unfair to suggest more than that his original material was the same as Synge's. His originality is evident, for the mystic imagination that revealed to him such visions as *The Lifting of the Veil* and *Through the Rain* is nowhere perceptible in Synge — the one writer with whom he may legitimately be compared.

What should we deduce about the music that Bax wrote at this time in the light of his literary work? It certainly appears reasonable to accept that sources and imagery were common to the two arts he embraced. Perhaps, too, for a very brief time he may have been more successful in encapsulating mood and atmosphere in words rather than notes, but there can never have been any doubt that his primary allegiance was as composer.

Bax wrote four plays, two of which were published. The earliest was *Déirdre: a Saga-drama in Five Scenes and a Prologue*, written over Bax's real name, and dated 'Glencolumcille, November 30th 1907'. Bax's second play — *On the Hill* — was a brief one-acter, published by Dermot O'Byrne in the *Irish Review* in February 1913. Also published was the three-acter *Red Owen*, which appeared from The Talbot Press, Dublin, in 1919, and was dedicated to Lennox Robinson. Finally, another one-acter that remains unpublished, *The Grey Swan*, dated 29 April 1919. In the latter we can see the mature composer, then at the height of his musical powers, still closely concerned with the legends and spirit of Eire.

Bax's interest in Irish drama originated in his attempts to write an Irish opera, attempts which got as far as two libretti. The first was *Déirdre*. The other, the first act of *Red Owen* — 'The Twisting of the Rope'.[12] Bax's play is about the wandering poet Red Owen Hanrahan, and this first act is very similar to Douglas Hyde's well-known bilingual playlet of the same title. The name of Douglas Hyde is important, however, as a key figure in the development of Bax's interest in the Irish language: Bax was certainly in correspondence with Hyde on matters Irish in 1908.[13] It is probably from Hyde, too, that Bax obtained the story of *Déirdre*.

The typescript of Bax's *Déirdre* has on its flyleaf this quotation:

> Old unhappy far-off things
> And battles long ago

and the dedication 'To the spirits on the Ulster Mountains'. Bax's play tells the story chronologically in a Prologue and five scenes as follows:

Prologue:	On the Road to Emain Macha
Scene I:	Sixteen Years Later
Scene II:	Two Years Later. The Hall of Feasts in Emain
Scene III:	By the Shore of Loch Etive
Scene IV:	Emain Macha
Scene V:	On the sea-shore.

Bax prefaces his script with an extended discussion of his sources and the nature of Irish mythology. In this context it is important to note how vivid was the small amount of music for *Déirdre* that Bax actually completed. (See pp. 50–2.)

Herbert Vern Fackler[14] has listed some thirty literary versions of the Déirdre legend by Anglo-Irish writers, though not including Bax. The progenitors of Bax's version were probably those by William Sharp,[15] AE[16] and Douglas Hyde's *Literary History of Ireland*.[17] The most famous version, though treated very differently, was that by Yeats which was first produced the year before Bax wrote his own play though probably in ignorance of the Yeats at that time. Synge's *Déirdre of the Sorrows*, which has inspired a number of composers to write operatic treatments,[18] appeared two years later. None of the early, pre-Yeats, versions were very good, and Bax's blank verse drama compares favourably with them. As Dorothy Hoare remarked, 'it is a difficult tale to re-tell, and especially re-tell dramatically'. The story of Déirdre, with its themes of doomed and eternal love, heroism and stark tragedy has intrigued many, and is one of the favourite Irish legends.

Bax's second play was a short atmospheric piece, *On the Hill*, written for Padraic Colum. Bax referred to it as 'my tinker sketch', and it is very much in the manner of Synge. So too, though on a much bigger canvas, is *Red Owen*, which finally saw the light of day after the First World War. *The Grey Swan* sticks to this idiom, though in a much more tragic vein.[19] On the typescript of this last play Bax still signs himself 'Dermot O'Byrne'.

Bax was not alone among his circle of friends in his choice of subject-matter. For example, there is a parallel in Herbert Farjeon's delightfully Irish one-act comedy *Friends*, which belongs to the same genre as Lady Gregory's *Spreading the News* and *The Rising of the Moon*. Farjeon's play was performed at the Abbey Theatre, Dublin, on 20 November 1917; so far as is known Bax's plays have never been produced. They deserve at least some attention: perhaps as radio plays they could well be worth a hearing.

The scenario of *King Kojata*

(From the opening of the manuscript score, Bax Memorial Room, University College, Cork)

Once upon a time there was a certain King in Muscovy whose beard was of such an inordinate length that it became a country tale for miles around. Now this King Kojata was greatly addicted to the chase and was in the habit of wandering far from his home in Moscow for many months together. One day having been abroad in the east of the land for nearly a year he lost his way during a long hunt and it fell out that he was wandering long in the forest without anything to quench his thirst. However, he chanced at last upon a pool of the clearest water upon which a golden bowl rocked temptingly. He tried to seize the bowl but it ever eluded him so he fell on his knees at the brink and putting his mouth to the water so that his long beard was submerged began to drink greedily. But alas! When he tried to lift his head again he found that he could nowise do so, and the same moment he heard a hoarse chuckling in the depths and looking through the water beheld the horrible beaked face of a hideous water demon. The King wrenched this way and that but he could not free himself and at last he was obliged to promise the demon to grant him any request if only he might regain his freedom. So the poor King swore that after twenty one years he would surrender to the demon whatever new thing he would find on his return from this foray. And with that and with a great dread in his heart he was allowed to go, only to find on his return to Moscow that during his absence his wife the Queen had born him a baby son.

After the twenty one years were passed the young prince Igor set out to fulfil his father's promise and in due time came to the brink of the same pool where his father the King had been entrapped. But the princess Tamara one of the enchanter's daughters knew of the prince's fate and was already waiting to warn him. No sooner did the two young people meet than they were altogether in love with one another and the princess tells him that a great ordeal is at hand for him. He must choose her from among her thirty sisters who are all exactly like her, on failing that must forfeit his life to the enchanter's evil whim. But she tells him to have no fear for he will recognise her among the others because of a tiny fly which he will seek on her cheek. The princess disappeared after that and the prince was taken down into the pool in the arms of naiads and undines. All fell out as the princess promised. Prince Igor chose her correctly from among them all and was just about to carry off the beautiful Tamara when her father in a fit of baffled fury suddenly metamorphozed her into a little blue flower. The prince in despair falls on his knees before the tiny blossom but is driven out scornfully by the water people. But one of the sisters was sorry for the unhappy lovers and plucking the blue flower when no-one was observing her, hid it in her bosom.

King Kojata was of course overjoyed when his son was restored to him none the worse and made a great feast in the palace to which all the boyars and nobility were invited. But through all the merriment Prince Igor remained brooding and melancholy and thought only of his beautiful Tamara whom he had won only to lose instantly. Suddenly there was a knock on the door, and a little old woman entered bearing a basket of flowers on her arm. She begs the King to buy some of her flowers saying that the only payment she will ask is a kiss on the cheek. All laugh, but she turns to Prince Igor and fumbling in her basket draws forth the little blue flower he knows so well. Then Prince Igor in a transport of delight embraced the old woman heartily. And lo! the rags fell from her and a beautiful water-nymph appeared, exactly like Tamara though it is not she. She made a pass then over the blue flower and the little blossom disappeared in a blue mist while the real princess Tamara took its place. After that the revelry continued until morning when Igor and Tamara were wedded and lived happily ever after.

The Happy Forest by Herbert Farjeon

It was in a green place of the forest that I lay, deep among long, growing things. I remember first the gray rustle of preparation, and next the wetness under my hands, and after that the brushing of my forehead by some stirred grass. And when I opened my eyes, the yellow light was darting like a needle among the blades, and the blue bindweed dappled into sudden transparencies. I sat up, and there were flowers all about, red lupins, and bryony I fancy, and columbine, and many more familiar flowers whose names I do not know. How blithely they bore their little coloured banners in the morning! And the forest was all around, and beyond I could see the high rim of a hill against the sky, and between the hill and where I lay, below me, was a little clearing, like a cup of light.

There came suddenly into this cup a running deer. I do not know what could have startled it, or perhaps it was about its business as the herald of the day. There had seemed in its flight (for it was gone now) and in the momentary poise of neck – I mean when it turned for an instant to glance behind – a certain trembling delight, a sort of sorrowful ecstasy that reached into the very heart of the morning. For there was somehow a pang in the wood that I do not understand, painful and glad like the pang of birth, or I might say it was all expressed in the slender legs of the animal, though to explain this further is beyond me. It was as if a man took the deer strongly by the horns and smote the sweet mouth of her; or as if this had not been, but yet might be.

Now I lay that morning in the forest until the sun was very hot, I think it must have been midday quite; when there came into the clearing two shepherds, and each made wood and water ring with the praises of his beloved. I call them shepherds for they were dressed as such, but they spoke in rhyme like poets, breaking into the most extravagant flatteries, one against the other – as when the first declared that his love's smile was so radiant that beside it the sun seemed as a little beam, and the second answered that when his love smiled the sun became all the brighter for joy and the blossoms rocked and the birds delighted at such a gay intrusion. At last they ceased from speaking, and a third shepherd, who was very brown and tall and who had been listening and twining a wreath of ivy, placed the chaplet on the locks of one of them and set to playing on a pipe. Instantly there was a great ado among the leaves and branches and into the cup sprang a little fellow, half boy, half goat, that I knew to be a satyr. I wish you could have seen him, how he beat the air and stamped the earth, how he darted faster than sight could follow and rolled over and over, kicking his legs in such infectious mirth that I was constrained to stuff my mouth with grass, lest they should hear me gurgling. Now he would hug himself for love, now leap into the air as if to snatch the sun, now slap his sides, making a lively sound. It seemed to me that it was fellows of this kind made a round thing out of the world.

It was late now, for time fleets in the forest, and the dancer paused for a moment in his capers, and I noticed in this pause that his eyes seemed pricked with light. (I tell all that I remember.) Then he signalled with a little curl of the arm to the two shepherds that had been making verses — the one crowned and the other his rich black hair quite unadorned — and to the piper, who still continued to pipe, and up they rose and followed him in single file. At first he seemed very solemn (but I could see that he was not so), rocking slowly from side to side, and they did the same; and then, a curious movement, three little steps forward and one back, the arms dancing. The piper was a good fellow, suiting his tune ably to the measure, which kept changing in a most laughable manner, and when at last they all disappeared from sight, it was with hands on hips, stepping like fine stallions (and the black-headed fellow ridiculously out of it). I thought they were clean gone, but soon the music came louder again upon my ears, and they returned with one more behind them, a laughing virgin. And they kept coming and going in and out of the cup, as if to trick someone who was not there, and each time they reappeared one was added to their number, a wise man with a staff, a child with corn-coloured hair, a swimmer, three tire-women holding hands, and an idiot. It was with great difficulty that I kept from following myself. And then, at last, they went without returning, and I was heavy at heart, thinking to myself that I had been over-timid. But I could still hear the piping, far away, and crept to the fringe of the wood, over in that part which seemed toward the music. The moon was up, quite full and yellow, and then I saw them for the last time, far off and up on the high rim of the hill dancing away with flinging arms and flying steps, now bobbing against the moon, now almost ceasing from movement altogether, twisting and swaying — the merry little satyr, the two love-sick shepherds, the long piper, with a golden treasury of breath, the laughing virgin, the old man twirling his staff, the child, the swimmer, and the three tire-women and the idiot — dancing away out of sight, I know not whither, unless it was to some fair city.

Bax's Symphonies at the Proms

Bax's first Prom performance was in 1910 (*In the Faery Hills*). From 1919 onwards, during his lifetime Bax featured every year except for 1921, 1926 and 1939.

Bax Symphonies at the Proms

1928 (21/8)	Symphony No. 1 (Wood & his SO)
1929 (24/8)	Symphony No. 1 (Wood & his SO)
1930 (14/8)	Symphony No. 1 (Wood/BBCSO)
1930 (25/9)	Symphony No. 3 (Wood/BBCSO)
1931 (20/8)	Symphony No. 3 (Wood/BBCSO)
1932 (11/8)	Symphony No. 3 (Wood/BBCSO)
1933 (14/9)	Symphony No. 3 (Wood/BBCSO)
1934 (25/9)	Symphony No. 3 (Wood/BBCSO)
1936 (27/8)	Symphony No. 3 (Wood/BBCSO)
1937 (24/8)	Symphony No. 4 (Wood/BBCSO)
1942 (21/6)	Symphony No. 3 (Wood/BBCSO)
1943 (22/7)	Symphony No. 7 (Boult/BBCSO)
1945 (11/9)	Symphony No. 5 (Boult/BBCSO)
1946 (11/9)	Symphony No. 7 (Cameron/BBCSO)
1947 (4/9)	Symphony No. 7 (Cameron/LPO)
1948 (3/9)	Symphony No. 7 (Cameron/LSO)
1949 (11/8)	Symphony No. 4 (Cameron/LSO)
1951 (29/8)	Symphony No. 7 (Cameron/LPO)
1952 (10/9)	Symphony No. 4 (Cameron/LPO)
1953 (26/8)	Symphony No. 6 (Barbirolli/Hallé)
1984 (24/7)	Symphony No. 5 (Leppard/BBC Philharmonic Orch.)

NOTES

Of the source materials used in this study, two categories in particular have been largely found in private hands: letters and press cuttings. Of the letters quoted, those addressed to the following are still in the hands of the addressees or their families:

Aloys and Tilly Fleischmann
Mary Gleaves
Julius Harrison
John Simons
Meta Malins
Henri van Marken
Christopher Whelen

Those addressed to Patrick Hadley, Harry Isaacs and Ernest Newman were loaned to me during their recipients' lifetimes, and although I do not now know where the originals are, I do hold copies which I was given permission to make.

Major institutional collections of letter include:

BBC Written Archives
British Library (Edward Clark; Cecil Gray; some Philip Heseltine; Colin Taylor; Sir Henry Wood)
Humanities Research Center, University of Texas at Austin (Clifford Bax; Richard Church; John Masefield)
Library of Congress (Philip Hale; Serge Kussevitsky; Nikolai Medtner)

Letters to the following are in the author's collection:

Arthur Alexander ('Sasha')
Harry Farjeon
Philip Heseltine (2)
Christine Ryan
Winifred Small
Freda Swain
Rosalind Thorneycroft
Richard Tildsley

Owners of the other letters have been identified in the text when they are cited. As far as cuttings are concerned I consulted those collections compiled by:

Felix Aprahamian
BBC Written Archives
York Bowen
Edwin Evans (Central Music Library)

Mary Gleaves
Sir Dan Godfrey (Bournemouth Public Libraries)
Edmund Rubbra
Patric Stevenson
Freda Swain

I have tried to keep superior numbers to designate notes or sources to a minimum, and have therefore not indicated sources for every letter quoted, which should be assumed to be as above. Where it has been possible to deduce a date for a letter (Bax rarely dated his correspondence) it is normally quoted in the text.

Sources that are quoted repeatedly are referred to by the following sigla:

(a) *Published sources*
BMOT Bacharach, A. L. *ed: British Music of Our Time.* Pelican Books, 1946. (Bax chapter by Julian Herbage pp. 113–29.)
BOT   Cohen, Harriet: *A Bundle of Time.* Faber, 1969.
CHH   Church, Richard: *The Voyage Home.* Heinemann, 1969.
CIF   Bax, Clifford: *Inland Far.* Heinemann, 1925; Lovat Dickson, 1933.
CLD   Colum, Mary: *Life and the Dream.* Macmillan, 1947.
CSS   Scott-Sutherland, Colin: *Arnold Bax.* Dent, 1973.
EBB   Bax, Ernest Belfort: *Reminiscences and Reflexions of a Mid and Late Victorian.* Allen & Unwin, 1918.
FDB   Foreman, Lewis: *Dermot O'Byrne – selected poems of Arnold Bax.* Thames Publishing, 1979.
FET   Farjeon, Eleanor: *Edward Thomas, the last four years – Book one of the Memoirs of Eleanor Farjeon.* OUP, 1958.
FWMY Bax, [Sir] Arnold: *Farewell, My Youth.* Longmans, Green & Co., 1943.
IAP   Bax, Clifford: *Ideas and People.* Lovat Dickson, 1936.
MIR   Fleischmann, Aloys *ed: Music in Ireland – a symposium.* Cork University Press, 1952.
ODB   'O'Byrne, Dermot': *A Dublin Ballad and other poems.* Dublin, The Candle Press, 1918.

(b) *Unpublished and institutional sources*
AAR   Alexander, Arthur: 'Arnold Bax – Some Personal Recollections' [unpublished essay] (courtesy Freda Swain).
BL   British Library (formerly British Museum), Department of Manuscripts.
BMR   Bax Memorial Room, University College, Cork.
BT   Bax, Sir Arnold: Broadcast Talk, BBC, Series 'British Composers' 6 May 1949 (BBC Sound Archives, disc X 13389).
BWA   BBC Written Archives Centre, Caversham, Berks.
FRB   Fleischmann, Tilly: *Some Reminiscences of Arnold Bax.* Unpublished typescript, Aug. 1955.

Those correspondents who are cited more than once or twice are abbreviated as follows in the citations, with the exception of the many names with the initials AB (Adrian Boult, Arthur Bliss, Arthur Benjamin etc.) and in these cases the surname is given in full; the abbreviation AB always means Arnold Bax. (The abbreviation 'pm' stands for postmark.)

AA   Arthur Alexander   EC   Edward Clark
AB   Arnold Bax   HC   Harriet Cohen
CB   Clifford Bax   PC   Padraic Colum

RC   Richard Church   JH   Julius Harrison
AE   George Russell   PH   Philip Heseltine ('Peter Warlock')
EE   Edwin Evans   VHH   Victor Hely-Hutchinson
AF   Aloys Fleischmann   HvM   Henri van Marken
LF   *the present author*   MM   Meta Malins
TF   Tilly Fleischmann   EN   Ernest Newman
BG   Balfour Gardiner   FS   Freda Swain
CG   Cecil Gray   RT   Rosalind Thorneycroft
MG   Mary Gleaves   CW   Christopher Whelen

Chapter I. 1883–1900. **The Background**

1 *EBB* pp. 27 and 65.
2 Sharp, Elizabeth: *William Sharp (Fiona Macleod) – a memoir compiled by his wife.* Heinemann, 1912, vol. I, p. 49.
3 Colmer, Francis: 'A few remarks on certain traits of character belonging to Arnold and Clifford Bax.' (Unpublished notes sent to Colin Scott-Sutherland, May 1963.)
4 Arnold Edward Trevor Bax, birth certificate.
5 *FWMY* p. 14.
6 Thompson, F. M. L.: *Hampstead – building a borough 1650–1964.* Routledge & Kegan Paul, 1974, p. 335.
7 Ivy Bank was originally built as Glen House. It was rebuilt in 1875, and from 1885 to 1893 was owned by Mrs Eliza D. Hill, the widow of one Charles Hill. The *Hampstead and Highgate Express* dated 5 Aug. 1893 records that 'on Friday last week, Messrs Baker & Sons, of 11, Queen Victoria-street, E.C., held another successful sale at the Mart. The Ivy Bank Estate, Haverstock Hill, comprising 3¾ acres with residence, realized £10,075.' Alfred Ridley

Bax is recorded as only being in residence from 1897 to 1911, and the property, in fact was not rated until 1899. However, when Arnold's brother Aubrey died in 1895 he was buried locally at Highgate. The Camden Public Libraries local history department owns a detailed model of Ivy Bank.
8 Alexander, Arthur: *Memoirs* [unpublished] (Courtesy of Freda Swain).
9 *CIF* p. 20.
10 Colmer *op. cit.*
11 *FWMY* p. 11.
12 *FWMY* p. 12.
13 Bax, [Sir] Arnold: '...A Physical Giant'. In *Homage to Sir Henry Wood – a world symposium.* (LPO Booklets.) LPP Ltd., 2nd enlarged edition, nd [1944?], pp. 13–14.
14 *FWMY* p. 18.
15 *BT*
16 *CIF* pp. 18–19; 21–2.
17 I quoted a number of music-type extracts from Bax's juvenilia in my article, 'The Musical Developments of Arnold Bax', *Music & Letters* Jan. 1971, pp. 59–68.

Chapter II. 1900–1905. **The Royal Academy of Music**

1 *FWMY* p. 18.
2 MacDonald, Calum: 'Parry and Liszt' [letter to the editor], *The Listener* 3 Aug. 1978, p. 148.
3 Corder, Frederick: *Ferencz (Francois) Liszt.* Kegan Paul, Trench, Trubner & Co., 1925.
4 The tone-poem *The Flowing Tide* was written at the end of Dale's life, its composer dying during the final rehearsal for its first performance in 1943. It has not been played since, though the score and parts are still available from Boosey & Hawkes.
5 *CIF* p. 35.

6 *FWMY* p. 27.
7 Tobin, J. Raymond: 'Great Teachers – No. 1 Frederick Corder', *Musical Opinion* Jan. 1912, p. 249.
8 The composer W. H. Bell, also a pupil of Corder, wrote in his unpublished reminiscences: 'looking back on the five years I spent in his class I don't think that at that time he had gained the experience or skill as a teacher that was afterwards to make him, together with Sir Charles Stanford, one of the finest teachers of composition England ever had' (*Reminiscences* ch. 3, p. 57, University Library, Cape Town).

9   *AAR.*

10 Corder, Frederick: *Modern Musical Composition – a manual for students*, J. Curwen & Sons, nd, [p. 1].

11 *op. cit*. p. 5.

12 See, for example, Corder, Frederick: *The Orchestra and How To Write for It – a practical guide*, J. Curwen & Sons, nd [1896?].

13 AB to E. J. Dent; letter in Rowe Music Library, Cambridge.

14 Alexander, Arthur: 'I Remember Matthay'. *RAM Magazine* Oct. 1958, pp. 52–3.

15 *RAM Club Magazine* May 1903, p. 12; Oct. 1903, p. 13.

16 *FWMY* pp. 29–30.

17 Bax, Sir Arnold: 'Foreword', *Prospectus for 57th Season of Promenade Concerts* 1951, p. 3.

18 *FWMY* p. 24.

19 *RAM Club Magazine* Jan. 1904, p. 17.

20 *BT.*

21 *FWMY* p. 44.

22 Undated letter ('Saturday'); collection Colin Scott-Sutherland.

23 Patterson, Edward M.: *The County Donegal Railways*. David & Charles, 1962; Pan Books, 1972, pp. 60–1.

24 *FWMY* p. 45.

25 Gogarty, Oliver St. John: *As I Was Going Down Sackville Street*. Rich & Cowan, rev. ed., 1937, pp. 142, 190.

26 'O'Byrne, Dermot' *pseud*: 'Wrack'. In his *Wrack and Other Stories*. Dublin, The Talbot Press/London, T. Fisher Unwin, 1918, pp. 1–2.

27 *FWMY* pp. 49–50.

28 'O'Byrne, Dermot' *pseud*: 'The Servant of the Bishop'. *Orpheus* No. 16, Oct. 1911, p. 345.

29 Synge, J. M.: *The Aran Islands*. Dublin, Maunsel & Co./London, Elkin Mathews, 1907, pp. 1–28.

30 *Musical Standard* 10 Dec. 1904, p. 369.

31 Bax, Arnold: programme note. Patron's Fund Concert, Aeolian Hall, 6 Dec. 1904.

32 *RCM Magazine* Vol. 1, no. 1, Christmas Term 1904, p. 21.

33 Clarke, Rebecca: *Memoirs* [unpublished] (Courtesy of Christopher Johnson).

34 *CIF* p. 34.

35 *FWMY* pp. 26–7.

36 *Musical News* 26 Nov. 1904, p. 470.

37 Archives of J. & W. Chester, London.

38 *Music & Letters* Jan. 1954, p. 5.

39 *AAR.*

40 *ibid.*

41 *Musical Times* May 1905, p. 330.

42 *RAM Club Magazine* Oct. 1905, p. 15.

43 Corder, Frederick: *A History of the Royal Academy of Music from 1822 to 1922*. The author, 1922. p. 93.

44 *FWMY* p. 47.

Chapter III. 1905–1909. **Many Influences**

1   Corder, Frederick: 'Benjamin Dale's Pianoforte Sonata in D' *Musical Times* April 1918, p. 164.

2   *AAR*

3   Three issues bound together in Birmingham Public Library; 1907/8: Bodleian Library (Per. 258751 e.5); 1912: British Library (Ac. 5168).

4   This title may well have been suggested to Bax by Frederick Cowen's *A Phantasy of Life and Love*, first given at Gloucester in Sept. 1901; subsequently at the Queen's Hall, and 1903 Proms.

5   Evans, Edwin: [Letter to the editor.] *Musical Opinion* Dec. 1920, p. 226. ('Some works of his [Bax] came under my notice as one of the founders of the Society of British Composers about the Spring of 1905.')

6   Calvocoressi, M. D.: *Musicians Gallery – music and ballet in Paris and London*. Faber, 1933, p. 282–3.

7   *CIF* p. 116.

8   *CIF* p. 126.

9   Delany, Paul: *D. H. Lawrence's Nightmare*. Hassocks, Sussex, Harvester Press, 1979, p. 122.

10 *CIF* pp. 160–1.

11 David Garnett, letter to LF, 3 Sept. 1979.

12 Bax, Sir Arnold: 'Richard Strauss'. In *Music Magazine* edited by Anna Instone and Julian Herbage. Rockliffe, 1953, pp. 76–7.

13 Published by G. Schirmer, New York, 1908. (British Library H. 1794. dd. (17).) The third of *Fünf Lieder für eine Singstimme und Klavier, op. 5*.

14 Bournemouth Municipal Orchestra programme, 13 Dec. 1906.

15 The *Bournemouth Guardian* for Saturday 15 Dec 1906 described the overture as 'a brilliant and light-hearted representation of several sides of Irish character' and added that it was 'per-

sonally conducted by the composer
Mr Trevor Bax, who is already favour-
ably known as the writer of several
Celtic pieces based more or less upon
Folk melodies'. Did the reviewer at-
tend the concert or not?

16 Bax: programme note, Hallé Concert
    7 Jan 1915 (the notes are by Ernest
    Newman who quotes Bax, p. 342).
17 *Irish Statesman* 11 Sept. 1926, p. 11.
18 Bax: programme note, Hallé Concert
    op. cit.
19 *FWMY* p. 39.
20 *FWMY* p. 38.
21 Maitland, J. A. Fuller: *Grove's Diction-
    ary of Music and Musicians*. Macmillan,
    1910; Vol. V and Appendix p. 162.
22 Manuscript introduction to the auto-
    graph short score preserved in the Bax
    Memorial Room, University College,
    Cork.
23 The short score sketches for *Déirdre*
    are preserved in the Bax Memorial
    Room, and comprise just the movement
    later orchestrated as *Roscatha* and 'Cuid
    5' (i.e. part 5). See also: Parlett, Gra-
    ham: 'Deirdre and Rosc-Catha' *Bax
    Society Bulletin* Nov. 1970, pp. 18–21.
24 *CIF* p. 132.
25 *CIF* p. 132–133.
26 'Concerts – Mr Arnold Bax's Compo-
    sitions' *The Times* 20 July 1908 p. 6.
    (This review appeared only in the early
    edition. It will not be found in editions
    on sale in microform, nor in the editions
    filed by *The Times* itself. I obtained a
    transcript from the set preserved at
    Exeter Public Library. It appears in full
    in my article 'The Musical Development
    of Arnold Bax' *Music & Letters* Jan.
    1971, pp. 65–6.)
27 Lloyd, Stephen: *H. Balfour Gardiner*.
    Cambridge University Press, 1984.

28 *AAR.*
29 *ibid.*
30 *ibid.*
31 *Le Sacre* was first published for piano,
    four hands, in 1913. The orchestral
    score did not appear for another eight
    years.
32 *AAR.*
33 Acton, Charles: 'Fleischmann conducts
    the RTESO'. *Irish Times* 12 June 1971.
34 Fleischmann. Aloys: programme note.
    Radio Telefís Éireann studio concert
    11 June 1971.
35 *FWMY* p. 90.
36 Bell became Principal of the South Af-
    rican College of Music in 1912, and re-
    mained there until his death in 1946.
    Thus we have no experience of his
    music, which includes several symph-
    onies, five operas based on Japanese
    Noh-plays, and six conventional operas
    (including a setting of Clifford Bax's
    libretto for *The Wandering Scholar* only
    four years after Holst set it). *See* Taylor,
    L. E.: *Catalogue of the Music Manu-
    scripts of William Henry Bell 1873–
    1946*. Cape Town, University of Cape
    Town Libraries, 1948.
37 *FWMY* p. 89.
38 *FWMY* p. 89.
39 Nathan, M. Montagu: 'Reminiscences
    of Arnold Bax' *Musical Times* Nov.
    1953, pp. 507–8.
40 Sale catalogue No. 102 of Richard
    MacNutt (Tunbridge Wells), p. 7, item
    9.
41 *Orpheus* No. 10, April 1910: supple-
    ment.
41 'Appendix – Three Prehistoric Matches'
    In *The Old Broughtonians Cricket
    Weeks*, Vol. 4, Kensington, The Favil
    Press, 1930, pp. 87–93.

Chapter IV. 1909–1910. **Ireland and Russia**

1 Stravinsky, Igor, *and* Craft, Robert:
   Expositions and Developments. Faber,
   1962, p. 148.
2 Taped interview with the late Anne
   Crowley, 1976. Miss Crowley read and
   translated Bax's comments from letters
   written to her by him in Gaelic.
3 Bax: programme note, Promenade Concert, Queen's Hall, 30 Aug. 1910.
4 Yeats, W. B.: 'The Wanderings of Us-
   heen'. In his *Poems*. T. Fisher Unwin,
   nd, pp. 249–50.

5 Kennedy, Michael: *Portrait of Elgar*.
   OUP, 1968, pp. 178–9.
6 Philip Heseltine's annotations to his
   copy of the printed full score, now in
   the author's collection.
7 See: Bray, Trevor: *Bantock – Music in
   the Midlands before the First World
   War*. Triad Press, 1973.
8 *FWMY* p. 56.
9 *FWMY* p. 57.
10 Bax: programme note, Queen's Hall,
   27 March 1912.

11 Carey, Hugh: Duet for Two Voices. CUP, 1979, p. 71.
12 *FWMY* p. 63.
13 Identification by Olga Antonietti's daughter, Jessica Morton. The real name appears as the dedication on the ms of the First Violin Sonata.
14 Bax, Arnold: [On Inspiration]. In *On Inspiration*. J. & W. Chester, nd [1929], pp. 17–18. See pp. 192–3.
15 White, Felix: 'Arnold Bax's Violin Sonata'. *Musical News & Herald* 14 Jan. 1922, p. 49.
16 *FWMY* pp. 66–7.
17 *FWMY* p. 70.

18 *FWMY* p. 71.
19 See: 'Dermot O'Byrne's' poem 'A Summer in Exile'. *FDB* p. 49.
20 Cooper, Martin: 'Gogol's Pictures of Ukrainian Life in a Masterly Setting.' Notes to the recording of Rimsky-Korsakov's *May Night* on DGG 2530 687/9.
21 Cohen, Harriet, quoted in *BMOT* p. 124.
22 Merrick, Frank: Sleeve note to his recording of Bax's First Piano Sonata. Frank Merrick Society, ALO 10779 (FMS 7).
23 *FWMY* p. 72.

Chapter V. 1910–1911. **Marriage**

1 Garnett, David: *The Golden Echo*. Chatto & Windus, 1953, p. 261.
2 *FET* p. 2.
3 *ibid*.
4 Bax, Sir Arnold: 'Tribute to Sir Henry Wood', unpublished script in BBC Script Registry: broadcast BBC Home Service, 4 March 1944.
5 *Pall Mall Gazette*, quoted in *Musical Standard* 3 Sept. 1910, p. 154.
6 Wilson, Dorothy: *The Orchestral Development of Arnold Bax*. MA Thesis, University College of Wales, Bangor, 1975, p. 21.
7 I am grateful to Graham Parlett for the explanation of this Irishism. He writes: The tag "Pós bean ó'n tsléibh is pósfair an tsléibh go léir", translates as "marry a mountainy woman and you marry the whole mountain", meaning that mountainy people are more sociable and hospitable than plain-dwellers.
8 Balfour Gardiner note books; transcripts supplied by Stephen Lloyd.
9 PH to Colin Taylor; British Library Add. MS 54197.
10 Bax: programme note, Queen's Hall, 13 March 1912.
11 Pirie, Peter J.: 'The Unfashionable Generation' *High Fidelity Magazine* Jan. 1966, p. 62.

12 Bax: programme note, Queen's Hall, 13 March 1912.
13 *Athenaeum* 16 March 1912, p. 320.
14 Woolf, Virginia: 'Mr Bennet and Mrs Brown'. In her *The Captain's Deathbed and other essays*. Hogarth Press, 1950, p. 96.
15 *CSS* p. 30.
16 *FWMY* p. 77.
17 *FET* p. 243. (This illustration does not appear in the paperback edition.)
18 Quoted in *CSS* pp. 30–1.
19 *FWMY* p. 94.
20 Dedication on the ms short score of *King Kojata (Tamara)* preserved in the Bax Memorial Room, University College, Cork.
21 *CIF* p. 231.
22 *CIF* p. 188–93.
23 *FET* pp. 3–4.
24 Bax, Clifford: *Vintage Verse*. Hollis & Carter, 1945, p. 293.
25 *CIF* p. 231.
26 *FWMY* p. 95.
27 *FWMY* p. 100.
28 Dodds, E. R.: *Missing Persons – an autobiography*. Oxford, Clarendon Press, 1977, pp. 55–6.
29 *CLD* p. 302.
30 *FWMY* p. 100.
31 *FWMY* pp. 100–1.
32 *CSS* p. 29.

Chapter VI. 1912–1914. **Rathgar and London**

1 Dermot Bax died in December 1976.
2 Warlock, Peter [Philip Heseltine]: *Frederick Delius* – reprinted with additions, annotations and comments

by Hubert Foss. Bodley Head, 1952, pp. 157–8.
3 *ibid.*
4 *ibid.*

5 *Athenaeum* 16 March 1912, p. 320.
6 Bax: programme note, Queen's Hall, 4 March 1913.
7 *FWMY* p. 86.
8 Gogol, Nikolay: 'A May Night'. In his *Evenings on a Farm Near Dikanka*, translated by Constance Garnett. Chatto & Windus, 1926, pp. 84–5.
9 Bax: ms inscription on the autograph piano score in the British Library, Add Ms 54737.
10 *The Times* 1 June 1961.
11 Bax: ms inscription on the autograph full score, collection Chappell & Co.
12 Swinburne, Algernon Charles: 'A Nympholept' In his *Poems ... in Six Volumes*, vol. 6, Chatto & Windus, 1905, pp. 127–40.
13 Sackville, Margaret: 'The Nympholept' *Orpheus* No. 9, Jan 1910, pp. 108–9.
14 *FDB* p. 55.
15 AB to AA nd [Sept. 1913?].
16 Bax: programme note, Queen's Hall, 23 Sept. 1913.
17 *The Times* 24 Sept. 1913.
18 Bax: programme note, Queen's Hall, 20 March 1914.
19 *ibid.*
20 *FWMY* pp. 102–3.
21 *ibid.*
22 Bax, Clifford: *Some I Knew Well.* Phoenix House, 1951, p. 90.
23 *CIF* p. 216.
24 *FET* p. 10.
25 *CLD* p. 188.
26 AB to PC; letter in the Colum Collection, SUNY at Binghamton.
27 *ibid.*
28 *ibid.*
29 'On the Hill' *Irish Review* Feb. 1913, pp. 638–63.
30 Contemporary programmes do not include the work, though its performance may well have been a last minute arrangement through a change of programme.

31 AB to AA, nd [July 1913?].
32 AB to AA, nd [July 1913?].
33 Colin Taylor to PH, British Library Add. MS 54197.
34 Bax: programme note, Queen's Hall, 28 Feb. 1916. (Performance not given.)
35 AB to RT, nd [1913?].
36 AB to MG, nd [pm: 1933].
37 Taped interview with the late Anne Crowley.
38 Bax: programme note printed in the published score.
39 Blom, Eric: programme note, Queen's Hall, 13 Nov. 1922.
40 Bax, Arnold: contribution to the article on harmony in *Dictionary of Modern Music and Musicians*. Dent, 1924, p. 221.
41 *FWMY* p. 93.
42 *FWMY* p. 94.
43 *Music & Letters* Jan. 1954, p. 13.
44 Bax: programme note, Queen Mary Memorial Concert, Royal Festival Hall, 15 April 1953.
45 *Orpheus* No. 18, April 1912, pp. 34–5.
46 Nathan, M.M.: 'Reminiscence of Arnold Bax'. *Musical Times* Nov. 1953, p. 507.
47 Aprahamian, Felix: 'Genuine Pearls'. *Sunday Times* 7 Oct. 1973, p. 30.
48 Palmer, Christopher: 'Bax' [notice of concert]. *Musical Times* Nov. 1973, p. 1149.
49 Payne, Anthony: 'Crisis-Ridden Bax Quintet'. *Daily Telegraph*, 1 Oct. 1973.
50 Palmer *op. cit.*
51 Pirie, Peter J.: 'More Than A Brazen Romantic'. *Music & Musicians*, Jan. 1971, p. 33.
52 LF interview with the late Vivian Langrish, 1975.
53 Rubbra, Edmund: 'Arnold Bax's Technics – a new flowering of old traditions'. *Daily Telegraph*, 14 Oct. 1933.
54 Dent, Edward J.: [Bax Quintet]. *The London Mercury* June 1920, p. 232.

Chapter VII. 1914–1916. **The Great War**

1 *FWMY* p. 94.
2 *The Bard of the Dimbovitza.* [First series.] James R. Osgood, McIlvaine & Co., 1892.
3 *The Bard of the Dimbovitza.* Second Series. James R. Osgood, McIlvaine & Co., 1897. (Advertisement on the front flyleaf.)
4 *AAR.*

5 This copy now in the present writer's collection.
6 *FWMY* p. 84.
7 AB to PH; British Library Add. MS 57772 NN.
8 Harrison, May: 'Delius'. In *A Delius Companion* ed. Christopher Redwood. Calder, 1976, p. 102.

9   AB to PH; British Library Add. MS 57772 NN.
10 *FET* p. 123.
11 AB to PH; British Library Add. MS 53809 I.
12 Heseltine, Philip: 'Classic Concert Society'. *Daily Mail* 25 March 1915, p. 2.
13 Heseltine, Philip: 'Vodka Shop in Music'. *Daily Mail* 19 May 1915, p. 3.
14 *FWMY* p. 6.
15 LF interview with Sir Melford Stevenson, 1977.
16 Alexander, Arthur: *Memoirs* [unpublished]. (Courtesy of Freda Swain.)
17 Heseltine, Philip: 'British Music Festival' *Daily Mail* 17 May 1915, p. 3.
18 Evans, Edwin: 'Modern British Composers – II: Arnold Bax'. *Musical Times* March 1919, pp. 103–5.

19 Concert handbill, Wigmore Hall, 25 April 1922. (Reproduced in facsimile on the cover of *Bax Society Bulletin* no. 5, May 1969.)
20 Rosenberg, Maeve to LF, 8 Nov. 1976.
21 *FET* p. 243.
22 Bax, Clifford: 'Musician'. In his *Farewell My Muse*. Lovat Dickson, 1932, pp. 50–1.
23 *FWMY* pp. 106.
24 AB to TF, see p. 379.
25 'O'Byrne, Dermot': 'In Memoriam My Friend Patrick H. Pearse'. *ODB* p. 8.
26 The title might be variously translated from the unpublished manuscript, where it appears as: 'I gcuimhne ar bpádraig mac Piarais'.
27 Bax, Elsita (3 The Vale, Golders Green, NW4 to AA; nd [*ca* last week of March, 1918]).

Chapter VIII. 1916–1918. Harriet Cohen

1   Newmarch, Rosa: programme note, Queen's Hall, 23 Nov. 1920.
2   see *CSS* pp. 53–4.
3   Sorabji, Kaikhosru Shapurji: *Around Music*. Unicorn Press, 1932, p. 70.
4   Quoted in Podro, Paul: 'Bax and his critics', Bax Society Bulletin, no. 1, Feb. 1968, p. 4.
5   Scott-Sutherland, Colin: 'Sir Arnold Bax – Symphonic Variations' [a review]. *Music Review* May 1967, pp. 156–7.
6   *ibid.*
7   *CHH* p. 51.
8   Parlett, Graham: 'The Metamorphosis of Deirdre'; unpublished essay.
9   *CSS* p. 54.
10 Bax: programme note.
11 AB to A. Boult; BBC Written Archives.
12 HC to AA, Sept. 21 [1917].
13 Bax: programme note, Leeds Musical Festival 1922, Saturday morning 7 Oct.
14 Palmer, Christopher: 'England' In his *Delius – portrait of a cosmopolitan*. Duckworth, 1976, pp. 151–2.

15 *BT.*
16 Herbage, Julian: 'Sir Arnold Bax'. In *BMOT* p. 116.
17 AB to EN, transcript courtesy the late Vera Newman.
18 In his notebook for 1929, Philip Heseltine compiled a list of Bax's works including 'The Frog Skin ballet 1918'. (British Library Add. MS 57969 H.)
19 *The Stage* 13 Dec. 1917.
20 AB to A Boult (10 Heath West Road, Hampstead NW3), Wed. [6 March 1918], quoted in *Music and Friends: seven decades of letters to Adrian Boult*, annotated by Jerrold Northrop Moore. Hamish Hamilton, 1979, p. 30.
21 Typescript of a copy in the Bantock archives made available by Dr. Trevor Bray.
22 It is not known which piece by Harriet Cohen was played, but it is worth noting that she published *Four Russian Pieces* for piano, with Augener, in 1916.

Chapter IX. 1918–1920. Peace and Success

1   The work's two 78 rpm recordings were on 6 and 8 sides respectively. Yet both start the last side with the first statement of the tune, clearly the selling point of the records.
2   *CSS* p. 80.

3   Hughes published the song in the first volume of his *Irish Country Songs* (Boosey & Co., 1909, p. 55) as 'The Fanaid Grove'. When Beatrice Harrison recorded it (HMV D 1195) the title became 'The Lament of Fanaid Grove'.

4   Lyle, Watson: 'Musician of the North'. *Bookman* Feb. 1932, p. 268.
5   Evans, Edwin: 'Modern British Composers – II: Arnold Bax'. *Musical Times* March 1919, p. 103.
6   *The Times* 7 June 1919, p. 10.
7   Alexander, Arthur: *Memoirs* [unpublished]. (Courtesy Freda Swain.)
8   AB to AA, nd.
9   Merrick, Frank: Sleeve note to his recording of the Second Piano Sonata. (Frank Merrick Society ALO 10500/1 (FMS 6)).
10 Cohen, Harriet: quoted in *BMOT* p. 124.
11 Dated 29 April 1919. Collection author.
12 Abraham, G. E. H.: 'Six British Piano Sonatas – III: the two Bax sonatas'. *Music Teacher* July 1926, p. 419.
13 Blom, Eric: programme notes, Queen's Hall, 13 Nov. 1922.
14 *Musical Times* March 1919, p. 128.
15 *ibid.*
16 *Musical Times* April 1919, p. 179.
17 *CHH* p. 52.
18 *BOT* p. 48.
19 *BOT* p. 46.
20 *Musical Times* Oct. 1919, p. 57.

21 Goossens, Eugène: *Overture and Beginners.* Methuen, 1951, p. 299.
22 AB to Harry Isaacs, nd [1945].
23 Karsavina, Tamara: 'The Truth About the Russian Dancers'. *Dance Perspectives* 14 Spring 1962, p. 8.
24 Karsavina, Tamara: transcript from a BBC Midland feature, 1969, that was prepared but never broadcast.
25 AB (155 Fellows Road NW3, Monday) to Harry Farjeon [March 1920].
26 'Picnic at Tintagel' by Ashton. See: Watt, D.: 'Musical Events – nothing gained'. *New Yorker* 8 March 1952, pp. 91–2.
27 'The Death of Cuchullian' by Marie Rambert. See: *BMOT* p. 125.
28 *Old English Ditties*, selected from W. Chappell's 'Popular Music of the Olden Time'. The long ballads compressed and occasionally new words written by J. Oxenford. The symphonies and accompaniments by G. A. Macfarren. Chappell, nd, p. 24.
29 *BOT* p. 72.
30 *BOT* p. 73.
31 *BOT* p. 59.

Chapter X. 1921–1923. Triumph

1   *BOT* p. 52.
2   *ibid.*
3   BL Add. MS 52256.
4   Morris, Margaret: *The Art of J. D. Fergusson.* Blackie, 1974, p. 135. 'Boonie' was Goossens' wife.
5   Bax, Arnold: 'E. J. Moeran 1894–1950' *Music & Letters* April 1951, pp. 125–7.
6   *Musical News & Herald* 30 April 1921.
7   *FRB* p. 40.
8   *CSS* p. 39.
9   Hull, Robin: *The English Music Society Volume Two – Arnold Bax* (Booklet with Columbia 78 rpm records.), p. 11.
10 Eggar, Katharine: 'The Piano Pieces of Arnold Bax' *Music Student* Nov. 1921, p. 67.
11 *ibid.*
12 *ibid.*
13 Newman, Ernest: 'The Philharmonic Concert' *Sunday Times* 19 Dec. 1920, p. 5.
14 'Bournemouth Symphony Concerts' *Bournemouth Guardian* 22 Oct. 1921.
15 *ODB* p. 18.
16 *BT.*
17 *Music & Letters* Jan. 1954, p. 3.

18 Bax, Arnold: 'On Inspiration' in *On Inspiration.* J. & W. Chester nd [1929], pp. 17–18.
19 Bax: programme note, Cleveland Orchestra, Masonic Auditorium, Cleveland, Ohio 7–9 Jan. 1926.
20 *ibid.*
21 Francis, C. M.: *The Musical Language of Arnold Bax.* Unpublished BA research essay; University of Bristol, 1970, p. 24.
22 'C': 'Arnold Bax's Symphony'. *Musical Times* Jan. 1923, p. 60.
23 Blom, Eric: programme notes, Queen's Hall, 13 Nov. 1922, pp. v–vi.
24 Evans, Edwin: 'The Arnold Bax Concert' *Musical Times* Dec. 1922, p. 874.
25 Karsavina, Tamara: *Theatre Street.* rev. edition, Constable, 1948, pp. 163–4.
26 Demuth, Norman: 'Sir Arnold Bax' in his *Musical Trends in the 20th Century.* Rockliffe, 1952, pp. 166–7.
27 Moore, Jerrold: *Elgar on Record.* OUP, 1974, p. 49.
28 'The Philharmonic Choir – St Patrick's Breastplate' *The Times* 23 May 1925, p. 14.
29 *ibid.*

Chapter XI. 1924–1925. Crisis

1 *IAP* p. 193.
2 *ibid.*
3 Hannah, Barbara: *Jung – his life and work.* Michael Joseph, 1977, p. 140.
4 Clifford Bax implies the conversation dates from 1926; circumstantial evidence would suggest some two years earlier.
5 *IAP* p. 194.
6 *IAP* p. 202.
7 *IAP* p. 204.
8 Harriet Cohen bequeathed her personal papers to the BL on condition that they remain unopened for 30 years.
9 *BT.*
10 AB to RC, nd.
11 Jelka Delius to Percy Grainger, Grainger Museum, Melbourne.
12 *BOT* p. 95.
13 *BOT* p. 93.
14 *The Old Broughtonians Cricket Weeks.* Volume 3 (cf III/41). Kensington, The Favil Press, 1922, p. 7.
15 AB to CG, BL Add. MS 57784.
16 AB to Philip Hale, 22 Nov. 1929; original in Library of Congress, quoted in programme notes for first perform-ance, Symphony Hall, Boston 13 and 14 Dec. 1929, p. 610.
17 Cox, David: 'Arnold Bax' in *The Symphony* Vol. 2, edited by Robert Simpson. Penguin, 1967, p. 157.
18 'Arnold Schoenberg'. *Music & Letters* Oct. 1951, p. 307.
19 'The Philharmonic Choir – St Patrick's Breastplate'. *The Times* 23 May 1925, p. 14.
20 Murdoch, James: *Australia's Contemporary Composers.* Melbourne (Australia), Macmillan, 1972, p. 183.
21 Margaret Sutherland: typescript statement in Library of Congress.
22 Sutherland, Margaret: 'Young Days in Music'. *Overland* no. 40, Dec. 1968, p. 27.
23 Godwin Baynes' second marriage, to Hilda Davidson, niece of the then Archbishop of Canterbury, had failed.
24 The private significance of Arnold's signature to his brother is unexplained.
25 Referring to Balfour Gardiner's financing of Holst's holiday with AB and CB in Spain, as recounted in CIF, then newly published.

Chapter XII. 1926–1928. New Directions

1 Gray, Cecil: *Peter Warlock – a memoir of Philip Heseltine.* Cape, 1934; 1938, pp. 265–6.
2 At letter H and the three following bars, p. 15, in the full score published by Murdoch, 1928.
3 *The Old Codger* in 'Cod Pieces' (British Library Add. MS 48303); published in an arrangement for piano duet by Fred Tomlinson by Thames Publishing, 1972.
4 AB to PH; British Library Add. MS 57772 NN.
5 'Savoy Theatre'. *The Times* 29 July 1926, p. 10.
6 AB to John Simons, nd [pm: 13 May 1935].
7 Suckling, Norman: 'Bax and his Piano Sonatas'. *The Listener* 17 June 1954, p. 1069.
8 Bax: programme note, Queen's Hall, 3 Oct. 1929.
9 BT.
10 Kennedy, Michael: *Barbirolli – conductor laureate.* MacGibbon & Kee, 1971, p. 68.
11 'Concerts – Chamber Music by Arnold Bax'. *The Times* 22 Oct. 1927, p. 10.
12 *Oxford English Dictionary*, vol. VII, OUP 1933, p. 995. 'Planxty' is now the name of a celebrated Irish folk group.
13 Bax file, BWA: Imperial Concert Agency to Pedro Tillett, BBC, Savoy Hill, 30 Nov. 1927.
14 *op. cit.,* 20 Dec. 1927.
15 Eric Fenby to LF, 30 July 1976.
16 AB to MG, 'Thursday' [pm: 19 May 1927].
17 'Concerts – Chamber Music by Arnold Bax'. *The Times* 22 Oct. 1927, p. 10.
18 Foss, Hubert J.: 'Some Chamber Music by Arnold Bax'. *The Dominant* Dec. 1927, pp. 16–19.
19 *CHH* pp. 50–2.
20 'AKH': 'New Bax Sonata'. *Musical Times* Jan. 1928, p. 67.
21 Unidentified cutting signed 'PW' in Edwin Evans' cuttings book.
22 'The Promenade Concerts – A Postwar Symphony'. *The Times* 22 Aug. 1923, p. 10.
23 'H.H.': 'Promenade Concerts – Mr

Bax's Symphony'. *Daily Telegraph* 22
Aug. 1928.
24   *MIR* p. 272.

25   *FRB* pp. 1–3.
26   Bax, Arnold: 'I am a Brazen Romantic'.
     Musical America 7 July 1928, p. 9.

Chapter XIII. 1928–1929. **Dreams and Reality**

1   Hadley, Patrick: [obituary tribute]
    Music & Letters Jan. 1954, p. 8.
2   Shore, Bernard: 'Bax's Third Sym-
    phony' In his *Sixteen Symphonies*.
    Longmans, Green & Co., 1949, p. 350.
3   Hull, Robert A.: *A Handbook on Bax's
    Symphonies*. Murdoch, nd [1932],
    p. 33.
4   Bax: programme note, Queen's Hall,
    14 March 1930.
5   James, Burnett: unpublished essay on
    Bax.
6   Shore, Bernard: *op. cit.,* p. 351.
7   RCA SB 6806 or GL 42247.
8   Demuth, Norman: 'Bax – Symphony
    No. 3 in C'. In his *Record Collector's
    Series. No. 2 Symphonies*. EMI, 1950,
    p. 55.
9   *FWMY* p. 10.
10 Hadley, Patrick: *op. cit.*
11 McCabe, John: 'Bax – Symphony No.
    3'. *Records & Recordings* Oct. 1969,
    p. 62.
12 Foss, Hubert: *Ralph Vaughan Williams*.
    Harrap, 1950, p. 142.
13 British Library Add. MS 50385.
14 Kennedy, Michael: *The Works of
    Ralph Vaughan Williams*. OUP, 1964,
    p. 236.

15 *op. cit.,* p. 237.
16 Threlfall, Robert: 'The Finale Problem
    and Vaughan Williams' Piano Concerto'.
    Musical Opinion Feb. 1975, pp. 237–8.
17 *Musical Opinion* Feb. 1929.
18 *BT.*
19 Robertson, Rae: quoted in 'Notes on
    the New Issues'. *Gramophone* Sept.
    1930, pp. 179–80.
20 Dunton-Green, L.: 'Arnold Bax' [in
    French]. In the programme book for
    the 1930 ISCM Festival at Liège;
    specially   translated   by   Maureen
    Gooding.
21 AB to Balfour Gardiner, Gardiner
    Estate.
22 PH to Balfour Gardiner.
23 Hadley, Patrick: *op. cit.*
24 Bax: programme note, Queen's Hall,
    10 Feb. 1932.
25 *BOT* p. 182.
26 Newman, Ernest: 'Bax's New Work'.
    Sunday Times 14 Feb. 1932, p. 7.
27 Lyle, Watson: 'Musician of the North'.
    Bookman Feb. 1932, p. 268.
28 AB to A. Boult, nd [15 Oct. 1931],
    BWA.

Chapter XIV. 1930–1932. **Going Northern**

1   HC to A Boult, BWA.
2   Hull, Robert H.: *A Handbook to Arnold
    Bax's Symphonies*. Murdoch, nd [1932],
    p. 44.
3   *ibid.*
4   Payne, Anthony: 'Problem of a Lyric
    Composer'. *Music & Musicians* Jan.
    1965, p. 17.
5   *ibid.*
6   AB to CW, nd.
7   *Gramophone* Feb. 1930, p. 404.
8   *Gramophone* March 1930, pp. 437–8.
9   Wood, Sir Henry: *My Life of Music*.
    Gollancz, 1938, p. 425.
10 *ibid.*
11 *Daily Express* 21 May 1930.
12 *ibid.*
13 *Morning Post* 21 May 1930.
14 AB to EC, 'Saturday', BWA.
15 BBC internal memo, BWA.

16 AB to A. Boult, BWA.
17 AB to A. Boult, BWA.
18 Dale Smith singing *As Ever I Saw, My
    Gostly Fader, Heraclitus, Lullaby,
    Rantum Tantum*; Megan Foster singing
    *The Distracted Maid, The Bayley
    Berith the Bell away, Johnny wi' the
    tye, A Sad Song, The Shoemaker*; Dale
    Smith singing *Away to Twiver, 'Bethle-
    hem Down', The Toper's Song, Roister
    Doister*; John Armstrong singing *Con-
    sider* and *Sweet and Twenty*.
19 Fenby, Eric: *Delius as I Knew Him*.
    Icon Books, 1966, p. 199. (Footnote,
    only in this edition.)
20 *BOT* p. 65.
21 Bax: programme note, 12 April 1934.
22 Newman, Ernest: 'The Philharmonic
    Concert'. *Sunday Times* 15 April
    1934, p. 7.

23 AB to CW, nd.

24 Newman, Ernest: 'Bax Symphony No. 5'. *Sunday Times* 21 Jan. 1934.

25 Hull, Robert H.: 'Bax's Fifth Symphony'. Unidentified cutting in Patric Stevenson's cuttings book.

26 Bax, Arnold: 'Celtic Twilight in Moderation'. *The National and English Review* Dec. 1950, p. 51.

27 Wilson, Jane: *C. W. Orr – the unknown song writer*. Thesis: MM, University of Adelaide, 1976, p. 50.

28 Hughes, Herbert ed.: *The Joyce Book*. The Sylvan Press, nd [1932].

29 Lloyd, Stephen: *H. Balfour Gardiner*. Cambridge University Press, 1984.

30 *BOT* pp. 206–9.

31 AB to TF, nd, 'Thursday'.

32 AB to A. Boult, BWA.

33 AB to AA, nd, 'Tuesday Eve'.

34 AB to BBC, Bax file, BWA.

35 AB to A. Boult, BWA.

Chapter XV. 1933–1936. **Past Fifty**

1 AB to Anne Crowley, 6 Jan. 1944.

2 AB to MG (as are all the remainder of the quotations on this page).

3 Fleischmann, Aloys: 'In conversation with Michael Dawney'. *Composer* Winter 1975/76 no. 56, p. 29.

4 *ibid.*

5 Fleischmann, Aloys, *op. cit.*, p. 30.

6 AB to AA, nd. 'Monday'.

7 'Harriet Cohen and Thelma Reiss'. *Musical Opinion* April 1934, p. 624.

8 AB to Julian Herbage, BWA.

9 AB to Julian Herbage, BWA.

10 *BOT* p. 258.

11 'The Encaenia at Oxford'. *The Times* 21 June 1934, p. 8. I am grateful to Graham Parlett for specially preparing this translation for me.

12 Pirie, Peter J.: 'The Unfashionable Generation'. *High Fidelity* Jan. 1966, p. 62.

13 Hammond, Philip: 'The Hallé Years and After' In *Hamilton Harty – his life and music*, edited by David Greer. Belfast, Blackstaff Press, nd [1979], p. 49.

14 AB to John Simons, nd [pm: 13 May 1935].

15 *FRB* p. 6.

16 *BOT* p. 258.

17 Kennedy, Michael: *The Works of Ralph Vaughan Williams*. OUP, 1964, 1966, pp. 247–8.

18 *FRB* p. 5.

19 Bax, Arnold: quoted in *Radio Times* for 16 May 1937, issue dated 14 May 1937, p. 20.

20 *ibid.*

21 AB to N. Medtner, nd, letter in Library of Congress.

22 *BOT* p. 267.

Chapter XVI. 1937–1939. **'I Can't Grow Up'**

1 AB to Kenneth Wright, 30 Aug. [1936], BWA.

2 AB to Clarence Raybould, nd.

3 HC to A. Boult, nd, BWA.

4 *ibid.*

5 Newman, Ernest: 'BBC Concert'. *Sunday Times* 21 Feb. 1937, p. 7.

6 Stevenson, Patric: 'Some Anecdotes About Arnold Bax'. *Bax Society Bulletin* May 1969, p. 77.

7 Taped interview with the late Anne Crowley, 1976.

8 *FRB* pp. 21–22.

9 *BOT* p. 269.

10 Mann, William: 'Some English Concertos'. In *The Concerto* ed. Ralph Hill. Penguin Books, 1952, p. 402.

11 Latham, Peter: [obituary tribute]. *Music & Letters* Jan. 1954, p. 11.

12 Pirie, Peter J.: *The British Musical Renaissance*. Gollancz, 1979, p. 158.

13 AB to MG, nd.

14 *FWMY* p. 5.

15 AB to A. Boult nd, BWA.

16 AB to A. Boult, quoted in *Music and Friends: seven decades of letters to Adrian Boult*, annotated by Jerrold Northrop Moore, Hamish Hamilton, 1979, p. 128.

17 Crichton, Ronald: 'Shropshire Lad and Sun King'. *Financial Times* 22 Jan. 1976, p. 3.

18 Yeats died on 28 January 1939.

Chapter XVII. 1939–1945. **The Second War — Storrington**

1 AB (155 Fellows Road), to EE 24 July [1939]; letter in Central Music Library, London.
2 HC to BBC, BWA.
3 AB to CG; British Library Add. MS 57784.
4 Interview with the late Marjorie McTavish, 1976.
5 AB to RT, nd.
6 AB to A. Boult, nd, BWA.
7 AB to RT, nd.
8 'The Master of the King's Music'. *Picture Post* 28 March 1942, p. 21.
9 Mellers, Wilfrid: 'Master of the King's Music 1942'. In his *Studies in Contemporary Music.* Dobson, 1947, pp. 179–82.
10 AB to CB, nd.
11 Autograph full score now in the National Library of Malta.
12 AB to MG, nd.

13 HC to BBC, BWA.
14 BBC internal memo, BWA.
15 BBC internal memo, BWA.
16 BWA.
17 Harriet Cohen finally performed the Kabalevsky early in 1944.
18 HC to Julian Herbage, 8 Jan. 1942, BWA.
19 HC to Julian Herbage, BWA.
20 HC to Cecil Madden, BWA.
21 HC to A. Boult, BWA.
22 A. Bliss – BBC internal memo, HC file, BWA.
23 HC to VHH, BWA.
24 BBC internal memo, HC file, BWA.
25 AB to MM, nd.
26 *Musical Times* Dec. 1944.
27 AB to Ralph Hill, 8 Oct. [1944]; collection Tom Clarke.
28 Inscription on published score, Chappell, 1946.
29 AB to CB, nd.

Chapter XVIII. 1945–1953. **Last Years**

1 'Harry Isaacs Trio – New Work by Arnold Bax'. *The Times* 23 March 1946, p. 8.
2 'FB' [i.e. F Bonavia]: 'New Bax Trio'. *Daily Telegraph* 22 March 1946, p. 5.
3 Quoted in Harry Isaacs Trio publicity brochure for 1946.
4 AB to CG; British Library Add. MS 57784.
5 AB to VHH, nd, BWA.
6 Anderson, W. R.: [Bax]. *Gramophone* June 1947, p. 6.
7 'A Tribute'. *The Irish Times* 16 July 1947, p. 5.
8 HC (55 Park Lane, London W. 1.) to Julian Herbage; 5 Jan. 1942); BWA.
9 Keller, Hans: 'Bax's "Oliver Twist"'. *Music Review* Aug. 1948, pp. 198–9.
10 AB to HvM, nd.
11 AB to JH, 1 March [1949].
12 Whelen, Christopher: 'An Approach to Bax'. *The Mercury* July 1950, pp. 5–9.
13 LF interview with FS, 1976.
14 AB to MG, nd.

15 Searle, Muriel V.: *John Ireland – the man and his music.* Tunbridge Wells, Midas Books, 1979, p. 138.
16 AB to CB, nd.
17 AB to MG, nd.
18 AB to MG, nd.
19 AB to FS, 28 Sept. [1952].
20 Fenby, Eric, quoted in *CSS* p. 40.
21 Walker, Richard: 'A Reminiscence of Bax'. *Bax Society Bulletin* Oct. 1968, p. 41.
22 *FWMY* p. 6.
23 *FRB* pp. 35–6.
24 Wentz, W. Y. Evans: *The Fairy-Faith in Celtic Countries.* London, 1911, pp. 332–3.
25 Puffett, Derrick: 'In the Garden of Fand: Arnold Bax and the 'Celtic Twilight'. In *Art Nouveau Jugendstil und Musik:* Herausgegeben aus Anlass des 80. Geburtstages von Willi Schuh, von Jürg Stenzl. Zurich, Atlantis Musikbuch-Verlag, 1980, pp. 193–210.

Chapter XIX. After 1953. **Decline and Revival**

1 AB to Lady Jessie Wood, 2 Feb. [1953]; British Library Add. MS 56419.
2 'MC': 'Bax's Violin Concerto'. *Daily Telegraph* 2 Sept. 1950, p. 5.

3 BBC internal memo, [Feb.] 1953, Harriet Cohen file, BWA.
4 HC file, BWA.

5 Blom, Eric: 'Obituary'. *Observer* 11 Oct. 1953, p. 13.
6 Shore, Bernard: [obituary tribute]. *Music & Letters* Jan. 1954, p. 13.
7 Coates, Eric: [obituary tribute]. *Music & Letters* Jan. 1954, p. 7.
8 Fleischmann, Aloys: 'The Arnold Bax Memorial'. *UCC Record* Easter 1956, p. 25.
9 *The Times* 21 Oct. 1953, p. 10.
10 Fleischmann, *ibid.*
11 *op. cit.,* p. 26.
12 *op. cit.,* p. 26 and 28.
13 HC to BBC, BWA.
14 Shawe-Taylor, Desmond: 'The Arts and Entertainment – Cheltenham'. *New Statesman* 24 July 1954, p. 100.
15 HC to BBC, BWA.
16 HC to BBC, BWA.
17 Whelen, Christopher: broadcast script 8 Nov. 1953; BBC Script Registry.
18 Mitchell, Donald: 'Crowds Kept Away by British Music'. *Daily Telegraph* 31 Jan. 1962.
19 Cohen, Harriet: 'Grave Wrong to Composer – BBC and Bax's Music'. *Daily Telegraph* 5 Aug. 1965.
20 Porter, Andrew: 'Contemporary Piano Music'. *Gramophone* May 1960, p. 597.

21 James, Burnett: 'Arnold Bax (1883–1953)'. In *Music on Record – a critical guide*, vol. I 'Orchestral Music A–L' by Peter Gammond with Burnett James. Anchor Books, 1962, pp. 32–3.
22 Mitchell, Donald: 'Talented New Conductor – college scheme's first results'. *Daily Telegraph* 6 Dec. 1961.
23 'Students Revive Bax Symphony'. *The Times* 3 Feb. 1967, p. 5.
24 Layton, Robert: 'Bax Symphony No. 6'. *Gramophone* July 1977, p. 167.
25 Harvey, Trevor: 'Bax Symphony No. 3'. *Gramophone* Oct. 1969, p. 555.
26 Layton, Robert: 'Bax Symphony No. 3'. *Gramophone* July 1977, p. 167.
27 Christopher, John: 'Rewarding Evening'. *Liverpool Daily Post* 7 Feb. 1969.
28 AEP [i.e. Anthony Payne]: 'Second Symphony Revived'. *Daily Telegraph* 7 Feb. 1969, p. 21.
29 Hopkins, Bill: 'Bax Fifth Symphony'. *Music & Musicians* Jan. 1969.
30 BT.
31 Handley, Vernon: 'Conducting Bax's Music'. *Bax Society Bulletin* no. 5 May 1969, pp. 74–5.
32 Vaughan Williams, Ralph: 'A Matter of Opinion'. *Radio Times* 6 Jan. 1933, p. 13.

Appendix A. **Dermot O'Byrne**

1 Yeats, W. B.: 'Preface'. In *Cuchulain of Muirthemne* by Lady Gregory. Gerards Cross, Colin Smythe, 1970, pp. 16–17.
2 *CSS* p. 19.
3 'The Peasant' and 'Sonnet (To A French Composer of Songs)' *Transactions ...* no. 3, June 1908, pp. 15 and 18.
4 *CLD* p. 302.
5 AB to TF quoted in Fleischmann, A.: 'The Arnold Bax Memorial'. *UCC Record* Easter 1956, p. 25.
6 *Eire: Bulletin of the Department of External Affairs* no. 729: 15 Feb. 1966, p. 4.
7 Foreman, Lewis: 'Dermot O'Byrne – background and sources'. *FDB*, p. 13.
8 The song is published in *FDB*, pp. 80–95.
9 *CLD* p. 301.
10 *Lyra Celtica.* [1896]. John Grant, 1924, p. 405.
11 O'Byrne, Dermot: 'The Sisters'. In his *The Sisters and Green Magic*, pp. 5–49.
12 The acts of *Red Owen* are separately titled as follows: I 'The Twisting of the Rope'; II 'The Bargaining' – 'Red

Owen's Fever-Dream'; III 'The Payment'.
13 A letter from Douglas Hyde to Bax, dating from 1908, is preserved in the Bax Memorial Room, at University College, Cork.
14 Fackler, Herbert Vern: *The Deirdre Legend in Anglo-Irish Literature, 1834–1937.* University of North Carolina at Chapel Hill, thesis: Ph. D., 1972: 'Appendix'.
15 Sharp, William: *The House of Usna.* Portland (Maine), T. B. Mosher, 1903.
16 Russell, George William: 'Deirdre' In his *Imaginations and Reviews.* Dublin, Maunsell, 1916.
17 Hyde, Douglas: *A Literary History of Ireland.* T. Fisher Unwin, nd [1899?].
18 Cecil Gray (1925); Healey Willan (1943); Karl Rankl (1948); Havergal Brian (opera abandoned, but *Sinfonia Tragica* (1948) completed); John J. Becker (1956); Leon Stein (1957).
19 The mythological assumptions incorporated into this play are outlined by Bax in an introductory note, published in *FDB* pp. 14–15.

(a) Literary works written under the pseudonym of Dermot O'Byrne

IR   *Irish Review*
OS   The Orpheus Series [of booklets]
ORPH   *Orpheus: a quarterly magazine of mystical art* [commenced publication
        in 1907 as *Transaction of the Theosophical Art-Circle*, became *Orpheus,
        the Transactions* ..., and continued as cited above. The numbering
        continues consecutively throughout.]
SF   *Seafoam and Firelight* (see citation below)
LPM   *Love Poems of a Musician* (see citation below)

Abbreviations from the notes on pp. 389–90 have also been used.

Published Sources

The Birth of a Song: a Celtic Idyll: ORPH no. 24, Oct. 1913, pp. 113–25.

Certainty [a poem beginning: 'I heard an old man mumble']: *ORPH* no. 14,
April 1911, p. 282.

*Children of the Hills: tales and sketches of Western Ireland in the Old Time and
the Present Day.* Dublin, Maunsel & Co. Ltd., n.d. [1913]. Contains:
Hunger (from *IR* May 1912, pp. 140–51); Through the Rain (from *ORPH* no.
15, July 1911, pp. 301–5); The Call of the Road (from *IR* December 1912,
pp. 519–33); 'seanoidin'; The Lifting of the Veil ('August 1912') (from *ORPH*,
no. 20, Oct. 1912, pp. 105–10); Ancient Dominions; The Death of Macha
Gold-Hair (from *ORPH* no. 12, July 1910, pp. 211–17).

Dermot O'Byrne: selected poems of Arnold Bax, edited by Lewis Foreman.
Thames Publishing, 1979. Contains:
The Enchanted Fiddle (words of the song of the same title); Dedication; A
Summer Memory (from *LPM* pp. 9–10); A Ghost (from *LPM* p. 35); The Aran
Islands (from *SF* p. 30; also quoted in CSS pp. 19–20); On the Strand (from *SF*
p. 23); A Poet's Immortality (from *SF* p. 12); Déirdre's Spinning Song (from the
'saga-drama' *Déirdre*); An Old Man's Chatter (from *LPM* pp. 53–4); At the
Last; The Glen of Starry Peace (from *SF* p. 17); The Lake of Stars; Sundered
Dreams; The Song of the Old Fiddler; The Emigrant (from *LPM* p. 49); By a
Faery Lough (from *SF* p. 11); To the Beloved (from *SF* p. 15); From Old Days;
On Pipe-Music Heard in a London Street (from *SF* p. 28); Green Magic (from
Green Magic pp. 64–5); To My Little Friend Donnall Gillespie (from *Orpheus*
No. 10 April 1910, p. 144; it was the first use of 'Dermot O'Byrne' in that
journal); Allurement; To a Russian Girl (from *LPM* p. 11); Out of Faeryland

('*To Natasha*' – from *Orpheus* No. 18 April 1912, p. 41); In the Night (from *LPM* p. 15); A Lullaby (the words of Bax's song *Slumber Song*, in which the words are attributed to 'Shiela MacCarthy'); A Summer in Exile; Certainty; The End of a Romance; Morning in Connemara; The Burden of Memory (also known as 'The Shadow of Memory'); Woman and Artist (from *LPM* p. 25); Tryst; Nympholept (from *LPM* pp. 12–13); Consolation (from *LPM* p. 40); The New Devil; A Girl's Music (from *LPM* p. 41); Crisis; The Guest House (from *LPM* p. 28); The Irish Mail; A Dublin Ballad – 1916 (from *ODB* pp. 5–7); In Glencullen (from *ODB* pp. 14–15); Shells at Oranmore (from *ODB* p. 16); Kilmasheogue – 1916 (from *ODB* pp. 17–18); In a Back-Street; Amersham; Darkness; Man and Wife; Tintagel Castle (from *LPM*); The Grey Swan: final chorus (from Dermot O'Byrne's play *The Grey Swan*); To F.

*A Dublin Ballad and Other Poems.** Dublin, The Candle Press, 1918. (Poetry Booklets – no. 2). Contains:
A Dublin Ballad – 1916 (reprinted in *Nineteen-Sixteen: an anthology*, compiled by Edna C. Fitzhenry, Dublin, Browne & Nolan, 1935, 1966, p. 41; and again in *Poetry Ireland* no. 13, April 1951, p. 18); In Memoriam *My Friend* Patrick H. Pearse (*Ruler of Ireland for one week*); After; In Glencullen; Shells at Oranmore (*April 1916*) (reprinted in *Nineteen-Sixteen*, p. 45; and again, in part in *Eire: weekly Bulletin of the Dept. of External Affairs*, no. 729, 15 Feb. 1966, p. 4); Kilmasheogue (reprinted in *Nineteen-Sixteen*, p. 48); Martial Law in Dublin (reprinted in *Nineteen-Sixteen*, p. 44); The East Clare Election 1828–1917; The East Clare Election 1917 (reprinted in *Nineteen-Sixteen*, p. 99).

The End of Oodh Costello. ORPH no. 8, Oct. 1909, pp. 80–2 and no. 9, Jan. 1910, pp. 116–20.

Exile [a poem beginning: 'Tonight in grey Glencolumcille'] *IR* April 1913, p. 68.

Firelight see 'Seafoam and Firelight'.

Glamour [a poem beginning: 'As I walked at dusk in Eyrè Square'] *ORPH* no. 12, Oct. 1910, pp. 202–3. (Set to music by Bax, *FDB* pp. 80–95.)

Green Magic see 'The Sisters and Green Magic'.

In a Bohemian Forest [a poem beginning: 'On my strange virgin bridal night'] extract in *CSS* pp. 14–15.

Love and the Sea [a poem beginning 'For all my heart's warm blood is mixed with surf and green sea-flame'] extract in *CSS* pp. 70–71.

Love Poems of a Musician [published anonymously]. Cecil Palmer, 1923. Contains: A Summer Memory; To a Russian Girl; Nympholept; Mirrors (from *ORPH* no. 26, Jan. 1914, p. 34); In the Night; Heart's Desire; Sanctuary; At 'Tristan and Isolde'; At Parting; The Battle of the Somme; Stephen's Green; In Donegal; Love and Reason; Woman and Artist; The Immortality of Form; The Guest House; The Prison House; Oblation; A Moment; Love; Epithalamium; A Ghost; The Labour of Love; Enigma; Transitional; Shiplake; Consolation; A Girl's Music; Panic; Irony; Cherry Blossom; Illusion; Helplessness; Tintagel Castle; Too Late; The Emigrant (a variant text previously appeared in the *Irish Review* April 1913, p. 68); Glamour (the words of Bax's song of the same name, in *FDB* pp. 80–95, previously published in *ORPH* no. 12, Oct. 1910, pp. 202–3); A Thought of Ireland at Sunset; An Old Man's Chatter.

On the Hill: a play. IR Feb. 1913, pp. 648–63.

* *A Dublin Ballad – 1916* was never published officially as it was suppressed by the British censor in Ireland. However, it was widely circulated.

Red Owen: a drama. Dublin, The Talbot Press, 1919.

Seafoam and Firelight [verse]. *OS* no. 2, 1909. Contains:
In Carna (from *ORPH* no. 7, June 1909, p. 60); To Ireland; The Peasant (from *ORPH* no. 3, 26 June 1908, p. 15); By A Faery Lough; A Poet's Immortality; To Eire; In Galway Bay (from *ORPH* no. 6, April 1909, p. 33); To the Beloved; The Glen of Starry Peace (from *ORPH* no. 4, Oct. 1908, p. 11); Sonnet (*To a Foreign Singer*)* (from *ORPH* no. 3, 26 June 1908, p. 18); The Music of Man (from *ORPH* no. 6, April 1909, p. 43); A Quiet Landscape; On the Strand; The Valley of the Bells; The Proud Harper; The Emigrants; On Pipe-Music Heard in a London Street (later reprinted in the *Hallé Magazine*, Aug. 1950, p. 24); A Country Song; The Aran Islands; Behind the Wind; Fintan, the Spirit of Irish Song; The Ships.

The Servant of the Bishop. ORPH no. 16, Oct. 1911, pp. 345–54.

The Sisters and Green Magic. OS no. 8, 1912.

The Soul's Answer [a poem beginning: 'I and my soul, while shadows grew'] *ORPH* no. 5, Jan. 1909, p. 16.

The Strayed Soul ('Glencolumcille, December 1910') ORPH no. 18, April 1912, pp. 42–54.

This for the maiden with the daffodil [poem beginning thus]. *CSS* p. 47.

To Déirdre [a poem beginning: 'O Holy Spirit of love ...'] *ORPH* no. 13, Jan. 1911, p. 249.

When we are Lost [a song with words by Dermot O'Byrne, setting by Arnold Bax]. in *FDB* pp. 75–9.

Wrack and other stories. Dublin, The Talbot Press; London, T. Fisher Unwin, 1918. Contains:
Wrack; Before Dawn; 'From the Fury of the O'Flahertys!'; A Coward's Saga; The Invisible City of Coolanoole; The King's Messenger; The Vision of St Molaise.

Unpublished Sources

Poems (June 1907). A 64-page typescript collection. A disbound incomplete top copy was sold by Sotheby in 1977. Bax's own bound carbon copy with a large number of additional poems in manuscript remains in private hands; a photocopy is in the author's possession.

Déirdre: a saga-drama in five scenes and a prologue by Arnold Bax. Typescript 30 Nov. 1907, 107 pp. ('Déirdre's Spinning Song', Sc. I, published in *FDB*, p. 30.)

The Grey Swan by Dermot O'Byrne. Typescript, 29 April 1919, 26 pp. (The introduction and final chorus published in *FDB*, pp. 14–15, 71.)

A collection of miscellaneous typescript and longhand poems.

Various unpublished stories.

(b) Writings by Bax over his real name

'Arnold Bax' [on music], *Musical Standard*, 11 April 1914, p. 342 (reprinted in *Bax Society Bulletin*, Jan. 1973, p. 48).

'More "Victory" Year Messages', *Musical Standard*, 18 Jan. 1919, p. 22.

'Lionel Tertis: an appreciation', *Musical News and Herald*, 27 May 1922, p. 656.

Love Poems of a Musician [published anonymously], Cecil Palmer, 1923, 54 pp.

---

* In *ORPH* subtitled: *To a French Composer of Songs.*

'Harmony' [contribution to the section in] *A Dictionary of Modern Music and Musicians*, Dent, 1924, pp. 214–24.

'The "Korshjem-Saga" translated from the Icelandic by AB with notes by Sir Gaga Thompson', in *The Old Broughtonians Cricket Weeks*, vol. 3 [edited by Clifford Bax]. Kensington, The Favil Press, 1927, pp. 44–9.

'Arnold Bax' in *A Book of Greetings from British Musicians to their friends and colleagues members of the Music Supervisors National Conference Chicago*, [18 April] 1928, [Collected by Percy A. Scholes]. OUP/Aeolian Co., 1928, pp. 31–2.

'I am a Brazen Romantic', *Musical America*, 7 July 1928, p. 9. The celebrated brief description of himself that Bax sent to R. H. Wollstein's "The Turn of the Dial" musical gossip column, published under the heading "Bax defines his music – 'I am a Brazen Romantic' he says". (See p. 240.)

'On Inspiration', *Chesterian*, Sept./Oct. 1928, pp. 2–3 (reprinted in *On Inspiration*, J. & W. Chester, nd [1929], pp. 17–18). (See pp. 192–3.)

'At Melksham' in *The Old Broughtonians Cricket Weeks*, vol. 4 [edited by Clifford Bax]. Kensington, The Favil Press, 1930, pp. 80–1.

'Frederick Corder', *The Times*, 27 Aug. 1932.

'Melksham', in *The Old Broughtonians Cricket Weeks*, vol. 5 [edited by Clifford Bax]. Kensington, The Favil Press, 1933, pp. 56–7.

'Sir E. Elgar: artist of balance and finish', *Daily Telegraph*, 26 Feb. 1934, p. 10.

Farewell My Youth. Longman, Green & Co., 1943, 1949, 112 pp. Reissued in facsimile reprint: Westport, Conn., Greenwood Press, 1970. (Extracts reprinted: 'Mackenzie – Parry – Stanford', 'Atonalism', in *Musicians on Music*, ed. F. Bonavia, Routledge & Kegan Paul, 1956, pp. 50–2.)

'... A Physical Giant' in *Homage to Sir Henry Wood: a world Symposium* (LPO Booklets). 2nd enlarged edition, nd [*ca* 1944] LPP Ltd., pp. 13–14.

'He is a National Institution' [Sir Henry Wood] in *Sir Henry Wood: Fifty years of the Proms*, ed. Ralph Hill and C. B. Rees, BBC, nd [1944], pp. 26–9.

'Edwin Evans: September 1, 1874 – March 3, 1945', *Musical Times*, April 1945, p. 107.

'Give British Music a Chance!', *Radio Times*, 6 April 1945, p. 3.

'My Strongest Musical Impression of 1946', *Music Teacher*, Jan. 1947, p. 13.

'My Strongest Musical Impression of 1947', *Music Teacher*, Jan. 1948, p. 13.

[Film Music] in *British Film Music* by John Huntley, Skelton Robinson, 1947, p. 160.

'My Strongest Musical Impression of 1948', *Music Teacher*, Jan. 1949, p. 13.

[Bax on Malta GC and Oliver Twist] in 'The Music of Hamlet and Oliver Twist', *Penguin Film Review*, no. 8, 1949, pp. 110 and 114 (reprinted Scolar Press, 1977).

'Sir Edward Elgar', introduction to the programme for the Elgar Festival, Royal Albert Hall, 30 May – 15 June 1949, pp. 2–5.

'My Strongest Musical Impression of 1949', *Music Teacher*, Jan. 1950, p. 15.

'On Pipe Music Heard in a London Street', *Hallé Magazine*, Aug. 1950, p. 24. (See also: catalogue of Bax's writings as 'Dermot O'Byrne', pp. 402–4.)

'Celtic Twilight in Moderation', [a review of] *Turf Beneath My Feet* by Garry Hogg, *National and English Review*, Dec. 1950, pp. 510 and 512.

'E. J. Moeran: 1894–1950', *Music & Letters*, April 1951, pp. 125–7.

'Foreword' in *Eight Concerts of Music by British Composers 1300–1750*, "Commemorative book of programmes and text. Arts Council of Great Britain (on the occasion of the Festival of Britain), 1951.

'Foreword', *Prospectus for 57th Season of Promenade Concerts*, BBC, 1951, p. 3.

'Arnold Schoenberg', *Music & Letters*, Oct. 1951, p. 307.

'Tang of Turf-Smoke', [a review of] *Sweet Cork of Thee* by Robert Gibbings, *National and English Review*, Dec. 1951, pp. 237–8.

'New Light on a Genius', [a review of] *Letters of Richard Wagner – the Burrell Collection, National and English Review*, March 1952, pp. 172–4.

'Foreword' in *Music in Ireland*, ed. Aloys Fleischmann, Cork University Press, 1952, pp. iii–iv.

'Ralph Vaughan Williams: a tribute on behalf of the musicians of Britain', [introduction to the programme for the] Celebration Concert on the occasion of the 80th birthday of Dr Ralph Vaughan Williams, Royal Festival Hall, 12 Oct. 1952, pp. 3–4.

'Music at the Coronation', *National and English Review*, June 1953, pp. 345–7.

'Richard Strauss' in *Music Magazine*, ed. Anna Instone and Julian Herbage, Rockliffe, 1953, pp. 76–8 (script of radio talk broadcast on 2 Oct. 1949).

(c) Bax's programme notes to his own works

In chronological order of composition. Halls are assumed to be in London unless stated.

Concert Piece for Viola and Piano. Aeolian Hall (Patron's Fund Concert): 6 Dec. 1904. Includes musical examples.

Symphony in F. Introductory longhand note to the third movement appears in the autograph MS in BMR. See pp. 47–8.

Fatherland. Bax's programme notes included in Ernest Newman's programme note. Hallé Concert, Manchester: 7 Jan. 1915. Includes musical examples, and the text.

In the Faery Hills. Queen's Hall (Promenade Concert): 30 Aug. 1910. Version with musical examples, Queen's Hall: 20 Nov. 1913.

Festival Overture. Queen's Hall: 27 March 1912. Includes musical examples.

Enchanted Summer. Queen's Hall: 13 March 1912. Includes the text.

King Kojata (Tamara). Scenario written at the beginning of the MS short score in BMR. See pp. 383–4.

Christmas Eve on the Mountains. Queen's Hall: 14 March 1913. Additional note in FWMY, p. 86.

Nympholept. Brief note in MS full score, collection Chappell & Co. For Herbert Farjeon story on which it was based see Appendix C, pp. 385–6.

Four Orchestral Sketches. Queen's Hall: 20 March 1914.

The Garden of Fand. Programme quoted at the beginning of the published full and miniature scores (Murdoch/Chappell).

Spring Fire. Queen's Hall: 28 Feb. 1916. Includes the Swinburne poems inscribed by Bax before each movement.

Three Songs with Orchestra (Celtic Lullaby, A Christmas Carol, Slumber Song). Queen's Hall: 27 March 1914. Just the words of the songs.

The Happy Forest. Autograph MS annotation to the piano solo version, BL Add. MS 50176. Programme note, Royal Festival Hall (Queen Mary Memorial Concert) 15 April 1953.

Violin Sonata No. 2. Handbill for the first performance, Wigmore Hall: 25 April 1922. Reprinted in reduced facsimile on the cover of *Bax Society Bulletin* no. 5, May 1969.

November Woods. Bax's letter to Ernest Newman on the origins of this work partly quoted in Newman's programme note. Hallé Orchestra, Manchester, 18 Nov. 1920.

Summer Music. Bax's one sentence description of this work (see p. 149) is taken from an unidentified cutting from a concert programme, *ca* 1932–7.

Tintagel. Programme note quoted at the beginning of the published full and miniature scores (Murdoch/Chappell). A slightly longer note appears in the programme book for the Leeds Festival, 7 Oct. 1922, where it is quoted in Herbert Thompson's notes, p. 14.

Phantasy (Concerto) for Viola and Orchestra. Queen's Hall: 17 Nov. 1921. Includes musical examples.

Symphony No. 1. Bax's programme notes included in Arthur Shepherd's programme note. Masonic Auditorium, Cleveland, Ohio: 7–9 Jan. 1926. Includes musical examples.

Symphony No. 2. Bax's letter to Philip Hale on the origins of this work (see p. 208) is partly quoted in Hale's programme notes for the first performance, Symphony Hall, Boston: 13 and 14 Dec. 1929, p. 610. Also quoted by Slonimsky. (See bibliography of published letters, below.)

Overture, Elegy and Rondo. Queen's Hall: 13 March 1930. Includes musical examples.

Violin Sonata No. 3. Wigmore Hall: 8 Dec. [1935?].

Northern Ballad No. 1. Queen's Hall: 3 Dec. 1931.

Symphony No. 3. Queen's Hall: 14 March 1930. Includes musical examples. A later, shorter note (Queen's Hall: 27 Aug. 1936) does not include examples.

Nonet. Bradford Triennial Festival: 30 Sept. 1930. Includes musical examples.

Winter Legends. Queen's Hall: 10 Feb. 1932. Includes musical examples.

String Quartet No. 3. Bax is quoted in *Radio Times'* (issue dated 14 May 1937) billing of the first performance: 16 May 1937, p. 20.

A Legend. Guildhall, Cambridge: 20 Oct. 1944.

The Tale the Pine-Trees Knew. Queen's Hall: 12 April 1934. Includes musical examples.

(d) Published letters by Bax

The following list of Bax's letters is broadly in chronological order. The same abbreviations are used as in the Notes (pp. 389—90). Quotations from letters reproduced in sale and auction catalogues have not been included.

ca 1912   to Rosalind Thorneycroft (extract only), *CSS*, p. 84.

ca 1912   to Padraic Colum (extracts from letters), *CSS*, pp. 29, 30—1.

6 March 1918 to Adrian Boult, in *Music and Friends: seven decades of letters to Adrian Boult*, annotated by Jerrold Northrop Moore. Hamish Hamilton, 1979, p. 30.

3 March 1921 to Sir Edward Elgar, in *Elgar OM* by Percy M. Young, Collins, 1955, p. 214.

30 April 1921 to *Musical News & Herald*.

?1923   to Rutland Boughton (brief extract) in *Immortal Hour* by Michael Hurd, Routledge and Kegan Paul, 1962, p. 83.

1924   to *The Sackbut*, Feb. 1924, p. 24 (brief extract listing recent works as requested).

9 Nov. 1924 (?) to Æ, *FDB* p. 13.

1925   to Philip Heseltine.

Sept. 1926   to *The Irish Statesman*, 11 Sept. 1926, pp. 11—12.

1927   to L. Dunton-Green, in *Letters of Composers: an anthology 1603—1945*. Compiled by Gertrude Norman and Miriam Lubell Shrifte, New York, Knopf, 1946, pp. 358—9.
              (In fact Bax's essay 'On Inspiration' from *The Chesterian*; see pp. 192—3.)

1928   to *The Gramophone* [on Moy Mell] Feb. 1928, p. 397.

22 Nov. 1929 to Philip Hale (extract only), in *Music Since 1900* by Nicholas Slonimsky, 3rd rev. & enl. ed., New York, Coleman & Ross, 1949, p. 320.

1930   to Harriet Cohen, *CSS*, pp. 37 and 68.

Jan. 1931   to *Daily Telegraph*, 13 Jan. 1931.

1935   To Tilly Fleischmann (extract only) in 'The Arnold Bax Memorial' by Professor Aloys Fleischmann, *UCC Record*, Easter 1956, no. 31, p. 29.

27 May 1937   to John Horgan (extract only) in 'The Arnold Bax Memorial', *op. cit.*, p. 29.

1940   to Adrian Boult in *Music and Friends, op. cit.*, p. 128.

1945   to Adrian Boult, *ibid.*, p. 145.

April 1946   to *The Times*, 9 April 1946.

1947   to Rex Harris (extract only) in 'The Influence of Jazz on English Composers', *The Penguin Music Magazine*, II. Penguin, 1947, p. 30.

July 1947   to *The Irish Times*, 12 July 1947.

1949   to John Horgan (extract only) in 'The Arnold Bax Memorial', *op. cit.*, p. 29.

31 Aug. 1953 to Clifford Gillam, *Bax Society Bulletin*, Oct. 1968, p. 40.

CATALOGUE OF BAX'S WORKS

Introduction

This catalogue is presented in as few sequences as possible, in the belief that this makes its use simpler. Full details of first performances are given in the case of the orchestral and chamber works, but in the case of solo piano pieces and the songs, where this information is much more elusive it is only presented selectively.

The primary sequence is dictated by date of composition (taken from the surviving mss where possible). In the case of a few works it has been necessary to establish a title and spelling (e.g. I have used *Roscatha* in preference to *Rosc Catha*).

Orchestrations have not depended on previously published lists, but are the result of examination of the actual scores. In particular the need for doublings or extra players are indicated, as are numbers of percussion players required and what instruments they play. Durations, where timing has been possible, are based on actual performances, of which the author has kept records over twenty years. For Bax this can be of particular interest as extraordinary variations are sometimes experienced in the case of some of Bax's works. The slowest and fastest are given in each case.

The catalogue incorporates additions and corrections from the classified catalogue in Graham Parlett's forthcoming PhD thesis *The Unpublished Music of Arnold Bax* (University of London).

Abbreviations

Orchestrations are given in the usual sequence:

flutes, oboes, clarinets, bassoons, horns, trumpets, trombones, tuba(s), timpani, harp, percussion, other instruments, strings.

Piccolo and bass-flute follow flutes; cor anglais and heckelphone follow oboes; E♭ and bass-clarinet follow clarinets; contra-bassoon follows bassoons. Where these are in parentheses the extra instrument doubles on one of the players of the principal instrument. Where it is indicated by a + sign, then an extra player is required. Additional instruments indicated after trumpets, are cornets (as in *Cortège*).

The following abbreviations are used:

b fl	bass-flute		perc	percussion
bd	bass drum		SATB	Soprano/Alto/Tenor/Bass (voices)
cym	cymbals		sd	side drum
db	double bass		tamb	tambourine
E♭	E♭ clarinet		timp	timpani
fag	bassoon		tr	triangle
fl	flute		t	tenor
glock	glockenspiel		v & p	voice and piano
hp	harp		vla	viola
hpn	heckelphone		vlc	cello
md	military drum		xyl	xylophone

Add ms	Additional manuscript			
BMIC	British Music Information Centre		orch	Orchestra(tion)
			pc	private collection
f. sc.	full score		RAM	Royal Academy of Music
ICA	Institute of Contemporary Arts		RCM	Royal College of Music
			RPS	Royal Philharmonic Society
m. sc.	miniature score		v. sc.	vocal score
NSO	New Symphony Orchestra		wds	words

Manuscripts still in the collections of private individuals are just marked 'pc'. Other locations are given as follows:

Århus, National Library of Denmark	DK A	London, University Library (Senate House)	Lu
Åbo (Turku), Sibelius Museum	SF A	Montreal, Montreal University (Boyd Neel Loan)	C Mu
Copenhagen, University Library	DK Ku	New Haven, Yale University Library	US NH
Cork, University Library (Bax Memorial Room)	EIRE C	New York, New York Public Library	US NYp
Dublin, University College Library	EIRE Duc	Oxford, Bodleian Library	GB Ob
Durham, University Library	DRu	Paris, Bibliothèque Nationale	F Pn
London, British Broadcasting Corporation Music Library	Lbbc	Stanford, California, University Memorial Library of Music	US STu
London, British Library	Lbm	Valletta, National Library of Malta	MALTA Vn
London, Central Music Library	Lcml	Washington, Library of Congress	US Wc
London, Royal Academy of Music Library	Lam		

(a) Orchestral Music (including all concerti, works for voices and orchestra, and dramatic works)

(b) Chamber and Instrumental Music (including all sonatas and solo works, except those for piano solo, but including works for two pianos and choral works with chamber accompaniment)

(c) Songs with piano accompaniment

(d) Piano solos

(e) Unaccompanied choral works and those with organ accompaniment

(f) Works for pianola, harpsichord and organ

(g) Juvenilia (works written up to the end of 1902)

(a) Orchestral Music

10 June 1904
Variations for Orchestra (Improvisations)
Orch. 2+1 222 4331 timp hp 2perc (sd cym tr) strings
MS pc (unpublished)
First perf. Runthrough RCM / Summer 1904; otherwise unplayed

1905
A Connemara Revel
MS lost (unpublished)
First perf. Queen's Hall / RAM Student Orch. / Mackenzie: 4 April 1905

1905
An Irish Overture
MS lost (unpublished)
First perf. Only known performance: Winter Gardens Bournemouth / Bournemouth Municipal Orch. / Godfrey: 13 Dec. 1906
(May possibly be the work also known as *A Connemara Revel.*)

July 1905
Cathaleen-ni-Hoolihan
(Orchestrated from the middle movement of the String Quartet in E major.)
Orch. 2222 2100 timp hp strings (parts: LF)
MS EIRE C (unpublished)
Dur. 10'32"–12'20"
First perf. RCM / Student Assn. Orch. / David Chatwin: 22 Oct. 1970

1905?
A Song of Life and Love – 'tone poem for full orchestra'
MS lost (unpublished)

1905
A Song of War and Victory – tone poem for full orchestra
Orch. 2+1 2+1 2+1 2 4 2+2 31 timp 2perc (sd cym bd) strings
MS pc (unpublished)
Ded. Godwin H. Baynes
Unperformed

1905
Rune of Age (Fiona Macleod) – song for voice and orchestra
MS lost (unpublished)

March 1907
Fatherland – for tenor, chorus and orchestra; Op. 5 (wds: Runeberg)
(revised 1934)
Orch. (revised version) t solo / SATB chorus / 2+1 2+1 2+1 2+1 4331 timp
hp 3 perc (sd cym bd glock) strings (parts: Chappell)
MS pc: Chester. Published: Novello (Avison Ed.) v.sc. 1909; later Chester, assigned Chappell 1985
Dur. ca. 10'
Ded. Arne von Erpecum
First perf. Philharmonic Hall, Liverpool / J. Coates (t) / Welsh Choral Union / Orch. / Harry Evans: 25 Sept. 1909

3 April 1907
Symphony in F minor and major Op. 8

Orch. pf score only — never orchestrated
MS movements I & II: pc; movements III & IV: EIRE C (unpublished)
III *Intermezzo* (for piano)
Dur. 11'32"
First perf. BMIC/David Owen Norris (pf)/3 Feb. 1983

1908
Into the Twilight ('Eire — Prologue')
Orch. 3 2+1 3+1 2+1 4040 2hp celesta strings (parts: Fleischmann)
MS pf and f.sc: EIRE C (unpublished)
Dur. 12'32"—13'20"
First perf. Queen's Hall/NSO/Beecham: 19 April 1909

[1908]
[**Deirdre** — sketches for opera]
1. *The Gathering of the Chiefs: 2. 'Cuid v'*
Orch. pf. score
MS EIRE C (unpublished)
1 orchestrated as **Roscatha** (1910) q.v.
2 orchestrated by Graham Parlett as **On the Sea-Shore**
Orch. 3(1) 2+1 2+1 2+1 4331 timp 3perc (sd cym (suspended) bd gong) strings
(parts: G.P.)
Dur. 6'22"—7'25"
First perf. St John's Smith Sq/KSO/Head: 7 Feb. 1984

28 June 1909
In the Faery Hills (An Sluagh Sidhe — 'Eire part 2')
Orch. 3(1) 2+1 3+1 2 4331 timp 2hp 2perc (sd cym tamb glock) celesta
strings (parts: Chappell)
MS Lbm, Add ms 54733; another score, EIRE C. Published: Murdoch f. sc.
1926 m. sc. ca 1934 / now Chappell
Dur. 14'48"—16'30"
Ded. H. Balfour Gardiner
First perf. Queen's Hall (Prom) / QH Orch. / Wood: 30 Aug. 1910

Oct. 1909, orchestrated 1911
Festival Overture (revised 1918)
Orch. (revised version) 3(1)2+1 3+1 2+1 4331 timp hp 4perc (sd cym bd tr
tamb glock) strings (parts: Chappell)
MS pc: Lbm, Add ms 50173/4 (piano score and full score) (unpublished)
Dur. 14'53"
Ded. H. Balfour Gardiner
First perf. Queen's Hall / NSO / Gardiner: 27 March 1912
(revised version Queen's Hall / Orch. / Boult: 27 Feb. 1919)

— arranged two pianos
MS pc (unpublished)
Dur. 13'11"
First perf. BBC broadcast/Howard Shelley & Hilary MacNamara (pfs)/16 Dec.
1983

1910
Roscatha ('Eire part 3')

Orch. 3(1) 2+1 3+1 2+1   4331   timp   3perc (sd cym bd md)   strings   (parts: LF)
MS Lbm, Add ms 54734 (unpublished)
Dur. 10'43"−11'22"
Ded. To the 'Mountainy men of Glencolumcille'
First perf. St John's Smith Sq / KSO / Head: 5 March 1974

December 1910
Enchanted Summer, for 2 sopranos, chorus and orchestra (wds: Shelley)
Orch. 2 s soli / SATB chorus / 3(1) 2+1 3+1 2+1   4331   timp   2hp   3perc (cym
bd tr tamb glock)   celesta   strings   (parts: Chappell)
MS Lbm, Add ms 54772. Published: Riorden v. sc. 1912; assigned Chappell
Dur. 26'49"−26'52"
Ded. 'F. Corder esq my ever true friend'
First perf. Queen's Hall / Hatchard, Tubb (sops) / London Choral Soc / NSO /
Fagge: 13 March 1912

April 1911
Nocturnes for soprano and orchestra
1. *Aufblick* (wds: Richard Dehmel) (18 April 1911)
Orch. sop (c-Bb) 3(1) 2+1 2+1 2   4231   timp   hp   2perc (glock gong)   celesta
strings
MS Lbm, Add ms 54735 (unpublished/parts: BBC)
Dur. 3'47"
First perf. (arr. v. & pf. Stephen Banfield. University of Keele/John Potter(t)/
Stephen Banfield (pf) (5'15"): 6 Nov. 1980) Orchestral version: BBC Studio
Seven, Manchester/Rita Cullis (sop)/BBC NSO/Downes: rec. 23 Sept. 1982; bc.
18 Nov. 1983

2. *Liebesode* (wds: O. E. Hartleben)
Orch. sop (d-A)   3(1) 2 2+1 2   4200   timp   hp   celesta   strings
MS Lbm, Add ms 54735 (unpublished/parts: BBC)
Dur. 3'24"
First perf. BBC Studio Seven, Manchester/Rita Cullis (sop)/PBC NSO/Downes:
rec. 23 Sept. 1982; bc. 18 Nov. 1983

July−November 1911
Tamara: a Little-Russian Faery Tale in Action and Dance (King Kojata)
Piano score only − never orchestrated
MS EIRE C (unpublished)
Ded. 'To the divine dancer Madame Tamara Karsavina, whose wonderful art
inspired this work.'
Unperformed

Jan. 1912
Christmas Eve on the Mountains
Orch. 3(1) 3+1 3+1 2+1   4331   timp   2hp   1perc (cym bd glock)   celesta
organ   strings
MS Lbm, Add ms 54735 (unpublished, no parts)
Dur. ca 19'
First perf. Queen's Hall / NSO /Gardiner: 4 March 1913

Revised as:
Christmas Eve

Orch. 3(1) 2+1 2+1 2+1* 4331 timp hp 1perc (cym bd glock) celesta organ strings (* contra-bassoon: *ad lib*) (parts: LF or BBC)
MS Lbm, Add ms 54735 (unpublished)
Dur. 17'12"–18'16"
First perf. St Peter's, Eaton Sq. / KSO / Head: 8 Nov. 1979

1912
Prelude to Adonais
MS lost (unpublished)
First perf. Haymarket Theatre / Orch. / O'Neill: 25 June 1912

1912–13
Four Orchestral Sketches
1. *Pensive Twilight*
2. *Dance in the Sun*
3. *In the Hills of Home* (or *From the Mountains of Home*)
4. *Dance of Wild Irravel*
Orch. 1: 3(1) 232   2000   hp   strings; 2: 3(1) 232   4000   timp   hp   2perc (cym tamb glock)   strings; 3: hp   strings; 4: 3(1) 2+1 3+1 2+1   4331   timp   hp   3 or 4 perc (cym bd tamb glock castanets)   strings
MS Lbm, Add ms 50175 (unpublished, no parts)
Dur. 4. 5'28"; 1–3. See revisions below.
First perf. 1 and 4: Queen's Hall (Prom) / QH Orch. / Wood: 23 Sept. 1913; complete: Queen's Hall / QH Orch. / Toye: 20 March 1914

Revised as: **Three Pieces for Small Orchestra** (1928)
1. *Evening Piece*
Orch. 2222   2000   hp   strings   (parts: Chappell)
MS pc: Chappell (unpublished)
Dur. 6'57"
2. *Irish Landscape*
Orch. hp   strings   (parts: Chappell)
MS pc: Chappell (unpublished)
Dur. 5'31"–7'50"
3. *Dance in the Sunlight*
Orch. 2(1) 222   4000   timp   hp   1perc (cym tamb)   strings   (parts: Chappell)
MS pc: Chappell (unpublished)
Dur. 4'16'–5'31"
First perf. 1 and 3: Central Hall, Westminster / orch. / Sargent: 1 Dec. 1928

July 1912 (orchestrated 1915)
Nympholept
Orch. 3(1) 2+1 3+1 2+1   4331   timp   2hp   2perc (sd cym bd glock xyl)   strings (parts: Chappell)
MS pc: Chappell (unpublished)
Dur. 14'15"–17'56"
Ded. Constant Lambert
First perf. RAM / Strolling Players / Lovett: 31 May 1961

1913
Spring Fire (based upon the first chorus in Swinburne's 'Atalanta in Calydon')
Orch. 3(1)3(1) 3+1 2+1   6 [or 4] 331   timp   2hp   3perc (cym tamb bd glock) celesta   piano   strings   (parts: Chappell)
MS Lbm, Add ms 54738/9 (unpublished)

Dur. 28'25"–31'40"
Ded. Sir Henry J. Wood
First perf. Kensington TH / KSO / Head: 8 Dec. 1970

1913
Scherzo for Orchestra (orchestrated 1917, revised 1933)
1. 1917 version
Orch. 3+1 2+1 3+1 2+1 4331 timp hp 3perc (sd cym bd tamb glock) celesta
strings (parts: Chappell)
MS pc (unpublished)
First perf. Queen's Hall / New QH Orch. / Wood: 3 Sept. 1919
2. 1933 revision as **Symphonic Scherzo**
Orch. 4(1) 2+1 3+1 2+1 4331 timp hp 3perc (sd cym bd tamb) celesta
strings
MS Lbm, Add ms 54742 (parts: Chappell)
Dur. 6'57"–7'18"
First perf. All Saints, Tooting (Chandos recording session)/RPO/Handley: 3 Jan.
1986
(*See also*: versions for piano and pianola roll)

1913 (orchestrated 1916)
The Garden of Fand
Orch. 3+1 2+1 3+1 2+1 4331 timp 2hp 3perc (cym bd tamb glock) celesta
strings (parts: Chappell)
MS short score: EIRE C; f. sc. lost. Published: Murdoch f. sc. 1922, m. sc. 1933;
st. sc. Chappell 1948
Dur. 15'19"–16'38"
First perf. Chicago / Chicago SO / Stock: 29 Oct. 1920. First UK perf. Kingsway
Hall / British S.O. / Boult: 11 Dec. 1921

1914
Three Songs with Orchestra
1904 (orchestrated 1914)
1. *Celtic Lullaby* (No. 4 from *A Celtic Song Cycle*; wds: 'Fiona Macleod')
Orch. s(b♭–A♭') 222(1) 2 4000 hp strings (v & p/parts: Chester)
(orch. score unpublished)
Dur. 7'00"
Ded. Gladys Lees, 1904
First perf. Queen's Hall / Dilys Jones (s) / QH Orch. / F. B. Ellis: 27 March 1914

1909 (orchestrated 1914)
2. *A Christmas Carol* (pub. v & p in 'Seven Bax Songs', wds: 15th century)
Orch. s(d–A') 2222 4000 strings (v & p parts: Chester)
(orch. score unpublished)
Dur. 3'47"–4'06"
Ded. To my Sister Evelyn
First perf. Queen's Hall / Dilys Jones (s) / QH Orch. / F. B. Ellis: 27 March 1914

1910 (orchestrated 1914)
3. *Slumber Song* (v & p: Enoch, wds: 'Shiela MacCarthy' – i.e. Arnold Bax)
Orch. s(C♯–F) 2022 0000 hp strings
MS Lbm, Add ms (orch. score unpublished, parts: BBC); v & p (as *A Lullaby*):
Enoch

Dur. 3'56"
Ded. To Gladys Ross
First perf. Queen's Hall / Dilys Jones (s) / QH Orch. / F. B. Ellis: 27 March 1914

15 March 1914 (orchestrated 1921)
The Happy Forest
Orch. 2+1 2+1 2+E♭+1 2+1   4330   timp   hp   3perc (cym bd tamb xyl)   celesta
strings   (parts: Chappell)
MS Lost. Published: Murdoch f. sc. 1925
Dur. 9'52" — 10'13"
Ded. Eugène Goossens
First perf. Queen's Hall / Goossens Orch. / Goossens: 3 July 1923

14 Dec. 1914
The Bard of the Dimbovitza (original settings of the Rumanian peasant verse
collected by 'Hélène Vacaresco')
Original version:
1. *The Well of Tears*
2. *Gipsy Song*
3. *My Girdle I Hung on a Tree Top Tall*
4. *Spinning Song*
5. *Misconception*
Orch. ms (ranges as below) 3(1) 2+1 3+1 2   4000   hp   strings
MS Lbm, Add ms 54773 v & p 54779 (orch. score unpublished, no parts)
Dur. See below
First perf. Queen's Hall / Ethel Fenton (ms) / Orch. / Edward Clark: 8 April 1921
6. *Song of the Dagger* (not part of the cycle)
Orch. bar (F♯ —D')   3(1) 2+1 2+E♭+1 2+1   4331   timp   hp   2perc (cym bd
tamb)   strings
MS Lbm, Add ms 54773, fragment v & p 54779 (unpublished, no parts)

1941 Revised version:
1. *Gipsy Song* (d—G') (not revised)
2. *The Well of Tears* (c♯—G')
3. *Misconception* (b♯—F')
4. *My Girdle I Hung on a Treetop Tall* (d—G')
5. *Spinning Song* (d—G')
Orch. 2322   3000   hp   strings   (parts: Chappell)
MS pc: Chappell. Published: Chappell, v & p 1948
Dur. 38'15" (7'40", 8'11", 9'09", 5'50", 7'25")
Ded. 'To my friend Gou Constantinesco'
First perf. BBC Third Programme / Emelie Hooke (ms) / BBC SO / Boult: 26
March 1949

9 Aug. 1916
In Memoriam, Pádraig Pearse
('I gcuimhne ar bPádraig mac Piarais')
Piano score only — never orchestrated
MS EIRE Du
unperformed

8 Feb. 1917 (orchestrated 1918)
Symphonic Variations for piano and orchestra
Orch. solo pf   3(1) 2+1 2 2+1   4231   timp   2perc (cym bd tamb)   strings

(parts: Chappell)
MS f. sc. Chappell, ms copy Lbm, Add. ms 54741, pf. score Add ms 54740.
Published (2pf. arr.): Chappell 1963
Dur. Pt. 1: 21'22" – 23'46"; pt. 2: 24'47" – 24'56". (A note in the score times
the 1938 Prom performance of the cut version at 38')
First perf. Queen's Hall / Cohen / Orch. / Wood: 23 Nov. 1920

1917
November Woods
Orch. 3+1 2+1 3+1 2+1 4331 timp 2hp 1perc (cym glock) celesta strings
(parts: Chappell)
MS pf. sc.: Lbm Add ms 54743, f. sc. lost. Published: Murdoch, f. sc. 1921, m.
sc. ca. 1933
Dur. 18'25" – 20'28"
First perf. Manchester / Hallé Orch. / Harty: 18 Nov. 1920. First London perf.
Queen's Hall (Royal Philharmonic Society) / Orch. / Harty: 16 Dec. 1920

1917 (orchestrated 1920)
Summer Music
Original version: unseen
MS Lost (unpublished, no parts)
First perf. Queen's Hall / LSO / (Margaret Collins Orchestral Concert) / Harty: 1
Nov. 1921
Revised version: (1932)
Orch. 3(1) 1+1 22 4100 timp hp strings (parts: Chappell)
MS pf. sc. Lbm Add ms 54746, f. sc. lost. Published: Murdoch f. sc. 1932
Dur. 8'53" – 9'05"
Ded. Sir Thomas Beecham

June 1917
From Dusk till Dawn (originally *Between Twelve and Three*): ballet in one act
Orch. 2(1) 122 4230 timp hp 2perc (cym tamb sd) wind machine strings
(parts: Lam)
MS f. sc. and pf. sc. RAM (unpublished/parts: RAM)
First perf. Palace Theatre / Charity matinee / O'Neill: Dec. 1917
First complete concert perf. St Mary's Parish Church, Petworth/Southern
Philharmonic Orch./Aaron Tighe: 25 Sept. 1982

Oct. 1917 (orchestrated Jan. 1919)
Tintagel
(also available in cued version for smaller orchestra)
Orch. 3+1 2+1 2+1 2+1 4331 timp hp 1 (or 2) perc (cym bd tri glock)
strings (parts: Chappell)
MS f. sc. Lam. Published: Murdoch f. sc. 1923; m. sc. ca. 1933; st. sc. Chappell
1973
Dur. 12'22" – 14'55"
Ded. 'Darling Tania with love from Arnold'
First perf. Winter Gardens, Bournemouth / Bournemouth Municipal Orch. /
Godfrey: 20 Oct. 1921
First London perf. Queen's Hall / RPS / Coates: 27 Nov. 1922

1918
The Frog-Skin ballet
MS lost
No performance traced

Orchestrated 1919
Dance Prelude and **Lament of the Swan-Princess**
(by Anatol Liadov)
Orchestrated by Bax for Diaghilev's ballet *Children's Tales (Les Contes Russes)*
MS lost (unpublished)
First perf. London Coliseum / 8 Dec. 1919

Orchestrated 1919
Russian Suite (piano pieces orchestrated as interludes for Diaghilev's 1919 season)
1. *Gopak*
Orch. 3(1) 222   4331   timp   hp   3perc (cym bd tamb)   strings   (parts now available from Chappell)
MS pc. Chappell (unpublished)
Dur. 5'55"
First perf. Earliest traced performance Alhambra Theatre/Orch./Ansermet/ca. May 1919

2. *May Night in the Ukraine*
Announced but possibly never orchestrated

3. *In a Vodka Shop*
Orch. 3(1) 222(1) 4231 timp hp 2perc (cym bd tamb tri) strings
MS pc (unpublished) (parts: Chappell)
First perf. Alhambra Theatre/Orch./Ansermet/25 July 1919

5 Feb. 1920
The Truth About the Russian Dancers
(complete score)
Orch. 3(1) 2+1 22   4331   timp   hp   2perc (cym bd tamb)   bells   strings
available cued to: *Orch.* 2(1) 2(1) 22   2230   timp   hp   2perc (cym bd tamb) bells   strings
(parts: Chappell)
MS Lbm: Add ms 54744. (Unpublished) (parts: Chappell)
Dur. without dialogue ca. 42'
First. perf. London Coliseum: 15 March 1920

Various suites are playable comprising some or all of:
1. *Overture [Ceremonial Dance]*
Orch. 3(1) 2+1 22   4331   timp   hp   1perc (cym bd tamb)   strings; cued version: 2(1) 222   2221   timp   hp   1perc (cym bd tamb) strings
Dur 3'11"–3'23"
2. *Karissima Plays Golf*
(can start with 30" clarinet solo used in full work or cut straight to the piece.)
Orch. 3(1) 2+1 22   4000   timp   hp   1perc (tamb)   strings; cued version: 2(1) 222   2000   timp   hp   1perc (tamb)   strings
Dur. 2'37"–3'00"
3. *Bridal Procession (Wedding)*
(can start with 16" bells or cut straight to the piece)
Orch. 3(1) 2+1 22   4331   timp   hp   2perc (cym tamb tri)   bells; cued version: 2(1) 222   2230   timp   hp   2perc (cym tamb tri)   strings
Dur. 2'35"–2'47"
4. *Dance of Motherhood [Water Music]*

Orch. 3(1) 2+1 22   4331   timp   hp   strings; cued version: 2(1) 222   2220
timp   hp   strings
Dur. 5'33"−5'45"
5. *Funeral of Karissima*
Orch. 2 2+1 22   4200   timp   hp   strings; cued version: 2222   2000   timp   hp
Orch. 2 2+1 22 4200 timp hp strings; cued version: 2222 2000 timp hp strings
6. *Child's Dance*
Orch. 2+1 2+1 22   4200   timp   hp   1perc (tamb)   strings; cued version: 2(1)
222   2220   timp   hp   1perc (tamb)   strings
Dur. 1'57"−2'18"
7. *Karissima's Farewell* [*Serpent Dance*]
(can preface by 5-bar lead-in and can segue to finale at p. 165, 2 bars before 70)
Orch. 3(1) 2+1 22   4330   timp   hp   1perc (tamb)   strings; cued version: 2(1)
222   2330   timp   hp   1perc (tamb)   strings
Dur. 3'32"
8. *Finale*
Orch. 3(1) 2+1 22   4331   timp   hp   2perc (cym bd tamb)   strings; cued
version: 2(1) 222   2230   timp   hp   2perc (cym bd tamb)   strings
Dur. 3'41"−3'50"

1920
Phantasy [concerto] for viola and orchestra
Orch. solo viola   3(1) 2+1 22   4200   timp   hp   1perc (cym)   strings (parts:
Chappell)
MS f. sc. Lbm: Add ms 54745. Published: Murdoch vla & pf 1922; f. sc. 1938
Dur. 18'54"−21'34"
Ded. Lionel Tertis
First perf. Queen's Hall: Tertis / RPS / Coates: 17 Nov. 1921

Variations sur Cadet-Rousselle by Arnold Bax, Frank Bridge, John Ireland and
Eugène Goossens. Orchestrated by Eugène Goossens (1930). (See also songs.)
Orch. 2221   2100   timp   hp   1perc (sd cym tamb tri glock xyl)   bells   strings
(parts: Chester)
MS pc: Chester; published: Chester f. sc. 1931
Ded. 'To our good friend, Edwin Evans, who suggested this collaboration'

1921
Ballade in A♭ , op. 47 (Chopin orchestrated by Bax)
MS Lost (unpublished)
First perf. London Coliseum / Orch. / Alfred Dove / 4 July 1921
(danced by Laurent Novikoff and Tamara Karsavina)

1921
Fanfare for A Hosting at Dawn
Orch. 'for wind and brass'
MS Lost pf. sc. published in *Fanfare* No. 3, 1 Nov. 1921, p. 50, f. sc. lost
First perf. Queen's Hall / Orch. / Goossens: 12 Dec. 1921
— arr. brass: 4331   (parts: Kneller Hall)
— arr. Arthur Cohn: 1020   232 (2nd ad lib) 1   cym   bd   (parts: Fleischer
Collection)
MS US: Edwin Fleischer Collection, Philadelphia
— arr. Graham Parlett full orchestra (*ad lib.*) (parts: Graham Parlett)
MS pc

Dur. 33"
First perf. St John's, Smith Square / KSO / Head: 2 March 1979

8 Oct. 1922
Symphony No. 1 in E♭ (pf. sc. 30 June 1921)
Orch. 4(1+b fl) 2+1+h'pn 3(E♭)+1 2(contrabass sarrusaphone or c fag)   4331
timp   2hp   3perc (sd cym bd tamb tri td glock xyl gong)   celesta   strings
(parts: Chappell)
MS pf. sc. Lbm Add ms 54724; f. sc. Lbm Add ms 54725. Published: Murdoch
f. sc. 1923, m. sc. ca. 1933
Dur. I: 13'13"–15'09", II: 10'17"–12'31", III: 8'10"–9'06"
Ded. John Ireland
First perf. Queen's Hall / LSO / Coates: 4 Dec. 1922

Oboe Concerto (Oboe Quintet arr. Sir John Barbirolli)
Orch. solo oboe, strings (parts: Chappell)
Dur. I: 5'19", II: 7'58", III: 4'28"
First perf. Free Trade Hall Manchester / E. Rothwell / Hallé / Barbirolli: 21 April
1969

Orchestrated 1922
Mediterranean (orchestration of piano piece)
Orch. 22+1 22 4000 timp hp 2(or 3)perc (tamb castanets glock) strings
(parts: Chappell)
MS Lost. Published: Murdoch f. sc. 1923
Dur. 3'05"–4'10"
Ded. Gustav Holst
First perf. Queen's Hall / Goossens Orch. / Goossens: 13 Nov. 1922

16 March 1923
To the Name Above Every Name Soprano chorus and orchestra (wds: Crashaw)
Orch. Solo s/SATB chorus / 3(1) 2+1 2+1 2+1   4331   timp   hp   3perc (glock
bd sd tri gong cym)   organ   strings (parts: Chappell)
MS v. sc. Lbm Add ms 50179, f. sc. SF A. Published: Murdoch v. sc. 1923
Dur. 20'12"–21'22"
First perf. Worcester Cathedral (Three Choirs Festival) Agnes Nicholls (s) / Choir
and Orch. / Atkins: 5 Sept. 1923

Dec. 1923
St Patrick's Breastplate for chorus and orchestra
Orch. SATB chorus / 3(1) 2+1 2+1 2+1   4331   timp   hp   1perc (sd cym bd)
strings (parts: Chappell)
MS f. sc. pc: Chappell. Published: Murdoch v. sc. 1924
Dur. 15'06"–17'51"
First perf. Queen's Hall / Philharmonic Choir / Orch. / Kennedy Scott: 21 May
1925

1925
Cortège
Orch. 3(1) 2+1 3+1 2+1   4 3+2 31   timp   hp   2perc (sd cym bd tr tamb glock)
strings (parts: Chappell)
MS pc: Chappell (unpublished)
Dur. 5'07"–5'43"

Ded. Herbert Hughes
First perf. St Johns Smith Square / KSO / Head: 29 Jan. 1972

26 March 1926
Symphony No. 2 in E minor and C (pf. sc. 10 Oct. 1924)
Orch. 3(1) 2+1 3+1 2+1   4332   timp   2hp   3perc (sd cym bd tamb glock xyl gong)   piano   celesta   organ   strings   (parts: Chappell)
MS pf. sc. Lbm Add ms 54726, f. sc. Add ms 54727. Published: Murdoch f. sc. 1929, m. sc. 1933
Dur. I: 14'46"–16'17", II: 11'06"–12'56", III: 9'47"–12'15"
Ded. Serge Kussevitsky
First perf. Boston / BSO / Kussevitsky: 13 Dec. 1929
First London perf. Queen's Hall / Orch. / Goossens: 20 May 1930

April 1926
Romantic Overture for chamber orchestra
Orch. 2(1) 122   2100   pf   strings   (parts: Chappell)
MS pf. sc. Lbm Add ms 54748; f. sc. Add ms 54749. Published: Murdoch f. sc. 1928
Dur. 12'26"–13'17"
Ded. Frederick Delius
First perf. New Chenil Galleries / Rae Robertson (pf) / Chenil Chamber Orch. / Barbirolli: Jan. 1927

May 1926
Walsinghame
Orch. ten solo / SATB chorus + obbligato soprano / 2222   4331   timp   hp   celesta   strings   (parts: Chappell)
MS v. sc. Lbm Add ms 54774, f. sc. pc Chappell. Published: Murdoch, v. sc. 1927
Dur. 18'02"
Ded. Philip Heseltine
First perf. Queen's Hall / Philharmonic Choir / Orch. / Kennedy Scott: 6 June 1929

Summer 1927
Overture, Elegy and Rondo
Orch. 3(1) 2+1 2+1 2+1   4331   timp   hp   3perc (sd cym bd tamb glock xyl gong*)   strings   (parts: Chappell)
(* tri asked for at beginning of 1 and 3 but does not appear in the score)
MS Lost. Published: Murdoch f. sc. 1938
Dur. I: 7'44"–8'12", II: 10'11", III: 7'53"
Ded. Eugène Goossens
First perf. Queen's Hall (Prom) / [BBC Symphony] Orch. / Wood: 3 Oct. 1929

26 Oct. 1927 (orchestrated Feb. 1933)
Prelude for a Solemn Occasion (Northern Ballad No. 3?)
Orch. 3(1) 2+1 3+1 2+1   4331   timp   hp   2perc (sd cym bd tri glock gong)   organ   strings
MS st. sc. Lbm Add ms 54750, f. sc. Add ms 54756 (unpublished/parts: BBC)
Dur. 7'24"–8'33"
First perf. BBC Studio Seven, Manchester/BBC NSO/Downes: 22/9/82

Nov. 1927
Northern Ballad No. 1 ('1st Northern Ballad')
Orch. 3(1) 2+1 2+1 2+1   4331   timp   2hp   2perc (sd cym tamb gong)   strings

(parts: Chappell)
MS st. sc. Lbm Add ms 54750, f. sc. pc Chappell (unpublished)
Dur. 9'55'–10'46"
Ded. Basil Cameron
First perf. Glasgow / Scottish Orch. / Basil Cameron: 14 Nov. 1931
First London perf. Queen's Hall / Orch. / Basil Cameron: 3 Dec. 1931

Feb. 1929
Symphony No. 3
Orch. 3(1) 2+1 3(E♭)+1 2+1 4331 timp 2hp (2nd *ad lib.*) 4perc (sd cym bd tamb gong glock xyl td anvil) celesta strings (parts: Chappell)
MS st. sc. Lbm Add ms 54728, f. sc. Add ms 54729. Published: Murdoch f. sc. 1931, m. sc. nd (1933?)
Dur. I: 17'30"–21'19", II: 12'11"–12'57", III: 12'59"–16'06"
Ded. Sir Henry J. Wood
First perf. Queen's Hall / [BBC Symphony] Orch. / Wood: 14 March 1930

3 April 1930
Winter Legends for piano and orchestra
Orch. solo pf / 3(1) 2+1 3+1 2+1 4331 timp hp 3perc (sd cym bd tamb glock xyl gong tri) strings (parts: Chappell)
MS st. sc. Lbm Add ms 54751, f. sc. Add ms 54752 (unpublished)
Dur. I: 13'10"–14'51", II: 13'26"–15'08", III: 12'00"–13'59"
Ded. Harriet Cohen (originally Sibelius)
First perf. Queen's Hall / Cohen / BBC SO / Boult: 10 Feb. 1932

1930
Fanfare for a Cheerful Occasion
Orch. 2 E♭ sop. cornets; 4 B♭ trumpets; 3 ten trombs; 1 bass tromb; timp; cym
MS Copyist's f. sc: Royal Military School of Music, Kneller Hall
First. perf. Savoy Hotel (Musicians' Benevolent Fund Annual Dinner) / Kneller Hall Musicians / Adkins / 8 May 1930.

13 Oct. 1930
Overture to a Picaresque Comedy
Orch. 3(1) 2+1 3+1 2+1 4331 timp hp 3perc (sd cym bd tamb tb glock xyl gong rattle) celesta strings
MS Lost. Published: Murdoch f. sc. 1932, m. sc. Chappell 1945
Dur. 8'36"–9'48"
Ded. Sir Hamilton Harty
First perf. Manchester / Hallé Orch. / Harty: 19 Nov. 1931
First London perf. Queen's Hall / LSO / Harty: 15 Feb. 1932

Feb. 1931
Symphony No. 4
Orch. 3(1) 2+1 3+1 2+1 6332 timp hp 3perc (sd cym bd tamb tri glock xyl gong) celesta organ strings (parts: Chappell)
MS f. sc. Ob: ms don c. 48. Published: Murdoch f. sc. 1932, m. sc. 1932
Dur. I: 15'19"–16'16", II: 12'37"–12'48", III: 10'33"–10'45"
Ded. Paul Corder
First perf. San Francisco / SFSO / Basil Cameron: 16 March 1932
First London perf. Queen's Hall / LPO / Sargent: 5 Dec. 1932

Dec. 1931
The Tale the Pine-Trees Knew
Orch. 3(1) 2+1 2(E♭)+1 2+1 4331 timp 2hp 4perc (sd cym bd tamb td gong glock xyl) strings (parts: Chappell)
MS st. sc. Lbm Add ms 54753, f. sc. Add ms 54754. Published: Murdoch f. sc. 1933
Dur. 15'08"−17'22"
Ded. John Barbirolli
First perf. Queen's Hall / RPS concert / Beecham: 12 April 1934

March 1932
Symphony No. 5
Orch. 3(1) 2+1 3+1 2+1 4331 timp hp 3perc (cym bd tamb td tri glock gong) strings (parts: Chappell)
MS pf. sc. SF A, f. sc. Lbm Add ms 57430. Published: Murdoch f. sc. 1933, m. sc. nd (ca. 1934)
Dur. I: 15'30"−17'23", II: 10'07"−10'39", III: 12'06"−12'30"
Ded. Jean Sibelius
First perf. Queen's Hall / Orch. / Beecham: 15 Jan. 1934

May 1932
Sinfonietta (Symphonic Fantasy)
Orch. 3(1) 2+1 3+1 2+1 4331 timp hp 1(or 2)perc (cym tamb glock) strings (parts: BBC)
MS pc (unpublished)
Dur. 23'35"
First perf. BBC Concert Hall (Studio One), Cardiff/BBC Welsh SO/Handley: rec. 25 June 1983; bc. 23 Dec. 1983.

June 1932
Cello Concerto
Orch. Vlc solo / 3(1) 2+1 2 2+1 4200 timp hp strings (the second trumpet is not required in the first movement) (parts: Chappell)
MS Lbm Add ms 54755. Published: Murdoch f. sc. 1934, v/c & pf 1934
Dur. I: 13'10"−15'25", II: 8'55"−10'34", III: 7'50"−8'18"
Ded. Gaspar Cassadó
First perf. Queen's Hall / Cassadó / LSO / Harty: 5 March 1934

Sept. 1932
Saga Fragment (orch. of Piano Quartet *qv*)
Orch. pf solo tmpt 2perc (sd cym bd) strings (parts: Chappell (use the solo piano part from the published Piano Quartet))
MS (neither Bax's autograph) US Wc; Lbm Add ms 54747 (unpublished)
Dur. 10'53"−11'29"
Ded. Harriet Cohen
First perf. Queen's Hall / Cohen / Orch. / Constant Lambert: 21 Oct. 1933

Orchestrated Jan. 1934
Northern Ballad No. 2
Orch. 3(1) 2+1 3+1 2+1 4331 timp hp 4perc (sd cym bd tamb glock xyl gong tri) strings (parts: Chappell)
MS f. sc. pc (Chappell) unpublished
Dur. 15'12" − 16'17"
Ded. Adam Carse
First perf. Royal Albert Hall / LPO / Cameron: 16 Feb. 1946

Orchestrated Feb. 1934
Three Songs for voice and orchestra:
1. **A Lyke-Wake** [Dirge] ('This Ae Night', v & p 1908)
Orch. voice (C–B) 3(2) 2+1 2+1 4330 timp hp 2perc (cym bd gong) strings
2. **Wild Almond** (wds: Trench, v & p 1924)
3. **The Splendour Falls** (wds: Tennyson, v & p 1917)
1. *MS* LU; 2 & 3 orchestral scores lost
All unpublished / no parts
Unperformed

16 Nov. 1934
Eternity for voice and orchestra (wds: Herrick, v & p 1925)
Orch. voice (F–A) 3 2+1 2+1 2+1 4331 timp strings
MS f. sc. Lbm Add ms 54774 (unpublished). (Solo song published: Murdoch, 1925)
Ded. Original v & p, W. Grant Oliver
Unperformed

1934
Symphony No. 6
Orch. 3(1) 2+1 3+1 2+1 4331 timp hp 3perc (sd cym bd tamb glock gong tri td) celesta strings (parts: Chappell)
MS f. sc. (1st mvt only) pc (Chappell). Published: Murdoch f. sc. 1935; m. sc. nd (ca. 1935)
Dur. I: 8'58"–10'12", II: 7'30"–10'39", III: 16'30"–17'53"
Ded. [Sir] Adrian Boult (originally Szymanowski)
First perf. Queen's Hall / RPS / Harty: 21 Nov. 1935

1935
The Morning Watch for chorus and orchestra
Orch. chorus SATB / 3(1) 2+1 3+1 2+1 4331 timp hp 2perc (sd cym bd glock gong tri td) strings (parts: Chappell)
MS pc: Chappell. Published: Murdoch, v. sc. 1935
Dur. 19'13"
Ded. 'Sir Ivor Atkins (in memory of very old days)'
First perf. Worcester Cathedral (Three Choirs Festival) / Choir and orch. / Atkins: 4 Sept. 1935

Feb. 1936
Rogue's Comedy Overture
Orch. 3(1) 2+1 3+1 2+1 4331 timp hp 4perc (sd cym bd tamb glock gong tri rattle) strings (parts: Chappell)
MS pc: Chappell (unpublished)
Dur. 9'06"
Ded. Julius Harrison
First perf. Liverpool / RLPO / Harrison: 13 Oct. 1936

March 1936
Threnody and Scherzo (for bassoon, harp and string sextet)
Played by solo bassoon, harp and string orchestra (ordinary Chamber version parts: Chappell)
Dur. I: 9'34", II: 6'16"
Ded. Patrick Hadley
First perf. Keene, New Hampshire / John Millar (fag) / New Hampshire SO / James Bolle: 1 Dec. 1977

Oct. 1936
Overture to Adventure
Orch. 3(1) 222 4331 timp 2perc (sd cym bd tamb glock tri) strings
MS Lost. Published: Murdoch f. sc. 1937
Dur. 8'55"–9'03"
Ded. Richard Austin
First perf. Winter Gardens, Bournemouth / Bournemouth Municipal Orch. /
Austin: 23 Feb. 1937

1937
London Pageant[ry] march and trio for orchestra
Orch. 3(1) 2+1 3 2+1 43+2 31 timp (2nd player desirable) 3perc (sd cym bd
glock tri gong bells (*ad. lib.*)) organ strings (parts: Chappell)
MS pc: Chappell (unpublished)
Dur. 10'08"–10'49"
Ded. 'To my friends of the BBC Orchestra'
First perf. BBC broadcast/BBC SO/Coates: 4 May 1937
First public perf. Queen's Hall / (Prom) / BBC SO / Wood: 2 Oct. 1937

March 1938
Violin Concerto (in E major)
Orch. vln 3(1) 2+1 2 2+1 4200 timp hp 2perc (cym bd tamb td) strings
(parts: Chappell)
MS Lbm Add ms 54757. Published: Chappell vln & pf, 1946
Dur. I: 14'24"–15'38", II: 10'49"–11'04", III: 7'34"–8'05"
Ded. Jascha Heifetz (on ms only)
First perf. BBC Home Service/Eda Kersey (vln)/BBC SO/Wood: 22 Nov. 1943

Orchestrated 14 April 1938
Paean (orchestration of piano piece, 1920)
Orch. 3(1) 3 2+1 2+1 43+2 31 timp 3perc (sd cym bd gong bells) organ
strings (parts: Chappell)
MS pc: Chappell (unpublished)
Dur. 3'02"–3'10"
First perf. Royal Albert Hall / Orch. / Sargent: 24 May 1938

Jan. 1939
Symphony No. 7
Orch. 3(1) 2+1 3+1 2+1 4331 timp hp 4perc (sd cym bd tamb glock tri
gong td) strings (parts: Chappell)
MS pf. sc. US Wc ML96.B36; f. sc. Lbm Add ms 57253. Published: Chappell
st. sc. 1972
Dur. I: 15:04"–16'07", II: 12'29"–14'04", III: 13'05"–14'58"
Ded. 'To the People of America' (originally to Basil Cameron)
First perf. New York World Fair / NYPSO / Boult: 9 June 1939
First British perf. Colston Hall, Bristol / BBC SO / Boult: 21 June 1940
First London perf. Royal Albert Hall (Prom) / Orch. / Wood: 22 Aug. 1943

24 July 1939
Concertino for piano and orchestra
Orch. unfinished
MS mvts 1 & 2 only (draft st. sc.) Lbm Add ms 54758; III (?) 54752
Ded. [Harriet Cohen]

Sept. 1942
Malta GC
complete film score
Orch. 2222 2231 timp perc (sd cym) strings (parts: Chappell)
MS MALTA Vn (unpublished). (Extracts for piano solo and organ, qv.)
Dur. The actual film timed at 21'00", the BBC discs of the 'Suite' (actually the
complete score including bits cut from the film) timed at 23'12"
Ded. 'To Heroic Malta, GC'
First perf. (for sound track). St Johns Wood, HMV Studio / RAF Orch. /
Mathieson: ca Dec. 1942

1942
Five Fantasies on Polish Christmas Carols (wds: trans. Jan Sliwinski)
1. *God is Born* (Bóg Się Rodzi)
2. *In Nightly Stillness* (Wśród Nocnej Ciszy)
3. *In the Manger He is Lying* (W żłobie Leży)
4. *Lullay, Dear Jesus* (Lulajże Jezuniu)
5. *Merrily to Bethlehem* (Przybieżeli do Betlejem)
Orch. Unison voices / strings (parts: Chappell)
MS pc: Chappell. Published: Chappell v. sc. 1945, f. sc. 1946
Ded. To the Children of Poland
First perf. Royal Albert Hall/Joan Cross(s), in 4/children's choir and orch./
Cundell: 28 Feb. 1945

1943
A Solemn Fanfare
Orch. brass
MS Lost
First perf. Royal Albert Hall / Trumpets of the Household Cavalry: 21 Feb.
1943

31 March 1943
Salute to Sydney fanfare
Orch. brass (parts: BBC)
MS pc: BBC
First perf. BBC Overseas Broadcast ('Calling Sydney'): 19 April 1943

Nov. 1943
Work in Progress (Concert Overture for ENSA)
Orch. 2222 4231 timp 2perc (cym tamb) strings (parts: Chappell)
MS pc: Chappell (unpublished)
Dur. 7'41"
Ded. Walter Legge
First perf. 'A factory near London' / LSO / Weldon: 24 Feb. 1944

3 Feb. 1944 (v & p Jan. 1944)
To Russia (wds: Masefield)
Orch. bar solo / SATB chorus / 3222 4330 timp 2perc (sd cym bd) strings
(parts: Chappell)
MS v. sc., f. sc. pc: Chappell (unpublished)
Dur. 3'51"–4'22"
First perf. Royal Albert Hall / Roy Henderson (bar) / Royal Choral Soc. / LSO
plus section of BBC SO / Sargent: 23 Feb. 1944

2 May 1944
A Legend for Orchestra
Orch. 3(1) 222 4331 timp hp 2perc (sd cym bd glock tamb gong) strings
(parts: Chappell)
MS pc: Chappell (unpublished)
Dur. 13'14"
Ded. Julian Livingstone Herbage
First perf. Guildhall Cambridge (BBC Home Service) / BBC SO / Boult: 28 Oct.
1944

June 1945
Variations on the Name Gabriel Fauré (written for pf as *Suite for Fauré*, 1945,
orch. 1949)
Orch. harp and strings (parts: Chappell)
MS f. sc. C Mu xerox Lbm facs 595 (unpublished)
Dur. 18'17"
Ded. Boyd Neel
First perf. BBC Third Programme / Boyd Neel O / Boyd Neel: 31 Jan. 1961

8 Sept. 1945
Victory March (extended version of the march from *Malta GC*)
Orch. 2222 4231 timp 1perc (sd cym) strings (parts: Chappell)
Dur. 7'36"
— Arr. military band W. J. Duthoit
Published: Chappell's Army Journal (766)

Jan. 1946
Golden Eagle (incidental music to a play by Clifford Bax)
1. *Prelude*
Orch. pf and strings
2. *Rizzio's Song of Ronsard*
Orch. bar (D♭–E♭) sop, con hp strings
3. *Dance* harpsichord
Orch. harpsichord
Dur. 1'11"
4. *Pavane* (Prelude Act II sc. 1)
Orch. pf and strings
5. *Rizzio*
Orch. harp
Dur. 0'36"
6. *Song* (Rizzio)
Orch. v and harp
7. *Prelude* Act III sc. 2
Orch. piano and strings
8. *Act III* sc. i
Orch. tmpt pf sd strings
9. *Prelude* Act III sc. 2
Orch. pf sd strings
Dur. 1'01"
10. *Mary Stuart's Prayer*
Orch. tmpt pf strings
Dur. 2'07"

MS (all) pc: Chappell (unpublished). (Parts: Chappell); see also under *Songs*
First perf. Westminster Theatre: 29 Jan. 1946

1946
Morning Song ('Maytime in Sussex')
Orch. pf solo 2(1) 222 2000 timp strings (parts: Chappell)
MS Lost. Published: Chappell, f. sc. 1946
Dur. 8'16"–8'38"
Ded. HRH Princess Elizabeth
First perf. (for recording) Cohen (pf) / Orch. / Sargent: 7 Feb. 1947
First public perf. Royal Albert Hall / Cohen / LSO / Sargent: 13 Aug. 1947

Nov. 1947
Two Fanfares for the Royal Wedding
Orch. brass
Dur. 1. 0'55", 2. 1'32"
First perf. Westminster Abbey / RMSM Trumpeters / Roberts: 20 Nov. 1947

1947
The Pageant of St George
(wds: John Masefield)
Unfinished. Never orchestrated
MS sketches (see p. 341 for details): Lbm Add ms 54775
Unperformed

1948
Oliver Twist: music for the film
complete film score
Orch. pf solo 3(1) 2+1 22 4331 timp hp 2perc (sd cym bd tamb glock)
strings
MS pc (incomplete) (unpublished)
First perf. (for soundtrack): Denham Recording Theatre / Cohen (pf) / Philharmonia Orch. / Mathieson: May 1948
– *Storm* (not used)
Orch. 2+1 2+1 22 4331 timp 2perc (cym bd) strings (parts: Chappell)
MS pc (unpublished)
First perf. (for recording) RPO/Kenneth Alwyn: 8 Jan. 1986

– Suite (parts: Chappell)
1. *Prelude*
Orch. 3 2+1 22 4330 timp hp 1perc (bd) strings
MS Lost
Dur. 2'12"–2'15"
2. *The Fight*
Orch. 3(1) 222 4331 timp 1perc (cym) strings
MS pc: Chappell
Dur. 1'24"–1'34"
3. Two Piano Pieces (together also known as 'The Oliver Theme')
a. *Oliver's Sleepless Night*
Orch. pf solo 2022 2000 strings
MS Lost
Dur. 1'50"–3'02"
b. *Oliver and Brownlow*
Orch. pf solo 2022 1000 strings
MS Lost

Dur. 2'42"–3'33"
4. *The Chase (Oliver's Flight)*
Orch. 3(1) 222 4331 timp hp 2perc (sd cym bd) strings
MS Lost
Dur. 2'09"
5. *Fagin's Romp*
Orch. 3(1) 222 4331 timp 1perc (sd cym tamb glock) strings
MS Lost
Dur. 2'18"
6. *Finale*
Orch. 2 2+1 22 4331 timp hp 2perc (sd cym bd) strings
MS Lost
Dur. 3'23"–4'33"

1 Jan. 1949
Concertante for Three Wind Instruments
Orch.   I CA solo / 0000 0130 timp hp 1perc (sd cym) strings
   II CLAR solo / 0000 0130 timp 1perc (td cym) strings
   III HRN solo / 0000 0130 timp hp strings
   IV 3(1) 2+1 22 4230 timp hp 1perc (sd tamb glock) strings
MS destroyed, film survives (unpublished). Parts: Chappell
Dur. I: 8'24"–8'53", II: 6'02"–6'06", III: 6'32"–6'55", IV: 4'57"–5'48"
First perf. Royal Albert Hall/Helen Gaskell (cor anglais), Ralph Clarke (cl), Aubrey Thonger (horn)/BBC SO/Sargent: 2 March 1949

3 June 1949
Concertante for orchestra with piano (LH) ('Concerto for piano (LH)')
Orch. pf solo / 3(1) 2+1 22 4331 timp hp 2perc (sd cym bd tamb glock td) strings (parts: Chappell)
MS Lbm pf. sc. Add ms 54759 (unpublished)
Arr. of slow mvt. pub, pf. solo, Chappell, 1950
Dur. I: 9'22", II: 8'32", III: 7'53"
Ded. Harriet Cohen
First perf. Cheltenham Festival / Cohen / Hallé Orch. / Barbirolli: 4 July 1950
First London perf. Royal Albert Hall (Prom) / Cohen / BBC SO / Sargent: 25 July 1950

28 Aug. 1949
Variations on the Name Gabriel Fauré: see 1945

March 1951
Two Fanfares for 'Show Business'
Orch. 3 tmpts, 2 ten-trombs, 1 bass-tromb.
– arr. Chappelle: 2 hrns. 2 tmpts. 3 tombs. sd.
First perf. BBC broadcast 'Show Business' / Billy Ternent and his Orch.: 18 May 1951
MS BBC (unpublished)

1952
Journey Into History: music for the film
MS Lost (unpublished, parts lost); sketches Lbm Add ms 54775
Dur. film runs for 11'00"
First perf. Philharmonia Orch. / Mathieson (sound track)

29 Nov. 1952
Coronation March
Orch. 3(1) 222   4331   2perc (sd cym glock) bells *ad lib* organ   strings
(parts: Chappell)
MS pc: Chappell (unpublished)
Dur. 6'34"
First perf. Westminster Abbey / Orch. / Boult: 2 June 1953
First concert perf. Dukes Hall (RAM) / RAM Orch. / Raybould: 10 June 1953

(b) Chamber and Instrumental music (including music for two pianos)

23 Nov. 1903
String Quartet in E major
MS pc (unpublished)
Dur. I: −, II: ca. 12', III: −
(II orchestrated as the tone poem *Cathaleen-ni-Hoolihan*, qv)

1904
Concert Piece for Viola and Piano (also referred to as *Fantasy*)
MS EIRE (unpublished)
Dur. 11'21"−16'
First perf. Aeolian Hall (Patron's Fund Concert): L. Tertis (vla) / A. Bax (pf) /
6 Dec. 1904

[1904]
Phantasie for violin and piano
(Known only from the listing in the Society of British Composers' *Yearbook for*
1907/8. May well be violin version of the *Concert Piece* for viola.)

1905
From the Uplands to the Sea (wds: William Morris)
for voice and two pianos
MS pc (unpublished) (parts: BBC)
Dur. 11'18"−12'59"
First perf. BBC broadcast (Radio 3): Howard Shelley and Hilary MacNamara
(pfs)/Michael Goldthorpe (t)/bc. 23 Nov. 1983
First public perf. ICA, London/Keith Williams and Clive Williamson (pfs)/
Alasdair Elliott (t)/24 March 1984

1906
Trio in One Movement for violin, viola (or clarinet) and piano
MS Lost. Avison edition, 1907; J. & W. Chester, 1925
Ded. A. J. Rowan-Hamilton
Dur. 18'22"

1908
String Quintet in G for two violins, viola and two cellos
MS pc (unpublished, but slow movement arranged as *Lyrical Interlude*, q. v.)
First perf. Aeolian Hall: Wesserly Quartet + R. W. Tabb (vlc) / 16 July 1908

Oct. 1909
Festival Overture, arranged for two pianos. See under (a) Orchestral music

2 Aug. 1910
Violin Sonata No. 1 in E

(a) original version:
MS Lbm, Add ms 54765 (third movement a copy)
Ded. Natalia Skarginski
First perf. (1st mvt. only) Steinway Hall/Winifred Smith (vln)/Myra Hess (pf)/ 18 June 1914. (2nd mvt. only) BMIC/Bernard Partridge (vln)/Andrew Pledge (pf)/21 April 1983/(*Dur.* 9'41")

(b) revised version (with new 2nd and 3rd movements, March 1915)
MS Lbm, Add ms 54765. Published: Murdoch, 1921
Ded. Paul Kochanski
Dur. I: 13'25", II: 7'39", III: 11'19"
First perf. Queen's Hall / Paul Kochanski (vln) / A. Bax (pf) / 22. Nov. 1920

(c) final revision (cuts in the outer movements, revised tempo and dynamic markings)
Published: Chappell, 1946

[1910]
Aspiration (song, wds Friedrich Rückert, for sop. and piano trio)
MS EIRE C (unpublished) (published as *Song with Piano*, q.v.)

[1912]
Four pieces for flute and piano
(I: 'Shadow Dance', II: 'The Princess Dances', III: 'Naiad', IV: 'Grotesque')
MS Lost. Published: Chappell, 1947
Ded. 'Dedicated to Joseph Slater'
Dur. I: 3'09"–3'42", II: 1'21"–1'31", III:4'16"–5'00", IV: 1'44"–2'18"
First perf. Aeolian Hall / A. Fransella (fl) / H. Cohen (pf) / 28 June 1916
(Early performances dub the work 'Four Dances')

1912
Red Autumn (originally for piano solo — *see* 1933 for arr. for 2 pianos)

Feb. 1915
Legend for violin and piano
MS Lbm, Add ms 54395. Published: Augener, 1915
Ded. Miss Winifred Smith
Dur. 8'48"
First perf. Aeolian Hall / Winifred Small (vln) / Harriet Cohen (pf) / 28 June 1916

13 April 1915
Quintet in G minor for piano and string quartet
MS Lbm, Add ms 54761
Ded. Edwin Evans
Dur. I: 14'30"–21'10", II: 8'50"–10'45", III: 11'46"–13'23"
First perf. Music Club Concert at the Savoy Hotel/English String Quartet/ H. Cohen (pf)/19 Feb. 1917; first public performance: Queen's Hall/Bohemian Quartet/Fanny Davies (pf)/12 May 1920

13 Aug. 1915
Violin Sonata No. 2 (revised 1921)
MS Lbm, Add ms 54766. Published: Murdoch, 1923

Dur. I: 7'24", II: 5'15", III: 8'39", IV: 8'41"
First perf. Wigmore Hall / Bessie Rawlins (vln) / A. Bax (pf) / 25 April 1922

1915
Gopak (arranged, 1937, for violin and piano, q.v.)

1916
Ballad for violin and piano
MS pc. Published: Murdoch, 1935
Dur. 7'49"
Ded. Winifred Small
Earliest traced perf. Aeolian Hall / Winifred Small (vln) / Harriet Cohen (pf) / 28 June 1916

1916
Moy Mell: an Irish Tone Poem for two pianos
MS Lbm, Add ms 53735. Published: J. & W. Chester, 1918.
Dur. 9'06"–9'21"
Ded. Myra Hess and Irene Scharrer
First perf. Aeolian Hall / Myra Hess & Irene Scharrer (pfs) / 5 Dec. 1916

1916
Elegiac Trio for flute, viola and harp
MS pc: Chester. Published, score and parts, 1920, 1979
Dur. 9'21"–9'25"
First perf. Aeolian Hall / A. Fransella (fl) / H. Waldo Warner (vln) / M. Timothy (hp) / 26 March 1917

1917
In Memoriam (Sextet): An Irish Elegy for cor anglais, harp and string quartet
MS Lost. Published: Murdoch, score and parts, 1935
Dur. 8'06"
First perf. Plough Club (32 Holland Park Ave.) / E. Dubrucq (cor anglais) / G. Mason (hp) / Philharmonic Quartet / 10 March 1918

1918
String Quartet No. 1 in G major
MS Lost. Published: Murdoch, score and parts, 1921
Dur. I: 8'24"–9'00", II: 8'01"–9'36", III: 6'05"–6'52"
Ded. Sir Edward Elgar
First perf. Aeolian Hall / Philharmonic Quartet / 7 June 1918

1918
Folk-Tale (conte-populaire)
MS Lost. Published: J. & W. Chester, 1920
Dur. 8'37"–9'07"
Ded. Felix Salmond
First perf. Wigmore Hall / F. Salmond (vlc) / G. O'Connor Morris (pf) / 27 April 1918

1919
Harp Quintet for harp and string quartet
MS Lost. Published: Murdoch, 1922
Dur. 12'23"–13'36"
Ded. Raymond Jeremy

First perf. Hampstead Centre / G. Mason (hp) / Philharmonic Quartet / 24 Feb. 1921

1920
Of a Rose I Sing a Song for tenor solo, small choir, harp, cello and double bass
MS Lost. Published: Murdoch, 1921
Dur. 6'58"
Ded. Leigh Henry
First perf. Queen's Hall / M. Goossens (hp) / C. Sharpe (vlc) / V. Watson (db) /
Oriana Madrigal Society/Kennedy Scott/13 Nov. 1922

1921
Now is the Time of Christymas for men's voices, flute and piano
MS Lost. Published: Murdoch, 1921
Dur. 3'02"
Ded. Hamilton Harty
First perf. Queen's Hall / R. Murchie (fl) / A Bax (pf) / Oriana Madrigal Society /
Kennedy Scott/13 Nov. 1922

9 Jan. 1922
Sonata in G major for viola and piano
MS DRu. Published: Murdoch, 1923
Dur. I: 9'21"–11'31", II: 5'58"–7'04", III: 5'57"–8'28"
(In his recording with Tertis, Bax's own timings are: I: 7'42", II: 5'36", III: 6'30")
Ded. Lionel Tertis
First perf. Aeolian Hall / Lionel Tertis (pf) / A. Bax (pf) / 17 Nov. 1922

1922
Piano Quartet (see also Saga Fragment for piano and orchestra) for piano, violin, viola, cello
MS Lbm, Add ms 54762. Published, score and parts, Murdoch, 1924
Dur. 11'53"–13'08"
Ded. Miss Bessie Rawlins
First perf. Aeolian Hall / Meredyll Quartet, 9 Feb. 1923

1 Nov. 1922
Oboe Quintet for oboe and string quartet
MS EIRE C. Published: Murdoch, score and parts, 1925
Dur. I:5'49"–6'07", II: 6'05"–8'58", III: 4'33"–4'36"
Ded. Leon Goossens
First perf. Hyde Park Hotel (Mrs Adele Maddison Chamber Concert) / Leon
Goossens (ob) / Kutcher Quartet / 11 May 1924

1922
Lyrical Interlude (arranged from the slow movement of the String Quintet, 1908) for two violins, two violas and cello
MS Lost. Published: Murdoch, score and parts, 1923
Dur. 11'50"
Ded. R. Vaughan Williams

[1922]
Two Songs for Voice and String Quartet
(1. *My eyes for Beauty pine*; 2. *O mistress mine*)

MS Britten-Pears Library, Aldeburgh (unpublished) (parts: LF)
Dur. I: 3'13", II: 2'01"
First perf. BMIC/Janet Linsé (s)/Bernard Partridge (vln)/Antonina Bialos (vln)/
Michael Ponder (vla)/Elizabeth Wilson (vlc)/14 Oct. 1983

7 Nov. 1923
Cello Sonata in E♭
MS Lbm, Add ms 50180. Published: Murdoch, 1925
Dur. I: 12'24", II: 11'07", III: 10'23"
Ded. Beatrice Harrison (changed in the late 1940s to Henri van Marken)
First perf. Wigmore Hall / B. Harrison (vlc) / H. Cohen (pf) / 26 Feb. 1924

5 Feb. 1925
String Quartet No. 2
MS Lbm, Add ms 54763. Published: Murdoch, score and parts, 1927
Dur. I; 13'02", II: 8'18", III: 7'47"
Ded. Ralph Vaughan Williams
First perf. Grotrian Hall / New Philharmonic Quartet / 16 March 1929

1927
Hardanger for two pianos
MS Lost. Published: Murdoch, 1929
Dur. 3'09"–3'38"
First perf. Aeolian Hall/Ethel Bartlett and Rae Robertson (pfs)/2 Feb. 1929

1927
Violin Sonata No. 3 in G minor
MS Lost. Published: Murdoch, 1929
Dur. I: 8'31"–12'52", II: 9'16"–11'40"
Ded. Emil Telmanyi
First perf. Arts Theatre / E. Telmanyi (vln) / A. Bax (pf) / 4 Feb. 1929

8 May 1927
Concerto in D minor (Vivaldi, R.V.540, arranged by Bax) for harp and string
quartet
MS pc. Published: (parts only) Lyra Music Co., N.Y., 1978
First perf. Grotrian Hall/M. Korchinska (hp)/Harp Ensemble/10 June 1927

1927
Fantasy Sonata for harp and viola
MS EIRE C. Published: Murdoch, 1927
Dur. 19'59"–25'11"
Ded. Madame Maria Korchinska
First perf. Wigmore Hall/M. Korchinska (hp)/Raymond Jeremy (vla)/30 Oct.
1927

1928
The Poisoned Fountain for two pianos
MS Lost. Published: Murdoch, 1928
Dur. 3'53"–4'53"
Ded. Ethel Bartlett and Rae Robertson
First perf. Aeolian Hall / Ethel Bartlett and Rae Robertson (pfs) / 19 June 1928

1928
The Devil That Tempted St. Anthony for two pianos
MS Lost. Published: Murdoch, 1928
Dur. 6'00"–6'36"
First perf. Aeolian Hall / Ethel Bartlett and Rae Robertson (pfs) / 19 June 1928

Sept. 1928
Violin Sonata in F (later arranged as Nonett, q.v.)
MS Lbm, Add ms 54766
Dur. I: 9'38", II: 10'10"
First perf. BMIC/Bernard Partridge (vln)/Andrew Pledge (pf)/21 April 1983

1928
Sonata for harp and flute
MS destroyed (photocopy survives) (unpublished)
Dur. I: 5'57"– 6'47", II: 6'35"–7'15", III: 4'33"–4'53"
Ded. 'To Count K. Benckendorff'
First. perf. Ipswich Central Library / K. Kony (fl) / M. Korchinska (hp) / 19 Jan. 1929
First London perf. Wigmore Hall / K. Kony (fl) / M. Korchinska (hp) / 28 Jan. 1929

July 1929
Legend for viola and piano
MS US Wc ML 29c.B 34. Published: Murdoch, 1930
Dur. 10'31"
First perf. Aeolian Hall: L. Tertis (vla) / A. Bax (pf) / 7 Dec. 1929

1929
Sonata for Two Pianos
MS Lost. Published: Murdoch, 1930
Dur. I: 7'20"–10'42", II: 7'00"–7'35", III: 3'49"–5'32"
Ded. 'To Ethel Bartlett and Rae Robertson'
First perf. Music Club (Westminster) / Ethel Bartlett and Rae Robertson (pfs) /
10 Dec. 1929

Jan. 1930
Nonett for flute, oboe, clarinet, harp, string quartet and double bass
MS Lbm, Add ms 54760. Published: Murdoch, score and parts, 1932
Dur. I: 8'23"–9'29", II: 6'25"–7'41"
Ded. 'To the memory of Eric Verney-Cohen'
First perf. Bradford Triennial Festival / J. Slater (fl) / L. Goossens (ob) / R. Clarke
(cl) / M. Korchinska (hp) / Brósa Quartet / V. Watson (db) / 30 Sept. 1930
First London perf. Sunday Evening Concert Society, Working Men's College,
Camden Town / March 1931

1931
Red Autumn for two pianos
MS Lost. Published: Murdoch, 1933
Dur. 5'17"
Ded. 'To Ethel Bartlett and Rae Robertson'
First perf. College of Nursing Hall, Henrietta Street / Ethel Bartlett and Rae
Robertson (pfs) / 3 Oct. 1933

5 Sept. 1931
Valse for harp
MS pc (unpublished)

Dur. ca. 4'15"
Ded. Sidonie Goossens
First perf. Wigmore Hall / Sidonie Goossens / 1932

21 Jan. 1933
String Quintet in one movement for two violins, two violas and cello
MS pc: Chappell. Published: Murdoch, score and parts, 1935
Dur. 11'46"
Ded. Stratton String Quartet
First perf. Aeolian Hall / Stratton String Quartet / R. Jeremy (vla) / 1 March 1935

29 Sept. 1933
Sonatina in D for cello and piano
MS US NYp. Published: Murdoch, 1934
Dur. I: 7'21", II: 6'54", III: 4'07"
Ded. Pablo Casals
First perf. Wigmore Hall / Thelma Reiss (vlc) / H. Cohen (pf) / 8 March 1934

June 1934
Clarinet Sonata in D major
MS DRu. Published: Murdoch, 1935
Dur. I: 8'32"–8'47", II: 4'27"–5'19"
Ded. Hugh Prew
First perf. London Contemporary Music Centre (at Cowdray Hall) / F. Thurston (cl) / H. Cohen (pf) / 17 June 1935

31 Oct. 1934
Octet for horn, piano and string sextet (2 vlns, 2 vlas, vlc, db)
MS (short score, entitled 'Serenade') US Wc; (full score) US Wc, xerox copy in Lbm, Ms Facs 639; unpublished (hire from Chappell)
Dur. I: 8'48"–10'36", II: 6'04"
Ded. 'To Mrs Elizabeth Sprague Coolidge with kindest birthday wishes'
First perf. London Contemporary Music Centre (at Aeolian Hall) / A. Brain (hrn) / H. Cohen (pf) / Griller Quartet / 11 Dec. 1936

1935
Mediterranean, arranged for violin and piano by J. Heifetz
MS Lost. Published: Murdoch, 1936
Dur. ca. 3'30"
Ded. 'To Firenze' [i.e. Heifetz]

14 March 1936
Threnody and Scherzo for bassoon, harp and string sextet
MS pc (Chappell); unpublished (hire from Chappell)
Dur. I: 9'34", II: 6'16"
Ded. Patrick Hadley
First perf. London Contemporary Music Centre (at Aeolian Hall) / A. Camden (fag)/M. Korchinska (hp)/F. Riddle (vla)/E. Cruft (db)/Griller Quartet/11 Dec. 1936

19 April 1936
Concerto for flute, oboe, harp and string quartet ('Septet')
MS pc (Chappell); unpublished (hire from Chappell)
Dur. I: 7'36", II: 7'18", III: 5'17"
Ded. Count K. Benckendorf

First perf. London Contemporary Music Centre (at Aeolian Hall) / J. Francis (fl) / H. Gaskell (ob) / M. Korchinska (hp) / Griller Quartet / 11 Dec. 1936
This work was arranged from the sonata for Harp and Flute (1928)

23 Sept. 1936
String Quartet No. 3
MS Lbm, Add ms 54763. Published: Murdoch, score and parts, 1941
Dur. I: 9'56", II: 11'33", III: 9'19", IV: 7'41"
Ded. The Griller Quartet
First perf. BBC National Programme / Griller Quartet / 16 May 1937
First public perf. Aeolian Hall / Griller Quartet / 29 Oct. 1937

1937
Gopak, arranged for violin and piano by Louis Godowsky
MS Lost. Published: J. Williams, 1937
Dur. ca. 5'30"

3 June 1939
Rhapsodic Ballad for unaccompanied cello
MS EIRE C. Published: Chappell, 1969
Dur. 12'41"
Ded. Beatrice Harrison
First perf. Cork Municipal School of Music / Bernard Vocadlo / 25 May 1966
First London perf. Purcell Room/Rohan de Saram/10 May 1967

Feb. 1943
Legend-Sonata in F♯ minor for cello and piano
MS pc. Published: Chappell, 1944
Dur. I: 9'11"–10'18", II: 8'42"–9'57", III: 7'22"–7'41"
Ded. Florence Hooton
First perf. Wigmore Hall / Florence Hooton (vlc) / Harriet Cohen (pf) / 10 Nov. 1943

9 Jan. 1946
Trio in B♭ for violin, cello and piano
MS Lbm, Add ms 54764. Published: Chappell, score and parts, 1947
Dur. I: 6'37", II: 9'01", III: 6'39"
Ded. Harry Isaacs
First perf. Wigmore Hall / Harry Isaacs Trio / 21 March 1946

(c) Songs for voice and piano
(Those written before 1903 are listed under juvenilia)

29 June 1903
The Grand Match (wds: Moira O'Neill from *Songs of the Glens of Antrim*)
MS pc (unpublished)
First perf. St. James's Hall / RAM Concert / George Clowser (bar.) / ?pf / 23 July 1903

July 1904
To My Homeland (wds: Stephen Lucius Gwynn)
MS pc (unpublished)

July/Aug. 1904
A Celtic Song Cycle (Fiona Macleod)
(1. Eilidh my Fawn, 2. Closing Doors, 3. Thy Dark Eyes to Mine, 4. A Celtic Lullaby, 5. At the Last.)
MS Lost. Published: Avison Edition, 1906; revised edition, J. & W. Chester 1922. (Chester's hold the set of amended pulls from the plates of the first edition, from which the later one was prepared.)
Ded. The first version bears no dedication; in the later one each song is separately inscribed 'To Miss Gladys Lees'.
First perf. (incomplete) Queen's Hall / RAM Concert / Miss Ethel M. Lister (s) ?(pf) / 21 Nov. 1904

27 Jan. 1905
When We Are Lost ('Roundel') (wds: Dermot O'Byrne)
MS Lbm, Add ms 54778; a fair copy of a slightly variant text, pc. Published: as an appendix in *FDB*
Dur. 3'51"
First perf. BMIC/Jeff Weaver (t)/David Owen Norris (pf)/3 Feb. 1983

Feb. 1905
From the Uplands to the Sea (wds: William Morris: 'Poems by the Way')
MS Lbm, Add ms 54778 (unpublished)
– also arranged for voice and two pianos: pc (unpublished). See (b) Chamber and Instrumental Music

May 1905
Leaves, Shadows and Dreams (wds: Fiona Macleod)
MS Lbm, Add ms 54776 (unpublished)

2 June 1905
In the Silences of the Woods (wds: Fiona Macleod)
(also known as *The Multitudes of the Wind*)
MS Lbm, Add ms 54777; a second autograph Add ms 54776 (unpublished)

6 June 1905
Green Branches (wds: Fiona Macleod)
MS Lbm, Add ms 54777; a second autograph: EIRE C (unpublished)

Oct. 1905
The Fairies (wds: William Allingham)
MS Lost. Published: Avison Edition, 1907; J. & W. Chester, 1922
Dur. 5'01"–5'56"
Ded. 'To "Little Bridget"'
Earliest traced perf. Bechstein Hall / Luisa Sobrino (s) / Carlos Sobrino (pf) / 20 June 1908

Nov. 1905
Golden Guendolen: a Pre-Raphaelite song (wds: William Morris)
MS Lost. Published: Avison Edition, 1907.
Ded. 'To Christabel Marillier'

8 Dec. 1905
The Song in the Twilight (wds: Freda Bax)
MS Lost. Published: Avison Edition, 1907

Dur. 3'58"
Ded. 'To Freda' [Bax]

1905
Mircath [**Viking-Battle-Song**] (wds: Fiona Macleod)
MS pc and Lbm, Add ms 54777 (unpublished)
Of the two mss, pc is entitled 'Mircath' and the voice is in the bass clef, while
Lbm (a ms copy) is entitled 'Viking-Battle-Song' and has the voice in the treble
clef.

March 1906
A Hushing Song (wds: Fiona Macleod)
MS Lbm, Add ms 54777 (unpublished)
Ded. 'To D.P.'

15 June 1906
I Fear Thy Kisses Gentle Maiden (wds: P. B. Shelley)
MS Lbm, Add ms 54778 (unpublished)

20 Sept. 1906
Ballad: The Twa Corbies (From 'Border Minstrelsy') (Recitation with piano)
MS pc (unpublished)
Ded. 'To Roland Bocquet'

Xmas 1906
Magnificat (After a picture by D. G. Rossetti) (wds: St Luke's Gospel I.46–55)
MS Lost. Published: Avison Edition, 1907; J. & W. Chester, 1922
Ded. 'To Dorothy Pyman'
(later arranged for chorus, SATB, q.v.)

[1906]
The Blessed Damozel (wds: D. G. Rossetti) (Recitation; 'piano arrangement')
MS pc
Ded. 'Miss Dorothy Pyman'

[1906]
Echo
Lost

March 1907
The Fiddler of Dooney (wds: W. B. Yeats)
MS Lbm, Add ms 54778
Unpublished in this form. J. & W. Chester own a set of proofs of this song
corrected in Bax's hand, with new words substituted for those by Yeats, and the
title changed to *The Enchanted Fiddle*. The words would appear to be by Bax
himself. See facsimile of the proofs in *FDB*.
Dur. 1'59"
First perf. BMIC/Janet Linsé (s)/David Owen Norris (pf)/14 Oct. 1983

The Enchanted Fiddle (wds: Arnold Bax, 1919)
Dur. 2'00"
Ded. J. B. McEwen
See above entry. Published: J. & W. Chester, 1919

8 May 1907
Longing (wds: Fiona Macleod)
MS Lbm, Add ms 54777 (unpublished)
Ded. 'To. D. P.'

8 July 1907
Ideala (The Flute) (from 'Anna' of Björnstjerne Björnsen, translated into English by Edmond Gosse)
MS Lbm, Add ms 54778. Published: Murdoch, 1923
(The manuscript is in Norwegian and is headed 'Ideala', the published version is called 'The Flute' and includes words in English and Norwegian.)
Dur. 4'28"
Ded. (ms) 'To GNL'; (printed copy) 'To Madame Elisabeth Munthe-Kaas'

2 Sept. 1907
Du blomst i Dug (O Dewy Flower) (wds: digt fra 'Mogens' by J. B. Jacobsen)
MS Lbm, Add ms 54778 (unpublished)

6 Sept. 1907
From the Hills of Dream (wds: Fiona Macleod)
MS Lbm, Add ms 54777 (unpublished)
Ded. 'To G.N.L.'

23 Sept. 1907
A Milking Sian (wds: Fiona Macleod)
MS Lbm, Add ms 54777. Published: J. & W. Chester, 1919
Ded. 'To D.P.'

26 Sept. 1907
The White Peace (wds: Fiona Macleod)
MS Lbm, Add ms 54777; another ms: pc. Published: J. & W. Chester, 1919
Dur. 2'14"
Ded. (ms) 'To Dorothy'; (published) 'To my mother'
The Lbm ms is a later copy in Bax's hand, and is erroneously dated '1906'

30 Sept. 1907
Heart O'Beauty (wds: Fiona Macleod)
MS Lbm, Add ms 54777; another ms: pc. (unpublished)
Ded. 'To G.N.L.'

[1907]
The Kingdom (wds: Friedrich Rückert)
Lost

25 Jan. 1908
A Lyke-Wake [Dirge] (Border Ballad)
MS Lbm, Add ms 54778; incomplete ms Lu, Ms 435 (unpublished)
The ms in Lbm is a copy, and is entitled 'A Lyke-Wake Dirge'; the incomplete ms in Lu and the later orchestration is called 'A Lyke-Wake'.
Dur. 6'18"
First perf. BMIC/Jeff Weaver (t)/David Owen Norris (pf)/3 Feb. 1983

15 July 1908
Landskab (Landscape) (J. P. Jacobsen)
MS DK A; copy ms Lbm, Add ms 54778 (unpublished)

30 July 1908
Shieling Song (Fiona Macleod)
MS Lbm, Add ms 54777. Published: J. & W. Chester, 1919
Dur. 1'35"
Ded. 'To Mrs William Sharp'

[1908]
Isla (Fiona Macleod)
MS Lbm, Add ms 54777 (unpublished)

[1908]
The Wood-Lake (Der Waldsee) (H. Leuthold)
Lost

8 June 1909
Marguerite (William Morris)
MS Lbm, Add ms 54778 (unpublished)

26 Oct. 1909
The Garden by the Sea (William Morris)
MS Lbm, Add ms 54778 (unpublished)
Ded. 'To G'

1909
Aspiration (Adapted from Dehmel by Clifford Bax)
MS Lost. Published: Murdoch, 1921
A version with piano trio accompaniment also exists, ms: EIRE C, q.v.

Dur. 2'28"
Ded. 'To Paul Corder'
First perf. (piano trio version) BMIC/Janet Linse (s)/Bernard Partridge (vln)
Elizabeth Wilson (vlc)/David Owen Norris (pf)/14 Oct. 1983

[1909]
Beloved, Even in Dreams (Friedrich Rückert — No. 64 from *Liebesfrühling*)
Lost

[1909]
The Dance-Ring (O. Bierbaum)
Lost

[1909]
Home (Heimat) (Richard Dehmel)
Lost

[1909]
Enlightenment (Richard Dehmel)
Lost

[1909]
Ideala (Richard Dehmel)
Lost

[1910]
Love-Ode (Liebesode) (O. E. Hartleben)
Voice and piano version lost; but orchestration as No. 2 of Three Nocturnes, ms:
Lbm, Add ms 54735

Christmas 1909
A Christmas Carol (15th Century)
MS pc: Chester; Lbm, Add ms 54778. Published: J. & W. Chester, 1919
Dur. 4'12"
Ded. 'To my sister Evelyn'

22 March 1910
Lullaby ('Sheila MacCarthy' = Arnold Bax)
MS Lbm, Add ms 54778. Published: Enoch, 1920
The version for voice and orchestra (26 Feb. 1914) uses the title 'Slumber-song'.
Ded. 'To Gladys Ross' (not on ms)
Bax spells 'Sheila' as above on the printed score, but 'Shiela' on the ms

1910
To Eire (J. H. Cousins)
MS Lost. Published: J. & W. Chester, 1919
Dur. 3'42"

21 Dec. 1910
Spring Rain (Frühlingsregen) (Friedrich Rückert)
MS EIRE Published: Thames Publishing, 1986
Originally set in German; English text and title added later
Dur. 2'21"–3'33"
First perf. BMIC/Jeff Weaver (t)/David Owen Norris (pf)/3 Feb. 1983

23 Dec. 1910
Treue Liebe (Volkslied)
MS pc (unpublished)
Dur. 2'51"

5 Jan. 1911
Das Tote Kind (The Dead Child) (J. P. Meyer)
MS Lbm, Add ms 54779 (unpublished)

18 April 1911
Aufblick (Richard Dehmel)
Voice and piano version lost; but orchestration as No. 1 of Three Nocturnes, ms:
Lbm, Add ms 54735. Piano reduction by Stephen Banfield, 1980

[1911]
The Bridal Prayer (Nachtgebet der Braut) (Richard Dehmel)
Lost

[1911]
Faith (Vertrauen) (Friedrich Rückert)
Lost

[1911]
Flight (Im Fluge) (Richard Dehmel)
Lost

[1911]
Freimund (Friedrich Rückert)
Lost

[1911]
The Journey (Die Reise) (Richard Dehmel)
Lost

14 Aug. 1914
Roundel (*Three Rondels by Chaucer*, No. 1) (Geoffrey Chaucer) ('Your eyen
two')
MS Lbm, Add ms 54779, another ms: pc Chester. Published: J. & W. Chester,
1919
Dur. 3'31"

20 Oct. 1914
Welcome Somer (Geoffrey Chaucer) (*Three Rondels by Chaucer*, No. 2)
MS Lbm, Add ms 54779 (unpublished)
Ded. 'To Joan Thorneycroft'

31 Oct. 1914
Of her Mercy (Geoffrey Chaucer) (*Three Rondels by Chaucer*, No. 3)
MS Lbm, Add ms 54779 (unpublished)

1914
The Bard of the Dimbovitza ('Rumanian peasant verse')
(1. The Well of Tears, nd; 2. Gipsy Song, f. sc, 14 Dec. 1914; 3. My Girdle I
Hung on a Tree Top Tall, nd; 4. Spinning Song, 15 Oct. 1914; 5. Misconception,
1914.)
MS v & pf, Lbm, Add ms 54773, 54779; v & orch, Lbm 54773 (rev. version, pc,
Chappell). Published (v & pf): Chappell, 1948
Dur. see (a) Orchestral Music
Ded. 'To my friend Gou Constantinesco'

1914
The Song of the Dagger (The Bard of the Dimbovitza)
MS v & p (incomplete), Lbm, Add ms 54779. F. sc: Add ms 54773 (unpublished)

[1916]
A Leader (AE)
Lost

[1916]
A Patriot (AE)
Lost

[1916]
I Know Myself No More, My Child (A New Being) (AE)
Lost

[1916]
O Mistress Mine (Shakespeare)
MS Britten-Pears Library, who also have a version with string quartet accompani-
ment
Dur. 2'01"
First perf. (string quartet version) BMIC/Janet Linsé (s)/Bernard Partridge (vln)/
Antonina Bialos (vln)/Michael Ponder (vla)/Elizabeth Wilson (vlc)/14 Oct. 1983

1916
Parting (AE)
MS Lost. Published: Murdoch, 1921

Jan. 1917
The Splendour Falls on Castle-walls (Tennyson)
MS Lbm, Add ms 54779 (dated 'Nov. 1912–Jan. 1917')

[1917]
Go Lovely Rose (Edmund Waller)
Lost

1918
Far in a Western Brookland (A. E. Housman)
MS Lost. Published: Enoch, 1920
Ded. 'To Frederic Austin'

1918
Green Grow the Rashes O! (Character Sketch) (Robert Burns)
MS Lost. Published: Murdoch, 1920
Dur. 2'34"
Ded. 'To John Coates'

1918
I Have House and Land in Kent (modernised from Thomas Ravenscroft's
'Melismata' (1611)) (Trad. tune, arr. Bax)
MS pc: Chester. Published: J. & W. Chester, 1920
Dur. 2'43"

1918
The Maid and the Miller (Trad. tune arr. Bax)
MS pc: Chester, Published: J. & W. Chester, 1920

1918
Jack and Jone (Thomas Campion arr. Bax)
MS pc: Chester. Published: J. & W. Chester, 1920

[1918]
Midsummer (Clifford Bax)
Lost

1918
O dear! What can the matter be? (Trad. tune arr. Bax)
MS pc: Chester. Published: J. & W. Chester, 1920
Dur. 1'18"

1918
Trois Enfantines (Three Songs for Children) (trad. French, English words by
Edward Agate)
(Trad. tunes arr. Bax)
(1. Jean P'tit Jean; 2. Berceuse: Petit enfant, déjà la brume; 3. Une petite fille
Agée d'environ cinq ans.)
MS pc: Chester. Published: J. & W. Chester, 1920
First perf. Aeolian Hall / Raymonde Collignon (s) / Edwin Evans (pf) / 27 April
1918

[1918]
Variations sur Cadet-Rousselle (trad.)
(Alternate verses arranged by Bax, Frank Bridge, Eugène Goossens, and John
Ireland. Later orchestrated by Goossens q.v.)
MS Lost. Published: J. & W. Chester, 1920
Dur. 3'32"
Ded. 'To our friend Edwin Evans who suggested this collaboration'
First perf. Aeolian Hall / Raymonde Collignon (s) / Harriet Cohen (pf) / 6 June
1919

[1918]
When I was One-and-Twenty (A. E. Housman)
MS Lost. Published: Enoch, 1920
Ded. 'To Harriet Cohen'

1918
Youth (wds: Clifford Bax)
MS Lost. Published: Murdoch, 1920
Dur. 2'57"–3'52"

24 July 1920
Le Chant D'Isabeau (French Canadian Melody; wds: M. Uzanne's 'French Songs
of Old Canada')
MS Lost. Published: Murdoch, 1921
First perf. (as one of the *Traditional Songs of France*) Grafton Galleries (A
Music Club Concert) / Anne Thursfield (m-s) / A. Bax (pf) / 13 Feb. 1921

26 July 1920
La Targo (Provençal) (Traditional Songs of France, No. 5)
MS Lost. Published: Murdoch, 1921

27 July 1920
Me Soui Meso en Danso (Me suis mise en danse) (Bas Quercy) (Traditional Songs
of France, No. 3) (printed score misprinted as *Me Soui Mesocu . . .*)
MS Lost. Published: Murdoch, 1921

28 July 1920
Sarabande (Amours, amours, tant tu me fais de mal) (Old French Melody)
(Traditional Songs of France, No. 1)
MS Lost. Published: Murdoch, 1921
Dur. 3'32"

31 July 1920
Langueo D'Amours, Ma Doulce Fillette (Old French Poem and Melody) (Trad-
itional Songs of France, No. 2)
MS Lost. Published: Murdoch, 1921

16 Aug. 1920
A Rabelaisian Catechism (La Foi d'la loi)
MS Lbm, Add ms 54779 (unpublished)

21 Aug. 1920
Femmes, Battez vos Marys (Old French) (Traditional Songs of France, No. 4)
MS Lost. Published: Murdoch, 1921

[1920]
My Eyes for Beauty Pine (Robert Bridges)
MS Lbm, Add ms 54779 (unpublished); another ms in Britten-Pears Library, who also have a version for string quartet accompaniment
Dur. 3'13"
First perf. (string quartet version) BMIC/Janet Linsé (s)/Bernard Partridge (vln)/ Antonina Bialos (vln)/Michael Ponder (vla)/Elizabeth Wilson (vlc)/14 Oct. 1983

18 Feb. 1921
Across the Door (wds: Padraic Colum)
MS Lost. Published: Murdoch (*Five Irish Songs* – 4), 1922

19 Feb. 1921
Beg-Innish (J. M. Synge)
MS Lost. Published: Murdoch (*Five Irish Songs* – 5), 1922
Dur. 2'02"

28 Feb. 1921
As I Came Over The Grey, Grey Hills (Joseph Campbell)
MS Lost. Published: Murdoch (*Five Irish Songs* – 2), 1922
Dur. 3'05"

1 March 1921
The Pigeons (wds: Padraic Colum)
MS Lost. Published: Murdoch (*Five Irish Songs* – 1), 1922
Dur. 2'28"

11 March 1921
Glamour ('As I Walked at Dusk in Eyre Square' – 'Dermot O'Byrne')
MS Lbm, 54779. Published: as an appendix in *FDB*
Dur. 8'13"

[1921]
I Heard A Piper Piping (Joseph Campbell)
MS Lost. Published: Murdoch (*Five Irish Songs* – 3), 1922
Dur. 2'53"

Feb. 1922
Three Irish Songs (Padraic Colum)
(1. Cradle Song; 2. Rann of Exile; 3. Rann of Wandering)
MS Lost. Published: Murdoch, 1922
Dur. I: 2'52"–3'21", II: 2'45"–3'29", III: 1'29"–2'20"

1 March 1922
Dermot Donn McMorna (Padraic Colum)
MS pc (unpublished)

[1922]
The Market Girl (Thomas Hardy)
MS Lost. Published: Murdoch, 1922
Dur. 1'35"

[1923]
Morfydd (Lionel Johnson)
Lost

[1923]
To An Isle in the Water (W. B. Yeats)
Lost

31 March 1924
I Heard A Soldier (Herbert Trench)
MS Lbm, Add ms 54779. Published: Murdoch, 1926
Dur. 3'33"
Ded. 'To W. Grant Oliver'

April 1924
Wild Almond (Scherzo) (wds: Herbert Trench)
MS pc (unpublished); another ms in Britten-Pears Library

6 Aug. 1925
Carrey Clavel (Thomas Hardy)
MS Lbm, Add ms 50181. Published: Murdoch, 1926
Ded. 'To W. Grant Oliver'

6 Sept. 1925
Eternity (wds: Herrick)
MS Lbm, Add ms 54779. Published: Murdoch, 1926
Dur. 3'39"
Ded. 'To W. Grant Oliver'

[1926]
In the Morning (wds: A. E. Housman)
MS Lost. Published: Murdoch, 1926
Ded. 'To W. Grant Oliver'

[1926]
On the Bridge (wds: Thomas Hardy − 'Sitting on the Bridge (Echo of an Old Song)')
MS Lost. Published: Murdoch, 1926

1926
[Three carol arrangements] : **Haut, haut, Peyrot** (from Béarn) for bar & pf, **Laisse quy tas affaires** for con & pf; **Guillô, pran ton tamborin** (from Burgundy) for voice, pf, flute & tambourine
MS Lost. (unpublished)
First perf. Aeolian Hall (Oriana Madrigal Soc. Concert) / 14 Dec. 1926

[1926]
Out and Away (wds: James Stephens)
MS Lost. Published: Murdoch, 1926
Ded. 'To W. Grant Oliver'

[1926]
Blow Northern Wind (wds: Clifford Bax)
Lost

20 April 1927
Lad Vaaren Komme (J. P. Jacobsen) (Three Songs from the Norse No. 2)
MS DK Ku, ms copies DK A; Lbm, Add ms 54779 (unpublished)
Ded. Set dedicated 'To Lydia'

16 April 1927
Irmelin Rose (J. P. Jacobsen) (Three Songs from the Norse No.1)
MS DK Ku, ms copies DK A; Lbm, Add ms 54779 (unpublished)
Ded. Set dedicated 'To Lydia'

June 1927
Venevil (wds: Björnstjerne Björnsen) (Three Songs from the Norse No. 3)
MS DK Ku, ms copies DK A; Lbm, Add ms 54779 (unpublished)
Ded. Set dedicated 'To Lydia'

[1932]
Watching the Needleboats (James Joyce)
MS Lost. Published: 'The Joyce Book', 1932
Dur. 1'37"

1946
Rizzio's Songs (wds: Clifford Bax)
MS pc: Chappell (unpublished); autograph copies of the two songs (*My Faithful Fair One* and *Rizzio's Song*) in Britten-Pears Library
Included as part of the incidental music to 'Golden Eagle', q.v.

1947
Dream Child (Val Newton)
MS Lost. Published: Chappell, 1957
Dur. 2'12"

(d) Piano solos

16 Feb. 1910
Concert Valse in E♭
MS Lost. Published: Boosey, 1911
Ded. 'To Miss Myra Hess'
Apparently the first of two concert valses, the second of which may never have been written.
Dur. 5'21"

[1910]
Romantic Tone Poem
(Probably the same as *Symphonic Phantasy*.)
Lost

[1910]
Symphonic Phantasy
Lost
(The Original version of the First Piano Sonata.)

1911
Piano Sonata in D minor
Lost

10 Feb. 1912
Two Russian Tone Pictures: No. 1: Nocturne 'May-Night in the Ukraine'
MS pc. Published: Joseph Williams, 1913
Ded. 'To Olga and Natasha 1910'
Dur. 7'18"
First perf. Royal Academy Musical Union / Myra Hess (pf) / 12 Nov. 1912

[1912]
Two Russian Tone Pictures: No. 2: 'Gopak'
MS pc. Published: Joseph Williams, 1913
Ded. 'To Tobias Matthay affectionately dedicated'
Dur. 5'22"
First perf. Bechstein Hall / Myra Hess / 9 April 1913

July 1912
Nympholept: poem for piano
MS Lbm, Add ms 54737
Ded. 'To Tobias Matthay affectionately dedicated'
Dur. 11'06"
First perf. BBC Manchester/Martin Roscoe (pf)/rec. 17 Sept. 1986; broadcast 14 Feb. 1987. Later orchestrated, q.v.

[1912]
Mask
Lost

[1912]
Red Autumn
Lost
Later arranged for two pianos, q.v.

17 Oct. 1913
Sonata in F: No. 2 Scherzo
MS Lbm, Add ms 54767 (unpublished)
Dur. 9'03"

Only this movement known. Later orchestrated, and also arranged for pianola roll, q.v.

[1913]
Capriccio
(possibly the same as *Toccata*, below)
Lost

[1913]
Toccata
MS Lost. Published: Murdoch, 1920
Ded. 'To Hamilton Harty'
Dur. 5'24"

13 May 1914
The Happy Forest

MS Lbm, Add ms 50176 (unpublished)
Later orchestrated, q.v.

6 Nov. 1914
In the Night: passacaglia
MS Lbm, Add ms 54769 (unpublished)
Dur. 5'34"–6'10"
First perf. BBC Manchester/Martin Roscoe (pf)/rec. 17 Sept. 1986; broadcast
14 Feb. 1987

10 Jan. 1915
The Princess's Rose Garden: Nocturne
MS (ms entitled 'Berceuse') as 'Berceuse', Lbm, Add ms 54769, dated 9 Jan., 13
Jan. 1915. Published: Augener, 1915
Ded. (ms) 'To Tania' (printed score) 'To Miss Harriet Cohen'
Dur. 5'43" – 6'58"

22 Jan. 1915
In a Vodka Shop
MS Lbm, Add ms 54769. Published: Augener, 1915
Ded. (ms) 'To Tania' (printed score) 'To Miss Myra Hess'
Dur. 3'35"–3'50"
First perf. Grafton Galleries / Myra Hess (pf) / 29 April 1915

23 Jan. 1915
Idyll: The Maiden with the Daffodil
MS L cml (035718); also Lbm, Add ms 54769. Published: Joseph Williams, 1915
Ded. 'To Tania'
Dur. 4'05"
First perf. Aeolian Hall / Myra Hess (pf) / 24 March 1915

May 1915
Apple-Blossom-Time
MS Lost. Published: Augener, 1915
Dur. 3'45"
Ded. 'To S. H. Braithwaite'
First perf. Steinway Hall / Phyllis Emanuel (pf) / 18 Nov. 1915

24 May 1915
Sleepy Head
MS Lost. Published: Augener, 1915
Ded. 'To Elsita'
Dur. 4'48"

2 Sept. 1915
A Mountain Mood: melody and variations
MS pc: Chester. Published: J. & W. Chester, 1918
Ded. 'To Miss Harriet Cohen' (on ms: 'To Tania who plays it perfectly')
Dur. 4'34"

5 Sept. 1915
Winter Waters: tragic landscape
MS pc: Chester. Published: J. & W. Chester, 1918
Ded. 'To Arthur Alexander'
Dur. 6'22"

Feb. 1916
Dream in Exile: intermezzo (previously entitled 'Capriccio', then 'Intermezzo')
MS pc: Chester. Published: J. & W. Chester, 1918
Ded. 'Affectionately dedicated to Tobias Matthay'
Dur. 8'17"

24 March 1916
Nereid (ms entitled 'Ideala')
MS pc: Chester (ms as 'Ideala': Lbm, Add ms 54769). Published: J. & W. Chester, 1919
Ded. 'To Harriet Cohen'

[1918]
Love Song
(The same as *A Romance* below?)
Lost

[1918]
On A May Evening
MS Lost. Published: Ascherberg, Hopwood & Crew, 1919
Ded. 'To C. Albanesi Esq'
Dur. 5'05"

[1918]
A Romance
MS Lbm, Add ms 50178. Published: Ascherberg, Hopwood & Crew, 1919
Ded. 'To Miss Harriet Cohen'
Dur. 5'10"

1 July 1919
Whirligig
MS pc: Chester. Published: J. & W. Chester, 1919
Ded. 'To Miss Irene Scharrer'
Dur. 2'18"

26 July 1919
Piano Sonata No. 2 in G
MS Lbm, Add ms 54767. Published: Murdoch, 1921
Ded. 'To Miss Harriet Cohen'
First perf. Aeolian Hall / Arthur Alexander / 24 Nov. 1919; final version: Queen's Hall / Harriet Cohen / 15 June 1920
Dur. 24'02"–27'21"

[1919]
What the Minstrel Told Us (Ballad)
MS pc: Chester (another ms: Lbm, Add ms 54769). Published: Anglo-French Music Co., 1920
Ded. 'To Harriet Cohen'
Dur. 9'34"
First perf. Wigmore Hall / Harriet Cohen (pf) / 15 June 1920

[1919]
The Slave-Girl

MS Lost. Published: Anglo-French Music Co., 1920
Ded. 'To Madame Tamara Karsavina'
Dur. 4'05"
First perf. London Coliseum / H. Cohen (pf) / 29 Nov. 1920

27 April 1920
Lullaby (Berceuse)
MS Lost. Published: Murdoch, 1920
Ded. 'To Madame Tamara Karsavina'
Dur. 3'35"–3'41"
First perf. Wigmore Hall / Harriet Cohen (pf) / 15 June 1920

[1920]
Burlesque
MS Lost. Published: Murdoch, 1920
Ded. 'To Iso Elinson'
Dur. 3'01"–3'31"

[1920]
Country-Tune
MS Lost. Published: Murdoch, 1920
Dur. 2'02"

[1920]
The Devil That Tempted St Anthony
Lost
Later arranged for two pianos, q.v.

[1920]
A Hill Tune
MS Lost. Published: Murdoch, 1920
Dur. 3'07"–4'44"

[1920]
Mediterranean
MS Lost. Published: Murdoch, 1921
Dur. 3'07"
Later arranged for orchestra, and violin and piano, q.v.

[1920]
Pæan (Passacaglia)
MS Lost. Published: Murdoch, 1929
Ded. 'To Frank Merrick'
Dur. 3'07"
Later orchestrated, and arranged for organ, q.v.

[1920]
The Truth About the Russian Dancers [three excerpts for piano solo]
1. Ceremonial Dance; 2. Serpent Dance; 3. Water Music (see p. 000)
MS Lost. Published: Murdoch, 1929
Ded. 1: no dedication; 2: 'To Reginald Paul'; 3: 'To Lady George Cholmondeley'
Dur. 1: 3'26", 2: 3'22", 3: 4'27"–4'59"

[1921]
First Piano Sonata in F♯ minor
(1910–1917–1921)
MS Lost. Published: Murdoch, 1922
Dur. 18'26"–20'01"
First perf. (of final version) Wigmore Hall / Harriet Cohen / 12 April 1921

[May 1922]
Lento con Molto Espressione
MS Lbm, Add ms 54724 (unpublished)
Dur. 7'56"–9'15"
This is the original slow movement of the first symphony (written as Bax's third piano sonata), replaced by the more orchestral middle movement now known, when Bax decided to orchestrate the work. It is a fine and viable concert work on its own.

23 Nov. 1926
Third Piano Sonata in G♯ minor
MS Lbm, Add ms 54767. Published: Murdoch, 1929
Ded. 'To Miss Harriet Cohen'
Dur. I: 10'02"–10'59", II: 6'50"–8'19", III: 6'05"–6'51"
First perf. Liverpool Centre of the British Music Society / Harriet Cohen / 18 Nov. 1927

[1932]
Fourth Piano Sonata [in G major]
MS Lost. Published: Murdoch, 1934
Ded. 'To Charles Lynch'
Dur. I: 5'49", II; 5'24", III: 5'23"
First perf. Town Hall / New York / Harriet Cohen / 1 Feb. 1934
First UK perf. Wigmore Hall / Harriet Cohen / 18 May 1934

[1932]
Fantasia (Bach, transcribed Bax)
MS Lost. Published: OUP, 1932 (A Bach Book for Harriet Cohen)
Ded. 'For Harriet Cohen'
Dur. 5'56"
First perf. Queen's Hall / Harriet Cohen / 17 Oct. 1932

[1935]
Legends No. 1 [Legend]
MS pc (unpublished) (Dyeline copies of the ms were circulated privately by the dedicatee.)
Ded. 'To John Simons'
Dur. 6'19"–8'48"
First perf. BBC broadcast/John Simons (pf)/28 Aug. 1969
First public perf. BMIC/John Simons (pf)/14 Oct. 1983

[1936]
Piano Sonata in B♭ major. 'Salzburg' ('author unknown')
MS Lbm, Add ms 54769 (unpublished)
First perf. (II *Lento Espressivo* only) BMIC/Jonathan Higgins (pf)/21 April 1983/(*Dur.* 7'19")

[1945]
Suite for Fauré
MS F Pn, ms 9887; ms copy Lbm, Add ms 54770 (unpublished)
Later orchestrated, as *Variations on the Name Gabriel Fauré* q.v.

Dec. 1945
O Dame Get Up and Bake Your Pies: variations on a Northern Country carol
MS Lost. Published: Chappell, 1947
Ded. 'To Anna and Julian Herbage in acknowledgement of pies baked and enjoyed "on Christmas Day in the Morning" 1945'
Dur. 2'37"

30 Jan. 1947
Fantastic March
MS Lbm, Add ms 54770 (unpublished)
Dur. 4'46"
First perf. BMIC/Jonathan Higgins (pf)/21 April 1983

11 Feb. 1947
Romanza
MS Lbm, Add ms 54770 (unpublished)
Dur. 5'18"
First perf. BMIC/Jonathan Higgins (pf)/21 April 1983

19 Feb. 1947
Idyll: Allegretto Pastorale
MS Lbm, Add ms 54770 (unpublished)
Dur. 3'52"
First perf. BMIC/Jonathan Higgins (pf)/21 April 1983

12 March 1947
Phantasie (Allegro)
MS Lbm, Add ms 54770 (unpublished)
Dur. 5'01"
First perf. BMIC/Jonathan Higgins (pf)/21 April 1983

[1948]
Two Lyrical Pieces (from Oliver Twist)
MS Lost. Published: Chappell, 1948

[1950]
Slow Movement of the Left Hand Concertante
(Abridged version: arranged for piano solo (both hands) by Lloyd Webber)
MS Lost. Published: Chappell, 1950
Dur. 5'40"

[1951]
March: Malta GC
(Arranged for piano solo by Lloyd Webber)
MS Lost. Published: Chappell, 1951

(e) Choral music (unaccompanied or organ accompaniment)

1921
Mater Ora Filium (for unaccompanied double choir) (Carol — from a Manu-
script at Balliol College, Oxford)
MS Lost. Published: Murdoch, 1926
Ded. 'To C. Kennedy Scott'
Dur. 10'21"–10'24"
First perf. Queen's Hall / Oriana Madrigal Society / Scott / 13 Nov. 1922

13 March 1922
This Worldes Joie: motet for unaccompanied choir
(Spelt 'This World's Joy' on the ms)
MS EIRE C. Published: Murdoch, 1923
Ded. 'To W. G. Whittaker'
Dur. 5'50"
First perf. Queen's Hall / Philharmonic Choir / Scott / 5 June 1924

Jan. 1923
The Boar's Head for male voice choir (trad.)
(Testpiece for Blackpool music festival, 1923)
MS Lost. Published: Murdoch, 1923
Dur. 2'31"
First perf. Old Opera House, Blackpool / 20 Oct. 1923

[1923]
I Sing of a Maiden that is Makeless: unaccompanied part-song for five voices
(15th century)
MS Lost. Published: Murdoch, 1926
Ded. 'J. B. McEwen'
Dur. 5'13"

[1931]
Wonder ('Lord, Thou Hast Told Us That There Be Two Dwellings') (hymn tune)
(Wds: Thomas Washbourne)
Published: *Songs of Praise*, OUP 1931

[1944]
Five Greek Folksongs for SATB
(1. The Miracle of St Basil; 2. The Brides Maid's Song; 3. In Far-Off Malta; 4. The
Happy Tramp; 5. A Pilgrim's Chant.)
MS Lost. Published: Chappell, 1947
Dur. 11'01"
First perf. Cowdray Hall / BBC Singers / 11 Nov. 1946

[1945]
Nunc Dimittis for SATB and organ
MS Lost. Published: Chappell, 1945
Ded. 'To Eric Gillett'
Dur. 2'58"

[1945]
Te Deum for SATB and organ

MS Lost. Published: Chappell, 1945
Ded. 'To Sir Stanley Marchant'

21 Aug. 1945
Gloria (communion service) for SATB and organ
MS Lost. Published: Chappell, 1947
Ded. 'Horace A. Hawkins'
Dur. 5'20"

2 Sept. 1947
Epithalamium for SATB (in unison) and organ (wds: Edmund Spenser)
MS Lost. Published: Chappell, 1947

1948
Magnificat for SATB and organ
MS US NH; photostat Lbm, Ms facs 656. Published: Chappell, 1949
Ded. 'Dr Harold Darke'
Dur. 5'57"

Feb. 1953
What is it Like to be Young and Fair? (wds: Clifford Bax)
(Bax's contribution to 'A Garland for the Queen')
MS Draft, Lbm, Add ms 54775; ms lost, but photocopy held by the Arts Council of Great Britain. Published: Stainer & Bell (in *A Garland for the Queen*), 1953
Dur. 2'15"–2'21"
First perf. Royal Festival Hall / Cambridge Madrigal Society and The Golden Age Singers / Boris Ord / 1 June 1953

(f) Works for Pianola, Harpsichord and Organ

1920
Scherzo for pianola
(The scherzo of 1913, abridged for pianola roll)
Published: Piano rolls – Aeolian 1951; Universal Music Co. 513620; Broadwood Piano Co. 513620; Artistyle 93519

1945
Funeral March for organ ('Ruins' from *Malta GC*, arranged by W. H. Harris)
Published: Chappell, 1945

1946
Dance for harpsichord (from 'Golden Eagle' music)
MS pc: Chappell (unpublished)
Dur. 1'11"

1949
Pæan for organ
(The piano solo of 1920, arranged by Wm. Barr)
Published: Chappell, 1949
Dur. 3'07"

(g) Juvenilia

The following works by Bax, written in the period up to 1902, survive. This list does not attempt to classify, but merely lists them in chronological order of composition with their present location.

189?   Butterflies all white (song)

1897   Minuet for piano solo
           (31 Oct.) Variations on an air in G minor for piano solo; *MS* EIRE C

1898   Two Hungarian Dances for piano solo
           Three Mazurkas for piano solo
           Two Scherzi for piano solo
           Prelude in G major for piano solo   *MS* Lbm, Add
           Nocturne in B major for piano solo   ms 54768
           Sonata in D minor for piano
              ('No. 5' incomplete)
           Minuet in E minor, for eight instruments
              (?small orchestra)

1898   Sonata for piano [unnumbered]; *MS* EIRE C
           Symphonische Dichtung nach 'Rubaiyat' von Omar Khayyam, for orch.
              (piano score only); *MS* EIRE C

1900   Songs: (25 March) Wanting is — what? (Browning)
                 (4 April) To Daffodils (Herrick)
                 (7 April) A Serenade of Spring-Time ('Come out with me, come
                      out with me')
                      Ded. 'To my dear Nannie'
                 (13 May) I Love Thee! (Hans Andersen)
                 (25 May) Cytherea's Day (from *The Progress of Poesy*)
                 (10 Aug.) To the Moon (Shelley)
                 (10 Aug.) A Widow Bird sat mourning (Shelley)
                 (14 Aug.) To the Cuckoo (Wordsworth); *MS* Lbm, Add ms
                    54776
                 (15 Aug.) An Indian Serenade (Shelley)
                 (20 Aug.) To Phyllis (Sir Edward Dyers)
                 (20 Aug.) Phillida and Corydon (Nicholas Breton)
                 (23 Aug.) Why we Love and Why we Hate (Ambrose Philips)
                 —   Music When Soft Voices Die (Shelley)
                 —   The Soldier's Dream ('Our bugles sang') (?Thomas
                      Campbell)
           (28 Oct.) Fantasia in A minor for two pianos
           (26 April) Marcia Trionfale (short score only); *MS* Lbm, Add ms 54769

1901   (April) Intermezzo for clarinet and pianoforte; *MS* pc
           Violin Sonata in G minor (in one movement); *MS* pc
              Dur. 8'40"
              First perf. Aeolian Hall / Ivy Angove (vln) / A. Bax (pf) / 1st week in
              June 1907
           Ballet Suite: (1) lost; (2) Humoresque; (3) Russian Dance. Piano score
              MS Lbm, Add ms 54732
           (1 Sept.) Trio in B♭ minor: No. 1 Allegro Appassionata only; *MS* pc
           Songs: (4 Nov.) In Summer-time ('Songs of the Four Seasons' — No. 3)
                 —   It was a Lover and His Lass (Shakespeare) ('2 Songs of
                      the Springtime, No. 1) (plus sketch, vocal line only)
                      MS Lbm, Add ms 54776

          —   I will dream, I will dream, in my boat (Clifford Bax)
      Tegnér's Drapa (incomplete): voices and orchestra; *MS* Lbm, Add ms
          54775

1902   (21 Feb.) Love Song for Orchestra (piano score); *MS* Lbm, Add ms
       String Quartet in A; *MS* pc
       (Slow movement, *Andante in A*, performed at RAM Student Concert,
       St James's Hall, 23 Nov. 1903)

DISCOGRAPHY

This discography includes all known commercially-made recordings of Bax's music, with their various reissued numbers, so far as they are known. All records are taken to be 12 inch stereo LPs unless otherwise noted. Variants from this norm are abbreviated as follows:

(m)	mono	auto	auto-coupled set
78	78 rpm record	7"	7-inch record, revolving at 45 rpm
s	side(s)	10"	10-inch LP record, unless designated '78'
cas	cassette	CD	compact disc

Apple-Blossom-Time
Malcolm Binns (pf)
Pearl SHE 565

Ballad for Violin and Piano
Henry Holst (vln), Frank Merrick (pf)
Frank Merrick Society FMS 18(m)

The Boar's Head
Baccholian Singers
HMV CSD 3783

Burlesque, piano solo
Iris Loveridge (pf)
Lyrita RCS 26(m)

Richard Deering (pf)
Saga 5445

A Christmas Carol (words 15th century)
Jane Wilson (s), George Trovillo (pf)
US Decca DL 9554(m)

Dorothy Dorow (s), Susan Bradshaw (pf)
Jupiter JEP OC33(7"m)

— arr choir and organ
Canterbury Cathedral Choir/Stephen Darlington (org)/conducted by Allan Wicks
Grosvenor GRS 1034

Christmas Eve
London Philharmonic Orch/Malcolm Hicks (org)/Bryden Thomson
Chandos ABRD 1192; ABTD 1192 (cas); CHAN 8480 (CD)

Concerto for cello and orchestra
Raphael Wallfisch (vlc)/LPO/Bryden Thomson
Chandos ABRD 1204; ABTD 1204 (cas); CHAN 8494 (CD)

Coronation March (1953)
London Symphony Orch cond Sir Malcolm Sargent
Decca LXT 2793 (m); (reissued: LW 5057 (10"m); Ace of Clubs ACL 137(m);
Eclipse ECS 649; US-London LL804; LD 9046.)
London Festival Orch/Rogers
BR 1077
LPO/Sir Charles Mackerras
Reader's Digest RDS 8024
— arr organ (O'Brien)
Christopher Herrick (org)
Vista VPS 1055

Cortège
LPO/Bryden Thomson
Chandos ABRD 1204; ABTD 1204 (cas); CHAN 8494 (CD)

Country-Tune, piano solo
Iris Loveridge (pf)
Lyrita RCS 10(m)

Eric Parkin (pf)
Chandos ABRD 1206; ABTD 1206 (cas); CHAN 8496 (CD)

The Dance of Wild Irravel
LPO/Bryden Thomson
Chandos ABRD 1165; ABTD 1165 (cas); CHAN 8454 (CD)

The Devil That Tempted St Anthony
Ruth Harte & Vivian Langrish (2 pfs)
Bax Soc BAX LP 1(m)

Frank Merrick & Michael Round (2 pfs)
Cabaletta HRS 2004; CDN 5002

A Dream in Exile, piano solo
Iris Loveridge (pf)
Lyrita RCS 10(m)

Elegiac Trio
Martin Ruderman (fl), Milton Thomas (vla), Lois Craft (hp)
Alco ALP 1007(m); AC 205/3 (78,3s)
Christopher Hyde-Smith (fl), John Underwood (vla), Marisa Robles (hp)
Argo ZRG 574
Lucien Grujon (fl), Walter Mony (vla), Kathleen Alister (hp)
RPM RPM 1038S (reissued: Westminster WGS-8196)

The Enchanted Fiddle (words 'Dermot O'Byrne')
Norma Burrowes (s), Noel Skinner (pf)
Bax Society BAX LP 1(m)

The Fairies
Christopher Gillett (t), David Owen Norris (pf)
Ensemble TRI 002 (cas only)

Fanfare for a Cheerful Occasion
Kneller Hall Trumpeters/Capt H.E. Adkins
HMV C 2445 (78)

(2) Fanfares for the Royal Wedding
Trumpeters of the Royal Military School of Music/
Capt M. Roberts
HMV B 9616 (10" 78)
— No 1 only
Royal Marine Band/Dunn
Columbia TWO 285
Scots Guards/Ian Bent
EMI EMC 3179

— No 2 only
Philip Jones Brass Ensemble
Decca SDD 274; SPA 419; SPA 500 KCSP500 (cas)

Fantasy Sonata for Harp and Viola
Maria Korchinska (hp), Raymond Jeremy (vla)
National Gramophonic Society NGS 118/120 (78)

Maria Korchinska (hp), Watson Forbes (vla)
Decca AK 941/943 (78)

Margaret Ross (hp), Emanuel Vardi (vla)
Musical Heritage Society MHS 3613

Susann McDonald (hp), Milton Thomas (vla)
Klavier KS-570

Imogen Barford (hp), Michael Ponder (vla)
Ensemble ENS 136 (cas only)

Far in a Western Brookland (words Housman)
Graham Trew (bar), Roger Vignoles (pf)
Meridian E 77031/2

Five Fantasies on Polish Christmas Carols
St Angela's Singers/Divertimenti/Peter Broadbent
Ensemble ENS 136 (cas only)

Five Greek Folksongs
BBC Northern Singers/Stephen Wilkinson
Hyperion A 66092

Folk-Tale, cello and piano
Florence Hooton (vlc), Wilfrid Parry (pf)
Lyrita RCS 7 (m)

Moray Welsh (vlc), Roger Vignoles (pf)
Pearl SHE 571

Four Pieces for Flute and Piano
Kathleen Moy (fl), John Simons (pf)
Ensemble TRIAD 001 (cas only)

Frühlingsregen (Spring Rain)
Christopher Gillett (t), David Owen Norris (pf)
Ensemble TRI 002 (cas only)

The Garden of Fand
Royal Philharmonic Orchestra/Sir Thomas Beecham
HMV DB 6654/5 (78); HQM 1165(m); Odeon PHQM 1165(m)
Hallé Orch/Sir John Barbirolli
PYE CCT 31000(10''m); GGC4061(m); GSGC 14061; GSGC 15017; GSGC
2059; ZGGC 2059 (cas); Mercury MG 50115(m); MG 90115(m)
London Philharmonic Orch/Sir Adrian Boult
Lyrita SRCS 62; HNH sic 4034 and box 4080x; Musical Heritage Soc MHS 1769
Ulster Orch/Bryden Thomson
Chandos ABRD 1066; ABTD 1066; CHAN 8307 (CD)

Glamour
Christopher Gillett (t), David Owen Norris (pf)
Ensemble TRI 002 (cas only)

The Happy Forest
London Symphony Orch/Edward Downes
RCA SB 6806; GL 42247

Ulster Orch/Bryden Thomson
Chandos ABRD 1066; ABTD 1066; CHAN 8307 (CD)

Hardanger
Ethel Bartlett & Rae Robertson (2 pfs)
National Gramophonic Society NGS 158 (78)
Frank Merrick & Michael Round (2 pfs)
Cabaletta HRS 2004; CDN 5002

A Hill Tune, piano
Harriet Cohen (pf)
Columbia DX 1109 (78)
Iris Loveridge (pf)
Lyrita RCS 10(m)
Frank Merrick (pf)
Frank Merrick Society FMS 8(m); Rare Recorded Edition SRRE 129
Eric Parkin (pf)
Chandos ABRD 1207; ABTD 1207 (cas); CHAN 8497 (CD)

I Heard a Soldier
Peter Savidge (bar), David Owen Norris (pf)
Ensemble TRI 002 (cas only)

I Sing of a Maiden That is Makeless
Norwich Cathedral Choir/Michael Nicholas
Vista VPS 1084

BBC Northern Singers/Stephen Wilkinson
Hyperion A 66092
King's College Choir/Nicholas Cleobury
EMI EL 270440-1; EL 270440-4 (cas)

In a Vodka Shop
Iris Loveridge (pf)
Lyrita RCS 12

Eric Parkin (pf)
Chandos ABRD 1207; ABTD 1207 (cas); CHAN 8497 (CD)

In the Faery Hills
Ulster Orch/Bryden Thomson
Chandos ABRD 1133; ABTD 1133 (cas); CHAN 8367 (CD)

Into the Twilight
Ulster Orch/Bryden Thomson
Chandos ABRD 1133; ABTD 1133 (cas); CHAN 8367 (CD)

(5) Irish Songs
— No 3: I heard a Piper Piping (words Campbell)
Astra Desmond (c), Gerald Moore (pf)
Decca M 522 (10" 78)

Norma Burrowes (s), Noel Skinner (pf)
Bax Society: BAX LP 1 (m)

(3) Irish Songs (1 Cradle Song, 2 Rann of Exile, 3 Rann of Wandering)
(words Colum)
— complete: Mary O'Brien (s), Lincoln Mayorga (pf)
Town Hall S-22

— 1 and 2: Anne Thursfield (m-s) with piano
HMV E 410 (10" 78)

— 1: Kirsten Flagstad (s), Waldemar Almo (pf)
Golden Age of Opera EJS338(m)

— 1: Norma Burrowes (s), Noel Skinner (pf)
Bax Society: BAX LP 1 (m)

— 2: Peter Dawson (bar), Gerald Moore (pf)
HMV B 8866 (10" 78)

— 2: Peter Savidge (bar), David Owen Norris (pf)
Ensemble TRI 002 (cas only)

Legend for violin and piano
Henry Holst (vln), Frank Merrick (pf)
Frank Merrick Society FMS 21 (m)

Legend for viola and piano
Watson Forbes (vla), Leonard Cassini (pf)
Delta DEL 12028(m); Summit LSU 3058(m), TLS 6063; Concert Artist
SRCAM 5008; ATL-TC 5001 (cas) Hayward Recordings HCR 5260; Dover
5260; HCR 7012

Legend-Sonata for cello and piano
Florence Hooton (vlc), Wilfrid Parry (pf)
Lyrita RCS 6(m); Musical Heritage Society MHS 7(m)

Lento, piano (original slow movement of First Symphony) see *Sonata for piano in E♭*

John Simons (pf)
Ensemble TRI 002 (cas only)

Lullaby, piano
Frank Merrick (pf)
Frank Merrick Society FMS 7(m)

Iris Loveridge (pf)
Lyrita RCS 12(m)

Eric Parkin (pf)
Chandos ABRD 1206; ABTD 1206 (cas); CHAN 8496 (CD)

Magnificat
BBC Northern Singers/Keith Swallow (pf)/Stephen Wilkinson
Hyperion A 66092

The Maiden with the Daffodil, piano solo
Iris Loveridge (pf)
Lyrita RCS 12(m)

Malta GC: music for the film
— complete score
Royal Philharmonic Orch/Kenneth Alwyn
Cloud Nine CN 7012
— Quiet Interlude and Gay March (only)
London Symphony Orch/Muir Mathieson
London T 5054 (10" 78)
— 'Introduction and March'
City of Birmingham SO/Marcus Dods
HMV ASD 3797; ED 290109-1 ED 290109-14 (cas)

Mater Ora Filium
Leeds Festival Chorus (1925)/Albert Coates
HMV D 1044/5(78,3s)
BBC Chorus/Leslie Woodgate
Columbia ROX 179/82(78,4s); ROX 8041/39(78auto).
US Columbia 11156/7D, set M 386 (English Music Society Vol 2)

BBC Northern Singers/Stephen Wilkinson
Hyperion A 66092

King's College Choir/Nicholas Cleobury
EMI EL 270440-1; EL 270440-4 (cas)

Mediterranean, piano solo
Eugène D'Albert (pf)
Polydor 66032 (78); Veritas VM 110(m); Concert Artist CH4-TC-4013 (cas only)

Iris Loveridge (pf)
Lyrita RCS 10(m)
— arr 3 hands 2 pianos (Rich)

Cyril Smith and Phyllis Sellick (3 hands 2 pfs)
HMV CLP 3563(m); CSD 3563

— orchestrated by Bax
New Symphony Orchestra/Eugène Goossens
HMV C 1620(78); US Victor 9788(78)

LPO/Boult
Lyrita RCS 62; Musical Heritage Society MHS 1769; HNH HNH 4034 and box
4080x

LPO/Bryden Thomson
Chandos ABRD 1204; ABTD 1204 (cas); CHAN 8494 (CD)

— arranged by Jascha Heifetz for violin and piano
Jascha Heifetz (vln), Emmanuel Bay (pf)
Victor 10-1293(78) HMV EC 193(78). IN set ARM 4-0946(m)

Morning Song (Maytime in Sussex) for piano and orchestra
Harriet Cohen (pf)/orch/Sir Malcolm Sargent
Columbia DX 1361(78); DX 1838 (78); HMV HLM 7148(m)

A Mountain Mood, piano solo
Harriet Cohen (pf)
Columbia DX 1109(78)

John Clegg (pf)
Alpha 148c

Moy Mell, the Pleasant Plain
Ethel Bartlett and Rae Robertson (2 pfs)
National Gramophonic Society NGS 102 (78)

Frank Merrick and Michael Round (2 pfs)
Cabaletta HRS 2004; CDN 5002

— arranged 3 hands 2 pianos
Cyril Smith and Phyllis Sellick (3 hands at 2 pianos)
MK D-011283-4(m) D-003150(m)

Nonett
Joseph Slater (fl), Leon Goossens (ob), Frederick Thurston (cl), Maria Korchinska
(hp), Griller String Quartet, Victor Watson (db)
Columbia ROX 182/4(78 4s); (English Music Society Vol 2)

Northern Ballad No. 1
LPO/Boult
Lyrita SRCS 62; Musical Heritage Society MHS 1769; HNH HNH 4034, and box
4080x

Northern Ballad No. 2
RPO/Vernon Handley
Chandos ABRD 1180; ABTD 1180 (cas); CHAN 8464 (CD)

Northern Ballad No. 3 (Prelude for a Solemn Occasion)
LPO/Bryden Thomson
Chandos ABRD 1204; ABTD 1204 (cas); CHAN 8494 (CD)

November Woods
LPO/Boult
Lyrita SRCS 37

Ulster Orch/Bryden Thomson
Chandos ABRD 1066; ABTD 1066 (cas); CHAN 8307 (CD)

Nympholept
LPO/Bryden Thomson
Chandos ABRD 1203; ABTD 1203 (cas); CHAN 8473 (CD)

O Dame Get Up and Bake Your Pies, piano solo
Iris Loveridge (pf)
Lyrita RCS 12(m)

Of a Rose I Sing a Song
BBC Northern Singers/Charlotte Seal (hp), David Fletcher (vlc), Jeffrey Box
(db)/Stephen Wilkinson
Hyperion A 66092

Oliver Twist: music for the film
Prelude; The Storm; The Fight; Oliver's Sleepless Night; Oliver and the Artful
Dodger; Fagin's Romp; The Chase; Oliver and Brownlow; Nancy and Brown-
low: Finale
Eric Parkin (pf)/Royal Philharmonic Orch/Kenneth Alwyn
Cloud Nine CN 7012

'The Oliver Theme'; Pickpocketing; The Chase; Fagin's Romp; Finale
Harriet Cohen (pf)/Philharmonia Orch/Muir Mathieson
Columbia DX 1516/7 (78 4s); American Columbia MX 330(78); ML 2092
(10"m); Ariel CBF 13

— Fagin's Romp; Finale
National SO/Bernard Herrmann
Decca PFS 4363; Pf 54363 (cas); 411837-1 1DV; 411837-4DV (cas);
London SPC 21149

On the Sea-Shore (orch. realised Parlett)
Ulster Orch/Vernon Handley
Chandos ABRD 1184; ABTD 1184 (cas); CHAN 8473 (CD)

Overture, Elegy and Rondo
Forthcoming

Overture to a Picaresque Comedy
London Philharmonic Orch/Harty
Columbia LX 394 (78 2s)

New York Philharmonic Symphony Orch/Mitropoulos
Off The Air Record Club 8(m)

Royal Philharmonic Orch/Igor Buketoff
RCA Victor RB 6730(m) SB 6730 (US) LM 3005(m); LSC 3005

London Philharmonic Orch/Bryden Thomson
Chandos ABRD 1204; ABTD 1204 (cas); CHAN 8494 (CD)

Pæan, for orchestra
London Philharmonic Orch/Bryden Thomson
Chandos ABRD 1165; ABTD 1165 (cas); CHAN 8454 (CD)

Pæan, piano solo
Harriet Cohen (pf)
Columbia DB 1786 (10" 78)

Frank Merrick (pf)
Frank Merrick Society FMS 3 (m)

Iris Loveridge (pf)
Lyrita RCS 11 (m)

Piano Quartet
John McCabe (pf)/English String Quartet
Chandos ABRD 1113; ABTD 1113 (cas)

(3) Pieces for Orchestra
— 2 Irish Landscape
Royal Philharmonic Orch/Vernon Handley
Lyrita SRCS 99

— 3 Dance in the Sun
English Sinfonia/Neville Dilkes
HMV CSD 3696; Greensleeve ESD 7100; TC-ESD 7100 (cas)

The Poisoned Fountain
Arthur Whittemore and Jack Lowe (2 pfs)
Victor LM 1705 (m); WDM 1705 (7" m)

Arthur Whittemore and Jack Lowe (2 pfs)
Capitol P 8550 (m); SP 8550

Ruth Harte and Vivian Langrish (2 pfs)
Bax Society BAX LP 1 (m)

Frank Merrick and Michael Round (2 pfs)
Cabaletta HRS 2004; CDN 5002

Prelude for a Solemn Occasion see *Northern Ballad No. 3*

The Princess's Rose Garden, piano solo
Malcolm Binns (pf)
Pearl SHE 565

Quintet for Harp and Strings
Laura Newell (hp)/Stuyvesant String Quartet
Philharmonia PH 102 (m); PH 119 (m)

Skaila Kauga (hp)/English String Quartet
Chandos ABRD 1113; ABTD 1113 (cas)

Quintet for Oboe and Strings
Leon Goossens (ob)/International String Quartet
National Gramophonic Society NGS 76/7 (78 4s)

Earl Schuster (ob)/Classic String Quartet
Classic Editions CE 1030 (m)

I. Wilson (ob)/Hoffman String Quartet
Brolga [Australian] BZM 06 (m)

Helen Powell (ob), Sylvia Sutton (vln), Avril MacLennon (vln), Janet Schlapp (vla), Robert Glenton (vlc)
Bax Society BAX LP 1 (m)

Bert Lucarelli (ob)/Manhatten String Quartet
Musical Heritage Society MHS 3521

Sarah Francis (ob)/English String Quartet
Chandos ABRD 1114; ABTD 1114 (cas)

Rhapsodic Ballad
Rohan de Saram (vlc)
Pearl SHE 547

Raphael Wallfisch (vlc)
Chandos, ABRD 1209; CHAN 8499 (CD); ABTD 1209 (cas)

A Romance, piano solo
Iris Loveridge (pf)
Lyrita RCS 26 (m)

Roscatha
Ulster Orch/Bryden Thomson
Chandos ABRD 1133; ABTD 1133 (cas); CHAN 8367 (CD)

Roundel
Peter Savidge (bar), David Owen Norris (pf)
Ensemble TRI 002 (cas only)

(2) Russian Tone Pictures, piano solo
(1 Nocturne: May Night in the Ukraine; 2 Gopak)

1 and 2: Iris Loveridge (pf)
Lyrita RCS 26 (m)

Saga Fragment
Margaret Fingerhut (pf)/LPO/Bryden Thomson
Chandos ABRD 1195; ABTD 1195 (cas); CHAN 8484 (CD)

Scherzo, piano solo
Malcolm Binns (pf)
Pearl SHE 565

Scherzo, orchestrated as *Symphonic Scherzo*, q.v.

Sinfonietta
Slovak Philharmonic/Barry Wordsworth
Marco Polo 8.223 102 (CD)

The Slave-Girl, piano solo
Malcolm Binns (pf)
Pearl SHE 565

Sleepy Head, piano solo
Iris Loveridge (pf)
Lyrita RCS 26 (m)

Sonata in E♭ for cello and piano
Florence Hooton (vlc), Wilfrid Parry (pf)
Lyrita RCS 7 (m); Musical Heritage Society MHS 7016 (m)

Sonata in D major for Clarinet and Piano
Stanley Drucker (cl), Leonid Hambro (pf)
Odyssey Y 30492

John Denman (cl), Hazel Vivienne (pf)
Revolution RCF 009

Janet Hilton (cl), Keith Swallow (pf)
Chandos ABRD 1078; ABTD 1078 (cas); *also in set* DBRD 4001; DBTD 4001 (cas)

Sonata for Piano No. 1
Iris Loveridge (pf)
Lyrita RCS 10(m); Musical Heritage Society MHS 7011(m)

Frank Merrick (pf)
Frank Merrick Society FMS 7(m)

Joyce Hatto (pf)
Revolution RCF 010; FED-TC-011 (cas)

Eric Parkin (pf)
Chandos ABRD 1206; ABTD 1206 (cas); CHAN 8496 (CD)

Sonata for Piano No. 2
Frank Merrick (pf)
Frank Merrick Society FMS 6(m)

Iris Loveridge (pf)
Lyrita RCS 11(m); Musical Heritage Society MHS 7012(m)

Peter Cooper (pf)
PYE GGC 4045(m); GSGC 14045; GSGC 2061; ZGGC 2061 (cas)

Malcolm Binns (pf)
Pearl SHE 565

Eric Parkin (pf)
Chandos ABRD 1206; ABTD 1206 (cas); CHAN 8496 (CD)

Sonata for Piano in E♭ (original version of Symphony No. 1)
Noemy Belinkaya (pf)
Ensemble EMS 136 (cas only)

— *Lento con molto espressione* only
John Simons (pf)
Ensemble TRIAD 001 (cas only)

Sonata for Piano No. 3
Frank Merrick (pf)
Frank Merrick Society FMS 7(m)

Iris Loveridge (pf)
Lyrita RCS 12(m); Musical Heritage Society MHS 7013(m)

Eric Parkin (pf)
Chandos ABRD 1207; ABTD 1207 (cas); CHAN 8497 (CD)

Sonata for Piano No. 4
Iris Loveridge (pf)
Lyrita RCS 26(m); Musical Heritage Society MHS 7014(m)
Frank Merrick (pf)
Frank Merrick Society FMS 7(m)

Joyce Hatto (pf)
Revolution RCF 010; FED-TC-011 (cas)

Eric Parkin (pf)
Chandos ABRD 1207; ABTD 1207 (cas); CHAN 8497 (CD)

— slow movement only
John McCabe (pf)
Decca SDD 444

Sonata for Two Pianos
Ethel Bartlett and Rae Robertson (2 pfs)
National Gramophonic Society NGS 156/158 (78 5s)

Frank Merrick and Michael Round (2 pfs)
Cabaletta HRS 2004; CDN 5002

Sonata for Viola and Piano
Lionel Tertis (vla), Arnold Bax (pf)
Pearl GEMM 201(m)

William Primrose (vla), Harriet Cohen (pf)
Columbia ROX 179/182; ROX 8039/45auto; IN English Music Society Vol 2;
US Columbia 11181/4D, set M 386 (English Music Society Vol 2)

Herbert Downes (vla), Leonard Cassini (pf)
Delta DEL 12028(m); Summit LSU 3073(m); Revolution RCB 1

Emanuel Vardi (vla), Abba Bogin (pf)
Musical Heritage Society MHS 3613

Milton Thomas (vla), Doris Stevenson (pf)
Klavier KS-570

Michael Ponder (vla), John Alley (pf)
Ensemble ENS 123 (cas only)

Sonata for Violin and Piano No. 1
Henry Holst (vln), Frank Merrick (pf)
Concert Artist LPA 1099(m); Revolution RCB 20

Sonata for Violin and Piano No. 2
Henry Holst (vln), Frank Merrick (pf)
Frank Merrick Society FMS 18(m)

Sonata for Violin and Piano No. 3
Henry Holst (vln), Frank Merrick (pf)
Frank Merrick Society FMS 18(m)

Sonatina for cello and piano
Florence Hooton (vlc), Wilfrid Parry (pf)
Lyrita RCS 6(m)

Spring Fire
RPO/Vernon Handley
Chandos ABRD 1180; ABTD 1180 (cas); CHAN 8464 (CD)

String Quartet No. 1
Wilson String Quartet
National Gramophonic Society NGS 153/5 (78)

Griller String Quartet
Decca K 1009/12 (78)

English String Quartet
Chandos ABRD 1113; ABTD 1113 (cas)

String Quartet No. 3
Amici String Quartet
Gaudeamus KRS 31

Summer Music
Ulster Orch/Bryden Thomson
Chandos ABRD 1066; ABTD 1066 (cas); CHAN 8307 (CD)

Symphonic Scherzo
RPO/Vernon Handley
Chandos ABRD 1180; ABTD 1180 (cas); CHAN 8464 (CD)

Symphonic Variations for piano and orchestra
Joyce Hatto (pf)/Guildford Philharmonic Orch/Vernon Handley
Revolution RCF 001; FED-TC-001 (cas)

Symphony No. 1
LPO/Fredman
Lyrita SRCS 53; Musical Heritage Society MHS 1586
LPO/Bryden Thomson
Chandos ABRD 1192; ABTD 1192 (cas); CHAN 8480 (CD)
(see also: *Sonata for Piano in E♭*)

Symphony No. 2
LPO/Fredman
Lyrita SRCS 54; Musical Heritage Society MHS 1632
LPO/Bryden Thomson
Chandos ABRD 1203; ABTD 1203 (cas); CHAN 8493 (CD)

Symphony No. 3
Hallé Orch/Barbirolli
HMV C 3380/5(78); C 7593/8 (78auto); EX 290107-3; EX 290107-5 (cas)
LSO/Downes
RCA SB 6806; GL 42247

LPO/Bryden Thomson
Chandos ABRD 1165; ABTD 1165 (cas); CHAN 8454 (CD)

Symphony No. 4
Guildford Philharmonic Orch/Vernon Handley
Concert Artist LPA 1097; Revolution RCF 002; FED-TC-009 (cas)

Ulster Orch/Bryden Thomson
Chandos ABRD 1091; ABTD 1091 (cas); CHAN 8312 (CD)

Symphony No. 5
LPO/Raymond Leppard
Lyrita SRCS 58; Musical Heritage Society MHS 1652

Symphony No. 6
New Philharmonia Orch/Norman del Mar
Lyrita RCS 35(m); SRCS 35; Musical Heritage Society MHS 1198

Symphony No. 7
LPO/Raymond Leppard
Lyrita SRCS 83; HNH HNH 4010

The Tale the Pine-Trees Knew
Guildford Philharmonic Orch/Vernon Handley
Concert Artist LPA 2002; Revolution RCF 003

Ulster Orch/Bryden Thomson
Chandos ABRD 1133; ABTD 1133 (cas); CHAN 8367 (CD)

This Worldes Joie
BBC Northern Singers/Stephen Wilkinson
Hyperion A 66092

Tintagel
New Symphony Orch/Goossens
HMV C 1619/20(78 3s); Victor 9887/8 (78 3s)
LSO/George Weldon
Columbia 33SX 1010(m); CCT 655 (7½"ps tape) (m)
LPO/Boult
Decca LXT 5015(m); Ace of Clubs ACL 113(m); London LL 1169(m); CM
9122(m)
LSO/Barbirolli
HMV ALP 2305(m); ASD 2305; ESD 7092; TC-ESD 7092 (cas); Angel 36415
LPO/Boult
Lyrita SRCS 62; Musical Heritage Society MHS 7016; HNH HNH 4034, and box
4080x

Ulster Orch/Bryden Thomson
Chandos ABRD 1091; ABTD 1091 (cas); CHAN 8312 (CD)

To Eire
Peter Savidge (bar), David Owen Norris (pf)
Ensemble TRI 002 (cas only)

Toccata, piano solo
Joyce Hatto (pf)
Revolution RCF 010; FED-TC-011 (cas)

The Truth About the Russian Dancers (three dances arranged for piano)
(1 Ceremonial Dance; 2 Serpent Dance; 3 Water Music)
1–3: Iris Loveridge (pf)
Lyrita RCS 10(m)
— 3 Eric Parkin (pf)
Chandos ABRD 1207; ABTD 1207 (cas); CHAN 8497 (CD)
— 3 Joyce Hatto (pf)
Revolution RCF 010; FED-TC-011 (cas)

Traditional Songs of France
— 1 Sarabande
Peter Savidge (bar), David Owen Norris (pf)

Ensemble TRI 002 (cas only)
— 3 Me Suis Mise en Danse
Janet Baker (ms), Gerald Moore (pf)
HMV ASD 2929

Treue Liebe
Peter Savidge (bar), David Owen Norris (pf)
Ensemble TRI 002 (cas only)

Trio in B♭
Borodin Trio
Chandos ABRD 1205; ABTD 1205 (cas); CHAN 8495 (CD)

Trio in One Movement
Elizabeth Holborn (vln), Thomas Tatton (vla), Robert MacSparren (pf)
Ensemble TRIAD 001 (cas only)

What is it Like to be Young and Fair? (wds: Clifford Bax)
Cambridge University Madrigal Society/Boris Ord
Columbia 33CX 1063 (m)
Exultate Singers/Gareth O'Brien
RCA GL 25062; GK 25062 (cas)

What the Minstrel Told Us, piano solo
Iris Loveridge (pf)
Lyrita RCS 11 (m)
The White Peace (wds: 'Fiona Macleod')
John McCormack (t), Gerald Moore (pf)
HMV DA 1791 (10" 78); HMV Ireland IR 299 (10" 78); HQM 1176 (m); HLM 3037
Kirsten Flagstad (s), Waldemar Almo (pf)
Golden Age of Opera EJS 238 (m)
Frederick Harvey (bar), Gerald Moore (pf)
HMV CLP 3587 (m), CSD 3587
Norma Burrowes (s), Noel Skinner (pf)
Bax Society BAX LP 1 (m)

Winter Legends
Margaret Fingerhut (pf)/LPO/Bryden Thomson
Chandos ABRD 1195; ABTD 1195 (cas); CHAN 8484 (CD)

Winter Waters, piano solo
Iris Loveridge (pf)
Lyrita RCS 12 (m)
Eric Parkin (pf)
Chandos ABRD 1206; ABTD 1206 (cas); CHAN 8496 (CD)

Youth
Peter Savidge (bar), David Owen Norris (pf)
Ensemble TRI 002 (cas only)

BIBLIOGRAPHY

This bibliography does not completely supersede that in *Current Musicology* No. 10 (see below). Only the more important items from that work are relisted here, together with *all* the citations in its supplement, and all items noted since. Sources cited in the notes (see pp. 388–401) are not necessarily listed again here.

Abraham, G. E. H.: 'The Two Bax Sonatas' (Six British Piano Sonatas – 3). *Music Teacher*, July 1926, pp. 418–19.

Balanchine, G. *and* Mason, F.: 'Picnic at Tintagel' in their *Balanchine's Festival of Ballet*. W. H. Allen, 1978, pp. 429–32.
    The story of Ashton's ballet to *The Garden of Fand*.

Bannard, Y.: 'Arnold Bax, Magician'. *Musical Standard*, 13 Oct. 1917.
    With a photograph.

Barrie, J. M.: 'The Truth About the Russian Dancers; introduced by Tamara Karsavina'. *Dance Perspectives*, Spring 1962 – no. 14, 42 pp.
    Contains the full text of Barrie's play, published for the first time; also illustrations of the production and reprints of selected criticism. This issue is now out of print and very scarce, but a reprint was issued by the Johnson Reprint Corp., N.Y., 1970.

Bax, Clifford: *Inland Far*. Heinemann, 1925.
— *Ideas and People*. Lovat Dickson, 1936.
    Two autobiographical volumes by the composer's brother which also contain illuminating comment on Arnold Bax himself. In the former, Chapters XIV and XV (pp. 204–36) contain interesting references to the composer but also mention Holst and others. In the second, references to Bax will be found on pp. 60, 99, 123, 189–206, 235–6.

Bax Society Bulletin. Duplicated periodical of the Bax Society, 1968–1973. There were 11 issues.
    Important articles that have appeared in this publication are indexed under their respective authors.

Bliss, [Sir] A.: 'Recent Works of Arnold Bax'. *Musical News and Herald*, 21 May 1921, p. 625.
— 'Berners and Bax'. *League of Composers Review*, Feb. 1924, pp. 26–7.
    A short note by the composer who much later succeeded Bax as Master of the Musick.

— 'Arnold Bax 1883–1953'. *Music & Letters*, Jan. 1954, pp. 1–14.
  A collection of tributes published shortly after Bax's death. The nine musicians who contributed are: Sir Arthur Bliss, Arthur Benjamin (including part of a correspondence between Benjamin and Bax), York Bowen, Eric Coates, Patrick Hadley, Peter Latham, Bernard Shore, R. Vaughan Williams, and Sir William Walton.

Blom, E.: 'Arnold Bax'. *Chesterian*, Feb. 1920, pp. 136–9.
  Part of this article was reprinted by Norman Demuth in his *An Anthology of Musical Criticism*, Eyre & Spottiswoode, 1947, pp. 358–9.

— 'A Revival of the Carol' (Studies at Random – XVI). *Musical Opinion*, Nov. 1922, p. 144.

— *Programme of Concert of Recent Works of Arnold Bax*. Queen's Hall, London, Monday, 13 Nov. 1922. Programme notes by Eric Blom. vii, 24 pp.
  As well as a general introduction to Bax's music, it includes analyses of: *The Garden of Fand*; Songs: 'The Market Girl', 'I Heard a Piper Piping', 'Green Grow the Rashes O!'; *Piano Sonata No. 2; Mater Ora Filium; Phantasy* for Viola and Orchestra; *Four Traditional Songs of France*; Piano solos: 'A Hill Tune'; 'Lullaby'; 'Burlesque'; Carols: 'Of A Rose I sing'; 'Now is the Time of Christymas'; *Mediterranean* for Orchestra.

— 'Arnold Bax's [First] Symphony'. *Manchester Guardian*, 14 Jan. 1924.
  Reprinted in *Bax Society Bulletin*, Oct. 1968 – no. 3, pp. 44–5.

— 'The Carol Revived'. In his *Stepchildren of Music*, G. T. Foulis, nd [1926], pp. 277–83.

— 'Bax's Symphony No. 2'. *Music Teacher*, April 1931, pp. 195–6.

— 'Arnold Bax's Piano Sonatas'. *Listener*, 12 Oct. 1944, p. 417.

Brian, Havergal: 'The First Symphony of Arnold Bax'. *Musical Opinion*, Dec. 1922, pp. 253–4.
  In a letter addressed to the present writer, dated 3 Oct. 1966, the veteran composer Havergal Brian wrote: 'When he [Bax] finished his first symphony, I wrote an article about it which appeared in *Musical Opinion* ... Bax was pleased and at that time I was working on my Gothic symphony: I suggested to him that if ever the Gothic was published he should do the same for it as I had done for his first symphony. He agreed. Years later when the Gothic was published I posted a copy of the full score to him. ... Arnold returned the score and said "I am sorry – I should never dare write about such a work without first hearing it".'

Chester, J. & W. *publishers: Arnold Bax*. (Miniature Essay Series) 1921, 16 pp.
  Parallel English and French texts; this essay was reprinted in a German translation in the programme of the International Society for Contemporary Music, on the occasion of the performance of Bax's first symphony in Prague, 1 June 1924.

Church, R.: 'The Story of Tintagel in a Bax Tone Poem'. (Music Masterpieces of the Week – XXIV.) *Radio Times*, 24 April 1931, p. 189.

Cohen, H.: 'Arnold Bax – Nereid'. In her *Music's Handmaid*. Faber, 1936, pp. 153–60.

— *A Bundle of Time*. Faber, 1969.

Colum, Mary: *Life and the Dream*. Macmillan, 1947.
  Bax described on pp. 103, 185, 188, 301–2, 421.

Cooper, M.: 'John Ireland et Arnold Bax'. In his *Les Musiciens Anglais d'Aujourd'hui*, Paris, Plon, 1952, pp. 61–73.
  The section on Bax is on pp. 66–73; the English original from which this French version was translated was never published.

Cox, D.: 'Arnold Bax'. In *The Symphony*, ed. R. Simpson, vol. 2. Penguin Books, 1967, pp. 153–65.

Cronin, *Sister* K.: *The Celtic Literary Influence in the songs of Arnold Bax*. MA thesis, Mt St Mary College, Los Angeles, Calif., July 1967.
— Bax in the Modern Media. *Bax Society Bulletin*, Feb. 1969, no. 4, pp. 57–60.

Daily Telegraph: 'Italian Critics of Bax'. 25 Nov. 1935 (reprinted in *Bax Society Bulletin*, no. 6, Aug. 1969, pp. 103–4).

Dale, S. S.: 'Contemporary Cello Concerti XVI – Sir Arnold Bax'. *Strad*, Feb. 1974, pp. 591, 593, 595.

Demuth, N.: 'Sir Arnold Bax'. In his *Musical Trends in the Twentieth Century*, Rockliffe, 1952, pp. 155–67.
   At the time one of the best published accounts on Bax, particularly help-ful on the choral music.

Evans, E.: 'Arnold Bax's Piano Music'. *Chesterian*, June 1918, pp. 213–16.
— 'Arnold Bax'. (Modern British Composers no. 2) *Musical Times*, March 1919, pp. 103–5, April 1919, pp. 154–6.
   The April issue contains an important early list of works.
— 'November Woods'. *Sackbut*, Feb. 1922, pp. 33–4.
— 'Arnold Bax'. *Musical Quarterly*, April 1923, pp. 167–80.
— 'Bax, Arnold Edward Trevor'. In *A Dictionary of Modern Music and Musicians*, ed. A. Eaglefield-Hull and others. Dent, 1924, pp. 32–4.
— 'Arnold Bax'. *Modern Music*, Nov.–Dec. 1927, pp. 25–30.
— 'Bax'. In *Cobbett's Cyclopaedic Survey of Chamber Music*, OUP, 1929; 2nd. ed. 1963, vol. 1, pp. 67–78.
— 'Master of the King's Musick'. *Time & Tide*, 28 Feb. 1942, p. 172.
   A background to the office and discussion of Bax's prowess as a sight reader in scores like Strauss's *Ein Heldenleben*.
— 'The Bax Symphonies'. *Listener*, 29 Oct. 1942, p. 573.
— 'Arnold Bax, Hunter of Dreams'. *Listener*, 4 Jan. 1945, p. 25.
— 'Bax'. In *Grove's Dictionary of Music and Musicians*, Macmillan, 5th ed., 1954, vol. 1, pp. 509–12. Also supplement, 1961, p. 27.

Fleischmann, *Prof.* A.: 'The Arnold Bax Memorial'. *UCC Record* [University College, Cork], Easter 1956 – no. 31, pp. 25–30.
   Account of the Bax Memorial Room at Cork, with useful illustrations. The identification of 'The Concertante' mentioned in a letter quoted in the article as that for 'Piano, Left Hand, and Orchestra' is erroneous; it should be the one for three winds and orchestra.
— 'Arnold Bax'. *Recorded Sound*, Jan.–April 1968, pp. 273–6.
   One of the best general surveys of Bax and his problems.
— 'In Conversation with Michael Dawney'. *Composer*, no. 56, Winter 1975–6, pp. 29–31.

Foreman, R.L.E. [Lewis]: 'The Unperformed Works of Sir Arnold Bax'. *Musical Opinion*, July 1966, pp. 598–9.
— *Catalogue of the Unrecorded Works of Arnold Bax*. [A duplicated, quarto, list compiled for the British Institute of Recorded Sound] BIRS, Aug. 1966, 8 pp.
— 'Arnold Bax – a discography'. *Recorded Sound*, Jan.–April 1968, pp. 277–83.
   List complete up to April 1967, including unpublished recordings at the BBC, BIRS, and Library of Congress.

— 'Spring Fire – a major unperformed work by Sir Arnold Bax'. *Bax Society Bulletin*, June 1968 – no. 2, pp. 30–5.
    Written when the only score was thought to have been destroyed in Chappell's fire.

— 'A Time for Bax'. *Records and Recordings*, Oct. 1968, pp. 20–1.
    Includes previously unpublished early photographs of Bax.

— 'The Garden of Fand – a study of Arnold Bax'. *Audio and Record Review*, Jan. 1969, pp. 19 and 78.

— 'Sir Arnold Bax's Rhapsodic Ballad'. *Strad*, April 1969, pp. 505, 507.
See also R. B. Vocadlo's letter in the June 1969 issue, p. 71.

— 'Recording Bax 3'. *Bax Society Bulletin*, Aug. 1969 – no. 6, pp. 102–3.

— 'The quest for Bax'. *Brio*, Autumn 1969, pp. 28–31.

— 'Bax, the symphony and Sibelius'. *Musical Opinion*, Feb. 1970, pp. 245–6.

— 'Bax and the score of Malta G.C.'. *Bax Society Bulletin*, April 1970 – no. 8, pp. 7–9.

— 'Bibliography of writings on Arnold Bax'. *Current Musicology*, 10, 1970, pp. 124–40.
    Lists 210 references.

— 'The Musical Development of Arnold Bax'. *Music & Letters*, Jan. 1971, pp. 59–68.

— 'Symphonic Variations'. *Musical Opinion*, March 1971, pp. 291 and 293.

— 'A Catalogue of Autograph Manuscript Sources of Music by Sir Arnold Bax'. *RMA Research Chronicle*, no. 12, 1974, pp. 91–105.

— 'Bax and the Ballet'. *Proceedings of the RMA 104*, 1977–8, pp. 11–19.

— 'Dermot O'Byrne: background and sources' *and* 'The Poems' in *Dermot O'Byrne: poems by Arnold Bax*, edited by Lewis Foreman. Thames, 1979, pp. 11–15, 16–19.

[Forsyth, J. A.]: 'Pen Pictures of Personalities Past and Present, by the editor: No. 4 Arnold Bax'. *The RAM Club Magazine*, June 1927, pp. 3–5.

Foss, H. J.: 'Some Chamber Music by Arnold Bax'. *The Dominant*, Dec. 1927, pp. 16–19.

Handley, V.: 'Conducting Bax's music'. *Bax Society Bulletin*, May 1969 – no. 5, pp. 74–6.

Heim, N. M.: 'Sonata for Clarinet and Piano by Arnold Bax'. In his *The Use of the Clarinet in Published Sonatas for Clarinet and Piano by English Composers* ... Thesis: MM, Eastman School of Music, 1954, pp. 124–58.

Herbage, J.: 'Sir Arnold Bax'. In *British Music of Our Time*, ed. A. L. Bacharach. Pelican Books, 2nd ed., 1951, pp. 11–26.

Hill, R.: 'Colour Impressionism'. *Radio Times*, 13 Aug. 1943, p. 4.

Holbrooke, J.: 'Arnold Bax'. In his *Contemporary British Composers*. Cecil Palmer, 1925, pp. 53–60.

Holquist, R. A.: *An Analytical Study of Choral Music of Arnold Bax (1883–1953)*. Thesis: Wisconsin State University, MST, 1971.

Howes, F.: 'The Late Romantics'. In his *English Musical Renaissance*, Secker and Warburg, 1966, pp. 214–22.

Hull, R. H.: 'Bax's Third Symphony'. *Musical Times*, March 1930, pp. 217–20.

— 'Arnold Bax's Third Symphony'. *Monthly Musical Record*, Sept. 1930, pp. 259–60.

— 'In the Vanguard of British Composers'. *Radio Times*, July 11, 1930, 66 pp.

— 'Arnold Bax'. *Contemporary Review*, March 1931, pp. 343–8.

— 'Bax's Fourth Symphony'. *Daily Telegraph*, 9 Jan. 1932.
— *A Handbook of Arnold Bax's Symphonies*. Murdoch, 1932, 51 pp.
    Deals with symphonies nos. 1—4.
— 'Bax's Fourth Symphony'. *Spectator*, 9 Dec. 1932, p. 827.
— 'Arnold Bax's Fourth Symphony'. *Musical Mirror and Fanfare*, Dec. 1932, pp. 77—8.
— 'Arnold Bax — chamber music'. *Musical Mirror and Fanfare*, June 1933.
— 'Arnold Bax's Fifth Symphony'. *Monthly Musical Record*, Jan. 1934, pp. 7—9 [reprinted in *Bax Society Bulletin*, Feb. 1969 — no. 4, pp. 61—5].
— 'Arnold Bax's Fifth Symphony'. *Daily Telegraph*, 13 Jan. 1934.
— 'About "Cello Concerti" [Bax's Cello Concerto]'. *Radio Times*, 15 March 1935, p. 15. Includes an interesting cartoon of Bax.
— 'Bax's Cello Concerto'. *Radio Times*, 15 March 1935.
— 'Bax's Sixth Symphony'. *Musical Opinion*, Nov. 1935, pp. 115—16.
— 'Approach to Bax's Symphonies'. *Music & Letters*, April 1942, pp. 101—15.
— [The English Music Society, vol. 2] *Arnold Bax*. Columbia Records, *ca* 1942, 16 pp.
    Booklet issued with a set of Columbia 78 rpm records. Consists of a brief account of Bax's music, plus analyses of the Viola Sonata, Nonett and *Mater Ora Filium*.

Huntley, J.: 'The Film Music of Arnold Bax'. *The Cinema Studio*, vol. I, no. 10, 2 June 1948, p. 5.
— 'The Film Music of Bax — fanfares and anthems — the M.K.M. writes them from a room over the saloon bar'. *Musical Express*, 25 June 1948, p. 2.

Inman, D.: 'The Truth About the Russian Dancers — the play and the music'. *Bax Society Bulletin*, June 1968 — no. 2, pp. 21—3.

James, B.: 'Sir Arnold Bax...'. *Gramophone*, Nov. 1953, p. 179.

Lloyd, S.: 'Symphony No. 7'. *Bax Society Bulletin*, Jan. 1973, pp. 46—7.

McNaught, W.: '[Bax]'. In his *Modern Music and Musicians*. Novello, 2nd ed., 1938, pp. 38—40.

Maine, B.: 'Arnold Bax'. *Morning Post*, 21 Aug. 1931.

Mann, W.: 'Some English Concertos — Arnold Bax Violin Concerto'. In *The Concerto*, ed. R. Hill. Penguin, 1952, pp. 405—9.
    A general section on Bax's concertos, pp. 402—3.

Mellers, W.H.: 'Master of the King's Musick'. In his *Studies in Contemporary Music*, Dobson, 1947, pp. 179—86.
    A revised version of 'Comments and Reviews — Master of the King's Musick', *Scrutiny*, 1942, pp. 376—80.

Monthly Musical Record. 'Arnold Bax'. Nov. 1915, p. 322.
    The earliest article on the composer that has been traced, other than newspaper reviews and lists of his works. A portrait appears on p. 325.

Morris, M.: *The Art of J. D. Fergusson*. Glasgow, Blackie, 1974. Bax on pp. 102, 135—6.

Newman, E.: 'The Art of Mr Arnold Bax'. *Sunday Times*, 19 Nov. 1922.
— 'Bax's New Work'. [*Winter Legends*] *Sunday Times*, 14 Feb. 1932.
— 'The Week's Music: Bax and the Promenades'. *Sunday Times*, 30 Aug. 1936.
    Detailed discussion of Bax's imagery in the context of a performance of the Third Symphony.

Palmer, C.: 'The Post-Impressionists in England'. In his *Impressionism in Music*, Hutchinson, 1973, pp. 167—72.

— 'England [− Bax]' In his *Delius − portrait of a Cosmopolitan*, Duckworth, 1976, pp. 151−3.

Parlett, G.: 'Bax's Viola Concerto'. *Bax Society Bulletin*, June 1968 − no. 2, pp. 25−7.
    Useful survey of all Bax's music for the viola, with an analysis of the Viola Phantasy.
— 'Deirdre and Rosc-Catha'. *Bax Society Bulletin*, Nov. 1970, pp. 18−21.
— *Arnold Bax: a catalogue of his music*. Triad Press, 1972, 52 pp.
— 'Bax's Overtures'. *Bax Society Bulletin*, Jan. 1973, pp. 38−9.

Payne, A.: 'Problems of a Lyric Composer'. *Music and Musicians*, Jan. 1965, p. 17. *See also* P.J. Pirie's letter and Payne's reply in the March 1965 issue, p. 47.
— 'Bax, Sir Arnold (Edward Trevor)'. In *The New Grove*, vol. 2, pp. 306−10.
    Up-to-date, and well-informed survey, with a strongly personal view.

Picture Post: 'The Master of the King's Music'. 28 March 1942, p. 21.
    Includes three photographs.
— 'Bax composes a royal fanfare'. 22 Nov. 1947, p. 47.
    Includes two photographs.

Pirie, P.J.: 'The Nordic Element − Bax and Sibelius'. *Musical Opinion*, Feb. 1957, pp. 277−8.
— 'The Odd Case of Sir Arnold Bax'. *Musical Times*, Sept. 1961, pp. 559−60.
— 'The "Georgian" Composers'. *Music in Britain*, Summer 1965 − no. 69, pp. 23−7.
    Deals with Bax, Ireland, Bridge, Warlock, van Dieren, and Lambert.
— 'The Unfashionable Generation'. *High Fidelity Magazine*, Jan. 1966, pp. 59−62.
    Deals with Bax, Bridge, and Ireland, Section on Bax pp. 61−2.
— 'Some Thoughts on Hearing "The Truth About the Russian Dancers".' *Bax Society Bulletin*, June 1968 − no. 2, pp. 20−1.
— 'More than a Brazen Romantic'. *Music and Musicians*, Jan. 1971, pp. 32−6 and 38.
    Includes the first two pages of the *Rhapsodic Ballad*, pp. 40−1.
— *The English Musical Renaissance*. Gollancz, 1979.
    Extensive sympathetic references to Bax.

Puffett, D.: 'In the Garden of Fand − Arnold Bax and the "Celtic Twilight".' In *Art Nouveau, Jugendstil und Musik*, ed. Jürg Stenzl. Zürich, Atlantis Musik-buch-Verlag, 1980, pp. 193−210.

Rothstein, E.: *The Two-Piano Music of Arnold Bax*. Thesis: Eastman School of Music, 1945, 50 pp.

Rubbra, E.: 'Arnold Bax's Technics − a new flowering of old traditions'. *Daily Telegraph*, 14 Oct. 1933.
    Reprinted with minor alteration in *Bax Society Bulletin*, Feb. 1968 − no. 1, under title 'Arnold Bax's Music − a new flowering ...', pp. 11−13.

Saul, G.B.: 'Of Tales Half Forgotten'. *Arizona Quarterly*, Summer 1962, pp. 151−4.
    At the time the only published assessment of Bax's writings under the pseudonym Dermot O'Byrne.

Scott-Sutherland, C.: 'The Symphonies of Arnold Bax'. *Music Review*, Feb. 1962, pp. 20−3.

— 'Morar and the Master of the Queen's Music'. *Scotland's Magazine*, Nov. 1962, pp. 44–5.
    Contains an unusual portrait of the composer (1942) apparently at work on a score. He is actually posing with the score of the *Sinfonietta*, open at p. 4 of the manuscript.
— 'Arnold Bax'. *Musical Times*, Oct. 1963, p. 706.
    Illustrated by a photograph of Bax's grave; p. 707 contains an advertisement for Bax's music.
— 'Some Unpublished Works of Arnold Bax'. *Music Review*, Nov. 1963, pp. 322–6.
— 'Sir Arnold Bax — Symphonic Variations' [a review]. *Music Review*, May 1967, pp. 156–7.
— 'Bax and Melody'. *Bax Society Bulletin*, Feb. 1969 — no. 4, pp. 54–7.
— *Arnold Bax*. J.M. Dent, 1973, xviii, 214 pp.

Shore, B.: 'Arnold Bax'. In his *Sixteen Symphonies*, Longmans, 1949, pp. 341–8.
— 'Bax's Third Symphony'. In his *Sixteen Symphonies*. Longmans, 1949, pp. 349–65.

Suckling, N.: 'Bax and his Piano Sonatas'. *Listener*, 17 June 1954, p. 1069.

Thistlethwaite, B.: *The Bax Family*. Headly Bros., 1936.
    The section on Bax and his immediate family is pp. 172–3.

Whelen, C.: 'Arnold Edward Trevor Bax'. In *The Music Masters*, ed. A.L. Bacharach; vol. 4: *The Twentieth Century*. Cornell, 1954, Pelican, 1957, pp. 26–34.

White, F.: 'Arnold Bax's Violin Sonata'. *Musical News and Herald*, 14 Jan. 1922, pp. 49–50.

Willetts, P.: 'Autograph Music MSS of Arnold Bax'. *British Museum Quarterly*, 1961, vol. 23, pp. 43–5.
    Details the seven works in manuscript given to the museum by Miss Harriet Cohen in 1961, a total of nine manuscripts (Add. MSS 50173–81).

Williams, L.H.: 'The Philosopher's Musician'. *Sackbut*, March 1931, pp. 216–19.
    Part of this article reprinted by Norman Demuth in his 'An Anthology of Musical Criticism.' Eyre & Spottiswoode, 1947, pp. 359–62.

Wilson, D.: 'The Orchestral Development of Arnold Bax'. Thesis: University of Wales, MA, 1975.

SUPPLEMENTARY BIBLIOGRAPHY

Banfield, S.: 'The Celtic Twilight'. In his *Sensibility and English Song*, vol. I. CUP, 1985, pp. 248–74.
    Section on Bax pp. 253–63; most of this section previously published as 'Bax as song composer'. *Musical Times*, Nov. 1983, pp. 666–9.

Bax, C.: 'Silver and Bronze Trumpets'. *National & English Review*, June 1948, pp. 500–6. Account of the Baxes' childhood and youth.

Beechey, G.: 'The Legacy of Arnold Bax (1883–1953)'. *Musical Opinion*, Aug. 1983, pp. 348–51; Sept. 1983, pp. 357–63, 383.

Boyd, E.: *Ireland's Literary Renaissance*. Dublin & London, Maunsel & Co Ltd., 1916. Section on Dermot O'Byrne pp. 386–7, 407. This assessment of Bax's Dermot O'Byrne stories is cut in the later edition.

Bradbury, E.: 'Celtic Soul of Bax laid bare'. *Yorkshire Post*, 25 June 1983.

Chappell Music: *Sir Arnold Bax 1883–1953*. [A centenary folder of leaflets including 'Sir Arnold Bax' by Lewis Foreman; and 'A Guide to the Music of Arnold Bax' by Christopher Palmer] 1983.

Cooper, M.: 'The Dream World of Arnold Bax'. *Daily Telegraph*, 19 May 1973.

Crichton, R.: 'A Century of Bax'. *Financial Times*, 23 Sept. 1983, p. 19.

Elliott, C. K.: 'Rosalind and Godwin Baynes: a Wisbech Vignette 1913–15'. *The Wisbech Society: 46th Annual Report 1985*, pp. 7–10.

Foreman, L.: 'Celtic Nympholept'. *Listener*, 3 Nov. 1983, p. 36.
— 'Arnold Bax at the RAM'. *The Royal Academy of Music Magazine*, no. 233, pp. 11–17.
— 'Spring Fire'. [Programme for Royal Philharmonic Society concert] Royal Festival Hall, 5 Oct. 1983.
Includes short biographical sketch of Bax, pp. 3–4; programme note pp. 4–6; and 'Bax and the Royal Philharmonic Society' by Michael Pope, pp. 10–11.

Hoffpauir, J. C.: 'Three Tone-Poems by Arnold Bax'. MM thesis: University of Missouri – Kansas City, 1981.

Lloyd, S.: *H. Balfour Gardiner*. CUP, 1984.

MacDonald, C.: 'Burgeoning Bax'. *Listener*, 18 Oct. 1984, pp. 41–2.

Payne, A.: 'Bax- a Centenary assessment'. *Tempo* 180, Sept. 1984, pp. 29–32.

Protheroe, G.: 'The Choral Music of Arnold Bax (1883–1953)'. *Chorale*, March/April 1983, pp. 6–9.

[Prowse, J.]: 'Bax on 78s'; 'Instrumentalists connected with Bax'; 'Composers connected with Bax'. Desco Epsom Ltd., *Collectors List No. 39*, Summer 1984, pp. 65–8.

Rivers, J. L.: 'Formal Determinants in the Symphonies of Arnold Bax'. Ph.D. Thesis, University of Arizona, 1982.

Sommerich, P.: 'Bax to the fore: briefly'. *Hampstead & Highgate Express*, 11 Nov. 1983, p. 20.

Stevenson, R.: 'The Truth About Bax'. *Radio 3 Magazine*, Nov. 1983, pp. 2–3.

Taylor, J. R.: 'Arnold Bax'. *Music & Musicians*, Nov. 1983, pp. 12–13.

INDEX

488Bax: a composer and his times

Denman, John 469
Denmark 231
Dent, E. J. 16, 66, 121, 122, 180, 316
D'Erlanger, The Baroness 158
Dermot Donn McMorna 446
Desmond, Astra 463
Devil That Tempted St Anthony, The 252, 435, 452
Diaghilev; Sergei 94, 117, 158, 168, 172, 209, 418
Diaghilev Ballet 102
Dickens, Charles 346
Dilkes, Neville 467
D'Indy, Vincent 65; *Istar* 273
Divertimenti 461
Dodds, E. R. 90
Dods, M. 464
Donovan, Dr James 359
Dorow, Dorothy 459
Dove, Alfred 419
Dowdall, Mrs 362
Downes, Edward 245, 413, 421, 462, 471
Downes, Herbert 470
Dragon's Song see *Pageant of St George*
Draper, Muriel 176
Dream Child 448
Dream in Exile 140, 451, 460
Dresden 42, 46, 47, 50
Drinkwater, John 158
Drucker, Stanley 468
Du Blomst i Dug see *O Dewy Flower*
Dublin 69, 86, 89, 95, 108, 110, 111, 139, 166, 310, 321, 339, 341, 344, 345, 349, 354, 357, 358, 379, 381, 382; Gaity Theatre 61; Municipal Gallery 166; Radio Orchestra 350; University College 340, 357, 362, 416
Dublin Ballad, A 139, 379, 403
Dubrucq, Eugène 159, 180, 432
Duff, Arthur 344
Duggan, L. 362
Dukas, Paul 102
Dumas, Alexandre 288
Duncan, Mary *pl. 11*
Dunhill, Thomas 48; *Violin Sonata No. 2* 137
Dunn, Vivian 461
Durham 303, 343
Duthoit, W. J. 427
Dvořák, Antonin 15, 55, 115, 323; *American Quartet* 162; *Dumky Trio* 338; *Piano Concerto* 44; *Russalka* 67
Dyer, Louise 220
Dyers, Sir Edward 457

Easter Rising 91, 109, 138, 141, 148, 191, 257, 340, 379, 381
Echo 39, 439
Eden, John 141

Edward VIII, King 306
Eggar, Kathleen E. 186, 187, 396
Eglinton, John (i.e. W. K. Magee) 90, 91
Eigg 316
Eilidh my Fawn see *Celtic Song Cycle*
Eire 51, 52, 74, 75, 381, 412
Elegiac Trio 140, 148, 176, 432, 460
Elgar, Sir Edward 18, 64, 74, 75, 96, 103, 130, 160, 202, 239, 314, 323, 325, 326, 327, 405, 408, 432; *Enigma* 62; *Grania and Diarmid* 61; *Imperial March* 14; *Kingdom* 362; *Pomp and Circumstance* 14, 19, 305; *Symphony No. 2* 86, 98; *Violin Concerto* 154, 162
Elgar, Lady 18
Elizabeth of Roumania, Queen see Sylva, Carmen, *pseud.*
Elizabeth, H.R.H. Princess 342, 345, 428
Elliott, Alisdair 430
Ellis, F. Bevis 104, 115, 123, 142, 415, 416
Ely 130
Emmet, Robert 349
Enchanted Fiddle, The 439, 460; see also *Fiddler of Dooney*
Enchanted Summer 74, 78ff, 97, 98, 100, 102, 103, 173, 298, 374, 406, 413
English Sinfonia 467
English String Quartet 431, 467, 468, 471
Enlightenment 441
Ennis 350
E.N.S.A. 335, 426
Epithalamium 456
Epstein, Jacob 158
Erpecum see Von Erpecum, Arne
Eternity 208, 300, 424, 447
Eton 78, 109
Evans, Edwin 39, 117, 136, 164, 168, 171, 172, 173, 179, 197, 322, 388, 391, 397, 405, 419, 431, 444, 445, 476
Evans, Harry 65, 411
Exeter 342
Exultate Singers 473
Eynsford 223
Eyotkuhnen 70

Fabianism 41
Fackler, Herbert Vern 382
Fagge, Arthur 98, 413
Fagin's Romp see *Oliver Twist*
Fahy, Frank 165
'Fair Hills of Ireland, The' 162
Fairies, The 39, 82, 438, 461
Faith 84, 442
Falla, Manuel de 273
Fand 112, 151, 159, 359; see also *Garden of Fand*
Fanfare for a Cheerful Occasion 422, 461
Fanfare for A Hosting at Dawn 172, 419

The Sir Arnold Bax Trust

The Sir Arnold Bax Trust was established as a registered charity in 1985 (registered no. 326841). The Trust has been established to promote knowledge and performance of the music of Sir Arnold Bax.

The Trust has limited funds available to help promote selected activities, and donations from interested music lovers are also welcomed.

Initial activity has been in support of three Chandos recordings (tone poems Vol 2; *Spring Fire* and the First Symphony); the publication of a volume of Bax's piano music (Thames Publishing); and concert performances of various works.

The Legal Adviser is C. S. Stewart, Wray Smith & Co., 1 King's Bench Walk, Temple, London WC4Y 7DD